Amer
Casino
Guide

2020 Edition

<u>Written and Edited By</u>

Steve Bourie

<u>Assistant Editors</u>

Matt Bourie

<u>Contributing Writers</u>

Linda Boyd

John Grochowski

H. Scot Krause

Henry Tamburin

Jean Scott

<u>Research Assistant</u>

Zachary Krause

This book is dedicated to my wife and children.
Thank you for your love and support.

American Casino Guide - 2020 edition

Published By:
Casino Vacations Press, Inc.
P.O. Box 703
Dania, Florida 33004
(954) 989-2766

e-mail: info@americancasinoguidebook.com
website: americancasinoguidebook.com

ISBN-13: 978-1-883768-29-4
ISSN: 1086-9018

Table of Contents

About Your Guide

This guide has been written to help you plan your visit to casino gambling areas and also to help you save money once you are there. The first edition of this guide began 29 years ago as an eight-page newsletter and it has continued to grow each year as casino gambling has spread throughout the country. We have listed information on all of the states that offer any type of traditional casino table games or slot machines (including video lottery terminals). We have also included stories to help you understand how casinos operate; how video poker and slot machines work; how to make the best plays in blackjack, craps, roulette and baccarat; and how to take advantage of casino promotional programs. Additionally, we have included a casino coupon section that should save you many times the cost of this book.

Virtually every casino has a "comp" program whereby you can get free rooms, food, shows or gifts based upon your level of play. If you plan on gambling during your trip to the casino, you may want to call ahead and ask their marketing department for details on their programs. There are also stories in this book to help you understand how "comp" programs work and how to best take advantage of them.

One more suggestion to save you money when visiting a casino is to join their players club. It doesn't cost anything and you would be surprised at how quickly those points can add up to earn you gifts, cash, food or other complimentaries. Also, as a club member you will usually receive periodic mailings from the casino with money-saving offers that are generally not available to the public.

When using this guide please remember that all of the listed room rates reflect the lowest and highest prices charged during the year. During holidays and peak periods, however, higher rates may apply. Also, since the gambling games offered at casinos vary from state to state, a listing of available games is found at the start of each state heading. We hope you enjoy your guide and we wish you good luck on your casino vacation!

Your Best Casino Bets - Part I

by Henry Tamburin

The majority of casino players leave too much to chance when playing in a casino. To put it bluntly, they don't have a clue as to how to play. They are literally throwing their money away with little chance of winning. Luck most certainly has a lot to do with your success in a casino but what really separates the winners from the losers is the skill of the players. Granted, there is no guarantee that you will win, but on the other hand, there is no guarantee that you must lose. My objectivc in this article is to educate you on the casino games so that at the very least, you'll be able to enjoy yourself in the casino with maximum play time and minimum risk to your bankroll.

Let's begin our understanding of casino gambling by learning how casinos win as much as they do. They don't charge admission, and they certainly don't depend on the luck of their dealers to generate the income they need to pay their overhead. In fact, they guarantee themselves a steady income by having a built in advantage, or house edge, on every bet. Think of it as a very efficient hidden tax that generates them a guaranteed daily profit.

Here's an example of how this works. Suppose we take a coin and play heads or tails. Every time you lose a flip of the coin you pay me $1. Every time you win a flip, I pay you 90¢. Would you play? I hope you said no. Here's why. In this simple game I would have an advantage over you and I created that advantage by not paying you at the true odds of one-to-one (or $1).

Casinos do this very same thing to create their advantage. They simply pay off winning bets at less than the true odds. For example, the true odds of winning a bet on number 7 on roulette are 37-to-1 (the latter means you have 37 chances to lose vs. one chance to win). If you get lucky and the roulette ball lands in the number seven slot, you'd expect the casino to pay you 37 chips as winnings for the one chip you bet on number 7 (37- to-1 payoff). If they did that, the casino's advantage would be zero. However, as I mentioned above, the casinos create their advantage by paying off winning bets at less than true odds. In the case of our bet on number 7, the winning payoff is 35 chips (instead of 37 chips). The two chips the casino quietly kept is what pays their bills. Mathematically, the casino advantage is 5.26% on this bet which simply means day in and day out, the casino expects to win (or keep) 5.26% of all money wagered in roulette.

The casino games with the lowest casino advantage (less than 1.25%), and your best bets, are blackjack, craps, baccarat, and video poker. Now don't sell the ranch and run over to your nearest casino just yet. These games, plus table poker, are your best bets but you must learn how to play these games properly to enhance your chances of winning. Here are some tips to get you started:

BLACKJACK - This is your best casino game, but you must learn how to play your hands (when to hit, stand, double-down, split, etc.). This is known as the basic strategy. Learn it and you can reduce the casino's advantage to virtually zero. And if you learn how to keep track of the cards as they are played (i.e. card counting) you can actually turn the tables on the casino and have the edge over them! Do not try to play blackjack if you haven't learned the correct basic strategy. If you do, your chances of winning are slim. Also, it's wise not to make any side bets that may be offered on your table and please stay away from any game which only pays 6-to-5 for an untied blackjack. Blackjack tournaments are also popular and here players compete against other players with the player with the most chips at the end of the round advancing. Tournament prizes can be substantial. Playing and betting strategy for blackjack tournaments, however, is different than playing blackjack in a casino so bone up on your tournament skills before considering playing in a tournament.

CRAPS - The game of craps intimidates most casino players because of the complicated playing layout and the multitude of bets. In fact craps is an easy game to play. And it also has some of the best bets in the casino (and also some of the worst). Your best bet is the pass line with odds and come with odds. Next best is a place bet on six or eight. Stay away from all other bets on the layout because the casino's advantage is too high. If you really enjoy the game of craps you might consider learning dice control – it's not an easy skill to learn and it requires a lot of practice but if you get good at it, you can have the edge over the casino.

ROULETTE - Every bet on the American roulette layout (with 0 and 00 on the wheel) has a high casino advantage. That goes for bets straight up on numbers that pay 35-to-1, as well as even money wagers on red or black. Atlantic City players get a break. If you bet on an even money payoff bet and 0 or 00 hits, you lose only half your wager. This cuts the casino's advantage in half. Also, some casinos offer a European layout with only one zero. This is a better bet than wheels with 0 and 00.

BACCARAT - Many casinos offer a low stakes version called mini-baccarat. Not a bad game to play. If you bet on the bank hand, the casino's edge is only 1.17%. And when you play baccarat, there are no playing decisions to make which makes the game very easy to play. However, this game is fast with many decisions per hour. It's best to play slowly. One way is to only bet on the bank hand after it wins (meaning you won't be betting on every hand which will slow down your play).

BIG SIX WHEEL - Stay away from spending a lot of time (and money) at this game. The casino's advantage is astronomical (11% to 26%). Its drawing card for the novice player is the low minimum bet ($1). Save your money for the better games.

PAI GOW POKER - Strange name for a casino game. The game is a cross between Pai Gow, a Chinese game of dominoes, and the American game of seven-card poker. Players are dealt seven cards and they must arrange (or set) their cards into a five-card poker hand and a two-card poker hand. Skill is involved in setting the two hands which can help reduce the casino's advantage.

SLOT MACHINES - Casinos earn more money from slot machines than all the table games combined. The casino's advantage varies from one machine to another. Typically the higher denomination machines ($1 and up) pay back more than the nickel, quarter and fifty-cent machines. Slots are not your best bet in the casino, but here are a few tips: It's wise to play one coin only in machines where all the payouts increase proportionally to the number of coins played (i.e. there is no jackpot for playing maximum coins). However, if the machine has a substantial jackpot when you play maximum coins, then you should always play the maximum number of coins the machine will accept or you won't be eligible for a bonus payoff for the jackpot. Don't waste hours looking for a machine that's "ready to hit." Join the players clubs, always use your players club card when you play, and try to schedule your play time when the casino offers multiple points. Joining is free and you'll be rewarded with discounts and other freebies. Machines that have lower jackpots pay smaller amounts more frequently which means you normally get more playing time for your money. Playing machines that have bonus rounds and fancy graphics may be fun, but the house edge on these machines is usually higher than traditional reel spinning machines. Likewise, the house edge is higher for linked machines that have those life-changing mega jackpots. Some casinos now certify their machines to return 98% or more and these machines are your best bets. Also, consider playing in slot tournaments where you are competing against other players, rather than the house, and the prizes can be substantial.

VIDEO POKER - Your best bet if you enjoy playing slot machines. Skill is involved as well as learning to spot the better payoff machines. For example, on the classic jacks-or-better game, always check the full house and flush payoff schedule. The best machines on jacks or better pay nine coins for a full house and six coins for a flush for each coin played. These machines are known as 9/6 machines. They are readily available; seek them out. The same analogy holds for bonus poker, double bonus, deuces wild, jokers wild, etc. video poker games. There are good pay schedules and bad ones, and it's up to you to know the difference and play only the higher paying schedules with the correct playing strategy (readily available on the Internet, in books, and on strategy cards).

KENO - This casino game has a very high casino advantage (usually 20% and up). Stay away if you are serious about winning.

ULTIMATE TEXAS HOLD 'EM - This game is based on Texas Hold 'em and just like Let It Ride, players play against the house rather than against each other. Each player at the table must make two bets of the same amount on the ante and blind to play with an option "trips" side bet that pays with a three-of-a-kind or better. The player has to make the best five-card poker hand using their two cards and the five community cards, and has the option to bet or check at three different times throughout the hand. This game has a house edge of 2.19% with proper playing strategy. There are several pay tables for the trips bet, with the two most popular having house edges of 3.50% and 6.18%. So it is usually a good idea to avoid that bet.

MISSISSIPPI STUD - This game is different from other poker-based games because the player is paid based on the poker value of their hand made from two cards dealt to them, plus three community cards. They are not playing against another player or the dealer. The player makes an ante bet and receives two cards face down then makes a bet that must be one to three times their initial ante bet to see the first community card. They must then make another bet of one to three times their ante bet to see the second community card and then do it again a third time to see the final community card. The strategy for the first decision with two cards is rather simple. Make the big, 3x bet with any pair, and make the small 1x wager with either any face card, any two medium cards (6 through 10), or with a 5/6 suited or better. The other decisions are much more complex and can be found online.

LET IT RIDE - This casino table game is based on the all-American game of poker. Like Caribbean Stud Poker, players compete against the house rather than against each other. What makes this game so unique is that the players can remove up to two of their initial mandatory three bets if they don't think they can win. The objective is to end up with a five-card poker hand of at least 10's or higher. The higher the rank, the greater the payoff; up to 1,000-to-1 for the royal flush. The casino edge is about 3% and about 70% of the hands will be losing hands. If you are lucky enough to catch a high payoff hand, be smart, push your chair back, and take the money and run!

THREE CARD POKER - One of the more successful table games in recent years, you can wager on either the Ante/Play or Pair Plus. You win your Ante/Play bet if your three card poker hand beats the dealer's hand. If you wager Pair Plus, you win money if your three card hand contains at least a pair or higher (the higher the ranking hand, the greater the payout). There are different paytables – the best pays 4-1 for a flush rather than 3-1. The optimum playing strategy is to raise on Q-6-4 or higher and avoid playing the Pair Plus if the flush pays only 3-1.

Henry Tamburin, Ph.D., has over 50 years experience as a blackjack player, writer, author, and instructor. His latest book is the Ultimate Blackjack Strategy Guide, which is FREE to read on https://www.888casino.com/blog/blackjack-strategy-guide/. See his ad on page 24.

Your Best Casino Bets - Part II

by Steve Bourie

In the previous story Henry gave you his choices for your best casino bets based on which ones offer you the best mathematical odds. Now, Henry is a great mathematician who is truly an expert at crunching numbers to figure out what the theoretical odds are, but what about real life? By this I mean - at the end of the week, or the month, or the year, how much does a casino really make from blackjack, or craps, or roulette? Sure, you can do the math to calculate the casino advantage on a bank hand in mini-baccarat as 1.17%, but at the end of the day what percent of those bets on mini-baccarat actually wind up in the hands of the casino? Is it precisely 1.17%? Or is it less? Or is it more? And, if you knew how much the casino truly averaged on all of the games it offered, which one would turn out to be your best bet based on that information?

To find the answer to this question I began my search by looking at the annual gaming revenue report issued by Nevada's State Gaming Control Board. It lists the win percentages, based on the *drop* (an explanation of this term is provided later), for all of the games offered by the casinos and, as Henry stated in his story, blackjack, baccarat and craps were among the best casino bets. The first column below lists the actual win percentages based on the "drop" (an explanation of "drop" follows shortly) for Nevada's various games for the fiscal year from July 1, 2018 through June 30, 2019:

Game	Win %	Adjusted Win %
Keno	27.08	27.08
Race Book	15.90	15.90
Bingo	8.32	8.32
Slot Machines	6.87	6.87
3-Card Poker	31.91	6.38
Sports Pool	5.83	5.83
Let It Ride	25.11	5.02
Pai Gow Poker	20.78	4.16
Pai Gow	19.68	3.94
Roulette	19.07	3.81
Craps	15.12	3.02
Twenty-One	14.05	2.81
Baccarat	11.92	2.38
Mini-Baccarat	10.58	2.12

Before we go on to the other games though you'll need a brief explanation of how the win percentages are calculated and we'll start off with a basic lesson in how casinos do their accounting.

Casinos measure their take in table games by the drop and the win. The drop is the count of all of the receipts (cash and credit markers) that go into the drop box located at the table. Later, an accounting is made to see how much more (or less) they have than they started with. This amount is known as the win (or loss).

What the first column in the table shows you is how much the casinos won as a percentage of the drop. For example, on the roulette table for every $100 that went into the drop box the casino won $19.07 or 19.07%. What it doesn't tell you, however, is how much the casinos won as a percentage of all the bets that were made. In other words, the drop tells you how many chips were bought at that table, but it doesn't tell you how many bets were made with those chips. For example, if you buy $100 worth of chips at a blackjack table and play $10 a hand you don't bet for exactly 10 hands and then leave the table, do you? Of course not. You win some hands and you lose some hands and if you counted all of the times you made a $10 bet before you left the table you would see that your original $100 in chips generated many times that amount in bets. In other words, there is a multiplier effect for the money that goes into the drop box. We know that for every dollar that goes into the drop box there is a corresponding number of bets made. To find out exactly what that number is I asked Henry for some help. He replied that there is no exact answer, but during a 1982 study of the roulette tables in Atlantic City it was discovered that the total amount bet was approximately five times the amount of the buy-in. This means that for every $100 worth of chips bought at the table it resulted in $500 worth of bets being made.

The multiplier effect for the money that goes into the drop box is also dependent on the skill of the player. A blackjack player that loses his money quickly because he doesn't know good playing strategy will have a much lower multiplier than a player who uses a correct playing strategy. For purposes of this story, however, we'll assume that they balance each other out and we'll also assume that all games have the same multiplier of five. We can now return to our win percentage tables and divide by five the percentages for those games that have a multiplier effect. These new adjusted numbers let us know approximately how much the casinos actually won as a percentage of the amount bet on each of those games. Keep in mind, however, that besides bingo there are three other game categories that do not need to be adjusted: keno, race book and sports pool. They need no adjustment because there is no multiplier factor involved. On these particular games the casinos know the exact total of the bets they take in and the exact total of the bets they pay out.

After calculating our adjusted win numbers we can now go back and take another look at which games are your best casino bets. The worst game, by far, is keno with its 27.08% edge. Next comes the race book with 15.90% and then bingo at 8.32%.

Usually bingo would rank as one of the games with the worst odds, but not in Nevada where it's sometimes used as a "loss leader." Just like your local Kmart runs especially low prices on a couple of items to bring you into the store where they believe you'll buy some other items, Nevada casinos use bingo to bring people into their casinos, believing that while they're there they'll play other games and also develop a loyalty to that casino. So, if you're a bingo player Nevada casinos are the best places you'll ever find to play your game.

Next is slots at 6.87% and then three card poker at 6.38%. Sports betting has a casino win rate of 5.83% but that number actually deserves a closer look because there are really five different types of bets that make up that figure: football - 6.10%; basketball - 5.54%; baseball - 4.36%; sports parlay cards - 32.56%; and other sports (golf, car racing, etc.) - 6.35%. As you can see, all sports bets carry a relatively low house edge, except for sports parlay cards which you may want to avoid.

Next on our list is let it ride at 5.02%. That's followed by pai gow poker at 4.16%, pai gow at 3.94% , and roulette at 3.81%.

Finally, we come to the four best casino bets that all have roughly the same edge of three percent or less: craps at 3.02%; twenty-one (blackjack) at 2.81%; baccarat at 2.38%; and mini-baccarat at 2.12%.

So there you have it. Mini-baccarat is your best casino bet! Henry said it was a good game to play and he was right. But didn't he also say that blackjack was your best casino bet? Was he wrong about that? Not really, because he prefaced it by saying "you must learn how to play your hands."

You have to remember that of all the table games offered in a casino (other than poker) only blackjack is a game of skill. This means that the better you are at playing your cards, the better you will be able to beat the house average. The 2.81% figure shown is just an average and if you learn proper basic strategy you can cut it down even more which would then make it your best bet. Good luck!

Casino Comps

by Steve Bourie

In the world of casino gambling a "comp" is short for complimentary and it refers to anything that the casino will give you for free in return for your play in their casino.

Naturally, the more you bet, the more the casino will be willing to give you back. For the truly "high roller" (those willing to bet thousands, tens of thousands or even hundreds of thousands on the turn of a card) there is no expense spared to cater to their every whim, including: private jet transportation, chauffeur-driven limousines, gourmet chef-prepared foods, the finest wines and champagnes, plus pampered butler and maid service in a $10 million penthouse suite. But what about the lower-limit bettor?

Well, it turns out that pretty much any gambler can qualify for comps no matter what their level of play and if you know you're going to be gambling anyway, you might as well ask to get rated to see what you can get on a comp basis.

When you sit down to play be sure to tell the dealer that you want to be rated and they'll call over the appropriate floorperson who will take down your name and put it on a card along with information on how long you play and how much you bet. The floorperson won't stand there and constantly watch you, instead they'll just glance over every once in awhile to see how much you're betting and note it on the card. If you change tables be sure to tell the floorperson so that they can continue to track your play at the new table.

Usually a casino will want you to play for at least three hours and virtually all casinos use the same formula to calculate your comp value. They simply take the size of your average bet and multiply it by: the casino's advantage on the game you're playing; the decisions per hour in your game; and the length of your play in hours. The end result is what the casino expects to win from you during your play and most casinos will return anywhere from 10% to 40% of that amount to you in the form of comps.

So, let's say you're a roulette player that averages $20 a spin and you play for four hours. What's that worth in comps? Well, just multiply your average bet ($20), by the casino's advantage in roulette (5.3%) to get $1.06, which is the average amount the casino expects to make on you on each spin of the wheel. You then multiply that by the number of decisions (or spins) per hour (40) to get $42.40, which is the average amount the casino expects to make on you after one hour. Then, multiply that by the total hours of play (4) to get $169.60, which is the average amount the casino expects to make on you during your four hours of play. Since the casinos will return 10% to 40% of that amount in comps, you should qualify for a minimum of $16.96 to a maximum of $67.84 in casino comps.

One thing to keep in mind about comps is that you don't have to lose in order to qualify. The casino only asks that you put in the time to play. So, in our example if, after four hours of gambling, our roulette player ended up winning $100, they would still be eligible for the same amount of comps.

The last thing to mention about comps is that some casino games require skill (blackjack and pai gow poker), or offer various bets that have different casino advantages (craps) so those factors are sometimes adjusted in the equation when determining the casino advantage in those games. Just take a look at the chart below to see how the average casino will adjust for skill in blackjack and pai gow poker as well as for the types of bets that are made in craps.

Game	Game Advantage	Decisions Per Hour
Blackjack	.0025 (Card Counter) .01 (Good Basic Strategy) .015 (Soft Player)	70
Roulette	.053	40
Craps	.005 (Pass Line/Full Odds) .01 (Knowledgeable) .04 (Soft)	144
Baccarat	.012	70
Mini-Baccarat	.012	110
Pai Gow Poker	.01 (Knowledgeable) .02 (Average)	25

Players Clubs And Comps

by Steve Bourie

Before you start playing any kind of electronic gaming machine in a casino, you should first join the casino's players club to reap the rewards that your play will entitle you to. What is a players club you ask? Well, it's similar to a frequent flyer club, except that in these clubs you will earn cash or comps (free food, rooms, shows, etc.) based on how much money you put through the machines.

Virtually all casinos in the U.S. have a players club and joining is simple. Just go to the club's registration desk, present an ID, and you'll be issued a plastic card, similar to a credit card. When you walk up to a machine you'll see a small slot (usually at the top, or side) where you should insert your card before you start to play. The card will then record how much money you've played in that particular machine. Then, based on the amount you put through, you will be eligible to receive cash (sometimes) and comps (always) back from the casino. Naturally, the more you gamble, the more they will give back to you.

Some casinos will give you a free gift, or some other kind of bonus (extra slot club points, free buffet, etc.) just for joining and since there's no cost involved, it certainly makes sense to join even if you don't plan on playing that much. As a club member you'll also be on the casino's mailing list and you'll probably be receiving some good money-saving offers in the mail. Additionally, some casinos offer discounts to their club members on hotel rooms, meals and gift shop purchases.

While almost no casino will give you cashback for playing their table games, virtually all casinos will give you cashback for playing their machines. The amount returned is calculated as a percentage of the money you put through the machines and it basically varies from as low as .05% to as high as 1%. This means that for every $100 you put into a machine you will earn a cash rebate of anywhere from five cents to $1. This may not seem like a great deal of money but it can add up very quickly. Additionally, some casinos (usually the casinos with the lower rates) will periodically offer double, triple or quadruple point days when your points will accumulate much more rapidly.

One other point to make about cashback is that the vast majority of casinos (about 90%) offer a lower cash rebate on their video poker machines than they do on their slot machines. Generally, the rate is about one-half of what the casino normally pays on its slot machines. The reason for the reduced rate is that video poker is a game of skill and knowledgeable players can achieve a greater return on video poker games than they could on slots. Since the casino will make less money on video poker games they simply reduce their cash rebates accordingly. This is very important to keep in mind, especially if you're a bad video poker player, because you'll probably only be earning half the cash rebate you could be getting by just playing the slots.

Of course, the best situation is to be a smart video poker player in a casino that offers the same cash rebate to all of its player regardless of what kind of machine they play. This way you could be playing a good VP game, combined with a good rebate, and this will allow you to be playing at a near 100% level!

Not all casinos will give you cashback. Many casinos will send a freeplay offer to you and you must return to the casino on a specific date to use it. This is called a bounce back offer and it is the preferred method for most casinos. Keep in mind, if you won't be going back to that casino, a bounce back offer won't be of much use to you.

While not every casino's club will give you back cash it is standard for every club to allow you to earn "comps" for your machine play. "Comps" is short for complimentaries and it means various things that you can get for free from the casino: rooms, meals, shows, gifts, etc.

Once again, the comp you will earn is based on the amount of money you put through the machines but it is usually at a higher level than you would earn for cashback. After all, the real cost to a casino for a $15 meal is much less than giving you back $15 in cash so the casinos can afford to be more generous.

When it comes to players club comp policies they basically fall into one of three categories. Some casinos have clubs that allow you to redeem your points for either cash at one rate, or comps at a reduced rate that will cost you fewer points. In these clubs, for example, you might have a choice of redeeming your 1,000 points for either $10 in cash or $20 in comps.

Another option (one that is commonly used by many "locals" casinos in Las Vegas) is for the casino to set a redemption schedule for each particular restaurant, or meal. For example: breakfast is 800 points, lunch is 1,200 points and dinner is 1,600 points. These are popular programs because players know exactly what is required to earn their comp.

At the other extreme, many casinos base their comps on your total machine play but won't tell you exactly what's required to achieve it. At the MGM Resorts properties in Las Vegas, for example, you will earn cashback at a set schedule but you'll never quite know what you need to earn a food comp. You just have to go to the players club booth, present your card, and ask if you can get a buffet or restaurant comp. The staff will then either give it to you or say you need some more play on your card before they can issue you a food comp.

And which casinos have the best players clubs? Well, that would really be dependant on what's most important to you. If you're visiting from out of town you would probably want a club that's more generous with room comps so you could save money on your accomodations. However, if you're going to be playing at a casino near your home you would be more interested in which casino offers the best cashback rate and food comps. Whatever the situation, be sure to give most of your play to the casino that offers the best benefits for you and you'll soon be reaping the rewards of players club membership!

Sports Betting Expands Across The U.S. in 2020

by John Grochowski

The U.S. Supreme Court opened a brave new world to bettors and sports fans in May 2018 when it ruled the federal government may not discriminate between states by allowing sports betting in some while prohibiting it in others.

Since then, state legislatures throughout the United States have been busy, enacting legalized sports betting in nearly 20 states, with more sure to follow.

Until the Supreme Court cleared the way, Nevada had been the only state with legal, full-scale sports betting. Limited forms were legal in Delaware, Montana and through the state lottery in Oregon.

A dramatic change started soon after the Supreme Court decision. Within a few months, Mississippi and New Jersey had legal sports books open and running. So did Delaware, which expanded its minimal legal sports wagering to full-service books.

A year later, a number states had joined Nevada, Mississippi, New Jersey and Delaware. By late summer of 2019, you could place legal sports bets in West Virginia, New Mexico, Pennsylvania, Rhode Island, Arkansas and New York.

In addition, the following states and district had legalized sports betting and were awaiting either approval of regulations and / or licenses by state gaming boards or an effective date for their enabling acts: Montana (expected to go live by the end of 2019); Washington D.C. (legal as of May 2019, opening not yet announced); Indiana (expected to go live by the end of 2019); Iowa (legal as of May 2019, awaiting gaming commission licensing); Tennessee (legal effective July 2019, awaiting activation); Illinois (legal starting Jan. 1, 2020); New Hampshire (legal as of July 2019, awaiting activation).

One other state – Maine – has passed legislation to legalize sports betting, but the bill was vetoed by the state's governor. Others, including Michigan, Kentucky and Connecticut, have introduced but not yet passed bills. Others have impact studies underway.

The reason states had to wait for a Supreme Court ruling was the Professional and Amateur Sports Protection Act of 1992, which prohibited legalization of sports betting in any state that did not already have it. Nevada, with its full-scale sports gambling, and Montana, Delaware and Oregon, with their limited forms of sports wagering, were exempt from the restriction.

The major outside backers of PASPA were the major professional sports leagues and the National Collegiate Athletic Association. All had high-profile gambling scandals in the past and were worried a new proliferation of casinos would increase risk of gambling being associated with their sports. By the time of the bill, casinos had just begun to grow beyond their Nevada and New Jersey homes. Tribal casinos began spreading after the Indian Gaming Regulatory Act of 1988, riverboat casinos opened in Iowa and Illinois in 1990 and 1991, and Louisiana and Mississippi were right behind.

A former Princeton University and New York Knicks basketball star, Bill Bradley, was a U.S. Senator from New Jersey and was highly influential as the main Senate sponsor of the bill.

One provision gave New Jersey one year past enactment to legalize sports betting at Atlantic City casinos. The year passed and New Jersey did not act.

That's an odd little coincidence, because in the end, New Jersey did pass a bill legalizing sports gambling and it was New Jersey that went to court to upend the federal law.

Old hands who have wagered in Nevada or online already know the basics, but for those finding a new betting experience, here are a few of the basic ways to bet.

Point spreads: Most sports fans are familiar with spreads. On a sports book board, you might see a New England Patriots-Buffalo Bills NFL game listed with a +3.5 next to Buffalo. That means the Patriots are favored, and if you bet on them, they must win by more than 3.5 points for you to win the bet. If you bet on the Bills, you win if either they win the game or lose by less than 3.5 points.

An easy way to visualize is to add the point spread to the underdog's score. If the final score is Patriots 20, Bills 17, then for the purpose of the wager you add 3.5 points to the Bills' score. That makes it Bills 20.5, Patriots 20, and Bills bettors win.

Most sports books charge an extra 10 percent, called "vigorish" or just "vig" to make point-spread bets. To win $100, you need to bet $110, or to win $20, you must bet $22.

The 10-percent vig does not mean the house has a 10-percent edge. Instead, the house edge is 4.55 percent. Here's how it works:

Let's say you and I each bet $11 on opposite sides of a game. Between us, we risk $22. The winner gets his $11 back plus $10 in winnings, for a total of $21.

The house keeps $1. Divide that house profit by the $22 risked, then multiply by 100 to convert to percent, and you get 4.55 percent.

Oddsmakers set the spread to attract bettors to both sides of the wager. As long as somewhere close to the same amount of money is attracted on each side, the house is guaranteed a profit. That makes the spread not so much a prediction of what will happen in the game, but a reflection of bettor behavior.

Winning half your bets will not break even, it will leave you 4.55 percent in the red.

How successful at predicting games do you have to be to make a profit? The break-even point is just under 52.4 percent.

If I make 1,000 bets at $10 each, then with the 10 percent vig, I bet $11,000. If I win 524 bets, I keep the $5,764 I've risked on the winners, and collect $5,240 in winnings. That gives me $11,004, or a $4 profit per $11,000 risked at a 52.4-percent success rate.

A 52.4-percent win rate might not sound like too steep a hill to climb, but longtime sports bettors will tell you it's harder than it sounds. If it was easy, sports books would either go out of business or charge a steeper vig.

Over/under: This is a bet on the total points scored by two teams. If the over/under number on that Bills-Patriots game was set at 40.5, then over bettors would need the two teams to total 41 points or more, and under bettors would need 40 points or fewer.

As with point spreads, sports books typically collect a 10 percent vig on over/under.

Money line: This is a bet on who will win the game, with no point spreads involved. You'll see two numbers on the board, a negative number next to the favorite and a positive number next to the underdog. In our Patriots-Bills game, you might see -140 next to the Patriots and +120 next to the Bills.

Those represent payoff odds. To win $100 on the Patriots, you must bet $100, but if you bet $100 on the Bills, you can win $120.

No extra 10 percent is required on the money line. The different odds between favorite and underdog bets give the house its edge.

Money lines are available in all sports, and are the most common way to bet on baseball.

The house edge on the money line varies with the specific numbers. You can find a calculator at https://wizardofodds.com/games/sports-betting/straight-bet-calculator/. For the example above, in a game with a heavy favorite, if you saw the line at +300 and -400, the edge would be 4.76 percent. In a tossup, with both teams listed at -110, it would be 4.55 percent.

Parlays: There are times sports bettors think they've zeroed in on multiple winners and are tempted to bet parlays -- betting multiple teams, with all required to win for the bettor to collect. The temptation is in the payoffs. Let's use parlays on point-spread bets as an example.

Point-spread bets or over/unders pay at even-money, minus the 10 percent vigorish. Win three $11 point spread bets, and you win a total of $30.

What if you made just one $10 bet on a three-team parlay instead? Odds may vary from book to book, but at the Nevada books that are the model for states just beginning to offer sports betting, a three-team parlay usually pays at 6-1 odds, so your $10 bet would win $60.

That's tempting, but there's also danger. If any one of your team loses, you lose your $10. If you make three $11 bets instead and two teams win, you lose $11 on one game but win $10 on each of the other two, and have a $9 profit.

True odds of winning a three team parlay are 7-1. In each game, there are two possibilities -- win or lose. With three teams, the number of possibilities is 2x2x2, or 8. One of those is win-win-win, giving you one possible winner against seven possible losing outcomes.

By paying 6-1 instead of the true odds of 7-1, the house has a 12.5 percent edge. If you parlay four teams, the true odds are 15-1, a typical payoff is 10-1, and the house edge jumps all the way to 31.25 percent. Parlay five teams, and the true odds are 31-1. A 20-1 payoff yields a 34.38 percent house edge.

No matter how many teams you parlay, the house gets its edge by paying less than true odds. The closer the payoff is to true odds, the lower the house edge. It might pay to shop around at different casino sports books to find the best payoffs.

At any common pay table, you'll be facing a higher house edge on a parlay than on single-game bets. It's up to you to decide the possibility of a bigger payoff is worth risking an increased likelihood of losing.

For nearly 25 years, John Grochowski has been one of the most prolific gaming writers in the United States. He has written for casino industry professionals in Casino Executive and Casino Journal magazines, and for players in Casino Player, Strictly Slots and many other magazines. He is also the author of several best-selling books on gambling.

Are There Any Gambling Systems That Really Work?

by Jean Scott

The word "system" connected with gambling has a negative connotation and is often paired (incorrectly) with the words "loser" or "scam." However, you can't dismiss all systems. Blackjack card-counting and video poker correct-strategy play could be called systems—and they work. Even a system that tells you how to make the best bets in craps and which ones you should avoid helps you lose less. So, some systems can be valuable to gamblers.

So how can you spot the bad systems? This isn't always a simple task, but here are some of the characteristics of charlatan systems.

• It's easy! There's no easy way to beat casinos—never has been, never will be. If someone did happen to stumble on one that anyone could do, the casinos would change the games, the rules, or the policies to plug up the hole so fast your head would spin.

• It's secret! "Only 200 people in the whole world are being offered this surefire way to win at XXX." We get these letters in the mail frequently. Why us? As gambling-product buyers, our address is obviously on a lot of direct-mail lists. But I seriously doubt that only 200 people in the whole world are offered these "surefire" winning systems.

• You'll win every time you play! One ad on the Internet said its system was "like going to the bank for a withdrawal." Why is the seller sharing this information? Shouldn't he be out there madly making his own withdrawals before the casinos catch on?

• It costs more than $50. A number of years ago, before home computers were common and not much was written about gambling based on sound mathematics, some good blackjack systems for counting cards were worth the $100 or $200 being charged for them. However, today, a wealth of published information is available on every aspect of gambling and almost all of the really trustworthy materials (books, software, strategy aids) can be bought for less than $50, most of it much lower.

• It's a money-management system that promises you can beat a negative-expectation game. Most of these come-ons offer up complicated betting systems that don't (and can't) change the math over the long term. A few might change the win/loss pattern, so you'll have lots of small wins. But if you continue to use these systems, you'll lose; the fewer, but large, losing bets will wipe out all of those prior small wins.

• It's a progressive betting system based on raising your bets after a loss. In a popular version of this, called the Martingale, you double your bet after every losing hand. The dealer can't beat you every hand forever, goes the thinking. That's true, but there's a good chance he can beat you long enough for your system to crash, either by reaching casino bet limits or by your bankroll hitting zero. This is one of the surest systems to use if your goal is to go broke.

• It's a progressive betting system based on raising your bets after a win. Many progressive systems that require you to increase your wager modestly after a win can safely be used to break the monotony of flat betting. But again, they can't move a negative-expectation game into positive territory in the long term. You may have winning streaks, but over time, most assuredly, you'll lose an amount close to what the casino edge says you should, just as you would have if you'd been flat betting.

• It has quit-and-start-again requirements that ignore proven mathematical theories about the long term. Short-term goals can be a way of managing your bankroll and your state of mind. However, short-term sessions, all taken together, do add up to the long term, whether you want to believe it or not. The machines, cards, and dice don't know whether this is your first hand in a new session or your thousandth hand in an ongoing one. Thus, the odds of the game don't change.

• It advocates changing your machine or sizing or placing your bets only at specific times, again ignoring math principles. Some valid techniques are associated with this "choice" feature—blackjack card-counting, for example—but they're based on sound computer-validated principles of mathematics. The arbitrarily chosen systems have no math basis. Wait for a crapshooter to make three passes, then jump in? The odds against you aren't changed. Switch machines after you've won $150? In four hours of play on a slot machine, whether done all at one machine in one session or over a whole day of jumping from machine to machine, the casino edge remains the same.

I've seen scores, maybe hundreds, of systems over my 35 years of casino gambling. A few are useful. Some are harmless, but a waste of money to buy. But most of them are cruel, giving false hope that will be disastrous to your wallet. Don't be taken in; most of these system promoters are selling dreams and fantasies. Nothing takes the place of study, practice, and discipline.

With all that said, I'll now state that as long as you aren't fooled into believing that these "wait" or "jump-around" or "start-and-stop" techniques will make you a long-term winner at negative-expectation games, many of these snake-oil systems do have one redeeming factor.

I hear you: "I can't believe you said that, Ms. Stick-to-the-Math!"

It's true. I'm in favor of any system that slows down your rate of play on negative-expectation games. The more downtime you can schedule, the less you'll lose. When you're doing something other than putting money at risk, you're saving money. But you don't have to spend your hard-earned money for some complicated system advertised in a magazine to do this. Make up your own system! You'd be surprised how interesting that can be. Here are some examples.

Crapshooters bet only when an attractive person of the opposite sex has the dice; if an ugly shooter comes up, just stand by.

If you lose three spins straight on a slot machine, punish the machine by cashing out and looking for a friendlier one.

If you're playing video poker and lose your first bill in, put the machine in "time out" and play the next one for 15 minutes before you go back to the naughty one.

Play roulette only if there's a blonde dealer.

Sit down at a blackjack table only if the dealer looks older than you. Depending on your age, you might have to shop around a long time.

The point is, whenever you aren't actually in action at a negative-expectation game, you're "winning."

Jean Scott is a retired teacher who never stopped teaching, just switching her subject from high school English to smart casino gambling. She and her husband Brad have been extremely successful gamblers for 33 years. She has continuously shared their secrets on TV, in countless articles, and presently in the blog "Frugal Vegas" you can access at http://jscott.lvablog.com/. She has written five books in the Frugal Gambler series and the previous excerpt is from the "Show Me the Money" chapter of Jean's newest book: THE FRUGAL GAMBLER CASINO GUIDE, which updates the information in her previous books to help gamblers adjust to the changing casino environment.

Slot Machines

by Steve Bourie

Virtually anyone who visits a casino, even for the first time, is familiar with a slot machine and how it operates: just put in your money, pull the handle and wait a few seconds to see if you win. It isn't intimidating like table games where you really need some knowledge of the rules before you play and it's this basic simplicity that accounts for much of the success of slot machines in the modern American casino.

As a matter of fact, the biggest money-maker for casinos is the slot machine with approximately 65 percent of the average casino's profits being generated by slot machine play. As an example, in Nevada's fiscal year ending June 30, 2019 the total win by all of the state's casinos was a little more than $11.9 billion. Of that amount, $7.80 billion, or slightly more than 65 percent, was from electronic machine winnings.

With this in mind, you must ask yourself, "can I really win money by playing slot machines?" The answer is a resounding yes...and no. First the "no" part: in simplest terms a slot machine makes money for the casino by paying out less money than it takes in. In some states, such as Nevada and New Jersey, the minimum amount to be returned is regulated. In Nevada the minimum is 75 percent and in New Jersey it's 83 percent. However, if you look at the slot payback percentages for those particular states in this book you will see that the actual average payback percentages are much higher. In New Jersey it's close to 91 percent and in Nevada it's slightly more than 93 percent. Even though the actual paybacks are higher than the law requires, you can still see that on average for every $1 you play in an Atlantic City slot machine you will lose 9¢ and in a Las Vegas slot machine you will lose 7¢. Therefore, it doesn't take a rocket scientist to see that if you stand in front of a slot machine and continue to pump in your money, eventually, you will lose it all. On average, it will take you longer to lose it in Las Vegas rather than Atlantic City, but the result is still the same: you will go broke.

Gee, sounds kind of depressing, doesn't it? Well, cheer up because now we go on to the "yes" part. But, before we talk about that, let's first try to understand how slot machines work. All modern slot machines contain a random number generator (RNG) which is used to control the payback percentage for each machine. When a casino orders a slot machine the manufacturer will have a list of percentage paybacks for each machine and the casino must choose one from that list. For example, a manufacturer may have 10 chips available for one machine that range from a high of 98% to as low as 85%. All of these chips have been inspected and approved by a gaming commission and the casino is free to choose whichever chip it wants for that particular brand of machine.

In almost all instances, the casino will place a higher denomination chip in a higher denomination machine. In other words, the penny machines will get the chips programmed to pay back around 85% and the $25 machines will get the chips programmed to pay back around 98%. A casino can always change the payback percentage, but in order to do that it usually must go back to the manufacturer to get a new RNG that is programmed with the new percentage. For this reason, most casinos rarely change their payback percentages unless there is a major revision in their marketing philosophy.

And what exactly is a random number generator? Well, it's a little computer chip that is constantly working (as its name implies) to generate number combinations on a random basis. It docs this extremely fast and is capable of producing hundreds of combinations each second. When you pull the handle, or push the spin button, the RNG stops and the combination it stops at is used to determine where the reels will stop in the pay window. Unlike video poker machines, you have no way of knowing what a slot machine is programmed to pay back just by looking at it. The only way to tell is by knowing what is programmed into the RNG.

As an example of the differences in RNG payout percentages I have listed below some statistics concerning various slot manufacturers' payback percentages in their slot machines. Normally, this information isn't available to the public, but it is sometimes printed in various gaming industry publications and that is where I found it. The list shows the entire range of percentages that can be programmed into each machine:

AGS	
Fu Nan Fu Nu	86.00% - 95.00%
River Dragons	86.00% - 95.00%
Ainsworth Game Technology	
El Toro Wild	85.00% - 96.00%
Kong of Skull Island	85.00% - 96.00%
Mustang	82.00% - 96.00%
PAC MAN	86.00% - 94.00%
Aristocrat	
African Storm	87.86% - 94.84%
Britney Spears	86.00% - 96.00%
The Walking Dead	88.50% - 93.50%
Buffalo Diamond	88.00% - 95.00%
Wild Panda	88.00% - 95.00%
Sharknado	87.82% - 90.01%
Everi	
Smokin Hot Stuff Wicked Wheel	88.00% - 98.00%

Aruze Gaming

999.9 Gold Wheel Ultra Stack: Lion Gold	87.58% - 96.40%
999.9 Gold Wheel Ultra Stack: Dragon Gold	87.58% - 96.40%
Money Rush	87.02% - 97.94%

Scientific Games

Black & White 5 Times Pay	84.49% - 96.72%
Black & White Sevens	87.00% - 95.00%
Blazing 7's Double (reel)	88.00% - 95.98%
Cash Spin	85.72% - 88.38%
Heidi's Bier Haus	86.07% - 95.44%
Hot Shot Progressive	85.41% - 96.01%
Hot Spin	87.59% - 89.99%
Money Wheel	85.38% - 96.08%
Triple Cash Wheel with Quick Hit	85.49% - 93.95%
Spin & Win (3-Reel)	83.24% - 94.00%
Cash Crop	86.36% - 94.92%
James Bond: Goldfinger	85.92% - 94.96%
Quick Hit Ultra Pays	85.49% - 95.97%
Ultimate Fire Link	85.23% - 95.99%

IGT

Blake Shelton	85.90% - 96.00%
Diamond Jackpots	87.90% - 96.50%
Elephant King	85.03% - 98.04%
Enchanted Unicorn	85.00% - 98.00%
Gong Xi Fa Cai	85.09% - 96.01%
Ocean Magic	86.00% - 96.00%
Red White and Blue	85.03% - 97.45%
Texas Tea	87.00% - 97.00%
Wolf Run 2: Into The Wild	85.00% - 98.00%
IC Money	85.20% - 97.02%
Zuma	84.15% - 94.16%
Sphinx 3D	86.00% - 92.00%
Wheel of Fortune: Triple Double Diamond	85.90% - 96.00%

Konami Gaming

African Diamond	82.13% - 96.03%
Big Africa	85.50% - 98.10%
China Shores Great Stacks	82.00% - 96.00%
Triple Sparkle	82.00% - 96.00%

Incredible Technologies

Crazy Money Deluxe	85.20% - 94.00%
Money Roll	85.15% - 94.00%
Money Rain Deluxe	85.10% - 94.06%
Clinko Winning Wall	85.08% - 94.08%

Once again, keep in mind that casinos generally set their slot paybacks based on each machine's denomination. Therefore, penny machines will probably be set towards the lower number and $5-$25 machines will be set towards the higher number.

Okay, now let's get back to the "yes" part. Yes, you can win money on slot machines by using a little knowledge, practicing some money management and, mostly, having lots of luck. First, the knowledge part. You need to know what kind of player you are and how much risk you are willing to take. Do you want to go for the giant progressive jackpot that could make you a millionaire in an instant or would you be content walking away just a few dollars ahead?

An example of a wide-area progressive machine is Nevada's Megabucks where the jackpot starts at $10 million. These $1 machines are located at more than 125 Nevada casinos around the state and are linked together by a computer. It's fine if that's the kind of machine you want to play, but keep in mind that the odds are fairly astronomical of you hitting that big jackpot. Also, the payback percentage is lower on these machines than the average $1 machine. During Nevada's fiscal year ending June 30, 2019 Megabucks averaged a little more than 87% payback while the typical $1 machine averaged a little less than 94%. So, be aware that if you play these machines you'll win fewer small payouts and it will be very difficult to leave as a winner. Unless, of course, you hit that big one! If you really like to play the wide-area progressive machines your best bet is probably to set aside a small percentage of your bankroll (maybe 10 to 15 percent) for chasing that big jackpot and saving the rest for the regular machines.

One other thing you should know about playing these wide-area progressives is that on most of them, including Megabucks, you will receive your jackpot in equal payments over a period of years (usually 25). You can avoid this, however, by playing at one of the casinos that link slot machines at their own properties and will pay you in one lump sum. Be sure to look on the machine before playing to see how it says you will be paid for the jackpot.

Knowledge also comes into play when deciding how many coins to bet. You should always look at the payback schedule posted on the machine to see if a bonus is payed for playing the maximum number of coins that the machine will accept. For example, if it's a two-coin machine and the jackpot payout is 500 coins when you bet one coin, but it pays you 1,200 coins when you bet two coins, then that machine is paying you a 200-coin bonus for playing the maximum number of coins and you may want to bet the maximum two coins to take advantage of that bonus. However, if it's a two-coin machine that will pay you 500 coins for a one-coin bet and 1,000 coins for a two-coin bet, then there is no advantage to making the maximum bet on that machine and you should only bet the minimum amount. To see more on this subject, watch my video titled "The Slot Machine - When to bet Maximum Coins" on our YouTube channel at www.youtube.com/americancasinoguide.

Knowledge of which casinos offer the best payback percentages is also helpful. When available, we print that information in this book to help you decide where to go for the best return on your slot machine dollar. You may want to go to the Las Vegas Strip to see some of the sites, but take a look at the slot machine payback percentages for the Strip-area casinos in the Las Vegas section and you'll see that you can get better returns for your slot machine dollar by playing at the off-Strip area casinos.

The final bit of knowledge you need concerns players clubs. Every major casino has a players club and you should make it a point to join it before you insert your first coin. It doesn't cost anything to join and as a member you will be able to earn complimentaries from the casinos in the form of cash, food, shows, drinks, rooms or other "freebies." Just make sure you don't get carried away and bet more than you're comfortable with just to earn some extra "comps." Ideally, you want to get "comps" for gambling that you were going to do anyway and not be pressured into betting more than you had planned.

Now let's talk about money management. The first thing you have to remember when playing slot machines is that there is no skill involved. Unlike blackjack or video poker, there are no decisions you can make that will affect whether you win or lose. It is strictly luck, or the lack of it, that will determine whether or not you win. However, when you are lucky enough to get ahead (even if it's just a little) that's where the money management factor comes in. As stated earlier, the longer you stand in front of a machine and put in your money, the more likely you are to go broke. Therefore, there is only one way you can walk away a winner and that's to make sure that when you do win, you don't put it all back in. You really need to set a "win goal" for yourself and to stop when you reach it. A realistic example would be a "win goal" of roughly 25 percent of your bankroll. If you started with $400, then you should stop if you win about $100. The "win goal" you decide on is up to you, but keep in mind that the higher your goal, the harder it will be to reach it, so be practical.

And what if you should happen to reach your goal? Take a break! Go have a meal, see a show, visit the lounge for a drink or even just take a walk around the casino. You may have the urge to keep playing, but if you can just take a break from the machines, even it's just for a short time, you'll have the satisfaction of leaving as a winner. If, later on, you get really bored and find that you just have to go back to the machines you can avoid a total loss by not risking more than half of your winnings and by playing on smaller denomination machines. If you made your winnings on $1 machines, move down to quarters. If you won on quarters, move down to nickels. The idea now is basically to kill some time and have a little fun knowing that no matter what happens you'll still leave as a winner.

And now, let's move on to luck. As stated previously, the ultimate decider in whether or not you win is how lucky you are. But, is there anything you can do to help you choose a "winning" machine? Not really, because there is no such thing. Remember, in the long run, no machine will pay out more than it takes in. There are, however, some things you could try to help you find the more generous machines and avoid the stingy ones. Keep in mind that all slot machine payback percentages shown in this book are averages.

Like everything else in life, slot machines have good cycles where they pay out more than average and bad cycles where they pay out less than average. Ultimately, what you want to find is a machine in a good cycle. Of course if I knew how to find that machine I wouldn't be writing this story, instead I'd be standing in front of it with a $100 bill in my hand getting ready to play it. So, I guess you'll have to settle for my two recommendations as to how you might be able to make your slot bankroll last longer.

First, is the "accounting" method. With this method you start with a pre-determined number of credits and after playing them though one time, you take an accounting of your results. If you have more than you started with you stay at that machine and start another cycle. Just keep doing this until the machine returns less than you started with. As an example, let's say you start with a $10 credit voucher. After making 10 $1 bets you see how many credits you have left on the machine. If it's more than $10 you start over again with another 10 $1 bets and then do another accounting. If, after any accounting, you get back less than the $10 bankroll you started with, stop playing and move on to a different machine. This is an especially good method because you have to slow down your play to take periodic accountings and you will always have an accurate idea of how well you are doing.

The other method is even simpler and requires no math. It's called the "baseball" method and is based on the principle of three strikes and you're out. Just play a machine until it loses three times in a row, then move on to another machine. Both of these methods will prevent you from losing a lot in a machine that is going through a bad cycle. To see more on this subject, watch my video titled "10 Tips To Stretch Your Slot Machine Bankroll" on our YouTube channel at www.youtube.com/americancasinoguide

Slot Machine Trends - 2020

by John Grochowski

Slot machines have paid higher percentages back to players on higher denomination games for decades.

Game manufacturers and casinos would love to be able to signal that to players, who can't tell from the outside which games pay more than others.

Perhaps IGT will kick off a trend with its Fortune Link progressives, which started rolling into casinos in 2019 and should reach nationwide distribution in 2020. With initial themes Feline Fortune and Egyptian Fortune, Fortune Link games show players on their welcome screens just how playing higher denominations can benefit them.

A word of caution: Even though payback percentages are higher at high denoms, you put more money at risk and have higher average losses. Don't bet more than you can afford in the quest for higher payback percentages.

That aside, Fortune Link games tell you up front that if you play higher denomination games, you trigger the Fortune bonus more easily. One configuration was spotted that takes you to the bonus with six Fortune Link symbols on 1- or 2-cent games; five symbols on 5- or 10-cent games, and a mere four symbols on $1 and $2 games.

Machines have multiple denominations. You touch the screen to choose your coin denomination and your Fortune Link trigger requirements.

In the feature, the Fortune Link symbols lock in place and you get three respins to try to add more to the collection. If a respin adds on or more of the symbols, the respin meter resets to three – you can go on respinning until you either fill the screen with Fortune Links or go three respins in a row without adding any.

At the end, you get a bonus for every Fortune Link symbol on the screen.

During bonus rounds on video slots – and on those newer reel slots that have bonuses – you have the opportunity to win credits without risking extra money. Needing fewer symbols to trigger a bonus means higher-denomination players have more bonus play and less time when they are risking money.

If all else is equal, the difference in bonus triggers would mean higher payback percentages at higher coin denominations. We don't know that all else is equal, but revenue reports in various states consistently show higher paybacks at higher denominations.

Fortune Link games are among the latest and greatest to look for in 2020, but the slot machine landscape is ever-changing as manufacturers engage in a constant game of "Can you top this?"

As you explore slot floors, check out these new offerings:

Clinko games, Incredible Technologies: Clinko: King of Bling and Clinko: Winning Wall both feature the Clinko bonus trigger. A Clinko ball falls from the top of the screen on random spins, drops peg to peg, and if it lands on an icon for a game feature, it could bring pumped up symbols, added wild symbols or multipliers – all good news for your credit meter.

The first is the latest version of King of Bling, a longtime Incredible Technologies favorite with a nod toward hip-hop. The base game in the really gets hopping in the Pump Up da Club bonus, where players and a DJ can scratch the record for bigger wins. With three progressive-levels, it's a thrill-packed game.

Winning Wall also has three progressive levels. It adds to the intrigue by enabling you to win on the wall. Here, the Clinko pegs include jackpot icons. It takes only one Minor peg to win that pot, while you win the Major by accumulating two and the Grand by accumulating three pegs.

Asian themes, multiple manufacturers: The growth of games featuring the sights and sounds of the Far East is among the hottest trends going, and not just because of the enormous growth of overseas markets such as Macau. Americans flock to Asian-themed games, too. Here are some to watch:

Sky Dragons and Fireworks Festival, Incredible Technologies: Fireworks Festival is a 50-line game that makes explosive use of Incredible's Stack 2 Stack game dynamic. When two stacks of fireworks symbols touch, they pop, bang and sizzle to reveal instant credit awards. Players could also win up to 20 free spins.

The Red Envelope feature offers the chance to win credit awards. When Red Envelopes scatter on the reels, players may pick all but one, with a prize behind each. So if there are five envelopes on the screen, you have four picks to boost your bankroll.

Sky Dragons starts with a typical grid of five reels, each three symbols deep, but when dragons appear in the sky, they can expand the reels, with 5-by-7 as the maximum. All those extra symbols create extra opportunities to win on a game with three progressives and up to 20 free spins.

Jin Ji Bao Xi – Rising Fortunes, Scientific Games: The No. 1 game in Asia, Jin Ji Bao Xi making its North American debut with 5-reel, 243 ways game. Rising Fortunes includes the popular ALL UP bet structure where players can make an extra wager to buy higher-paying symbols.

One game highlight is the Jin Ji Bao Xi Feature where players pick icons to win one of four jackpots.

If six or more Red Gong symbols displaying credit prizes land on the reels, a Feature Selection is triggered and you can choose your bonus. The sum of the credit prizes creates the Shou Bonus, one of the feature selection options.

Players also can choose between a Top Up Bonus and Free Games Bonus where eight free games are awarded. During free games, players can win additional free games while each Gold Gong symbol that lands on the reels award the Shou Bonus.

In the Top Up Bonus, a lock and spin feature, Gold Gong symbols award the Shou Bonus and lucky Green Gong symbols award the sum of all Gong symbols, resulting in a rising fortune.

Shou Hu Shen Xtreme Jackpots, American Gaming Systems: The Asian-themed Shou Hu Shen is based on the good luck and guardian lions along with four progressive jackpot levels. Together, they promise fun and the chance to win big.

Featuring fireworks and sparks animations that add excitement to gameplay, Shou Hu Shen can award massive progressive jackpots. The Jackpot Pick Bonus is randomly triggered any time a Wild symbol lands on the reels during base-game play. Players touch and pick from 12 Lucky Fu symbols until they get three matching progressive symbols to win one of the four jackpots.

During the Free Games Bonus, the number of free spins that can be won depends on the reel configuration selected by the player – 243 ways to win gets 15 free spins; 1024 ways to win gets 10 free spins; and 3125 ways to win gets five free spins.

Pop culture themes: Slot makers have been mining TV, movies, music and board games for decades, with themes including Wheel of Fortune, Monopoly, Elvis and the Beach Boys.

Every year brings new Wheel of Fortune games, and slot players should be sure to look for the likes of Penn and Teller and The Game of Life, too.

Wheel of Fortune 4D Featuring Vanna White, IGT: No new year would be complete with out a new spin on Wheel of Fortune This 75-payline video slot comes on IGT's new CrystalCurve True 4D gaming machine.

The fourth dimension in "True 4D" is touch. You can reach out to three-dimensional images and get a touch sensation. Instead of touching the screen or pushing a button to spin a prize wheel, you can reach out to the 3D image in front of the screen and give the wheel a spin.

You can bet from 100 to 500 coins, so on a penny machine your bet range is $1-$5. With a bet of at least 300 credits, you qualify for a big-money wide-area progressive jackpot. For those unfamiliar with the terminology, wide-area progressives link multiple casinos so that portions of wagers at different casinos help build the same pot.

Among the game features are original audio and video featuring TV show hostess Vanna White. When you reach out to that 3D wheel to give it a spin, Vanna cheers you on.

The Game of Life – Career Day, Scientific Games: WMS Gaming, which now is under the Scientific Games corporate umbrella, had success with it's the Game of Life slots a while back, Now, under license from board game owner Hasbro, Scientific Games creates a new slot adventure with a new three-reel game, The Game of Life – Career Day.

Players spin the reels and travel through life while collecting credit prizes, bonuses, and jackpots. Career Day is a 3-reel, 9-line game on the TwinStar J43 with iReels cabinet. The game boasts a life-changing single-level, wide-area progressive jackpot that can be won in the base game and is part of Scientific Games' Cash Connection or Reel Adventures links.

The game's centerpiece is the Game of Life Bonus where players are assigned one of four careers - a firefighter, pro athlete, construction worker or culinary chef. You then spin for paydays, raises and spins of a wheel that award moves around the game board.

Stops along the way award credit prizes, additional spins of the wheel, and extra bonuses such as the Weekend Getaway with free spins where reel 2 is Wild and all pays are multiplied by three; or the Groundhog Day Bonus where the reels spin and stop until a winning combination is awarded.

The goal is to reach the Retirement Island Bonus board game where even more prizes, multipliers, and bonuses are available.

Penn & Teller, Everi: The magical duo team up in a 9-payline slot with three mechanical reels, targeted at 25-cent and $1 play.

Loaded with an innovative feature trigger and eight interactive bonuses, players get constant assistance from famous stage magicians Penn & Teller as they wonder what will happen next. Game play incorporates some of Penn & Teller's most famous tricks, including Vanish a Rabbit, Miser's Dream, and Shadows. And Everi has added some magic of its own.

In a nudge bonus, a reel nudge may be triggered after any losing reel stop where one "Penn," "&" or "Teller" lands one position away from a winning progressive combination or where one wheel symbol is one position away from awarding the wheel bonus. Then presto! The symbol nudges into place.

Smokin' Hot Stuff Wicked Wheel, Everi: Hot Stuff, the little devil of comic book fame, was a red-hot winner in the original Smokin' Hot Stuff slot. Now the mischievous imp with his asbestos diaper and trusty trident returns in a 243 ways to win slot, perfect for pennies, packed with multipliers, a progressive pick bonus and progressive jaclpots available at all bet levels

The progressive pick bonus is triggered randomly after any base game spin. Players pick from 25 coins to reveal either a progressive jackpot or pitchfork symbol. Hot Stuff removes the lowest remaining jackpot each time his pitchfork is revealed, thus guaranteeing higher prizes.

Extended game families: When a slot theme really resonates with players and becomes a popular favorite, you can rely on the manufacturer developing a follow-up game. Sometimes they develop into whole families of games.

Here are some newer games that follow up on player favorites:

Mayan Chief Great Stacks, Konami Gaming: Mayan Chief, a Konami favorite, gets a fresh look with six reels, each five symbols deeo, on the curved Concerto Crescent and tall Concerto Stack cabinets.

Mayan Chief Great Stacks is a 60-line game that features Action Stacked Symbols and top free game awards. Action Stacked Symbols are hidden at first, but once all reels are stopped they transform into matching symbols – part of the fun is waiting to see if your Action Stacks will match symbols already on the reels to form winning combos.

A free games feature gives you up to 15 free spins with a 2x multiplier. And for extra bonus excitement, players get to choose their event in the Balance of Fortune feature. When Balance of fortune launches, you can choose regular free games, a random credit prize, or super free games combinations with different combinations of more or fewer free games matched with lower or higher multipliers.

Lightning Zap Jackpots, Everi: With no reels, no paylines and no pay tables, Everi creates a new play experience that builds on the original Lightning Zap game.

Everi calls the jackpot games "innovation on video slots," available on three game themes: Electric Rush, Power Burst and Super Charge. Each has varying volatility levels and different features, and the series incorporates five linked progressives.

How does it work with no pay tables? Your prizes can vary. Check out the Electric Rush feature where an orb zaps everything to increase prizes by a random multiplier, then zaps away at prizes. In the Power Burst feature, the orb turns into a magnet and sucks in anywhere from four to 22 prizes. Each prize can be upgraded by a random multiplier. In the Super Charge feature, the orb selects four to eight prizes and increases them up to 1,000 times.

Latest innovations: Looking for new ways to play? Try these recent developments:

Blazing X Game Series, Scientific Games: With two game themes – Blazing X – Asia and Blazing X – Las Vegas, this innovative series ramps up player anticipation for the possibility of Blazing X Multipliers on each spin.

Both themes are five-reel, 40-line video slots. There are four progressive jackpot levels available in a jackpot pick feature in which players touch the screen not only to determine their jackpot level but also for a multiplier that can put jackpot winnings into hyperdrive.

The Blazing X Feature, triggered when a Wild Banner symbol lands on reel 3, awards a 2x multiplier for three spins. For every Wild Banner symbol that lands during the three spins, the Blazing X multiplier increases to 3x, 5x, 10x and up to 25x. Blazing X also can be triggered during a Free Games Bonus. And if the Free Games Bonus is awarded during the Blazing X Feature, the current Blazing X multiplier is applied to all Free Games wins. During the free games, additional Wild Banner symbols achieved within three spins increases the multiplier. A Blazing X multiplier streak can really set your credit meter soaring

Rakin' Bacon Xtreme Jackpots, American Gaming Systems: A cherubic pig in a gold coin-filled room is a central figure in this five-reel game with a multi-level progressive that's packed full of player-favorite features, including free spins, multipliers and scatter pays.

As the wins add up, the golden pig gets fatter and fatter, until the player wins the Free Game Bonus and the golden pig explodes to reveals a pick screen. That screen gives you the chance to choose three different reel layouts for up to 3125 ways to win.

Additional free spins can be won during the Free Game Bonus, making this game even more potentially lucrative. During the randomly awarded Jackpot Pick feature, you touch and select icons until you match three of a kind, which awards a guaranteed jackpot pay.

For nearly 25 years, John Grochowski has been one of the most prolific gaming writers in the United States. He has written for casino industry professionals in Casino Executive and Casino Journal magazines, and for players in Casino Player, Strictly Slots and many other magazines. He is also the author of several best-selling books on gambling.

Video Poker

by Steve Bourie

Okay, who knows the main difference between video poker and slot machines? C'mon now, raise your hands if you think you know it. If you said "a slot machine is a game of luck and video poker is a game of skill" then you are correct! When you play a slot machine there is no decision you can make which will affect the outcome of the game. You put in your money; pull the handle; and hope for the best. In video poker, however, it is your skill in playing the cards which definitely affects the outcome of the game.

Okay, who knows the other major difference between video poker and slot machines? Well, you're right again if you said "you never know what percentage a slot machine is set to pay back, but you can tell a video poker machine's payback percentage just by looking at it." Of course if you knew that answer then you also knew that video poker machines almost always offer you better returns than slot machines (provided you make the right playing decisions).

Now for those of you who didn't know the answers to those two questions, please read on. You others can skip the rest of this story as I am sure you're eager to get back to your favorite video poker machine.

First, let's cover the basics. Video poker has virtually the same rules as a game of five card draw poker. The only difference is that you have no opponent to beat and you can't lose more than your initial bet. First, you deposit from one to five coins in the machine to make your bet. You are then shown five cards on the video screen and your goal is to try to make the best poker hand possible from those cards. Since it is a draw game, you are given one opportunity to improve your hand. This is done by allowing you to discard from one, up to all five cards from your original hand. Of course, you don't have to discard any if you don't want to. After choosing which cards you want to keep (by pushing the button below each card), you then push the deal button and the machine will replace all of the other cards with new cards. Based on the resulting final hand the machine will then pay you according to the pay schedule posted on the machine. Naturally, the better your hand, the higher the amount the machine will pay you back.

That's pretty much how a video poker machine works from the outside, but what about the inside? Well, I had a few questions about that so I visited International Game Technology, which is the world's largest manufacturer of video poker machines (as well as slot machines), in January 2001 and spoke to their chief software engineer, James Vasquez. Here's what Jim had to say in answer to some questions about how his company's machines work:

Let's talk about the difference between video poker and slot machines. It's my understanding that with video poker you can't control the number of winning and losing combinations programmed into the computer chip, instead its based on a 52-card deck with a fixed number of combinations. Is that correct?

Vasquez: Yes, assuming there are no wild cards.

When the cards are dealt is it done on a serial basis where it's similar to cards coming off the top of a deck? Or, parallel where there are five cards dealt face up and one card is unseen underneath each of the initial five cards?

Vasquez: It's serial and the five later cards aren't determined until there is more player interaction at the time of the draw.

They aren't determined at the time of the deal?

Vasquez: No. They're determined at the time of the draw. That varies with the jurisdictional regulation actually. Some lottery jurisdictions tell you that you have to draw all 10 at once. Different jurisdictions write into their rules how they want it done, specifically on poker, because it's a simpler game and they understand it. They say they either want all 10 done at once, or however they want.

How is it done in Nevada? All ten at once, or five and five?

IGT: In Nevada it's five and five.

The talk with Jim Vasquez confirmed that in most regulated jurisdictions video poker machines use a Random Number Generator to shuffle a 52-card deck and then choose five cards to display to the player. (By the way, when played without wild cards, there are exactly 2,598,960 unique five-card poker hands that can be dealt to a player.) Then, when the deal button is pushed, the next group of cards is chosen and dealt to the player.

One point must be made here regarding random outcomes in video poker machines. Please note that gaming regulations always require video poker machines to have random outcomes. You should be aware that there are casinos operating in places that do not have gaming regulations. Examples are cruise ships which operate in international waters, some Indian reservations that are not subject to state regulations, and virtually all Internet casinos. You should also be aware that the technology exists for machines to be set so they do not act randomly. These machines can be actually programmed to avoid giving the players better hands and they wind up giving the house a much bigger advantage. These machines are illegal in Nevada, New Jersey, Colorado and all other states that pattern their gaming regulations after those states. You may, however, come across them in unregulated casinos.

One final point you should keep in mind - IGT is not the only manufacturer of video poker machines. There are quite a few others and they may engineer their machines to work in a different manner. Their RNG may not stop in the same way and their draw cards may be dealt differently. IGT, however, is by far the largest and it is the type of machine you will most often encounter in a casino.

Now that you understand how a video poker machine works let's learn how to pick out the best paying ones. In the beginning of this story it was mentioned that "you can tell a video poker machine's payback percentage just by looking at it." That's true, but it takes a little bit of knowledge to know the difference among all the different types of machines. An example of some of the different machines available are: Jacks or Better, Bonus, Double Bonus, Double Double Bonus, Joker Poker and Deuces Wild. To make it even more confusing, not only are there different machines, but each of those machines can have a different pay schedule for the same hand.

Fortunately, every video poker machine's payback percentage can be mathematically calculated. Not only does this let you know which machines offer you the best return, but it also tells you the best playing decisions to make on that particular machine based on the odds of that combination occurring. The bad news, however, is that it's fairly impossible to do on your own so you'll have to either buy a book that lists all of the percentages and strategies or buy a computer program that does the work for you. Take a look at the tables on the next few pages and you'll see some different types of video poker games and their payback percentages (when played with maximum coin and perfect strategy). For those of you with a computer there are several software programs on the market that can determine the exact payback percentage for any video poker machine. They retail for prices from $29.95 to $59.95, but can be purchased at discounted prices at www.americancasinoguidebook.com/video-poker-software.html. Besides calculating percentages, they also allow you to play different types of machines and analyze hands to show you the expected return for each play. You can set these games to automatically show you the best decision, or to just warn you if you make a wrong decision.

If you have no desire to get quite that serious about learning video poker then I'll try to provide some general tips to help you out. First, you'll need to find the machines that offer you the highest returns. One of the best is the 9/6 Jacks or Better machine. Of course, you're probably wondering "what is a 9/6 Jacks or Better machine?" Well, the Jacks or Better part refers to the fact that you won't win anything from the machine unless you have at least a pair of Jacks. The 9/6 part refers to the payback schedule on this kind of machine.

As stated earlier, each machine can have a different payback schedule and there are at least 20 different kinds of payback schedules available on Jacks or Better machines. In Las Vegas the two most common Jacks or Better machines you will find are 8/5 and 9/6. Here's a comparison of their pay schedules (per coin, for five-coin play):

Hand	9/6	8/5
Royal Flush	800	800
Straight Flush	50	50
4-of-a-Kind	25	25
Full House	**9**	**8**
Flush	**6**	**5**
Straight	4	4
3-of-a-Kind	3	3
Two Pair	2	2
Jacks or Better	1	1

As you can see, the schedules are identical except for the better payoffs on the 9/6 machines for Flushes and Full Houses. The payback on a 9/6 machine is 99.5% with perfect play, while the 8/5 machines return 97.3% with perfect play. Of course, it doesn't make any sense to play an 8/5 machine if a 9/6 machine is available. Yet, you'll often see lots of people playing an 8/5 when a 9/6 can often be found in the same casino. The reason they do that is because they don't know any better; you do. Always look for the 9/6 machines. They can be usually found in most downtown Las Vegas casinos at the quarter level and in many Strip casinos at denominations of $1 and higher. In other states they won't be found as easily, and sometimes, not at all.

One other common machine you will come across is an 8/5 Jacks or Better progressive. These feature the same 8/5 pay table as above except for the royal flush which pays a jackpot amount that is displayed on a meter above the machine. The jackpot will continue to build until someone hits a royal flush; then it will reset and start to build again. When the progressive jackpot (for five coins) on a 25¢ machine first starts out at $1,000 the payback is only 97.30%, but when it reaches $2,166.50, the payback is 100%.

Another good tip is to restrict your play to the same kind of machine all the time. Each video poker machine has its own particular strategy and what works best on a Jacks or Better machine is definitely much different from what works best on a Deuces Wild machine. I usually only play 9/6 Jacks or Better machines because that is what I practice on and I automatically know the best decision to make all the time. Keep in mind that when you calculate the payback percentage for a video poker machine the number you arrive at is based on perfect play. As an example, a 9/6 Jacks or Better video poker machine has a 99.5% payback with perfect play. This means that, theoretically, it will return $99.50 for every $100 played in the machine, but only if the player makes the correct decision every time. If you make mistakes, and most players do, the return to the casino will be higher. If you play several different kinds of machines it becomes increasingly harder to remember the correct play and you will make mistakes. Therefore, it only makes sense to memorize the correct decisions for one kind of machine and to always play on that same kind of machine (of course, in order to learn those proper strategies, you may want to buy that book or software).

Jacks or Better Pay Table Variations

(Per coin with maximum coin played and perfect strategy)

9/6

Royal Flush	800
Straight Flush	50
4-of-a-kind	25
Full House	***9***
Flush	***6***
Straight	4
3-of-a-kind	3
2 Pair	2
Jacks or Better	1
Payback	**99.54%**

9/5

Royal Flush	800
Straight Flush	50
4-of-a-kind	25
Full House	***9***
Flush	***5***
Straight	4
3-of-a-kind	3
2 Pair	2
Jacks or Better	1
Payback	**98.45%**

8/6

Royal Flush	800
Straight Flush	50
4-of-a-kind	25
Full House	***8***
Flush	***6***
Straight	4
3-of-a-kind	3
2 Pair	2
Jacks or Better	1
Payback	**98.39%**

8/5

Royal Flush	800
Straight Flush	50
4-of-a-kind	25
Full House	***8***
Flush	***5***
Straight	4
3-of-a-kind	3
2 Pair	2
Jacks or Better	1
Payback	**97.28%**

7/5

Royal Flush	800
Straight Flush	50
4-of-a-kind	25
Full House	***7***
Flush	***5***
Straight	4
3-of-a-kind	3
2 Pair	2
Jacks or Better	1
Payback	**96.15%**

6/5

Royal Flush	800
Straight Flush	50
4-of-a-kind	25
Full House	***6***
Flush	***5***
Straight	4
3-of-a-kind	3
2 Pair	2
Jacks or Better	1
Payback	**95.00%**

Bonus Poker Pay Table Variations

(Per coin with maximum coin played and perfect strategy)

8/5 Bonus

Royal Flush	800
Straight Flush	50
Four Aces	80
Four 2s 3s 4s	40
Four 5s-Ks	25
Full House	***8***
Flush	***5***
Straight	4
3-of-a-kind	3
2 Pair	2
Jacks or Better	1
Payback	**99.17%**

7/5 Bonus

Royal Flush	800
Straight Flush	50
Four Aces	80
Four 2s 3s 4s	40
Four 5s-Ks	25
Full House	***7***
Flush	***5***
Straight	4
3-of-a-kind	3
2 Pair	2
Jacks or Better	1
Payback	**98.02%**

10/7 Double Bonus

Royal Flush	800
Straight Flush	50
Four Aces	160
Four 2s 3s 4s	80
Four 5s-Ks	50
Full House	***10***
Flush	***7***
Straight	5
3-of-a-kind	3
2 Pair	1
Jacks or Better	1
Payback	**100.17%**

9/7 Double Bonus

Royal Flush	800
Straight Flush	50
Four Aces	160
Four 2s 3s 4s	80
Four 5s-Ks	50
Full House	***9***
Flush	***7***
Straight	5
3-of-a-kind	3
2 Pair	1
Jacks or Better	1
Payback	**99.11%**

10/6 Double Double Bonus

Royal Flush	800
Straight Flush	50
Four Aces w/ 2, 3 or 4	400
Four 2, 3 or 4 w/A-4	160
Four Aces	160
Four 2,3 or 4	80
Four 5-K	50
Full House	***10***
Flush	***6***
Straight	4
3-of-a-kind	3
2 Pair	1
Jacks or Better	1
Payback	**100.07%**

9/6 Double Double Bonus

Royal Flush	800
Straight Flush	50
Four Aces w/ 2, 3 or 4	400
Four 2, 3 or 4 w/A-4	160
Four Aces	160
Four 2,3 or 4	80
Four 5-K	50
Full House	***9***
Flush	***6***
Straight	4
3-of-a-kind	3
2 Pair	1
Jacks or Better	1
Payback	**98.98%**

Deces Wild Pay Table Variations

(Per coin with maximum coin played and perfect strategy)

Full Pay

Natural Royal Flush	800
Four Deuces	200
Wild Royal Flush	25
5-of-a-kind	15
Straight Flush	9
4-of-a-kind	***5***
Full House	3
Flush	2
Straight	2
3-of-a-kind	1
Payback	**100.76%**

Short Pay

Natural Royal Flush	800
Four Deuces	200
Wild Royal Flush	25
5-of-a-kind	15
Straight Flush	9
4-of-a-kind	***4***
Full House	3
Flush	2
Straight	2
3-of-a-kind	1
Payback	**94.34%**

Deuces Deluxe

Natural Royal Flush	800
Four Deuces	200
Natural Straight Flush	50
Wild Royal Flush	25
5-of-a-kind	15
Natural 4-of-a-kind	10
Wild Straight Flush	9
Wild 4-of-a-kind	4
Full House	4
Flush	3
Straight	2
3-of-a-kind	1
Payback	**100.34%**

Not So Ugly (NSU) Deuces

Natural Royal Flush	800
Four Deuces	200
Wild Royal Flush	25
5-of-a-kind	***16***
Straight Flush	***10***
4-of-a-kind	***4***
Full House	***4***
Flush	***3***
Straight	2
3-of-a-kind	1
Payback	**99.73%**

Now that you've decided which machines to play, you'll need some help with strategy. On the next page is a chart that will give you an excellent simple strategy to use for both 9/6 and 8/5 video poker machines. For each dealt hand, start at the top of the chart, and hold the cards for the first available hand type.

The chart was derived from calculations using the video poker software program called Optimum Video Poker by Dan Paymar. The chart does not take into account any penalty card situations (where the holding of some cards can lessen your chance of getting a straight or a flush), but it will still give you an expected return of 99.5429%, which is within 0.001% off of perfect play. Most players would lose more through inadvertent deviations from a chart with several penalty considerations. Although the chart was created specifically for 9/6 paytables, it can also be used for 8/5 games for a return of 99.29% (within 0.002% of perfect play).

Optimum Strategy Chart For 9/6 Jacks or Better

1. Royal Flush
2. Straight Flush
3. 4 of a kind
4. Any 4 card Royal Flush
5. Full House
6. Flush
7. 3 of a kind
8. Straight
9. 4 card Open-ended Straight Flush
10. Two Pairs
11. 4 card Inside Straight Flush
12. High Pair (Jacks or higher)
13. 3 card Royal Flush
14. 4 card Flush
15. 4 card Open-ended Straight with 3 high cards
16. Low Pair (2's through 10's)
17. 4 card Open-ended Straight with 1 or 2 high cards
18. 3 card Inside Straight Flush with 2 high cards
19. 3 card Open-ended Straight Flush with 1 high card
20. 4 card Open-ended Straight with no high cards
21. 3 card Double Inside Straight Flush with 2 high cards
22. 3 card Inside Straight Flush with 1 high card
23. 3 card Open-ended Straight Flush with no high cards
24. 2 card Royal Flush (Q-J)
25. 4 high cards (A-K-Q-J)
26. 2 card Royal Flush with no 10
27. 4 card Inside Straight with 3 high cards
28. 3 card Double Inside Straight Flush with 1 high card
29. 3 card Inside Straight Flush with no high card
30. 3 high cards with no Ace (K-Q-J)
31. 2 high cards (Q-J)
32. 2 card Royal Flush (J-10)
33. 2 high cards (K-Q or K-J)
34. 2 card Royal Flush (Q-10)
35. 2 high cards (A-K, A-Q or A-J)
36. 1 high card (J or Q)
37. 2 card Royal Flush (K-10)
38. 1 high card (A or K)
39. 3 card Double Inside Straight Flush with no high card
40. Redraw (All New Cards)

To use the chart just look up your hand and play it in the manner that is closest to the top of the chart. For example: you are dealt (6♣,6♦,7♥,8♠,9♣). You keep (6♣,6♦) rather than (6♦,7♥,8♠,9♣) because a low pair (#16) is higher on the chart than a four-card straight with no high cards (#20). Remember to always look for the highest possible choice on the chart when there are multiple ways to play your hand. As another example: you are dealt (8♣,8♦, J♥,Q♥,K♥). You keep (J♥,Q♥,K♥) rather than (8♣,8♦) because a three-card royal flush (#13) is higher on the chart than a low pair (#16). As a final, but radical, example of how to play your hand by the chart what would you do if you're dealt (6♥,10♥,J♥,Q♥,K♥)? Yes, you have to break up your flush by discarding the 6♥ and go for the royal flush because the four-card royal flush (#4) is higher on the chart than the pat flush (#6). When looking at the 9/6 chart there are a few things that should seem rather obvious:

1) A low pair is relatively good. Of the 40 possible hands, a low pair is #16 which means there are 24 hands worse than a low pair. If you look at the 15 hands that are better than a low pair nine of them are pat hands that require no draw. Of the other six hands, five of them are four card hands and the remaining hand is a three-card royal flush.

2) Don't hold three cards trying to get a straight or flush. Nowhere on the chart do you see that you should hold three cards to try for a straight or flush. In some instances you should hold three cards to try for a straight flush, but never a straight or flush.

3) Rarely draw to an inside straight. Inside straights (6,7,_,9,10) appear only twice on the chart and only in rather bad positions: #27 (with three high cards) and #25 (with four high cards). It is much easier to draw to an outside straight (_7,8,9,10_) where you can complete your straight by getting the card you need on either end. Open end straights appear three times on the chart and in much higher positions than inside straights: #20 (with no high cards), #17 (with one or two high cards) and #15 (with three high cards).

4) Don't hold a kicker. A kicker is an unpaired card held with a pair. For example (8,8,K) or (K,K,9) are examples of hands where an extra card (the kicker) is held. Never hold a kicker because they add no value to your hand!

If you want to make your own video poker strategy charts there are some special video poker programs that can do this for you. For information on buying these programs, go to americancasinoguidebook.com/video-poker-software.html With these specialized video poker software programs you can then print out the strategy charts and bring them with you into the casino.

For your information there are exactly 2,598,960 unique poker hands that can be dealt on a video poker machine (when played without a joker). Depending on the strategy that is used, on a 9/6 Jacks or Better machine a royal flush will occur about once every 40,000 hands; a straight flush about every 9,000 hands; four-of-a-kind about every 425 hands; a full house about every 87 hands; a

Other Video Poker Game Pay Tables

(Per coin with maximum coin played and perfect strategy)

Pick'Em Poker (five coin payout)

Royal Flush	6,000
Straight Flush	1,199
4-of-a-kind	600
Full House	90
Flush	75
Straight	55
3-of-a-kind	25
Two Pair	15
Pair 9's or Better	10
Payback	**99.95%**

All American Poker

Royal Flush	800
Straight Flush	200
4-of-a-kind	40
Full House	8
Flush	8
Straight	8
3-of-a-kind	3
Two Pair	1
Pair Jacks or Better	1
Payback	**100.72%**

Double Joker Full-Pay

Natural Royal Flush	800
Wild Royal Flush	100
5-of-a-kind	50
Straight Flush	25
4-of-a-kind	***9***
Full House	5
Flush	4
Straight	3
3-of-a-kind	2
2 Pair	1
Payback	**99.97%**

Double Joker Short-Pay

Natural Royal Flush	800
Wild Royal Flush	100
5-of-a-kind	50
Straight Flush	25
4-of-a-kind	***8***
Full House	5
Flush	4
Straight	3
3-of-a-kind	2
2 Pair	1
Payback	**98.10%**

flush about every 91 hands; a straight about every 89 hands; three-of-a-kind about every 14 hands; two pairs about every 8 hands; and a pair of Jacks or better about every 5 hands. The interesting thing to note here is that both a flush and a straight are harder to get than a full house, yet a full house always has a higher payback. The majority of the time, about 55% to be exact, you will wind up with a losing hand on a 9/6 machine.

The next bit of advice concerns how many coins you should bet. You should always bet the maximum amount (on machines returning 100% or more) because it will allow you to earn bonus coins when you hit the royal flush. Example: for a royal flush on a 9/6 machine with one coin played you receive 250 coins; for two coins you get 500; for three coins you get 750; for four coins you get 1,000 and for five (maximum) coins you get 4,000 coins. This translates into a bonus of 2,750 coins! A royal flush can be expected once every 40,400 hands on a 9/6 Jacks or Better machine and once every 40,200 hands on an 8/5 Bonus Poker machine. The odds are high, but the added bonus makes it worthwhile. If you can't afford to play the maximum coins on a positive machine then move down to a lower denomination machine. And, if you absolutely insist on playing less than the maximum, be sure to play only one at a time. It doesn't make any sense to play two, three or four coins, because you still won't be eligible for the bonus.

One important thing to keep in mind when you look at the total payback on these video poker machines is that those numbers always include a royal flush and the royal flush plays a very big factor in the total return. As a matter of fact, the royal flush is such a big factor on video poker machines that you are actually expected to lose until you get that royal flush. Yes, even by restricting your play to video poker machines with a more than 100% payback you are still expected to lose money until you hit a royal flush. Once you hit that royal flush it will bring your cash back up to that 100% level but until it happens you should be fully aware that you are statistically expected to lose money.

According to video poker expert Bob Dancer, "on a 25¢ Jacks or Better 9/6 machine you will lose at a rate of 2.5% while you are waiting for the royal to happen. Another way to look at this is quarter players who play 600 hands per hour can expect to lose about $18.75 per hour, on average, on any hour they do not hit a royal." You really have to keep in mind that there are no guarantees when you play video poker. Yes, you are expected to get a royal flush about once every 40,000 hands but there are no guarantees that it will happen and if you don't get that royal flush it could cost you dearly.

A final tip about playing video poker concerns players clubs. Every major casino has a club and you should make it a point to join the players club before you insert your first coin. It doesn't cost anything to join and as a member you will have the opportunity to earn complimentaries from the casinos in the form of cash, food, shows, drinks, rooms or other "freebies." When you join the club you'll be issued a card (similar to a credit card) that you insert in the machine before you start to play and it will track how much you bet, as well as how long you play. Naturally, the more money you gamble, the more freebies you'll earn. Just make sure you don't get carried away and bet more than you're comfortable with just to earn some extra comps. Ideally, you want to get comps for gambling that you were going to do anyway and not be pressured into betting more than you had planned. Many clubs will also give you cash back for your play and that amount should be added into the payback percentage on the kind of machine you'll be playing. For example, let's say a slot club rebates .25% in cash for your video poker play. By only playing 9/6 Jacks or Better machines with a return of 99.54% you can add the .25% rebate to get an adjusted figure of 99.79%. This means that you are, theoretically, playing an almost even game, plus you're still eligible for other room and food discounts on top of your cash rebate.

"Not So Ugly Deuces" Optimum Strategy

by Steve Bourie

The following strategy chart was created with a software program called Optimum Video Poker by Dan Paymar. The program can be used to practice video poker just like a regular game. However, it can also show you how to use the best strategies, analyze any video poker game, plus it can create customized strategy charts for any video poker game.

To buy this program at a discounted price, or to learn more about it, plus other similar programs, go to: www.americancasinoguidebook.com/video-poker-software.html

There are numerous pay tables for Deuces Wild games, but keep in mind that this chart only applies to the "NSUD" pay table found in the previous story.

If followed accurately, the expected return (when playing maximum coin) is 99.71%, which is less than 0.012% off of perfect play.

To use the chart, count the number of deuces in the hand that you are originally dealt. Then, hold the first hand-type available in that group.

Four Deuces

1. Just the Deuces

Three Deuces

1. Wild Royal
2. 5 of a Kind
3. Just the Deuces

Two Deuces

1. Wild Royal
2. 5 of a Kind
3. Straight Flush (SF)
4. 4 of a Kind
5. 4 card Royal Flush
6. 4 card SF
7. 4 card Inside SF
8. 4 card SF (2-2-5-6)
9. 4 card SF (2-2-4-5)
10. Just the Deuces

One Deuce

1. Wild Royal
2. 5 of a Kind
3. Straight Flush (SF)
4. 4 of a Kind
5. Full House
6. 4 card Royal Flush
7. Flush
8. 4 card SF
9. 4 card Inside SF
10. Straight
11. 4 card Double-Inside SF
12. 3 of a Kind
13. 4 card SF (Ace low)
14. 3 card Royal Flush
15. 3 card SF
16. 3 card Inside SF
17. Just the Deuce

No Deuces

1. Royal Flush
2. 4 card Royal Flush
3. Straight Flush (SF)
4. 4 of a Kind
5. Full House
6. Flush
7. Straight
8. 4 card SF
9. 3 of a Kind
10. 4 card Inside SF
11. 3 card Royal Flush
12. 3 card Inside SF (Ace low)
13. 4 card Flush
14. 2 Pairs
15. 3 card SF
16. 1 Pair
17. 4 card Straight
18. 3 card Inside SF
19. 3 card Double-Inside SF
20. 2 card Royal Flush (no Ace)
21. 3 card Inside SF (Ace low)
22. 4 card Inside Straight
23. Redraw

Dan Paymar, the creator of Optimum Video Poker, also offers the following advice for using this strategy chart.

Note that any deuces in the dealt hand are included in the hand type description. For example, "4 card Straight Flush" in the "1 Deuce" group could be 2-5♥-6♥-7♥ or 2-9♥-10♥-J♥ (where the non-deuces are all the same suit), but not 2-10♥-J♥-Q♥ since that would be a 4 card Royal Flush which is higher in the chart. A hand such as 2-6♥-8♥-9♥ would not qualify since that would be a 4 card Inside Straight Flush which is lower in the chart.

This strategy is optimized. That is, there are no penalty considerations, and it's simplified in situations that occur infrequently and have very small EV difference. The total net "cost" of this optimization is less than 0.012% off of perfect play and less than 0.005% off of the best published professional strategy for this game. Most players will actually achieve better payback with this strategy than they would with a professional strategy due to many fewer inadvertent deviations from the chart.

Why is this game called "Not So Ugly Deuces"? The original full pay Deuces Wild has the per-coin payoff schedule 1-2-2-3-5-9-15-25-200-800. A game analysis shows that the 5-for-1 payoff for four of a kind contributes over 32% of the game's payback. Many casinos offer this game, but with the quads payoff reduced to 4-for-1. With no strategy change, this reduces the payback by 1/5 of that 32% or more than 6%. This game has the 4-for-1 quads payoff, but increases the payoffs for four other hands. The result, assuming perfect strategy, is 99.726% payback, so many players clubs benefits put it to just about 100%. Multiple points days and/or off-point comps can also make it attractive to advantage players.

Video Poker Vs. Table Poker

by Linda Boyd

Years ago, in the mid-seventies, video poker (VP) was just a novelty device gamblers played for a few minutes on their way to the "real' game at the tables. Times have changed! Now players must determine whether they want to play online, at a felt table or at a VP machine inside a casino. I'll summarize the online and live tables games but focus on video poker in this analysis.

Online Poker

I can clearly remember major shockwaves rippling through the poker world when Chris Moneymaker won the main event at the 2003 WSOP after qualifying online. Thus began the global fascination with online poker, highlighted by Full Tilt Poker and Poker Stars (both owned by the Rational Group until it sold to the Amaya Group for $4.9 billion on August 1, 2014) and they became a mega competitor to casinos for poker players. In 2011 the US Department of Justice lowered the boom on online poker sites by confiscating the money that belonged to the players and assessing hefty fines to site owners. Now that Amaya owns the company and $850 million was paid to the feds in fines (plus who knows how much under the table) online gaming has once more become a legitimate contender for gaming dollars. Already it's legal in New Jersey and Nevada, plus Pennsylvania is scheduled to approve a deal almost certainly by early-2020 and I expect Delaware to be close behind. In fact, look for several states to enter the re-opening doors to online gambling in 2020 and 2021. (Note that this will be on a state, not a federal level and will require an affiliation with an existing land-based casino entity.)

Highlights: Nowadays expect the approved venues to be as well-regulated as the casinos with which they're affiliated and it will be safe to deposit and withdraw money from your account. In addition, you can play 24/7 and even safely download the app to your phone allowing you to play during lunch or breaks at work. Look for legitimate incentives like a 100% joining match of up to $600 with 120 days in which to use it. Some players are even unashamed to laud the pleasure of playing unshaven in their underwear while swigging a beer.

Cautions: Be aware that some games are new and you need to proceed with care. For example, Zoom Poker (also known as Snap Poker, Rush Poker or Fast-Fold) is popular online, especially with action junkies. You can immediately fold your hand after the deal and be re-seated at another table and dealt a new hand. Be careful if you paid the big blind or even the small blind in some cases because you have a forced investment and need to evaluate what's going on before folding. Some play as many as 250 hands per hour and a few play as many as four tables at once. You may know nothing about the other players, including tells and their strategy. Opting for Zoom Poker could cost you a bundle.

Table Poker

Doyle Brunson said, "Show me your eyes and you may as well show me your cards". That statement alone is why online poker (unlike Bunker Hill, you never see the whites of their eyes) and the live felt game version are very different. Table poker inside a reputable casino is regulated but you're still the odd man out when you know nothing about the other players and they have played together in the past. There are many differences between VP and live poker including the concept of "bad beats" and, of course, game strategy.

Video Poker

I choose to play VP over both Online Poker and Table Poker, especially given the unknown variables in the felt and internet versions. Others, of course, may disagree but having knowledge of the differences along with smart strategies is always a good thing.

Poker Bad Beats: If you're playing live poker you know a "bad beat" is when you lose with a great hand. But, again quoting Doyle Brunson: "Try to decide how good your hand is at a given moment. Nothing else matters. Nothing.". In poker it doesn't matter how strong or weak your hand is but whether or not it's enough to win by hook or by crook. To compensate for the frustration of players in table poker after losing with an excellent hand several incentives have been implemented by the house. Years ago, there were bonuses paid for special high-ranking hands, like four aces, a straight flush or a royal flush and you didn't have to pay extra for them. (I played at the old Sam's Town in Laughlin, now River Palms, before noon to get paid for high hands but the Colorado Belle and many Vegas casinos had similar incentives.) Now casinos charge to participate in "bad beat" jackpots but it definitely removes the angst.

VP Bad Beats: One of the good things people cite about video poker is that there are no possible "bad beats". In other words, you know the winning combinations along with the payout before the cards are dealt. Does this mean there are no feelings of despair akin to bad beats when you play video poker? The way I see it, the close but no cigar feeling you get from poker bad beats can also happen in video poker. I'm not referring to leaving a machine and watching the next person sit at that device and get a royal either. In that case it's highly unlikely that you would have gotten the same hand due to the way an RNG (random number generator) works. I'm talking about being dealt four to a royal or trips but coming up empty handed on the draw. This is especially annoying when it happens repeatedly over a relatively short period of time as well as over many sessions. We've all experienced the constant close calls in a session where we can't seem to draw a thing. Rest assured that if you've been through several royal cycles (the number of hands it takes to get a royal, statistically speaking) and are repeatedly shut out it doesn't mean the machine is gaffed. I consider the mercurial nature of VP results in conjunction with the mathematical odds to be analogous to poker's bad beats. You should still play according to Zamzow (that's Dean Zamzow, the creator of outstanding VP tutorial software called WinPoker).

Poker Strategy: Whether you're playing online or live poker it's important to study the topic before you lay your money down. There are close to 500 poker books to choose from on Amazon so I'll narrow down the list to a half a dozen that I recommend along with a brief annotation. The must haves for any serious poker player, in my opinion, are "Super System" by Doyle Brunson and several other contributors ("Texas Dolly's" poker "bible" might be the best book ever written on the topic) and "The Theory of Poker" by David Sklansky (a brilliant book written by one of the contributors to Brunson's "Super System"). Other books you should read are "Little Green Book" by Phil Gordon, "Kill Phil" by Blair Rodman and Lee Nelson (promotes aggressive Hold'em play, especially in tournaments, and the "Phils" refer to great players like Phil Ivey, Phil Hellmuth and Phil Gordon), Harrington on Hold'em" by Dan Harrington (excellent strategy book), "Every Hand Revealed" by Gus Hansen (an original but unorthodox approach to tournament play) and "The Mathematics of Poker" by Bill Chen and Jerrod Ankenman (advanced mathematics and not for beginners). There are other outstanding poker books but these are my personal choices for smart poker players.

VP Strategy: If you're going to gamble then you must be prepared for an emotional roller coaster and some sad (at least to you) possibilities. It's important, however, to consistently play the odds mathematically correct and make rational decisions to minimize the negative impact of close calls. If you're psychologically unable to take some bad licks in stride then you probably should end your session or quit gambling altogether. My book, "The Video Poker Edge", gives you specific strategy tips for the 8 core games that you'll find in almost every casino. In addition, I include free removable strategy cards in the back of my book for each of the 8 core video poker games. It's important that you stick to these strategies and avoid playing hunches to have the best long run results.

According to Zamzow: The adage "according to Hoyle" means the final authority on card game rules and strategy just like "according to" recognition for world records goes to Guinness and for the accuracy of urban legends refer to Snopes. For video poker the honor definitely belongs to software pioneer Dean Zamzow. He's the video poker guru who wrote WinPoker, the 100% accurate way to play individual video poker games mathematically perfect. Before Zamzow experts were fiddling around with statistical data to develop game strategy, but it was inexact. Dean Zamzow wrote software for individual video poker games that changes when the pay schedule changes and indicates the correct holds for every possible dealt hand. (If you're playing video poker you should be practicing at home using Zamzow's tutorial software.) In fact, I used his software to ensure the accuracy of the video poker strategy cards I wrote for the 8 VP core games. Others have software for video poker that is close to correct but chose to trade off difficulty of remembering quirky hands with overall ease of play. Some may also have correct software but Dean was first and the genius with the computer tutorial that is final authority on whether or not the hand was played correctly. (Also, be aware that there is a lot of junk on the market that allows you to have fun playing but has no tutorial function;

some software has tutorial features but poor graphics.) You may hear stories of long shot and even foolish video poker holds that resulted in a big win, but if it's not according to Zamzow you're simply not playing accurately.

Does this mean you won't have some painful bad beats from time-to-time as discussed earlier? Unfortunately, no. Without a crystal ball there's no way to predict future deals or draws based on past hands. This concept is difficult to comprehend for mathematically challenged players because they want to talk about the results of a single hand instead of statistical odds.

The next sections will put things into perspective.

Possible Versus Probable: One of the most misunderstood concepts in video poker is possibility versus probability. The best holds in video poker are those that maximize your long run results based on the coins returned in relation to the odds of achieving the hand. This is a difficult concept for many players to comprehend, but the examples below will help put it in perspective.

The easiest way to understand video poker probabilities is to use an extreme example and then bring it down to closer calls. If you are dealt three aces any six and any seven in 10/7 Double Bonus (10/7 DB), you would keep just the three aces, a correct and intuitive move. I could argue that you could possibly have kept any one of the aces and gotten a royal on the draw. You would correctly respond that it was too much of a long shot to consider. You have just made a good argument for not always going for the highest hand if the odds are so remote that you will lose more money over time by playing that way. You understand the probability is so stacked against drawing the royal that you'll spend more money trying for it over time than keeping the three aces. The same is true in every instance when you must choose between two possible winning hand outcomes. The problem is many aren't intuitive holds like the example because the odds versus the payout are closer. That's why you play according to Zamzow!

Deviations for Non-Purists: Personally, I'm from the school of thought that says play right and accept the consequences with a poker face. If you can't do this then gambling probably just isn't for you.

Others look at it differently. For example, they may take a shot at playing above their means, say a $5 denomination when they normally play quarters. This means that each game costs $25 instead of $1.25. If they're dealt a sure thing hand, a flush worth $150 in 9/6 JOB, but four to a royal, the correct play is hold four to the royal. Some argue the odds are so long and they rarely play this denomination so it makes sense to keep the flush. This is not a math argument and I think you should avoid playing above your means. You'll probably feel some pain regardless of what you decide because if you keep the flush you'll never know if you got beat out of $20,000, an extremely bad beat by playing with scared money. A similar scene happens when you play multi-hands and are dealt a winner, like a straight, with four to a royal. My view is go for the royal, but I can understand why some would keep the sure payout. Mathematically, however, they made a bad decision.

Getting Beat Up: If you're playing correctly you may still be taking a major drubbing. Just because you're supposed to get four-of-a-kind (quads) around once every 400 hands and you've played several times that number of hands doesn't mean you're due. Before the deal your odds never change regardless of whether you've been winning or losing. In a sense the overall picture of going through several royal cycles (the odds of getting a royal are approximately one in 40,000) or quad cycles (around once every 400 hands) and coming up blank are like bad beat poker hands. Mathematically it shouldn't happen but it can and will if you play long enough. That's because the long run refers to many hands, with experts arguing as to a good number to place on it. Several royal cycles for sure and the closer to infinite, assuming correct play, the closer actual results will resemble statistical expectations. If you continue to play accurately and if the theoretical expectation is positive, then there is absolutely no logical math reason to quit.

Mistakes: Gambling is definitely an emotional activity regardless of your chosen form. If you're getting a series of bad beats, say an inordinate number of trips without converting any into quads or dealt four-flushes and no flushes after the draw, you may become frustrated. That's when you can get sloppy and fail to hold all the cards you intended to or not even see all the cards and make hold mistakes. It's also a good signal to stop playing table and online poker as well as VP and lick your wounds.

Bankroll: Sometimes you simply run out of the money you set aside for the session even though you may have played far fewer hands than you expected. I'm referring to risk of ruin tables that give you an idea of how many betting units you should be able to play with a given amount of money and pay schedule. If you lose all the money you wanted to risk for a session, especially if the video poker choice has an expected return of less than 100%, then it's probably a good time to call it a day.

Promotion Equity: Sometimes it's worth giving a casino a significant amount of business during a promotion. That's because they usually have virtual entries sorted by a computer and the number you earn is based on the amount of play you give them. You can't know your exact odds since there are too many variables, like the number of other players and the amount of entries they have. You can, however, have a ballpark indicating whether this promotion is worth you spending a lot of time playing in this casino. You should look at the value of the prizes to you (cash is the best for most) as well as the number of winners. I try to avoid drawings where there are only a few winners.

Be There or Be Square: Before investing a lot of time going for entry tickets get a copy of the contest flyer. Make sure the drawing is at a time and on a date when you can be there. Also consider the game's volatility to maximize the number of tickets, assuming the ER (expected returns) are comparable. A less volatile game, say 9/6 JOB (ER 99.5439%, variance 19.51468) versus 9/6 DDB (ER 98.9808 %, variance 41.98498) is a better choice in terms of earning more entries. It's a bad feeling when you invest a lot of energy and money in acquiring tickets only to discover that you can't possibly be present, a typical requirement.

Final Thoughts: Years ago, the name of my poison was 7-card stud (sometimes 5-card), Texas Hold'em or Blackjack (single or double deck, no shuffling up when the buses arrived, no automatic shufflers; forget card-counting when these are in operation and the dealer stands on a soft seventeen). There was no such thing as bad beat jackpots; if you lost with a big hand you just had to live with it. Players got some mitigation by choosing to play during slow times, like weekday mornings, in the form of specific high-hand bonuses. Best of all, it wasn't necessary to contribute to a side pot to be eligible. Honestly, these hands are so infrequent that the casino can well afford to offer incentives without charging extra or increasing the rake. Table game options are just like retirement choices, it's always better to take the "old system" than opt for the glittery new offering. That doesn't mean I can't appreciate the draw of the felt games, both online and live at your local casino. It is, however, the reason that I personally consider my odds at VP significantly more predictable than those at the poker table where, to quote Amarillo Slim, "Look around the table. If you don't see a sucker, get up, because you're the sucker."

Please note: If you are interested in purchasing the software from Dean Zamzow, it retails for $29.95, but can be purchased at a discount at www.americancasinoguidebook.com/video-poker-software.html.

Linda Boyd, a long-time table game player before turning to video poker, writes for numerous gaming magazines. Her book, "The Video Poker Edge," includes free removable pay schedules and her free strategy cards for the eight most popular games. The second edition is available at amazon.com, Square One Publishers and major bookstores. www.squareonepublishers.com.

Blackjack

by Steve Bourie

Blackjack is the most popular casino game in America and one of the biggest reasons for that is its relatively simple rules that are familiar to most casino visitors. Blackjack also has a reputation as being "beatable" and although that is true in some cases, the vast majority of players will always be playing the game with the house having a slight edge over them.

At most blackjack tables there are seven boxes, or betting areas, on the table. This means that up to seven people can play at that table and each player has their own box in front of them in which they'll place their bet. Now, before you take a seat at any blackjack table the first thing you should do is to take a look at the sign that's sitting on each table because it will tell you the minimum amount that you must bet on each hand. If you're a $5 player you certainly wouldn't want to sit at a table that has a $25 minimum so, once again, be sure to look before you sit down.

Once you're at the table you'll need chips to play with and you get them by giving your cash to the dealer who will exchange it for an equal amount of chips. Be careful, however, that you don't put your cash down into one of the betting boxes because the dealer might think you're playing it all on the next hand!

After everyone has placed their bets in their respective boxes the dealer will deal out two cards to each player. He will also deal two cards to himself; one of those cards will be face up and the other face down. Now, if you've ever read any brochures in a casino they'll tell you that the object of the game of blackjack is to get a total of cards as close to 21 as possible, without going over 21. However, that really isn't the object of the game. The true object is to beat the dealer and you do that by getting a total closer to 21 than the dealer, or by having the dealer bust by drawing cards that total more than 21.

The one thing that's strange about blackjack is that the rules can be slightly different at each casino and this is the only game where this happens. If you play baccarat, roulette or craps you'll find that the rules are virtually the same at every casino in the U.S. but that isn't the case with blackjack. For example, in most jurisdictions all of the casinos use six or eight decks that are always dealt from a rectangular box called a *shoe* and the cards are always dealt face up. In Las Vegas, some casinos will offer that same kind of game while others will offer games that use only one or two decks that are dealt directly from the dealer's hand and all of the cards will be dealt face down. To make it even stranger, some casinos in Las Vegas will offer both kinds of games in their casinos and the rules will probably change when you move from one table to

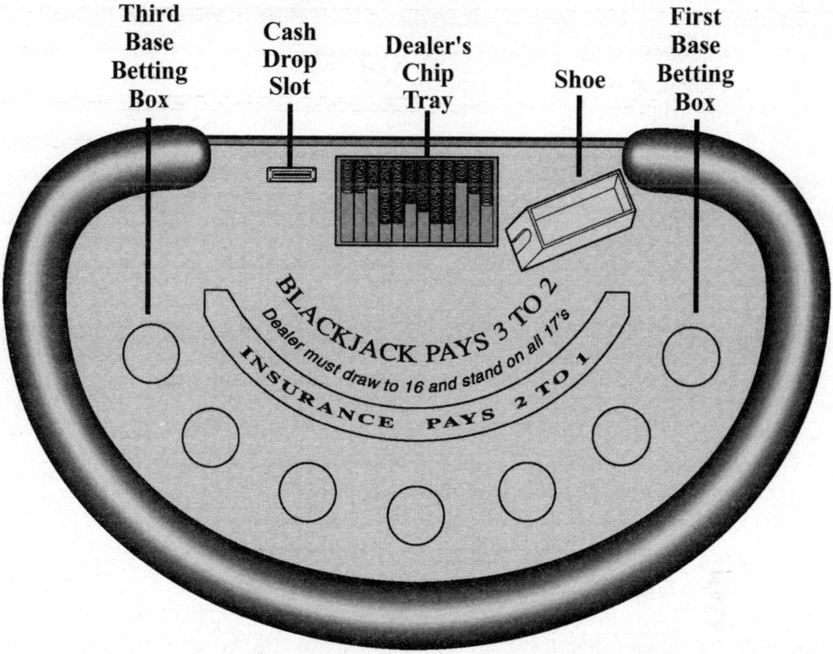

Typical Blackjack Table Layout

another. There can also be other rule variations concerning doubling down and splitting of pairs but we'll talk about those later. For now, just be aware that different casinos can have different blackjack rules and some of those rules will be good for you while others will be bad for you. Hopefully, after reading this story you'll know the good rules from the bad ones and which tables are the best ones to play at.

For our purposes, we'll assume we're playing in a casino that uses six decks of cards that are dealt out of a shoe and all of the player's cards are dealt face up. By the way, whenever you play blackjack in a casino where the cards are dealt face up don't touch the cards. In that kind of game the dealer is the only who is allowed to touch the cards and if you do happen to touch them they'll give you a warning not to do it again - so, don't touch the cards!

After the cards are dealt the players must determine the total of their hand by adding the value of their two cards together. All of the cards are counted at their face value except for the picture cards - jack, queen and king which all have a value of 10 - and the aces which can be counted as either 1 or 11. If you have an ace and any 10-value card you have a blackjack which is also called a natural and your hand is an automatic winner, unless the dealer also has a blackjack in which case the hands are tied. A tie is also called a ***push*** and when that happens it's a standoff and you neither win nor lose. All winning blackjacks should be paid at 3-to-2, so if you bet $5, you would be paid $7.50. You should avoid playing at any game that pays 6-to-5 (or even money) for blackjacks.

If the dealer has an ace as his up card the first thing he'll do is ask if anyone wants to buy ***insurance***. When you buy insurance you're betting that the dealer has a blackjack by having a 10 as his face down card. To make an insurance bet you would place your bet in the area just above your betting box that says "insurance pays 2-to-1" and you're only allowed to make an insurance bet of up to one-half the amount of your original bet. So, if you originally bet $10 you could only bet a maximum of $5 as your insurance bet. After all the insurance bets are made the dealer will check his face down card and if it's a 10 he'll turn it over and all of the insurance bets will be paid off at 2-to-1. If he doesn't have a 10 underneath, the dealer will then take away all of the losing insurance bets and the game will continue. By the way, according to basic strategy, insurance is a bad bet and you should never make an insurance bet.

If the dealer has a 10 as his up card the first thing he'll do is check to see if he has an ace underneath which would give him a blackjack. If he does have an ace he'll turn it face up and start collecting the losing bets that are out on the table. If he doesn't have an ace underneath the game will continue. In some casinos, however, the dealer won't check his hole card until after all of the hands are played out.

If the dealer doesn't have an ace or a 10 as his up card the game continues and the dealer will start with the player to his immediate left to see if they want another card. If a player wants another card they indicate that with a hand signal by tapping or scratching the table with their finger to show they want another card. Taking a card is also known as ***hitting*** or taking a hit. If a player doesn't want another card they would just wave their hand palm down over their cards. Not taking another card is known as ***standing***. The reason hand signals are used is because it eliminates any confusion on the part of the dealer as to exactly what the player wants and it also allows the security people to follow the game on the closed-circuit cameras that are hung from the ceiling throughout the casino.

Keep in mind that the hand signals will be slightly different if you're playing in a casino where the cards are dealt face down and you're allowed to pick them up. In that situation a player would signal that they wanted another card by scratching the table with the edges of the two cards they're holding. If they didn't want another card, they would simply place their two cards under the bet in their box.

In either case, if a player draws another card the value of that card is added to the total of the other cards and the player can continue to draw cards unless he gets a total of more than 21 in which case he busts and loses his bet.

When a player doesn't want any more cards, or stands, the dealer then moves on to the next player and after all of the players are finished then it's the dealer's turn to play. While each player can decide whether or not they want another card the dealer doesn't have that option and he must play by a fixed set of rules that require him to draw a card whenever his total is 16 or less and to stop when his total is 17 or more. If the dealer goes over 21 then he has busted and all of the players remaining in the game will be paid 1-to-1, or even money, on their bet.

If the dealer doesn't bust then each player's hand is compared to the dealer's. If the player's total is higher than the dealer's then they win and are paid even money. If the player's hand has a total that is lower than the dealer's hand then the player loses his bet. If the player and the dealer have the same total then it's a tie, or a push and neither hand wins. After all of the bets have been paid off, or taken by the dealer, a new round begins and new hands are dealt to all of the players.

When deciding how to play your hand there are also three other options available to you besides standing or hitting. The first is called ***doubling down*** and most casinos will allow a player to double their bet on their first two cards and draw only one more card. To do this you would place an amount equal to your original bet right next to it and then the dealer would give you one more card, sideways, to indicate that your bet was a double down. To double down in a game where the cards are dealt face down you would turn up your original two cards and tell the dealer you wanted to double down. Then, after you double your bet, the dealer would give you one more card face down. Some casinos may have restrictions on this bet and may only allow you to double down if the total of your two cards is 10 or 11, but it's always to your advantage if they allow you to double down on any two cards.

Another thing you can do is ***split*** your cards if you have a pair and then play each card as a separate hand. For example, if you had a pair of 8's you would place a bet equal to your original bet right next to it and tell the dealer you wanted to split your pair. The dealer would then separate your two 8's and give you one card on your first 8. Unlike doubling down, however, you are not limited to only getting one card and you can play your hand out normally. When you were finished with your first hand the dealer would then give you a card on your other 8 and you would play that hand out. Although you aren't usually limited to just one card on your splits, there is one instance where that will happen and that happens when you split aces. Almost all casinos will give you just one card on each ace when you split them. Also, if you get a 10-value card with your ace it will only count as 21 and not as a blackjack so you'll only get even money on that bet if you win. Besides splitting pairs you can also split all 10-value cards such as jack-king or 10-queen but it would be a very bad idea to do that because you would be breaking up a 20 which is a very strong hand and you should never split 10's. By the way, if you wanted to split a pair in a casino where the cards are dealt face down you would simply turn your original two cards face-up and tell the dealer that you wanted to split them.

The last option you have is not available in most casinos but you may come across it in some casinos and it's called ***surrender***. With the surrender option you're allowed to lose half of your bet if you decide you don't want to play out your hand after looking at your first two cards. Let's say you're dealt a 10-6 for a total of 16 and the dealer has a 10 as his face-up card. A 16 is not a very strong hand, especially against a dealer's 10, so in this case it would be a good idea to surrender your hand and when the dealer came to your cards you would say "surrender." The dealer would then take half of your bet and remove your cards. Surrender is good for the player because in the long run you will lose less on the bad hands you're dealt and you should always try to play in a casino that offers the surrender option.

All right, we've covered the basics of how to play the game of blackjack and all of the possible options a player has, so the next question is how do you win? Well, the best way to win is to become a card counter, but for the average person that isn't always possible so let's start off by taking a look at basic blackjack strategy.

Computer studies have been done on the game of blackjack and millions of hands have been analyzed to come up with a basic formula for how to play your hand in any given situation. The main principle that these decisions are based on is the dealer's up card because, remember that the dealer has no say in whether or not he takes a card - he must play by the rules that require him to draw a card until he has a total of 17 or more. Now, according to these computer calculations the dealer will bust more often when his up card is a 2,3,4,5 or 6 and he will complete more hands when his up card is a 7,8,9,10-value card or an ace. Take a look at the following chart that shows how each up-card affects the dealer's chance of busting:

Chance The Dealer's Up Card Will Bust

2	35%
3	38%
4	40%
5	43%
6	42%
7	26%
8	24%
9	23%
10	21%
Ace	11%

As you can see, the dealer will bust most often when he has a 5 or 6 as his upcard and he will bust the least amount, approximately 11% of the time, when his upcard is an ace. This means it's to your advantage to stand more often when the dealer's upcard is a 2 through 6 and hope that the dealer will draw cards that make him bust. It also means that when the dealer's upcard is a 7 through ace he will complete more of his hands and in that situation you should draw cards until you have a total of 17 or more.

Now let's show you how to play your hands by using the basic strategy and we'll start off with the ***hard hand*** strategy and hard hand means a two-card total without an ace. A hand with an ace is known as a **soft hand** because the ace can be counted as either a 1 or an 11. So, if you had an ace-6 you would have a soft 17 hand and if you had a 10-6 you would have a hard 16 hand. Later on we'll take a look at how to play soft hands, but for now we'll concentrate on the hard hand totals. Oh yes, one more thing, the following basic strategy applies to casinos where they deal more than one deck at a time and the dealer stands on soft 17, which is the situation you'll find in the majority of casinos today. So, keep in mind that the strategy would be slightly different if you were playing against a single deck and it would also be slightly different if the dealer hit a soft 17.

Whenever your first two cards total 17 through 21, you should stand, no matter what the dealer's up card is.

If your cards total 16, you should stand if the dealer has a 2 through 6 as his upcard otherwise, draw a card. By the way, 16 is the worst hand you can have because you will bust more often with 16 than with any other hand. So, if that's the case then why would you want to ever hit a 16? Well, once again, those computer studies have shown that you should hit a 16 when the dealer has 7 through ace as his upcard because in the long run you will lose less often. This means that yes, 16 is a terrible hand, but you should hit it because if you don't you will lose even more often than when you do take a card.

If your cards total 15, you should also stand if the dealer has a 2 through 6 as his upcard otherwise, draw cards until your total is 17 or more.

The same rules from 15 and 16 also apply if your cards total 14. Stand if the dealer has a 2 through 6, otherwise draw cards until your total is 17 or more. The same rules also apply if your cards total 13. Stand if the dealer has a 2 through 6, otherwise draw cards until your total is 17 or more.

When your cards total 12 you should only stand when the dealer has a 4,5 or 6 as his upcard, remember - those are his three weakest cards and he will bust more often with those cards, so you don't want to take a chance on busting yourself. If the dealer's upcard is a 2 or a 3, then you should take just one card and stop on your total of 13 or more. Finally, if the dealer has a 7 through ace as his upcard then you should draw cards until your total is 17 or more.

When your cards total 11 you would always want to hit it because you can't bust, but before you ask for a card you should consider making a double down bet. If the casino allows you to double down then you should do that if the dealer has anything but an ace as his upcard. After you double down the dealer would give you just one additional card on that hand. If the dealer's upcard is an ace then you shouldn't double down. Instead, you should hit the hand and continue to draw until your total is 17 or more. If the casino doesn't allow you to double down then you should just hit your hand and then, depending on your total, play it by the rules you were given for the hands that totaled 12 through 21. Meaning, if you had an 11 and the dealer had a 5 as his upcard, you should take a card. Then let's say you draw an ace which gives you a total of 12. Well, as noted before, if you have a 12 against a dealer's 5 you should stand and that's how you should play that hand.

If your total is 10 you would, once again, want to double down unless the dealer showed an ace or a 10. If the dealer had an ace or a 10 as his upcard you should hit your hand and then use the standard rules for a hand valued at 12 through 21. Therefore, if you had a 10 and the dealer had an 8 as his up card you would want to double down and take one more card. If you weren't allowed to double, then you would take a hit and let's say you got a 4 for a total of 14. You should then continue to hit your hand until your total is 17 or more.

If your total is 9 you would want to double down whenever the dealer was showing a 3,4,5 or 6 as his upcard. If the dealer had a 2 as his upcard, or if he had a 7 through ace as his upcard, you should hit your hand and then use the standard playing rules as discussed before. So, let's say you had a 9 and the dealer had a 4 as his upcard you would want to double down and take one more card. If you weren't allowed to double then you should take a hit and let's say you got a 2 for a total of 11, you would then take another hit and let's say you got an ace. That would give you a total of 12 and, as mentioned previously, you should stand on 12 against a dealer's 4.

Finally, if your total is 8 or less you should always take a card and then use the standard playing rules that were already discussed.

Now, let's take a look at splitting pairs, but keep in mind that the rules for splitting will change slightly depending on whether or not the casino will allow you to double down after you split your cards. Most multiple-deck games allow you to double down after splitting so that's the situation we'll cover first and then we'll talk about the changes you need to make if you're not allowed to double down after splitting.

Basic Strategy - Single Deck

Dealer stands on soft 17 • Double on any 2 cards • Double allowed after split

Your Hand	Dealer's Upcard									
	2	3	4	5	6	7	8	9	10	A
17	ALWAYS STAND ON HARD 17 (OR MORE)									
16	-	-	-	-	-	H	H	H	H*	H
15	-	-	-	-	-	H	H	H	H*	H
14	-	-	-	-	-	H	H	H	H	H
13	-	-	-	-	-	H	H	H	H	H
12	H	H	-	-	-	H	H	H	H	H
11	ALWAYS DOUBLE									
10	D	D	D	D	D	D	D	D	H	H
9	D	D	D	D	D	H	H	H	H	H
8	H	H	H	D	D	H	H	H	H	H
A,8	-	-	-	-	D	-	-	-	-	-
A,7	-	D	D	D	D	-	-	H	H	-
A,6	D	D	D	D	D	H	H	H	H	H
A,5	H	H	D	D	D	H	H	H	H	H
A,4	H	H	D	D	D	H	H	H	H	H
A,3	H	H	D	D	D	H	H	H	H	H
A,2	H	H	D	D	D	H	H	H	H	H
A,A	ALWAYS SPLIT									
10,10	ALWAYS STAND (NEVER SPLIT)									
9,9	Sp	Sp	Sp	Sp	Sp	-	Sp	Sp	-	-
8,8	ALWAYS SPLIT									
7,7	Sp	Sp	Sp	Sp	Sp	Sp	**Sp**	H	-*	H
6,6	Sp	Sp	Sp	Sp	Sp	**Sp**	H	H	H	H
5,5	NEVER SPLIT (PLAY AS 10 HAND)									
4,4	H	H	**Sp**	**Sp**	**Sp**	H	H	H	H	H
3,3	**Sp**	**Sp**	Sp	Sp	Sp	Sp	Sp	H	H	H
2,2	**Sp**	H	Sp	Sp	Sp	Sp	H	H	H	H

- =Stand **H=Hit** **D=Double** **Sp=Split** ***= Surrender if allowed**

Basic Strategy - Single Deck

Dealer stands on soft 17 • Double on any 2 cards • Double NOT allowed after split

Your Hand	Dealer's Upcard									
	2	3	4	5	6	7	8	9	10	A
17	ALWAYS STAND ON HARD 17 (OR MORE)									
16	-	-	-	-	-	H	H	H	H*	H*
15	-	-	-	-	-	H	H	H	H*	H
14	-	-	-	-	-	H	H	H	H	H
13	-	-	-	-	-	H	H	H	H	H
12	H	H	-	-	-	H	H	H	H	H
11	ALWAYS DOUBLE									
10	D	D	D	D	D	D	D	D	H	H
9	D	D	D	D	D	H	H	H	H	H
8	H	H	H	D	D	H	H	H	H	H
A,8	-	-	-	-	D	-	-	-	-	-
A,7	-	D	D	D	D	-	-	H	H	-
A,6	D	D	D	D	D	H	H	H	H	H
A,5	H	H	D	D	D	H	H	H	H	H
A,4	H	H	D	D	D	H	H	H	H	H
A,3	H	H	D	D	D	H	H	H	H	H
A,2	H	H	D	D	D	H	H	H	H	H
A,A	ALWAYS SPLIT									
10,10	NEVER SPLIT (ALWAYS STAND)									
9,9	Sp	Sp	Sp	Sp	Sp	-	Sp	Sp	-	-
8,8	ALWAYS SPLIT									
7,7	Sp	Sp	Sp	Sp	Sp	Sp	H	H	-*	H
6,6	Sp	Sp	Sp	Sp	Sp	H	H	H	H	H
5,5	NEVER SPLIT (PLAY AS 10 HAND)									
4,4	NEVER SPLIT (PLAY AS 8 HAND)									
3,3	H	H	Sp	Sp	Sp	Sp	H	H	H	H
2,2	H	Sp	Sp	Sp	Sp	Sp	H	H	H	H

- =Stand H=Hit D=Double Sp=Split *= Surrender if allowed

Basic Strategy - Multiple Decks

Dealer stands on soft 17 • Double on any 2 cards • Double allowed after split

Your Hand	Dealer's Upcard									
	2	3	4	5	6	7	8	9	10	A
17	ALWAYS STAND ON 17 (OR MORE)									
16	-	-	-	-	-	H	H	H*	H*	H*
15	-	-	-	-	-	H	H	H	H*	H
14	-	-	-	-	-	H	H	H	H	H
13	-	-	-	-	-	H	H	H	H	H
12	H	H	-	-	-	H	H	H	H	H
11	D	D	D	D	D	D	D	D	D	H
10	D	D	D	D	D	D	D	D	H	H
9	H	D	D	D	D	H	H	H	H	H
8	ALWAYS HIT 8 (OR LESS)									
A,8	ALWAYS STAND ON SOFT 19 (OR MORE)									
A,7	-	D	D	D	D	-	-	H	H	H
A,6	H	D	D	D	D	H	H	H	H	H
A,5	H	H	D	D	D	H	H	H	H	H
A,4	H	H	D	D	D	H	H	H	H	H
A,3	H	H	H	D	D	H	H	H	H	H
A,2	H	H	H	D	D	H	H	H	H	H
A,A	ALWAYS SPLIT									
10,10	ALWAYS STAND (NEVER SPLIT)									
9,9	Sp	Sp	Sp	Sp	Sp	-	Sp	Sp	-	-
8,8	ALWAYS SPLIT									
7,7	Sp	Sp	Sp	Sp	Sp	Sp	H	H	H	H
6,6	Sp	Sp	Sp	Sp	Sp	H	H	H	H	H
5,5	D	D	D	D	D	D	D	D	H	H
4,4	H	H	H	Sp	Sp	H	H	H	H	H
3,3	Sp	Sp	Sp	Sp	Sp	Sp	H	H	H	H
2,2	Sp	Sp	Sp	Sp	Sp	Sp	H	H	H	H

- =Stand   H=Hit   D=Double   Sp=Split   *= Surrender if allowed

Basic Strategy - Multiple Decks

Dealer stands on soft 17 • Double on any 2 cards • Double NOT allowed after split

Your	Dealer's Upcard									
Hand	2	3	4	5	6	7	8	9	10	A
17	ALWAYS STAND ON HARD 17 (OR MORE)									
16	-	-	-	-	-	H	H	H*	H*	H*
15	-	-	-	-	-	H	H	H	H*	H
14	-	-	-	-	-	H	H	H	H	H
13	-	-	-	-	-	H	H	H	H	H
12	H	H	-	-	-	H	H	H	H	H
11	D	D	D	D	D	D	D	D	D	H
10	D	D	D	D	D	D	D	D	H	H
9	H	D	D	D	D	H	H	H	H	H
8	ALWAYS HIT 8 (OR LESS)									
A,8	ALWAYS STAND ON SOFT 19 (OR MORE)									
A,7	-	D	D	D	D	-	-	H	H	H
A,6	H	D	D	D	D	H	H	H	H	H
A,5	H	H	D	D	D	H	H	H	H	H
A,4	H	H	D	D	D	H	H	H	H	H
A,3	H	H	H	D	D	H	H	H	H	H
A,2	H	H	H	D	D	H	H	H	H	H
A,A	ALWAYS SPLIT									
10,10	ALWAYS STAND (NEVER SPLIT)									
9,9	Sp	Sp	Sp	Sp	Sp	-	Sp	Sp	-	-
8,8	ALWAYS SPLIT									
7,7	Sp	Sp	Sp	Sp	Sp	Sp	H	H	H	H
6,6	**H**	Sp	Sp	Sp	Sp	H	H	H	H	H
5,5	NEVER SPLIT (PLAY AS 10 HAND)									
4,4	H	H	H	**H**	**H**	H	H	H	H	H
3,3	**H**	**H**	Sp	Sp	Sp	Sp	H	H	H	H
2,2	**H**	**H**	Sp	Sp	Sp	Sp	H	H	H	H

- =Stand   H=Hit   D=Double   Sp=Split   *= Surrender if allowed

shaded boxes show strategy changes from chart on previous page

Basic Strategy - Multiple Decks

Dealer hits soft 17 • Double on any 2 cards • Double allowed after split

Your Hand	Dealer's Upcard									
	2	3	4	5	6	7	8	9	10	A
17	STAND ON ALL - EXCEPT SURRENDER* AGAINST DEALER'S ACE									
16	-	-	-	-	-	H	H	H*	H*	H*
15	-	-	-	-	-	H	H	H	H*	H*
14	-	-	-	-	-	H	H	H	H	H
13	-	-	-	-	-	H	H	H	H	H
12	H	H	-	-	-	H	H	H	H	H
11	D	D	D	D	D	D	D	D	D	D
10	D	D	D	D	D	D	D	D	H	H
9	H	D	D	D	D	H	H	H	H	H
8	ALWAYS HIT 8 (OR LESS)									
A,8	STAND ON ALL - EXCEPT DOUBLE AGAINST DEALER'S 6									
A,7	D	D	D	D	D	-	-	H	H	H
A,6	H	D	D	D	D	H	H	H	H	H
A,5	H	H	D	D	D	H	H	H	H	H
A,4	H	H	D	D	D	H	H	H	H	H
A,3	H	H	H	D	D	H	H	H	H	H
A,2	H	H	H	D	D	H	H	H	H	H
A,A	ALWAYS SPLIT									
10,10	ALWAYS STAND (NEVER SPLIT)									
9,9	Sp	Sp	Sp	Sp	Sp	-	Sp	Sp	-	-
8,8	ALWAYS SPLIT - EXCEPT SURRENDER* AGAINST ACE IF ALLOWED									
7,7	Sp	Sp	Sp	Sp	Sp	Sp	H	H	H	H
6,6	Sp	Sp	Sp	Sp	Sp	H	H	H	H	H
5,5	D	D	D	D	D	D	D	D	H	H
4,4	H	H	H	Sp	Sp	H	H	H	H	H
3,3	Sp	Sp	Sp	Sp	Sp	Sp	H	H	H	H
2,2	Sp	Sp	Sp	Sp	Sp	Sp	H	H	H	H

- =Stand H=Hit D=Double Sp=Split *= Surrender if allowed

Basic Strategy - Multiple Decks

Dealer hits soft 17 • Double on any 2 cards • Double NOT allowed after split

Your Hand	Dealer's Upcard									
	2	3	4	5	6	7	8	9	10	A
17	STAND ON ALL - EXCEPT SURRENDER* AGAINST DEALER'S ACE									
16	-	-	-	-	-	H	H	H*	H*	H*
15	-	-	-	-	-	H	H	H	H*	H*
14	-	-	-	-	-	H	H	H	H	H
13	-	-	-	-	-	H	H	H	H	H
12	H	H	-	-	-	H	H	H	H	H
11	D/H	D/H	D/H	D/H	D/H	D/H	D/H	D/H	D/H	D/H
10	D/H	D/H	D/H	D/H	D/H	D/H	D/H	D/H	H	H
9	H	D/H	D/H	D/H	D/H	H	H	H	H	H
8	ALWAYS HIT 8 (OR LESS)									
A,8	ALWAYS STAND - EXCEPT D/S AGAINST A DEALER 6									
A,7	D/S	D/S	D/S	D/S	D/S	-	-	H	H	H
A,6	H	D/H	D/H	D/H	D/H	H	H	H	H	H
A,5	H	H	D/H	D/H	D/H	H	H	H	H	H
A,4	H	H	D/H	D/H	D/H	H	H	H	H	H
A,3	H	H	H	D/H	D/H	H	H	H	H	H
A,2	H	H	H	D/H	D/H	H	H	H	H	H
A,A	ALWAYS SPLIT									
10,10	ALWAYS STAND (NEVER SPLIT)									
9,9	Sp	Sp	Sp	Sp	Sp	-	Sp	Sp	-	-
8,8	ALWAYS SPLIT - EXCEPT SURRENDER* AGAINST ACE IF ALLOWED									
7,7	Sp	Sp	Sp	Sp	Sp	Sp	H	H	H	H
6,6	H	Sp	Sp	Sp	Sp	H	H	H	H	H
5,5	D/H	D/H	D/H	D/H	D/H	D/H	D/H	D/H	H	H
4,4	H	H	H	H	H	H	H	H	H	H
3,3	H	H	Sp	Sp	Sp	Sp	H	H	H	H
2,2	H	H	Sp	Sp	Sp	Sp	H	H	H	H

- =Stand   H=Hit   D=Double   Sp=Split   *= Surrender if allowed

D/H=Double if allowed, otherwise hit   D/S=Double if allowed, otherwise stand

As noted earlier, when your first two cards are the same most casinos will allow you to split them and play them as two separate hands so let's go over the basic strategy rules on when you should do this.

The first thing you should remember is that you always split aces and 8's. The reason you split aces is obvious because if you get a 10 on either hand you'll have a perfect 21, but remember that you won't get paid for a blackjack at 3-to-2, instead it'll be counted as a regular 21 and you'll be paid at even money. If you have a pair of 8's you have 16 which is a terrible hand and you can always improve it by splitting your 8's and playing them as separate hands.

The next thing to remember about splitting pairs is that you never split 5's or 10's. Once again, the reasons should be rather obvious, you don't want to split 10's because 20 is a great hand and you don't want to split 5's because 10 is a great hand to draw to. Instead, you would want to double down on that 10, unless the dealer was showing a 10 or an ace as his upcard.

2's, 3's and 7's should only be split when the dealer is showing a 2 through 7 as his upcard. Split 4's only when the dealer has a 5 or 6 as his upcard (remember 5 and 6 are his weakest cards!), 6's should be split whenever the dealer is showing a 2 through 6 and finally, you should always split 9's unless the dealer is showing a 7, 10 or ace. The reason you don't want to split 9's against a 10 or an ace should be rather obvious, but the reason you don't want to split them against a 7 is in case the dealer has a 10 as his hole card because in that case your 18 would beat out his 17.

If the casino will not allow you to double down after splitting then you should make the following three changes: For 2's and 3's only split them against a 4,5,6 or 7; never split 4's; and for a pair of 6's only split them against a 3,4,5 or 6. Everything else should be played the same.

Now, let's take a look at how to play ***soft hands*** and, remember, a soft hand is any hand that contains an ace that can be counted as 1 or 11. For a soft hand of 19 or more you should always stand.

For soft 18 against a 2,7 or 8 you should always stand. If the dealer shows a 9, 10 or an ace you should always take a hit and for a soft 18 against a 3,4,5 or 6 you should double down, but if the casino won't allow you to double then you should just hit.

For soft 17 you should always take a hit, but if the casino allows you to double down, then you should double against a dealer's 3,4,5 or 6.

For soft 16 or a soft 15 you should always take a hit, but if the casino allows you to double down then you should double against a dealer's 4, 5 or 6.

For soft 14 you should always take a hit, but if the casino allows you to double down then you should double against a dealer's 5 or 6.

Finally, for a soft 13 you should always take a hit, but if the casino allows you to double down then you should double against a dealer's 5 or 6.

The last thing we need to cover is surrender which, as noted before, isn't offered in many casinos but it is an option that does work in your favor and if available, you should play in a casino that offers it. The surrender rules are very simple to remember and only apply to hard totals of 15 or 16. If you have a hard 16 you should surrender it whenever the dealer has a 9, 10 or ace as his upcard and if you have a hard 15 you should surrender it whenever the dealer has a 10 as his upcard. That's all there is to surrender.

Now that you know how to play the game and you have an understanding of the basic strategy let's take a quick look at how the rule variations can affect the game of blackjack. As noted before, various computer studies have been made on blackjack and these studies have shown that each rule change can either hurt or help the player by a certain amount. For example, a single-deck game where you can double on any first 2 cards (but not after splitting pairs), the dealer stands on soft 17 and no surrender is allowed has no advantage for the casino when using the basic strategy. That's right, in a game with those rules in effect the game is dead even and neither the casino nor the player has an edge!

Take a look at the following chart and you'll see how some rules changes can hurt you or help you as a player. Minus signs in front mean that the casino gains the edge by that particular amount while plus signs mean that you gain the edge by that amount.

RULES THAT HURT YOU		RULES THAT HELP YOU	
Two decks	-0.32%	Double after split	+0.13%
Four decks	-0.49%	Late surrender	+0.06%
Six decks	-0.54%	Resplit Aces	+0.14%
Eight decks	-0.57%	Double anytime	+0.20%
Dealer hits soft 17	-0.20%		
No soft doubling	-0.14%		
BJ pays 6-to-5	-1.40%		
BJ pays 1-to-1	-2.30%		

As you can see, it's always to your advantage to play against as few decks as possible. The house edge goes up substantially as you go from 1 deck to 2, but the change is less dramatic when you go from 2 to 4, or from 4 to 6, and it's barely noticeable when you go from 6 to 8. You can also see that you would prefer not to play in a casino where the dealer hits a soft 17 because that gives the dealer a slight edge. You would also want to play in a casino where you're allowed to double down on your soft hands or else you would be giving another added edge to the casino.

You can also see from these charts that you would want to play in a casino where you were allowed to double down after splitting cards and you would also want to play in a casino that offered surrender. The other two rule variations that help the player are somewhat rare but they were put in to show you how these rules changes can affect your odds in the game. Some casinos will allow you to resplit aces again if you draw an ace to one of your original aces and this works to your advantage. Also, some casinos will allow you to double down on any number of cards rather than just the first two. In other words, if you got 2-4-3-2 as your first four cards you would then be allowed to double down on your total of 11 before receiving your 5th card. If they allow you to do this then, once again, you have a rule that works in your favor.

The point of showing you these charts is to help you understand that when you have a choice of places to play you should always choose the casino that offers the best rules. So, if you find a single-deck game with good rules you could be playing an even game by using the basic strategy, or at worst be giving the casino an edge of less than one-half of 1%.

Now, there is one way that you can actually have the edge working in your favor when you play blackjack and that's by becoming a card counter. As mentioned before, card counting is not for the average person but it really is important that you understand the concept of card counting and if you think you'd like to learn more about counting cards then it's something you can follow up on later.

Many people think that to be a card counter you have to have a photographic memory and remember every single card that's been played. Fortunately, it's not quite that difficult. Actually, the main concept behind card counting is the assumption that the dealer will bust more often when there are a lot of 10's in the deck and that he will complete more hands when there are a lot of smaller cards in the deck. Now, if you stop to think about it, it makes sense doesn't it? After all, the dealer has to play by set rules that make him take a card until he has a total of 17 or more. If there are a lot of 2's, 3's and 4's in the deck the dealer won't bust very often when he draws cards, but if there are a lot of 10's in the deck then chances are he will bust more often when he is forced to draw cards.

The card counter tries to take advantage of this fact by keeping a running total of the cards that have been played to give him an idea of what kind of cards remain in the deck. If there are a lot of 10 cards remaining in the deck then the counter will bet more money because the odds are slightly in his favor. Of course, if there are a lot of small cards remaining then the counter would only make a small bet because the odds would be slightly in favor of the dealer. Another thing that the card counter can do is to change his basic strategy to take advantage of the differences in the deck.

There are at least a dozen different card counting systems but let's take a quick look at a relatively simple one (it's also the most popular) and it's called the ***high-low*** count. With this system you assign a value of +1 to all 2's, 3's, 4's, 5's and 6's, while all 10's, Jacks, Queens, Kings and Aces are assigned a value of -1. The remaining cards: 7, 8 and 9 have no value and are not counted.

+1 = 2, 3, 4, 5, 6
-1 = 10, J, Q, K, A

When you look at these numbers you'll see that there are an equal number of cards in each group: there are five cards valued at +1 and five cards valued at -1. This means that they balance each other out and if you go through the deck and add them all together the end result will always be a total of exactly zero.

What a card counter does is to keep a running total of all the cards as they're played out and whenever the total has a plus value he knows that a lot of small cards have appeared and the remaining deck is rich in 10's which is good for the player. But, if the total is a minus value then the counter knows that a lot of 10-value cards have appeared and the remaining deck must be rich in low cards which is bad for the player. To give you an example of how to count let's say the following cards have been dealt on the first hand from a single deck:

2, 3, 3, 4, 5, 5, 5, 6, = +8
J, K, Q, A, = -4
Total = +4

As you can see, there were eight plus-value cards and four minus-value cards which resulted in a total count of +4. This means that there are now four more 10-value cards than low cards remaining in the deck and the advantage is with the player. Naturally, the higher the plus count, the more advantageous it is for the player and counters would be proportionally increasing their bets as the count got higher. The card counter would also be using the same basic strategy we spoke about previously, except for certain instances where a slight change would be called for.

On the other hand, if the count is negative, a card counter will always bet the minimum amount. Of course, they would prefer not to bet at all, but the casinos don't like you to sit at their tables and not bet so the counter has to bet something and the minimum is the least they can get by with.

There is one more important thing to explain about card counting and it's called the ***true count***. The true count is a measure of the count per deck rather than a ***running count*** of all the cards that have been played and to get the true count you simply divide the running count by the number of decks remaining to be played. As an illustration, let's say you're playing in a six-deck game and the count is +9. You look at the shoe and estimate three decks remain to be played. You then divide the count of +9 by three to get +3 which is the true count. As another example, let's say you're in an eight-deck game with a count of +12 and there are six decks left to be played. You divide +12 by six to get +2 which is the true count. To put it another way, a +2 count in a double-deck game with one deck left to be played is the same as a +4 count in a four-deck game with two decks left to be played, which is the same as a +6 count is a six-deck game with three decks left to be played, which is the same as a +12 count in an eight-deck game with six decks left to be played.

For the card counter, it is crucial to always take the running count and then divide it by the number of decks remaining in order to get the true count because all betting and playing decisions are based on the true count rather than the running count.

Of course, if you're playing in a single-deck game the running count and the true count are initially the same. The more you get into the deck, however, the more weight is given to the running count because there is less than one deck remaining. So, if the running count was +3 and only a 1/2-deck remained you would calculate the true count by dividing +3 by 1/2 (which is the same as multiplying by 2/1, or 2) to get a true count of +6. As another example, if the running count was +2 and about 2/3 of the deck remained you would divide +2 by 2/3 (the same as multi-plying by 3/2 or, 1 and 1/2) to get +3.

As you can see, the count becomes much more meaningful as you get closer to the last cards in the deck and that's why casinos never deal down to the end. Instead, the dealer will insert a plastic card about 2/3 or 3/4 of the way in the deck and when that card is reached the dealer will finish that particular round and then shuffle the cards. How far into the deck(s) that plastic card is inserted is known as the ***penetration point*** and card counters always look for a dealer that offers good penetration. The card counter knows that the further into the deck(s) the plastic card is placed the more meaningful the true count will be and the more advantageous it will be for the card counter.

So, now that you know how those card counters keep track of the cards, what kind of advantage do you think they have over the casino? Well, not too much. Depending on the number of decks used, the rules in force, and the skill of the counter, it could be as much as 2% but that would be at the high end. Probably 1% would be closer to the actual truth. This means that for every $1,000 in bets that are made the card counter will win $10. Not exactly a huge amount but there are people out there who do make a living playing the game.

18 Things To Never Do When You Play Blackjack

by Henry Tamburin

The casino game of blackjack has its procedures, codes of conduct and playing strategies. The procedures are essential to ensure the security and integrity of the game. The codes of conduct encompass the playing etiquette so you don't attract the ire of your fellow players, or the dealer. The playing strategies help you win. When you don't follow any of the above, you are not going to play your best game. So avoid making these 18 faux pas.

1. **Handing money directly to the dealer.** All cash transactions must be visible to the security cameras, so always place your cash on the layout outside of your betting spot, and then tell the dealer what denomination chips you want.

2. **Touching the cards when they are dealt face up.** When four or more decks of cards are used, they are dealt face up to each player from a dealing shoe. The reason the cards are dealt face up is twofold. First, it eliminates the potential for player cheating (by either marking or switching the cards), and secondly, it speeds up the game, because the dealer can quickly announce the total of each player's hand. There is no reason to touch the cards, so don't do it.

3. **Holding the cards with two hands.** In games where the cards are dealt face down (usually single and two-deck games), pick the cards up with one hand please, not two.

4. **Removing the cards from the table.** Your cards must always be in full view of the dealer and the security cameras. Therefore, you should never, for example, hold them in your lap.

5. **Placing objects on the table.** Purses, wallets, bags and other items should be placed on your person or next to you (except ladies' purses, which should be held in the lap). It's OK to have a drink on the table, but use the drink holders provided by the casino to avoid spilling anything on the layout.

6. **Telling the dealer that you want a "hit."** Saying, "Hit me" might be OK when you play blackjack with friends back home, but in the casinos, it won't fly. For security reasons, you must always use hand signals to signify whether you want to hit or stand.

7. **Touching your chips after you've made your bet and the cards are dealt.** Your original bet must stay on the layout untouched until it either wins, loses or ties. Once the dealer starts dealing the cards, that's your cue to not touch your wager.

8. **Placing a higher denomination chip on top of a lower denomination chip in your betting spot.** If you are wagering two or more different denomination chips, always place the higher denomination chip on the bottom of the stack.

9. **Taking your bad luck out on the dealer or fellow players.** They are not the reason why you are losing; most likely it's just a bad run of cards, which happens to all blackjack players.

10. **Telling your fellow players how to play their hands.** It's their money and they have the right to play their hand any way they want to. However, if a fellow player asks you for advice, then it's OK to offer it.

11. **Inserting the cut card a few cards from either end of the shuffled deck(s) of cards.** On six and eight-deck games, most casinos require that players place the cut card at least a half-deck from either end of the stack (some require a full-deck). If you place it less than that, you'll get a rebuke from the dealer and a request to cut again.

12. **Sitting down and making a bet in the middle of a shoe.** In some casinos, this is forbidden and there will be a "No Mid-Shoe Entry" sign posted on the table. If you are not sure, ask the dealer.

13. **Not using the basic playing strategy.** The basic playing strategy is the mathematically correct way to play every hand dealt to you. This playing strategy is readily available in books, on the Internet, and on strategy cards, which you can take with you when you play (they are legal to use in a casino). Even if you are a regular player, there really is no reason to guess how to play a hand when you can have the answers at your fingertips by using a strategy card.

14. **Playing a 6-to-5 game.** Some blackjack tables will pay only 6-to-5 when you get an untied blackjack, rather than the traditional 3-to-2 payoff. Getting paid 6-to-5 is bad. How bad? The house edge in a single-deck, 6-to-5 game is increased as much as seven-fold! Usually there will be a sign on the table stating that blackjacks pay 6-to-5. Some casinos have it imprinted on the layout. If you are not sure, ask the dealer. By avoiding these awful 6-to-5 games, you'll take a big step to improving your bottom line.

15. **Playing on a table that uses a Continuous Shuffling Machine (CSM).** Don't confuse a CSM with a traditional automatic shuffling machine. A CSM is a device that randomly shuffles the discards after every round has been played. The net result is the game plays faster (no downtime for reshuffling) and you will play about 20 percent more hands per hour. Since the house has the edge on every hand, playing more hands dealt per hour will increase your theoretical loss by 20 percent. For average players, playing on a table that uses a CSM is bad news and should be avoided.

16. **Never getting rated when you play.** The casinos give away a lot of comps to players in the hopes that they become loyal players. You won't get your fair share of these comps unless you ask to be rated when you play blackjack. If you don't know how to go about this, get the details at the players' club or ask a casino host (VIP or Marketing Department).

17. **Using a progressive betting system.** I know, I know, many players use them and swear they work. But trust me, they don't. Never have, and never will, because your chance of winning the next hand is completely independent of whether or not you won (or lost) the previous hand. The secret to winning at blackjack (actually the secret has been known for 55 or so years) is to bet more money only when the unplayed cards are rich in 10s and aces. So if you want to increase your bet, you'd be wise to watch the cards as they are played and bet more only after you've seen a fair number of small vs. high cards played in previous rounds. Better yet, use one the simple card counting system that I explain in my Ultimate Blackjack Strategy Guide. (See end of story.)

18. **Never tipping the dealer.** You tip a waiter or waitress for good service, don't you? You should consider doing the same for a blackjack dealer. It's not mandatory to tip a dealer; however, if the dealer has been pleasant and helpful, it's customary to tip to show your appreciation for a job well done. Of course, tipping won't miraculously change the cards in your favor, but think of this -- it might put you in a favorable light with the floor supervisor, who is the person that has some leeway in approving your comp and the amount (get the picture?).

If you avoid making these 18 mistakes, you'll find that you will enjoy the game better, play better, get more comps, and wind up with fewer losses and more wins. Now, aren't those the reasons that you play blackjack?

Henry Tamburin, Ph.D., has over 50 years experience as a blackjack player, writer, author, and instructor. His latest book is the Ultimate Blackjack Strategy Guide, which is FREE to read on https://www.888casino.com/blog/blackjack-strategy-guide/. *See his ad on page 24.*

Roulette

by Steve Bourie

Virtually all American casinos use a double-zero roulette wheel which has pockets numbered from 1 to 36, plus 0 and 00 for a total of 38 pockets. This is in contrast to Europe where a single-zero wheel is used and the game has always been the most popular in the casino.

There are usually six seats at the roulette table and to help the dealer differentiate what each player is betting every player is assigned a different color chip which they purchase right at the table. Each table has its own minimum chip values and that information is usually posted on a sign at the table. As an example let's say a table has a $1 minimum chip value. This means that when you give the dealer your money the colored chips he gives you in return must have a minimum value of $1 each. So, if you gave the dealer $50 he would ask what value you wanted on the chips and if you said $1 he would give you 50 colored chips.

If you prefer, you could say you wanted the chips valued at $2 each and he would just give you 25 chips rather than 50. You can make the value of your colored chips anything you want and you'll notice that when the dealer gives you your chips he'll put one of your chips on the railing near the wheel with a marker on top to let him know the value of your chips. Later on when you're done playing at that table you must exchange your colored chips for regular chips before leaving. The colored chips have no value anywhere else in the casino so don't leave the table with them.

Besides the minimum chip value, there is also a minimum amount that must be bet on each spin of the wheel. Once again, the minimums are probably posted on a sign at the table. If it says $2 minimum inside/$5 minimum outside this means that when betting on any of the 38 numbers that pay 35-to-1 the total of all your bets must be $2. You could make two different $1 bets or one $2 bet, it doesn't matter except that the total of all your bets on the numbers must be at least $2. The $5 minimum outside means that any of the outside bets that pay 2-to-1, or even money, require that you bet $5 each time. On the outside bets you can't make a $3 bet and a $2 bet to meet the minimums - you have to bet at least $5 every time. After you've exchanged your cash for colored chips you're ready to place your first bet so, let's see what your options are:

You can make a ***straight*** bet where you only bet on one number and if it comes in you'll be paid 35-to-1. The casino advantage on this bet is 5.26% and by the time you're done with this roulette section I'm sure you'll be very familiar with that number.

Another choice you have is to do a ***split***. This is where you put a chip on the line that separates two numbers. If either number comes up you'll be paid at 17-to-1. The casino advantage on this bet is 5.26%.

If you put a chip in an area that splits 4 numbers this is called a ***corner*** bet and if any one of those 4 numbers comes in you will be paid off at 8-to-1. The casino advantage on this bet is 5.26%.

If you put a chip at the beginning of a row of 3 numbers, this is called a ***street*** bet and if any one of those 3 numbers shows up you will be paid off at 11-to-1. The casino advantage on this bet is 5.26%.

You can also put a chip on the line between two streets so that you have a ***double street*** covered and if any one of those 6 numbers come in you'll be paid off at 5-to-1. The casino advantage on this bet is?... you guessed it...5.26%.

The only other bet you can make on the inside numbers is the ***5- number*** bet where you place one chip in the upper left corner of the number 1 box. If any one of those 5 numbers comes in you'll be paid off at 6-to-1 and what do you think the casino advantage is on this bet? 5.26%? Nope, I gotcha... it's 7.89%. Actually, this is the worst possible bet on the roulette table and the only bet you'll come across that doesn't have a 5.26% house edge on the double-zero roulette wheel. You should never make this bet.

One quick word here about "to" and "for" when discussing odds. Whenever the odds are stated as "to" this means that in addition to the stated payoff you also receive your original bet back. In other words, if you won your single number bet in roulette you would receive 35-to-1, which is a 35-chip payoff, plus you'd still keep your original one-chip bet, so you end up with 36 chips. Now if the odds are stated as "for" that means you do not receive back your original bet. If the odds in your single number bet were 35-*for*-1 you would still receive a 35-chip payoff but the casino would keep your original one-chip bet so you would only end up with 35 chips. The only place in a casino where the odds are always stated as "for" is in video poker. You might also come across it on a couple of craps bets where the odds are stated as "for-one" rather than "to-one" in order to give the casino a slightly better edge.

Now, getting back to our roulette examples, let's look at all of the outside bets that you can make and keep in mind that the house edge on all of these outside bets is...do you remember the number?...that's right...5.26%.

There are three bets you can make that will pay you even money, or 1-to-1, which means that if you win, you will get back one dollar for every dollar you bet:

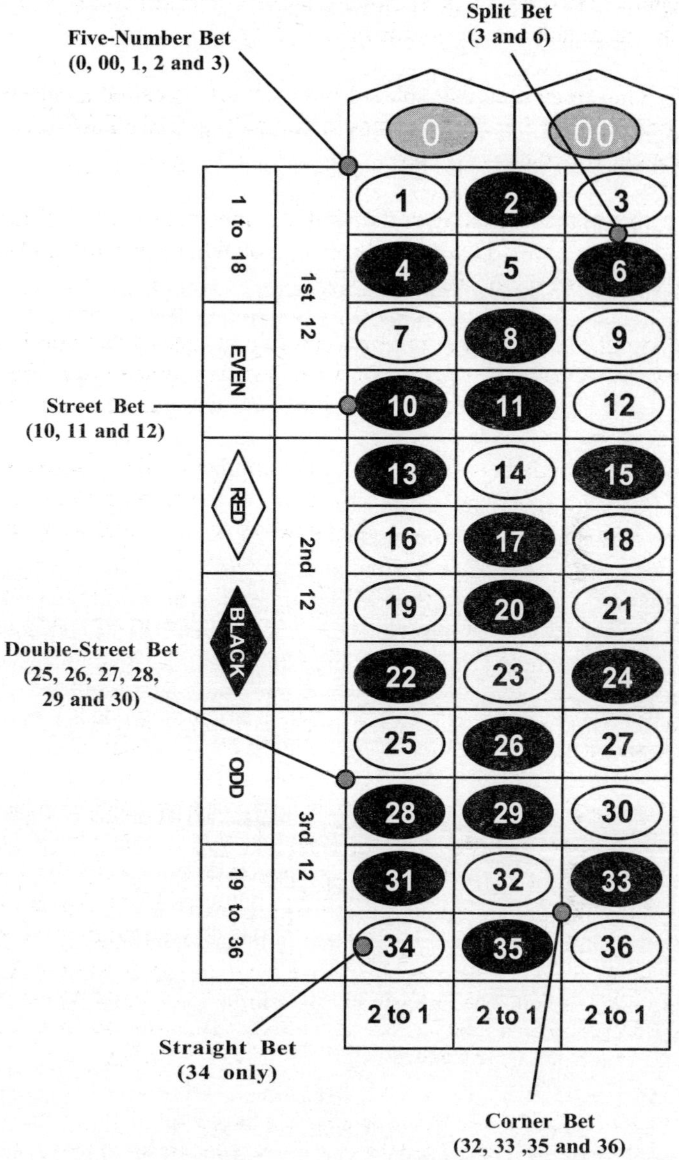

Typical felt layout for placing bets on American double-zero roulette wheel

Red or black - If you put a chip on red then a red number must come up in order for you to win. If the ball lands on a black number, 0 or 00 - you lose. The same thing goes for black - you lose if it comes in red, 0 or 00 and you win if the ball lands on a black number.

Odd or even - If you put a chip on odd then the ball must land on an odd number in order for you to win. If it lands on 0, 00, or an even number - you lose. If you bet on even, you win if an even number shows up and lose if the ball lands on 0, 00 or an odd number.

1 through 18 and 19 through 36 - If you bet on 1 through 18, then you win if a number from 1 through 18 comes in and you lose if the ball lands on 0, 00 or a number higher than 18. Similarly, if you bet on 19 through 36, you win if one of those numbers comes in and you lose on 0, 00 or any number lower than 19.

The only other bets left are the ***dozens*** and columns bets. If you look at the roulette betting layout you can see three areas that each correspond to 12-number sections on the table. The one marked 1st 12 covers the numbers from 1 to 12, the one marked 2nd 12 covers the numbers from 13 to 24 and the other one that's marked 3rd 12 covers the last section of numbers from 25 to 36. If you bet on the 1st 12 you would win if a number from 1 to 12 came in and you would lose if anything else came in, including 0 or 00. The same principle holds true for each of the other dozen bets where you would win if a number in that section came in and you would lose if anything else showed up. All dozens bets pay 2-to-1.

The last bet to look at is the ***column*** bet and that is also a bet that pays 2-to-1. There are three possible column bets you can make and you'll notice that each area corresponds to the numbers in the column directly above it. So, if you put a chip under the first column you will win if any of the numbers in that column come in and you will lose if any other number, including 0 or 00 shows up. Once again, the same rule is in effect for each of the other columns where you would win if the number appears in the column above your bet and you would lose if it doesn't.

All right, now you know all the possible bets and you know how to make them at the table. So, the next question is "How do you win?" and the answer to that is very simple - You have to get lucky! And that's the ONLY way you can win at roulette. As you found out earlier, every bet, except for the 5-number bet, which I'm sure you'll never make, has a house edge of?...that's right...5.26%. So, feel free to put your chips all over the table and then just hope that you're lucky enough to have one of your numbers come up. You see, it just doesn't matter what you do because you'll always have that same house edge of 5.26% working against you on every bet you make.

Now, you may have heard of a system for roulette where you should place your bets only on the numbers that are evenly spaced out around the wheel. For example, if you wanted to play only four numbers, you could bet on 1,2,31 and 32 because when you looked at a roulette wheel, you would notice that if you divided it into four equal parts, you would have a number that appears in each of the four sections. So, is this a good system? Well, actually it's no better and no worse than any other roulette system. The fact is that it's purely a matter of chance where the ball happens to land and it makes no difference whether the numbers you choose are right next to each other or evenly spaced out on the wheel. Each number has an equal chance to occur on every spin of the wheel and the house edge always remains at 5.26%.

You can probably tell that I wouldn't recommend roulette as a good game to play because there are other games that offer much better odds, but if you really insist on playing the game I have three good suggestions for you. #1 - Go to Atlantic City! In Atlantic City if you make an even-money outside bet, like red or black, odd or even, 1 through 18 or 19 through 36 and if 0 or 00 come up, the state gaming regulations allow the casino to take only half of your bet. Because you only lose half of your bet this also lowers the casino edge on these outside bets in half to 2.63%. This rule is only in effect for even-money bets so keep in mind that on all other bets the house edge still remains at that very high 5.26%.

The second suggestion I have for you also involves some travel and here it is: Go to Europe! The game of roulette began in Europe and many casinos over there use a single-zero wheel which makes it a much better game because the house edge on a single-zero roulette wheel is only 2.70%. To make it even better, they have a rule called "en prison" which is similar to the Atlantic City casino rule. If you make an even-money outside bet and the ball lands on 0 you don't lose right away. Instead, your bet is "imprisoned" and you have to let it ride on the next spin. Then, if your bet wins, you can remove it from the table. Because of this rule, the casino edge on this bet is cut in half to 1.35% which makes it one of the best bets in the casino and almost four times better than the same bet when it's made on a standard double-zero roulette wheel in the United States.

Now, if you're not into traveling and you don't think you can make it to Atlantic City or Europe, then you'll just have to settle for suggestion #3 which is: Win quickly! Naturally, this is easier said than done, but in reality, if you want to win at roulette the best suggestion I can give you is that you try to win quickly and then walk away from the table because the longer you continue to bet the longer that big 5.26% house edge will keep eating away at your bankroll. One major principle of gambling is that in order to win you must only play the games that have the lowest casino edge and, unfortunately, roulette is not one of them.

Before closing out this look at roulette, let's take a minute to examine one of the most famous betting systems of all time and the one that many people frequently like to use on roulette. It's called the Martingale system and it is basically a simple system of doubling your bet whenever you lose. The theory behind it is that sooner or later you'll have to win and thus, you will always come out ahead. As an example, let's say you're playing roulette and you bet $1 on red, if you lose you double your next bet to $2 and if you lose that then you double your next bet to $4 and if you lose that you double your next bet to $8 and so forth until you eventually win. Now, when you finally do win you will end up with a profit equal to your original bet, which in this case is $1. If you started the same system with a $5 bet, you would have to bet $10 after your first loss, $20 after your second loss and so forth, but whenever you won you would end up with a $5 profit.

In theory, this sounds like a good idea but in reality it's a terrible system because eventually you will be forced to risk a great amount of money for a very small profit. Let's face it, even if you only wanted to make a $1 profit on each spin of the wheel, sooner or later you will hit a major losing streak where you will have to bet an awful lot of money just to make that $1 profit. For example, if you go eight spins without a winner, you would have to bet $256 on the next spin and if that lost then you'd have to bet $512. Would you really want to risk that kind of money just to make $1? I don't think so. You may think that the odds are highly unlikely that you would lose that many bets in a row, but eventually it will happen and when it does you will suffer some astronomical losses. One other problem with this system is that eventually you won't be able to double your bet because you will have reached the casino maximum, which in most casinos is $500 on roulette. Just keep in mind that the Martingale system works best when it's played for fun on paper and not for real money in a casino. If it was truly a winning system it would have bankrupted the world's casinos years ago.

Baccarat

by Steve Bourie

When you think of Baccarat you probably think of a game that's played by the casino's wealthiest players who sit at a private table and can afford to bet tens of thousands of dollars on the flip of a card and you know what? You're right! The game of Baccarat has always had a reputation as being for the richest gamblers and that usually scared off the average player, but nowadays more and more people are discovering that Baccarat is really a good game for the small stakes player because 1. It has a relatively small advantage for the casino and 2. It's very simple to play.

The mini-Baccarat table is the kind of Baccarat table you're most likely to find in the standard American casino and the game is played pretty much the same as regular Baccarat except that in the mini version all of the hands are dealt out by the dealer and the players never touch the cards. Other than that, the rules are virtually the same. Oh yes, one other difference you'll find is that the betting minimums will always be lower on mini-Baccarat and it's usually pretty easy to find a table with a $10 minimum.

Now, as noted before, the game of Baccarat is very simple to play and that's because the only decision you have to make is what bet you want to make from the three that are available: player, banker or tie. After the players make their bets the game begins and two 2-card hands are dealt from a shoe that contains 8 decks of cards. One hand is dealt for the banker and another hand is dealt for the player. The values of the two cards in each hand are added together and the object of the game is to have a total as close to 9 as possible. After the values of the first two cards in each hand are totaled, a third card can be drawn by either the player, the banker or both. But, the decision as to whether or not a third card should be drawn is not decided by the dealer or the players - it is only decided by the rules of the game.

All of the 10's and all of the face cards are counted as zeros, while all of the other cards from ace though 9 are counted at their face value. So, a hand of Jack, 6 has a total of 6; 10,4 has a total of 4; king, 7 has a total of 7; and ace, queen which would be a great hand in blackjack, only has a total of 1. The other thing about adding the cards together is that no total can be higher than 9. So, if a total is 10 or higher you have to subtract 10 to determine its value. For example, 8,8 totals 16 but you subtract 10 and your total is 6; 9,5 has a total of 4; 8,3 has a total of 1; and 5,5 has a total of 0.

Once again, the object of the game of Baccarat is to have a total as close to 9 as possible, so after the first two cards are dealt if either the player or banker hand has a total of 9 then that's called a "natural" and that hand is the winner. If neither hand has a total of 9 then the next best possible hand is a total of 8 (which is also called a "natural") and that hand would be the winner. If both the player and the banker end up with the same total then it's a tie and neither hand wins.

Now, if neither hand has an 8 or a 9 then the rules of the game have to be consulted to decide whether or not a third card is drawn. Once that's done, the values of the cards are added together again and whichever hand is closest to a total of 9 is the winner. If both hands end up with the same total then it's a tie and neither hand wins.

If you want to bet on the player hand just put your money in the area marked "player" and if you win you'll be paid off at even-money, or $1 for every $1 you bet. The casino advantage on the player bet is 1.36%. If you want to bet on the banker hand you would place your bet in the area marked "banker" and if you win, you'll also be paid off at even-money, but you'll have to pay a 5% commission on the amount you win. So, if you won $10 on your bet, you would owe a 50¢ commission to the house. The 5% commission is only required if you win and not if you lose. The dealer will keep track of the amount you owe by putting an equal amount in a small area on the table that corresponds to your seat number at the table. So, if you're sitting at seat #3 and won $10 on the bank hand the dealer would pay you $10 and then put 50¢ in the #3 box. This lets him know how much you owe the casino in commissions and when you get up to leave the table you'll have to pay the dealer whatever amount is in that box. After adjusting for that 5% commission the casino advantage on the banker bet is 1.17%

Finally, if you want to bet on a tie you would place your bet in the area marked "tie" and if you win you'll be paid off at 8-to-1, or $8 for every $1 you bet. The big payoff sounds nice but actually this is a terrible bet because the casino advantage is a very high 14.1% and this bet should never be made.

As you've seen, the casino advantage in Baccarat is very low (except for the tie bet) and the rules are set in advance so no decisions are made by either the players or the dealer about how to play the cards. This means that, unlike blackjack where you have to decide whether or not you want another card, you have no decisions to make and no skill is involved. This also means that Baccarat is purely a guessing game, so even if you've never played the game before you can sit at a table and play just as well as anyone who's played the game for 20 years! This is the only game in the casino where this can happen and that's why I tell people that Baccarat is an especially good game for the beginning player because you need no special knowledge to take advantage of those low casino edge bets.

The only part of Baccarat that gets a little confusing is trying to understand the rules concerning the draw of a third card, but remember, the rules are always the same at every table and they'll usually have a printed copy of the rules at

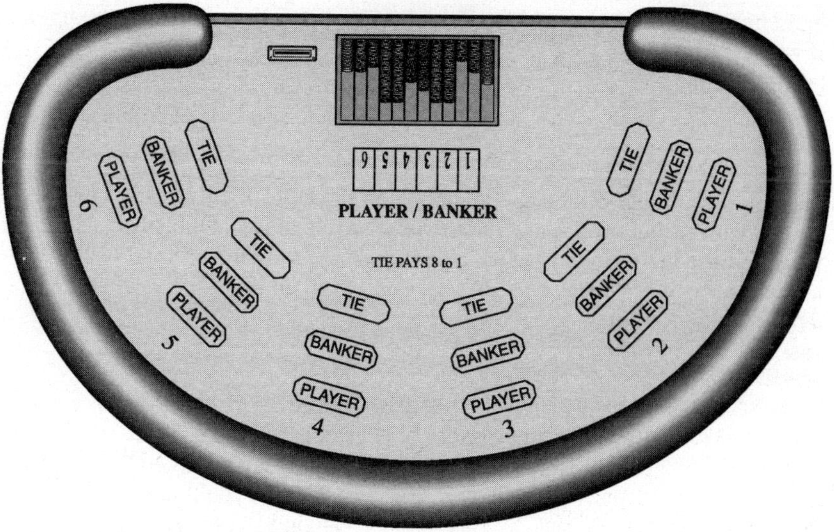

A Sample Mini-Baccarat Table Layout

the table and will give you a copy if you ask for it. After playing the game for awhile you'll start to remember the rules on your own, but until then here's a rundown on how it works:

As noted before, if the first two cards in either hand total 8 or 9, then the game is over and the highest total wins. If the totals are both 8 or both 9 then it's a tie and neither hand wins. For any other total the rules have to be consulted and it's always the player hand that goes first. If the player hand has a total of 6 or 7, it must stand. The only other totals it can possibly have are 0,1,2,3,4 or 5 and for all of those totals it must draw a card.

PLAYER HAND RULES

8,9	STANDS (Natural)
6,7	STANDS
0,1,2,3,4,5	DRAWS

There, that wasn't too hard to understand was it? If the player hand has a total of 6 or 7 it stands and for anything else it has to draw a card. Well, that was the easy part because now it gets a little complicated.

After the player hand is finished the banker hand must take its turn and if its first 2 cards total 0,1 or 2 it must draw a card. If its two cards total 7 it must stand and if the total is 6 it will stand, but only if the player hand did not take a card.

BANK HAND RULES

8,9	STANDS (Natural)
0,1,2	DRAWS
6	STANDS (If player took no card)
7	STANDS

The only other possible totals the bank can have are 3,4,5 or 6 and the decision as to whether or not a 3rd card is drawn depends on the 3rd card that was drawn by the player hand.

When the banker hand has a total of 3 it must stand if the player's 3rd card was an 8 and it must draw if the player's 3rd card was any other card.

IF BANK HAS 3 and

Player's third card is 8 - BANK STANDS
Player's third card is 1,2,3,4,5,6,7,9,10 - BANK DRAWS

When the banker hand has a total of 4 it must stand if the player's 3rd card was a 1,8,9, or 10 and it must draw if the player's 3rd card was any other card.

IF BANK HAS 4 and

Player's third card is 1,8,9,10 - BANK STANDS
Player's third card is 2,3,4,5,6,7 - BANK DRAWS

When the banker hand has a total of 5 it must draw if the player's 3rd card was a 4,5,6 or 7 and it must stand if the player's 3rd card was any other card.

IF BANK HAS 5 and

Player's third card is 1,2,3,8,9,10 - BANK STANDS
Player's third card is 4,5,6,7 - BANK DRAWS

When the banker hand has a total of 6 it must draw if the player's 3rd card was a 6 or 7 and it must stand if the player's 3rd card was any other card.

IF BANK HAS 6 and

Player's third card is 1,2,3,4,5,8,9,10 - BANK STANDS
Player's third card is 6 or 7 - BANK DRAWS

There you have it - those are the rules of Baccarat concerning the draw of a third card. As you saw they were a little complicated, but remember that you don't have to memorize the rules yourself because the dealer will know them and play each hand by those rules, but you can always ask for a copy of the rules at the table to follow along.

Now let's try some sample hands: The player hand has queen,9 for a total of 9 and the banker hand has 4,4 for a total of 8. Which hand wins? Both hands are naturals, but the player hand total of 9 is higher than the banker hand total of 8, so the player hand is the winner.

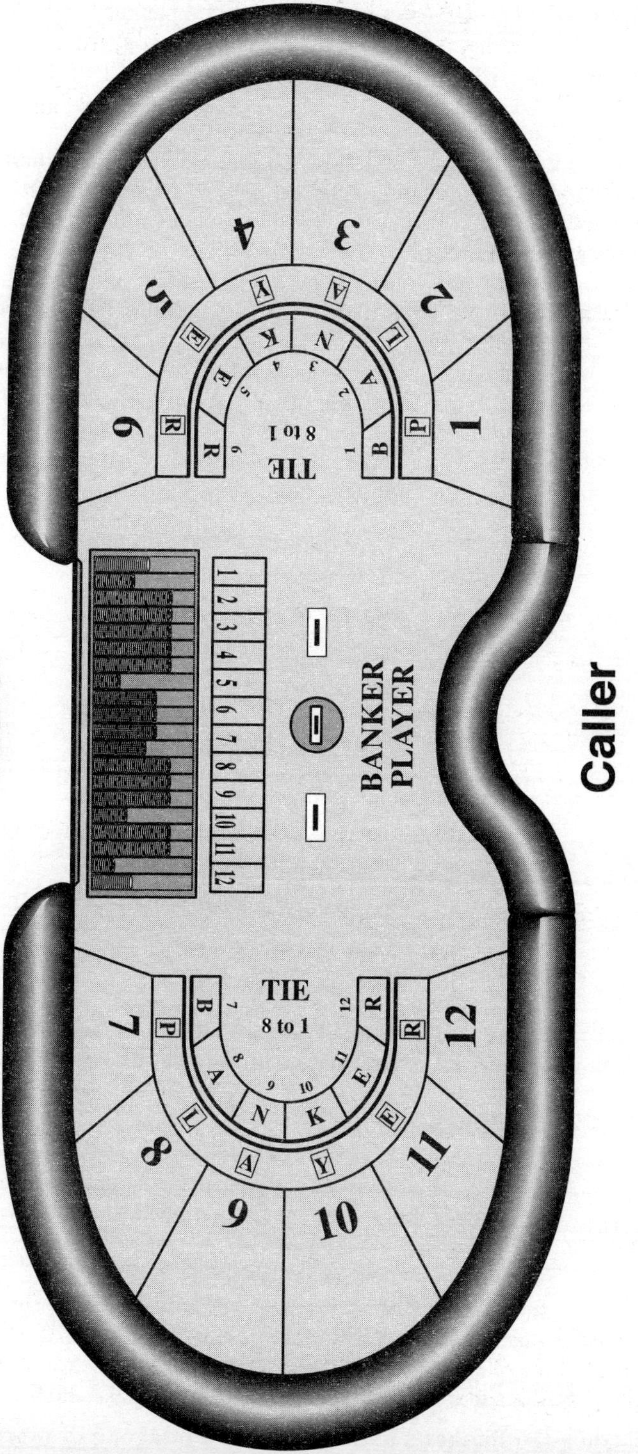

A 12-Seat Baccarat Table Layout

If the player hand has 4,2 for a total of 6 and the banker hand has ace, jack which totals 1, what happens? The player hand must stand on its 6 and the banker hand must always draw when it has a total of 0,1 or 2. Let's say the bank draws a 7 and wins 8 to 6.

What happens when the player hand has king, 5 and the bank hand has 2,4? The player hand must draw and let's say it gets a 7 for a total of 2. The banker hand has a total of 6 and if it could stand on that total it would win because its 6 is higher than the 2 held by the player. Of course, if you were betting on banker that's exactly what you would want to happen but, unfortunately for you, the rules require the bank hand to draw another card whenever its first two cards total 6 and the third card drawn by the player is a 7. So now, instead of having a winning hand you have to hope that the card you draw isn't a 4, giving you a total of 0 or a 5, giving you a total of 1. If either of those cards show up then your winning hand becomes a loser.You also wouldn't want to draw a 6 because that would give you a total of 2 which would give you a tie. In this case let's say that the bank hand goes on to draw an 8 which gives it a total of 3 and it wins 4 to 2.

Baccarat Rules Summary

Player Hand

Total of First Two Cards	
0-1-2-3-4-5	Draws
6-7	Stands
8-9	Natural (Banker cannot draw)

Banker Hand

Total of First Two Cards	DRAWS When Player's Third Card is	STANDS When Player's Third Card is
0-1-2	**Always Draws**	
3	**1-2-3-4-5-6-7-9-0**	**8**
4	**2-3-4-5-6-7**	**1-8-9-0**
5	**4-5-6-7**	**1-2-3-8-9-0**
6	**6-7**	**1-2-3-4-5-8-9-0**
7		**Stands**
8-9		**Stands (Natural)**

If the Player's hand does not draw a third card,

then the Banker's hand stands on a total of 6 or more.

If the player hand has 3, ace for a total of 4 and the banker hand has 8,7 for a total of 5, what happens? The player hand must draw and say it gets a 9 for a total of 3. Once again, the banker hand would like to stand on its total because it would win, but the rules have to be consulted first and in this case when the banker's first 2 cards total 5 and the player's third card drawn is a 9 the banker hand must stand, so the banker hand wins 5 to 3.

Finally, let's say the player hand has 4,3 for a total of 7 and the banker hand has 6,10 for a total of 6. The player hand must always stand on totals of 6 or 7 and the banker hand must also stand on its total of 6 because the player hand didn't take a third card. The player hand wins this one 7 to 6.

All right, now that you know how to play Baccarat we come to the important question which is - how do you win? Well, as I said before, if you bet on player you'll only be giving the casino a 1.36% edge and if you bet on banker you'll be giving the casino an even more modest edge of just 1.17%. While both of these are pretty low edges to give the casino you're still stuck with the fact that the casino will always have an edge over you and in the long run the game of Baccarat is unbeatable. So, if that's the case then how do you win? Well, the answer to that is very simple - You have to get lucky! And that's the ONLY way you can win at Baccarat. Of course, this is easier said than done, but fortunately, in the game of Baccarat, you have the option of making two bets that require no skill and both offer the casino a very low edge especially when you compare them to roulette where the house has a 5.26% advantage on a double-zero wheel and slot machines where the edge is about 5% to 15%. I always stress the point that when you gamble in a casino you have to play the games that have the lowest casino edge in order to have the best chance of winning and with that in mind you can see that Baccarat is not that bad a game to play for the recreational gambler.

Now let's take a quick look at one of the most common systems for betting on Baccarat. One thing that many Baccarat players seem to have in common is a belief in streaks and the casinos accommodate these players by providing scorecards at the table that can be used to track the results of each hand. Many players like to bet on whatever won the last hand in the belief that it will continue to come in and they hope for a long streak.

The thinking for these players is that since Baccarat is purely a guessing game it's just like guessing the outcome of a coin toss and chances are that a coin won't alternately come up heads, tails, heads, tails, heads, tails but rather that there will be streaks where the same result will come in for awhile. So, is this a good system? Well, actually, it's no better and no worse than any other system because no matter what you do you'll still have the same casino edge going against you on every bet you make: 1.36% on the player and 1.17% on the banker. The one good thing about a system like this though is that you don't have to sit there and guess what you want to play each time. Instead, you go into the game knowing how you're going to play and you don't have to blame yourself if your guess is wrong, instead you get to blame it on your system!

Craps

by Steve Bourie

At first glance the game of craps looks a little intimidating because of all the various bets you can make but actually the game itself is very simple, so first let me explain the game without any reference to the betting.

Everyone at the craps table gets a turn to roll the dice, but you don't have to roll if you don't want to. The dice are passed around the table clockwise and if it's your turn to roll you simply take two dice and roll them to the opposite end of the table. This is your first roll of the dice which is also called the "come-out" roll. If you roll a 7 or 11 that's called a "natural" and you win, plus you get to roll again. If you roll a 2,3 or 12 those are all called "craps" and you lose, but you still get to roll again. The only other possible numbers you can roll are 4,5,6,8,9 or 10 and if one of those numbers shows up, then that number becomes your "point" and the object of the game is to roll that number again before you roll a 7.

If a 7 shows up before your "point" number does then you lose and the dice move on to the next shooter. If your "point" number shows up before a 7 does, then you have made a "pass." You then win your bet and you get to roll again. That's all there is to the game of craps.

Now that you know how to play the game, let's find out about the different kinds of bets you can make. Two of the best bets you'll find on the craps table are in the areas marked "pass" and "don't pass". When you bet on the "pass" line you're betting that the shooter will win. To make a pass line bet you put your bet right in front of you on the pass line. Pass line bets are paid even-money and the house edge on a pass line bet is 1.41% You can also bet on the "don't pass" line in which case you're betting that the shooter will lose. To make a don't pass bet you put your bet in front of you in the don't pass area. Don't pass bets are also paid even-money and the house edge on them is 1.40%.

In reality, the odds are always 1.41% against the shooter and in favor of the "don't pass" bettor by that same amount. Of course, if you're a "don't pass" bettor the casinos don't want to give you a bet where you have an edge so they have a rule in effect on "don't pass" bets where on the come out roll if the shooter throws a 12, you don't win. You don't lose either, the bet is just considered a "push," or tie, and nothing happens. In some casinos they may make 2 instead of 12 the number that's a push. Just look on the don't pass line and you'll you see the word "bar" and then the number that the casino considers a push. In our illustration it says bar 12, so in this casino your bet on the don't pass line will be a push if the come-out roll is a 12. This rule is what gives the casino its advantage on don't pass bets and it doesn't matter whether the casino bars the 2 or 12 the result is the same 1.40% advantage for the house.

All right, let's say you put $10 on the pass line and you roll the dice. If you roll 7 or 11 you win $10 and if you roll 2,3 or 12 you lose $10. So, what happens if you roll any of the other numbers? Well, as I said before, that number becomes your point and you have to roll that number again before you roll a 7 in order to win your pass line bet.

Once your point is established the dealer at each end of the table will move a marker into the box that corresponds to your point number to let everyone at the table know what your point is. The marker that's used has two different sides. One side is black with the word "off" and the other side is white with the word "on." Before any point is established the marker is kept in the Don't Come box with the black side facing up until you roll a point number and then the dealer turns it over to the white side and moves it inside the box that contains your point number.

For example let's say your come-out roll is a 4. The dealer simply turns the marker over to the white side that says "on" and places it in the 4 box. This lets everyone know that 4 is your point and that you will continue to roll the dice, no matter how long it takes, until you roll a 4, which will make you a winner, or a 7, which will make you a loser.

Now, keep in mind that once your point is established you can't remove your pass line bet until you either win, by throwing your point, or lose, by rolling a 7. The reason for this is that on the come out roll the pass line bettor has the advantage because there are 8 ways to win (by rolling a 7 or 11) and only 4 ways to lose (by rolling a 2, 3 or 12). If a point number is rolled, no matter what number it is, there are then more ways to lose than to win and that's why the bet can't be removed. If you were allowed to remove your bet everyone would just wait for the come-out roll and if they didn't win they would take their bet back which would give them a big advantage over the house and, as you know, casinos don't like that, so that's why you can't remove your bet.

As previously noted, the pass line is one of the best bets you'll find, but there is a way to make it even better because once your point number is established the casino will allow you to make another bet that will be paid off at the true odds. This is a very good bet to make because the casino has no advantage on this bet.

In this instance, since your point was 4, the true odds are 2-to-1 and that's what your bet will be paid off at: $2 for every $1 you bet. This is called an "odds bet," "taking the free odds" or "betting behind the line" and to make this bet you simply put your chips directly behind your pass line bet. There is a limit to how much you're allowed to bet and for many years most casinos allowed a maximum of 2 times the amount of your pass line bet. Nowadays, however, many casinos offer 5 times odds and some casinos are even allowing up to 100 times odds. In the U.S. the Horseshoe casinos offer 100X odds at all of their locations.

Because the casino has no advantage on these bets you are effectively lowering the house edge on your total pass line bet by taking advantage of these free odds bets. For example, the normal house edge on a pass line bet is 1.41% but if you also make a single odds bet along with your pass line bet you will lower the house edge on your total pass line bets to .85%. If the casino offers double odds then the edge on your bets is lowered to .61%. With triple odds the edge is lowered to .47% and if you were to play in a casino that allowed 10 times odds the edge would be lowered to only .18% which means that, statistically speaking, over time, that casino would only make 18¢ out of every $100 you bet on that table. As you can see, the more the casino allows you to bet behind the line, the more it lowers their edge, so it's always a good idea to take advantage of this bet. By the way, free odds bets, unlike regular pass line bets, can be removed or reduced, at any time.

All right, let's make our free odds bet on our point number of 4 by putting $20 behind the line. Then we continue to roll until we either roll a 4 or a 7. If a 4 came up we would get even money on the pass line bet, plus 2-to-1 on the free odds bet, for a total win of $50. But, if we rolled a 7, we would lose both the pass line bet and the free odds bet for a total loss of $30.

In this example we used 4 as our point number, but there are 5 other numbers that could appear and here are the true odds for all of the possible point numbers: the 4 and 10 are 2-to-1; the 5 and 9 are 3-to-2; and the 6 and 8 are 6-to-5. You'll notice that the numbers appear in pairs and that's because each paired combination has the same probability of occurring.

7 = 6 ways	1+6,6+1,2+5,5+2,3+4,4+3
6 = 5 ways	1+5,5+1,2+4,4+2,3+3
8 = 5 ways	2+6,6+2,3+5,5+3,4+4

As you can see there are 6 ways to make a 7 and only 5 ways to make a 6 or 8. Therefore, the true odds are 6-to-5.

7 = 6 ways	1+6,6+1,2+5,5+2,3+4,4+3
4 = 3 ways	1+3,3+1,2+2
10 = 3 ways	4+6,6+4,5+5

There are 6 ways to make a 7 and only 3 ways to make a 4 or 10, so the true odds are 6-to-3, which is the same as 2-to-1;

7 = 6 ways	1+6,6+1,2+5,5+2,3+4,4+3
5 = 4 ways	1+4,4+1,2+3,3+2
9 = 4 ways	3+6,6+3,4+5,5+4

and finally, there are 6 ways to make a 7, but just 4 ways to make a 5 or 9, so the true odds here are 6-to-4 which is the same as 3-to-2.

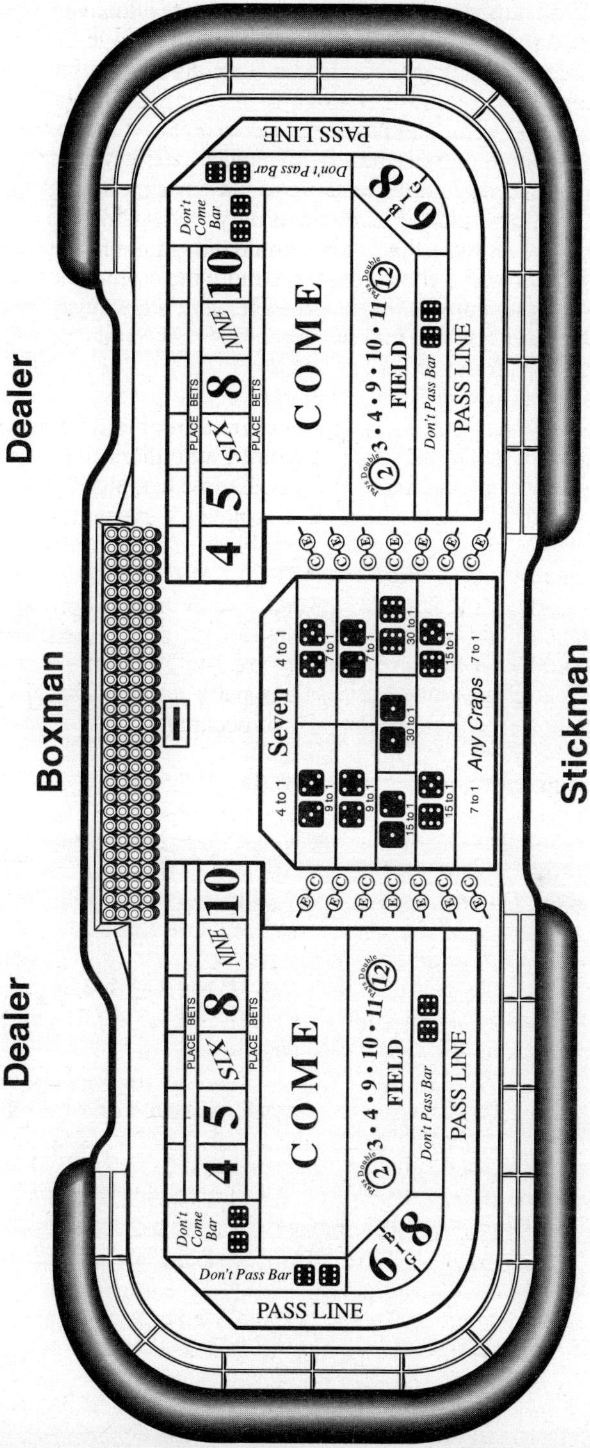

Typical craps table layout

It's important that you remember these numbers, because 1.You want to make sure that you're paid the right amount when you do win and 2. You want to make sure that when you make your odds bets you make them in amounts that are paid off evenly.

As an example, if your point is 5 and you have $5 on the pass line, you wouldn't want to bet $5 behind the line because at 3-to-2 odds the casino would have to pay you $7.50 and they don't deal in change. When making the odds bet on the 5 or 9 you should always bet in even amounts and in the situation just mentioned most casinos would allow you to add an extra $1 so you would have $6 out and they could pay you $9, if you won. The only other situation where this occurs is on the 6 and 8 where the payoff is 6-to-5. So, in that instance you want to make your bets in multiples of $5. Also, if your pass line bet is $15, most casinos will allow you to bet $25 behind the line because, if you win, it's quicker for them to pay you $30, rather than dealing in $1 chips to give you $18 for $15. When situations like this exist, it's good to take advantage of them and bet the full amount you're allowed because that helps to lower the casino edge even more.

We've spent all this time talking about pass line betting, so what about don't pass betting? Well, everything applied to pass line betting works pretty much just the opposite for don't pass betting. If you put $10 on don't pass you would win on the come out roll if the shooter rolled a 2 or 3, you would tie if the shooter rolled a 12, and you would lose if the shooter rolled a 7 or 11. If any other number comes up then that becomes the shooter's point number and if he rolls a 7 before he rolls that same point number, you will win. If he rolls his point number before he rolls a 7, you will lose.

Don't pass bettors are also allowed to make free odds bets to back up their original bets, however, because the odds are in their favor they must lay odds rather than take odds. This means that if the point is 4 or 10, the don't pass bettor must lay 2-to-1, or bet $10 to win $5; on 5 or 9 he must lay 3-to-2, or bet $6 to win $4; and on 6 or 8 he must lay 6-to-5, or bet $6 to win $5. By taking advantage of these free odds bets the casino advantage is slightly lowered on the total don't pass bets to .68% with single odds; .46% with double odds; .34% with triple odds and .12% with 10 times odds. If you want to you can remove, or reduce the amount of your free odds, bet at any time. To make a free odds bet on don't pass you should place your odds bet right next to your original bet and then put a chip on top to connect the two bets. Keep in mind that when you make a free odds bet on don't pass the casino will allow you to make your bet based on the payoff, rather than the original amount of your don't pass bet. In other words, if the casino offered double odds, the point was 4 and you had $10 on don't pass, you would be allowed to bet $40 because you would only win $20 which was double the amount of your original $10 bet. Since you have to put out more money than you'll be getting back, laying odds is not very popular at the craps table and you'll find that the vast majority of craps players would rather bet with the shooter and take the odds. Statistically speaking, it makes no difference whether you are laying or taking the odds because they both have a zero advantage for the house.

One last point about don't pass betting is that once the point is established, the casino will allow you to remove your don't pass bet if you want to - but don't do it! As noted before, on the come out roll the pass line bettor has the advantage because there are 8 rolls that can win and only 4 that can lose, but once the point is established, there are more ways the shooter can lose than win, so at that point the don't pass bettor has the advantage and it would be foolish to remove your bet.

Now, let's take a look at the area marked come and don't come. Since you already know how to bet pass and don't pass, you should easily understand come and don't come because they're the exact same bets as pass and don't pass, except for the fact that you bet them after the point has already been established.

Let's say that the shooter's point is 6 and you make a come bet by putting a $5 chip anywhere in the come box. Well, that's just like making a pass line bet, except that the shooter's next roll becomes the come-out roll for your bet. If the shooter rolls a 7 or 11, you win. If a 2,3, or 12 is rolled you lose, and if anything else comes up then that becomes your point and the shooter must roll that number again before rolling a 7 in order for you to win. In this example if the shooter rolled a 4 the dealer would move your $5 come bet up into the center of the 4 box and it would stay there until either a 4 was rolled, which would make you a winner, or a 7 was rolled which would make you a loser. The house edge on a come bet is the same 1.41% as on a pass line bet. You are allowed free odds on your come bet and you make that bet by giving your chips to the dealer and telling him you want to take the odds. The dealer will then place those chips slightly off center on top of your come bet to show that it's a free odds bet. By the way, if you win, the dealer will put your winnings back in the come bet area so be sure to pick them up off the table or else it will be considered a new come bet.

One other point to note here is that when you make a come bet your bet is always working on every roll, even a come-out roll. However, when you take the odds on your come bets they are never working on the come-out roll. That may sound a little confusing, but here's what it means. In our example the shooter's initial point was 6 and then we made a $5 come bet. The shooter then rolled a 4 which became the point for our come bet. The dealer then moved our $5 come bet to the middle of the 4 box at the top of the table. We then gave $10 to the dealer and said we wanted to take the odds on the 4. On the next roll the shooter rolls a 6 which means he made a pass by rolling his original point number. The next roll will then become the shooter's come-out roll and the odds bet on our 4 will not be working. If the shooter rolls a 7 the pass line bettors will win and we will lose our $5 come bet because he rolled a 7 before rolling a 4. The dealer will then return our $10 odds bet because it wasn't working on the come-out roll. Now, if you want to, you can request that your odds bet be working on the come-out roll by telling the dealer. Then he'll put a marker on top of your bet to show that your odds bet is in effect on the come-out roll.

Naturally, don't come betting is the same as don't pass betting, except again for the fact that the bet isn't made until after the point is established. In this case let's say the point is 5 and you make a don't come bet by placing a $5 chip in the don't come box. Well, once again, that's just like making a don't pass bet except that the shooter's next roll becomes the come-out roll for your bet. If the shooter rolls a 2 or 3, you win. If a 7 or 11 is rolled, you lose. If a 12 is rolled it's a standoff and if anything else comes up then that becomes your point and the shooter must seven-out, or roll a 7, before rolling that point number again in order for you to win. In this example if the shooter rolled a 10 the dealer would move your $5 don't come bet into the upper part of the 10 box and it would stay there until either a 7 was rolled, which would make you a winner, or a 10 was rolled which would make you a loser. The house edge on a don't come bet is the same 1.40% as on a don't pass bet and you can make a free odds bet on your don't come bet by giving your chips to the dealer and telling him you want to lay the odds. The dealer will then place those chips next to and on top of your don't come bet to show that it's a free odds bet. The final point to note here is that don't come bets, as well as the free odds bets on them, are always working - even on the come-out roll.

Now let's talk about place betting and that refers to the 6 numbers you see in the area at the top of the table: 4,5,6,8,9 and 10. Anytime during a roll you can make a bet that one of those numbers will appear before a 7 and if it does you will receive a payoff that is slightly less than the true odds. For example: the true odds are 2-to-1 that a 4 or 10 will appear before a 7. However, if you make a place bet on the 4 or 10 you will only be paid off at 9-to-5 and that works out to a casino advantage of 6.67%.

The true odds of a 5 or 9 appearing before a 7 are 3-to-2, but on a place bet you would only receive a payoff of 7-to-5 which works out to a casino edge of 4.0%. Finally, on the 6 and 8 the true odds are 6-to-5 that one of those numbers will appear before a 7, but on a place bet you would only be paid off at 7-to-6 which means the casino would have an edge of 1.52% on this bet.

As you can see, making a place bet on the 6 or 8 gives the casino its lowest edge and this means that a place bet on the 6 or 8 is one of the best bets you will find on the craps table.

When you want to make a place bet you aren't allowed to put the bet down yourself, you have to let the dealer do it for you. To do this you would just drop your chips down onto the table and tell the dealer what bet you wanted to make. For example you could put three $5 chips down and say "Place the 4,5 and 9." The dealer would then put $5 on the edge of the 4 box, $5 on the edge of the 5 box and $5 on the edge of the 9 box. You'll notice that when the dealer puts your bets on the edge of the boxes they will always be placed in an area that corresponds to where you're standing at the table and this helps the dealer to remember who placed that bet.

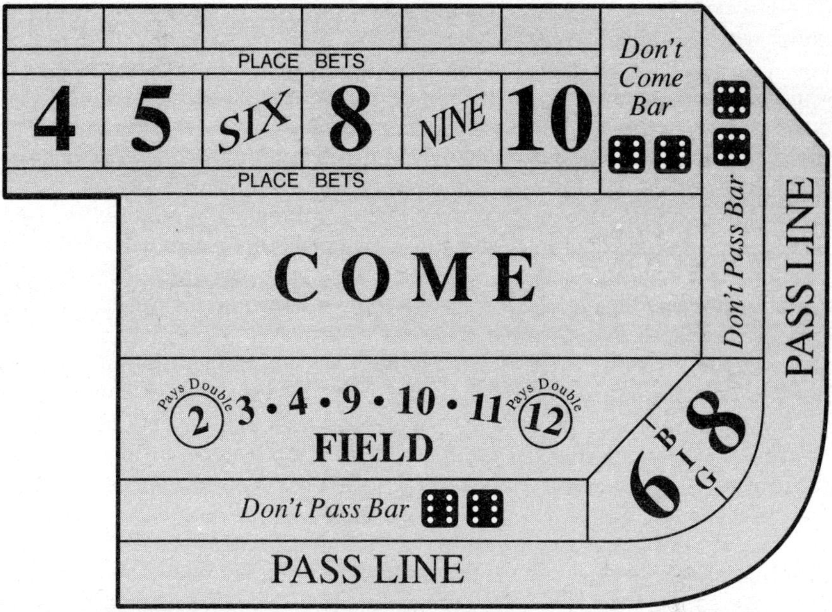

Enlargement of right side of craps layout

When making a place bet you don't have to bet more than one number and you don't have to bet the same amount on each number. You should, however, make sure that you always bet in multiples of $5 whenever you bet on the 4,5,9 or 10 and in multiples of $6 whenever you bet the 6 and 8. This will allow you to always get the full payoff on your bet. If, for example, you bet $3 on the 6 and you won you would only get back even-money, or $3, rather than the $3.50 which your bet should have paid and this results in an even bigger advantage for the casino. Another thing about place bets is that, unlike pass line bets, you can remove your place bets at any time and you do that by telling the dealer you want your bet down and he will take your chips off the table and return them to you. You could also tell the dealer that you didn't want your bet to be working on any particular roll or rolls and you do this by saying for example "off on the 5." The dealer would then put a little button on top of your bet that said "off" and he would remove it when you told him you wanted that number working again.

When we spoke about come bets before I mentioned that come bets are always working on every roll, but that's not the case with place bets because place bets are never working on the come-out roll. If you wanted to, however, you could ask for your place bet to be working on the come out roll by telling the dealer you wanted it working and he would place a button on top of your bet that said "on" to show that your bet was working on the come-out roll.

One last point about place bets is that when you win the dealer will want to know what you want to do for your next bet and you have three choices: if you want to make the same bet just say “same bet” and the dealer will give you your winning chips and leave your original place bet on the table. If you don’t want to bet again, just say “take it down” and the dealer will return your place bet along with your winnings. And if you want to double your bet just say “press it” and the dealer will add your winning chips to your other place bet and return any extra chips to you. For example, if you won a $10 place bet on the 5 the dealer would have to give you back $14 in winning chips. If you said “press it” the dealer would add $10 to your place bet and return the remaining $4 in chips to you.

Besides, place betting there is also another way to bet that one of the point numbers will show up before a 7 does and that’s called buying a number. A buy bet is basically the same as a place bet except you have to pay a commission of 5% of the amount of your bet and then if you win, the casino will pay you at the true odds. When making a buy bet you should always remember to bet at least $20 because 5% of $20 is $1 and that’s the minimum amount the casino will charge you. The reason for the $1 minimum is because that’s the smallest denomination chip they have at the craps table and they won’t make change for anything under $1. The casino edge on any buy bet for $20 works out to 4.76% so let’s take a look at a chart that shows the difference between buying and placing the point numbers.

Point Number	Casino Edge Buy Bet	Casino Edge Place Bet
4 or 10	4.76%	6.67%
5 or 9	4.76%	4.00%
6 or 8	4.76%	1.52%

As you can see the only numbers that you would want to buy rather than place are the 4 and 10 because the 4.76% edge on a buy bet is lower than the 6.67% edge on a place bet. For 5 and 9 the 4.76% edge on a buy bet is slightly worse than the 4.00% edge on a place bet and for the 6 and 8 the 4.76% is a hefty three times higher than the 1.52% edge on the place bet.

To buy the 4 or 10 you would just put your chips down on the layout and tell the dealer what bet you wanted to make. For example, if you put down $21 and said “buy the 10.” The dealer will then keep the $1 chip for the house and put your $20 in the same area as the place bets but he’ll put a button on top that says “buy” to let him know that you bought the number rather than placed it. Buy bets, just like place bets, can be removed at any time and are always off on the come-out roll. Also, if you do remove your buy bet you will get your 5% commission back.

Besides buy bets where you're betting with the shooter and hoping that a point number will appear before a 7 does, there are also lay bets where you're doing just the opposite - you're betting against the shooter and hoping that a 7 will appear before a point number does.

Lay bets are also paid at the true odds and you have to pay a 5% commission of the amount you will win rather than the amount you're betting. Once again, when making a lay bet you should always remember to make them based on a minimum payoff of $20 because 5% of $20 is $1 and that's the minimum amount the casino will charge you.

Lay Number	Payoff	Casino Edge
4 or 10	$40 for $20	2.44%
5 or 9	$30 for $20	3.23%
6 or 8	$24 for $20	4.00%

For 4 and 10 you'll have to lay $40 to win $20 and the casino edge is 2.44%; for the 5 and 9 you'll have to lay $30 to win $20 and the casino edge is 3.23%; and for the 6 and 8 you'll have to lay $24 to win $20. The casino edge on that bet is 4.00%.

To make a lay bet you would just put your chips down on the layout and tell the dealer what you wanted to bet. For example, if you put down $41 and said "lay the 10." The dealer would then keep the $1 chip for the house and put your $40 in the same area as the don't come bets but he'll put a button on top that says "buy" to let him know that it's a lay bet. Lay bets, unlike buy bets, are always working on come-out rolls. Lay bets are, however, similar to buy bets in that they can be removed at any time and if you do remove your lay bet you will also receive your 5% commission back.

There are only a few other bets left located on the ends of the table to discuss and two of them are the big 6 and the big 8 which are both very bad bets. To bet the big 6 you place a chip in the big 6 box and then if the shooter rolls a 6 before rolling a 7 you win even money, or $1 for every $1 you bet. To bet the big 8 the same rules would apply: you put your bet in the box and then hope that the shooter rolls an 8 before rolling a 7 so you could win even money on your bet. The big 6 and big 8 can both be bet at any time and both are always working, even on the come-out roll. The casino edge on both the big 6 and the big 8 is 9.1%, which is the biggest edge we've seen so far. But, if you think back about some of the other bets we discussed doesn't this bet sound familiar? It should. This bet is the exact same as a place bet on the 6 or 8, but instead of getting paid off at 7-to-6 we're only getting paid off at even-money! Why would you want to bet the big 6 or big 8 at a house edge of more than 9% instead of making a place bet on the 6 or 8 at a house edge of only 1.5%? The answer is you wouldn't - so don't ever make this bet because it's a sucker bet that's only for people who don't know what they're doing.

The last bet we have to discuss on the player's side of the table is the field bet which is a one-roll bet that will pay even money if a 3,4,9,10 or 11 is rolled and 2-to-1 if a 2 or 12 is rolled. To make a field bet you would just place your chip anywhere in the field box and at first glance it doesn't seem like a bad bet. After all, there are 7 numbers you can win on and only 4 numbers you can lose on! The only problem is that there are 20 ways to roll the 4 losing numbers and only 16 ways to roll the 7 winning numbers and even after factoring in the double payoff for the 2 and 12 the casino winds up with a hefty 5.6% advantage. In some casinos they pay 3-to-1 on the 2 (or the 12) which cuts the casino edge in half to a more manageable 2.8%, but as you've seen there are still much better bets you can make. By the way, if you win on a field bet the dealer will put your winning chips right next to your bet so it's your responsibility to pick them up, or else they'll be considered a new bet!

Now, let's take a look at some of the long-shots, or proposition bets in the center of the table. When you look at these bets one of the first things you'll notice is that, unlike the bets on the other side of the table, the winning payoffs are clearly labeled. The reason they do that is so you can see those big payoffs and want to bet them, but as you'll see, although the payoffs are high, so are the casino advantages.

All of the proposition bets are controlled by the stickman and he is the person who must make those bets for you. So, if you wanted to make a $1 bet on "any craps" you would throw a $1 chip to the center of the table and say "$1 any craps" and the stickman would place that bet in the proper area for you. Then if you won, the stickman would tell the dealer at your end of the table to pay you. You should also be aware that they will only pay you your winnings and keep your original bet in place. If you don't want to make the same bet again, you should tell the stickman that you want your bet down and it will be returned to you.

There are only four proposition bets that are not one-roll bets and they are known as the "hardways." They are the hard 4, hard 6, hard 8 and hard 10. To roll a number the hardway means that the number must be rolled as doubles. For example 3 and 3 is a hard 6, but a roll of 4-2, or 5-1 are both called an easy 6, because they are easier to roll than double 3's.

To win a bet on hard 10 the shooter has to roll two 5's before rolling a 7 or an easy 10 such as 6-4 or 4-6. To win a bet on hard 4 the shooter has to roll two 2's before rolling a 7 or an easy 4 such as 3-1 or 1-3. The true odds of rolling a hard 4 or hard 10 are 8-to-1, but the casino will only pay you 7-to-1 which works out to a casino advantage of 11.1% on both of these bets.

To win a bet on hard 6 the shooter must roll two 3's before rolling a 7 or an easy 6 such as 5-1, 1-5; or 4-2, 2-4. To win a bet on hard 8 the shooter must roll two 4's before rolling a 7 or an easy 8 such as 6-2, 2-6 or 5-3, 3-5. The true odds of rolling a hard 6 or hard 8 are 10-to-1, but the casino will only pay you 9-to-1 which works out to a casino advantage of 9.1% on both of these bets.

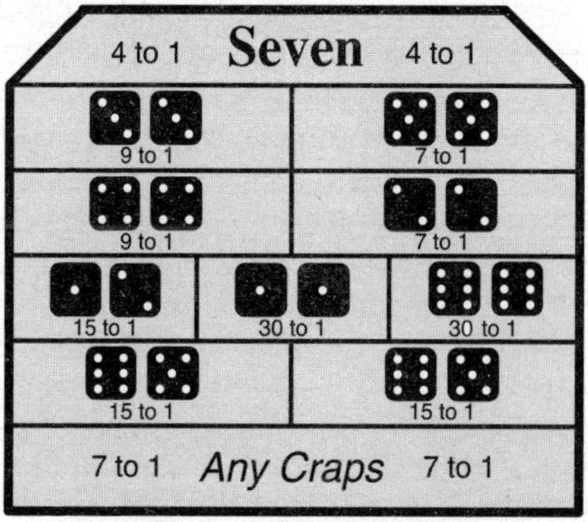

Two different types of proposition bets layouts

As noted before, all of the other proposition bets are one-roll bets which means that the next roll of the dice will decide whether you win or lose. As you'll see, the house edge on all of these bets is very high and they should all be avoided.

For the any craps bet you will win if a 2,3,or 12 is thrown on the next roll and lose if any other number comes up. The true odds are 8-to-1 but the casino will only pay you at 7-to-1 which gives them an edge of 11.1% on this bet and you'll notice that the stickman can put your bet either in the any craps box or, more likely, he'll put it on the circled marked "C" which stands for craps. The reason your bet will be placed in the "C" circle is that it's put in the circle that corresponds to where you're standing at the table and it makes it easier for the stickman to know who that bet belongs to.

For a craps 2 bet you win if the next roll is a 2 and lose if any other number shows up. The true odds are 35-to-1 but the casino will only pay you 30-to-1 which means that the edge on this bet is 13.9% In some casinos the odds for this bet will be shown as 30-for-1 which is actually the same as 29-to-1 and this results in an even bigger edge of 16.7% for the casino.

A craps 12 bet works the same as a craps 2 bet, except that now you will only win if a 12 is thrown. Again, the true odds are 35-to-1 but you will only be paid at 30-to-1 which means the casino edge on this bet is the same 13.9% as in the last craps 2 bet. Also if the bet is shown on the layout as 30-for-1 the casino edge is raised to 16.7%.

For a craps 3 bet you will only win if the next throw is a 3. The true odds are 17-to-1, but the casino will only pay you 15-to-1 which results in a casino advantage of 11.1% Once again, in some casinos the payoff will be shown as 15-for-1 which is the same as 14-to-1 and the house edge in that casino is an even higher 16.7%.

The 11 bet is similar to the craps 3 bet, except that now the only number you can win on is 11. The true odds of rolling an 11 are 17-to-1, but the casino will only pay you 15-to-1 which gives them an 11.1% advantage. Additionally, if the payoff is shown on the layout as 15-for-1 rather than 15-to-1 the casino edge will be even higher at 16.7%. By the way, because 11 sounds so much like 7 you will always hear 11 referred to at the table as "yo" or "yo-leven" to eliminate any confusion as to what number you are referring to. So, if you wanted to bet $5 on 11 you would throw a $5 chip to the stickman and say "$5 yo" and then he will either place it in the 11 box or place it on top of the "E" circle that corresponds to where you're standing at the table.

With a horn bet you are betting on the 2,3,11 and 12 all at once. A horn bet has to be made in multiples of $4 because you're making 4 bets at one time and you'll win if any one of those 4 numbers shows up on the next roll. You'll be paid off at the odds for the number that came in and you'll lose the rest of your chips. For example, if you make an $8 horn bet, this is the same as betting $2 on the 2, $2 on the 3, $2 on the 11 and $2 on the 12. If the number 2 came in you would get paid off at 30-to-1 so you would get back $60 in winnings and the casino would keep the $6 that you lost for the three $2 bets on the 3,11 and 12. The only advantage of a horn bet is that it allows you to make 4 bad bets at once rather than one at a time.

The last proposition bet we have to look at is also the worst bet on the craps table and it's the any 7 bet. With this bet you win if a 7 is rolled and lose if any other number comes up. The true odds are 5-to-1, but the casino will only pay you at 4-to-1 which gives them an edge of 16.7%

So there you have it! We've gone over all the possible bets you can make and now it's time to tell you how to win at the game of craps. Unfortunately, as you've seen, craps is a negative expectation game which means that every bet you make has a built-in advantage for the house. Actually, there is one bet that the casino has no advantage on and do you remember the name of that one? That's right it's the free odds bet and it's great that the casino has no advantage on that bet but the only way you're allowed to make that bet is to first make a negative expectation bet on pass/don't pass or come/don't come, so in essence, there are no bets you can make where you have an advantage over the house and in the long run the game of craps is unbeatable.

So, if that's the case then how do you win? Well, in reality there is only one way to win in craps and that way is to get lucky! Of course, this is easier said than done, but you will find it much easier to come out a winner if you only stick to the bets that offer the casino its lowest edge and those are the only bets you should ever make.

If you want to bet with the shooter I suggest you make a pass line bet, back it up with the free odds and then make a maximum of two come bets that are also both backed up with free odds. For example if double odds are allowed, you could start with a $5 pass line bet and say a 4 is rolled. You would then put $10 behind the line on your 4 and make a $5 come bet. If the shooter then rolled an 8 you would take $10 in odds on your come bet on the 8 and make another $5 come bet. If the shooter then rolled a 5 you would take $10 in odds on your come bet on the 5 and then stop betting. The idea here is that you always want to have a maximum of three numbers working and once you do, you shouldn't make anymore bets until one of your come numbers hits, in which case you would make another come bet, or if your pass line bet wins and then you would follow that up with another pass line bet. The important thing to remember is not to make more than two come bets because you don't want to have too much out on the table if the shooter rolls a 7. By using this betting system you'll only be giving the casino an edge of around .60% on all of your bets and with just a little bit of luck you can easily walk away a winner.

If you wanted to be a little more aggressive with this betting system there are some modifications you could make such as making a maximum of three come bets rather than two, or you could add place bets on the 6 and 8. Remember that a place bet on either the 6 or 8 only gives the casino a 1.52% advantage and that makes them both the next best bets after pass/don't pass and come/don't come. To add the place bets you would start off the same as before, but after you've made your second come bet you would look at the 6 and 8 and if they weren't covered you would then make a $6 place bet on whichever one was open or on both. By adding the place bets on the 6 and 8 you would always have at least three numbers in action and you could have as many as five covered at one time.

One final option with this system is to gradually increase the amount of your pass line and come bets by 50%, or by doubling them, and then backing them up with full odds, but I would only suggest you do this if you've been winning for a while because it could get very expensive if the table was cold and no one was rolling many numbers. Of course, if the table got real cold you could always change your strategy by betting against the shooter and the strategy for that is basically just the opposite of the one I just told you about.

To bet against the shooter you would start with a $5 don't pass bet which you would back up with single free odds and then bet a maximum of two don't come bets that are both backed up with single odds. The reason you don't want to back up your bets with double odds is because when you're betting against the shooter you have to lay the odds which means you're putting up more money than you'll be getting back and, once again, it could get very expensive if a shooter got on a hot roll and made quite a few passes.

For an example of this system let's say you start with a $5 don't pass bet and a 4 is rolled. You would then lay the odds by putting $10 next to your $5 don't pass bet and then make a $5 don't come bet. If the shooter then rolled an 8 you would lay $6 in odds on your don't come bet on the 8 and make another $5 don't come bet. If the shooter then rolled a 5 you would lay $9 in odds on your come bet on the 5 and then stop betting. The idea here is that you always want to have a maximum of three numbers working and once you do that, you shouldn't make anymore bets until, hopefully, the shooter sevens out and all of your bets win. If that does happen, then you would start all over again with a new don't pass bet. Once again, the important thing to remember is not to make more than two don't come bets because you don't want to have too much out on the table if the shooter gets hot and starts to roll a lot of numbers. With this system you'll always have a maximum of three numbers in action and you'll only be giving the casino an edge of about .80% on all of your bets. Some options to bet more aggressively with this system are to increase your free odds bets to double odds rather than single odds and also to make three don't come bets, rather than stopping at two. The choice is up to you but remember that because you must lay the odds and put out more money than you'll be getting back you could lose a substantial amount rather quickly if the roller got hot and made a lot of point numbers.

Now, one last point I want to make about betting craps is that the bankroll you'll need is going to be much bigger than the bankroll you'll need for playing any other casino game. If you're betting with the shooter you'll have one $5 pass line bet with double odds and two come bets with double odds which means that you could have as much as $45 on the table that could be wiped out with the roll of a 7. If you're betting against the shooter you'll have $5 on don't pass with single odds and two don't come bets with single odds which means you could have as much as $44 on the table that could be wiped out if the shooter got on a "hot" roll and made a lot of numbers. As I said before, you need to have an adequate bankroll to be able to ride out the losing streaks that will eventually occur and you need to be able to hold on until things turn around and you start to win.

So how much of a bankroll is enough? Well, I would say about 7 times the maximum amount of money you'll have out on the table is adequate and 10 times would be even better. In both of our examples then you should have a bankroll of at least $300. If you don't have that much money to put out on the table then you might want to consider having less money out on the table by making only one come or don't come bet rather than two or maybe even just limiting your bets to pass and don't pass along with the free odds.

Just remember that it doesn't matter whether you want to bet with the shooter or against the shooter - both of these systems will give you the best chance of winning because they allow the casino only the slightest edge and with a little bit of luck you can easily come out a winner. Good luck!

A Few Last Words

by Steve Bourie

When I sit down to put this book together each year I try to make sure that everything in here will help to make you a better and more knowledgeable gambler when you go to a casino.

I try to include stories that will help you understand how casinos operate, how to choose the best casino games and also how to play those games in the best way possible.

My philosophy with this book is that gambling in a casino is a fun activity and, according to research studies, for about 98% of the people who visit casinos this statement is true. The vast majority of people who gamble in casinos are recreational players who enjoy the fun and excitement of gambling. They know that they won't always win and they also realize that over the long term they will most likely have more losing sessions than winning ones. They also understand that any losses they incur will be the price they pay for their fun and they only gamble with money they can afford to lose. In other words, they realize that casino gambling is a form of entertainment, just like going to a movie or an amusement park, and they are willing to pay a price for that entertainment. Unfortunately, there are also some people who go to casinos and become problem gamblers.

According to Gamblers Anonymous you may be a problem gambler if you answer yes to at least seven of the following 20 questions:

1. Do you lose time from work due to gambling?
2. Does gambling make your home life unhappy?
3. Does gambling affect your reputation?
4. Do you ever feel remorse after gambling?
5. Do you ever gamble to get money with which to pay debts or to otherwise solve financial difficulties?
6. Does gambling cause a decrease in your ambition or efficiency?
7. After losing, do you feel you must return as soon as possible and win back your losses?
8. After a win, do you have a strong urge to return and win more?
9. Do you often gamble until your last dollar is gone?
10. Do you ever borrow to finance your gambling?
11. Do you ever sell anything to finance your gambling?
12. Are you reluctant to use your "gambling money" for other expenses?
13. Does gambling make you careless about the welfare of your family?
14. Do you ever gamble longer than you planned?

15. Do you ever gamble to escape worry or trouble?
16. Do you ever commit, or consider committing, an illegal act to finance your gambling?
17. Does gambling cause you to have difficulty sleeping?
18. Do arguments, disappointments, or frustrations create within you an urge to gamble?
19. Do you have an urge to celebrate good fortune by a few hours of gambling?
20. Do you ever consider self-destruction as a result of your gambling?

If you believe you might have a gambling problem you should be aware that help is available from The National Council on Problem Gambling, Inc. It is the foremost advocacy organization in the country for problem gamblers and is headquartered in Washington, D.C. It was formed in 1972 as a non-profit agency to promote public education and awareness about gambling problems and operates a 24-hour nationwide help line at (800) 522-4700, plus a website at www.ncpgambling.org. Anyone contacting that organization will be provided with the appropriate referral resources for help with their gambling problem.

Another good source for anyone seeking help with a gambling problem is Gambler's Anonymous. They have chapters in many cities throughout the U.S. as well as in most major cities throughout the world. You can see a list of all those cities on their website at www.gamblersanonymous.org or contact them by telephone at (213) 386-8789.

A third program, Gam-Anon, specializes in helping the spouse, family and close friends of compulsive gamblers rather than the gamblers themselves.If you are adversely affected by a loved one who is a compulsive gambler, then Gam-Anon is an organization that may benefit you. They have a website at www.gam-anon.org that lists the cities which host meetings. They can also be contacted by telephone at (718) 352-1671.

I sincerely hope that none of you reading this book will ever have a need to contact any of these worthwhile organizations, but it was an issue that I felt should be addressed.

ALABAMA

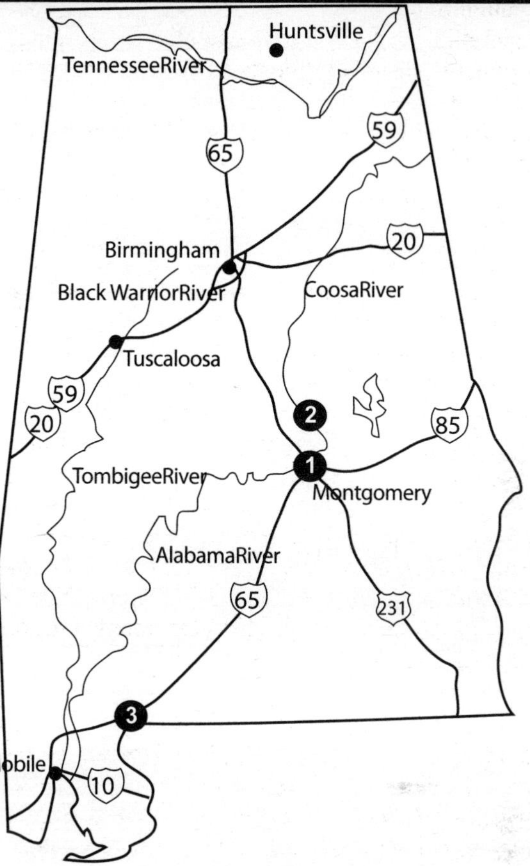

Alabama has three Indian casinos that offer Class II video gaming machines.

Class II video gaming devices look like slot machines, but are actually bingo games and the spinning reels are for "entertainment purposes only." No public information is available concerning the payback percentages on any gaming machines in Alabama. Legislation has been introduced to legalize sports betting and that may happen in 2020.

The minimum gambling age is 21 and all of the casinos are open 24 hours. For Alabama tourism information call (800) 252-2262, or go to: www.alabama.travel.

Wind Creek Casino & Hotel - Atmore
303 Poarch Road
Atmore, Alabama 36502
(251) 446-4200
Website: www.windcreekatmore.com
Map: **#3** (55 miles NE. of Mobile)

Toll-Free: (866) 946-3360
Rooms: 236 Price Range: $109-$219
Suites: 36 Price Range $159-$299
Casino Size: 80,000 Square Feet
Restaurants: 4 (1 open 24 hours) Valet: Free
Buffets: B- $20.00 (Sat)/$14.00 (Sun)
L- $14.00/$20.00 (Sat)/$14.00 (Sun)
D- $20.00/$24.00(Fri/Sat)/$14.00(Sun)
Overnight RV Parking: No
Special Features: 24-space RV park $38/night.

Wind Creek Casino & Hotel - Montgomery
1801 Eddie Tullis Drive
Montgomery, Alabama 36117
(866) 946-3360
Website: www.windcreekmontgomery.com
Map: **#1**

Rooms: 123 Price Range: $109-$119
Suites: 8 Price Range: $199- $219
Casino Size: 65,000 Square feet
Restaurants: 3
Overnight RV Parking: Free
Senior discount: Various Mon 12pm-4pm if 50+

Wind Creek Casino & Hotel - Wetumpka
100 River Oaks Drive
Wetumpka, Alabama 36092-3084
(866)-946-3360
Website: www.windcreekwetumpka.com
Map: **#2** (20 miles N. of Montgomery)

Rooms: 270 Price Range: $119-$179
Suites: 13 Price Range: $199-$259
Casino Size: 85,000 Square Feet
Restaurants: 3 (1 open 24 hours)
Buffets: B- $13.00 (Thu)/$20.00 (Sat/Sun)
L- $14.00/$20.00 (Sat/Sun)
D- $20.00/$35.00 (Fri-Sun)
Overnight RV Parking: No
Senior Discount: Free breakfast after earning 10 player's club points on Thu if 50+

ARIZONA

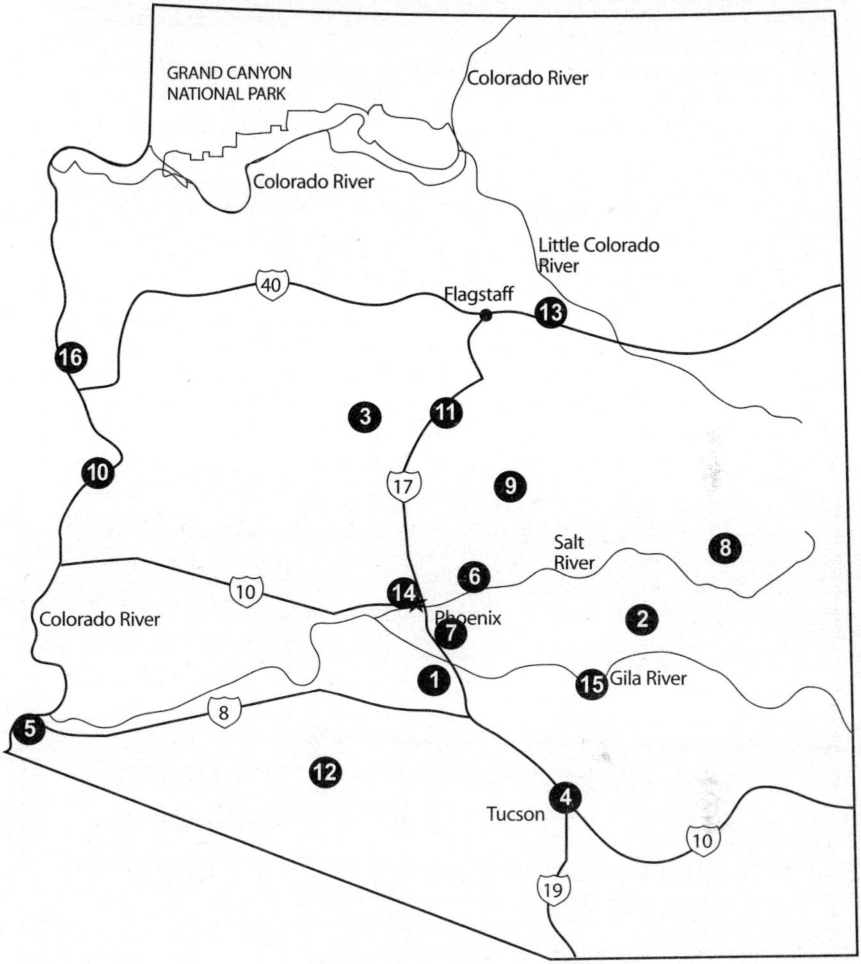

All Arizona casinos are located on Indian reservations and all of them offer slot machines, video poker and video keno. Optional games include: blackjack (BJ), Spanish 21 (S21), let it ride (LIR), casino war (CW), pai gow poker (PGP), three card poker (TCP), Mississippi stud (MS), poker (P), live keno (K), and bingo (BG). Legislation has been introduced to legalize sports betting and that may happen in 2020.

Arizona tribes aren't required to release information on their slot machine percentage paybacks, however, according to the Arizona Department of Gaming, the terms of the compact require each tribes' machines to return the following minimum and maximum paybacks: video poker and video blackjack - 83% to 100%, slot machines - 80% to 100%, keno - 75% to 100%. Each tribe is free to set its machines to pay back anywhere within those limits.

The minimum gambling age is 21 and all casinos are open 24 hours. For more information on visiting Arizona call the state's Office of Tourism at (866) 275-5816 or visit their website at: tourism.az.gov

Apache Gold Casino Resort
777 Jeronimo Springs Boulevard
San Carlos, Arizona 85550
(928) 475-7800
Map: **#2** (90 miles E. of Phoenix)
Website: www.apache-gold-casino.com

Toll-Free Number: (800) 272-2438
Rooms: 146 Price Range: $79-$149
Suites: 2 Price Range: $149-$179
Restaurants: 3 Liquor: Yes
Buffets: L- $14.99 (Sat/Sun)
D- $14.99/$19.99 (Fri-Sun)
Casino Size: 10,000 Square Feet
Other Games: BJ, TCP BG (Fri-Sun),
P (Fri/Sat)
Overnight RV Parking: Yes
Special Features: 18-hole golf course. Convenience store. 60-space RV Park ($30 per night) w/full hookups and dump station. Table games open at 3pm.

Apache Sky Casino
777 Apache Sky Boulevard
Winkelman, Arizona 85192
(800) 272-0077
Website: www.apacheskycasino.com
Map: **#15** (70 miles N. of Tucson)

Restaurants: 1
Casino Size: 15,000 Square Feet
Other Games: BJ (Sun-Thu 2pm-10pm/
Fri/Sat 2pm-12am)
Overnight RV Parking: No
Special Features: Affiliated with Apache Gold casino.

Blue Water Casino
11300 Resort Drive
Parker, Arizona 85344
(928) 669-7000
Website: www.bluewaterfun.com
Map: **#10** (160 miles W. of Phoenix)

Toll-Free Number: (888) 243-3360
Rooms: 200 Price Range: $94-$114
Suites: 25 Price Range: $144-$195
Restaurants: 4 Liquor: Yes
Buffet: L-$12.95
D-$26.95/$13.95 (Fri/Sat)
Other Games: BJ, TCP, P, BG
Casino Size: 30,000 Square Feet
Overnight RV Parking: Free (only 1 night)
RV Dump: No
Senior Discount: Various buffet discounts.
Special Features: 100-slip marina with Wakeboard park. Four-screen movie theater.

Bucky's Casino & Resort
1500 E. Highway 69
Prescott, Arizona 86301
(928) 776-5695
Website: www.buckyscasino.com
Map: **#3** (91 miles S.W. of Flagstaff)

Toll-Free Number: (800) 756-8744
Rooms: 81 Price Range: $160-$189
Suites: 80 Price Range: $169-$229
Restaurants: 1 Liquor: No
Other Games: BJ, P
Casino Size: 24,000 Square Feet
Overnight RV Parking: No
Special Features: Located in Prescott Resort Hotel. Free on-site shuttle service.

Casino Arizona
524 N. 92nd Street
Scottsdale, Arizona 85256
(480) 850-7777
Website: www.casinoarizona.com
Map: **#6** (15 miles N.E. of Phoenix)

Toll-Free Number: (877) 724-4687
Restaurants: 5 (1 open 24 hours) Liquor: Yes
Buffets: B-$20.95(Sun)
L-$12.95
D-$18.95/$29.95(Wed/Thu)/
$23.50(Fri/Sat)
Casino Size: 40,000 Square Feet
Other Games: BJ, LIR, TCP, K, PGP, CW, BG
Overnight RV Parking: $25/night Check in with Security
Special Features: 500-seat showroom.

Casino Del Sol
5655 W. Valencia
Tucson, Arizona 85757
(520) 883-1700
Website: www.casinodelsol.com
Map: **#4**

Toll-Free Number: (800) 344-9435
Rooms: 200 Price Range: $99-$149
Suites: 15 Price Range: $259-$289
Restaurants: 9 Liquor: Yes
Buffets: B-$12.00/$30.00 (Sat/Sun)
L-$15.00 (Mon-Fri)/$28.00 (Sat/Sun)
D-$35.00 (Thu)/$25.00 (Fri-Sat)/
$28.00 (Sun)
Casino Size: 50,500 Square Feet
Other Games: BJ, P, BG, TCP, S21, PGP
Overnight RV Parking: $40/day/RV Dump: No
Special Features: 4,400-seat amphitheater.

Casino of the Sun
7406 S. Camino De Oeste
Tucson, Arizona 85746
(800) 344-9435
Website: www.solcasinos.com
Map: **#4**

Restaurants: 1 Liquor: Yes
Other Games: BJ
Overnight RV Parking: Free/RV Dump: No
Special Features: Smoke shop. Gift shop.

Cliff Castle Casino Hotel
555 Middle Verde Road
Camp Verde, Arizona 86322
(928) 567-7999
Website: www.cliffcastlecasinohotel.com
Map: **#11** (50 miles S. of Flagstaff)

Toll-Free Number: (800) 381-7568
Rooms: 122 Price Range: $149-$189
Suites: 36 Price Range: $169-$209
Restaurants: 7 Liquor: Yes
Buffets: B- $8.00 L- $12.00/$14.00 (Sun)
D- $14.00/$16.99 (Sat)
Casino Size: 47,000 Square Feet
Other Games: BJ, P
Overnight RV Parking: Free/RV Dump: No
Special Features: Casino is in Cliff Castle Lodge. Bowling alley. Childcare facility.

Cocopah Resort
15318 S. Avenue B
Somerton, Arizona 85350
(800) 237-5687
Map: **#5** (13 miles S.W. of Yuma)
Website: www.cocopahresort.com

Rooms: 101 Price Range: $77-$107
Suites: 7 Price Range: $127-197
Restaurants: 3 Liquor: Yes
Buffets: B- $8.99 D- $20.99 (Fri/Sat)
Casino Size: 24,000 Square Feet
Other Games: BJ, BG
Overnight RV Parking: $6 per night
Special Features: 18-hole golf course.

Desert Diamond Casino - Sahuarita
1100 West Pima Mine Road
Sahuarita, Arizona 85629
(520) 294-7777
Website: www.ddcaz.com
Map: **#4**

Toll-Free Number: (866) 332-9467
Restaurants: 3 Liquor: Yes
Buffets: L- $8.99/$16.99 (Sun)
D- $9.99/$10.99 (Fri)/$14.99 (Sat/Sun)
Casino Size: 15,000 Square Feet
Other Games: BJ, S21, K
Overnight RV Parking: Free/RV Dump: No
Special Features: 2,500-seat event center.

Desert Diamond Casino - Tucson
7350 S. Nogales Highway
Tucson, Arizona 85706
(520) 294-7777
Website: www.ddcaz.com
Map: **#4**

Toll-Free Number: (866) 332-9467
Rooms: 140 Rates: $86-$196
Suites: 8 Rates: $266-$350
Restaurants: 3 Liquor: Yes
Buffets: B- $7.99/$14.99 (Sat/Sun)
L- $10.99 (Tue)/$14.99 (Sat/Sun)
D- $14.99 ()/$16.99 (Fri)/
$18.99 (Sat)
Casino Size: 15,000 Square Feet
Other Games: BJ, P, TCP, PGP, K, BG, S21
Overnight RV Parking: Free/RV Dump: No
Special Features: No bingo Tuesday

Desert Diamond West Valley
91st Ave and Northern Ave
Glendale, Arizona 85305
(520) 294-7777
Website: www.ddcaz.com
Map: **#14** (Suburb of Phoenix)

Restaurants: Food Court Liquor: No
Casino Size: 35,000 Square Feet
Special Features: Free self-serve soft drinks. New casino with table games expeced to open early 2020.

Desert Diamond Casino - Why
Highway 86 Mile Post 55
Ajo, Arizona 85321
(866) 332-9467
Website: www.ddcaz.com
Map: **#12** (125 miles S.W. of Phoenix)

Restaurants: 1 Snack Bar
Other Games: Only Gaming Machines
Overnight RV Parking: No
Special Features: Located on State Highway 86 at mile post 55 near Why, Arizona. Convenience Store.

Fort McDowell Casino
10424 North Fort McDowell Road
Fountain Hills, Arizona 85264
(480) 837-1424
Website: www.fortmcdowellcasino.com
Map: **#6** (25 miles N.E. of Phoenix)

Toll-Free Number: (800) 843-3678
Rooms: 246 Rates: $129-$229
Suites: 23 Rates: $375-$499
Restaurants: 5 Liquor: Yes
Buffets: L- 11.95/$14.50 (Sun)
D-$21.95 (Tue)/$16.95 (Wed/Thu)/
$33.95 (Fri)/$24.95 (Sat/Sun)
Other Games: BJ, P, K, BG, TCP, P
Overnight RV Parking: No
Special Features: Free local shuttle. Gift shop.

Harrah's Ak Chin Casino Resort
15406 Maricopa Road
Maricopa, Arizona 85239
(480) 802-5000
Website: www.harrahsakchin.com
Map: **#1** (25 miles S. of Phoenix)

Toll-Free Number: (800) 427-7247
Rooms: 142 Price Range: $80-$215
Suites: 4 Price Range: $160-$280
Restaurants: 4 Liquor: Yes
Buffets: L-$14.99/$21.99 (Sun)
D-$19.99/$29.99 (Fri/Sat)
Casino Size: 43,000 Square Feet
Other Games: BJ, P, K, BG (Wed-Sun), MS,
TCP, LIR, PGP
Overnight RV Parking: Free/RV Dump: No
Senior Discount: Various Mon/Thu if 50+
Special Features: Free local shuttle.

Hon-Dah Resort Casino
777 Highway 260
Pinetop, Arizona 85935
(928) 369-0299
Website: www.hon-dah.com
Map: **#8** (190 miles N.E. of Phoenix)

Toll-Free Number: (800) 929-8744
Rooms: 126 Price Range: $109-$129
Suites: 2 Price Range: $179-$199
Restaurants: 1 Liquor: Yes
Buffets: B- $6.99/$24.99 (Sun)
L- $7.99/$24.99 (Sun)
D- $13.99/$24.99 (Fri)/$17.99 (Sat)
Casino Size: 20,000 Square Feet
Other Games: P, BJ
Overnight RV Parking: Must use RV park
Special Features: 258-space RV park ($34.77 per night). Convenience store. Gas station.

Lone Butte Casino
1077 South Kyrene Road
Chandler, Arizona 85226
(520) 796-7777
Website: www.wingilariver.com
Map: **#7** (10 miles S.W. of Phoenix)

Toll-Free Number: (800) 946-4452
Restaurants: 2 Liquor: Yes
Casino Size: 10,000 Square Feet
Other Games: BJ, BG, PGP, TCP
Overnight RV Parking: Free 4 day max/
RV Dump: No
Special Features: Food Court with 6 fast food locations.

Mazatzal Hotel & Casino
Highway 87 Mile Post 251
Payson, Arizona 85541
(928) 474-6044
Website: www.mazatzal-casino.com
Map: **#9** (90 miles N.E. of Phoenix)

Toll-Free Number: (800) 777-7529
Suites: 40 Prices: $120-$180
Restaurants: 2 Liquor: Yes
Buffets: L- $12.00/$20.00 (Sun)
D- $14.00 (Fri)
Casino Size: 38,000 Square Feet
Other Games: BJ, P, K, BG (Mon-Thu)
Overnight RV Parking: Free/RV Dump: No
Special Features: Offers Stay & Play packages (Sun-Thu) with local motels. Free shuttle. Table games open at 10am

Paradise Casino Arizona
450 Quechan Drive
Yuma, Arizona 85364
(760) 572-7777
Website: www.paradise-casinos.com
Map: **#5** (244 miles W. of Tucson)

Toll-Free Number: (888) 777-4946
Restaurants: 2 Liquor: Yes
Casino Size: 11,600 Square Feet
Other Games: BG
Overnight RV Parking: $10/RV Dump: No
Special Features: Part of casino is located across the state border in California. Poker offered in CA casino. 10% food discount with players club card.

Spirit Mountain Casino
8555 South Highway 95
Mohave Valley, Arizona 86440
(928) 346-2000
Website: www. runtothemountain.com
Map: **#12** (15 miles S. of Bullhead City)

Toll-Free Number: (888) 837-4030
RV Reservations: (928) 346-1225
Restaurants: 1 Liquor: Yes
Casino Size: 12,000 Square Feet
Other Games: Only Gaming Machines
Overnight RV Parking: Must use RV park.
Special Features: Convenience store. Gas station.

Talking Stick Resort
9800 E. Talking Stick Way
Scottsdale, Arizona 85256
(480) 850-7777
Website: www.talkingstickresort.com
Map: **#6** (15 miles N.E. of Phoenix)

Toll-Free Number: (866) 877-9897
Rooms: 470 Prices: $139-$189
Suites: 27 Prices: $449-$799
Restaurants: 6 Liquor: Yes
Buffet Prices: B-$12.95/ $37.95 (Sun)
L-$15.95
D-$23.95/ $38.95 (Fri/Sat)
Other Games: BJ, P, TCP, LIR,
CW, K, PGP, BG
Overnight RV Parking: Free 6 day max/
RV Dump: No

Twin Arrows Navajo Casino Resort
22181 Resort Blvd
Twin Arrows, Arizona 86004
(928) 856-7200
Website: www.twinarrows.com
Map: **#13** (40 miles E. of Flagstaff)

Toll-Free Number: (855) 946-8946
Rooms: 85 Price Range: $159-$189
Suites: 5 Price Range: $379-$489
Restaurants: 4
Buffets: L-$10.49 D-$14.69/$19.99 (Wed)
Other Games: BJ, TCP, PGP, K, P, BG, S21
Special Features: Located at Twin Arrows exit of Interstate 40. Alcohol is only served in dining areas.

Vee Quiva Hotel & Casino
15091 S. Komatke Lane
Laveen Village, Arizona 85339
(520) 796-7777
Website: www.playatgila.com
Map: **#7** (10 miles S.W. of Phoenix)

Toll-Free Number: (800) 946-4452
Rooms: 82 Price Range: $79-$149
Suites: 8 Price Range: $189-$258
Restaurants: 2 Liquor: Yes
Casino Size: 15,000 Square Feet
Other Games: BJ, P, BG, TCP, PGP, S21
Overnight RV Parking: Free 4 day max/
RV Dump: No

Wild Horse Pass Hotel & Casino
5040 Wild Horse Pass Blvd
Chandler, Arizona 85226
(520) 796-7727
Website: www.playatgila.com
Map: **#7** (25 miles S.E. of Phoenix)

Toll-Free Number: (800) 946-4452
Rooms: 223 Rates: $99-$299
Suites: 19 Rates: $169-$369
Restaurants: 2 Liquor: Yes
Casino Size: 100,000 Square Feet
Other Games: BJ, PGP, LIR, TCP, P
Overnight RV Parking: Free 4 day max/ RV Dump: No
Senior Discount: Various Mon if 55+.
Special Features: 1,400-seat showroom.

Yavapai Casino
1505 E. Highway 69
Prescott, Arizona 86301
(928) 445-5767
Website: www.buckyscasino.com
Map: **#3** (91 miles S.W. of Flagstaff)

Toll-Free Number: (800) 756-8744
Casino Size: 6,000 Square Feet
Restaurants: 1 Liquor: Yes
Overnight RV Parking: No
Special Features: Located across the street from Bucky's Casino. Free local-area shuttle bus.

ARKANSAS

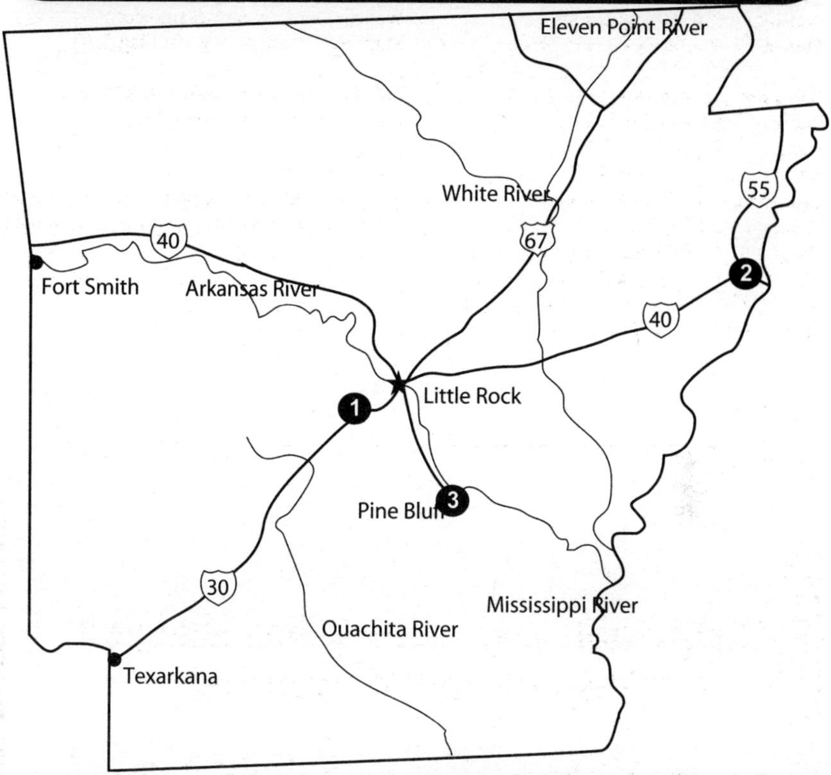

There are two racetrack casinos in Arkansas. They both offer electronic gaming machines, as well as live table games. Pari-mutuel wagering on live racing is also offered seasonally.

In late 2018 Arkansas voters approved a referendum to allow one casino in both Jefferson and Pope Counties. The Quapaw Indian Tribe is building a $350 million casino resort in Jefferson County near Pine Bluff (map location **#3**). The Saracen Casino Resort, which will have a 300-room hotel and 80,000 square feet of gaming space, is expected to open by late 2020. However, a smaller temporary casino may be opened in that location by early 2020. A license for the Pope County casino location had not been approved as of late 2019.

Gaming regulations require that all Arkansas machines return a minimum of 83%. For the one year period from July 1, 2018 through June 30, 2019, the average gaming machine's return at Oaklawn was 92.81% and at Southland it was 92.72%

Both Arkansas casinos offer: slots, video poker, video keno. blackjack, craps, roulette, three card poker, Ultimate Texas Hold'em and sports betting. Southland also offers Mississippi Stud.

The minimum gambling age is 21 for slots and 18 for pari-mutuel wagering. For more information on visiting Arkansas call the state's tourism office at (800) 628-8725 or visit their website at: www.arkansas.com.

Oaklawn Racing Casino Resort
2705 Central Avenue
Hot Springs, Arkansas 71901
(501) 623-4411
Website: www.oaklawn.com
Map: **#1** (55 miles S.W. of Little Rock)

Toll-Free Number: (800) 625-5296
Restaurants: 5
Hours: 10am-3am /6am(Fri/Sat)
Other Games: P, TCP, UTH
Admission: Free Parking: Free
Overnight RV Parking: No
Special Features: Live throroughbred racing seasonally. Daily simulcasting of horse racing. New 200-room hotel expected to open mid-2020.

Southland Casino Racing
1550 North Ingram Boulevard
West Memphis, Arkansas 72301
(800) 467-6182
Website: www.southlandcasino.com
Map: **#2** (130 miles E. of Little Rock)

Restaurants: 4
Other Games: P, LIR, TCP
Preferred Parking: $3/Valet Parking: Free
Buffets: B- $11.99 (Sat)
L- $12.99 (Mon)/$14.99 (Tue-Thu)/ $13.99 (Fri)/$28.99(Sat)/ $16.99(Sun)
D-$16.99 (Mon)/$17.99(Tue-Thu)/ $28.99(Fri/Sat)/ $16.99 (Sun)
Overnight RV Parking: No
Special Features: Live greyhound racing seasonally. Daily simulcasting of greyhound and horse racing. Buffet discount for players club members.

CALIFORNIA

All California casinos are located on Indian reservations and all are legally allowed to offer electronic gaming machines, blackjack, and other house-banked card games. The games of craps and roulette are not permitted. However, some casinos do offer modified versions of craps and roulette that are played with cards rather than dice or roulette wheels.

Most California card rooms also offer some form of player-banked blackjack, but because they are prohibited by law from playing blackjack, the game is usually played to 22 rather than 21. Additionally, players must pay a commission to the house on every hand they play. The amount will vary depending on the rules of the house but, generally, it's about two to five percent of the total amount bet. There are about 90 card rooms in California and you can see a listing of them on the Internet at: *http://www.cgcc.ca.gov.*

California's tribes aren't required to release information on their slot machine percentage paybacks and the state of California does not require any minimum returns.

Unless otherwise noted, all California casinos are open 24 hours and offer: slots, video poker, and video keno. Optional games offered include: baccarat (B), blackjack (BJ), Spanish 21 (S21), mini-baccarat (MB), poker (P), pai gow poker (PGP), Caribbean stud poker (CSP), let it ride (LIR), three card poker (TCP), four card poker (FCP) bingo (BG), sic bo (SIC) casino war (CW), Mississippi stud (MS) and off track betting (OTB). Please note that legislation has been introduced to legalize sports betting and that may happen in 2020.

The minimum gambling age is 21 at most casinos (at some it's 18) and 18 for bingo or pari-mutuel betting. Look in the "Special Features" listing for each casino to see which allow gambling at 18 years of age.

Although most of the casinos have toll-free numbers be aware that some of those numbers will only work for calls made within California. Also, many of the casinos are in out-of-the-way locations, so it is advisable to call ahead for directions, especially if you will be driving at night.

For more information on visiting California contact the state's department of tourism at (800) 862-2543 or www.visitcalifornia.com.

Agua Caliente Casino
32250 Bob Hope Drive
Rancho Mirage, California 92270
(760) 321-2000
Website: www.hotwatercasino.com
Map: **#3** (115 miles E. of L. A.)

Toll-Free Number: (888) 999-1995
Gambling Age: 21
Rooms: 340 Price Range: $99-$209
Suites: 22 Price Range $239-$419
Restaurants: 4 Liquor: Yes
Buffets: B- $12.99/$21.99 (Sun)
L- $12.99
D-$17.99/$21.99 (Fri-Sat)
Other Games: BJ, MB, TCP, MS
S21, LIR, P, PGP
Overnight RV Parking: Only offered at adjacent Flying J truck stop
Special Features: Associated with Spa Casino. Offers card version of craps.

Augustine Casino
84001 Avenue 54
Coachella, California 92236
(760) 452-0047
Website: www.augustinecasino.com
Map: **#8** (125 miles E. of L. A.)

Toll-Free Number: (888) 752-9294
Gambling Age: 21
Restaurants: 3 Liquor: Yes
Buffets: B- $10.95/$14.95 (Sat)/$16.95 (Sun)
L- $10.95
D- $14.95/$34.95 (Fri/Sat)
Other Games: BJ, TCP, S21
Overnight RV Parking: No

Barona Valley Ranch Resort and Casino
1932 Wildcat Canyon Road
Lakeside, California 92040
(619) 443-2300
Website: www.barona.com
Map: **#1** (15 miles N.E. of San Diego)

Toll-Free Number: (888) 722-7662
Room Reservations: (877) 287-2624
Gambling Age: 18
Rooms: 397 Price Range: $129-$189
Suites: 9 Price Range: Private Use Only
Restaurants: 8 Liquor: Yes
Buffets: B/L/D-$44.99
Other Games: BJ, B, MB, P, CSP, UTH
PGP, MS,TCP, LIR, FCP
CW, OTB, FCP, SIC
Overnight RV Parking: Free 3 day Max/
RV Dump: No
Special Features: Offers card versions of roulette and craps. Food court. Wedding chapel. 18-hole golf course. Buffet discounts for players club members.

Bear River Casino Hotel
11 Bear Paws Way
Loleta, California 95551
(707) 733-9644
Website: www.bearrivercasino.com
Map: **#38** (10 miles S. of Eureka)

Toll-Free Number: (800) 761-2327
Gambling Age: 21
Rooms: 140 Prices: $143-$249
Suites: 3 Prices: $170-$220

Restaurants: 3 Liquor: Yes
Buffet: B- $15.99 (Sun)
Casino Size: 31,000 Square Feet
Other Games: BJ, S21, PGP, TCP
Overnight RV Parking: Free, but must
check in with security first
Special Features: Card versions of craps and roulette.

Black Oak Casino
19400 Tuolumne Road North
Tuolumne, California 95379
(209) 928-9300
Website: www.blackoakcasino.com
Map: **#5** (100 miles S.E. of Sacramento)

Toll-Free Number: (877) 747-8777
Gambling Age: 21
Rooms: 148 Price Range: $129-$189
Suites: 16 Price Range: $309-$549
Restaurants: 5 Liquor: Yes
Buffet: B- $13.99 (Sat)/$14.99 (Sun)
L- $9.99/$14.99 (Sun)
D- $27.99 (Fri/Sat)/$16.99 (Sun)
Casino Size: 42,000 Square Feet
Other Games: BJ, TCP, LIR, PGP, FCP,
S21, FCP, MB, P
Overnight RV Parking: No
Special Features: Casino has electronic poker tables, 85-space RV Park $60-$70 per night.

Blue Lake Casino & Hotel
777 Casino Way
Blue Lake, California 95525
(707) 668-9770
Website: www.bluelakecasino.com
Map: **#34** (10 miles N. of Eureka)

Toll-Free Number: (877) 252-2946
Gambling Age: 21
Rooms: 102 Rates: $140-$165
Suites: 10 Rates: $210-$335
Restaurants: 3 Liquor: Yes
Buffet: B-$15.99 (Sun)
Other Games: BJ, S21, P, TCP, PGP
Overnight RV Parking: 2 nights Free with player's club card/RV Dump: No

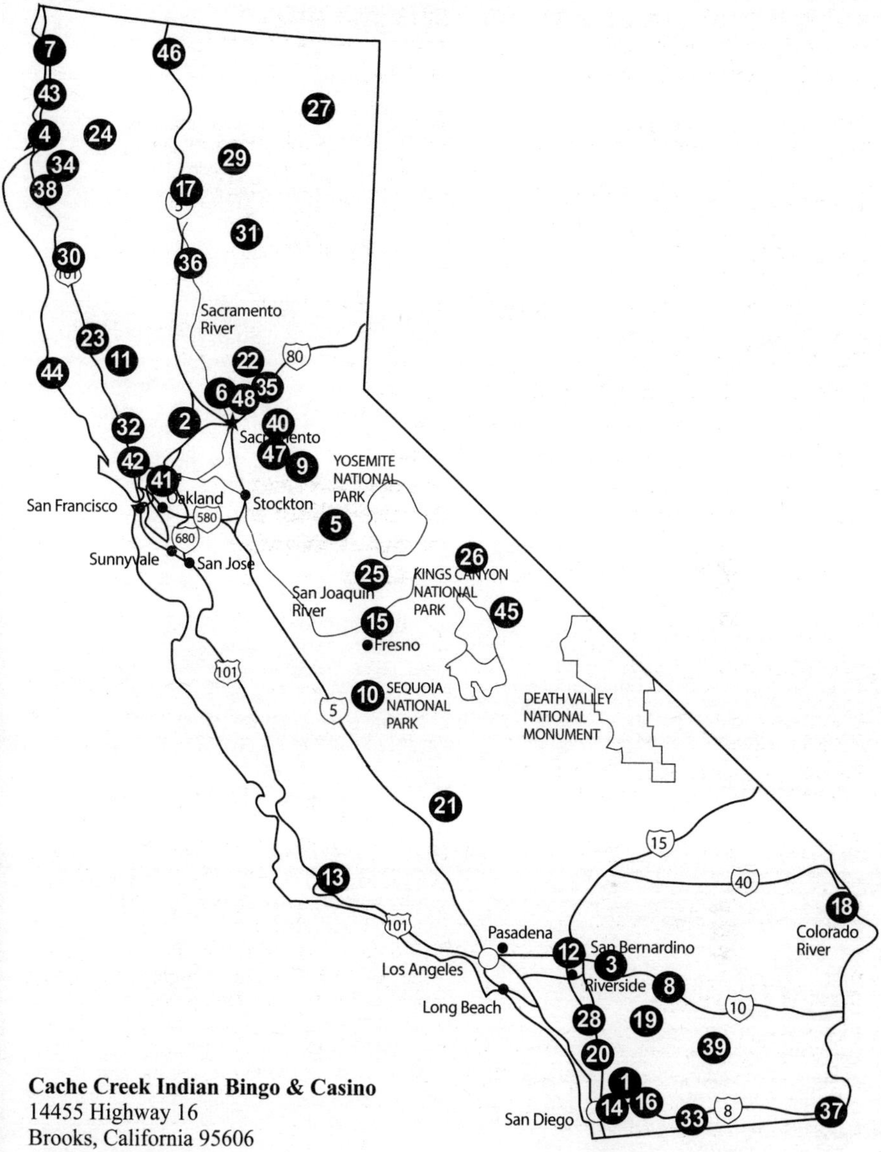

Cache Creek Indian Bingo & Casino
14455 Highway 16
Brooks, California 95606
(530) 796-3118
Website: www.cachecreek.com
Map: **#2** (35 miles N.W. of Sacramento)

Toll-Free Number: (800) 992-8686
Gambling Age: 21
Rooms: 563 Prices: $159-$309
Suites: 96 Prices: $159-$349
Restaurants: 9 Liquor: Yes
Buffets: L- $15.95 (Fri-Tue)
D- $17.95 (Sun-Tue)/$31.99 (Fri)/ $27.99 (Sat)
Casino Size: 75,000 Square Feet
Other Games: BJ, P, CSP, LIR, PGP, MS, TCP, B, MB, FCP, CW, PG
Overnight RV Parking: Free/RV Dump: No
Special Features: Offers card versions of craps and roulette. Full-service spa. No buffet on Tuesday or Wednesday. $3 buffet discount for players club members. Suites only available for premier casino patrons.

Cahuilla Casino
52702 Highway 371
Anza, California 92539
(951) 763-1200
Website: www.cahuillacasino.com
Map: **#19** (30 miles S. of Palm Springs)

Toll-Free Number: (888) 371-2692
Gambling Age: 21
Restaurants: 1 Liquor: Yes
Overnight RV Parking: No

Casino Pauma
777 Pauma Reservation Road
Pauma Valley, California 92061
(760) 742-2177
Website: www.casinopauma.com
Map: **#20** (35 miles N.E. of San Diego)

Toll-Free Number: (877) 687-2862
Gambling Age: 18 Restaurants: 3 Liquor: Yes
Buffet: L-$10.95/$14.95 (Sat/Sun)
D-$14.95$19.95 (Sat)/$24.95 (Fri)
Casino Size: 35,000 Square Feet
Other Games: BJ, P, PGP, TCP, MB,
LIR, UTH,MS
Overnight RV Parking: Free/RV Dump: No
Senior Discount: Various Thu if 55+
Special Features: Offers card versions of craps and roulette.

Cher-Ae Heights Casino
27 Scenic Drive
Trinidad, California 95570
(707) 677-3611
Website: www.cheraeheightscasino.com
Map: **#4** (25 miles N. of Eureka)

Toll-Free Number: (800) 684-2464
Gambling Age: 21
Restaurants: 3 Liquor: Yes
Casino Size: 50,000 Square Feet
Other Games: BJ, S21, PGP, TCP, BG
Overnight RV Parking:
Free with Players club card/RV Dump: No
Special Features: Bingo is 18+

Chicken Ranch Bingo
16929 Chicken Ranch Road
Jamestown, California 95327
(209) 984-3000
Website: www.chickenranchcasino.com
Map: **#5** (100 miles S.E. of Sacramento)

Toll-Free Number: (800) 752-4646
Gambling Age: 18
Restaurants: 2 Liquor: No
Hours: 9am-1am/24 hrs (Wed-Sun)
Casino Size: 30,000 Square Feet
Other Games: Slots only, BG (Wed-Sun)
Overnight RV Parking: No

Chukchansi Gold Resort & Casino
711 Lucky Lane
Coarsegold, California 93614
(559) 692-5200
Website: www.chukchansigold.com
Map: **#25** (35 miles N. of Fresno)

Toll-Free Number: (866) 794-6946
Gambling Age: 21
Rooms: 190 Prices: $155-$313
Suites: 6 Prices: Casino Use Only
Restaurants: 7 Liquor: Yes
Casino Size: 56,000 Square Feet
Buffets: B- $17.95 (Sun)
L- $14.95/$17.95 (Sun)
D- $19.95/$24.95 (Fri/Sat)
Other Games: BJ, S21, TCP, PGP, UTH
FCP, MS, MB
Overnight RV Parking: Free/RV Dump: No
Senior Discount: Various Tue if 50+

Chumash Casino Resort
3400 East Highway 246
Santa Ynez, California 93460
(805) 686-0855
Website: www.chumashcasino.com
Map: **#13** (40 miles N.W. of Santa Barbara)

Toll-Free Number: (800) 248-6274
Gambling Age: 18
Room Reservations: (800) 248-6274
Rooms: 320 Prices: $135-$335
Suites: 58 Prices: $380-$550
Restaurants: 3 Liquor: Yes
Buffet: D- $24.95
Casino Size: 115,000 Square Feet
Other Games: S21, BJ, P, BG (Sun-Wed), PGP,
TCP, FCP, LIR, MB, MS, UTH
Overnight RV Parking: No
Special Features: Spa.

Colusa Casino Resort
3770 Highway 45
Colusa, California 95932
(530) 458-8844
Website: www.colusacasino.com
Map: **#6** (75 miles N. of Sacramento)

Toll-Free Number: (800) 655-8946
Gambling Age: 21
Rooms: 50 Prices: $99-$139
Suites: 10 Prices: $199-$219
Restaurants: 3 Liquor: Yes
Other Games: BJ, P, TCP, PGP,
BG (Sun-Wed)
Overnight RV Parking: Free/RV Dump: No
Senior Discount: Various Tue/Thu if 50+

Coyote Valley Casino
445 coyote Valley Boulevard
Redwood Valley, California 95470
(707) 485-0700
Website: www.coyotevalleycasino.com
Map: **#23** (115 miles N. of San Francisco)

Toll-Free Number: (800) 332-9683
Gambling Age: 21
Restaurants: 1 Cafe Liquor: Yes
Other Games: BJ, P
Overnight RV Parking: Free/RV Dump: No
Senior Discount: Various Mon if 55+

Desert Rose Casino
901 County Road 56
Alturas, California 96101
(530) 233-3141
Website: www.desertrosecasino.net
Map: **#27** (300 miles N.E. of Sacramento)

Gambling Age: 21
Restaurants: 1 Snack Bar Liquor: Yes
Hours: 10am-11pm/2am (Fri/Sat)
Casino Size: 5,000 Square Feet
Overnight RV Parking: Free/RV Dump: No
Senior Discount: Mon 10am-6pm if 55+

Diamond Mountain Casino Hotel Brewery
900 Skyline Drive
Susanville, California 96130
(530) 252-1100
Website: www.dmcah.com
Map: **#31** (160 Miles N.E. of Sacramento)

Toll-Free Number: (877) 319-8514
Gambling Age: 21
Rooms: 63 Prices: $91-$109
Suites: 7 Prices: $154-$189
Restaurants: 2 Liquor: Yes
Casino Size: 26,000 Square Feet
Other Games: BJ, BG (Tue)
Overnight RV Parking: Free/RV Dump: No
Senior Discount: 50% off in Lava Cafe for 55+ from 2-5 pm.

Eagle Mountain Casino
681 South Reservation Road
Porterville, California 93257
(559) 788-6220
Website: www.eaglemtncasino.com
Map: **#21** (60 miles S.E. of Fresno)

Toll-Free Number: (800) 903-3353
Gambling Age: 18
Restaurants: 3 Liquor: No
Buffets: L- $7.99 (Wed/Thu)/$9.99 (Fri-Sun)
D- $20.99 (Fri)/$7.49 (Sat)/
$10.99 (Sun)
Casino Size: 9,600 Square Feet
Other Games: BJ, P, S21, PGP
Overnight RV Parking: Free/RV Dump: No
Special Features: Food court with four fast food stations.

Elk Valley Casino
2500 Howland Hill Road
Crescent City, California 95531
(707) 464-1020
Website: www.elkvalleycasino.com
Map: **#7** (84 miles N. of Eureka)

Toll-Free Number: (888) 574-2744
Gambling Age: 21 Restaurants: 1 Liquor: Yes
Buffets: D- $9.99 (Tue)/$19.99 (Wed)
Casino Size: 23,000 Square Feet
Other Games: BJ, P, BG (Mon/Thu/Fri/Sun)
Overnight RV Parking: No

Fantasy Springs Casino
82-245 Indio Springs Drive
Indio, California 92203
(760) 342-5000
Website: www.fantasyspringsresort.com
Map: **#8** (125 miles E. of Los Angeles)

Toll-Free Number: (800) 827-2946
Gambling Age: 21
Rooms: 250 Prices: $99-$209
Suites: 11 Prices: $350-$599
Restaurants: 6 Liquor: Yes
Buffets: L- $15.99/$24.99 (Sun)
D- $19.99/$24.99 (Sat)
Casino Size: 95,000 Square Feet
Other Games: BJ, S21, MB, LIR, PGP, UTH, TCP, FCP, BG, OTB
Overnight RV Parking: No
Special Features: 24-lane bowling center. 5,000-seat special events center. Card version of craps. Golf course.

Feather Falls Casino
3 Alverda Drive
Oroville, California 95966
(530) 533-3885
Website: www.featherfallscasino.com
Map: **#22** (100 miles N. of Sacramento)

Toll-Free Number: (877) 652-4646
Gambling Age: 21
Rooms: 74 Prices: $99-$200
Suites: 10 Prices: $200-$450
Restaurants: 2 Liquor: Yes
Buffets: B- $8.95/$13.95 (Sat/Sun)
L- $11.95 D- $16.95/$19.95 (Fri/Sat)
Casino Size: 55,000 Square Feet
Other Games: BJ, P
Overnight RV Parking: Must use RV Park
Senior Discount: Various on Mon/Wed if 55+

Garcia River Casino
22215 Windy Hollow Rd
Point Arena, California 95468
(707) 467-5300
Website:www.thegarciarivercasino.com
Map: **#44** (130 miles N. of San Francisco)

Restaurants: 1
Other Games: Gaming Machines Only
Casino Size: 11,000 Square Feet
Hours: 9am - 11pm/1am (Fri/Sat)

Gold Country Casino
4020 Olive Highway
Oroville, California 95966
(530) 538-4560
Website: www.goldcountrycasino.com
Map: **#22** (100 miles N. of Sacramento)

Toll-Free Number: (800) 334-9400
Gambling Age: 21
Rooms: 87 Prices: $99-$169
Restaurants: 3 Liquor: Yes
Buffets: L- $14.95(Sun)
D-$24.95 (Fri/Sat) $14.95 (Sun)
Other Games: BJ, TCP, PGP, FCP, BG (Wed-Sun)
Overnight RV Parking: Free/RV Dump: No
Senior discount: 10% off buffet if 55+.
Special Features: 1,200-seat showroom. 77-space RV park ($52-$64 per night)

Golden Acorn Casino and Travel Center
1800 Golden Acorn Way
Campo, California 91906
(619) 938-6000
Website: www.goldenacorncasino.com
Map: **#33** (40 miles S.E. of San Diego)

Toll-Free Number: (866) 794-6244
Gambling Age: 18
Restaurants: 2 Liquor: Yes
Other Games: BJ
Overnight RV Parking: Free/RV Dump: No
Special Features: 33-acre auto/truck stop and convenience store. Table games open at 2pm/10am Sat/Sun.

Graton Resort & Casino
630 Park Court
Rohnert Park, California 94928
(707) 588-7100
Website: www.gratonresortcasino.com
Map: **#42** (50 miles N. of San Francisco)

Rooms: 200 Prices: $235-$510
Gambling age: 21
Restaurants: 4 Liquor: Yes
Casino Size: 18,000 Square Feet
Other Games: BJ, PGP, TCP, B, FCP, P
Overnight RV Parking: Free/RV Dump: No
Special Features: Casino features a food court with seven fast food restaurants and a Starbucks.

Hard Rock Sacramento at Fire Mountain
3317 40 Mile Road
Wheatland, California 95961
Website: www.hardrockhotelsacramento.com
Map: **#22** (35 miles N. of Sacramento)

This casino expected to open in Fall-2019.

Special Features: All machines are Class-II gaming machines based on bingo.

Harrah's Resort Southern California
777 Harrah's Rincon Way
Valley Center, California 92082
(760) 751-3100
Website: www.harrahssocal.com
Map: **#20** (35 miles N.E. of San Diego)

Toll-Free Number: (877) 777-2457
Gambling Age: 21
Rooms: 552 Prices: $120-$360
Suites: 101 Prices: $150-$609
Restaurants: 7 Liquor: Yes
Buffets: B- $26.99 (Sat/Sun) L-$19.99
D- $27.99/$32.99 (Fri/Sat)
Casino Size: 55,000 Square Feet
Other Games: BJ, PGP, MB, P, MS,
UTH, TCP, LIR, FCP
Overnight RV Parking: Free/RV Dump: No
Special Features: Card version of craps and roulette.

Harrah's Northern California
4640 Coal Mine Road
Ione, California 95640
(209) 790-4500
Website: www.caesars.com
Map: **#47** (50 miles S.E. of Sacramento)

Toll-Free Number: (866) 915-0777
Restaurants: 1 Liquor: Yes
Casino Size: 75,000 Square Feet
Gambling Age: 21
Other Games: BJ, PGP
Overnight RV Parking: No
Special Features: Food court with three fast food outlets. Card-based versions of Craps and Roulette.

Havasu Landing Resort & Casino
5 Main Street
Havasu Lake, California 92363
(760) 858-4593
Website: www.havasulanding.com
Map: **#18** (200 miles E. of L. A.)

Gambling Age: 21
Restaurants: 1 Liquor: Yes
Hours: 8:30am-12:30am/2:30am (Fri/Sat)
Other Games: BJ, TCP
Overnight RV Parking: Must use RV park
Casino Size: 7,000 Square Feet
Special Features: Tables open 11:30 am/12:30 pm (Mon-Thu). Marina, RV park ($35-$65 per night), campground rentals. Mobile homes available for daily rental.

Hidden Oaks Casino
76700 Covelo Road
Covelo, California 95428
(707) 983-6898
Website: www.hiddenoakscasino.com
Map: **#30** (150 miles N.W. of Sacramento)

Restaurants: 1
Other Games: Gaming machines only
Casino Hours: 12:00pm to 12:00am
Senior Discount: Various Mon if 55+

Jackson Rancheria Casino & Hotel
12222 New York Ranch Road
Jackson, California 95642
(209) 223-1677
Website: www.jacksoncasino.com
Map: **#9** (60 miles S.E. of Sacramento)

Toll-Free Number: (800) 822-9466
Gambling Age: 21
Rooms: 77 Price Range: $99-$149
Suites: 9 Price Range: $189-$409
Restaurants: 4 Liquor: Yes
Buffets: L- $11.95/$36.95 (Fri-Sun)
D- $18.95/$36.95 (Fri-Sun)
Other Games: BJ, PGP, LIR, TCP, CW,
FCP, MB, P
Overnight RV Parking: No
Special Features: Offers card versions of craps and roulette. 805-seat showroom. 100 space RV park ($55-$60 per night)

Jamul Casino
14145 Campo Road
Jamul, California 91935
(619) 315-2250
Map: **#14** (10 miles E. of San Diego)

Gambling Age: 21
Restaurants: 6
Buffets: L- $49.99 (Sun)
Restaurants: 6
Casino Size: 50,000 Square Feet
Other Games: BJ, TCP, FCP, MB, LIR, MS, UTH, PGP

Konocti Vista Casino Resort & Marina
2755 Mission Rancheria Road
Lakeport, California 95453
(707) 262-1900
Website: www.konocti-vista-casino.com
Map: **#11** (120 miles N. of San Francisco)

Toll-Free Number: (877) 577-7829
Gambling Age: 21 Restaurants: 1 Liquor: Yes
Rooms: 74 Prices: $99-$139
Suites: 2 Prices: $169-$189
Other Games: BJ, PGP
Overnight RV Parking: Must use RV park
RV Dump: Free
Special Features: Marina with 90 slips. 74-space RV park ($38-$41 per night).

Lucky Bear Casino
12510 Highway 96
Hoopa, California 95546
(530) 625-5198
Map: **#24** (30 miles N.E. of Eureka)

Gambling Age: 18 Restaurants: 1 Liquor: No
Hours: 10am-12am/1am (Fri/Sat)
Other Games: BJ, BG
Overnight RV Parking: No
Special Features: Non-smoking casino.

Lucky 7 Casino
350 N. Indian Road
Smith River, California 95567
(707) 487-7777
Website: www.lucky7casino.com
Map: **#7** (100 miles N. of Eureka)

Toll-Free Number: (866) 777-7170
Gambling Age: 21
Restaurants: 1 Liquor: Yes
Casino Size: 24,000 Square Feet
Other Games: BJ, BG (Sun/Tue/Wed), P (Tue-Sun)
Senior Discount: Various Thu 11:30-2pm
Overnight RV Parking: Free/RV Dump: No

Mono Wind Casino
37302 Rancheria Lane
Auberry, California 93602
(559) 855-4350
Website: www.monowind.com
Map: **#25** (30 miles N.E. of Fresno)

Gambling Age: 21
Restaurants: 1 Liquor: Yes
Casino Size: 10,000 Square Feet
Overnight RV Parking: Free/RV Dump: No

Morongo Casino Resort and Spa
49500 Seminole Drive
Cabazon, California 92230
(951) 849-3080
Website: www.morongocasinoresort.com
Map: **#3** (90 miles E. of L. A.)

Toll-Free Number: (800) 252-4499
Gambling Age: 18
Rooms: 310 Prices: $109-$319
Suites: 32 Prices: $289-$549
Restaurants: 6 Liquor: Yes
Buffets: B- $26.99 (Sat/Sun)
L- $14.95/$20.95 (Wed/Thu)/ $21.95 (Fri/Sat)/$26.95 (Sun)
D- $16.95/$25.95 (Wed/Thu)/ $24.95 (Fri/Sat)/$23.95 (Sun)
Casino Size: 145,000 Square Feet
Other Games: BJ, P, TCP, FCP, MS, LIR, MB, PGP, BG
Overnight RV Parking: Free/RV Dump: No
Special Features: Card version of craps.

Paiute Palace Casino
2742 N. Sierra Highway
Bishop, California 93514
(760) 873-4150
Website: www.paiutepalace.com
Map: **#26** (130 miles N.E. of Fresno)

Toll-Free Number: (888) 372-4883
Gambling Age: 21
Restaurants: 1 Liquor: Yes
Other Games: BJ, P
Overnight RV Parking: $10/RV Dump: No
Senior Discount: 10% off in restaurant if 50+
Special Features: 24-hour gas station and convenience store.

Pala Casino Spa and Resort
11154 Highway 76
Pala, California 92059
(760) 510-5100
Website: www.palacasino.com
Map: **#20** (35 miles N.E. of San Diego)

Toll-Free Number: (877) 946-7252
Gambling Age: 21
Room Reservations: (877) 725-2766
Rooms: 425 Prices: $139-$299
Suites: 82 Prices: $189-$389
Restaurants: 9 Liquor: Yes
Buffets: B-$30.74 (Sat/Sun)
L-$23.74
D-$30.74/$46.00 (Thu)/
$35.74 (Fri/Sat)
Other Games: BJ, B, MB, TCP, PGP,
MS, LIR, P, BG (Thu)
Overnight RV Parking: Free (park in west lot)
RV Dump: No
Senior Discount: Various food if playing bingo
Special Features: Offers card versions of craps and roulette. Fitness center and spa. Discount on buffet if players club member. 100-space RV park ($50-$80).

Pechanga Resort and Casino
45000 Pechanga Parkway
Temecula, California 92592
(951) 693-1819
Website: www.pechanga.com
Map: **#28** (50 miles N. of San Diego)

Toll-Free Number: (877) 711-2946
Gambling Age: 21
Room Reservations: (888) 732-4264
Rooms: 458 Price Range: $109-$349
Suites: 64 Price Range: $179-$750
Restaurants: 8 Liquor: Yes
Buffets: B- $27.99 (Sat/Sun) L- $21.99
D- $26.99/$32.99 (Fri/Sat)
Other Games: BJ, MB, P, PGP, LIR, TCP, BG
Overnight RV Parking: Must use RV park
RV Dump: $14.00 charge to use
Casino Size: 88,000 Square Feet
Special Features: 206-space RV park ($50-$80 per night). Offers card versions of craps and roulette. Food court with six food outlets.

Pit River Casino
20265 Tamarack Avenue
Burney, California 96013
(530) 335-2334
Website: www.pitrivercasino.com
Map: **#29** (190 miles N. of Sacramento)

Toll-Free Number: (888) 245-2992
Gambling Age: 21
Restaurants: 1 Liquor: No
Casino Hours: 9am-12am/2am (Fri/Sat)
Other Games: BJ, P
Overnight RV Parking: Free/RV Dump: No
Senior Discount: Earn 10 points Mon,
get 50% off food, if 55+
Special Features: Tables open at 4pm/2pm (Sun).

Quechan Casino Resort
525 Algodones Road
Winterhaven, California 92283
(760) 572-3900
Website: www.playqcr.net
Map: **#37** (170 miles E. of San Diego)

Toll-Free Number: (877) 783-2426
Rooms: 158 Price Range: $95-$119
Suites: 8 Price Range: $159-$299
Gambling Age: 21
Restaurants: 3 Liquor: Yes
Buffet: L: $5.95/$12.95(Sat & Sun)
D: $19.95(Fri & Sat)
Other Games: BJ, P, PGP, TCP, UTH
Overnight RV Parking: $10 per night/
RV Dump: No
Special Features: Part of casino is located across the state border in Arizona. Offers video versions of craps and roulette. 10% off food with players club card.

Rain Rock Casino
777 Sharps Road
Yreka, California 96097
(530) 777-7246
Website: www.rainrockcasino.com
Map: **#46** (250 miles N. of Sacramento)

Restaurants: 2
Gambling Age: 21 Liquor: Yes
Casino Size: 36,000 square feet
Other Games: BJ, TCP, PGP, UTH
Overnight RV Parking: Free/RV Dump: No
Special Features: All machines are Class-II gaming machines based on bingo.

Red Earth Casino
3089 Norm Niver Road
Salton Sea Beach, California 92274
(760) 395-1700
Website: www.redearthcasino.com
Map: **#39** (114 miles S.E. of Riverside)

Gambling Age: 21
Restaurants: 1 Liquor: Yes
Casino Size: 10,000 Square Feet
Overnight RV Parking: Free/RV Dump: $8

Red Fox Casino
300 Cahto Drive
Laytonville, California 95454
(760) 395-1200
Website: www.redfoxcasino.net
Map: **#30** (150 miles N.W. of Sacramento)

Toll-Free Number: (888) 473-3369
Gambling Age: 18
Restaurants: 1 Snack Bar Liquor: No
Overnight RV Parking: Free/RV Dump: No
Senior Discount: Various Mon if 55+

Red Hawk Casino
1 Red Hawk Parkway
Placerville, California 95667
(530) 677-7000
Website: www.redhawkcasino.com
Map: **#40** (40 miles E of Sacramento)

Toll-Free Number: (888) 573-3495
Gambling Age: 21
Restaurants: 6 Liquor: Yes
Buffets: L- $15.99/$17.99 (Sat)/$24.99(Sun)
D- $18.99/$39.99 (Fri/Sat)/$31.99 (Sun)
Other Games: BJ, P, PGP, TCP, LIR,
MB, FCP, B, MS
Special Features: Childcare facility. Shopping arcade. Offers a card version of craps and roulette.

Redwood Hotel Casino
171 Klamath Boulevard
Klamath, California 95548
(707) 482-1777
Website: www.redwoodhotelcasino.com
Map: **#43** (65 miles N of Eureka)

Toll-Free Number: (855) 554-2946
Gambling Age: 21
Rooms: 60 Price Range: $99-$199
Restaurants: 1 Liquor: Yes
Overnight RV Parking: No
Special Features: The only hotel located within the Redwood National & State Parks. Hotel is affiliated with Holiday Inn Express.

River Rock Casino
3250 Hwy 128 East
Geyserville, California 95441
(877) 883-7777
Website: www.riverrockcasino.com
Map: **#32** (75 miles N. of San Fran.)

Gambling Age: 21
Restaurants: 2 Liquor: Yes
Buffets: L- $9.99/$12.99 (Sun)
D- $12.99/$28.99 (Fri)/$21.99 (Sat)
Other Games: BJ, MB, PGP, TCP, S21, UTH
Overnight RV Parking: No
Senior discount: 10% off buffet Thu if 55+
Special Features: Buffet closed Tue/Wed

Robinson Rancheria Resort & Casino
1545 East Highway 20
Nice, California 95464
(800) 809-3636
Website: www.rrrc.com
Map: **#11** (115 miles N.W. of Sacramento)

Gambling Age: 21
Rooms: 49 Price Range: $119-$169
Suites: 2 Price Range: $119-$295
Restaurants: 2 Liquor: Yes
Buffets: B - $9.95 (Sun) D- $8.95 (Wed)
Casino Size: 37,500 Square Feet
Other Games: BJ, P, PGP, LIR, TCP,
MB, BG (Wed-Sun)
Overnight RV Parking: Free (one night only)
RV Dump: No
Senior Discount: Various Wed if 55+.

Rolling Hills Casino
2655 Everett Freeman Way
Corning, California 96021
(530) 528-3500
Website: www.rollinghillscasino.com
Map: **#36** (115 miles N. of Sacramento)

Toll-Free Number: (888) 331-6400
Gambling Age: 21
Rooms: 90 Price Range: $119-$169
Suites: 21 Price Range: $159-$215
Restaurants: 2 Liquor: Yes
Buffet: B- $12.95/$15.95 (Sun) L- $13.95
D- $19.95/$24.95 (Fri)/$21.95 (Sat)
Casino Size: 60,000 Square Feet
Other Games: BJ, PGP, TCP, UTH
Overnight RV Parking: Free in truck lot
Senior Discount: Various Tue/Thu if 50+.
Special Features: 72-space RV park ($35/night)

Running Creek Casino
635 East Highway 20
Upper Lake, California 95485
(707) 275-9209
Website: www.runningcreekcasino.com
Map: **#11** (120 miles N.W. of Sacramento)

Gambling Age: 21
Restaurants: 3 Liquor: Yes
Buffet: L- $9.99 (Sun/Tue)
D- $9.95 (Tue)/$24.95 (Fri)
Other Games: BJ
Casino Size: 33,000 Square Feet

San Manuel Casino
5797 North Victoria Avenue
Highland, California 92346
(909) 864-5050
Website: www.sanmanuel.com
Map: **#12** (65 miles E. of L. A.)

Toll-Free Number: (800) 359-2464
Gambling Age: 21
Restaurants: 9 Liquor: Yes
Buffet: B-$9.99 L- $15.99/$39.99 (Fri-Sun)
D- $26.99/$34.99 (Thu/Fri)
Casino Size: 75,000 Square Feet
Other Games: BJ, MB, P, PGP, LIR, TCP,
FCP
Overnight RV Parking: Free/RV Dump: No
Special Features: Food Court with four fast food outlets. Buffet discounts for players club members. Offers card versions of craps and roulette.

San Pablo Lytton Casino
13255 San Pablo Avenue
San Pablo, California 94806
(510) 215-7888
Website: www.sanpablolytton.com
Map: **#41** (15 miles N of Oakland)

Gambling Age: 21
Restaurants: 2
Other Games: BJ, TCP, B, PGP
Special Features: All machines are Class-II gaming machines based on bingo. All table game players must place $1 ante for every $100 bet.

Sherwood Valley Casino
100 Kawi Place
Willits, California 95490
(707) 459-7978
Website: www.svrcasino.com
Map: **#11** (130 miles N. of San Francisco)

Gambling Age: 18
Restaurants: 1 Liquor: No
Casino Size: 6,000 Square Feet
Other Games: Slots Only
Overnight RV Parking: Free/RV Dump: No

Soboba Casino
22777 Soboba Road
San Jacinto, California 92583
(951) 665-1000
Website: www.soboba.com
Map: **#3** (90 miles E. of L. A.)

Toll-Free Number: (866) 476-2622
Gambling Age: 21
Restaurants: 3 Liquor: Yes
Casino Size: 52,000 Square Feet
Other Games: BJ, S21, PGP, TCP, FCP
Overnight RV Parking: Free/RV Dump: No
Special Features: Offers card version of roulette.

Spa Resort Casino
401 East Amado Road
Palm Springs, California 92262
(888) 999-1995
Website: www.sparesortcasino.com
Map: **#3** (115 miles E. of L. A.)

Gambling Age: 21
Restaurants: 3 Liquor: Yes
Buffets: B- $10.99 (Sat/Sun)
L- $9.99 (Mon/Thu/Fri/Sat)/
$24.99 (Sun)
D- $14.99 (Mon/Thurs/Fri/Sat)
Casino Size: 15,000 Square Feet
Other Games: BJ, MB, PGP, TCP, UTH
Overnight RV Parking: No
Special Features: Offers card version of roulette.

Spotlight 29 Casino
46200 Harrison Place
Coachella, California 92236
(760) 775-5566
Website: www.spotlight29.com
Map: **#8** (130 miles E. of L. A.)

Toll-Free Number: (866) 377-6829
Gambling Age: 21
Restaurants: 3 Liquor: Yes
Buffets: L-$12.95/$13.95 (Sat/Sun)
D-$16.95/$20.95 (Sat)
Other Games: BJ, S21, UTH, PGP, TCP
Overnight RV Parking: Free/RV Dump: No
Special Features: Three fast-food outlets including McDonald's. 2,200-seat showroom.

Sycuan Resort & Casino
5469 Casino Way
El Cajon, California 92019
(619) 445-6002
Website: www.sycuan.com
Map: **#14** (10 miles E. of San Diego)

Toll-Free Number: (800) 279-2826
Gambling Age: 21
Room Reservations: (800) 457-5568
Restaurants: 10 Liquor: Yes
Buffets: L- $17.95/$26.95 (Sat/Sun) D- $26.95
Casino Size: 73,000 Square Feet
Other Games: BJ, B, S21, P, BG, CW, TCP,
CSP, FCP, OTB, PGP, MS
Overnight RV Parking: Free/RV Dump: No
Senior Discount: Various Sun if 55+.
Special Features: Offers card/tile versions of roulette and craps. Three 18-hole golf courses. 500-seat showroom.

Table Mountain Casino & Bingo
8184 Table Mountain Road
Friant, California 93626
(559) 822-7777
Website: www.tmcasino.com
Map: **#15** (15 miles N. of Fresno)

Toll-Free Number: (800) 541-3637
Gambling Age: 18
Restaurants: 3 Liquor: No
Buffet: L- $12.99/$17.99 (Tue)/$12.99 (Fri)
D- $13.99/$21.99 (Tue)/
$15.99 (Fri-Sun)
Other Games: BJ, S21, P, PGP, TCP,
BG, CW, FCP
Overnight RV Parking: Free/RV Dump: No
Senior Discount: Buffet discount Mon-Fri if 55+

Tachi Palace Hotel and Casino
17225 Jersey Avenue
Lemoore, California 93245
(559) 924-7751
Website: www.tachipalace.com
Map: **#10** (50 miles S. of Fresno)

Toll-Free Number: (800) 942-6886
Gambling Age: 18
Room Reservations: (800) 615-8030
Rooms: 215 Price Range: $79-$159
Suites: 40 Price Range: $149-$259
Restaurants: 8 Liquor: Yes
Buffets: B-$19.99 (Sat/Sun)
L- $14.99
D- $19.99/$22.99 (Fri)
Casino Size: 50,000 Square Feet
Other Games: BJ, P, PGP, TCP, S21,
FCP, MB, BG
Overnight RV Parking: Free/RV Dump: No
Senior Discount: $5.99 lunch buffet if 55+.
Special Features: Offers a card-based version of roulette. No buffet Tue/Wed

Thunder Valley Casino
1200 Athens Ave
Lincoln, California 95648
(916) 408-7777
Website: www.thundervalleyresort.com
Map: **#35** (35 miles N.E. of Sacramento)

Toll-Free Number: (877) 468-8777
Gambling Age: 21
Rooms: 297 Price Range: $115-$210
Suites: 40 Price Range: $300-$399
Restaurants: 4 Liquor: Yes
Buffets: B/L-$17.95/$19.95 (Sun)
D-$16.99/$32.49 (Fri)/$32.99 (Sat)
Other Games: BJ, MB, PGP, P, MS,
LIR, TCP, FCP
Overnight RV Parking: No
Special Features: Affiliated with Station Casinos of Las Vegas. Five fast-food outlets. Buffet discount with players club card. Card versions of craps and roulette.

Tortoise Rock Casino
Baseline Road
Twentynine Palms, California 92277
(760) 367-9759
Website: www.tortiserockcasino.com
Map: **#8** (125 miles E. of L. A.)

Restaurants: 1 Liquor: Yes
Gambling Age: 18
Casino Size: 30,000 Square Feet
Other Games: P, S21, TCP
Overnight RV Parking: Free/RV Dump: No

Twin Pine Casino & Hotel
22223 Highway 29 at Rancheria Road
Middletown, California 95461
(707) 987-0197
Website: www.twinpine.com
Map: **#32** (100 miles N. of San Francisco)

Toll-Free Number: (800) 564-4872
Rooms: 59 Price Range: $89-$109
Suites: 3 Price Range: $149-$250
Gambling Age: 21
Restaurants: 1 Liquor: Yes
Other Games: BJ, P, TCP
Overnight RV Parking: No/RV Dump: No
Senior Discount: Various Tue/Thu if 50+.

Valley View Casino Resort
16300 Nyemii Pass Road
Valley Center, California 92082
(760) 291-5500
Website: www.valleyviewcasino.com
Map: **#20** (35 miles N.E. of San Diego)

Toll-Free Number: (866) 843-9946
Gambling Age: 21
Rooms: 100 Price Range: $119-$239
Suites: 8 Price Range: $299-$439
Restaurants: 6 Liquor: Yes
Buffets: L- $14.99/$32.99 (Sat/Sun)
D- $24.99/$32.99 (Fri-Sun)
Other Games: BJ, PGP, TCP, UTH
Overnight RV Parking: No
Special Features: Players club members receive $3 off buffets. Offers card-based version of roulette.

Viejas Casino
5000 Willows Road
Alpine, California 91901
(619) 445-5400
Website: www.viejas.com
Map: **#16** (25 miles E. of San Diego)

Toll-Free Number: (800) 847-6537
Rooms: 237 Price Range: $129-$289
Suites: 35 Price Range: $260-$500
Gambling Age: 21
Restaurants: 7 Liquor: Yes
Buffets: L/D- $28.99/$43.99(Mon)/
$39.99 (Fri-Sun)
Other Games: BJ, B, MB, LIR, TCP
FCP, CW, PGP, BG, OTB
Overnight RV Parking: Free/RV Dump: No
Special Features: 51-store factory outlet shopping center. Buffet discounts for players club members. Card-based versions of craps and roulette.

Win-River Casino
2100 Redding Rancheria Road
Redding, California 96001
(530) 243-3377
Website: www.winrivercasino.com
Map: **#17** (163 miles N. of Sacramento)

Toll-Free Number: (800) 280-8946
Gambling Age: 21
Restaurants: 1 Liquor: Yes
Buffets: B- $24.95 (Sun)
Casino Size: 37,000 Square Feet
Other Games: BJ,TCP, PGP, FCP,
S21, P, BG (Tue-Thu/Sun)
Overnight RV Parking: Free/RV Dump: No
Special Features: Comedy club. Food discounts for players club members. 1,000-seat showroom.

Winnedumah Winn's Casino
135 South Highway 395
Independence, California 93526
(760) 878-2483
Map: **#45** (90 miles E. of Fresno)

Restaurants: 1 Liquor: No
Gambling Age: 18
Other Games: Only Gaming Machines
Special Features: All machines are Class-II gaming machines based on bingo.

COLORADO

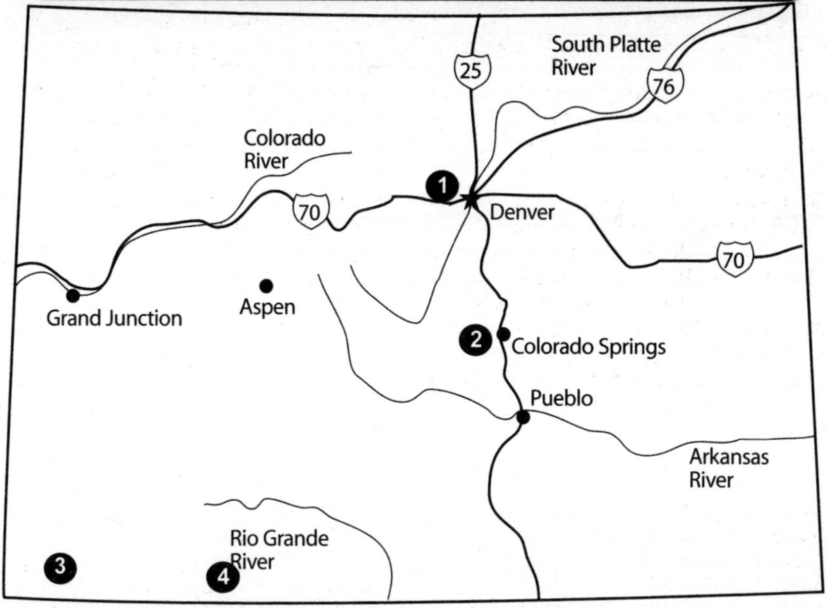

Colorado casinos can be found in the mountain towns of Black Hawk, Central City and Cripple Creek. There are also two Indian casinos (which abide by Colorado's limited gaming rules) in Ignacio and Towaoc.

When casino gambling was initially introduced in 1991 it was limited in that only electronic games (including slots, video poker, video blackjack and video keno) and the table games of poker, blackjack, let it ride and three-card poker were allowed. Plus, a single wager could not exceed $5.

All that changed, however, on July 2, 2009 when the maximum bet was raised to $100, plus the games of craps and roulette were added to the mix. Additionally, the casinos were allowed to stay open for 24 hours, rather than having to be closed between 2 a.m. and 8 a.m.

Here's information, as supplied by Colorado's Division of Gaming, showing the slot machine payback percentages for each city's casinos for the one-year period from July 1, 2018 through June 30, 2019:

	Black Hawk	Central City	Cripple Creek
1¢ Slots	89.80%	90.43%	**91.89%**
5¢ Slots	92.85%	**93.93%**	93.50%
25¢ Slots	92.30%	94.06%	**95.45%**
$1 Slots	93.69%	94.82%	**94.83%**
$5 Slots	93.69%	93.76%	**95.03%**
All	92.35%	92.30%	**93.53%**

These numbers reflect the percentage of money returned on each denomination of machine and encompass all electronic machines including video poker and video keno. The best returns for each category are highlighted in bold print.

The minimum gambling age at all Colorado casinos is 21, including Indian casinos. For general information on Colorado contact the state's tourism board at (800) 433-2656 or www.colorado.com.

For information on visiting Central City, call (303) 582-5251 or visit their website at: www.colorado.gov/centralcity

For information on visiting Black Hawk, call (303) 582-5221, or visit their website at: www.cityofblackhawk.org.

All casinos offer electronic games (slots, video poker, video blackjack and video keno). Some casinos also offer: blackjack (BJ), craps (C), roulette (R), poker (P), let it ride (LIR), Mississippi stud (MS) and three card poker (TCP). Please note that legislation has been introduced to legalize sports betting and that may happen in 2020.

Black Hawk

Map Location: **#1** (35 miles west of Denver. Take U.S. 6 through Golden to Hwy 119. Take Hwy 119 to Black Hawk. Another route is I-70 West to exit 244. Turn right onto Hwy. 6. Take Hwy 6 to 119 and into Black Hawk.)

The casinos in Black Hawk and Central City are located one mile apart. The Black Hawk Shuttle Service provides free transportation throughout Black Hawk and Central City.

Ameristar Black Hawk
111 Richman Street
Black Hawk, Colorado 80422
(720) 946-4000
Website: www.ameristar.com

Rooms: 472 Price Range: $149-$289
Suites: 64 Price Range: $249-$539
Restaurants: 5
Buffets: B- $19.99 (Sat/Sun)
L-$13.99/$19.99 (Sat/Sun)
D- $21.95/$33.95 (Sat/Sun)
Casino Size: 46,534 Square feet
Other Games: BJ, P, C, R, MS
Special Features: Buffet closed Mon/Tuesday.

Bull Durham Saloon & Casino
110 Main Street
Black Hawk, Colorado 80422
(303) 582-0810
Website: www.bulldurhamcasino.com

Restaurants: 1 (Sack Bar)
Casino Size: 2,579 Square Feet

Gilpin Hotel Casino
111 Main Street
Black Hawk, Colorado 80422
(303) 582-1133
Website: www.thegilpincasino.com

Restaurants: 1
Other Games: BJ, C, R
Casino Size: 11,087 Square Feet
Senior Discount: Specials on Tue if 50+.

Golden Gates Casino
261 Main Street
Black Hawk, Colorado 80422
(303) 582-1650
Website: www.thegoldengatescasino.com

Restaurants: 3
Casino Size: 8,004 Square Feet (Golden Gates)
Casino Size: 3,440 Square Feet (Golden Gulch)
Other Games: P, BJ
Special Features: Connected to **Golden Gulch Casino**. Skybridge to **Golden Mardi Gras Casino.**

Golden Mardi Gras Casino
333 Main Street
Black Hawk, Colorado 80422
(303) 582-5600

Restaurants: 1
Casino Size: 17,888 Square Feet
Other Games: BJ, C
Special Features: Skybridge to **Golden Gates Casino**.

The Isle Casino - Black Hawk
401 Main Street
Black Hawk, Colorado 80422
(303) 998-7777
Website: www.isleblackhawk.com

Rooms: 108 Price Range: $90-$189
Suites: 130 Price Range: $139-$299
Restaurants: 3
Buffets: B-$9.99 L-$14.99/$21.99 (Sat/Sun)
D- $22.99/$26.99 (Fri)/$33.99 (Sat/Sun)
Senior Discount: Various Sun if 50+.
Other Games: BJ, TCP, UTH, P, C, R, MS

Lady Luck Casino
340 Main Street
Black Hawk, Colorado 80422
(303) 582-3000
Website: www.isleofcapricasinos.com

Toll-Free Number (800) 843-4753
Rooms: 140 Price Range: $99-$229
Suites: 24 Price Range: $169-$279
Restaurants: 1 Valet parking: Free
Casino Size: 17,726 Square Feet
Other Games: BJ, P, C, R
Special Features: Affiliated with Isle Hotel Casino.

The Lodge Casino at Black Hawk
240 Main Street
Black Hawk, Colorado 80422
(303) 582-1771
Website: www.thelodgecasino.com

Rooms: 47 Price Range: $109-$179
Suites: 3 Price Range: Casino Use Only
Restaurants: 3
Buffets: B-$7.99 L-$11.49/$16.99 (Sat/Sun)
D-$20.99/$24.49 (Fri/Sat)
Senior Discount: 50% off breakfast or lunch buffets Mon/Tue if 50+.

Monarch Casino Black Hawk
488 Main Street
Black Hawk, Colorado 80422
(303) 582-1000
Website: www.monarchblackhawk.com

Restaurants: 2
Buffet: B- $8.99/$21.99 (Sat/Sun)
L- $12.99/$21.99 (Sat/Sun)
D- $22.99/$28.99 (Fri/Sat)
Casino Size: 25,860 Square Feet
Other Games: BJ, TCP, R, C, PGP
Senior Discount: Various Mon if 50+

Red Dolly Casino
530 Gregory Street
Black Hawk, Colorado 80422
Website: www.thereddollycasino.com
(303) 582-1100

Restaurants: 1
Casino Size: 1,992 Square Feet
Casino Hours: 8am-2am

Saratoga Casino
101 Main Street
Black Hawk, Colorado 80422
(303) 582-6100
Website: www.saratogacasinobh.com

Toll-Free Number: (800) 538-5825
Restaurants: 2
Casino Size: 17,129 Square Feet
Other Games: BJ, C, R, TCP, S21

Sasquatch Casino
125 Gregory Street
Black Hawk, Colorado 80422
(303) 582-5582
Website: www.sasquatchcasino.com

Casino Size: 1,827 Square feet
Restaurants: 2
Casino Hours: 8am-2am

Wild Card Saloon & Casino
112 Main Street
Black Hawk, Colorado 80422
Website: www.wildcardcasino.net
(303) 582-3412

Restaurants: 1
Casino Size: 2,750 Square Feet
Special Features: Grocery store.

Z Casino
101 Gregory Street
Black Hawk, Colorado 80422
(303) 271-2500
Website: www.zcasinobh.com

Toll-Free Number: (800) 924-6646
Restaurants: 2
Casino Size: 10,471 Square Feet
Other Games: BJ, C

Central City

Map location: **#1** (same as Black Hawk). Central City is located one mile from Black Hawk. Turn left at the third stoplight on Hwy. 119 and proceed up Gregory Street.

Century Casino & Hotel - Central City
102 Main Street
Central City, Colorado 80427
(303) 582-5050
Website: www.cnty.com

Rooms: 22 Price Range $109-$159
Restaurants: 2
Casino Size: 13,899 Square Feet
Senior Discount: Various Wed/Thu if 50+
Other Games: BJ, C, R

Dostal Alley Casino & Microbrewery
1 Dostal Alley
Central City, Colorado 80427
(303) 582-1610
Website: www.dostalalley.net

Restaurants: 1
Casino Size: 1,041 Square Feet
Casino Hours: 10am-2am
Special Features: Microbrewery.

Famous Bonanza/Easy Street
107 Main Street
Central City, Colorado 80427
(303) 582-5914
Website: www.famousbonanza.com

Restaurants: 1
Casino Size: 5,056 Square Feet (F. Bonanza)
Casino Size: 4,289 Square Feet (Easy Street)
Other Games: BJ, TCP
Casino Hours: 8am-2am/3am (Fri/Sat)

The Grand Z Casino Hotel
321 Gregory Street
Central City, Colorado 80427
(303) 582-0800
Website: www.reservecasinohotel.com

Restaurants: 3
Toll-Free Number: (800) 924-6646
Rooms: 118 Price Range $119-$219
Suites: 6 Price Range $199-$349
Other Games: BJ, P, TCP, C, R
Senior Discount: Various Mon/Tue if 60+

Johnny Z's Casino
132 Lawrence Street
Central City, Colorado 80427
(303) 582-5623
Website: www.johnnyzscasino.com

Restaurants: 1
Casino Size: 35,000 Square Feet
Other Games: BJ, C, TCP
Overnight RV Parking: Free/RV Dump: No
Senior Discount: Various Mon/Tue if 60+

Cripple Creek

Map Location: **#2** (47 miles west of Colorado Springs. Take exit 141 at Colorado Springs off I-25. Go west on Hwy. 24 to the town of Divide. Turn left onto Hwy. 67 and go 18 miles to Cripple Creek.)

All casinos offer electronic games (slots, video poker, video blackjack and video keno). Some casinos also offer: blackjack (BJ), poker (P), let it ride (LIR) and three card poker (TCP).

Brass Ass Casino
264 E. Bennett Avenue
Cripple Creek, Colorado 80813
(719) 689-2104
Website: www.triplecrowncasinos.com

Restaurants: 1
Casino Size: 7,486 Square Feet
Other Games: BJ, TCP, C, R
Special Features: Connected to **Midnight Rose** and **J.P. McGill's**. Covered parking garage.

Bronco Billy's Casino
233 E. Bennett Avenue
Cripple Creek, Colorado 80813
(719) 689-2142
Website: www.broncobillyscasino.com

Toll Free Number: (877) 989-2142
Restaurants: 5
Other Games: BJ, TCP, C, R
Casino Size: 6,086 Square Feet (Bronco's)
Casino Size: 5,991 Square Feet (Buffalo's)
Senior Discount: Specials Mon/Wed/Fri 8am-6pm if 50+
Special Features: Includes **Buffalo Billy's** Casino.

Century Casino - Cripple Creek
200-220 E. Bennett Avenue
Cripple Creek, Colorado 80813
(719) 689-0333
Website: www.cnty.com

Toll-Free Number: (888) 966-2257
Rooms: 21 Price Range: $109-$119
Suites: 3 Price Range: $119-$219
Restaurants: 1
Casino Size: 5,609 Square Feet
Other Games: BJ, R
Senior Discount: Various Mon/Wed if 50+

Christmas Casino & Inn
279 E Bennett Avenue
Cripple Creek, Colorado 80813
(719) 689-2142
Website: www.christmascasinoandinn.com

Rooms: 12 Price Range: $49-$99
Restaurants: 1
Casino Size: 4,000 Square Feet
Special Features: Affiliated with Bronco Billy's Casino.

Colorado Grande Casino
300 E. Bennett Avenue
Cripple Creek, Colorado 80813
(719) 689-3517
Website: www.coloradogrande.com

Toll Free Number: (877) 244-9469
Rooms: 5 Price Range: $59-$99
Suites: 2 Price Range: $119-$199
Restaurants: 1
Casino Size: 2,569 Square Feet
Senior Discount: Dining discounts if 50+
Special Features: Covered parking garage.

Double Eagle Hotel & Casino
442 E. Bennett Avenue
Cripple Creek, Colorado 80813
(719) 689-5000
Website: www.decasino.com

Toll-Free Reservations: (800) 711-7234
Rooms: 146 Price Range: $89-$139
Suites: 12 Price Range: $159-$500
Restaurants: 3
Casino Size: 14,631 Square Feet
Other Games: BJ, TCP, R
Special Features: Players club members get room discount. Covered parking garage. 48-space RV park ($15/$40 with hookups).

Johnny Nolon's Casino
301 E. Bennett Avenue
Cripple Creek, Colorado 80813
(719) 689-2080
Website: www.johnnynolonscasino.com

Restaurants: 1
Casino Size: 3,505 Square Feet

McGill's Hotel & Casino
232 E. Bennett Avenue
Cripple Creek, Colorado 80813
(719) 689-2446
Website: www.triplecrowncasinos.com

Toll-Free Number: (888) 461-7529
Rooms: 36 Price Range: $100-$135
Suites: 5 Price Range: $175-$240
Restaurants: 1
Casino Size: 7,386 Square Feet
Special Features: Connected to **Midnight Rose** and **Brass Ass**. 10% room/food discount for players club members. Covered parking garage.

Midnight Rose Hotel & Casino
256 E. Bennett Avenue
Cripple Creek, Colorado 80813
(719) 689-2865
Website: www.triplecrowncasinos.com

Toll-Free Number: (800) 635-5825
Rooms: 19 Price Range: $110-$139
Restaurants: 2
Casino Size: 9,590 Square Feet
Other Games: P
Special Features: Connected to Brass Ass and McGill's. Covered parking garage.

Wildwood Casino At Cripple Creek
119 Carbonate Sreet
Cripple Creek, Colorado 80813
(719) 244-9700
Website: www.wildwoodcasino.net

Toll-Free Number: (877) 945-3963
Valet Parking: Free
Restaurants: 2
Casino Size: 18,965 Square Feet
Other Games: BJ, P, C, R, LIR
Senior Discount: Various Sun-Thu if 50+
Special Features: Covered parking garage.

Indian Casinos

Sky Ute Casino and Lodge
14826 Highway 172 N.
Ignacio, Colorado 81137
(970) 563-3000
Website: www.skyutecasino.com
Map Location: **#4** (345 miles S.W. of Denver, 20 miles S.E. of Durango)

Toll-Free Number: (888) 842-4180
Rooms: 140 Price Range: $137-$184
Suites: 8 Price Range: $279-$299
Restaurants: 4 Liquor: Beer/Wine
Other Games: BJ, TCP, LIR, C, P, R, BG (Wed/Thu/Sun)
Senior Discount: Various Wed 9am-9pm if 50+
Special Features: 24-space RV park on property ($41 per night). 24-lane bowling alley. Southern Ute Cultural Center and Museum. Free local shuttle.

Ute Mountain Casino & RV Park
3 Weeminuche Drive
Towaoc, Colorado 81334
(970) 565-8800
Website: www.utemountaincasino.com
Map Location: **#3** (425 miles S.W. of Denver, 11 miles S. of Cortez on Hwys. 160/166)

Toll-Free Number: (800) 258-8007
Other Games: BJ, R, TCP, UTH
Rooms: 70 Price Range: $80-$109
Suites: 20 Price Range: $175-$275
Senior Discount: Earn 100 pts. for $10 food voucher on Tue, if 50+
Special Features: 84-space RV Park ($35 per night). Ute Tribal Park tours available.

CONNECTICUT

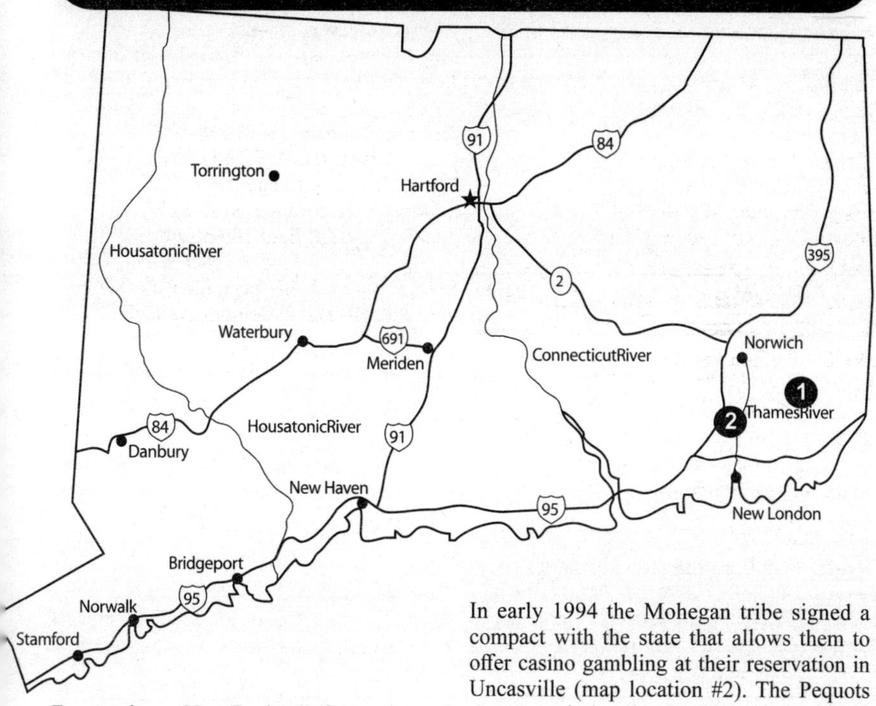

Foxwoods was New England's first casino and it is now the second largest casino in the world.

The Mashantucket Pequot Tribe which operates Foxwoods had to sue the state to allow the casino to open. They argued that since the state legally permitted "Las Vegas Nights," where low-stakes casino games were operated to benefit charities, then the tribe should be entitled to do the same. Eventually, they won their case before the U.S. Supreme Court and began construction of their casino which was financed by a Malaysian conglomerate (after 22 U.S. lenders turned down their loan requests).

When the casino first opened in February 1992, slot machines were not permitted. In January 1993 a deal was made between Governor Weicker and the Pequots which gave the tribe the exclusive right to offer slot machines in return for a yearly payment of 25% of the gross slot revenue. The agreement was subject to cancellation, however, if the state allowed slot machines anywhere else in Connecticut.

In early 1994 the Mohegan tribe signed a compact with the state that allows them to offer casino gambling at their reservation in Uncasville (map location #2). The Pequots gave permission for the Mohegans to have slot machines in their casino. The same 25% of the gross slot revenue payment schedule also applies to the Mohegans. The payment schedules are subject to cancellation, however, if the state legalizes any other form of casino gambling. The Mohegan casino opened in October 1996.

The minimum gambling age at both properties is 18 for bingo and 21 for the casino. Both casinos are open 24 hours. For information on visiting Connecticut call the state's Vacation Center at (800) 282-6863 or visit their website at www.ctbound.org.

The games offered at Foxwoods are: blackjack, craps, roulette, baccarat, mini-baccarat, midi baccarat, big six (money wheel), pai gow poker, pai gow tiles, Caribbean stud poker, let it ride, casino war, Spanish 21, three-card poker, Crazy 4 poker and poker; in addition to bingo, keno and pull tabs. There is also a Race Book offering off-track betting on horses, greyhounds and jai-alai.

Foxwoods Resort Casino+ has over 300,000 square feet of gaming space. The property features three hotels, over 30 food and beverage outlets, 24 retail shops, an outlet mall with 80 stores, six casinos, Ultimate Race Book, various high limit gaming areas, a 3,600-seat bingo room, a state of the art, smoke-free World Poker Room™ and more than 4,800 electronic gaming machines.

Foxwoods Resort Casino
350 Trolley Line Boulevard
Mashantucket, Connecticut 06338
(860) 312-3000
Website: www.foxwoods.com
Map Location: **#1** (45 miles S.E. of Hartford; 12 miles N. of I-95 at Mystic). From I-95 take exit 92 to Rt. 2-West, casino is 7 miles ahead. From I-395 take exit 79A to Rt. 2A follow to Rt. 2-East, casino is 2 miles ahead.

Toll-Free Number: (800) 369-9663
Rooms: 1,398 Price Range: $109-$699
Suites: 209 Price Range: $229-$1,500
Restaurants: 28 (3 open 24 hours)
Buffets: B- $15.00 L-$25.00 D-$29.00
Casino Size: 323,376 Square Feet
Overnight RV Parking: Free (self-contained only) RV Dump: No
Special Features: Daily resort fee charged in addition to room rate. Three hotels with pool, Grand Pequot Tower hotel spa and beauty salon, golf. Headliner entertainment, The Club and Atrium Lounge. Gift shops. Dream Card Mega Store. Hard Rock Cafe. Dream Card members earn complimentaries at table games, slots, poker and race book. 10% room discount for AAA and AARP members. Two Rees Jones designed golf courses.

In May, 2008 a new casino was added at Foxwoods. Originally called the MGM Grand at Foxwoods, in 2013 it was renamed the Fox Tower. It is connected to the Foxwoods Casino Resort by a covered, moving, walkway.

The property has its own casino offering electronic gaming machines, plus the following games: blackjack, craps, roulette, Spanish 21, and three-card Poker.

The following information is from Connecticut's Division of Special Revenue regarding Foxwoods' slot payback percentages:

Denomination	Payback %
1¢	90.09
2¢	91.38
5¢	90.73
25¢	91.34
50¢	90.77
$1.00	92.99
$5.00	93.67
$25.00	96.51
$100.00	94.14
Average	**91.95**

These figures reflect the total percentages returned by each denomination of slot machine from July 1, 2018 through June 30, 2019.

The games offered at Mohegan Sun are: blackjack, craps, roulette, poker, baccarat, mini-baccarat, pai gow, wheel of fortune, pai gow poker, Caribbean stud poker, let it ride, Spanish 21, Mississippi stud, sic bo, three card poker, four card poker, Texas hold 'em bonus and keno. There is also a race book offering off-track betting on horses, greyhounds and jai-alai.

Mohegan Sun Casino
1 Mohegan Sun Boulevard
Uncasville, Connecticut 06382
(860) 862-8000
Website: www.mohegansun.com
Map Location: **#2** (Take I-95 Exit 76/I-395 North. Take Exit 79A (Route 2A) East. Less than 1 mile to Mohegan Sun Boulevard)

Toll-Free Number: (888) 226-7711
Room Reservations: (888) 777-7922
Sky Tower Rooms: 1,020 Prices: $169-$449
Sky Tower Suites: 180 Prices: $209-$3,500
Earth Tower Rooms: 361 Prices: $179-$699
Earth Tower Suites: 39 Prices: $309-$2,500
Restaurants: 29 (3 open 24 hours)
Buffets (Seasons): B-$15.00 L-$25.00
D-$29.00
Casino Size: 295,000 Square Feet
Overnight RV Parking: Free/RV Dump: No
Special Features: Daily resort fee charged in addition to room rate. Food court with specialty food outlets. Kids Quest supervised children's activity center. On-site gas station. 37-store shopping arcade.

Here's information from Connecticut's Division of Special Revenue regarding Mohegan Sun's slot payback percentages:

Denomination	Payback %
1¢	88.86
2¢	86.65
5¢	92.08
25¢	91.01
50¢	91.73
$1.00	92.94
$5.00	94.41
$10.00	97.41
$25.00	95.50
$100.00	94.55
Average	**91.90**

These figures reflect the total percentages returned by each denomination of slot machine from July 1, 2018 through June 30, 2019.

DELAWARE

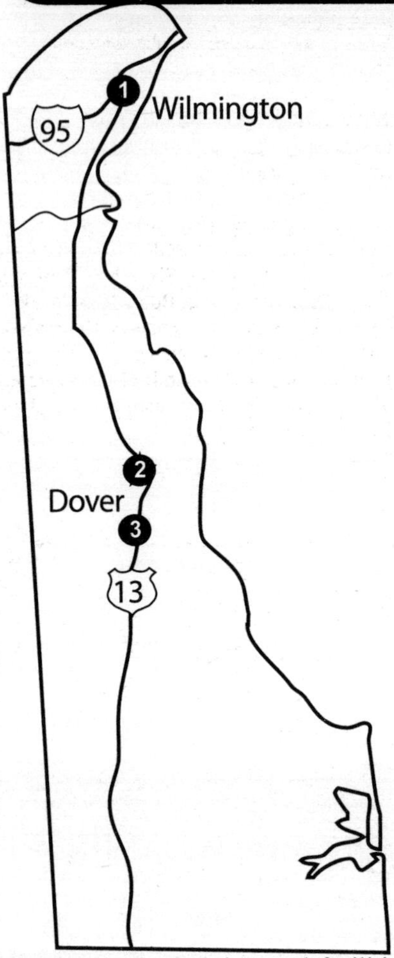

Delaware's three pari-mutuel facilities all feature slot machines. Technically, the machines are video lottery terminals (VLT's) because they are operated in conjunction with the Delaware Lottery. The VLT's also play other games including: video poker, video keno and video blackjack.

By law, all video lottery games must return between 87% and 95% of all wagers on an annual basis. Games can return above 95% but only with the Lottery Director's approval.

According to figures from the Delaware Lottery for the twelve-month period from July 1, 2018 through June 30, 2019 the average VLT return at Dover Downs was 92.59%, at Delaware Park it was 92.12%, and at Harrington Raceway it was 92.03%.

In January 2010 the Delaware legislature approved the addition of table games for the state's casinos. All Delaware casinos offer: blackjack, roulette, craps, slots and video poker. Some casinos also offer: mini-baccarat (MB), poker (P), pai gow poker (PGP), Caribbean stud poker (CSP), let it ride (LIR), big 6 (B6), bingo (BG), keno (K), three card poker (TCP), Mississippi stud (MS), casino war (CW), four card poker (FCP), Spanish 21 (S21) and sports betting (SB).

All casinos are open 24 hours, however, both Harrington and Delaware Park are closed on Christmas day. Additionally, Harrington is closed on Easter Sunday.

If you want to order a drink while playing, be aware that Delaware gaming regulations do not allow casinos to provide free alcoholic beverages. The minimum gambling age is 21 for slots or sports betting and 18 for horse racing.

For more information on visiting Delaware call the state's tourism office at (800) 441-8846 or visit their website at: www.visitdelaware.com.

Delaware Park Racetrack & Slots
777 Delaware Park Boulevard
Wilmington, Delaware 19804
(302) 994-2521
Website: www.delawarepark.com
Map: **#1**

Toll-Free Number: (800) 417-5687
Restaurants: 8
Buffets: Brunch: $29.95 (Sun)
Other Games: P, TCP, FCP, PGP, MS, S21
Overnight RV Parking: Free/RV Dump: No
Special Features: Live thoroughbred racing seasonally. Daily simulcasting of horse racing.

Dover Downs Hotel Casino
1131 N. DuPont Highway
Dover, Delaware 19901
(302) 674-4600
Website: www.doverdowns.com
Map: **#2**

Toll-Free Number: (800) 711-5882
Rooms: 206 Price Range: $99-$279
Suites: 26 Price Range: $195-$805
Restaurants: 8
Buffets: B-$11.50/$16.50 (Sat/Sun)
L-$15.50 D-$18.50/$26.95 (Fri/Sat)
Casino Size: 91,000 Square Feet
Other Games: S21, TCP, PGP, B, LIR, MS
Overnight RV Parking: Free/RV Dump: Free
(Not free during NASCAR events)
Special Features: Casino is non-smoking. Live harness racing seasonally. Daily simulcasting of horse racing. Motorsports speedway with NASCAR racing.

Harrington Raceway & Casino
Delaware State Fairgrounds
15 W Rider Road
Harrington, Delaware 19952
(302) 398-4920
Website: www.harringtonraceway.com
Map: **#3** (20 miles S. of Dover)

Toll-Free Number: (888) 887-5687
Restaurants: 6
Buffets: L- $13.95
D- $17.95/$29.95 (Wed)/
$21.95 (Fri-Sat)
Other Games: MB, P, PGP, TCP, Four Card Poker, Spanish 21, Big Six Wheel, Ultimate Texas Hold 'em, Sports Book, Race Book
Overnight RV Parking: Free/RV Dump: No
Special Features: Live harness racing April-June and August-October. Daily simulcasting of horse racing. Table games open 9am-2am/24-hours (Fri/Sat).

FLORIDA

Florida has three forms of casino gambling: casino boats, Indian casinos and gaming machines at pari-mutuels in two south Florida counties.

The casino boats offer gamblers the opportunity to board ships that cruise offshore where casino gambling is legal. From the west coast the boats travel nine miles out into the Gulf of Mexico. From the East coast they travel three miles out into the Atlantic Ocean.

Unless otherwise noted, all Florida casino boats offer: blackjack, craps, roulette, slots and video poker. Some casinos also offer: mini-baccarat (MB), poker (P), pai gow poker (PGP), three-card poker (TCP), Caribbean stud poker (CSP), let it ride (LIR), bingo (BG) and sports book (SB).

Due to security restrictions, you must present a photo ID at all casino boats or you will not be allowed to board.

For Florida visitor information call (888) 735-2872 or visit their website at: www.visitflorida.com.

Cape Canaveral

Map: **#7** (60 miles S.E. of Orlando)

Victory Casino Cruises - Cape Canaveral
180 Christopher Columbus Drive
Cape Canaveral, Florida 32920
(321) 799-0021
Website: www.victorycasinocruises.com

Toll-Free Number: (855) 468-4286
Gambling Age: 18 Price: $13
Food Service: A la Carte
Schedule: 11am-4pm (Mon-Sat)
12pm-6pm (Sun)
7pm-12am (Sun-Thu)
7pm-12:30am (Fri/Sat)
Buffet Price: $15/$20 (Fri-Sun)
Port Charges: Included Parking: Free
Other Games: BJ, C, R, MB, TCP, SB, LIR, UTH, MS, BG
Special Features: 1,200-passenger Victory I departs from Port Canaveral. 6-hour cruise on Sundays.

Port Richey

Map: **#6** (37 miles N.W. of Tampa)

Tropical Breeze Casino
7917 Bayview Street
Port Richey, Florida 34668
(727) 848-3423
Website: www.portricheycasino.com

Toll-Free Number: (844) 386-2789
Gambling Age: 18
Food Service: A la Carte
Sailing times and prices vary. Call for details.
Port Charges: Included Parking: Free
Other Games: BJ, C, R, LIR, TCP
Special Features: 465-passenger Royal Casino departs on high tide, from dock on Pithlachascotee River off of US 19 in Port Richey. Cruises Thursday through Monday.

Indian Casinos

Florida has eight Indian gaming locations. The Seminole Tribe has seven and the eighth is on the Miccosukee Tribe's reservation.

The Seminoles signed a compact with the state that allows them to offer traditional Class III gaming machines. As part of their compact, five Seminole casinos are also allowed to offer blackjack (BJ), poker (P), baccarat (B), mini-baccarat (MB), Mississippi stud (MS), three card poker (TCP), let it ride (LIR) and pai gow poker (PGP).

The Miccosukee Tribe has not signed a compact and they only offer Class II gaming machines at their casino.

Class II video gaming devices look like slot machines, but are actually bingo games and the spinning reels are for "entertainment purposes only." No public information is available concerning the payback percentages on any gaming machines in Florida's Indian casinos. All of the casinos are open 24 hours (except Big Cypress) and the minimum gambling age is 18 at all Indian casinos for bingo or poker and 21 for electronic gaming machines and table games.

Miccosukee Resort & Gaming
500 S.W. 177 Avenue
Miami, Florida 33194
(305) 222-4600
Website: www.miccosukee.com
Map: **#1**

Toll-Free Number: (800) 741-4600
Room Reservations: (877) 242-6464
Rooms: 256 Price Range: $109-$149
Suites: 46 Price Range: $129-$209
Restaurants: 4 Liquor: Yes
Games Offered: Class-II Electronic Gaming Machines, Poker, Bingo
Buffets: B-$14.55 L-$16.16 D-$17.78
Overnight RV Parking: Free/RV Dump: No
Note: Class II video gaming devices look like slot machines, but are actually bingo games and the spinning reels are for "entertainment purposes only."

Seminole Brighton Casino
17735 Reservation Road
Okeechobee, Florida 34974
(863) 467-9998
Website: www.seminolebrightoncasino.com
Map: **#8** (75 miles N.W. of West Palm Beach)

Toll-Free Number: (866) 222-7466
Restaurants: 1 Liquor: Yes
Casino Size: 27,000 Square Feet
Other Games: BJ, TCP, BG(Wed-Sun)
Overnight RV Parking: No

Seminole Casino Coconut Creek
5550 NW 40th Street
Coconut Creek, Florida 33073
(954) 977-6700
Website: seminolecoconutcreekcasino.com
Map: **#2**

Toll-Free Number: (866) 222-7466
Restaurants: 7 Liquor: Yes
Buffet: B-$28 (Sat/Sun)
L-$19 D- $27/$33 (Fri/Sat)
Casino Size: 30,000 Square Feet
Other Games: BJ, MB, TCP, PGP, LIR, S21, CW, MS, UTH, P
Overnight RV Parking: Call ahead.
Special Features: Non-smoking casino on second floor.

Seminole Casino Immokalee
506 South 1st Street
Immokalee, Florida 34142
(239) 658-1313
Website: seminoleimmokaleecasino.com
Map: **#4** (35 miles N.E. of Naples)

Toll-Free Number: (800) 218-0007
Rooms: 80 Price Range: $179-$299
Suites: 19 Price Range: $479-$599
Restaurants: 3 Liquor: Yes
Casino Size: 22,000 Square Feet
Other Games: BJ, MB, TCP, PGP, LIR, P, S21, MS, UTH
Overnight RV Parking: Free/RV Dump: No

Seminole Classic Casino
4150 N. State Road 7
Hollywood, Florida 33021
(954) 961-3220
Website: www.seminoleclassiccasino.com
Map: **#2** (1 miles S. of Fort Lauderdale)

Toll-Free Number: (800) 323-5452
Restaurants: 1 Liquor: Yes
Casino Size: 73,500 Square Feet
Other Games: BJ, MB, TCP, PGP, BG, S21, CW, MS, UTH
Overnight RV Parking: Free/RV Dump: No
Special Features: Located one block south of Hard Rock Hotel & Casino Hollywood. Food court with three fast food outlets.

This rendering shows the new Seminole Hard Rock Hotel & +Casino in Hollywood. The $1.5 Billion expansion, which opened Ocotber 24, 2019, features a 40-story, 638-room, guitar-shaped hotel, 30 restaurants, lounges and bars, plus a 6,500-seat Hard Rock Live entertainment venue.

Seminole Hard Rock Hotel & Casino - Hollywood
1 Seminole Way
Hollywood, Florida 33314
(954) 327-7625
www.seminolehardrockhollywood.com
Map: **#2** (1 mile S. of Fort Lauderdale)

Toll-Free Number: (866) 502-7529
Rooms: 1,175 Price Range: $219-$499
Suites: 63 Price Range: $539-$1,199
Restaurants: 16 Liquor: Yes
Buffets: Brunch-$79.99 (Sun) Other buffet pricing not available at press time.
Casino Size: 160,000 Square Feet
Other Games: BJ, MB, TCP, PGP, LIR, P, S21, CW, MS
Overnight RV Parking: No
Special Features: 450-foot guitar shaped hotel. Food court with six fast-food outlets. 13-acre lagoon-style pool. 42,000 square foot health spa. 6,500-seat Hard Rock Live entertainment venue.

Seminole Hard Rock Hotel & Casino - Tampa
5223 Orient Road
Tampa, Florida 33610
(813) 627-7625
www.seminolehardrocktampa.com
Map: **#3**

Toll-Free Number: (866) 388-4263
Rooms: 760 Price Range: $279-$429
Suites: 46 Price Range: $359-$599
Restaurants: 5 Liquor: Yes
Buffets: B-$34.95 (Sat/Sun) L-$21.95 D- $29.95
Casino Size: 90,000 Square Feet
Other Games: BJ, MB, TCP, PGP, LIR, P, S21, PG, CW, MS, UTH, P
Overnight RV Parking: Call ahead.
Special Features: Elvis Presley's 24-karat gold-leaf piano on display. Food court with four fast food outlets. 2,000-seat entertainment venue. $5 buffet discount for player's club members. Spa.

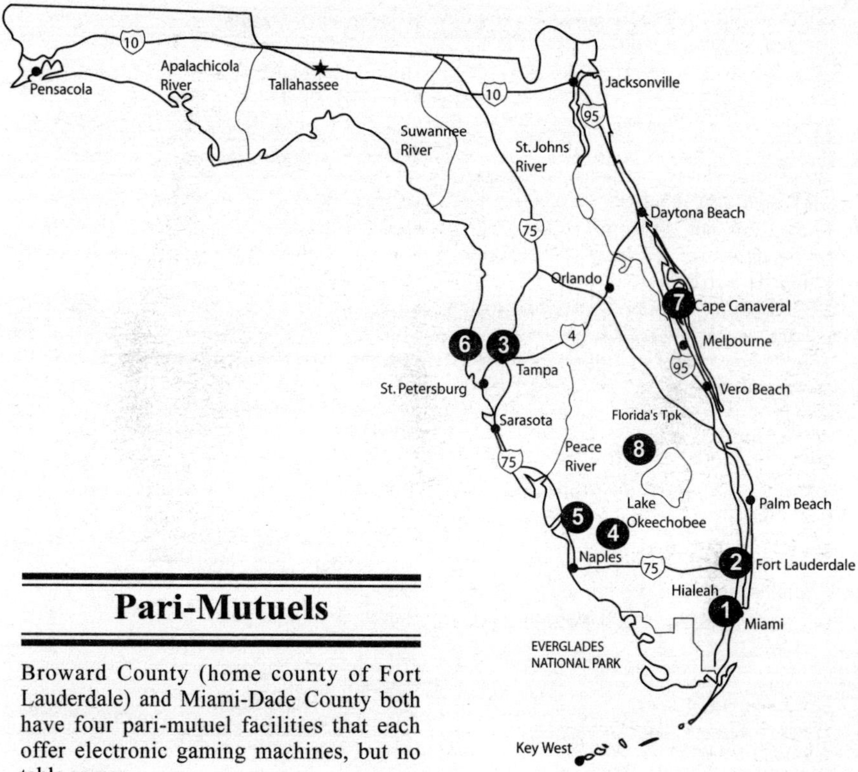

Pari-Mutuels

Broward County (home county of Fort Lauderdale) and Miami-Dade County both have four pari-mutuel facilities that each offer electronic gaming machines, but no table games.

Florida gaming regulations require a minimum payback of 85% on all gaming machines. From July 1, 2018 through June 30, 2019 the gaming machines at Hialeah Park returned 93.55%, Magic City returned 93.43%, Dania Casino returned 92.68%, Casino Miami returned 92.34%, Gulfstream Park returned 92.16%, Big Easy returned 91.50%, Calder returned 91.32%, and The Isle returned 90.22%.

South Florida's pari-mutuel facilities (as well as most pari-mutuels throughout the state), also offer poker. Admission to all casinos is free and they are allowed to be open a maximum of 18 hours per day during the week and 24 hours on the weekends and some holidays.

If you want to order a drink while playing, be aware that Florida gaming regulations do not allow pari-mutuel casinos to provide free alcoholic beverages.

The minimum gambling age is 18 for pari-mutuel betting or poker and 21 for gaming machines.

Big Easy Casino
831 N. Federal Highway
Hallandale Beach, Florida 33009
(954) 924-3200
Website: www.thebigeasycasino.com
Map: **#2**

Toll-Free Number: (877) 557-5687
Hours: 9am-3am/24 Hours (Fri/Sat)
Restaurants: 1 Liquor: Yes
Overnight RV Parking: No
Special Features: Daily simulcasting of dog, thoroughbred and harness races.

Calder Casino & Race Course
21001 N. W. 27th Avenue
Miami Gardens, Florida 33056
(305) 625-1311
Website: www.caldercasino.com
Map: #**1**

Toll Free: (800) 333-3227
Hours: 9am-3am/24 hours (Fri/Sat)
Restaurants: 2
Buffets: D-$21.99
Special Features: Live jai-alai played seasonally.

Casino Miami
3500 N.W. 37th Avenue
Miami Florida 33142
(305) 633-6400
Website: www.playcasinomiami.com
Map: #**1**

Hours: 10am-4am/24 hours (Fri/Sat)
Special Features: Live jai-alai seasonally. Daily simulcasting of jai-alai and harness racing.

The Casino @ Dania Beach
301 E. Dania Beach Boulevard
Dania Beach, Florida 33004
(954) 920-1511
Website: www.casinodaniabeach.com
Map: #**2**

Toll-Free Number: (844) 794-6244
Restaurants: 3
Buffet: B/L $24.95 (Sun) D- $29.95 (Fri/Sat)
Overnight RV Parking: No
Special Features: Live jai-alai seasonally. Daily simulcasting of thoroughbred/harness racing and jai-alai.

Gulfstream Park Racing & Casino
901 S. Federal Highway
Hallandale Beach, Florida 33009
(954) 454-7000
Website: www.gulfstreampark.com/casino
Map: #**2**

Hours: 9am-3am/ 24 Hours (Fri/Sat)
Restaurants: 4
Overnight RV Parking: No
Special Features: Live thoroughbred racing seasonally. Daily simulcasting of thoroughbred

Hialeah Park Casino
2200 East 4th Avenue
Hialeah, Florida 33013
(305) 885-8000
Website: www.hialeahparkcasino.com
Map: #1

Restaurants: 3
Casino Hours: 9am-3am/24 hours (Fri/Sat)
Special Features: Live quarter-horse racing seasonally.

Isle Casino Racing Pompano Park
777 Isle of Capri Circle
Pompano Beach, Florida 33069
(954) 972-2000
Website: www.theislepompanopark.com
Map: #**2**

Toll-Free Number: (800) 843-4753
Hours: 9am-3am/24 hours (Fri/Sat)
Restaurants: 4
Buffet: B- $23.99 (Sun) L- $16.99
D- $26.99/ $28.99 (Fri/Sat)
Overnight RV Parking: No
Special Features: Live evening harness racing seasonally. Daily simulcasting of thoroughbred/harness racing and jai-alai.

Magic City Casino
450 NW 37th Avenue
Miami, Florida 33126
305-649-3000
Website: www.magiccitycasino.com
Map: #**1**

Toll-free Number: (888) 566-2442
Hours: 10am-4am/5am (Fri/Sat)
Restaurants: 1
Buffet: B/L-$16.00 (Sun) D- $19.00 (Fri/Sat)
Special Features: Live jai-alai seasonally. Daily simulcasting of dog and harness racing. Buffet discount with players club card.

GEORGIA

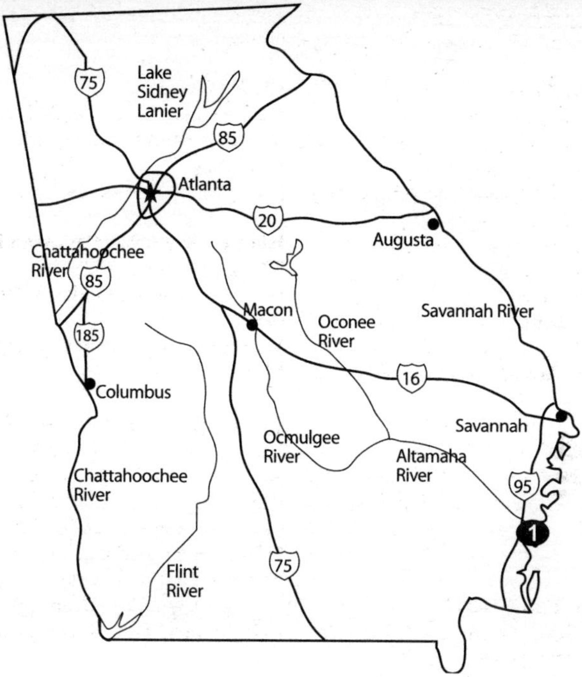

There is one casino boat in Georgia which sails three miles out into international waters where casino gambling is permitted.

The boat offers blackjack, craps, roulette, poker, slots and video poker. Due to security restrictions, you must present a photo ID or you will not be allowed to board.

For information on visiting Georgia call the state's tourism department at (800) 847-4842 or visit their website at www.georgia.org.

Emerald Princess Casino
1 Emerald Princess Drive
Brunswick, Georgia 31523
(912) 265-3558
Website: www.emeraldprincesscasino.com
Map Location: **#1** (75 miles S. of Savannah)

Reservation Number: (800) 842-0115
Gambling Age: 21 Parking: Free
Schedule
11:00am - 4:00pm (Fri)
1:00pm - 6:00pm (Sat/Sun)
7:00pm - 12:00am (Tue-Thu)
7:00pm - 1:00am (Fri/Sat)
Price: $10 Port Charges: Included
Special Features: 400-passenger Emerald Princess II sails from Gisco Point, at the southern end of the Sidney Lanier Bridge. Reservations are required for all cruises. Packages with hotel accommodations are available. No one under 21 permitted to board.

IDAHO

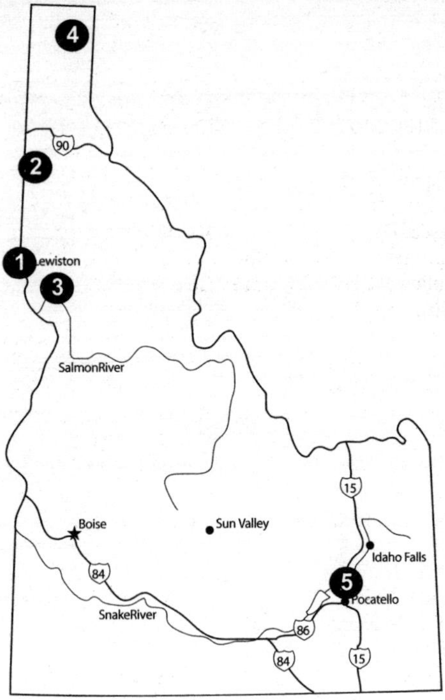

Idaho has seven Indian casinos that offer electronic pull-tab machines and other video games. Some casinos also offer bingo (BG), off-track betting (OTB) and poker (P).

The terms of the compact between the tribes and the state do not require any minimum payback percentage that the gaming machines must return to the public.

The minimum gambling age at all casinos is 18 and they are all open 24 hours. For Idaho tourism information call (800) 635-7820 or visit their website: www.visitid.org.

Bannock Peak Casino
1707 W. Country Road
Pocatello, Idaho 83204
(208) 235-1308
Website: www.shobangaming.com
Map: **#5** (5 miles N. of Pocatello)

Restaurants: 1 Snack Bar Liquor: No
Hours: 10am-12am/1am (Fri/Sat)
Casino Size: 5,000 Square Feet
Overnight RV Parking: Free/RV Dump: No

Clearwater River Casino and Lodge
17500 Nez Perce Road
Lewiston, Idaho 83501
(208) 746-0723
Website: www.crcasino.com
Map: **#1** (250 miles N. of Boise)

Toll-Free Number: (866) 719-3885
Rooms: 47 Price Range: $89-$139
Suites: 3 Price Range $189-$169
Restaurants: 1 Liquor: Yes
Casino Size: 30,000 Square Feet
Hours: 7am-12am
Other Games: BG (Select Days)
Overnight RV Parking: Free/RV Dump: No
Special Features:Gambling age is 21. 23-space RV park ($28 per night).

Coeur D'Alene Casino Resort Hotel
37914 South Nukwalow
Worley, Idaho 83876
(800) 523-2464
Website: www.cdacasino.com
Map: **#2** (350 miles N. of Boise)

Rooms: 202 Price Range: $85-$210
Suites: 8 Price Range $160-$450
Restaurants: 7 Liquor: Yes Valet Parking: Free
Buffet: B- $16.99 (Fri-Mon)
D-$16.99/$39.99(Fri/ Sat)
Casino Size: 30,000 Square Feet
Other Games: BG (Fri-Sun), OTB, K
Overnight RV Parking: $20/RV Dump: No
Special Features: 18-hole golf course. Spa.

Fort Hall Casino
Simplot Road
Fort Hall, Idaho 83203
(208) 237-8778
Website: www.shobangaming.com
Map: **#5** (14 miles N. of Pocatello)

Toll-Free Number: (800) 497-4231
Rooms: 145 Price Range: $149-$229
Suites: 11 Price Range $275-$325
Restaurants: 2 Liquor: No
Casino Size: 15,000 Square Feet
Other Games: BG (Wed-Sun)
Overnight RV Parking: Must use RV Park
Special Features: 27-space RV park ($27 per night).

It'Se-Ye-Ye Casino
419 Third Street
Kamiah, Idaho 83536
(208) 935-7860
Website: www.crcasino.com
Map: **#3** (225 miles N. of Boise)

Restaurants: 1 Liquor: No
Hours: 7am-10pm/2am (Fri/Sat)
Casino Size: 6,000 Square Feet
Overnight RV Parking: Free/RV Dump: No

Kootenai Casino and Spa
7169 Plaza Street
Bonners Ferry, Idaho 83805
(208) 267 8511
Website: www.kootenairiverinn.com
Map: **#4** (450 miles N. of Boise)

Toll-Free Number: (888) 875-8259
Rooms: 65 Price Range: $169-$189
Suites: 4 Price Range $299-$399
Restaurants: 1 Liquor: Yes
Casino Size: 30,000 Square Feet
Other Games: BG(1st and 3rd Wednesdays)
Overnight RV Parking: Free/RV Dump: No
Special Features: Hotel is Best Western. Spa.

Sage Hill Travel Center & Casino
2 North Eagle Road
Blackfoot, Idaho 83221
Map: **#5** (14 miles N. of Pocatello)
Website: www.shobangaming.com
(208) 237-4998

Restaurants: 1
Casino Hours: 6:30am-2am/24 hours (Fri/Sat)
Casino Size: 13,200 Square Feet
Special Features: Convenience store and gas station.

ILLINOIS

Illinois was the second state to legalize riverboat casinos. Riverboat casinos began operating there in September 1991 with the launching of the first boat: the Alton Belle.

All Illinois riverboats remain dockside and do not cruise. Unlike Mississippi, however, the casinos are not open 24 hours and state law limits the number of gaming licenses to 10.

In mid-2019 a gambling expansion bill was passed which allows for six new casinos, plus casinos at the state's three racetracks, and an expansion of video gambling machines at non-casino locations. Be sure to read John Grochowski's article "The Best Places to Play in the Chicago Area" for more details.

Here's information from the Illinois Gaming Board showing each casino's average slot payback percentage for the one-year period from July 1, 2018 through June 30, 2019:

CASINO	PAYBACK %
Casino Queen	92.05
Harrah's Joliet	91.98
Hollywood - Joliet	91.18
Par-A-Dice	91.02
Grand Victoria	91.02
Argosy Alton	90.83
Hollywood - Aurora	90.42
Rivers Casino	90.35
Jumer's	89.94
Harrah's Metropolis	89.39

These figures reflect the total percentages returned by each casino for all of their electronic machines.

All casinos are non-smoking and, unless otherwise noted, all casinos offer: slots, video poker, blackjack, craps, roulette and three card poker. Some casinos also offer: let it ride (LIR), baccarat (B), mini-baccarat (MB), poker (P), Ultimate Texas hold em (UTH), Caribbean stud poker (CSP), Mississippi stud (MS), pai gow poker (PGP) and four card poker (FCP). Additionally, sports betting was legalized for Illinois casinos in late 2019 and it is expected to be offered at most casinos by early 2020.

If you want to order a drink while playing, be aware that Illinois gaming regulations do not allow casinos to provide free alcoholic beverages. The minimum gambling age is 21.

For more information on visiting Illinois contact the state's Bureau of Tourism at (800) 226-6632 or www.enjoyillinois.com

Argosy Casino Alton
1 Piasa Street
Alton, Illinois 62002
(618) 474-7500
Website: www.argosyalton.com
Map: **#1** (260 miles S.W. of Chicago, 25 miles N. of St. Louis, MO)

Toll-Free Number: (800) 711-4263
Restaurants: 3
Buffets: L-$14.99/$16.99(Sun)
D-$19.99/$22.99 (Fri)/$37.99(Sat)
Casino Hours: 8am-6am Daily
Casino Size: 23,000 Square Feet
Other Games: UTH
Overnight RV Parking: Yes
Special Features: Casino features a 1,200-passenger modern yacht and a barge docked on the Mississippi River. Table games open at 10am daily. Buffet discount for players club members.

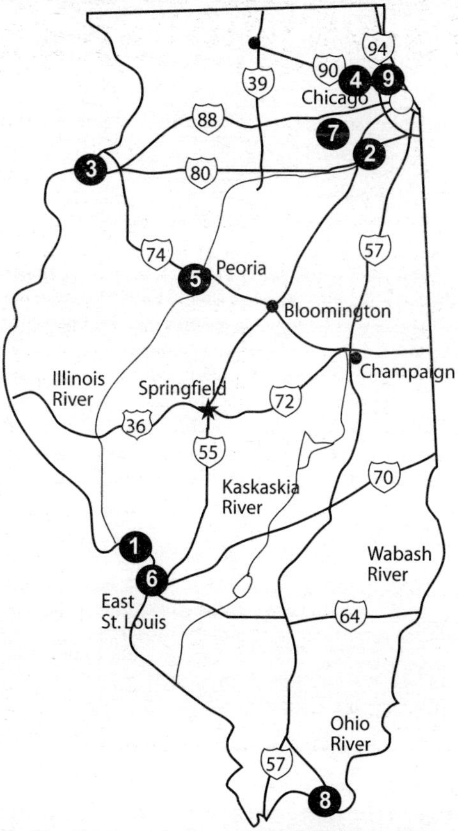

Casino Queen
200 S. Front Street
E. St. Louis, Illinois 62201
(618) 874-5000
Website: www.casinoqueen.com
Map: **#6** (290 miles S.W. of Chicago)

Toll-Free Number: (800) 777-0777
Rooms: 150 Price Range: $89-$169
Suites: 7 Price Range: $149-$699
Restaurants: 4
Buffets: B-$15.95(Sat/Sun)
L-$15.95/$16.95 (Sun)
D-$18.95/$23.95 (Sat)
Casino Hours: 8am-4am/6am (Thu-Sat)
Casino Size: 40,000 Square Feet
Other Games: UTH, MS, no Three Card Poker
Senior Discount: Various Tue 8am-7pm if 50+
Overnight RV Parking: Must use RV park
Special Features: Land-based casino. 140-space RV park ($59+ per night). Sports Bar. MetroLink light-rail station at doorstep.

Grand Victoria Casino
250 S. Grove Avenue
Elgin, Illinois 60120
(847) 468-7000
Website: www.grandvictoriacasino.com
Map: **#4** (41 miles N.W. of Chicago)

Toll Free Number: (888) 508-1900
Restaurants: 4
Buffets: L-$12.99/$15.99 (Sun)
D-$19.99/$38.99(Wed/Fri)/
$29.99(Sat/Sun)
Casino Hours: 8:30am-6:30am Daily
Casino Size: 29,850 Square Feet
Other Games: P, MS, MB
Overnight RV Parking: Yes
Special Features: 1,200-passenger paddle wheeler-replica docked on the Fox River. Buffet discount for player's club members. 100x odds on craps.

Harrah's Joliet
151 N. Joliet Street
Joliet, Illinois 60432
(815) 740-7800
Website: www.harrahsjoliet.com
Map: **#2** (43 miles S.W. of Chicago)

Toll-Free Number: (800) 427-7247
Rooms: 200 Price Range: $89-$249
Suites: 4 Price Range: Casino Use Only
Restaurants: 3
Buffets: L-$17.49/$23.99 (Sat)/$26.99 (Sun)
D-$22.99/$29.99 (Fri)/
$26.99 (Sat/Sun)
Casino Hours: 8am-6am Daily
Casino Size: 39,000 Square Feet
Other Games: MB, UTH, P, MS
Overnight RV Parking: No
Special Features: Casino is on a barge docked on the Des Plaines River. Buffet is closed Tue/Wed.

Harrah's Metropolis
100 E. Front Street
Metropolis, Illinois 62960
(618) 524-2628
Website: www.harrahsmetropolis.com
Map: **#8** (Across from Paducah, KY.)

Toll-Free Number: (800) 929-5905
Rooms: 252 Price Range: $55-$159
Suites: 6 Price Range: Casino Use Only
Restaurants: 3
Buffets: B-$16.99 (Sat/Sun)
D-$16.99 (Thu/Sun)/$21.99 (Fri/Sat)
Hours: 9am-5am/7am (Fri/Sat)
Other Games: MB, MS
Casino Size: 24,269 Square Feet
Overnight RV Parking: Free/RV Dump: No
Special Features: 1,300-passenger sidewheeler-replica docked on the Ohio River. Buffet closed Mon-Wed.

Hollywood Casino - Aurora
1 West New York Street
Aurora, Illinois 60506
(630) 801-1234
Website: www.hollywoodcasinoaurora.com
Map: **#7** (41 miles W. of Chicago)

Toll Free Number: (800) 888-7777
Restaurants: 3
Buffets: L-$13.99/$19.99 (Sun)
D-$17.99/$29.99 (Fri)/$20.99 (Sat)/
$19.99(Sun)
Casino Hours: 8:30am-4:30am/6:30 (Fri/Sat)
Casino Size: 41,384 Square Feet
Other Games: MB, MS, P
Overnight RV Parking: Yes
Senior Discount: 50% off buffet Wed if 55+
Special Features: Casino is on a barge docked on the Fox River. Buffet discount for players club members. Buffet closed Mon-Tue.

Hollywood Casino - Joliet
151 N. Joliet Street
Joliet, Illinois 60436
(815) 744-9400
Website: www.hollywoodcasinojoliet.com
Map: **#2** (43 miles S.W. of Chicago)

Toll-Free Number: (888) 436-7737
Rooms: 85 Price Range: $99-$149
Suites: 17 Price Range: $129-$179
Casino Hours: 7:30am-5:30am Daily
Restaurants: 4
Buffets: L-$13.99 (Wed-Sat)/$16.99 (Sun)
D-$17.99/$26.99 (Fri/Sat)
Casino Size: 50,000 square feet
Other Games: P, CSP, MB, MS
Overnight RV Parking: Must use RV park
Special Features: 2,500-passenger barge docked on the Des Plaines River. Buffet closed Mon-Tue. 80-space RV park ($36-$42 per night).

The Best Places To Play In The Chicago Area

by John Grochowski

Casinos in Illinois and on the Indiana side of the border on Lake Michigan have been very different experiences.

Those in Illinois have been restricted to 1,200 gaming positions and so far have had to be on water in keeping with the original riverboat gaming that launched in 1991. The new land-based Chicago casino introduction will break that pattern.

The definition of "on water" is very loose -- the Rivers Casino in northwest suburban Des Plaines, Illinois, was built over a shallow pit with a few inches of water.

Illinois casinos must close for at least two hours a day. Closing hours generally are early in the morning -- if you arrive between 6 and 8 a.m., you're likely to have a wait before you can get on the gaming floor.

Across the border east of Chicago, Indiana casinos are larger and open 24/7. There is no restriction on gaming positions. The only limitation is how many games they can get onto their Lake Michigan barges.

Beyond the full casino experience, there's a wild card in Illinois with up to five slot machines in licensed bars, restaurants, truck stops and service organizations. Though each operation is small scale, in a separate nook from the main businesses, there are thousands of outlets.

Riverboats no longer leave the dock, though Illinois and Indiana still do not permit land-based casinos. That leaves the following options for Chicago-area players, pending the awarding of licenses under the new Illinois law:

Rivers is the closest to Chicago, with Des Plaines neighboring O'Hare Airport about 16 miles from the north Loop. The others are in an arc about 40 to 50 miles from the Loop, with Elgin slightly northwest, Joliet to the southwest and Aurora in between.

All are smoke-free casinos under an Illinois ban on smoking in public venues. Typically, Illinois casinos use about 1,100 of those positions on slot machines and other electronic gaming devices such as video poker and video keno. Rivers has a larger than usual corps of table players, so its slot total is closer to 1,000. All that will be up for grabs as legal positions expand to 2,000.

Only the two Joliet casinos have hotels, though all have multiple restaurants, including buffet and steakhouse options. None have showrooms, and in Illinois, when a casino sponsors headliner entertainment, it usually is in cooperation with a partner in the host city.

Indiana casinos are actually closer to Chicago than all the Illinois casinos except Rivers. There are four Indiana casinos within the metro area. The largest, Horseshoe in Hammond, is only 16 miles from the South Loop. The others – Ameristar in East Chicago and Majestic Star I and II in Gary, are only a few miles farther east.

All may remain open 24/7, smoking is not banned and there is no limit on the number of games. The casinos there are much larger --- the largest facility, Horseshoe Hammond's barge, has more than 2,800 electronic games and 160-plus table games. One consequence is that there is a much larger selection of new table games in Indiana. If you want to try Blackjack Switch, High Card Flush, Pai-Gow tiles or even a Big Six wheel, you're more likely to find it in Indiana.

Ameristar and Majestic Star have hotels, while Horseshoe prefers to work with Chicago hotel partners.

Outlying casinos: A little outside the Chicago area, but within easy drives of about an hour and a half, are Blue Chip Casino in Michigan City, Ind., Four Winds Casino in New Buffalo, Mich., Potawatomi Bingo Casino in Milwaukee. Increase the range to a three-hour drive, and that brings in a couple of Illinois casinos, Par-A-Dice casino in Peoria and Jumer's Casino Rock Island.

Blue Chip operates under the same conditions as other Indiana properties and Par-A-Dice and Jumer's operate under Illinois regulations. Potawatomi in Wisconsin and Four Winds in Michigan are full-service, land-based showpieces for those with time to travel a little farther afield.

Illinois bars, restaurants, truck stops and service organizations: Unless prohibited by local ordinance, facilities that receive an Illinois Gaming Board license may operate up to five video gaming machines. Some communities, including the City of Chicago, have opted out, but even so, there are more than 30,000 machines in operation at such facilities across the state.

Each site is limited to five gaming terminals, and the terminals include both slot and video poker games. They are games with random number generators, and work just like casino slots, except there are some restrictions. Credit denominations must range between 5 cents and 25 cents, the maximum wager is $2, and the maximum payout for a single play is $500. A quarter video poker game in the bars, restaurants, et al can't pay the $1,000 jackpot players are used to on quarter machines.

Back in the casinos, let's look at some of the best of gaming in the Chicago area, subject to rapid change as venues are added starting in 2020.

VIDEO POKER: Chicago area players have little these days that resembles its video poker hey-day of the mid-2000s. Then, Chicagoans were used to a high volume of 99-percenters-plus payback games – not to mention the 100-percent plus 10-7-5 Double Bonus Poker games with progressive jackpots Empress offered until 2003. They were often shocked to find pay tables that didn't match up when they visited the Las Vegas Strip. Alas, the video poker oasis has dried up, though there remain some good plays.

Majestic Star in Gary stands as an oasis of high-paying video poker for players with moderate budgets. High payers once were confined to Majestic Star II, but now there's a collection of 99-percenters on Majestic Star I, too. They're not on every machine, so you have to check before you play, but there are 25-cent-50-cent-$1 single-hand machines with a 99.8-percent version of Triple Bonus Poker Plus; Not So Ugly Deuces Wild (99.7); 9-7 Triple Double Bonus (99.6), 9-6 Jacks or Better (99.5); 8-5 Bonus Poker (99.2), 9-5-5 Double Bonus (99.1) and more. One downside is that it takes $100 in play to earn one rewards point on these machines, as opposed to $10 per point on other machines, but the upgrade in payback at the machines is well worth it.

Horseshoe Hammond has a collection of good games for bigger players. You can find 8-5 Bonus Poker with all quads paying 35-for-1, a 99.76-percent game, on single-hand machines at $5, $10 and $25 level. There's 9-7 Triple Double Bonus (99.6) on $5-10-$25 single-hand games. There are more, but you get the idea: The good stuff is for big bettors.

Elsewhere, there are opportunities for dollar players, including 9-6 Double Double Bonus Poker (98.98 percent) at Hollywood Joliet, Harrah's Joliet and Ameristar East Chicago. All have $1 progressives, with the two Joliet casinos both offering three-way progressives --- progressive jackpots on royal flushes, four Aces with a low card kicker, and four Aces without the kicker. Ameristar and Hollywood Joliet also have 9-7-5 Double Bonus (99.1) at dollar level.

One longtime attraction is gone. For many years, Jumer's in Rock Island had 10-7-5 Double Bonus, full pay except that 250-coin payoffs on straight flushes and on 5 through King quads were reduced to 239-for-1. Alas, that 99.8-percent game is gone as Jumer's has reduced payouts throughout its video poker inventory.

Craps: The addition of Rivers gave the Chicago area a second casino catering to big craps players. Rivers offers 100x odds --- the same as Horseshoe in Hammond. Horseshoe had dramatically changed the face of Chicago area craps after Jack Binion bought the former Empress in 1999. Bringing in 100x odds and $10,000 maximums was a radical change for Chicago, which had been a double-odds kind of town through the mid-1990s.

Now 20x odds have become common among competitors, while Rivers makes it a 100x odds duo.

Blackjack: Most games in the Chicago area use either six or eight decks, usually with the dealer hitting soft 17 except at some high-limit tables.

The most common games throughout the area use six decks, have dealer hit soft 17, permit double downs on any first two cards, including after splits. The house edge against a basic strategy player is 0.63 percent. There are a few better deals, especially for bigger bettors. At $25 minimums, players can get the edge down to 0.34 percent at the Joliet casinos where, at that level, dealers stand on soft 17 and players may resplit Aces. Majestic Star drops that a fraction more to 0.33 percent by offering late surrender at its $25 tables.

Table minimums tend to be high, especially in Illinois where anything under $15 a hand is a rare treat for a midweek morning. Crossing into Indiana, even Majestic Star, long the last bastion of $5 tables, has gone to $10 minimums except for the sporadic opening of a $5 Blackjack Switch game.

If you want to play $5 blackjack and don't want to make the longer drive to Jumer's, Par-A-Dice or Blue Chip, your sole Illinois option is Harrah's Joliet, which pays only 6-5 on blackjacks at $5 tables. That adds 1.4 percent to the house edge for a total of 1.92 percent against basic strategy players. Smart players will avoid that -- average losses are less with $10 bets at 3-2 tables than betting $5 at 6-5 tables.

OTHER TABLE GAMES: As you might expect, there are more table options at the bigger casinos in Indiana. In Illinois, operators tend to stick to blackjack, craps, roulette and Three Card Poker, with Mississippi Stud making inroads. In Indiana, most operators have all those games, and also pick and choose from among mini-baccarat, Blackjack Switch, pai-gow poker, Spanish 21, High Card Flush, Ultimate Texas Hold'Em --- if there's a promising new game, someone in Indiana is likely to try it.

SLOT MACHINES: Along with the rest of the country, Chicago has seen a great expansion in video bonusing slot games, with the hottest trend being toward lower and lower coin denominations. All Chicago area casinos now have penny slots. Horseshoe had been reluctant to join the penny trend, but the nationwide growth and popularity of the games have even casinos that cater to big players clamoring for copper.

Traditional three-reel games remain a big part of the mix at dollars and above, with Majestic Star having the largest selection of quarter three-reelers.

One thing you'll not find in Illinois or Indiana is million-dollar jackpots. Wide-area progressives such as Megabucks that link several different properties to the same jackpot are illegal in Illinois and Indiana. If you're a jackpot chaser, you'll need to go to Potawatomi in Milwaukee or Four Winds in New Buffalo, which both are on the national Native American link.

Slot payouts tend to be higher in Illinois than in Indiana, from quarters on up, but the Indiana casinos pay as much or more than the Illinois operations in nickels and below. Illinois averages tend to hover around 95 percent on dollars, 93 percent on quarters and 88 percent on nickels, 85 percent on pennies while Indiana returns, are around 94 percent on dollars, 92 percent on quarters and 89 percent on nickels and 86 percent on pennies --- with variations from casino to casino, of course.

For nearly 25 years, John Grochowski has been one of the most prolific gaming writers in the United States. He has written for casino industry professionals in Casino Executive and Casino Journal magazines, and for players in Casino Player, Strictly Slots and many other magazines. He is also the author of several best-selling books on gambling.

Jumer's Casino & Hotel Rock Island
777 Jumer Drive
Rock Island, Illinois 61201
(309) 756-4600
Website: www.jumerscasinohotel.com
Map: **#3** (170 miles W. of Chicago)

Toll-Free Number: (800) 477-7747
Rooms: 205 Price Range: $109-$209
Suites: 7 Price Range: $159-$599
Restaurants: 4
Buffets: B-$11.99 L- $12.99/$21.99 (Sat/Sun)
D- $17.99/$19.99 (Fri/Sat)
Casino Hours: 7am-5am Daily
Casino Size: 42,300 Square Feet
Other Games: MS, P
Overnight RV Parking: Free/Dump: No

Par-A-Dice Hotel Casino
21 Blackjack Boulevard
East Peoria, Illinois 61611
(309) 699-7711
Website: www.paradicecasino.com
Map: **#5** (170 miles S.W. of Chicago)

Toll-Free Number: (800) 727-2342
Rooms: 195 Price Range: $99-$139
Suites 13 Price Range: $175-$500
Restaurants: 4
Buffets: B- $7.95 L-$10.99/$14.99 (Sat/Sun)
D-$13.99/$18.99 (Fri/Sat)/
$16.99 (Sun)
Casino Hours: 8am-4am/6am (Fri/Sat)
Casino Size: 26,116 Square Feet
Other Games: MB, CSP, LIR, MS, P, B6
Overnight RV Parking: Free/RV Dump: No
Special Features: 1,600-passenger modern boat docked on the Illinois River. Buffet closed Mon/Tue.

Rivers Casino
3000 S River Road
Des Plaines, Illinois 60018
(847) 795-0777
Website: www.playrivers.com
Map: **#9** (20 miles N.W. of Chicago)

Toll Free Number: (888) 307-0777
Restaurants: 5
Buffets: L-$19.95/$25.95 (Sun)
D-$29.95/$46.95 (Tue)
Casino Hours: 9am-7am Daily
Casino Size: 43,687 Square Feet
Other Games: MB, B, TCP, PGP,
S21, THB, MS
Overnight RV Parking: No
Special features: Closest casino to O'Hare airport. Free lounge entertainment nightly. 100x odds on craps.

INDIANA

In June 1993 Indiana became the sixth state to legalize riverboat gambling. All of the state's riverboat casinos offer dockside gambling and, unless otherwise noted, are open 24 hours. The minimum gambling age is 21.

Following is information from the Indiana Gaming Commission regarding average slot payout percentages for the one-year period from July 1, 2018 through June 30, 2019:

CASINO	PAYBACK %
French Lick	91.55
Blue Chip	91.40
Rising Star	91.38
Indiana Grand	90.88
Belterra	90.76
Majestic Star	90.25
Horseshoe SI	90.09
Horseshoe Hammond	90.07
Hoosier Park	90.05
Hollywood	89.96
Majestic Star II	89.84
Ameristar	89.92
Tropicana	89.61

These figures reflect the average percentage returned by each casino for all of their electronic machines including slot machines, video poker, video keno, etc.

Unless otherwise noted, all casinos offer: blackjack, craps, roulette, slots, video poker, video keno and Caribbean stud poker. Optional games include: baccarat (B), mini-baccarat (MB), poker (P), pai gow poker (PGP), three card poker (TCP), Mississippi stud (MS), pai gow (PG), four card poker (FCP), Spanish 21 (S21), big 6 wheel (B6) and let it ride (LIR). Additionally, sports betting was legalized for Indiana casinos in mid-2019 and it is expected to be offered at most casinos by early 2020.

If you want to order a drink while playing, be aware that Indiana gaming regulations do not allow casinos to provide free alcoholic beverages.

NOTE: If you happen to win a jackpot of $1,200 or more in Indiana, the casino will withhold 3.4% of your winnings for the Indiana Department of Revenue. You may, however, be able to get *some* of that money refunded by filing a state income tax return. The $1,200 threshold also applies to any cash prizes won in casino drawings or tournaments.

For more information on visiting Indiana call (800) 289-6646 or visit their website at www.enjoyindiana.com.

Ameristar East Chicago
777 Ameristar Boulevard
East Chicago, Indiana 46312
(219) 378-3000
Website: www.ameristar.com
Map: **#9** (12 miles E. of Chicago)

Toll-Free Number: (877) 496-1777
Hotel Reservations: (866) 711-7799
Rooms: 288 Prices: $109-$259
Suites: 7 Prices: Casino Use Only
Restaurants: 5
Buffets: B- $17.99 (Sun)
L- $15.99/$17.99
D- $19.99/$35.99 (Fri) /$27.99 (Sat)
Casino Size: 53,000 Square Feet
Other Games: B, MB, PGP, P, TCP, LIR, MS
Overnight RV Parking: No
Special Features: 3,750-passenger modern yacht docked on Lake Michigan.

Belterra Casino Resort
777 Belterra Drive
Florence, Indiana 47020
(812) 427-7777
Website: www.belterracasino.com
Map: **#1** (35 miles S.W. of Cincinnati, Ohio)

Toll-Free Number: (888) 235-8377
Rooms: 600 Price Range: $119-$329
Suites: 8 Price Range: $249-$499
Restaurants: 6
Buffets: B-$14.95 L-$21.95
D-$21.95/$39.95(Fri)/
$29.95 (Sat)/$21.95(Sun)
Casino Size: 38,000 Square Feet
Other Games: P, PGP, TCP, FCP, LIR,
MB, MS, UTH
Overnight RV Parking: Free (must park in back rows of parking lot)/RV Dump: No
Special Features: 2,600-passenger sidewheeler docked on the Ohio River. Health club and spa. 18-hole golf course. 1,500-seat showroom. Buffet is closed Monday- Friday for lunch and Monday & Tuesday for dinner.

Blue Chip Casino & Hotel
777 Blue Chip Drive
Michigan City, Indiana 46360
(219) 879-7711
Website: www.bluechip-casino.com
Map: **#7** (40 miles E. of Chicago)

Toll-Free Number: (888) 879-7711
Rooms: 180 Price Range: $79-$279
Suites: Casino Use Only
Restaurants: 5
Buffets: B-$11.99/$18.99 (Sat/Sun)
L- $15.99/$11.99 (Wed/Fri)
D- $19.99/$24.99 (Thu/Sun)/
$26.99 (Fri)/$31.99 (Sat)
Casino Size: 25,000 Square Feet
Other Games: MB, P, TCP, MS, UTH
Overnight RV Parking: Free/RV Dump: No
Senior Discount: Various Mon if 50+.
Special Features: 2,000-passenger barge docked in a man-made canal.

French Lick Resort & Casino
8670 West State Road 56
French Lick, Indiana 47432
(812) 936-9300
Website: www.frenchlick.com
Map: **#10** (108 miles S. of Indianapolis)

Toll-Free Number: (888) 936-9360
Rooms: 442 Price Range: $189-$339
Restaurants: 11
Buffets: B-$18.99/$22.99 (Sun)
Casino Size: 84,000 Square Feet
Other Games: MB, TCP, FCP, MS
Overnight RV Parking: No/RV Dump: No
Special Features: Two 18-hole golf courses. Full-service spa. 12-space RV park ($75 per night). Six-lane bowling alley. Buffet discount for players club members.

Hollywood Casino & Hotel - Lawrenceburg
777 Hollywood Boulevard
Lawrenceburg, Indiana 47025
(812) 539-8000
Website: www.hollywoodindiana.com
Map: **#3** (95 miles S.E. of Indianapolis)

Toll-Free Number: (888) 274-6797
Rooms: 440 Price Range: $89-$259
Restaurants: 5
Buffets: B-$21.99 (Sun)
L-$16.99/ $21.99(Sun)
D-$21.99/$37.99 (Fri)/
$32.99 (Sat)/$21.99 (Sun)
Casino Size: 80,000 Square Feet
Other Games: B6, MB, LIR, P, TCP, PGP,
FCP, B, MS
Overnight RV Parking: Free (only in lot across the street from the casino)/RV Dump: No
Special Features: 4,000-passenger modern yacht docked on the Ohio River. No dinner buffet Mon-Thu.

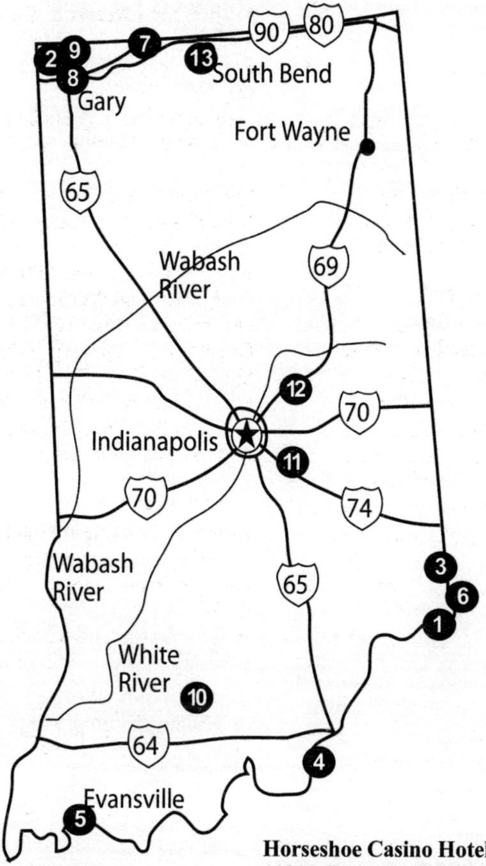

Horseshoe Casino Hammond
777 Casino Center Drive
Hammond, Indiana 46320
(219) 473-7000
Website: www.chicagohorseshoe.com
Map: **#2** (10 miles E. of Chicago)

Toll-Free Number: (866) 711-7463
Restaurants: 4
Buffets: L/D-$21.99 (Sat/Sun)
Casino Size: 43,000 Square Feet
Other Games: MB, TCP, LIR, P,
B6, PG, B, MS
Overnight RV Parking: Free/RV Dump: No
Special Features: 4,000-passenger barge docked on Lake Michigan. 100x odds on craps

Horseshoe Casino Hotel Southern Indiana
11999 Casino Center Drive SE
Elizabeth, Indiana 47117
(812) 969-6000
Website: www.horseshoe-indiana.com
Map: **#4** (20 miles S. of New Albany)

Toll-Free Number: (866) 676-7463
Reservation Number: (877) 237-6626
Rooms: 503 Prices: Price Range: $62-$229
Restaurants: 4
Buffets: B-$23.99 (Sat/Sun)
L-$15.99 D-$20.99/$34.99 (Fri)/
$29.99 (Sat)
Casino Size: 93,000 Square Feet
Other Games: S21, B, MB, MS,
P, PGP, LIR, TCP
Senior Discount: Various discounts Wed if 50+
Special Features: 5,000-passenger sidewheeler docked on the Ohio River. Buffet closed Mon-Thu. 18-hole golf course. Riverboat to be replaced with a land-based casino, Caesars Southern Indiana, by early 2020.

Majestic Star Casinos & Hotel
1 Buffington Harbor Drive
Gary, Indiana 46406
(219) 977-7777
Website: www.majesticstarcasino.com
Map: **#8** (15 miles E. of Chicago)

Toll-Free Number: (888) 225-8259
Rooms: 300 Price Range: $79-$139
Restaurants: 4
Buffets: B-$8.99 (Sat/Sun)
L-$9.99 (Mon-Sat)
D-$13.99 (Mon-Thu)
Casino Size: 43,000 Square Feet
Other Games: S21, B, MB, MS,
PGP, TCP, LIR, P, B6
Overnight RV Parking: Free/RV Dump: No
Special Features: Two boats: 1,300-passenger and 2,300-passenger modern yachts docked on Lake Michigan.

Rising Star Casino Resort
777 Rising Star Drive
Rising Sun, Indiana 47040
(812) 438-1234
Website: www.risingstarcasino.com
Map: **#6** (40 miles S.W. of Cincinnati)

Toll-Free Number: (800) 472-6311
Rooms: 294 Price Range: $79-$169
Restaurants: 4
Buffets: B-$16.99(Sat/Sun)
D-$13.99 (Fri) $14.99/
$16.99(Thu) $30.99(Fri)
Casino Size: 40,000 Square Feet
Other Games: TCP, B6, S21, MS,
CSP, LIR, FCP
Overnight RV Parking: Free/RV Dump: No
Senior Discount: Various Mon/Tue if 50+
Special Features: 3,000-passenger paddle wheeler docked on Ohio River. 56-space RV park ($19-$35 per night). Hotel is Hyatt. 18-hole golf course. 1,100-seat showroom.

Tropicana Evansville
421 N.W. Riverside Drive
Evansville, Indiana 47708
(812) 433-4000
Website: www.tropevansville.com
Map: **#5** (168 miles S.W. of Indianapolis)

Toll-Free Number: (800) 342-5386
Rooms: 243 Price Range: $99-$149
Suites: 10 Price Range: $239-$349
Restaurants: 4
Buffets: B-$10.95
L- $13.95/$14.95(Sat)/$16.95 (Sun)
D- $17.95/$21.95 (Fri/Sat)
Casino Size: 45,000 Square Feet
Other Games: MB, P, TCP, MS
Overnight RV Parking: No
Special Features: Land-based casino. Buffet closed Mon-Thu.

Pari-Mutuels

In April 2007, the Indiana state legislature authorized the state's two horse tracks to have up to 2,000 electronic gaming machines.

Both casinos are open 24 hours and the minimum gambling age is 21. The minimum age for pari-mutuel betting is 18.

Hoosier Park
4500 Dan Patch Circle
Anderson, Indiana 46013
(765) 642-7223
Website: www.hoosierpark.com
Map: **#12** (45 miles N.E. of Indianapolis)

Toll-Free Number: (800) 526-7223
Restaurants: 7
Buffets: B-$10.95/$22.95 (Sun)
L-$9.95/$22.95 (Sun)
D-$15.95/$26.95 (Fri/Sat)
Other Games: Only Gaming Machines
Casino Size: 92,000 Square Feet
Special Features: Live thoroughbred and harness racing seasonally. Year-round simulcasting of thoroughbred and harness racing.

Indiana Grand Casino
4300 N. Michigan Road
Shelbyville, Indiana 46176
(317) 421-0000
Website: www.indianagrand.com
Map: **#11** (32 miles S.E. of Indianapolis)

Toll-Free Number: (877) 386-4463
Restaurants: 4
Buffets: L- $13.95/$19.95 (Sun)
D- $18.95/$28.95 (Fri)/
$24.95 (Thu)/$21.95 (Sat)
Casino Size: 70,000 Square Feet
Other Games: Only Gaming Machines, P
Special Features: Live thoroughbred and harness racing seasonally. Year-round simulcasting of thoroughbred and harness racing.

Indian Casinos

Four Winds South Bend
Prairie Avenue and U.S. 31/20 Bypass
South Bend, Indiana
Website: www.fourwindscasino.com
Map: **#13**

Toll-Free Number: (866) 494-6371
Restaurants: 4 Liquor: Yes
Buffet: Buffet: B/L-$16.00 D-$22.00
Casino Size: 55,000 Square Feet
Other Games: Only Gaming Machines
Special Features: This casino offers Class II gambling which consist of electronic gaming machines which look like slot machines, but are actually games of bingo and the spinning video reels are for "entertainment purposes only." Buffet closed Monday - Wednesday.

IOWA

Iowa was the first state to legalize riverboat gambling. The boats began operating on April Fools Day in 1991 and passengers were originally limited to $5 per bet with a maximum loss of $200 per person, per cruise.

In early 1994 the Iowa legislature voted to eliminate the gambling restrictions. Additionally, gaming machines were legalized at three of the state's four pari-mutuel facilities. In mid-2004 a provision was added to allow table games at those three tracks. That same year the state also legalized casinos on moored barges that float in man-made basins of water and no longer required the casinos to be on boats. Iowa also has three Indian casinos.

Here's information, as supplied by the Iowa Racing and Gaming Commission, showing the electronic gaming machine payback percentages for all non-Indian locations for the one-year period from July 1, 2018 through June 30, 2019:

LOCATION	PAYBACK%
Prairie Meadows	91.67
Q Casino	90.63
Wild Rose - Emmetsburg	90.61
Wild Rose - Clinton	90.56
Wild Rose - Jefferson	90.52
Diamond Jo Worth	90.52
Diamond Jo Dubuque	90.49
Catfish Bend	90.42
Riverside	90.40
Grand Falls	90.36
Hard Rock Casino	90.29
Rhythm City	90.26
Casino Queen- Marquette	90.19
Ameristar	90.05
Isle of Capri - Bettendorf	90.04
Harrah's	89.77
Isle of Capri - Waterloo	89.73
Horsehoe Council Bluffs	89.66
Lakeside	88.91

These figures reflect the total percentages returned by each riverboat casino or pari-mutuel facility for all of its electronic machines including: slots, video poker, video keno, etc.

The minimum gambling age is 21 and, unless otherwise noted, all casinos are open 24 hours.

All Iowa casinos offer: blackjack, roulette, craps, slots and video poker. Some casinos also offer: mini-baccarat (MB), poker (P), pai gow poker (PGP), Caribbean stud poker (CSP), let it ride (LIR), big 6 (B6), bingo (BG), keno (K), ultimate Texas hold em (UTH), Mississippi stud (MS), three card poker (TCP), pai gow poker (PGP) four card poker (FCP), Spanish 21 (S21) and off-track betting (OTB). Sports betting was being introduced at Iowa casinos in mid-2019 and it is expected to be offered at most casinos by early 2020.

NOTE: If you happen to win a jackpot of $1,200 or more in Iowa, the casino will withhold 5% of your winnings for the Iowa Department of Revenue. If you want to try and get that money refunded, you will be required to file a state income tax return and, depending on the details of your return, you *may* get some of the money returned to you. The $1,200 threshold would also apply to any cash prizes won in casino drawings or tournaments.

For more information on visiting Iowa call the state's tourism department at (800) 345-4692 or visit their website at www.traveliowa.com.

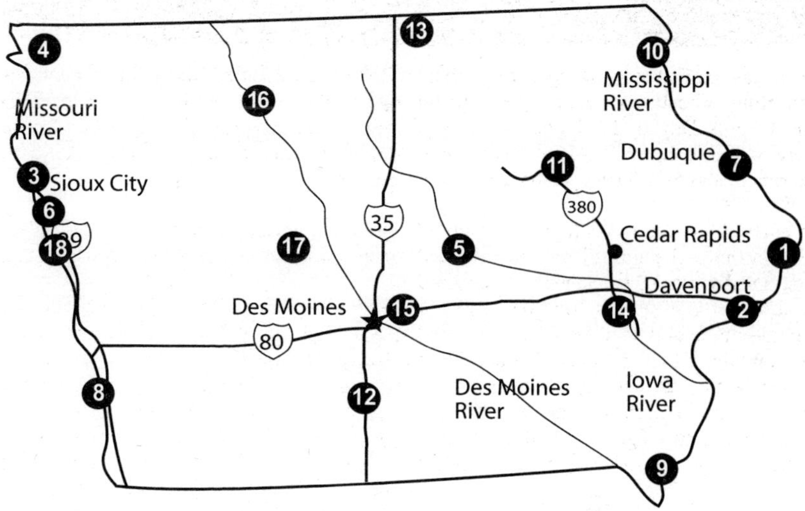

Ameristar Casino Hotel Council Bluffs
2200 River Road
Council Bluffs, Iowa 51501
(712) 328-8888
Website: www.ameristarcasinos.com
Map: **#8** (102 miles S. of Sioux City)

Toll-Free Number: (877) 462-7827
Rooms: 152 Price Range: $129-$259
Suites: 8 Price Range: $240-$349
Restaurants: 5
Buffets: B-$20.99 (Sat/Sun)
L-$13.99/$20.99 (Sat/Sun)
D-$17.99/$34.99(Fri)/$23.99 (Sat)
Casino Size: 35,125 Square Feet
Other Games: S21, TCP
Overnight RV Parking: No
Special Features: 2,700-passenger sidewheeler replica on the Missouri River.

Casino Queen Marquette
100 Anti Monopoly Street
Marquette, Iowa 52158
(563) 873-3531
Website: www.casinoqueen.com/marquette
Map: **#10** (60 miles N. of Dubuque)

Toll-Free Number: (800) 496-8238
Restaurants: 2
Buffets: B- $14.99 (Sat/Sun)
L- $10.99/$14.99 (Sat/Sun)
D- $14.99/$21.99 (Fri/Sat)
Hours: 9am-2am/24 Hours (Fri/Sat)
Other Games: MS, UTH
Casino Size: 17,514 Square Feet
Overnight RV Parking: Free/RV Dump: No
Senior Discount: Various Wed/Thu if 50+
Special Features: 1,200-passenger paddle wheeler on the Mississippi River.

Catfish Bend Casino - Burlington
3001 Winegard Drive
Burlington, Iowa 52601
(319) 753-2946
Website: www.thepzazz.com
Map: **#9** (180 miles S.E. of Des Moines)

Toll Free Number: (800) 372-2946
Rooms: 40 Price Range: $109-$179
Restaurants: 4
Hours: 9am-2am/3am (Tue-Thu)/4am (Fri/Sat)
Casino Size: 24,353 Square Feet
Other Games: S21, P, TCP, FCP,
MB, PGP, UTH
Overnight RV Parking: Free/RV Dump: No
Special Features: Casino is part of entertainment complex featuring laser tag, go karts, and water park.

Diamond Jo Casino Dubuque
301 Bell Street
Dubuque, Iowa 52001
(563) 690-4800
Website: www.diamondjodubuque.com
Map: **#7**

Toll-Free Number: (800) 582-5956
Restaurants: 4
Buffets: L-$10.99/$14.99 (Sun)
D-$15.99/$18.99 (Fri/Sat)
Casino Size: 43,508 Square Feet
Other Games: PGP, MS
Overnight RV Parking: Free RV Dump: No
Special features: Land-based casino. Buffet is closed Monday.

Diamond Jo Casino Worth
777 Diamond Jo Lane
Northwood, Iowa 50459
(641) 323-7777
Website: www.diamondjoworth.com
Map: **#13** (140 miles N. of Des Moines)

Toll-Free Number: (877) 323-5566
Restaurants: 2
Buffets: L-$7.99/$12.99 (Sat/Sun)
D-$9.99/$20.99 (Fri)/$19.99 (Sat)
Casino Size: 36,133 Square Feet
Other Games: TCP, P, MS, UTH
Overnight RV Parking: Free/RV Dump: No
Special Features: Land-based casino. Burger King and Subway.

Grand Falls Casino & Golf Resort
1415 Grand Falls Boulevard
Larchwood, Iowa 51241
(712) 777-7777
Website: www.grandfallscasinoresort.com
Map: **#4** (17 Miles SE of Sioux Falls, SD)

Toll-Free number: (877)511-4386
Rooms: 88 Price Range: $119-$229
Suites: 10 Price Range: $149-$469
Restaurants: 3
Buffets: B-$9.99 L-$11.99/$17.99 (Sun)
D-$17.99/$18.99 (Wed)/
$20.99 (Fri)/$19.99 (Sat)
Casino Size: 42,042 Square Feet
Other Games: P, PGP, MS, UTH
Overnight RV Parking: No
Special Features: Land-based casino. 1,200-seat event center. 14-space RV park ($25-$40 per night).

Hard Rock Hotel & Casino Sioux City
111 3rd Street
Sioux City, Iowa 51101
(712) 226-7600
Website: www.hardrockcasinosiouxcity.com
Map: **#3**

Toll Free Number: (844) 222-7625
Rooms: 50 Price Range: $149-$179
Suites: 4 Price Range: $209-$279
Restaurants: 3
Buffets: B-$14.99 (Sat/Sun)
L-$11.99/$14.99 (Sat/Sun)
D-$14.99/$15.99(Wed)
$19.99 (Fri/Sat)
Casino Size: 41,800 Square Feet
Overnight RV Parking: Yes
Other Games: TCP, PGP, MS, UTH
Special Features: Land-based casino.

Harrah's Council Bluffs
One Harrah's Boulevard
Council Bluffs, Iowa 51501
(712) 329-6000
Website: www.harrahscouncilbluffs.com
Map: **#8** (102 miles S. of Sioux City)

Toll Free Number: (800) 472-7247
Rooms: 240 Price Range: $129-$295
Suites: 11 Price Range: $250-$325
Restaurants: 3
Buffets: B-$14.99/$17.99 (Sat-Sun)
L-$14.99
D-$18.99/$22.99 (Fri/Sat)/
$20.99 (Sun)
Casino Size: 21,405 Square Feet
Other Games: TCP, PGP, MS
Overnight RV Parking: Free/RV Dump: No
Special Features: Land-based casino. Buffet discount for players club members.

Isle Casino Hotel - Bettendorf
1777 Isle Parkway
Bettendorf, Iowa 52722
(563) 441-7000
Website: www.islebettendorf.com
Map: **#2**

Toll-Free Number: (800) 843-4753
Rooms: 220 Price Range: $100-$260
Suites: 36 Price Range $159-$525
Restaurants: 3
Buffets: B- $14.99 (Sat/Sun)
L- $12.99/$15.99 (Sat)/ $19.99 (Sun)
D- $18.99/$19.99 (Sun) /
$21.99 (Fri) / $24.99 (Sat)
Other Games: TCP, PGP, MS
Casino Size: 36,659 Square Feet
Senior Discount: Various on Mon/Wed if 50+
Special Features: 53-slip marina.

Isle Casino Hotel - Waterloo
777 Isle of Capri Boulevard
Waterloo, Iowa 50701
(800) 843-4753
Website: www.islewaterloo.com
Map: **#11** (90 miles W. of Dubuque)

Rooms: 170 Price Range: $99-$200
Suites: 27 Price Range: $159-$280
Restaurants: 3
Buffets: B-$10.99 (Sat/Sun)
L-$12.99/$15.99 (Sun)
D-$17.99/$19.99 (Fri/Sat)
Other Games: P, MB
Casino Size: 39,788 Square Feet
Overnight RV Parking: Free/RV Dump: No
Special Features: Land-based casino.

Lakeside Hotel Casino
777 Casino Drive
Osceola, Iowa 50213
(641) 342-9511
Website: www.lakesidehotelcasino.com
Map: **#12** (50 miles S. of Des Moines)

Toll-Free Number: (877) 477-5253
Rooms: 150 Price: $99-$169
Restaurants: 2
Buffets: B- $7.99(Sun) $10.99 (Mon)
L - $16.99 (Sun)
D- $14.99/$18.99 (Thu/Sat)/
$21.99 (Fri)/$19.99 (Sun)
Casino Size: 26,199 Square Feet
Other Games: TCP, PGP
Overnight RV Parking: Free with players club card/
RV Dump: No
Senior Discount: Various on Mon if 50+.
Special Features: Casino is on a barge. 47-space RV park ($25 per night). Fishing/ boating dock.

Rhythm City Casino
7077 Elmore Avenue
Davenport, Iowa 52807
(563) 328-8000
Website: www.rhythmcitycasino.com
Map: **#2** (80 miles S.E. of Cedar Rapids)

Toll-Free Number: (844) 852-4386
Rooms: 106 Price: $120-$159
Suites: 8 Price: $211-$259
Restaurants: 3
Buffets: B-$8.99 L-$12.99/$17.99 (Sun)
D-$17.99/$19.99 (Fri/Sat)
Casino Size: 37,933 Square Feet
Other Games: TCP, PGP, P, MS, UTH
Overnight RV Parking: No
Senior Discount: Various Tue 7am-6pm if 50+
Special Features: Land-based casino.

Riverside Casino & Golf Resort
3184 Highway 22
Riverside, Iowa 52327
(319) 648-1234
Website: www.riversidecasinoandresort.com
Map: **#14** (81 miles W. of Davenport)

Toll-Free Number: (877) 677-3456
Rooms: 180 Price Range: $99-$139
Suite: 20 Price Range: $179-$219
Restaurants: 3
Buffets: B-$10.99/$11.99 (Sun)
L-$13.99/$18.99 (Sun)
D-$18.99/$21.99 (Tue/Fri/Sat)
Casino Size: 51,777 Square Feet
Overnight RV Parking: Free/RV Dump: No
Other Games: P, PGP, MS, UTH
Special features: Land-based casino. 18-hole golf course. 1,200-seat showroom.

Wild Rose Casino - Clinton
777 Wild Rose Drive
Clinton, Iowa 52732
(563) 243-9000
Website: www.wildroseresorts.com
Map: **#1** (90 miles E. of Cedar Rapids)

Toll-Free Number: (800) 457-9975
Rooms: 60 Price Range: $79-$119
Suites: 6 Price Range: $169-$199
Restaurants: 2
Buffets: B - $6.99 L-$8.99 (Mon/Tue)
D-$5.99/$12.99 (Fri) /$9.99 (Sat)
Hours: 8am-2am/24 hours (Fri/Sat)
Casino Size: 19,681 Square Feet
Additional Games: PGP, UTH, LIR,
OTB (Fri-Sun)
Overnight RV Parking: Free/RV Dump: No
Special Features: Land-based casino.

Wild Rose Casino - Emmetsberg
777 Main Street
Emmetsburg, Iowa 50536
(712) 852-3400
Website: www.wildroseresorts.com
Map: **#16** (120 miles N.E. of Sioux City)

Toll-Free Number: (877) 720-7673
Rooms: 62 Price Range: $69-$119
Suites: 8 Price Range: $179-$209
Restaurants: 2
Buffets: L-$9.95 (Tue)/$9.95 (Sat/Sun)
D- $12.95 (Fri)
Other Games: PGP, MS
Hours: 8am-2am/24 Hours (Fri/Sat)
Casino Size: 16,790 Square Feet
Overnight RV Parking: Must use RV park
Senior Discount: Various Tue if 50+
Special features: Land-based casino. 68-space RV park ($25 per night) includes breakfast in hotel lobby.

Wild Rose Casino - Jefferson
777 Wild Rose Drive
Jefferson, Iowa 50129
(515 386-7777
Website: www.wildroseresorts.com
Map: **#17** (70 miles N.W. of Des Moines)

Rooms: 74 Price Range: $119-$179
Restaurants: 1
Casino Hours: 8am-2am/24 Hours (Fri/Sat)
Casino Size: 16,686 Square Feet
Other Games: PGP, MS, UTH
Overnight RV Parking: Free/RV Dump: No

Indian Casinos

Blackbird Bend Casino
17214 210th Street
Onawa, Iowa 51040
(712) 423-9646
Website: www.blackbirdbendcasinos.com
Map: **#18** (40 miles S. of Sioux City)

Toll-Free Number: (844) 622-2121
Restaurants: 1
Buffets: B-$7.49/$9.99 (Sat/Sun)
L-$9.99/$11.99 (Wed/Fri)
D-$8.99/ $9.99 (Tue/Thu)/
$12.99 (Fri)/$15.99 (Sat)
Hours: 8am-2am/24 hours (Fri/Sat)
Casino Size: 6,800 Square Feet
Overnight RV Parking: No
Senior Discount: Various Tue if 50+
Special Features: Blackjack open noon-8pm Tue-Sat.

Meskwaki Bingo Casino Hotel
1504 305th Street
Tama, Iowa 52339
(641) 484-2108
Website: www.meskwaki.com
Map: **#5** (40 miles W. of Cedar Rapids)

Toll-Free Number: (800) 728-4263
Rooms: 390 Price Range: $79-$129
Suites: 14 Price Range: $149-$309
Restaurants: 4 Liquor: Yes
Buffets: B-$9.99/$13.99 (Sun)
L-$10.99/$13.99 (Sun)
D-$13.99/$15.99 (Mon/Wed/Thu)/
$22.99 (Fri)/$19.99 (Sat)
Other Games: MB, P, PGP, MS, UTH
K, BG, Off-Track Betting
Overnight RV Parking: Must Use RV Park
Senior Discount: Various every day if 55+
Special Features: 50-space RV park ($19 per night). Spa.

Prarie Flower Casino
1031 Avenue H
Carter Lake, Iowa 51510
(888) 946-6673
Website: www.prairieflowercasino.com
Map: **#5** (40 miles W. of Cedar Rapids)

Restaurants: 1 Snack Bar
Liquor: Yes
Casino Size: 9,500 Square Feet
Games offered: This casino offers Class II gambling which consist of electronic gaming machines which look like slot machines, but are actually games of bingo and the spinning video reels are for "entertainment purposes only."

WinnaVegas Casino
1500 330th Street
Sloan, Iowa 51055
(712) 428-9466
Website: www.winnavegas.biz
Map: **#6** (20 miles S. of Sioux City)

Toll-Free Number: (800) 468-9466
Rooms: 52 Price Range: $85-$122
Suites: 10 Price Range: $190-$220
Restaurants: 2 Liquor: Yes
Buffets: B- $12.70 (Sat/Sun)
L- $12.49 (Sat/Sun)
D- $8.99/$9.99 (Thu)/$19.49 (Fri)/
$16.49 (Sat)
Other Games: P, BG, PGP, MS
Overnight RV Parking: No/RV Dump: No
Special Features: 20-space RV park ($15/night).

Pari-Mutuels

Horseshoe Casino - Council Bluffs
2701 23rd Avenue
Council Bluffs, Iowa 51501
(712) 323-2500
Website: horseshoecouncilbluffs.com
Map: **#8** (102 miles S. of Sioux City)

Toll-Free Number: (877) 771-7463
Rooms: 158 Price Range: $149-$300
Restaurants: 3
Buffets: L-$15.99/$18.99 (Sat)/$20.99 (Sun)
D- $19.99/$25.99 (Fri/Sat
Casino Size: 59,937 Square Feet
Other Games: P, MB, S21, TCP, FCP
Overnight RV Parking: Free/RV Dump: No
Special Features: Hotel is Hilton Garden Inn. Buffet closed Mon/Tue. Free shuttle service from local hotels. Affiliated with Harrah's. 100x odds on craps.

Prairie Meadows Racetrack & Casino
1 Prairie Meadows Drive
Altoona, Iowa 50009
(515) 967-1000
Website: www.prairiemeadows.com
Map: **#15** (5 miles E. of Des Moines)

Toll-Free Number: (800) 325-9015
Rooms: 148 Price Range: $149-$219
Suites: 20 Price Range: $189-$349
Restaurants: 3
Buffets: B- $9.95/$10.95 (Tue)/$14.95 (Sat/Sun)
L- $10.95/$14.95 (Sat/Sun)
D- $14.95/$16.95 (Wed/Thu)/
$19.95 (Fri/Sat)/ $17.95 (Sun)
Casino Size: 82,247 Square Feet
Other Games: MB, P, TCP, PGP, MS, UTH
Overnight RV Parking: Yes
Special Features: Live thoroughbred and quarter-horse racing seasonally. Daily simulcasting of dog and horse racing. Discounts on Dining with club card.

Q Casino
1855 Greyhound Park Road
Dubuque, Iowa 52001
(563) 582-3647
Website: www.qcasinoandhotel.com
Map: **#7**

Toll-Free Number: (800) 373-3647
Rooms: 112 Price Range: $89-$189
Suites: 4 Price Range: $129-$349
Restaurants: 2
Buffets: L- $9.95/$10.95 (Sun)
D- $14.95/$16.95 (Fri/Sat)
Casino Size: 47,136 Square Feet
Other Games: P, PGP, MS, UTH
Overnight RV Parking: Free/RV Dump: No
Senior Discount: Various specials Wed if 50+.
Special Features: Live greyhound racing seasonally. Greyhound, harness and thoroughbred simulcasting all year. Hotel is Hilton Garden Inn.

KANSAS

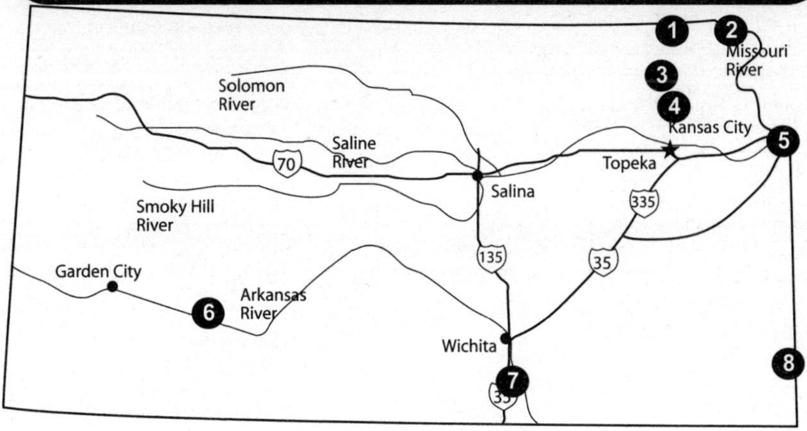

Kansas has four casinos that are state owned and operated. Additionally, there are five Indian casinos in Kansas.

The Kansas Racing & Gaming Commission does not release information about the payback percentages on electronic gaming machines at their casinos. However, gaming regulations require that all machines return no less than 87%.

Unless otherwise noted, all state-run casinos are open 24 hours and offer the following games: slot machines, video poker, video keno, blackjack, craps and roulette. Other games include: poker (P), pai gow poker (PGP), mini-baccarat (MB), let it ride (LIR), Mississippi stud (MS), three card poker (TCP) , Ultimate Texas Hold'em (UTH) and bingo (BG). The minimum gambling age is 21. Legislation to legalize sports betting was proposed in 2019, but it did not pass. However, it may be introduced again in 2020.

For information on visiting Kansas call the state's tourism department at (785) 296-2009 or visit their website at www.travelks.com

Boot Hill Casino & Resort
4000 W Comanche Street
Dodge City, Kansas 67801
(620) 682-7777
Website: www.boothillcasino.com
Map: **#6** (155 miles W of Wichita)

Toll-Free Number: (877) 906-0777
Restaurants: 2
Buffets: B - $24.99 (Sun)
Other Games: MB, P, TCP, MS, UTH
Overnight RV Parking: Free/RV Dump: No

Hollywood Casino at Kansas Speedway
777 Hollywood Casino Boulevard
Kansas City, Kansas 66111
(913) 288- 9300
Website: www.hollywoodcasinokansas.com
Map: **#5**

Restaurants: 4
Buffets: L - $14.99
D- $16.99/$19.99 (Wed)/
$38.99 (Fri)/$22.99 (Sat)
Casino Size: 80,000 Square Feet
Other Games: MB, P, PGP, TCP, MS, UTH
Overnight RV Parking: No/RV Dump: No

Kansas Crossing Casino + Hotel
1275 S. Highway 69
Pittsburg, Kansas 66762
(620) 240-4400
Website:www.kansascrossingcasino.com
Map: **#8** (160 miles E of Wichita)

Rooms: 123 Price Range: $99-$149
Restaurants: 1
Casino Size: 18,600 Square Feet
Other Games: TCP, UTH, MS
Senior Discount: Various Wed if 49+
Special Features: Hotel is Hampton Inn.

Kansas Star Casino Hotel
777 Kansas Star Drive
Mulvane, Kansas 67110
(316) 719-5000
Website: www.kansasstarcasino.com
Map: **#7** (20 miles S of Wichita)

Restaurants: 5
Buffets: L- $12.99 (Wed-Fri)/$14.99 (Sat/Sun)
D- $14.99/$17.99 (Sat)
Casino Size: 21,000 Square Feet
Other Games: P, TCP, LIR, MS, PGP, MB
Special Features: Buffet closed Mon/Tue.

Indian Casinos

There are five Indian casinos in Kansas and they are not required to release information on their slot machine payback percentages. However, according to officials at the Kansas State Gaming Agency, which is responsible for overseeing the tribal-state compacts, "the minimum payback percentage for electronic gaming devices is 80%."

Unless otherwise noted, all Kansas Indian casinos are open 24 hours and offer the following games: blackjack, craps, roulette, slots and video poker. Other games include: poker (P), Caribbean stud poker (CSP), mini-baccarat (MB), let it ride (LIR), pai gow poker (PGP), Mississippi stud (MS), three card poker (TCP) and bingo (BG). The minimum gambling age is 21.

Casino White Cloud
777 Jackpot Drive
White Cloud, Kansas 66094
(785) 595-3430
Website: www.casinowhitecloud.org
Map: **#2** (70 miles N.E. of Topeka)

Toll-Free Number: (877) 652-6115
Restaurants: 1 Liquor: Yes
Buffets: L-$12.00 D-$13.00/$15.00 (Sat)
Casino Size: 21,000 Square Feet
Casino Hours: 9am-1am/3am (Fri/Sat)
Other Games: Machines only, BG (Tue-Sun)
Overnight RV Parking: $5 a day/RV Dump: No
Special Features: Electronic blackjack and roulette.

Golden Eagle Casino
1121 Goldfinch Road
Horton, Kansas 66439
(785) 486-6601
Map: **#3** (45 miles N. of Topeka)
Website: www.goldeneaglecasino.com

Toll-Free Number: (888) 464-5825
Restaurants: 1 Liquor: No
Buffets: B- $7.95 (Sun) L- $8.75
D- $8.75 (Wed/Thu/Sun)/
$15.75(Fri-Sat)
Other Games: BG (Wed-Sun), No Roulette
Overnight RV Parking: Free/RV Dump: No
Special Features: RV hookups available ($10 per night).

Prairie Band Casino & Resort
12305 150th Road
Mayetta, Kansas 66509
(785) 966-7777
Website: www.pbpgaming.com
Map: **#4** (17 miles N. of Topeka)

Toll-Free Number: (888) 727-4946
Rooms: 297 Price Range: $89-$169
Suites: 8 Price Range: Casino Use Only
Restaurants: 3 Liquor: Yes
Buffets: B- $5.99/$14.99 (Sun)
L-$9.99/$14.99 (Sun)
D-$14.99/$34.99 (Fri)/$27.99 (Sat)
Casino Size: 33,000 Square Feet
Other Games: BG (Wed-Sun), MB, P, LIR,
TCP, MS, UTH, No Craps
Overnight RV Parking: Must use RV park.
Special Features: 67-space RV park ($30 per night).

Sac & Fox Casino
1322 U.S. Highway 75
Powhattan, Kansas 66527
(785) 467-8000
Map: **#1** (60 miles N. of Topeka)
Website: www.sacandfoxcasino.com

Toll-Free Number: (800) 990-2946
Restaurant: 2 Liquor: Yes
Buffets: L- $16.99 (Sun)
D-$18.99 (Thu)/$24.99 (Fri)/
$19.99 (Sat)/$12.99 (Sun)
Casino Size: 40,000 Square Feet
Other Games: TCP
Overnight RV Parking: Free/RV Dump: No
Senior Discount: Various Wed, if 50+
Special Features: 24-hour truck stop. Golf driving range. 12-space RV park ($10 per night).

7th Street Casino
777 North 7th Street
Kansas City, Kansas 66101
(913) 371-3500
Website: www.7th-streetcasino.com
Map: **#5**

Restaurant: 1 Liquor: Yes
Casino Size: 20,000 Square Feet
Other Games: Only Gaming Machines
Overnight RV Parking: No/RV Dump: No

LOUISIANA

Louisiana was the fourth state to approve riverboat casino gambling and its 1991 gambling law allows a maximum of 15 boats statewide. In 1992 a provision was added for one land-based casino in New Orleans.

The state also has three land-based Indian casinos and four slot machine-only (no video poker or video keno) casinos located at pari-mutuel facilities. Additionally, video poker is permitted at Louisiana truck stops, OTB's and bars/taverns in 31 of the state's 64 parishes (counties). All riverboat casinos in Louisiana are required to remain dockside and all are open 24 hours.

Gaming regulations require that gaming machines in casinos be programmed to pay back no less than 80% and no more than 99.9%. For video gaming machines at locations other than casinos the law requires a minimum return of 80% and a maximum return of 94%.

Louisiana gaming statistics are not broken down by individual properties. Rather, they are classified by region: Baton Rouge (BR), Lake Charles (LC), New Orleans (NO) and Shreveport/Bossier City (SB).

The Baton Rouge casinos consist of the Belle of Baton Rouge, Hollywood Casino, L'Auberge and Evangeline Downs. The Lake Charles casinos include: Isle of Capri, L'Auberge Resort, Golden Nugget and Delta Downs. New Orleans area casinos are: Amelia Belle, Boomtown, Harrah's (landbased), Treasure Chest and Fairgrounds Raceway. The Shreveport/Bossier city casinos include: Boomtown, Diamond Jack's, Sam's Town, Eldorado, Horseshoe, Margaritaville and Harrah's Louisiana Downs.

Here's information, as supplied by the Louisiana State Police-Riverboat Gaming Section, showing the average electronic machine payback percentages for each area's casinos for the 12-month period from June 1, 2018 through May 30, 2019:

	BR	LC	NO	SB
1¢	88.70%	88.57%	88.96%	**89.01%**
5¢	91.69%	**94.31%**	93.31%	93.12%
25¢	92.30%	**93.08%**	92.43%	90.73%
$1	**93.56%**	92.33%	92.72%	93.03%
$5	**94.49%**	92.99%	92.93%	92.70%
All	90.50%	**90.63%**	90.23%	90.43%

These numbers reflect the percentage of money returned on each denomination of machine and encompass all electronic machines including video poker and video keno. The best returns for each category are highlighted in bold print.

NOTE: If you happen to win a jackpot of $1,200 or more in Louisiana, the casino will withhold 6% of your winnings for the Louisiana Department of Revenue. If you want to try and get that money refunded, you will be required to file a state income tax return and, depending on the details of your return, you *may* get some of the money returned to you. The $1,200 threshold would also apply to any cash prizes won in casino drawings or tournaments.

All casinos offer: blackjack, craps, roulette, slots, video poker, three card poker and Mississippi stud. Optional games include: Spanish 21 (S21), baccarat (B), mini-baccarat (MB), poker (P), Caribbean stud poker (CSP), pai gow poker (PGP), let it ride (LIR), casino war (CW), four card poker (FCP), big 6 wheel (B6), keno (K), Texas hold 'em Bonus (THB), ultimate Texas hold em (UTH) and bingo (BG). The minimum gambling age is 21 for casino gaming and 18 for pari-mutuel betting.

Legislation to legalize sports betting was proposed in 2019, but it did not pass. However, it may be introduced again in 2020.

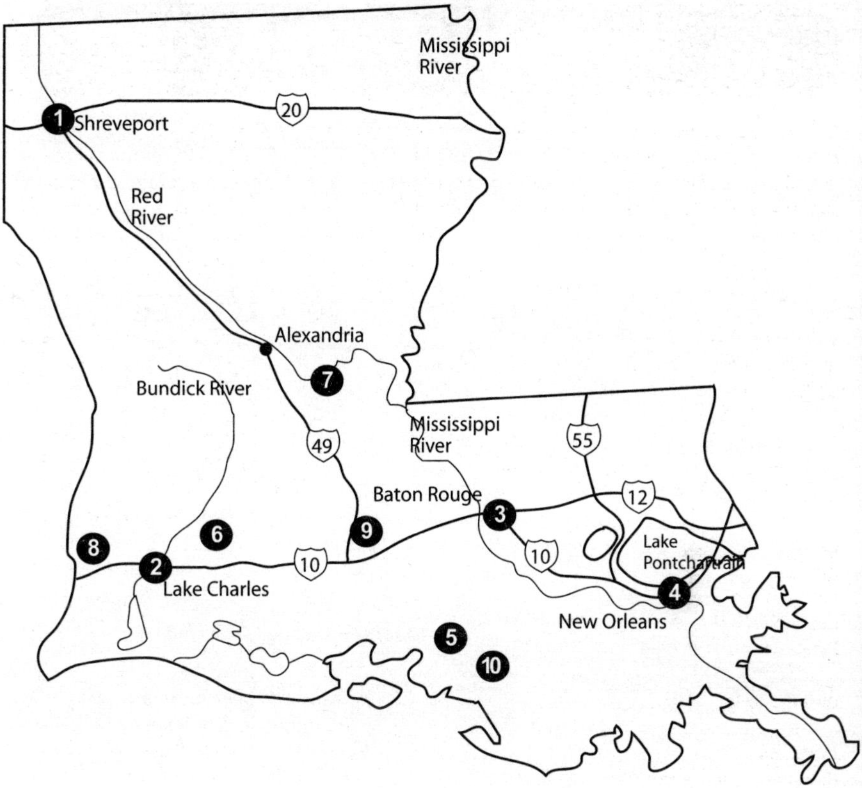

For more information on visiting Louisiana call the state's tourism department at (800) 633-6970 or visit www.louisianatravel.com

Amelia Belle Casino
500 Lake Palourde Road
Amelia, Louisiana 70380
(985) 631-1777
Website: www.ameliabellecasino.com
Map: **#10** (75 miles S. of Baton Rouge)

Restaurants: 2
Buffets: L- $6.99/$9.99 (Fri/Sat)
D- $6.99/$18.75 (Fri)/$9.99 (Sat)
Casino Size: 27,928 Square Feet
Other Games: TCP, MS, UTH
Overnight RV Parking: Free (Must park in employee lot)
Special Features: 1,200-passenger paddle wheeler on Bayou Boeuf.

Belle of Baton Rouge
102 France Street
Baton Rouge, Louisiana 70802
(225) 242-2600
Website: www.belleofbatonrouge.com
Map: **#3**

Toll-Free Number: (800) 676-4847
Rooms: 100 Price Range: $49-$109
Suites: 88 Price Range: $200-$550
Restaurants: 2
Buffets: B/L- $15.99 (Sun)
D- $15.99 (Fri/Sat)
Casino Size: 28,500 Square Feet
Other Games: MB, PGP
Overnight RV Parking: Yes/RV dump: No
Special Features: 1,500-passenger paddle wheeler on the Mississippi River.

Boomtown Casino & Hotel Bossier City
300 Riverside Drive
Bossier City, Louisiana 71111
(318) 746-0711
Website: www.boomtownbossier.com
Map: **#1** (across the Red River From Shreveport)

Toll-Free Number: (866) 462-8696
Rooms: 100 Price Range: $79-$185
Suites: 88 Price Range: $119-$219
Restaurants: 4
Buffets: B- $8.95 /$14.95 (Sat-Sun)
D- $18.95/$24.95 (Fri-Sat)/
$20.95 (Sun)
Casino Size: 25,635 Square Feet
Other Games: TCP, UTH
Overnight RV Parking: No
Special Features: 1,925-passenger paddle wheeler on the Red River.

Boomtown Casino New Orleans
4132 Peters Road
Harvey, Louisiana 70058
(504) 366-7711
Website: www.boomtownneworleans.com
Map: **#4** (a suburb of New Orleans)

Toll-Free Number: (800) 366-7711
Rooms: 150 Price Range: $129-$189
Suites: 17 Price Range: $149-$209
Restaurants: 5
Buffets: L- $13.99/$21.99 (Sun)
D- $24.99/$34.99 (Fri/Sat)
Casino Size: 29,027 Square Feet
Other Games: P, MB, PGP, TCP
Overnight RV Parking: Free/RV Dump: No
Senior Discount: Various Mon if 55+
Special Features: 1,600-passenger paddle wheeler on the Harvey Canal. Family arcade.

Diamond Jacks Casino - Bossier City
711 DiamondJacks Boulevard
Bossier City, Louisiana 71111
(318) 678-7777
Website: www.diamondjacks.com
Map: **#1** (across the Red River from Shreveport)

Toll-Free Number: (866) 552-9629
Suites: 570 Price Range: $59-$169
Restaurants: 3
Buffets: B- $10.99 (Sat/Sun)
L- $13.99 (Sat/Sun)
D- $16.99/$26.99 (Fri/Sat)
Casino Size: 29,921 Square Feet
Other Games: S21, FCP, LIR, MS, UTH
Overnight RV Parking: Must use RV park
Special Features: 1,650-passenger paddle wheeler on the Red River. 32-space RV park ($29/$34 Fri-Sat). Supervised childcare center. 1,200-seat showroom. Buffet discount for players club members. Buffet closed Mon-Wed.

Eldorado Casino Shreveport
451 Clyde Fant Parkway
Shreveport, Louisiana 71101
(877) 602-0711
Website: www.eldoradoshreveport.com
Map: **#1**

Toll Free: (877) 602-0711
Suites: 403 Price Range: $69-$229
Restaurants: 5
Buffet: L- $13.50/$17.99 (Sat)/$18.99 (Sun)
D- $22.50 (Mon)/$19.99 (Tue/Sun)/
$18.99 (Wed)/$21.50 (Thu)/
$23.99 (Fri)/$20.99 (Sat)
Casino Size: 28,226 Square Feet
Other Games: MB, P, CSP, LIR, PGP, CW, MS
Overnight RV Parking: Free (Weekdays only)
Special Features: 1,500-passenger paddle wheeler on the Red River.

Golden Nugget Casino - Lake Charles
2550 Golden Nugget Blvd
Lake Charles, Louisiana 70601
(337) 508-7777
Website: www.goldennuggetlc.com
Map: **#2** (220 miles W. of New Orleans)

Toll-Free Number: (844) 777-4653
Rooms: 736 Price Range: $169-$429
Suites: 20 Price Range: $699-$1,299
Restaurants: 11
Buffets: B- $13.99/$36.99 (Sat/Sun)
L-$16.99
D- $34.99/$36.99 (Fri/Sat)
Other Games: B, LIR, P, TCP, PGP, MS, UTH
Senior Discount: Various Wed if 50+
Special Features: 18 hole championship course.

Harrah's New Orleans
228 Poydras Street
New Orleans, Louisiana 70130
(504) 533-6000
Website: www.caesars.com
Map: **#4**

Toll-Free Number: (800) 427-7247
Rooms: 390 Price Range: $170-$259
Suites: 60 Price Range: $359-$699
Restaurants: 10
Buffet: B/L- $15.99/$34.99 (Sat/Sun)
D-$22.99(Mon)/$31.99 (Tue-Thu)/
$34.99 (Fri/Sat)/$29.99 (Sun)
Casino Size: 125,119 Square Feet
Other Games: MB, P, PGP, CSP, LIR,
B, FCP, B6, UTH, P
Overnight RV Parking: No
Special Features: Landbased, non-smoking casino. Five themed gaming areas. Fast food court. Daily live jazz music. Self-parking costs $5 to $30 depending on length of stay. Players club members playing for minimum of 30 rated minutes and earning 15 tier credits, can get validated for up to 24 hours of free parking. Buffet discount for players club members.

Hollywood Casino - Baton Rouge
1717 River Road North
Baton Rouge, Louisiana 70802
(225) 709-7777
Website: www.hollywoodbr.com
Map: **#3**

Toll-Free Number: (800) 447-6843
Restaurants: 3
Buffets: L- $14.95/$17.95 (Sat/Sun)
D- $29.95 (Thu/Fri)
Casino Size: 27,900 Square Feet
Overnight RV Parking: Free/RV Dump: No
Special Features: 1,500-passenger paddle wheeler on the Mississippi River.

Horseshoe Casino Hotel - Bossier City
711 Horseshoe Boulevard
Bossier City, Louisiana 71111
(318) 742-0711
Website: www.horseshoebossiercity.com
Map: **#1** (across the Red River from Shreveport)

Toll-Free Number: (800) 895-0711
Rooms: 606 Price Range: $89-$329
Restaurants: 5
Buffets: B- $16.99 (Sat/Sun)
L- $18.99/$24.99 (Fri)
D- $24.99/$29.99 (Fri)
Casino Size: 28,095 Square Feet
Other Games: MB, P, LIR, TCP, MS
Overnight RV Parking: Free/RV Dump: No
Special Features: 2,930-passenger paddle wheeler on the Red River. 100x odds on craps.

Isle of Capri Casino - Lake Charles
100 Westlake Avenue
Westlake, Louisiana 70669
(337) 430-0711
Website: www.isleofcapricasinos.com
Map: **#2** (220 miles W. of New Orleans)

Toll-Free Number: (800) 843-4753
Inn Rooms: 241 Price Range: $89-$199
Tower Rooms: 252 Price Range: $139-$249
Restaurants: 4
Buffets: B- $10.99
L- $13.99/$19.99 (Sat)/$17.99 (Sun)
D- $16.99/$22.99 (Fri)/
$19.99 (Sat)/$17.99 (Sun)
Casino Size: 51,569 Square Feet
Other Games: MB, P, TCP, LIR, MS
Overnight RV Parking: Must use RV park
Special Features: Two 1,200-passenger paddle wheelers on Lake Charles. 8-space RV park ($30 per night).

L'Auberge Casino Hotel Baton Rouge
777 L'Auberge Avenue
Baton Rouge, Louisiana 70820
(337) 395-7777
Website: www.lbatonrouge.com
Map: **#3**

Toll-Free Number: (866) 261-7777
Rooms: 205 Price Range: $159-$369
Suites: 99 Price Range: $499-$849
Restaurants: 4
Buffet: B- $12.99 L- $15.99/$22.99 (Sat/Sun)
D- $26.95/32.95 (Thu)/
$37.95 (Fri/Sat)
Casino Size: 29,876 Square Feet
Other Games: MB, B, PGP, P,
TCP, FCP, MS, THB
Overnight RV Parking: No
Senior Discount: Various Tue if 50+
Special Features: 1,600-seat event center

L'Auberge Casino Resort Lake Charles
3202 Nelson Road
Lake Charles, Louisiana 70601
(337) 395-7777
Website: www.llakecharles.com
Map: **#2** (220 miles W. of New Orleans)

Toll-Free Number: (866) 580-7444
Rooms: 636 Price Range: $189-$289
Suites: 99 Price Range: $599-$849
Restaurants: 8 Valet Parking: Free
Buffet: B- $8.99/$19.99 (Sat/Sun)
L- $16.99/$21.99 (Sat/Sun)
D- $34.99
Casino Size: 27,000 Square Feet
Other Games: MB, B, PGP, LIR, P,
TCP, FCP, THB
Overnight RV Parking: No
Special Features: 18-hole golf course. Spa. Pool with lazy river ride. 1,500-seat event center.

Margaritaville Resort Casino - Bossier City
777 Margaritaville Way
Bossier City, Louisiana 71111
(318) 698-7177
Website: www.margaritavillebossiercity.com
Map: **#1** (across the Red River from Shreveport)

Toll-Free Number: (855) 346-2489
Rooms: 354 Price Range: $79-$269
Suites: 36 Price Range: $319-$589
Restaurants: 4
Buffets: B- $11.99 L- $15.99/$26.99 (Sun)
D- $27.99
Casino Size: 26,624
Other Games: MB, B, TCP, LIR, MS, UTH
Overnight RV Parking: Yes/RV Dump: No

Sam's Town Hotel & Casino Shreveport
315 Clyde Fant Parkway
Shreveport, Louisiana 71101
(318) 424-7777
Website: www.samstownshreveport.com
Map: **#1**

Toll-Free Number: (877) 429-0711
Rooms: 514 Price Range: $79-$179
Restaurants: 4
Buffet: B/L-$14.99 (Sat/Sun)
D-$16.99/$19.99 (Sun)/
$23.99 (Thu-Sat)
Casino Size: 29,194 Square Feet
Other Games: MB, LIR, TCP
Overnight RV Parking: No
Special Features: 1,650-passenger paddle wheeler on the Red River.

Treasure Chest Casino
5050 Williams Boulevard
Kenner, Louisiana 70065
(504) 443-8000
Website: www.treasurechest.com
Map: **#4** (a suburb of New Orleans)

Toll-Free Number: (800) 298-0711
Restaurants: 2
Buffet: L-$11.99/$21.99 (Sat/Sun)
D- $17.99/$19.99 (Mon/Tue/Thu)/
$31.99 (Wed) /$33.99 (Fri)
Casino Hours: 8am-3am/24 hours (Fri/Sat)
Casino Size: 24,000 Square Feet
Other Games: MB, PGP, TCP, LIR, FCP
Overnight RV Parking: No
Special Features: 1,900-passenger paddle wheeler on Lake Pontchartrain. Hilton Garden Inn located next to casino (504-712-0504).

Indian Casinos

Coushatta Casino Resort
777 Coushatta Drive
Kinder, Louisiana 70648
(800) 584-7263
Website: www.coushattacasinoresort.com
Map: **#6** (35 miles N.E. of Lake Charles)

Hotel Rooms: 118 Price Range: $149-$229
Suites: 90 Price Range: Casino Use Only
Inn Rooms: 195 Price Range: $109-$159
Lodge Rooms: 92 Price Range: $89-$109
Restaurants: 8 Liquor: Yes
Buffets: B- $16.00
L- $18.00/$29.00 (Sat/Sun)
D- $30.00/$39.00 (Thu-Sun)
Casino Size: 100,000 Square Feet
Other Games: MB, PGP, LIR, P, TCP, FCP, MS, BG (Wed-Sun), OTB
Overnight RV Parking: No
Special Features: Land-based casino. 100-space RV park ($25-$65). Video arcade. 18-hole golf course.

Cypress Bayou Casino
832 Martin Luther King Road
Charenton, Louisiana 70523
(337) 923-7284
Website: www.cypressbayou.com
Map: **#5** (75 miles S. of Baton Rouge)

Toll-Free Number: (800) 284-4386
Rooms: 96 Price Range: $89-$139
Suites: 6 Price Range: $149-$299
Restaurants: 4 Liquor: Yes
Casino Size: 27,900 Square Feet
Other Games: MB, P, PGP, TCP, FCP, MS, BG
Overnight RV Parking: Free/RV Dump: No
Special Features: Land-based casino. Cigar bar. 30-space RV park ($15-$22 per night; $55 on holidays).

Jena Choctaw Pines Casino
149 Chahta Trails
Dry Prong, Louisiana 71423
(318) 648-7773
Website: www.jenachoctawpinescasino.com
Map: **#5** (75 miles S. of Baton Rouge)

Toll-Free Number: (855) 638-5825
Restaurants: 2 Liquor: Yes
Buffets: L- $11.95/$14.95 (Sun)
D- $16.95/$18.95 (Wed)/
$21.95 (Fri/Sat)
Other Games: P, No Table Games
Overnight RV Parking: Yes
Senior Discount: Various Tue/Wed if 55+

Paragon Casino Resort
711 Paragon Place
Marksville, Louisiana 71351
(318) 253-1946
Website: www.paragoncasinoresort.com
Map: **#7** (30 miles S.E. of Alexandria)

Toll-Free Number: (800) 946-1946
Rooms: 500 Price Range: $118-$159
Suites: 57 Price Range: $155-$355
Restaurants: 6 Liquor: Yes
Buffets: B-$9.99 L-$12.99/$13.99 (Sat/Sun)
D- $18.99/$28.99 (Fri)/$23.99 (Sat)
Casino Size: 103,520 Square Feet
Other Games: MB, TCP, PGP, MS, P
Overnight RV Parking: Must use RV park
Special Features: Land-based casino. 200-space RV Park ($25/$35 Fri-Sat). 18-hole golf course. Supervised childcare center.

Pari-Mutuels

Delta Downs Racetrack & Casino
2717 Delta Downs Drive
Vinton, Louisiana 70668
(800) 589-7441
Website: www.deltadowns.com
Map: **#8** (20 miles W. of Lake Charles)

Toll-Free Number: (800) 589-7441
Rooms: 367 Price Range: $89-$299
Suites: 33 Price Range: Casino use only
Restaurants: 4
Buffets: L- $13.99/$18.99 (Sat/Sun)
D- $18.99/$32.99 (Fri/Sat)
Casino Size: 14,901 Square Feet
Other Games: Only slots, no video poker
Overnight RV Parking: Free/RV Dump: No
Special Features: Live thoroughbred and quarter-horse racing seasonally. Daily simulcasting of horse racing.

Evangeline Downs Racetrack & Casino
2235 Creswell Lane Extension
Opelousas, Louisiana 70570
(866) 472-2466
Website: www.evangelinedowns.com
Map: **#9** (30 miles W. of Baton Rouge)

Toll-Free Number: (866) 472-2466
Rooms: 117 Price Range: $97-$159
Restaurants: 3
Buffets: L-$11.99
D-$16.99/$28.99 (Fri)/$18.99 (Sat)
Casino Size: 14,619 Square Feet
Other Games: Only slots, no video poker
Overnight RV Parking: Free/RV Dump: No
Senior Discount: Various Tue if 50 or older
Special Features: Live thoroughbred and quarter-horse racing seasonally. Daily simulcasting of horse racing.

Fair Grounds Racecourse & Slots
1751 Gentilly Boulevard
New Orleans, Louisiana 70119
(504) 944-5515
Website: www.fairgroundsracecourse.com
Map: **#4**

Restaurants: 2
Other Size: 15,000 Square Feet
Other Games: Only slots, no video poker
Casino Hours: 9am-12am/10am-12am (Sun)
Overnight RV Parking: No
Special Features: Live thoroughbred racing seasonally. Daily simulcasting of horse racing.

Harrah's Louisiana Downs
8000 E. Texas Street
Bossier City, Louisiana 71111
(318) 742-5555
Website: www.harrahslouisianadowns.com
Map: **#1**

Toll-Free Number: (800) 427-7247
Restaurants: 3
Casino Size: 12,855 Square Feet
Other Games: Only slots, no video poker
Overnight RV Parking: Free/RV Dump: No
Special Features: Live thoroughbred and quarter-horse racing seasonally. Daily simulcasting of horse racing.

MAINE

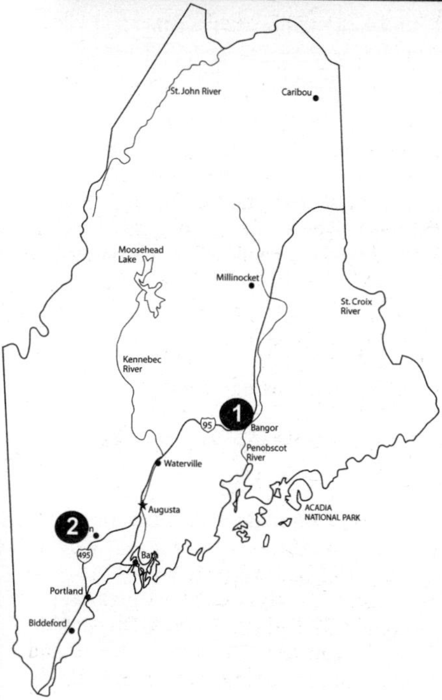

Maine has two racetrack casinos (racinos) that offer electronic gaming machines, as well as live table games.

State gaming regulations require a minimum return of 89% on all machines and during the one-year period from July 1, 2018 through June 30, 2019, the average return on gaming machines at Hollywood Casino was 90.15% and at Oxford Casino it was 90.01%.

Unless otherwise noted, all casinos offer: slots, video poker, video keno, craps, blackjack and roulette. Optional games include: three card poker (TCP) let it ride (LIR), mini baccarat (MB), Big 6 wheel (B6), spanish 21 (S21), ultimate Texas Hold 'em (UTH), Mississippi stud (MS) and Poker (P). Legislation was passed in mid-2019 to allow sports betting in Maine. However, it was not approved by the governor. The bill is expected to be revived in early 2020 when the legislature reconvenes.

The minimum gambling age is 21 for slots and 18 for pari-mutuel wagering.

For more information on visiting Maine call their Office of Tourism at (888) 624-6345 or visit their website at www.visitmaine.com.

Hollywood Casino - Bangor
500 Main Street
Bangor, Maine 04401
(207) 262-6146
Website: www.hollywoodcasinobangor.com
Map: **#1**

Toll-Free Number: (877) 779-7771
Rooms: 148 Price Range: $149-$219
Suites: 4 Price Range: $349-$449
Restaurants: 2
Buffets: L- $17.99 (Sun) D- $23.99
Other Games: TCP
Casino Hours: 8am-3am
Special Features: Live harness racing seasonally. Daily simulcasting of horse and harness racing.

Oxford Casino
777 Casino Way
Oxford, Maine 04270
(207) 539-6700
Website: www.oxfordcasino.com
Map: **#2** (55 miles S.W. of Agusta)

Rooms: 100 Price Range $139-$169
Suites: 7 Price Range $279-$299
Restaurants: 2
Other Games: MB, B6, S21, MS, UTH
Senior Discount: Various on Wed if 50+
Overnight RV Parking: Free (limit 24 hours)/
RV Dump: No

MARYLAND

Maryland has five casinos that are allowed to offer electronic gaming machines, as well as live table games. However, Ocean Downs has no table games.

No public information is available about the actual payback percentages on gaming machines in Maryland. However, gaming regulations require a minimum payback of 87% on any one machine and all machines within a casino must have an average payback of 90% to 95%.

All casinos are open 24 hours and, unless otherwise noted, offer: slots, video poker, video keno, craps, blackjack, roulette and three card poker. Optional games include: let it ride (LIR), pai gow poker (PGP), baccarat (B), Ultimate Texas Hold'em (UTH), Mississippi Stud (MS), Poker (P), four card poker (FCP) , big six (B6) and Texas Hold'em Bonus (THB). Legislation to legalize sports betting was proposed in 2019, but it did not pass. However, it may be introduced again in 2020.

If you want to order a drink while playing, be aware that Maryland gaming regulations do not allow casinos to provide free alcoholic beverages. The minimum gambling age is 21 for casinos and 18 for pari-mutuel wagering.

For Maryland tourism information, call (800) 543-1036, or visit their website at www.visitmaryland.com

Casino at Ocean Downs
10218 Racetrack Road
Berlin, Maryland 21811
(410) 641-0600
Website: www.oceandowns.com
Map: **#1** (110 miles SE of Annapolis)

Restaurants: 3
Overnight RV Parking: No
Other Games: UTH, MS
Special Features: Live harness racing seasonally. Daily simulcasting of thoroughbred and harness racing.

Hollywood Casino - Perryville
1201 Chesapeake Overlook Parkway
Perryville, Maryland 21903
(410) 378-8500
Website: hollywoodcasinoperryville.com
Map: **#2** (30 miles NE of Baltimore)

Restaurants: 2
Other Games: P, FCP, UTH
Casino Size: 35,000 Square Feet
Overnight RV Parking: No

Horseshoe Casino Baltimore
1525 Russell Street
Baltimore, Maryland 21230
(443) 931-4200
Website: www.caesars.com
Map: **#3** (10 miles SW of Baltimore)

Toll-Free Number: (844) 777-7463
Restaurants: 7
Other Games: B, PGP, FCP, MS, P, LIR, OTB, UTH
Senior Discount: Various Wed if 55+
Casino Size: 122,000 square feet
Special Features: 100x odds on craps.

Live! Casino - Maryland
7002 Arundel Mills Circle #7777
Handover, Maryland 21076
(443) 842-7000
Website: www.marylandlivecasino.com
Map: **#3** (10 miles SW of Baltimore)

Toll-free Number: (855) 563-5483
Rooms: 310 Price Range $199-$239
Suites: 53 Price Range: $299-$469
Restaurants: 8
Casino Size: 160,000 Square Feet
Other Games: B, FCP, PGP, B6, MS, UTH
Senior Discount: Various Mon-Thu if 55+
Special Features: 4,000 seat entertainment venue.

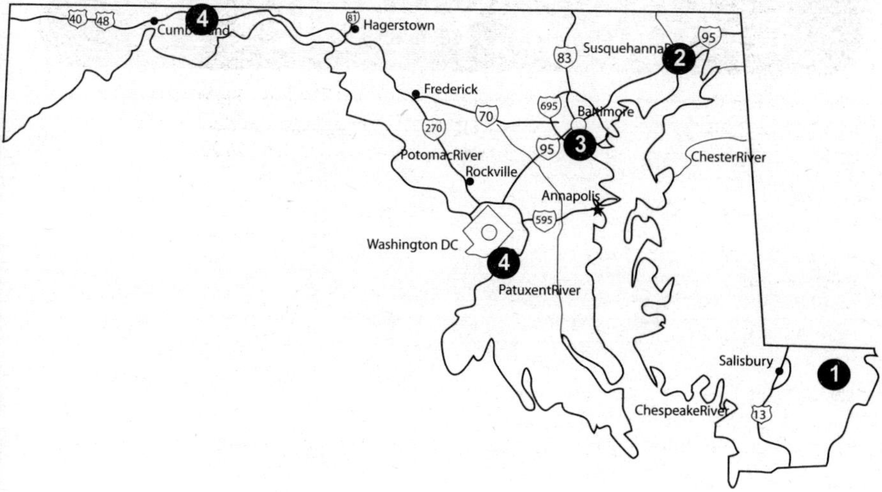

MGM National Harbor
101 MGM National Avenue
Oxon Hill, Maryland 20745
(301) 749-7500
Website: www.mgmnationalharbor.com
Map: **#4** (10 miles S of Washington, D.C.)

Toll-Free Number: (844) 646-6847
Rooms: 308 Price Range: $259-$559
Restaurants: 7
Casino Size: 125,000 Square Feet
Other Games: S21, MB, FCP, PGP, P, UTH
Senior Discount: Various Wed if 55+
Special Features: 3,000-seat theater. Luxury retail shops. Spa & fitness center.

Rocky Gap Casino Resort
16701 Lakeview Road
Flintstone, Maryland 21530
(301) 784-8400
Website: www.rockygapcasino.com
Map: **#4** (125 miles NW of Baltimore)

Toll-Free Number: (800) 724-0828
Rooms: 195 Price Range: $149-$219
Suites: 5 Price Range: $219-$265
Self-Parking: Free Valet: Free
Buffets: B- $12.99
D-$19.99/$21.99 (Fri/Sat)
Restaurants: 4
Other Games: P, B6, MS, UTH
Overnight RV Parking: No
Special Features: No buffet Mon/Tue

MASSACHUSETTS

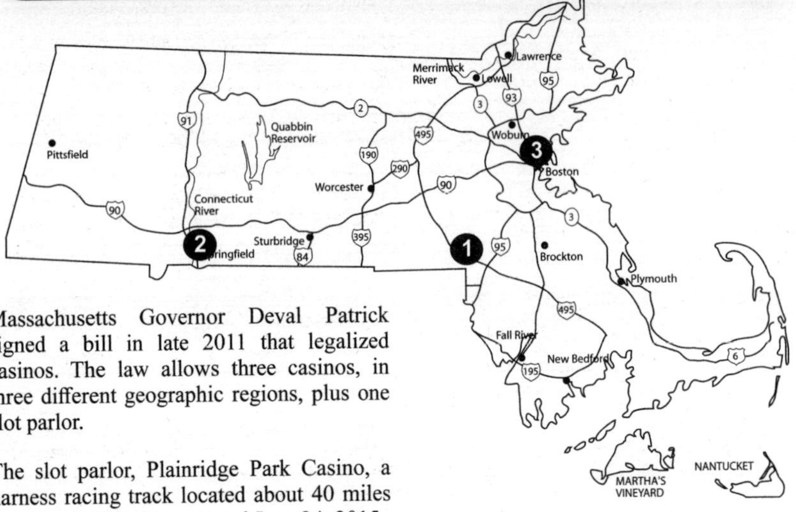

Massachusetts Governor Deval Patrick signed a bill in late 2011 that legalized casinos. The law allows three casinos, in three different geographic regions, plus one slot parlor.

The slot parlor, Plainridge Park Casino, a harness racing track located about 40 miles southwest of Boston, opened June 24, 2015.

The first resort-casino license in Region B (Western Massachusetts) was awarded to MGM Resorts and their $1.3 billion casino, MGM Springfield, opened August 24, 2018.

The second license for Region A (Eastern Massachusetts) was awarded to Wynn Resorts and their $2.6 billion, Encore Boston Harbor, opened June 23, 2019. The final license for Region C (Southeastern Massachusetts) had not yet been awarded as of August 2019.

Additionally, the Mashpee Wampanoag Tribe is planning to build a destination resort casino near Taunton. That facility, First Light Casino, was expected to open by late 2020. However, the project has been hampered by lawsuits which may stop it from being completed.

Legislation has been introduced to legalize sports betting and that may happen in 2020.

Massachusetts gaming regulations require a minimum payback of 80% on all gaming machines. From July 1, 2018 through June 30, 2019, the gaming machines at Plainridge Park returned 92.03%, 91.39% at MGM Springfield* and 91.49% at Encore**.

* Stats for MGM Springfield began August 23, 2018 when it opened.

** Stats for Encore are June 23- July 31 2019.

NOTE: If you happen to win a jackpot of $600 or more in Massachusetts, the casino will withhold 5% and send it to the Massachusetts Department of Revenue. You may, however, be able to get some of that money refunded by filing a state income tax return. The $600 threshold also applies to any cash prizes won in casino drawings or tournaments, as well as the fair market value of non-cash prizes such as cars, houses, and trips.

For information on visiting Massachusetts call (800) 447-6277 or visit their web site at www.massvacation.com

Encore Boston Harbor
98 Horizon Way
Everett, Massachusetts 02149
(857) 770-7000
Website: www.encorebostonharbor.com

Reservations Number: (888) 320-7125
Rooms: 567 Price Range: $350-$995
Suites: 104 Price Range: $750-$5000
Restaurants: 7
Buffets: B- $32.99 (Sat/Sun)
D- $38.99/$44.99 (Fri/Sat)
Casino Size: 210,000 Sq. Ft.
Games Offered: Slots, Video Poker, Blackjack, Craps, Roulette, Baccarat, Poker
Special Features: 19,000 Square foot spa. Six-acre Harborwalk. Buffet is located on casino floor and only available to guests 21+

MGM Springfield
1 MGM Way
Springfield, Massachusetts 01103
(413) 273-5000
Website: www.mgmspringfield.com

Rooms: 252 Price Range $179-$379
Suites: 16 Price Range $259-$659
Restaurants: 4
Buffet: B- $19.99 (Sun)
Casino Size: 125,000 Square feet
Games Offered: Slot Machines, Video Poker, Video Keno, Craps, Blackjack, Roulette, Spanish 21, Mini Baccarat, Three Card Poker, Four Card Poker, Pai Gow Poker, Poker, Ultimate Texas Hold 'Em
Special Features: South End Market food court with 6 casual dining options. Top Golf Swing Suite. Six screen Regal Cinema. 10-lane bowling alley. Spa.

Plainridge Park Casino
301 Washington Street
Plainville, Massachusetts 02762
(508) 643-2500
Website: www.plainridgeparkcasino.com
Map: **#1** (140 miles SW of Boston)

Toll-Free Number: (844) 327-4347
Restaurants: 2
Games Offered: Slots, Video Poker,
Video Blackjack
Special Features: Live harness racing seasonally. Daily simulcasting of horse racing. Food court with four fast food outlets.

MICHIGAN

One of Michigan's most popular casinos is actually in Canada. It's Caesars Windsor in Ontario which is just across the river from downtown Detroit.

All winnings are paid in Canadian currency and the minimum gambling age is 19. The casino is open 24 hours and offers the following games: blackjack, Spanish 21, craps, roulette, poker, baccarat, mini-baccarat, big six wheel, pai-gow poker, Caribbean stud poker, three-card poker and let it ride.

Caesars Windsor
377 Riverside Drive East
Windsor, Ontario N9A 7H7
(519) 258-7878
Website: www.caesars.com
Map: **#12**

PRICES ARE IN CANADIAN DOLLARS
Toll-Free Number: (800) 991-7777
Room Reservations: (800) 991-8888
Rooms: 758 Price Range: $169-$259
Suites: 40 Price Range: $239-$760
Restaurants: 5
Buffets: L-$20.99/$25.24 (Sun)
D-$27.24/$30.24 (Fri/Sat)
Casino Size: 100,000 Square Feet
Overnight RV Parking: Check with security/
RV Dump: No
Special Features: Entire casino is non-smoking. Buffet discount with players club card.

The only casinos in Michigan not on Indian reservations are located in downtown Detroit. All three are open 24 hours and offer the following games: slots, video poker, blackjack, craps, roulette, baccarat, mini-baccarat, Caribbean stud poker, three-card poker, pai gow poker, let it ride, big 6 wheel, Spanish 21, Mississippi stud and casino war. No public information is available about the payback percentages on Detroit's gaming machines. Sports betting was legalized for Michigan casinos in mid-2019 and it is expected to be offered at most casinos by early 2020.

The minimum gambling age at all Detroit casinos is 21 and all three casinos offer free valet parking.

Greektown Casino
555 E. Lafayette Avenue
Detroit, Michigan 48226
(313) 223-2999
Website: www.greektowncasino.com
Map: **#12**

Toll free Number: (888) 771-4386
Rooms: 400 Price Range: $129-$324
Suites: 20 Price Range: $295-$504
Restaurants: 5
Casino Size: 75,000 Square Feet
Other Games: Poker, no Spanish 21
Special Features: Starbucks coffeehouse.

MGM Grand Detroit Casino
1777 Third Avenue
Detroit, Michigan 48226
(313) 393-7777
Website: www.mgmgranddetroit.com
Map: **#12**

Toll-Free Number: (877) 888-2121
Rooms: 335 Price Range: $189-$460
Suites: 65 Price Range: $389-$699
Restaurants: 6
Casino Size: 75,000 Square Feet
Other Games: Poker, Four Card Poker
Overnight RV Parking: No

MotorCity Casino and Hotel
2901 Grand River Avenue
Detroit, Michigan 48201
(313) 237-7711
Website: www.motorcitycasino.com
Map: **#12**

Toll-Free Number: (866) 752-9622
Rooms: 359 Price Range: $199-$429
Suites: 41 Price Range: $439-$799
Restaurants: 4
Buffets: B-$17.00 (Sat/Sun) L-$23.00
D-$28.00/$49.00 (Mon)
Casino Size: 75,000 Square Feet
Other Games: Poker, Ultimate Texas Hold'em
Overnight RV Parking: Free/RV Dump: No

Indian Casinos

Indian casinos in Michigan are not required to release information on their slot machine payback percentages. However, according to officials at the Michigan Gaming Control Board, which is responsible for overseeing the tribal-state compacts, "the machines must meet the minimum standards for machines in Nevada or New Jersey." In Nevada the minimum return is 75% and in New Jersey it's 83%. Therefore, Michigan's Indian casinos must return at least 75% in order to comply with the law.

Unless otherwise noted, all Indian casinos in Michigan are open 24 hours and offer the following games: blackjack, craps, roulette, slots and video poker. Other games offered include: Spanish 21 (S21), craps (C), roulette (R), baccarat (B), mini-baccarat (MB), poker (P), Caribbean stud poker (CSP), let it ride (LIR), three-card poker (TCP), four-card poker (FCP), Ultimate Texas Hold'em (UTH), Mississippi stud (MS), keno (K) and bingo (BG). Sports betting was legalized for Michigan casinos in mid-2019 and it is expected to be offered at most casinos by early 2020.

Gambling age varies from casino to casino. Check listing for gambling age.

For more information on visiting Michigan call the state's department of tourism at (800) 543-2937 or go to www.michigan.org.

Bay Mills Resort & Casino
11386 Lakeshore Drive
Brimley, Michigan 49715
(906) 248-3715
Website: www.baymillscasinos.com
Map: **#3** (12 miles S.W. of Sault Ste. Marie)

Toll-Free Number: (888) 422-9645
Rooms: 143 Price Range: $79-$169
Suites: 4 Price Range: $150-$220
Restaurants: 3 Liquor: Yes
Buffets: D-$17.99 (Tue)/$36.99 (Fri)/
$24.99 (Sat)
Casino Size: 15,000 Square Feet
Gambling Age: 18
Other Games: P, LIR, TCP, UTH
Overnight RV Parking: Must use RV park
Special Features: 117-space RV park ($20/$25 with hookups). 18-hole golf course.

FireKeepers Casino
11177 East Michigan Ave
Battle Creek, Michigan 49014
(269) 962-0000
Website: www.firekeeperscasino.com
Map: **#18**

Toll-Free Number: (877) 352-8777
Restaurants: 5 Liquor: Yes
Buffets: L-$18.00/$23.00 (Sat)
D- $23.00/$35.00 (Fri-Sun)
Casino Size: 107,000 Square Feet
Gambling Age: 21
Other Games: MB, TCP, LIR, K, B6,
PGP, P, BG, MS, UTH
Overnight RV Parking: Free/RV Dump: No
Senior Discount: Various Tue if 50+
Special Features: Sports bar. Dance club. Food court. Buffet discount with players club card.

Four Winds Dowagiac
58700 M-51 South
Dowagiac, Michigan 49047
(866) 494-6371
Website: www.fourwindscasino.com
Map: **#21** (110 miles E. of Chicago)

Toll-Free Number: (866) 494-6371
Restaurants: 1 Liquor: Yes
Gambling Age: 21
Other Games: No craps, MS
Overnight RV Parking: Free/RV Dump: No
Senior Discount: Various Wed if 55+
Special Features: Table games open at 10am.

Four Winds Hartford
68600 Red Arrow Highway
Hartford, Michigan 49057
(866) 494-6371
Website: www.fourwindscasino.com
Map: **#21** (110 miles E. of Chicago)

Toll-Free Number: (866) 494-6371
Restaurants: 1 Liquor: Yes
Valet Parking: Free
Casino Size: 52,000 Square Feet
Gambling Age: 21
Other Games: TCP, MS
Overnight RV Parking: Free/RV Dump: No
Senior Discount: Various Wed if 55+

Four Winds New Buffalo
11111 Wilson Road
New Buffalo, Michigan 49117
(866) 494-6371
Website: www.fourwindscasino.com
Map: **#19** (60 miles E. of Chicago)

Toll-Free Number: (866) 494-6371
Rooms: 415 Price Range: $179-$349
Suites: 36 Price Range: $199-$549
Restaurants: 5 Liquor: Yes
Buffets: L- $11.50/$25.00 (Sat/Sun)
D-$29.00/$33.00 (Fri)/$47.00 (Sat)
Casino Size: 135,000 Square Feet
Gambling Age: 21
Other Games: MB, TCP, PGP, MS, K
Overnight RV Parking: Free/RV Dump: No
Senior Discount: Various Wed if 55+

Gun Lake Casino
1123 129th Ave
Wayland, Michigan 49348
(269) 792-7777
Website: www.gunlakecasino.com
Map: **#20** (23 miles S of Grand Rapids)

Toll-free Number: (866) 398-7111
Restaurants: 2 Liquor: Yes
Buffets: L-$13.00/$22.00 (Sat)/$28.00 (Sun)
D-$19.00/$28.00 (Thu/Sat/Sun)/
$28.00 (Fri)
Casino Size: 30,000 Square Feet
Gambling Age: 21
Other Games: TCP, MS
Overnight RV Parking: Free/RV Dump: No
Special Features: Food court with four fast food outlets.

Island Resort & Casino
W399 US Highway 2 and US Highway 41
Harris, Michigan 49845
(906) 466-2941
Website: www.islandresortandcasino.com
Map: **#1** (13 miles W. of Escanaba on Hwy. 41)

Toll-Free Number: (800) 682-6040
Rooms: 102 Price Range: $79-$122
Suites: 11 Price Range: $119-$379
Restaurants: 5 Liquor: Yes
Casino Size: 50,000 Square Feet
Gambling Age: 18
Other Games: S21, P, TCP, LIR, UTH, BG
Overnight RV Parking: Must use RV park
Senior Discount: Various Wed if 55+
Special Features: 42-space RV park ($23 per night). RV Park open seasonally May 1- Nov 30. Spa.

Kewadin Casino - Christmas
N7761 Candy Cane Lane
Christmas, Michigan 49862
(906) 387-5475
Website: www.kewadin.com/christmas
Map: **#9** (40 miles E. of Marquette)

Toll-Free Number: (800) 539-2346
Restaurants: 1 Liquor: Yes
Hours: 9am-1am Daily
Casino Size: 3,060 Square Feet
Gambling Age: 19
Other Games: LIR, UTH, No craps/roulette
Overnight RV Parking: Free/RV Dump: No
Senior Discount: Various Wed if 50+
Special Features: Free local-area shuttle service.

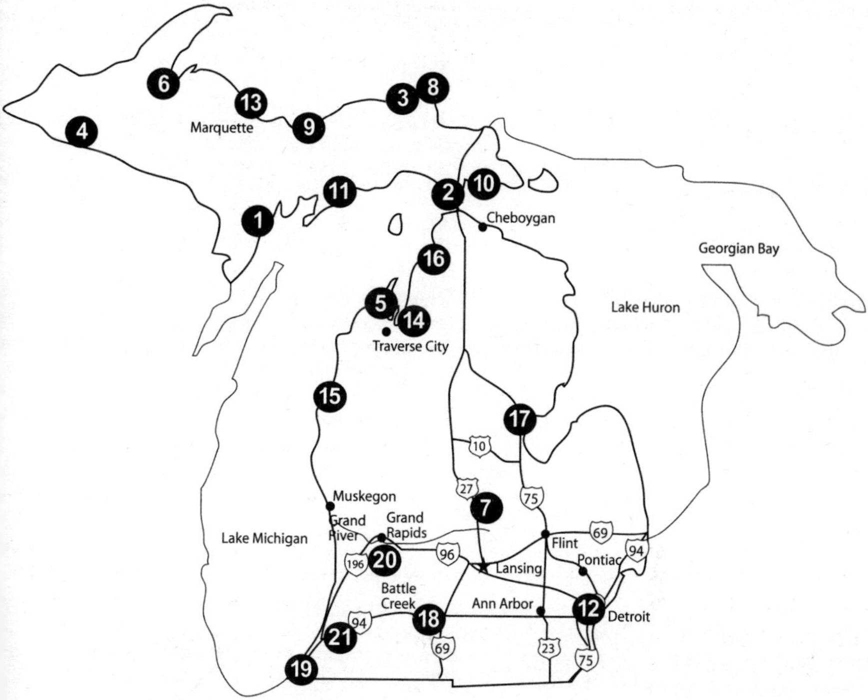

Kewadin Casino - Hessel
3 Mile Road
Hessel, Michigan 49745
(906) 484-2903
Website: www.kewadin.com /hessel
Map: **#10** (20 miles N.E. of St. Ignace)

Toll-Free Number: (800) 539-2346
Restaurants: 1 Deli Liquor: Yes
Hours: 9am-10pm/11pm (Fri/Sat)
Casino Size: 6,500 Square Feet
Gambling Age: 19
Other Games: Only Gaming Machines
Overnight RV Parking: Must use RV Park
Senior Discount: Various Wed if 50+
Special Features: 40-space RV park open May-October ($10/$15 with hook-ups per night).

Kewadin Casino - Manistique
5630 West U.S. Highway 2
Manistique, Michigan 49854
(906) 341-5510
Website: www.kewadin.com/manistique
Map: **#11** (95 miles S.E. of Marquette)

Toll-Free Number: (800) 539-2346
Restaurants: 1 Liquor: Yes
Hours: 9am-1am Daily
Casino Size: 25,000 Square Feet
Gambling Age: 19
Other Games: Only Gaming Machines
Overnight RV Parking: Free/RV Dump: No
Senior Discount: Various Wed if 50+
Special Features: Free shuttle service from local motels.

Kewadin Casino Hotel - Sault Ste. Marie
2186 Shunk Road
Sault Ste. Marie, Michigan 49783
(906) 632-0530
Website: www.kewadin.com/sault
Map: **#8**

Toll-Free Number: (800) 539-2346
Rooms: 300 Price Range: $79-$109
Suites: 20 Price Range: $99-$130
Restaurants: 3 Liquor: Yes
Buffets: B- $10.95 (Sat/Sun)
D-$10.95/$18.95 (Fri/Sat)
Casino Size: 37,000 Square Feet
Gambling Age: 19
Other Games: P, LIR, TCP, BG, K, UTH
Overnight RV Parking: Must use RV park
Senior Discount: Various Wed if 50+
Special Features: Free shuttle service to local motels and airport. Table games open at noon. 64-space RV park ($22 per night) open May-Oct.

Kewadin Casino - St. Ignace
3015 Mackinac Trail
St. Ignace, Michigan 49781
(906) 643-7071
Website: www.kewadin.com/st-ignace
Map: **#2** (50 miles S. of Sault Ste. Marie)

Toll-Free Number: (800) 539-2346
Rooms: 81 Prices: $115-$139
Suites: 11 Prices: $135-$169
Restaurants: 2 Liquor: Yes
Buffets: B- $10.95 (Sat/Sun)
D-$10.95/$18.99 (Fri/Sat)
Casino Size: 25,000 Square Feet
Gambling Age: 19
Other Games: P, LIR, TCP, UTH
Overnight RV Parking: Must use RV Park.
Senior Discount: Various Wed if 50+.
Special Features: Local motels/hotels offer packages with free shuttle service. Sports bar. 21-space RV park ($15 per night).

Kings Club Casino
11386 W. Lakeshore Drive
Brimley, Michigan 49715
(906) 248-3700
Website: www.4baymills.com
Map: **#3** (12 miles S.W. of Sault Ste. Marie)

Toll-Free Number: (888) 422-9645
Restaurants: 1 Liquor: Yes
Hours: 10am-12am/2am (Fri/Sat)
Casino Size: 6,500 Square Feet
Gambling Age: 18
Other Games: Only Gaming Machines
Overnight RV Parking: Must use RV park
Special Features: Two miles from, and affiliated with, Bay Mills Resort & Casino. 75-space RV park ($29/$39 w/hookup) at Bay Mills.

Leelanau Sands Casino & Lodge
2521 N.W. Bayshore Drive
Peshawbestown, Michigan 49682
(800) 922 - 2946
Website: www.leelanausandscasino.com
Map: **#5** (4 miles N. of Sutton's Bay)

Toll-Free Number: (800) 922-2946
Room Reservations: (800) 930-3008
Rooms: 51 Price Range: $120-$160
Suites: 2 Price Range: $160-$180
Restaurants: 2 Liquor: Yes
Casino Size: 29,000 Square Feet
Hours: 8am-2am Daily
Gambling Age: 18
Other Games: TCP, BG (Sun/Wed-Fri)
Overnight RV Parking: Free/RV Dump: No
Senior Discount: Various on Tue if 65+.
Special Features: RV hook-ups available for $10 per night.

Little River Casino Resort
2700 Orchard Drive
Manistee, Michigan 49660
(231) 723-1535
Website: www.lrcr.com
Map: **#15** (60 miles S.W of Traverse City)

Toll-Free Number: (888) 568-2244
Rooms: 271 Price Range: $119-$160
Suites: 20 Price Range: $189-$260
Restaurants: 4 Liquor: Yes
Buffets: B-$9.99 L-$11.99
D-$13.99/$29.99 (Fri/Sat)
Casino Size: 75,000 Square Feet
Gambling Age: 18
Other Games: LIR, TCP, MS, UTH
Overnight RV Parking: Free/RV Dump: Free
Senior Discount: Various Wed if 55+
Special Features: 95-space RV park open April-October ($25-$45 per night). Spa.

Northern Waters Casino Resort
N 5384 US 45 North
Watersmeet, Michigan 49969
(906) 358-4226
Website: www.lvdcasino.com
Map: **#4** (49 miles S.E. of Ironwood)

Toll-Free Number: (800) 583-3599
Room Reservations: (800) 895-2505
Rooms: 107 Price Range: $75-$110
Suites: 25 Price Range: $110-$135
Restaurants: 1 Liquor: Yes
Buffets: D- $14.95 (Wed)/$25.95 (Thu/Fri)/
$22.95 (Sat)
Casino Size: 25,000 Square Feet
Gambling Age: 18
Other Games: P
Overnight RV Parking: Must use RV park
Senior Discount: 10% off in restaurant if 55+
Special Features: 9-hole golf course. 14-space RV park ($15 per night). Gift Shop.

Odawa Casino Resort
1760 Lears Road
Petoskey, Michigan 49770
(231) 347-6041
Website: www.odawacasino.com
Map: **#16** (50 miles S.W of Cheboygan)

Toll-Free Number: (877) 442-6464
Rooms: 127 Price Range: $119-$169
Suites: 10 Price Range- $159-$249
Restaurants: 3 Liquor: Yes
Buffets: B- $9.95/$16.95 (Sun)
L- $12.99/$16.95 (Sun)
D- $18.95/ $21.95 (Fri/Sat)/
$34.95 (Thu)
Casino Size: 50,000 Square Feet
Gambling Age: 19
Other Games: LIR, TCP, P, UTH
Overnight RV Parking: Free/RV Dump: No
Senior Discount: Various Wed/Sun if 50+
Special Features: Hotel is 1/4-mile from casino. Free shuttle service to/from local hotels.

Odawa Casino Mackinaw
1080 S Nicolet Street
Mackinaw City, Michigan 49701
(877) 442-6464
Website: www.odawacasino.com
Map: **#2** (60 miles S. of Sault Ste. Marie)

Toll-Free Number: (877) 442-6464
Restaurants: 1 Snack Bar Liquor: No
Gambling Age: 19
Other Games: Class II gaming machines
based on bingo

Ojibwa Casino - Marquette
105 Acre Trail
Marquette, Michigan 49855
(906) 249-4200
Website: www.ojibwacasino.com
Map: **#13**

Toll-Free Number: (888) 560-9905
Restaurants: 1 Snack Bar Liquor: Yes
Gambling Age: 18
Other Games: LIR
Overnight RV Parking: No
Senior Discount: Various Mon if 55+
Special features: 7-space RV Park (Free). Table games open 2pm-2am/12pm-2am (Thu-Sun).

Ojibwa Casino Resort - Baraga
16449 Michigan Avenue
Baraga, Michigan 49908
(906) 353-6333
Website: www.ojibwacasino.com
Map: **#6** (30 miles S. of Houghton)

Toll-Free Number: (800) 323-8045
Rooms: 38 Price Range: $69-$89
Restaurants: 2 Liquor: Yes
Casino Size: 17,000 Square Feet
Gambling Age: 18
Other Games: LIR, BG
Overnight RV Parking: Must use RV park
Senior Discount: Various Mon if 55+
Special Features: 12-space RV Park ($20 per night). 8-lane bowling alley. Table games open 3pm-2am daily.

Saganing Eagles Landing Casino
2690 Worth Road
Standish, Michigan 48658
(888) 732-4537
Website: www.saganing-eagleslanding.com
Map: #**#17**

Toll-Free Number: (888) 732-4537
Rooms: 500 ($147-$500)
Suite: 25 ($215-$2400)
Restaurants: 2 Liquor: Yes
Casino Size: 32,000 Square Feet
Gambling Age: 18
Other Games: Only Gaming Machines
Overnight RV Parking: Must use RV park
Special Features: Electronic versions of blackjack and roulette. 50-space RV park ($20 per night) 60-slip marina.

Soaring Eagle Casino & Resort
6800 Soaring Eagle Boulevard
Mount Pleasant, Michigan 48858
(888) 732-4537
Website: www.soaringeaglecasino.com
Map: **#7** (65 miles N. of Lansing)

Toll-Free Number: (888) 732-4537
Room Reservations: (877) 232-4532
Rooms: 243 Price Range: $94-$385
Suites: 21 Price Range: $199-$449
Restaurants: 6 Liquor: Yes
Buffets: L-$17.75 D-$19.75/$24.95 (Mon/Fri)
Casino Size: 150,000 Square Feet
Gambling Age: 18
Other Games: P, TCP, BG (Wed-Sun)
Overnight RV Parking: Free/RV Dump: No
Senior Discount: Various Thu if 55+
Special Features: Casino is in two separate buildings. Gift shop. Art gallery. Off property RV park with free shuttle ($47-$65 per night). Water park located on property.

Turtle Creek Casino
7741 M-72 East
Williamsburg, Michigan 49690
(231) 534-8888
Website: www.turtlecreekcasino.com
Map: **#14** (8 miles E. of Traverse City)

Toll-Free Number: (800) 922-2946
Rooms: 127 Price Range: $159-$270
Suites: 10 Price Range: $350-$400
Restaurants: 3 Liquor: Yes
Gambling Age: 18
Buffets: B-$12.95 D- $22.95
Casino Size: 56,000 Square Feet
Other Games: P, TCP, UTH
Overnight RV Parking: Free/RV Dump: No
Senior Discount: Various Thu if 50+

MINNESOTA

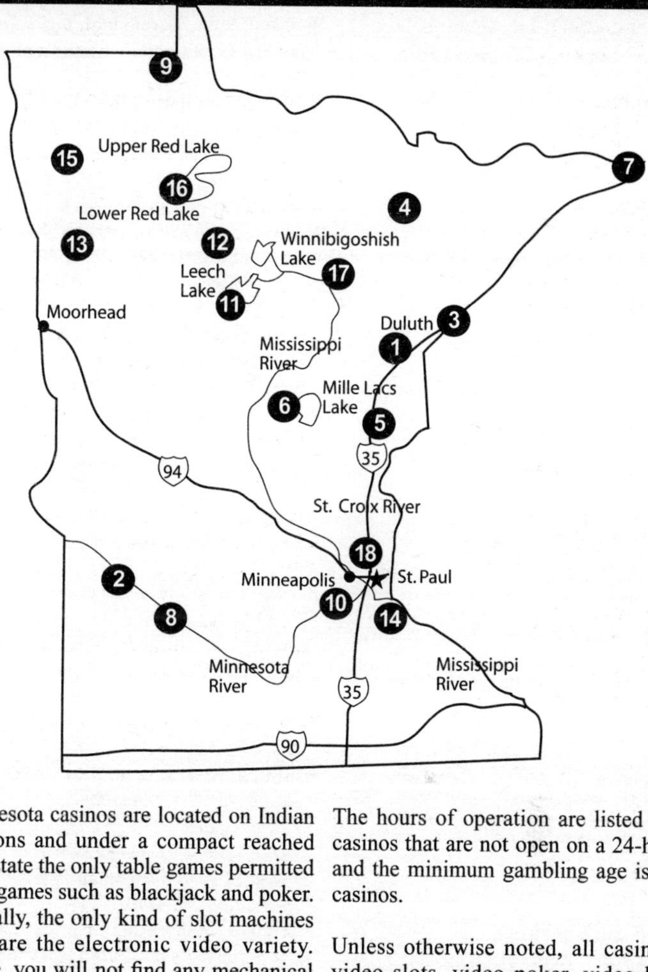

All Minnesota casinos are located on Indian reservations and under a compact reached with the state the only table games permitted are card games such as blackjack and poker. Additionally, the only kind of slot machines allowed are the electronic video variety. Therefore, you will not find any mechanical slots that have traditional reels - only video screens.

According to the terms of the compact between the state and the tribes, however, the minimum and maximum payouts are regulated as follows: video poker and video blackjack - 83% to 98%, slot machines - 80% to 95%, keno - 75% to 95%. Each tribe is free to set its machines to pay back anywhere within those limits and the tribes do not not release any information regarding their slot machine percentage paybacks.

The hours of operation are listed for those casinos that are not open on a 24-hour basis and the minimum gambling age is 18 at all casinos.

Unless otherwise noted, all casinos offer: video slots, video poker, video keno and blackjack. Optional games include: poker (P), Caribbean stud poker (CSP), pai gow poker (PGP), three-card poker (TCP), ultimate Texas hold'em (UTH), Mississippi stud (MS), let it ride (LIR) and bingo (BG). Legislation to legalize sports betting was proposed in 2019, but it did not pass. However, it may be introduced again in 2020.

For more information on visiting Minnesota call the state's office of tourism at (800) 657-3700 or go to www.exploreminnesota.com.

Black Bear Casino Resort
1785 Highway 210
Carlton, Minnesota 55718
(218) 878-2327
Website: www.blackbearcasinoresort.com
Map: **#1** (130 miles N. of Twin Cities)

Toll-Free Number: (888) 771-0777
Rooms: 348 Price Range: $91-$159
Suites: 60 Price Range: $101-$169
Restaurants: 4
Liquor: Yes
Buffets: B- $9.99/$11.99 (Sat/Sun)
L- $10.99/$11.99 (Sat/Sun)
D-$14.99/$19.99 (Thu)/
$19.99 (Fri)/$16.99 (Sat)
Casino Size: 65,000 Square Feet
Other Games: P, TCP, UTH, BG
Overnight RV Parking: Free/RV Dump: No
Special Features: 18-hole golf course.

Cedar Lakes Casino Hotel
6268 Upper Cass Frontage Road NW
Cass Lake, Minnesota 56633
(844) 554-2646
Website: www.cedarlakescasino.com
Map: **#12** (220 miles N.W. of Twin Cities)

Rooms: 80 Price Range: $119-$179
Suites: 20 Price Range $199-$219
Restaurants: 1 Liquor: No
Casino Size: 40,000 Square Feet
Other Games: UTH, BG (Thu/Fri/Sun)
Overnight RV Parking: Free/RV Dump: Free
Special Features: Food court with three fast food outlets.

Fond-du-Luth Casino
129 E. Superior Street
Duluth, Minnesota 55802
(218) 720-5100
Website: www.fondduluthcasino.com
Map: **#3** (150 miles N.E. of Twin Cities)

Toll-Free Number: (800) 873-0280
Restaurants: 0 Liquor: Yes
Casino Size: 20,000 Square Feet
Other Games: Only Blackjack and Slots
Overnight RV Parking: No
Senior Discount: Various Tue if 55+
Special Features: One hour free parking in lot adjacent to casino (must be validated in casino). Free shuttle to/from Black Bear Casino

Fortune Bay Resort Casino
1430 Bois Forte Road
Tower, Minnesota 55790
(218) 753-6400
Website: www.fortunebay.com
Map: **#4** (150 miles N.E. of Twin Cities)

Toll-Free Number: (800) 992-7529
Rooms: 83 Price Range: $119-$175
Suites: 33 Price Range: $155-$375
Restaurants: 4
Liquor: Yes
Buffets: B- $7.95/$13.95 (Sat/Sun)
L- $10.95/$13.95 (Sat/Sun)
D- $16.95/$22.95 (Fri/Sat)/
$28.95 (Mon)
Casino Size: 17,000 Square Feet
Other Games: P, MS, UTH
Overnight RV Parking: Must use RV park
Senior Discount: Various Wed if 50+.
Special Features: Located on S.E. shore of Lake Vermilion. 84-slip marina. 36-space RV Park ($20-$38 per night). Snowmobile and hiking trails. 18-hole golf course

Grand Casino Hinckley
777 Lady Luck Drive
Hinckley, Minnesota 55037
(320) 384-7777
Website: www.grandcasinomn.com
Map: **#5** (75 miles N. of Twin Cities)

Toll-Free Number: (800) 472-6321
Rooms: 485 Price Range: $109-$179 (Hotel)
Price Range: $99-$159 (Inn)
Price Range: $149-$179 (Chalet)
Suites: 52 Price Range: $129-$269
Restaurants: 5 Liquor: Yes
Buffets: L-$10.99
D-$15.99/$20.99 (Fri/Sat)/
$34.99 (Sun)
Casino Size: 54,800 Square Feet
Other Games: TCP, UTH, P, BG
Overnight RV Parking: Must use RV park
Senior Discount: Various Wed if 55+
Special Features: 271-space RV park ($34 per night/$43 Fri/Sat). 18-hole golf course. Free pet kennel.

Grand Casino Mille Lacs
777 Grand Avenue
Onamia, Minnesota 56359
(320) 532-7777
Website: www.grandcasinomn.com
Map: **#6** (90 miles N. of Twin Cities)

Toll-Free Number: (800) 626-5825
Rooms: 284 Price Range: $99-$159
Suites: 14 Price Range: $119-$389
Restaurants: 3 Liquor: Yes
Buffets: L- $10.00
D- $14.99/$15.99(Thu)/$34.99 (Fri)/
$20.99 (Sat)
Casino Size: 42,000 Square Feet
Senior Discounts: Various Tues if 55+
Other Games: UTH, TCP, FCP, MS, P, BG
Overnight RV Parking: Free/RV Dump: No
Special Features: Resort has two hotels (one is off-property). Free pet kennel.

Grand Portage Lodge & Casino
70 Casino Drive
Grand Portage, Minnesota 55605
(218) 475-2401
Website: www.grandportage.com
Map: **#7** (N.E. tip of Minnesota)

Reservation Number: (800) 543-1384
Rooms: 100 Price Range: $99-$175
Restaurants: 2 Liquor: Yes
Casino Size: 15,268 Square Feet
Overnight RV Parking: Must use RV park
Senior Discount: Various Thu if 50+
Special Features: On shore of Lake Superior. Hiking, skiing and snowmobile trails. Gift shop. Marina. 29-space RV park open May-Oct ($40/$45 per night). Free shuttle service to/from Thunder Bay, Ontario.

Jackpot Junction Casino Hotel
39375 County Highway 24
Morton, Minnesota 56270
(507) 697-8000
Website: www.jackpotjunction.com
Map: **#8** (110 miles S.W. of Twin Cities)

Toll-Free Number: (800) 946-2274
Rooms: 253 Price Range: $75-$97
Suites: 23 Price Range: $100-$175
Restaurants: 3 Liquor: Yes
Other Games: TCP, UTH, BG (Thu- Tue)
Senior Discount: Various Wed if 50+
Special Features: 30-space RV park ($45 to $55). 18-hole golf course.

Little Six Casino
2450 Sioux Trail N.W.
Prior Lake, Minnesota 55372
(952) 403-5525
Website: www.littlesixcasino.com
Map: **#10** (25 miles S.W. of Twin Cities)

Restaurants: 1 Liquor: Yes
Senior Discounts: Various Wed if 55+.
Special Features: 1/4-mile north of Mystic Lake Casino. Free shuttle from Mall of America.

Mystic Lake Casino Hotel
2400 Mystic Lake Boulevard
Prior Lake, Minnesota 55372
(952) 445-9000
Website: www.mysticlake.com
Map: **#10** (25 miles S.W. of Twin Cities)

Toll-Free Number: (800) 262-7799
Rooms: 510 Price Range: $129-$259
Suites: 76 Price Range: $179-$489
Restaurants: 7 Liquor: Yes
Buffets: L- $15.95/$21.95 (Sat/Sun)
D- $18.95/$19.95 (Fri/Sat)/$37.95 (Sun)
Casino Size: 102,000 Square Feet
Other Games: BG
Overnight RV Parking: Must use RV Park
Senior Discounts: Various Wed if 55+.
Special Features: Free shuttle bus service from Twin Cities area. 122-space RV park ($39/$47 per night spring/summer, $34 fall/winter). Health club. Childcare facility. Spa.

Northern Lights Casino & Hotel
6800 Y Frontage Rd NW
Walker, Minnesota 56484
(218) 547-2744
Website: www.northernlightscasino.com
Map: **#11** (175 miles N. of the Twin Cities)

Toll-Free Number: (844) 552-2646
Rooms: 105 Price Range: $115-$133
Suites: 4 Price Range: $169-$195
Restaurants: 2 Liquor: Yes
Buffets: B-$9.95
L-$10.95/$11.95 (Sat/Sun)
D-$12.95/$32.95 (Thu)/
$18.45 (Fri/Sat)/$14.95 (Sun)
Casino Size: 40,000 Square Feet
Other Games: P
Overnight RV Parking: Free/RV Dump: No
Senior Discount: Various Tue if 50+
Special Features: 90-foot dome simulates star constellations.

Prairie's Edge Casino Resort
5616 Prairie's Edge Lane
Granite Falls, Minnesota 56241
(320) 564-2121
Website: www.prairiesedgecasino.com
Map: **#2** (110 miles W. of Twin Cities)

Toll-Free Number: (866) 293-2121
Rooms: 79 Price Range: $75-$99
Suites: 10 Price Range: $129-$159
Restaurants: 2 Liquor: Yes
Buffets: B/L-$14.95 (Sun)
D-$13.95/$15.95 (Wed)/
$28.95 (3rd Friday of the month)
Casino Size: 36,000 Square Feet
Other Games: UTH
Overnight RV Parking: Must use RV Park
Special Features: 55-space RV park ($25 per night/$35 with hookups). Convenience store. No buffet Mon/Tue. Table games open at 10am daily.

Seven Clans Casino Red Lake
10200 Route 89
Red Lake, Minnesota 56671
(218) 679-2500
Website: www.sevenclanscasino.com
Map: **#16** (200 miles N.W. of Duluth)

Toll-Free Number: (888) 679-2501
Rooms: 56 Prices: $75-$165
Restaurants: 1 Liquor: No
Casino Size: 40,000 Square Feet
Other Games: Video Slots, Video Poker, Video Keno, Bingo (Sun)
Overnight RV Parking: Free/RV Dump: No
Senior Discount: Various Mon if 50 or older.

Seven Clans Casino Thief River Falls
20595 Center Street East
Thief River Falls, Minnesota 56701
(218) 681-4062
Website: www.sevenclanscasino.com
Map: **#15** (275 miles N.W. of Minneapolis)

Toll-Free Number: (888) 679-2501
Rooms: 56 Prices: $75-$165
Restaurants: 1 Liquor: No
Casino Size: 40,000 Square Feet
Other Games: BG(Sun), No Blackjack
Overnight RV Parking: Free/RV Dump: No
Senior Discount: Various Mon if 50+

Seven Clans Casino Warroad
34966 605th Avenue
Warroad, Minnesota 56763
(218) 386-3381
Website: www.sevenclanscasino.com
Map: **#9** (400 miles N.W. of Twin Cities)

Toll-Free Number: (800) 815-8293
Rooms: 34 Price Range: $90-$119
Suites: 7 Price Range: $159-$189
Restaurants: 2 Liquor: No
Casino Size: 13,608 Square Feet
Other Games: P(Thu-Sun)
Overnight RV Parking: Free/RV Dump: No
Senior Discount: Various Sunday if 50+
Special Features: Hotel is Super 8 located one mile from casino with free shuttle service provided.

Shooting Star Casino Bagley
13325 340th Street
Bagley, Minnesota 56676
(218) 935-2701
Website: www.starcasino.com
Map: **#13** (250 miles N.W. of Twin Cities)

Toll-Free Number: (800) 453-7827
Hours: 10am-2am/24 Hours (Fri/Sat)
Restaurants: 1 Liquor: Yes
Other Games: No Blackjack
Senior Discounts: Various Tue if 50+

Shooting Star Casino Hotel
777 Casino Road
Mahnomen, Minnesota 56557
(218) 935-2701
Website: www.starcasino.com
Map: **#13** (235 miles N.W. of Twin Cities)

Room Reservations: (800) 453-7827
Rooms: 360 Price Range: $79-$99
Restaurants: 4
Liquor: Yes
Buffets: B-$10.99/$12.99 L-$12.99
D-$25.99/$17.99(Thu)/$32.99 (Fri)/
$19.99 (Sat)/$16.99 (Sun)
Other Games: LIR, TCP, PGP, UTH, P, BG
Overnight RV Parking: Must use RV park
Senior Discounts: Various Tue if 50+
Special Features: Table Games open at 10am daily. 47-space RV park ($30 per night)

Treasure Island Resort & Casino
5734 Sturgeon Lake Road
Red Wing, Minnesota 55089
(651) 388-6300
Website: www.treasureislandcasino.com
Map: **#14** (40 miles S.E. of Twin Cities)

Toll-Free Number: (800) 222-7077
Rooms: 250 Price Range: $109-$159
Suites: 28 Price Range: $169-$239
Restaurants: 3 Liquor: Yes
Buffets: B- $14.50 (Sat/Sun)
L- $16.50
D- $18.50/$38.95 (Thu)/
$22.00 (Fri/Sat)/$26.99(Sun)
Casino Size: 110,000 Square Feet
Other Games:P, B, PGP, TCP, UTH, BG
Overnight RV Parking: Must use RV Park
Senior Discount: Various Wed if 50+
Special Features: 95-space RV park open April-October ($35-$65 per night). 137-slip marina. Dinner and sightseeing cruises.

White Oak Casino
45830 US Hwy 2
Deer River, Minnesota 56636
(218) 246-9600
Website: www.whiteoakcasino.com
Map: **#17** (5 miles N.W. of Grand Rapids)

Toll-Free Number: (844) 554-2646
Restaurants: 1 Liquor: Yes
Casino Size: 11,000 Square Feet
Overnight RV Parking: Free/RV Dump: No
Senior Discount: Various Tue if 50+

Pari-Mutuels

Minnesota has two racetracks that offer the card games of blackjack, poker, pai gow poker, let it ride, Mississippi stud, and four card poker.

The completely nonsmoking card rooms are open 24 hours and admission is free. Players must pay a commission to the card room on each hand played for all games except regular poker, where a rake is taken from each pot. The minimum gambling age is 18.

Canterbury Park
1100 Canterbury Road
Shakopee, Minnesota 55379
(952) 445-7223
Website: www.canterburypark.com
Map: **#10** (22 miles S.W. of Twin Cities)

Horse Track Toll-Free: (800) 340-6361
Card Room Toll-Free: (866) 667-6537
Restaurants: 2
Buffet: B-$26.95 (Sat)/$19.95 (Sun)
D- $27.95 (Thu)/$32.95 (Fri)
Casino Size: 18,000 Square Feet
Other Games: BJ, P, PGP, MS, TCP, UTH, B
Overnight RV Parking: Free/RV Dump: No
Special Features: Live horse racing seasonally. Daily simulcasting of horse racing. Free shuttle service to/from Mall of America.

Running Aces Casino Hotel & Racetrack
15201 Running Aces Boulevard
Columbus, Minnesota 55025
(651) 925-4600
Website: www.runaces.com
Map: **#18** (25 miles N.E. of Twin Cities)

Toll-Free: (877) 786-2237
Restaurants: 1
Other Games: B, MS, P, PGP, TCP, FCP, UTH
Special Features: New 116-room hotel expected to open early 2020.
Special Features: Live Horse racing seasonally. Daily simulcasting of horse racing.

MISSISSIPPI

Mississippi was the third state to legalize riverboat gambling when it was approved by that state's legislature in 1990. The law restricts casinos to coast waters (including the Bay of St. Louis and the Back Bay of Biloxi) along the Mississippi River and in navigable waters of counties that border the river.

Mississippi law also requires that riverboats be permanently moored at the dock and they are not permitted to cruise. This allows the riverboats to offer 24-hour dockside gambling. The Isle of Capri in Biloxi was the first casino to open on August 1, 1992 followed one month later by The President.

Since the law does not require that the floating vessel actually resemble a boat, almost all of the casinos are built on barges. This gives them the appearance of a land-based building, rather than a riverboat.

Due to the destruction caused by Hurricane Katrina in August 2005, the Mississippi legislature allowed the state's gulf coast casinos to be rebuilt on land within 800-feet of the shoreline and some casinos have been rebuilt in that manner.

The Mississippi Gaming Commission does not break down its slot statistics by individual properties. Rather, they are classified by region. The **Coastal** region includes Biloxi, Gulfport and Bay Saint Louis. The **North** region includes Tunica, Greenville and Lula. The **Central** region includes Vicksburg and Natchez.

With that in mind here's information, as supplied by the Mississippi Gaming Commission, showing the machine payback percentages for each area's casinos for the one-year period from July 1, 2018 through June 30, 2019:

	Coastal	North	Central
1¢ Slots	**91.99%**	91.95%	91.73%
5¢ Slots	94.78%	94.96%	**95.73%**
25¢ Slots	**93.91%**	92.41%	93.78%
$1 Slots	93.28%	93.51%	**94.10%**
$5 Slots	93.78%	95.16%	**95.52%**
All	92.18%	91.87%	**92.32%**

These numbers reflect the percentage of money returned on each denomination of machine and encompass all electronic machines including video poker and video keno. The best returns for each category are highlighted in bold print and you can see that all of the gaming areas offer rather similar returns on their machines.

Unless otherwise noted, all casinos are open 24 hours and offer: slots, video poker, blackjack, craps, roulette and three card poker. Other game listings include: Spanish 21 (S21), baccarat (B), mini-baccarat (MB), poker (P), pai gow poker (PGP), let it ride (LIR), Caribbean stud poker (CSP) Mississippi stud (MS), ultimate Texas hold'em (UTH), big six wheel (B6), four card poker (FCP), casino war (CW), keno (K) and sports book (SB). The minimum gambling age is 21.

Sports betting was legalized for Mississippi casinos in early 2018 and the Beau Rivage was the first casino to accept a sports bet on August 1, 2018.

NOTE: If you happen to win a jackpot of $1,200 or more in Mississippi, the casino will deduct 3% of your winnings and pay it to the Mississippi Tax Commission as a gambling tax. The tax is nonrefundable and the $1,200 threshold would also apply to any cash prizes won in casino drawings or tournaments.

For more information on visiting Mississippi call the state's tourism department at (866) 733-6477 or go to: www.visitmississippi.org

For Biloxi tourism information call (800) 237-9493 or go to: www.gulfcoast.org. For Tunica tourism information call (888) 488-6422 or go to: www.tunicatravel.com.

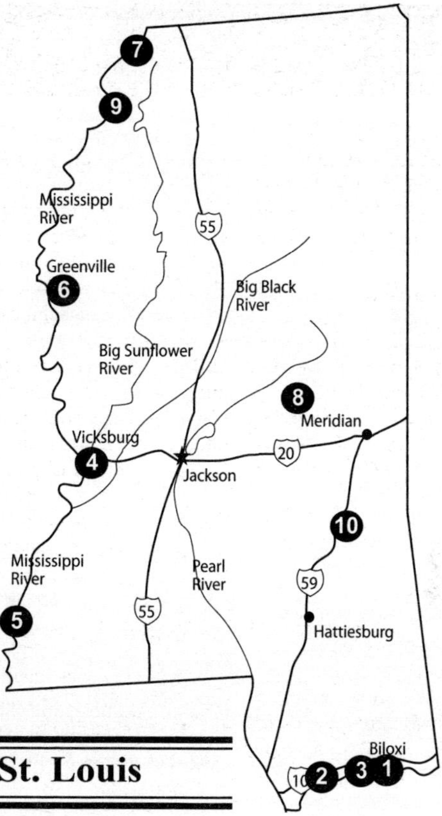

Bay St. Louis

Map: **#2** (on St. Louis Bay, 60 miles E. of New Orleans)

Hollywood Casino Gulf Coast
711 Hollywood Boulevard
Bay St. Louis, Mississippi 39520
(866) 758-2591
Website: www.hollywoodgulfcoast.com

Toll-Free Number: (866) 758-2591
Rooms: 498 Price Range: $89-$179
Suites: 78 Price Range: Casino Use Only
Restaurants: 3
Buffets: B- $10.99 (Sat/Sun)
Brunch- $34.99 (Sun) L-$12.99
D-$20.99/$26.99 (Thu)/
$34.99 (Fri-Sat)/$27.99 (Sun)
Casino Size: 56,300 Square Feet
Other Games: MB, PGP, P, MS, SB
Overnight RV Parking: Must use RV park
Special Features: 100-space RV Park (starting at$35/night). 18-hole golf course. Lazy river pool.

Silver Slipper Casino Hotel
5000 South Beach Boulevard
Bay St. Louis, Mississippi 39520
(228) 469-2777
Website: www.silverslipper-ms.com

Toll-Free Number: (866) 775-4773
Rooms: 129 Price Range: $119-179
Suites: 19 Price Range: $189-$249
Restaurants: 5
Buffets: L- $12.95/$34.95 (Sun) D- $34.95
Casino Size: 38,926 Square Feet
Other Games: K, MS
Overnight RV Parking: Must use RV park.
Special Features: Land-based casino. 24-space RV park ($25-$35 per night) $2 buffet discount for slot club members.

Biloxi

Map: **#1** (On the Gulf of Mexico, 90 miles E. of New Orleans)

Beau Rivage Resort & Casino
875 Beach Boulevard
Biloxi, Mississippi 39530
(228) 386-7111
Website: www.beaurivage.com

Toll-Free Number: (888) 750-7111
Rooms: 1,645 Price Range: $109-$300
Suites: 95 Price Range: $159-$450
Restaurants: 7
Buffets: B- $12.99/$15.99 (Sat)/$23.99 (Sun)
L- $15.99/$23.99 (Sun)
D- $22.99/$26.99 (Fri)/ $29.99 (Sat)
Casino Size: 84,819 Square Feet
Other Games: SB, MB, B, PGP, P, MS, UTH
Overnight RV Parking: No
Special Features: Casino is on a barge. Spa. Beauty salon. 13-store shopping arcade.

Boomtown Casino - Biloxi
676 Bayview Avenue
Biloxi, Mississippi 39530
(228) 435-7000
Website: www.boomtownbiloxi.com

Toll-Free Number: (800) 627-0777
Restaurants: 4
Buffets: L-$13.99/$29.99 (Sat)/$31.99 (Sun)
D- $19.99/$31.99 (Thu/Sun)/
$34.99 (Fri/Sat)
Casino Size: 37,891 Square Feet
Other Games: SB, MB, MS, PGP
Overnight RV Parking: Free/RV Dump: No
Special Features: Casino is on a barge. 50-space RV park ($29 to $45 per night).

Golden Nugget - Biloxi
151 Beach Boulevard
Biloxi, Mississippi 39530
(228) 435-5400
Website: www.goldennugget.com

Toll-Free Number: (800) 777-7568
Rooms: 541 Price Range: $59-$199
Suites: 200 Price Range: $99-$429
Restaurants: 5
Buffets: B- $11.99 L- $14.99
D- $19.99 /$21.99 (Thu)/
$24.99 (Fri-Sun)
Casino Size: 54,728 Square Feet
Other Games: SB, MB, B, MS, P, PGP, UTH
Overnight RV Parking: Free/RV Dump: No
Senior Discount: Various Wed if 50+
Special Features: Land-based casino. Spa. Beauty salon. Golf packages offered.

Hard Rock Hotel & Casino - Biloxi
777 Beach Boulevard
Biloxi, Mississippi 39530
(228) 374-7625
Website: www.hrhcbiloxi.com

Toll-Free Number: (877) 877-6256
Rooms: 306 Prices: $99-$229
Suites: 64 Prices: $249-$629
Restaurants: 6
Buffets: B-$21.99 (Sat/Sun)
L- $14.99/$21.99 (Sat/Sun)
D-$21.99/$25.99 (Fri/Sat)
Casino Size: 50,984 Square Feet
Other Games: SB, MB, PGP, MS
Overnight RV Parking: No
Special Features: Casino is on a barge. Spa. Nightclub. Collection of rock and roll memorabilia on display.

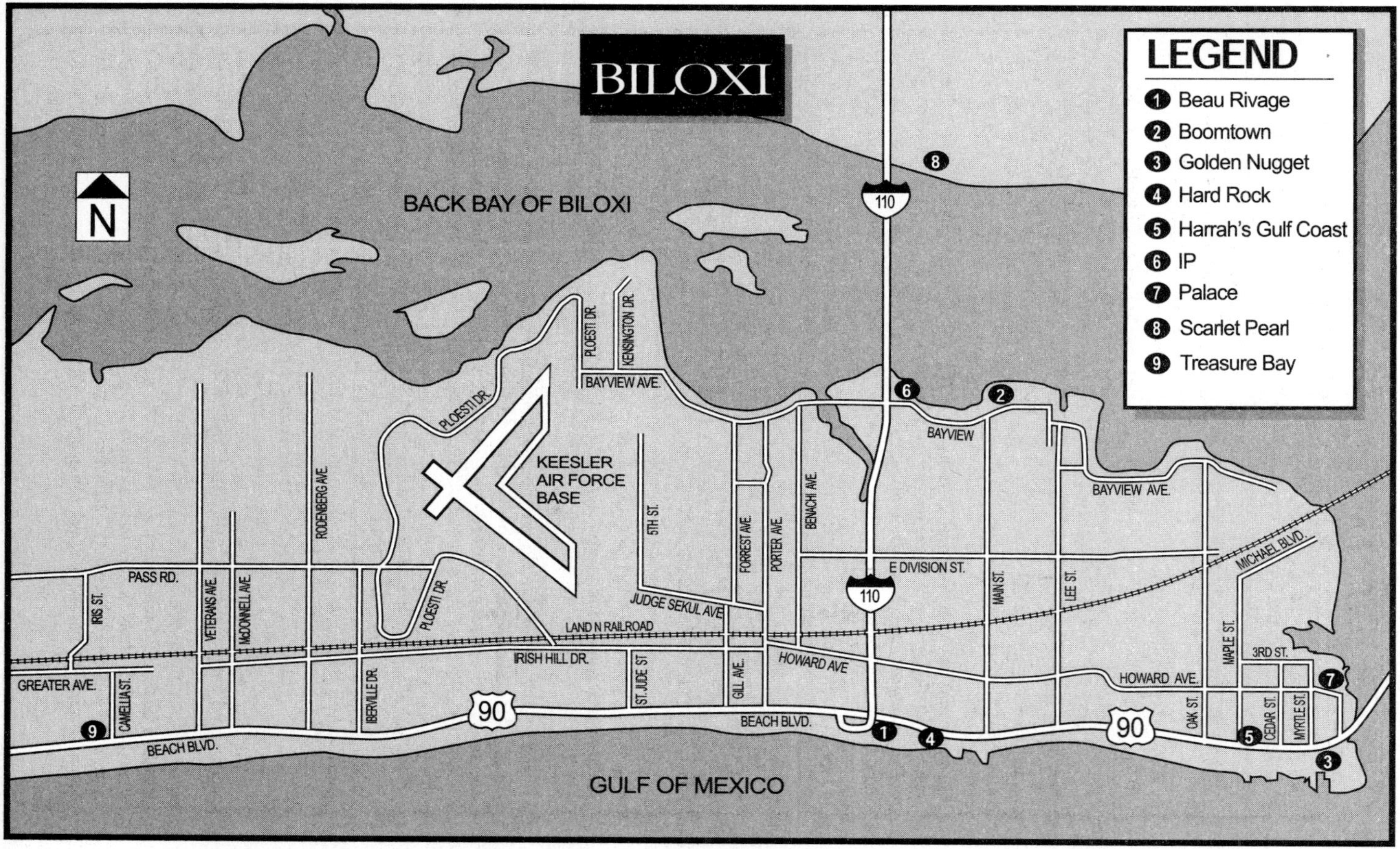
BILOXI
LEGEND
1 Beau Rivage
2 Boomtown
3 Golden Nugget
4 Hard Rock
5 Harrah's Gulf Coast
6 IP
7 Palace
8 Scarlet Pearl
9 Treasure Bay
N
BACK BAY OF BILOXI
110
KEESLER AIR FORCE BASE
PLOESTI DR.
KENSINGTON DR.
BAYVIEW AVE.
BAYVIEW
RODENBERG AVE.
5TH ST.
FORREST AVE.
PORTER AVE.
BENACHI AVE.
E DIVISION ST.
MAIN ST.
LEE ST.
MICHAEL BLVD.
MAPLE ST.
3RD ST.
PASS RD.
IRIS ST.
VETERANS AVE.
McDONNELL AVE.
JUDGE SEKUL AVE
LAND N RAILROAD
IRISH HILL DR.
HOWARD AVE
HOWARD AVE.
GREATER AVE.
CAMELLIA ST.
IBERVILLE DR.
ST. JUDE ST
GILL AVE.
OAK ST.
CEDAR ST.
MYRTLE ST.
90
BEACH BLVD.
GULF OF MEXICO

The Best Places To Play On The Gulf Coast
(Biloxi and Gulfport Only)

Roulette- The house edge on a single-zero wheel cuts the house edge from 5.26% down to a more reasonable 2.70%. Unfortunately, there are no casinos on the Gulf Coast that offer single-zero roulette.

Craps- IP is the most liberal of all gulf coast casinos by offering 20X odds on their craps games. All other casinos offer 10X odds.

Blackjack- All recommendations in this section apply to basic strategy players. You should always look for casinos that pay the standard 3-to-2 for blackjacks. Some casinos might only pay 6-to-5 for blackjack and this increases the casino edge to around 1.5% and they should be avoided.

Gulf Coast casinos offer some decent blackjack games with liberal rules, but all of the casinos hit soft 17, except for Scarlet Pearl, Treasure Bay and $100 tables at Beau Rivage. Hitting soft 17 results in an extra mathematical advantage of .20% for the house.

Treasure Bay offers the best double-deck game, with the following rules: stand on soft 17, double down on any first two cards, re-split any pair (including aces) and doubling allowed after splitting. This works out to a casino edge of just .14%. The minimum bet is $10. Scarlet Pearl and Beau Rivage offer a similar game, with the exception of resplitting aces and the casino edge on these games is .19%. The minimum bet is $50 at Scarlet Pearl and $100 at Beau Rivage.

Hard Rock and the Palace both have the same game as Treasure Bay, except they hit soft 17. which brings the casino edge up to .35%.

Boomtown, Golden Nugget, Harrah's, Scarlet Pearl, IP and Island View have the same rules as Hard Rock and Palace, but they do not allow re-splitting of aces and that game has a casino edge of .40%.

For six-deck shoe games the best places to play are Scarlet Pearl and Treasure Bay where they stand on soft 17, allow doubling down on any first two cards, doubling after splitting and re-splitting of aces. The casino advantage in this game is .34%.

Beau Rivage has an identical game as above but they don't allow resplitting of aces and the edge here is .41% with a $100 minimum bet.

Hard Rock, Island View, the Palace and Scarlet Pearl all offer a similar game, except they hit soft 17 and allow resplitting of aces that brings the casino edge up to .56%.

Video Poker- Some of the best video poker games on the Gulf Coast for lower limit players are 9/7 Double Bonus (99.11%), 9/6 Double Double Bonus (98.98%), 9/6 Jacks or Better (99.54%), 8/5 Bonus Poker (99.17%) and a version of Deuces Wild called Illinois Deuces (98.91%).

Beau Rivage has Illinois Deuces and 9/7 DB for $1.

The Golden Nugget offers a $1 version of Illinois Deuces, plus $1 9/6 Double Double Bonus.

Harrah's has 9/6 Double Double Bonus for 50-cents through $25, plus Illinois Deuces for 50-cents and $25.

The IP offers 9/6 Jacks for quarters, 50 cents and $1. There is also 9/6 Double Double Bonus in denominations from $2 to $100. Illinois Deuces is also offered in denominations from 25-cents through $25.

The Palace has 8/5 Bonus for quarters in 10-play, plus $1 and $2 Illinois Deuces.

Treasure Bay has 50-cent and $1 Bonus Poker, 9/6 Double Double Bonus for 50-cents and $1, 9/7 Double Bonus for 50-cents and $1. They also offer Illinois Deuces for 50-cents and $1.

Harrah's Gulf Coast
265 Beach Boulevard
Biloxi, Mississippi 39530
(228) 436-2946
Website: www.harrahsgulfcoast.com

Toll-Free Number: (800) 946-2946
Rooms: 500 Price Range: $89-$249
Suites: 40 Price Range: $239-$509
Restaurants: 4
Buffets: L- $12.99 (Sat/Sun)
D- $12.99/$17.99 (Fri-Sun)
Casino Size: 31,419 Square Feet
Other Games: SB, MB, B, TCP, PGP, MS
Overnight RV Parking: Free/RV Dump: No
Special Features: Land-based casino. Spa. Starbucks coffeehouse.

IP Casino Resort Spa
850 Bayview Avenue
Biloxi, Mississippi 39530
(228) 436-3000
Website: www.ipbiloxi.com

Toll-Free Number: (888) 946-2847
Rooms: 1,088 Price Range: $69-$229
Suites: 14 Price Range: $119-$475
Restaurants: 6
Buffets: B-$12.99/$20.99 (Sat)
L-$14.99/$20.99 (Sat)
D-$22.99/$23.99 (Wed)/
$25.99 (Fri-Sun)
Casino Size: 81,733 Square Feet
Other Games: P, SB, MB, PGP, LIR
Overnight RV Parking: Free/RV Dump: No
Senior Discounts: Various Mon/Wed if 50+
Special Features: Casino is on a barge. 20x odds on Craps

Palace Casino Resort
158 Howard Avenue
Biloxi, Mississippi 39530
(228) 432-8888
Website: www.palacecasinoresort.com

Toll-Free Number: (800) 725-2239
Rooms: 234 Price Range: $69-$119
Suites: 14 Price Range: $399-$500
Restaurants: 6
Buffets: B- $12.00 (Sat)/$23.00 (Sun)
L-$14.00
D- $23.00/$26.00 (Fri/Sat)
Casino Size: 38,000 Square Feet
Other Games: PGP, MS
Overnight RV Parking: No
Special Features: Land-based casino. 10-slip marina. 100% smoke-free casino.

Scarlet Pearl Casino Resort
9380 Central Avenue
D'Iberville, Mississippi 39540
(228) 392-1889
Website: www.scarletpearlcasino.com

Rooms: 234 Price Range: $79-$199
Suites: 66 Price Range: $259-$489
Restaurants: 5
Buffets:B/L- $19.99
L- $15.99/$13.99 (Fri)
D- $19.99/$27.99(Thu)/
$26.99 (Fri-Sun)
Casino Size: 60,445 Square Feet
Other Games: P, MB, PGP, MS, UTH, SB
Special features: 36-hole mini golf course.

Treasure Bay Casino and Hotel
1980 Beach Boulevard
Biloxi, Mississippi 39531
(228) 385-6000
Website: www.treasurebay.com

Toll-Free Number: (800) 747-2839
Rooms: 234 Price Range: $75-$189
Suites: 14 Price Range: $229-$259
Restaurants: 5
Buffets: B- $9.99 L- $12.49 D- $29.99
Casino Size:28,140 Square Feet
Other Games: PGP, CSP, LIR, MS, SB
Overnight RV Parking: No
Special Features: Land-based casino.

Greenville

Map: **#6** (On the Mississippi River, 121 miles N.W. of Jackson)

Harlow's Casino Resort
4280 Harlows Boulevard
Greenville, Mississippi 38701
(228) 436-4753
Website: www.harlowscasino.com

Toll-Free Number: (866) 524-5825
Rooms: 105 Price Range: $99-$159
Suites: 45 Price Range: $149-$219
Restaurants: 3
Buffets:B/L- $18.99 (Sun)
D- $18.99/$26.99 (Fri-Sun)
Casino Size: 33,000 Square Feet
Other Games: MS, B6, SB
Overnight RV Parking: Free/RV Dump: No
Senior Discount: Various Wed if 50+
Special Features: Land-based casino.

Trop Casino Greenville
199 N. Lakefront Road
Greenville, Mississippi 38701
(662) 334-7711
Website: www.tropgreenville.com

Suites: 30 Price Range: $99-$199
Restaurants: 1
Casino Size: 22,822 Square Feet
Senior Discount: Various Wed if 50+
Overnight RV Parking: Free/RV Dump: No

Gulfport

Map: **#3** (On the Gulf of Mexico, 80 miles E. of New Orleans)

Island View Casino Resort
3300 W. Beach Boulevard
Gulfport, Mississippi 39501
(228) 314-2100
Website: www.islandviewcasino.com

Toll-Free Number: (800) 817-9089
Rooms: 600 Price Range: $99-$199
Restaurants: 5
Buffets: B- $10.99 L- $12.99/$16.99 (Sun)
D- $22.99/$29.99 (Thu-Sat)
Casino Size: 126,000 Square Feet
Other Games: MS, SB
Overnight RV Parking: Free/RV Dump: No
Special Features: Land-based casino.

Lula

Map **#9** (On the Mississippi River, 70 miles S. of Memphis, TN)

Isle of Capri Casino & Hotel - Lula
777 Isle of Capri Parkway
Lula, Mississippi 38644
(610) 241-1627
Website: www.isleofcaprilula.com

Toll-Free Number: (800) 789-5825
Suites: 40 Price Range: Casino Use Only
Restaurants: 3
Buffets: L-$14.99
D- $14.99/$22.99 (Fri)/$26.99 (Sat)
Casino Size: 56,985 Square Feet
Other Games: MS, No TCP
Senior Discount: Various on Wed if 50+
Special Features: 28-space RV Park ($16 per night) Video arcade. Fitness center.

Natchez

Map: **#5** (on the Mississippi River, 102 miles S.W. of Jackson)

Magnolia Bluffs Casino Hotel
7 Roth Hill Road
Natchez, Mississippi 39120
(601) 861-4600
Website: www.magnoliabluffscasino.com

Toll-Free Number: 888-505-5777
Casino Size: 16,032
Restaurants: 3
Buffet: L- $9.00/$12(Sat/Sun)
D- $16/$26.99 (Fri/Sat)
Other Games: P, SB
Senior Discount: Various Wednesdays if 50+
Overnight RV Parking: Yes/RV Dump: No
Special Features: Buffet discount for Players Club members.

Tunica

Map: **#7** (on the Mississippi River, 28 miles S. of Memphis, TN)

1st Jackpot Casino
1450 Jackpot Boulevard
Robinsonville, Mississippi 38664
(662) 357-1500
Website: www.1stjackpot.com

Toll-Free Number: (866) 422-5597
Restaurants: 3
Buffet: B-$9.99 L-$10.99
D-$17.99/$26.99 (Fri/Sat)
Casino Size: 46,535 Square Feet
Other Games: MS, SB, No TCP
Overnight RV Parking: Free/RV Dump: No

Fitz Casino/Hotel
711 Lucky Lane
Robinsonville, Mississippi 38664
(662) 363-5825
Website: www.fitzgeraldstunica.com

Toll-Free Number: (800) 766-5825
Room Reservations: (888) 766-5825
Rooms: 507 Price Range: $69-$119
Suites: 70 Price Range: $99-$169
Restaurants: 3
Buffets: B- $10.99 L- $11.99/$17.99 (Fri/Sat)
D- $19.99/$30.99 (Fri/Sat)
Casino Size: 38,457 Square Feet
Other Games: SB
Overnight RV Parking: Free/RV Dump: No

Gold Strike Casino Resort
100 Casino Center Drive
Robinsonville, Mississippi 38664
(662) 357-1111
Website: www.goldstrike.com

Room Reservations: (888) 245-7829
Rooms: 1,130 Price Range: $79-$159
Suites: 70 Price Range: $179-$239
Restaurants: 4
Buffets: B-$14.99/$22.99 (Sat/Sun) L-$16.99
D-$17.99/$29.99 (Fri/Sat)
Casino Size: 50,000 Square Feet
Other Games: B, MB, CSP, LIR, FCP, MS, SB
Overnight RV Parking: Free/RV Dump: No
Special Features: Affiliated with MGM Resorts.

Hollywood Casino Tunica
1150 Casino Strip Resort Boulevard
Robinsonville, Mississippi 38664
(662) 357-7700
Website: www.hollywoodtunica.com

Toll-Free Number: (800) 871-0711
Rooms: 437 Price Range: $59-$179
Suites: 57 Price Range: $149-$269
Restaurants: 3
Buffets: B- $9.99 L- $10.99
D- $17.99/$26.99 (Fri/Sat)
Casino Size: 55,000 Square Feet
Other Games: P, MS, SB
Overnight RV Parking: Must use RV park
Special Features: Casino features a collection of Hollywood memorabilia. 123-space RV park ($35 per night). Indoor pool and jacuzzi. 18-hole golf course.

Horseshoe Casino & Hotel
1021 Casino Center Drive
Robinsonville, Mississippi 38664
(662) 357-5500
Website: www.horseshoetunica.com

Toll-Free Number: (800) 303-7463
Rooms: 200 Price Range: $65-$370
Suites: 311 Price Range: $129-$479
Restaurants: 5
Buffets: B- $25.99 (Sat/Sun)
L-$16.99 D-$23.99/$29.99 (Fri-Sun)
Casino Size: 63,000 Square Feet
Other Games: P, CSP, LIR, SB
Overnight RV Parking: Free/RV Dump: No
Special Features: Bluesville Nightclub. Starbucks. $2 buffet discount for players club members. 100x odds on craps.

Sam's Town Tunica
1477 Casino Strip Resorts Boulevard
Robinsonville, Mississippi 38664
(662) 363-0711
Website: www.samstowntunica.com

Toll-Free Number: (800) 456-0711
Room Reservations: (800) 946-0711
Rooms: 850 Price Range: $59-$149
Suites: 44 Price Range: $99-$199
Restaurants: 4
Buffet: B- $9.99/$14.99 (Sat/Sun) L- $10.99
D- $17.99/$21.99 (Fri)/$26.99(Sat)
Casino Size: 53,000 Square Feet
Other Games: MS, P, SB
Overnight RV Parking: Free/RV Dump: No
Special Features: 18-hole golf course. 100-space RV park ($25 per night).

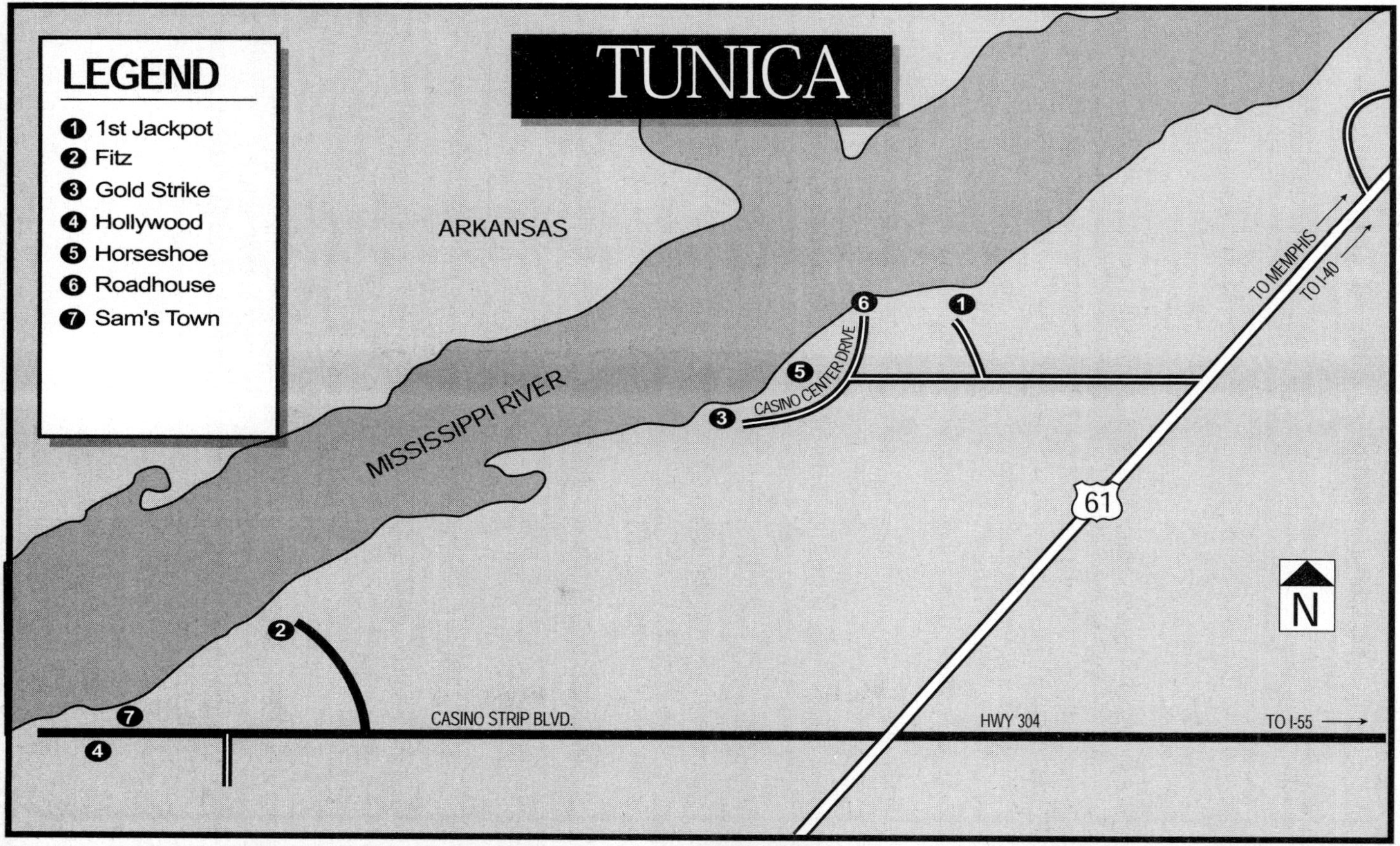
TUNICA
LEGEND
1 1st Jackpot
2 Fitz
3 Gold Strike
4 Hollywood
5 Horseshoe
6 Roadhouse
7 Sam's Town
ARKANSAS
MISSISSIPPI RIVER
CASINO CENTER DRIVE
TO MEMPHIS
TO I-40
61
N
CASINO STRIP BLVD.
HWY 304
TO I-55

The Best Places To Play in Tunica

Roulette - The house edge on a single-zero wheel cuts the house edge from 5.26% down to a more reasonable 2.70%. Unfortunately, there are no casinos in Tunica that offer single-zero roulette

Craps - All casinos offer 20X odds, except for the Horseshoe which offers 100X odds. Three casinos pay triple (rather than double) on 12 in the field, which cuts the house edge on this bet in half from 5.6 percent to 2.8 percent. The casinos offering this slightly better field bet are: Hollywood, Horseshoe and Gold Strike.

Blackjack- All recommendations in this section apply to basic strategy players. You should always look for casinos that pay the standard 3-to-2 for blackjacks. Some casinos might only pay 6-to-5 for blackjack and this increases the casino edge to around 1.5% and they should be avoided.

The blackjack games in Tunica are most similar to those offered in downtown Las Vegas. Most casinos offer both single and double-deck games, as well as six-deck shoe games. That's good. The bad part, however, is that dealers hit soft 17 at all casinos. This results in an extra advantage for the house of .20%.

1st Jackpot, Fitz, Gold Strike, Hollywood, and Roadhouse all offer the same double-deck games which have the following rules: double down on any first two cards, re-split any pair (including aces), and double down after split. This works out to a casino edge of .35%.

Horseshoe and Sam's Town both offer the same double-deck game as mentioned above, but they don't allow aces to be re-split and that brings the casino edge up slightly to .40%

The six-deck games found at 1st Jackpot, Fitz, Gold Strike, Hollywood and Horseshoe all have rules identical to the first two-deck games mentioned above and that results in a casino advantage of .56%. Sam's Town has a game similar, but with a slightly higher casino edge of .63% because they won't allow you to re-split aces.

Video Poker - Some of the best video poker games in Tunica for lower limit players are 9/7 Double Bonus (99.11%), 9/6 Double Double Bonus (98.98%), 9/6 Jacks or Better (99.54%), 8/5 Bonus Poker (99.17%) and a version of Deuces Wild called Illinois Deuces (98.91%).

1st Jackpot has both Illinois Deuces and 9/6 Double Double Bonus for $1.

Gold Strike and Horseshoe both have $1 9/7 Double Bonus and $1 9/6 Double Double Bonus. Horseshoe also offers both of those games in $5 denominations.

Roadhouse has 9/6 Jacks in a 100-coin penny game with a progressive and also the same game with an Illinois Deuces pay table. They also offer 9/7 Double Bonus, as well as 9/6 Double Bonus for both $1 and $5.

Sam's Town offers 9/6 Jacks for quarters, 50-cents and $1.

Vicksburg

Map: **#4** (on the Mississippi River, 44 miles W. of Jackson)

Vicksburg is one of the most historic cities in the South and is most famous for its National Military Park where 17,000 Union soldiers are buried. The Park is America's best-preserved Civil War battlefield and you can take a 16-mile drive through the 1,858-acre Park on a self-guided tour. In the Park you can also see the U.S.S. Cairo, the only salvaged Union Ironclad. Admission to the Park is $15 per car and allows unlimited returns for seven days.

There are about 10 historic homes in Vicksburg that are open to the public for narrated tours. Admission prices are about $10. Some of the homes also function as Bed and Breakfasts and rooms can be rented for overnight stays.

For more information on visiting Vicksburg call the city's Convention and Visitors Bureau at (800) 221-3536, or visit their website at: www.visitvicksburg.com/

Ameristar Casino Hotel - Vicksburg
4116 Washington Street
Vicksburg, Mississippi 39180
(601) 638-1000
Website: www.ameristar.com

Reservation Number: (800) 700-7770
Rooms: 146 Price Range: $89-$199
Suites: 4 Price Range: $129-$219
Restaurants: 4
Buffets: L- $11.95/$24.95 (Sun)
D-$17.95/$29.95 (Fri/Sat)
Casino Size: 72,210 Square Feet
Other Games: P, TCP, MB
Overnight RV Parking: Must use RV park.
Special features: Buffet closed Monday and Tuesday. Buffet discount for players club members. 67 space RV park ($30-$35 per night).

Lady Luck Casino Vicksburg
1380 Warrenton Road
Vicksburg, Mississippi 39180
(610) 241-1623
Website: www.isleofcapricasinos.com

Toll-Free Number: (800) 503-3777
Rooms: 82 Price Range: $69-$120
Suites: 7 Price Range: $99-$219
Restaurants: 3
Buffets: D- $22.99 (Fri/Sat)
Casino Size: 25,000 Square Feet
Overnight RV Parking: Yes
Senior Discount: Various Tues if 50+
Special Features: Affiliated with El Dorado Casinos.

Riverwalk Casino & Hotel
1046 Warrington Road
Vicksburg, Mississippi 39180
(601) 634-0100
Website: www.riverwalkvicksburg.com

Toll-Free Number: (866) 615-9125
Rooms: 80 Price Range: $79-$149
Suites: 4 Price Range: $109-$129
Restaurants: 2
Buffets: L- $19.99 (Sun)
D- $19.99/$22.99 (Thu)/$27.99 (Fri/Sat)
Casino Size: 25,000 square feet
Other Games: SB, No TCP

WaterView Casino And Hotel
3990 Washington Street
Vicksburg, Mississippi 39180
(601) 636-5700
Website: www.waterviewcasino.com

Toll-Free Number: (877) 711-0677
Rooms: 60 Price Range: $79-$129
Suites: 62 Price Range: $129-$229
Restaurants: 3
Buffets: L- $12.95 D- $15.95/$26.95 (Fri/Sat)
Casino Size: 28,000 Square Feet
Other Games: MS
Overnight RV Parking: No

Indian Casinos

Bok Homa Casino
1 Choctaw Road
Heidelberg, Mississippi 39439
Website: www.bokhomacasino.com

Toll-Free Number: (866) 447-3275
Restaurants: 1
Casino Size: 27,000 Square Feet
Other Games: MS, SB
Overnight RV Parking: Free/RV Dump: No
Special Features: Table games open 10am-4am/24 hours (Fri/Sat).

Pearl River Resort
Highway 16 West
Choctaw, Mississippi 39350
(601) 650-1234
Website: www.pearlriverresort.com
Map: **#8** (81 miles N.E. of Jackson)

Toll-Free Number: (800) 557-0711
Room Reservations (866) 447-3275
Silver Star Rooms: 420 Prices: $69-$259
Silver Star Suites: 75 Prices: $199-$780
G. Moon Rooms: 427 Prices: $99-$229
G. Moon Suites: 145 Prices: $329-$879
Restaurants: 12 Liquor: Yes
S. Star Buffet: L- $13.99/$21.99 (Sat/Sun)
D- $17.99/$19.99 (Fri)/$29.99 (Sat)
S. Star Casino Size: 90,000 Square Feet
Games Offered: MB, P, CSP, SB
Overnight RV Parking: Free/RV Dump: No
Special Features: Two separate hotels across the street from each other. Golden Moon has a 9,000-seat events arena. 18-hole golf course. 15-acre water park. Health spa. Beauty salon. Shopping arcade with nine stores.

MISSOURI

In November, 1992 Missouri voters approved a state-wide referendum to allow riverboat gambling. That made Missouri the fifth state to approve this form of gambling.

Since Missouri riverboats are not required to cruise, almost all casinos are built on a barge which gives them the appearance of a land-based building, rather than a riverboat.

Unlike dockside gaming in Mississippi, only Kansas City and St. Louis casinos are open 24 hours. The hours of operation are listed for the other casinos.

Here's information from the Missouri Gaming Commission regarding the payback percentages for each casino's electronic machines for the 12-month period from July 1, 2018 through June 30, 2019:

CASINO	PAYBACK %
Ameristar-St. Charles	91.0
River City	90.6
Hollywood	90.6
Ameristar-K.C.	90.4
Harrah's N.K.C.	90.1
Isle of Capri - Boonville	90.1
Lumiere Place	90.0
Argosy	89.9
Isle - Cape Girardeau	89.7
Lady Luck	89.3
Isle of Capri K.C.	88.9
St. Jo Frontier	88.9
Mark Twain	88.7

These figures reflect the total percentages returned by each casino for all of their electronic machines including slot machines, video poker, video keno, etc.

Unless otherwise noted, all casinos offer: slots, video poker, craps, blackjack and roulette. Optional games include: baccarat (B), mini-baccarat (MB), Caribbean stud poker (CSP), poker (P), three card poker (TCP), pai gow poker (PGP), let it ride (LIR), Spanish 21 (S21), Mississippi stud (MS), ultimate Texas hold 'em (UTH) and four card poker (FCP).

Legislation to legalize sports betting was proposed in 2019, but it did not pass. However, it may be introduced again in 2020.

If you want to order a drink while playing, be aware that Missouri gaming regulations do not allow casinos to provide free alcoholic beverages. The minimum gambling age is 21.

NOTE: If you happen to win a jackpot of $1,200 or more in Missouri, the casino will withhold 4% of your winnings for the Missouri Department of Revenue. If you want to try and get that money refunded, you will be required to file a state income tax return and, depending on the details of your return, you may get some of the money returned to you. The $1,200 threshold would also apply to any cash prizes won in casino drawings or tournaments.

For more information on visiting Missouri call the state's Travel Center at (800) 877-1234 or go to: www.visitmo.com.

Boonville

Map: **#5** (100 miles E. of Kansas City)

Isle of Capri Casino - Boonville
100 Isle of Capri Boulevard
Boonville, Missouri 65233
(610) 241-1625
Website: www.isleofcapriboonville.com

Toll-Free Number: (800) 843-4753
Rooms: 114 Price Range: $99-$159
Suites: 26 Price Range: $129-$199
Restaurants: 3
Buffets: B- $17.99 (Sun)
L- $12.99/$17.99 (Sun)
D- $18.99/$21.99 (Fri-Sat)
Hours: 8am-4:30am/24 Hours (Fri-Sat)
Casino Size: 28,000 Square Feet
Other Games: MB, LIR
Overnight RV Parking: No
Special Features: 600-passenger barge on the Missouri River. Affiliated with Eldorado Resorts.

Cape Girardeau

Map: **#7** (115 miles S. of St. Louis)

Isle of Capri Casino - Cape Girardeau
777 N. Main Street
Cape Girardeau, Missouri 63701
(800) 843-4753
Website: www.isleofcapricasino.com

Restaurants: 3
Casino Hours: 8am-4am/24 hours (Fri-Sat)
Other Games: B, MS, TCP, UTH
Overnight RV Parking: Free (Must check in with valet)/ RV Dump: No

Caruthersville

Map: **#4** (200 miles S. of St. Louis)

Lady Luck Caruthersville
777 East Third Street
Caruthersville, Missouri 63830
(573) 333-6000
Website: www.ladyluckcaruthersville.com

Toll-Free Number (800) 679-4945
Restaurants: 2
Hours: 9am-3am/24 hours (Fri-Sun)
Casino Size: 21,400 Square Feet
Other Games: MS, TCP
Overnight RV Parking: Free/RV Dump: Free
Special Features: 875-passenger sternwheeler on the Mississippi River. 27-space RV park ($40 per night); discounts for Good Sam and Fan Club members. Affiliated with Eldorado Resorts.

Kansas City

Map: **#1**

Ameristar Casino Hotel Kansas City
3200 North Ameristar Drive
Kansas City, Missouri 64161
(816) 414-7000
Website: www.ameristarkansascity.com

Toll-Free Number: (800) 499-4961
Rooms: 142 Price Range: $109-$259
Suites: 42 Price Range: $169-$529
Restaurants: 6
Buffets: B-$19.99 (Sun)
L-$15.99 (Wed/Fri/Sat)/$10.99 (Thu)
D- $19.99(Wed)/$14.99 (Thu)/
$39.99 (Fri/Sat)/$26.99 (Sun)
Casino Size: 140,000 Square Feet
Other Games: MB, P, LIR, TCP,
FCP, MS, PGP
Overnight RV Parking: Free/RV Dump: No
Special Features: 4,000-passenger barge adjacent to the Missouri River. Food court with four fast food outlets. 18-screen movie theater. 1,332-seat event center. Family arcade. Childcare center. Affiliated with Boyd Gaming.

Argosy Casino Hotel & Spa
777 N.W. Argosy Parkway
Riverside, Missouri 64150
(816) 746-3100
Website: www.argosykansascity.com

Toll-Free Number: (800) 270-7711
Rooms: 250 Price Range: $139-$349
Suites: 8 Price Range: $309-$649
Restaurants: 6
Buffets: B- $18.99 (Sat/Sun)
L- $10.99/$15.99 (Wed-Fri)
D- $15.99/$19.99 (Wed-Fri/Sun)/
$39.99 (Sat)
Casino Size: 62,000 Square Feet
Other Games: MB, P. PGP, MS, TCP
Overnight RV Parking: No
Special Features: 4,675-passenger single-deck Mediterranean-themed barge adjacent to the Missouri River.

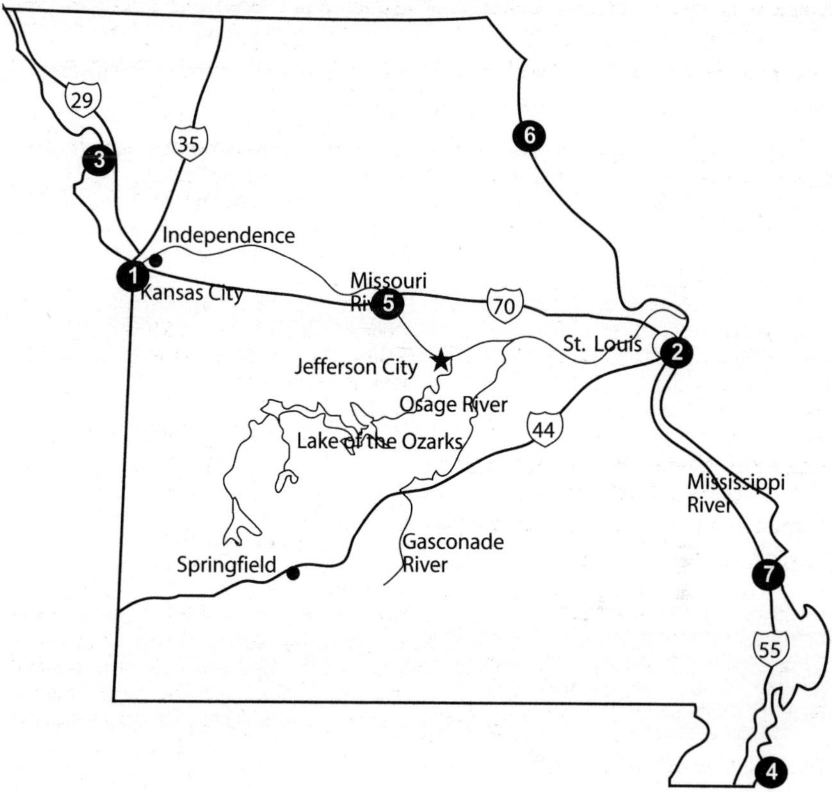

Harrah's North Kansas City
One Riverboat Drive
N. Kansas City, Missouri 64116
(816) 472-7777
Website: www.caesars.com

Toll-Free Number: (800) 427-7247
Rooms: 350 Price Range: $89-$249
Suites: 42 Price Range: $119-$279
Restaurants: 5
Buffets: B- $18.99 (Sat/Sun)
L- $18.99 (Sat/Sun)
D- $19.99/$15.99 (Tue)/$29.99 (Fri)/ $39.99 (Sat)/$26.99 (Sun)
Casino Size: 63,300 Square Feet
Other Games: P, MB, PGP
Overnight RV Parking: Free/RV Dump: No
Special Features: 1,700-passenger two-deck barge adjacent to the Missouri River. Casino closed 5am-8am Wednesdays. 100x odds on craps. Buffet discount for Players Club members.

Isle of Capri Casino - Kansas City
1800 E. Front Street
Kansas City, Missouri 64120
(816) 855-7777
Website: www.isleofcapricasinos.com

Toll-Free Number: (800) 843-4753
Restaurants: 2
Casino Size: 30,000 Square Feet
Other Games: UTH
Overnight RV Parking: Free/RV Dump: No
Special Features: 2,000-passenger two-deck Caribbean-themed barge docked in a man-made lake fed by the Missouri River. Closed Wednesdays from 5am to 6am. Affiliated with Eldorado Resorts.

La Grange

Map: **#6** (150 miles N.W. of St. Louis)

Mark Twain Casino
104 Pierce Street
La Grange, Missouri 63448
(573) 655-4770
Website: www.marktwaincasinolagrange.com

Toll-Free Number: (866) 454-5825
Restaurants: 2
Hours: 8am-2am/4am (Fri/Sat)
Casino Size: 18,000 Square Feet
Other Games: UTH
Overnight RV Parking: Must use RV park
Special Features: 600-passenger barge on the Mississippi River. 8-space RV park ($25 per night). Gift shop.

St. Joseph

Map: **#3** (55 miles N. of Kansas City)

St. Jo Frontier Casino
777 Winners Circle
St. Joseph, Missouri 64505
(816) 279-5514
Website: www.stjofrontiercasino.com

Toll-Free Number: (800) 888-2946
Restaurants: 2
Buffets: L- $14.99 (Sat/Sun)
D- $15.99/$17.99 (Wed)/
$21.99 (Thu/Sat)/$19.99 (Fri)
Hours: 8am-2am/5am (Fri/Sat)
Casino Size: 18,000 Square Feet
Other Games: MS, UTH
Overnight RV Parking: Free/RV Dump: No
Senior Discount: Various Mondays if 50+
Special Features: Table games open at noon (10:00 am Sat/Sun). Casino is on a barge in a moat adjacent to the Missouri River. Gift shop.

St. Louis

Map: **#2**

In addition to the four St. Louis-area casinos listed below, the Casino Queen in E. St. Louis, Illinois is also a nearby casino. It is located on the other side of the Mississippi river from downtown St. Louis.

Ameristar Casino St. Charles
1 Ameristar Boulevard
St. Charles, Missouri 63301
(636) 949-7777
Website: www.ameristarstcharles.com

Toll-Free Number: (800) 325-7777
Rooms: 400 Price Range: $149-$299
Restaurants: 7
Buffets: L-$16.95/$23.95 (Sat-Sun)
D-$21.95/$27.25 (Thu)/
$29.95 (Fri/Sat)/$24.95 (Sun)
Casino Size: 130,000 Square Feet
Other Games: MB, P, FCP, LIR, TCP,
PGP, UTH, MS
Overnight RV Parking: No
Senior Discount: Various Wednesday if 50+
Special Features: 2,000-passenger barge on the Missouri River. $2 buffet discount for Players Club members. Affiliated with Boyd Gaming.

Hollywood Casino St. Louis
777 Casino Center Drive
Maryland Heights, Missouri 63043
(314) 770-8100
Website: www.hollywoodcasinostlouis.com

Toll-Free Number: (855) 785-4263
Rooms: 455 Price Range: $119-$279
Suites: 47 Price Range: $169-$389
Restaurants: 6
Buffets: B- $19.99 (Sat/Sun)
L- $13.99/$15.99 (Mon)/
$19.99 (Sat/Sun)
D- $21.99 (Sun/Thu)$17.99 (Wed)/
$27.99 (Fri)/$25.99 (Sat)
Casino Size: 120,000 Square Feet
Other Games: B, MB, P, PGP, FCP, MS, UTH
Overnight RV Parking: Free/RV Dump: No
Senior Discount: Various Monday if 50+
Special Features: Two 3,200-passenger barges on the Missouri River. Affiliated with Penn National Gaming.

Lumière Place Casino Resort
999 North Second Street
St. Louis, Missouri 63102
(314) 881-7777
Website: www.lumiereplace.com

Toll-Free Number: (877) 450-7711
Suites: 300 Price Range: $139-$299
Restaurants: 5
Buffets: L- $14.95 D- $24.95
Casino Size: 75,000 Square Feet
Other Games: B, PGP, TCP, P, UTH
Special Features: 2,500-passenger barge floating in a man-made canal 700 feet from the Mississippi River. Property also features 200-room Four Seasons Hotel. Closed 6am-8am Wednesdays. Affiliated with Eldorado Resorts.

River City Casino & Hotel
777 River City Casino Boulevard
St. Louis, Missouri 63125
(314)388-7777
Website: www.rivercity.com

Toll-Free Number: (888)578-7289
Rooms: 186 Price Range: $129-$269
Suites: 7 Price Range: $169-$299
Restaurants: 4 Liquor: Yes
Buffets: L- $15.99/$21.95 (Sat/Sun)
D- $21.95/$34.95 (Fri/Sat)
Casino Hours: 24 hours daily
Casino Size: 90,000 Square Feet
Other Games: MB, SIC, TCP
Overnight RV Parking: No
Senior Discounts: Various Tuesdays if 50+
Special Features: $2 buffet discount for Players Club members.

MONTANA

Montana law permits bars and taverns to have up to 20 video gaming devices that play video poker, video keno, or video bingo.

The maximum bet on these machines is $2 and the maximum payout is limited to $800. Montana gaming regulations require these machines to return a minimum of 80%.

All of Montana's Indian casinos offer Class II video gaming devices that look like slot machines, but are actually bingo games and the spinning reels are for "entertainment purposes only."

The maximum bet on the machines in Indian casinos is $5 and the maximum payout is capped at $1,500. According to Montana's Gambling Control Division, there are no minimum payback percentages required for gaming machines on Indian reservations. The minimum gambling age is 18.

Sports betting was legalized for Montana in May 2019 and it is expected to be offered at some casinos by early 2020.

For Montana tourism information call (800) 847-4868 or go to: www.visitmt.com

Apsaalooke Nights Casino
71 Heritage Road
Crow Agency, Montana 59022
(406) 638-4440
Map: **#2** (60 miles S.E. of Billings on I-90)

Casino Hours: 10am-12am Daily
Casino Size: 4,000-square fee

Charging Horse Casino
1/2 US-212
Lame Deer, Montana 59043
(406) 477-6677
Map: **#3** (90 miles S.E. of Billings on Hwy. 212)

Restaurants: 1 Liquor: No
Hours: 8am-2am Daily
Overnight RV Parking: Free/RV Dump: No

Fort Belknap Casino
958 Agency Main Street
Harlem, Montana 59526
(406) 353-2235
Website: www.fortbelknapcasino.com
Map: **#8** (155 miles N.E of Great Falls)

Hours: 10am - 2am Daily

Glacier Peaks Casino
416 W Central Avenue
Browning, Montana 59417
(406) 338-2400
Website: www.glacierpeakscasino.com
Map: **#6** (140 miles N.W of Great Falls)

Toll-Free: (888) 848-8188
Rooms: 86 Price Range: $170-$185
Suites:14 Price Range: $198-$210
Restaurants: 1 Snack Bar Liquor: No
Hours: 8:00am-2:00am Daily
Overnight RV Parking: Free, check in with security first/RV Dump: Free

Gray Wolf Peak Casino
20750 US Highway 93 North
Missoula, Montana 59808
(406) 726-3778
Website: www.graywolfpeakcasino.net
Map: **#7**

Hours: 8am-3am/24 hours (Thu-Sat)
Restaurants: 2
Overnight RV Parking: Free/RV Dump: Free

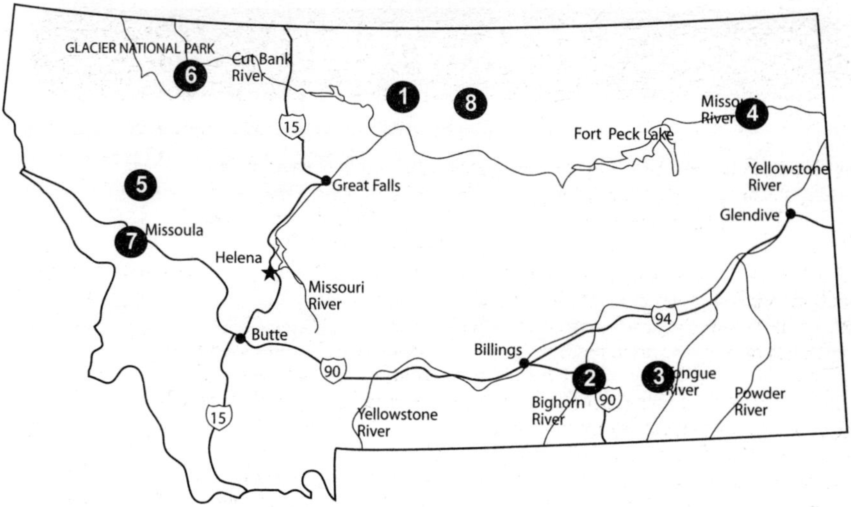

KwaTaqNuk Casino Resort
49708 Highway 93 East
Polson, Montana 59860
(406) 883-3636
Website: www.kwataqnuk.com
Map: **#5** (65 miles N. Of Missoula)

Room Reservations: (800) 882-6363
Rooms: 111 Price Range: $96-$145
Restaurants: 1 Liquor: Yes
Hours: 8am-3am daily
Overnight RV Parking: Free/RV Dump: Free
Special Features: Two casinos, one is non-smoking.

Northern Winz Hotel & Casino
11275 US Highway 87
Box Elder, Montana 59521
(406) 395-5420
Map: **#1** (90 miles N.E. of Great Falls)

Rooms: 10 Price Range: $59-$89
Restaurants: 2 Liquor: No
Overnight RV Parking: No
Casino Size: 10,000 sq ft
Hours: 10am-2am/24 hour (Fri/Sat)

Northern Winz II
Agency Road
Box Elder, Montana 59521
(406) 395-4863
Map: **#1** (90 miles N.E. of Great Falls)

Restaurants: 1 Liquor: No
Overnight RV Parking: No/RV Dump: No

Silver Wolf Casino
300 Highway 25 East
Wolf Point, Montana 59201
(406) 653-3475
Map: **#4** (180 miles N.E of Billings)

Restaurants: 1 Snack Bar Liquor: No
Hours: 10am-12am/2am (Fri-Sat)
Overnight RV Parking: Free/RV Dump: No

NEVADA

All Nevada casinos are open 24 hours and, unless otherwise noted, offer: slots, video poker, craps, blackjack, and roulette. The minimum gambling age is 21.

For Nevada tourism information call (800) 237-0774 or go to: www.travelnevada.com.

Other games in the casino listings include: sports book (SB), race book (RB), Spanish 21 (S21), baccarat (B), mini-baccarat (MB), pai gow (PG), poker (P), pai gow poker (PGP), Caribbean stud poker (CSP), crazy 4 poker (C4P), let it ride (LIR), three-card poker (TCP), Mississippi stud (MS), ultimate Texas hold'em (UTH), Texas hold'em bonus (THB), four card poker (FCP), sic bo (SIC), keno (K), big 6 wheel (B6) and bingo (BG).

Amargosa Valley

Map Location: **#8** (91 miles N.W. of Las Vegas on Hwy. 95)

Longstreet Inn Casino & RV Resort
4400 South Highway 373
Amargosa Valley, Nevada 89020
(775) 372-1777
Website: www.longstreetcasino.com

Rooms: 59 Price Range: $99-$119
Restaurants: 1
Overnight RV Parking: No
Senior Discount: 10% off food if 55+
Other Games: Machines only
Special Features: 51-space RV Park ($30 per night). 24-hour convenience store.

Battle Mountain

Map Location: **#9** (215 mile N.E. of Reno on I-80)

Owl Club Casino & Restaurant
72 E. Front Street
Battle Mountain, Nevada 89820
(775) 635-2444

Restaurants: 1
Casino Size: 840 Square Feet
Other Games: No table games
Overnight RV Parking: No

Beatty

Map Location: **#10** (120 miles N.W. of Las Vegas on Hwy. 95)

Stagecoach Hotel & Casino
900 East Highway 95
Beatty, Nevada 89003
(775) 553-2419

Reservation Number: (800) 424-4946
Rooms: 80 Price Range: $58-$78
Restaurants: 2 (1 open 24 hours)
Casino Size: 8,810 Square Feet
Other Games: SB, RB, P(Wed-Sat), B6, No Roulette
Overnight RV Parking: Free/RV Dump: No
Special Features: Denny's restaurant. Swimming pool and Jacuzzi. Seven miles from Rhyolite ghost town.

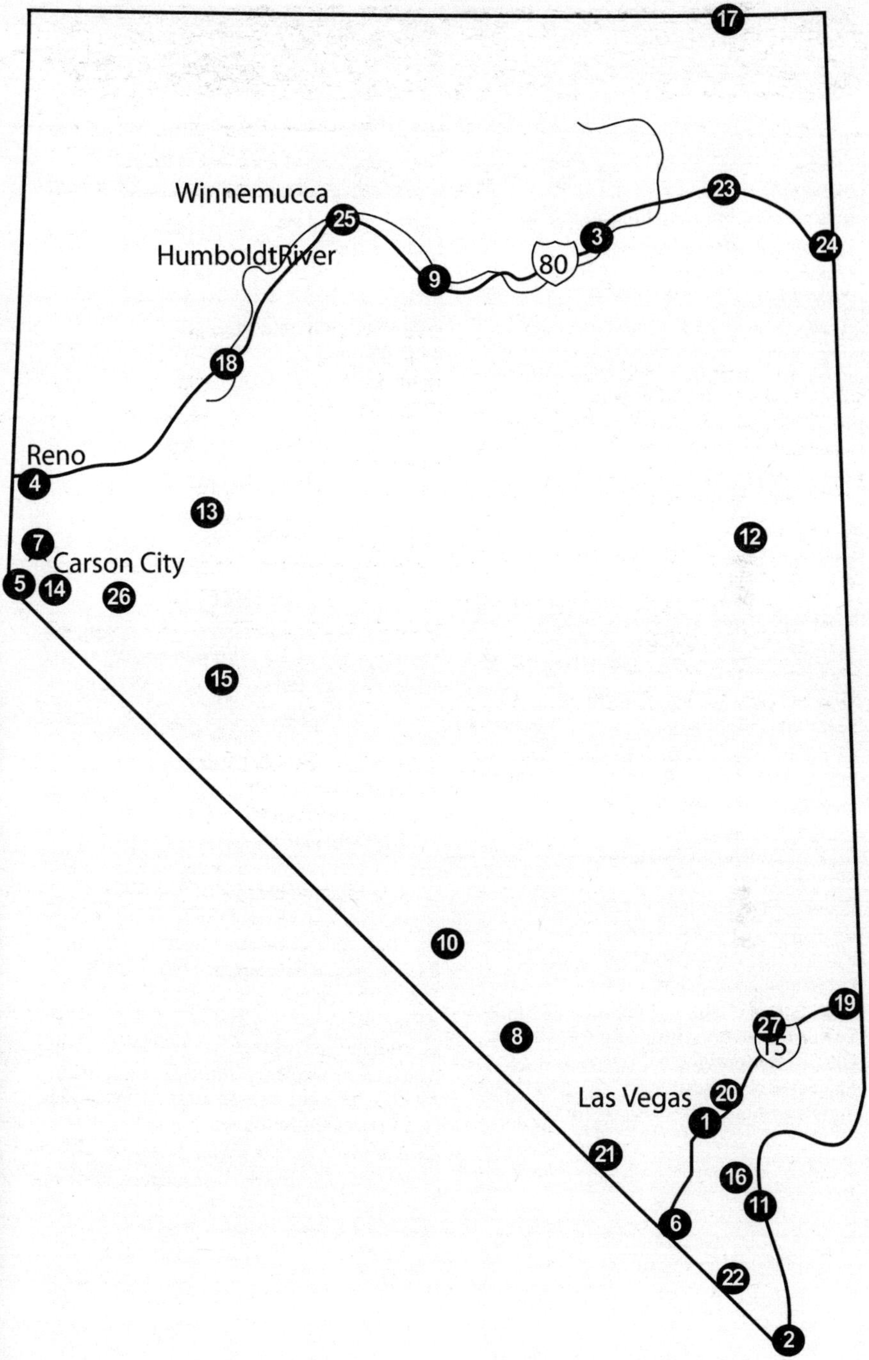
17
Winnemucca
25
HumboldtRiver
9
80
3
23
24
18
Reno
4
13
12
7
Carson City
5
14
26
15
10
19
27
8
15
Las Vegas
20
1
21
16
11
6
22
2

Boulder City

Map Location: **#11** (22 miles S.E. of Las Vegas on Hwy. 93)

Hoover Dam Lodge Hotel & Casino
18000 US Highway 93
Boulder City, Nevada 89005
(702) 293-5000
Website: www.hooverdamlodge.com

Reservation Number: (800) 245-6380
Rooms: 360 Price Range: $80-$125
Suites: 18 Price Range: $109-$160
Restaurants: 3 (1 open 24 hours)
Casino Size: 17,276 Square Feet
Games Offered: SB, no table games
Overnight RV Parking: No

Carson City

Map Location: **#7** (32 miles S. of Reno on Hwy. 395)

Carson Nugget Casino Hotel
507 N. Carson Street
Carson City, Nevada 89701
(775) 882-1626
Website: www.ccnugget.com

Rooms: 81 Price Range: $62-$89
Restaurants: 3 (1 open 24 hours)
Casino Size: 28,930 Square Feet
Other Games: SB, RB, P, TCP, K
Overnight RV Parking: Free/RV Dump: No
Special Features: Rare gold display. Free supervised childcare center. Rooms are three blocks away from casino.

Casino Fandango
3800 S. Carson Street
Carson City, Nevada 89701
(775) 885-7000
Website: www.casinofandango.com

Restaurants: 5
Casino Size: 42,943 Square Feet
Buffets: L-$12.99(Wed-Fri)/$15.99 (Sat/Sun)
D- $12.99 (Wed/Thu/Sun)/
$21.99 (Fri/Sat)
Other Games: SB, Race Book, Pai Gow Poker, Three Card Poker, Keno
Overnight RV Parking: Free/RV Dump: No
Senior Discount: Various discounts if 55+
Special Features: Buffet discount for players club members.

Gold Dust West - Carson City
2171 East William Street
Carson City, Nevada 89701
(775) 885-9000
Website: www.gdwcasino.com

Toll-Free Number: (877) 519-5567
Rooms: 120 Price Range: $109-$125
Suites: 22 Price Range: $125-$155
Restaurants: 2 (1 open 24 hours)
Casino Size: 18,100 Square Feet
Other Games: SB, RB, TCP, No Roulette
Overnight RV Parking: Must use RV park
Senior Discount: Various Wedif 50+
Special Features: 48-space RV park ($36-$39). 32-lane bowling center.

Max Casino Carson City
900 S. Carson Street
Carson City, Nevada 89701
(775) 883-0900
Website: www.maxcasinocc.com

Restaurants: 2
Casino Size: 12,750 Square Feet
Other Games: SB, RB, K, No Craps/Roulette
Overnight RV Parking: No
Senior Discounts: Various Wed if 50+

Elko

Map Location: **#3** (289 miles N.E. of Reno on I-80)

Commercial Casino
345 4th Street
Elko, Nevada 89801
(775) 738-3181
Website: www.northernstarcasinos.com

Toll-Free Number: (800) 648-2345
Casino Size: 6,744 Square Feet
Other Games: No table games
Overnight RV Parking: Yes/RV Dump: No
Special Features: Oldest continually operating casino in Nevada. 10-foot-tall stuffed polar bear in casino. Large gunfighter art collection.

Gold Dust West - Elko
1660 Mountain City Highway
Elko, Nevada 89801
(775) 777-7500
Website: www.gdwcasino.com

Restaurants: 2
Casino Size: 12,000 Square Feet
Other Games: SB, RB, TCP, No roulette
Senior Discount: Various Wed if 50+

Red Lion Hotel & Casino
2065 Idaho Street
Elko, Nevada 89801
(775) 738-2111
Website: www.redlionhotelelko.com

Rooms: 222 Price Range: $95-$159
Restaurants: 2 (1 open 24 hours)
Casino Size: 17,850 Square Feet
Other Games: SB, RB, P, TCP
Overnight RV Parking: No
Special Features: Starbucks.

Stockmen's Hotel & Casino
340 Commercial Street
Elko, Nevada 89801
(775) 738-5141
Website: www.northernstarcasinos.com

Reservation Number: (800) 648-2345
Rooms: 141 Price Range: $80-$95
Suites: 8 Price Range: $95-$195
Restaurants: 2
Casino Size: 8,441 Square Feet
Other Games: SB, RB, TCP
Overnight RV Parking: Free/RV Dump: No
Senior Discount: Food discount if 65 or older.
Special Features: 24-hour shuttle service.

Ely

Map Location: **#12** (317 miles E. of Reno on Hwy. 50)

Hotel Nevada & Gambling Hall
501 Aultman Street
Ely, Nevada 89301
(775) 289-6665
Website: www.hotelnevada.com

Rooms: 45 Price Range: $64-$125
Restaurants: 1 (open 24 hours)
Casino Size: 3,730 Square Feet
Other Games: No Table Games
Overnight RV Parking: Free/RV Dump: No
Special Features: Historical display of mining, ranching and railroad artifacts.

Fallon

Map Location: **#13** (61 miles E. of Reno on Hwy. 50)

Bonanza Inn & Casino
855 W. Williams Avenue
Fallon, Nevada 89406
(775) 423-6031

Rooms: 74 Price Range: $50-$65
Restaurants: 1
Casino Size: 5,830 Square Feet
Other Games: SB, RB, K, No Table Games
Overnight RV Parking: $20 per night

Stockman's Casino
1560 W. Williams Avenue
Fallon, Nevada 89406
(775) 423-2117
Website: www.stockmanscasino.com

Restaurants: 2 (1 open 24 hours)
Casino Size: 8,614 Square Feet
Other Games: SB, RB, BJ, K, no craps/roulette
Senior Discount: Various on Tue if 55+
Overnight RV Parking: Free in back

Gardnerville

Map Location: **#14** (45 miles S. of Reno on Hwy. 395)

Topaz Lodge & Casino
1979 Highway 395 South
Gardnerville, Nevada 89410
(775) 266-3338
Website: www.topazlodge.com

Rooms: 59 Price Range: $79-$125
Restaurants: 2 (1 open 24 hours)
Casino Size: 12,800 Square Feet
Other Games: SB, BG, TCP, no craps/roulette
Overnight RV Parking: Must use RV park
Special Features: Hotel is Super 8. 60-space RV park ($22/night).

Hawthorne

Map Location: **#15** (138 miles S.E. of Reno on Hwy. 95)

El Capitan Resort Casino
540 F Street
Hawthorne, Nevada 89415
(775) 945-3321
Website: www.northernstarcasinos.com

Toll Free: (800) 922-2311
Rooms: 103 Price Range: $88-$118
Restaurants: 1 (open 24 hours)
Casino Size: 12,860 Square Feet
Other Games: SB, RB, no table games
Overnight RV Parking: Free/RV Dump: Free

Henderson

Map Location: **#16** (15 miles S.E. of Las Vegas on Hwy. 93)

Club Fortune Casino
725 S Racetrack Drive
Henderson, Nevada 89015
(702) 566-5555
Website: www.clubfortunecasino.com

Restaurants: 1
Casino Size: 11,953
Other Games: P
Special Features: $1.99 breakfast special everyday from 6pm-11am. $3.49 lunch special Monday-Friday from 12pm-4pm.

Eldorado Casino
140 Water Street
Henderson, Nevada 89015
(702) 564-1811
Website: www.eldoradocasino.com

Restaurants: 1
Casino Size: 17,756 Square Feet
Other Games: SB, K, BG, no table games
Overnight RV Parking: No
Senior Discount: Various Wed if 50+

Fiesta Henderson Casino Hotel
777 West Lake Mead Parkway
Henderson, Nevada 89015
(702) 558-7000
Website: www.fiestahendersonlasvegas.com

Toll-Free Number: (866) 469-7666
Rooms: 224 Price Range: $39-$149
Suites: 8 Price Range: $135-$259
Restaurants: 4 (1 open 24 hours)
Buffets: B- $15.99 (Sat/Sun)
L- $12.99/$15.99 (Sun) D- $15.99
Casino Size: 73,450 Square Feet
Other Games: SB, RB, PGP, K, BG
Overnight RV Parking: No
Senior Discount: Join Fun Club if 50+
Special Features: Buffet Discount with players club card.

Green Valley Ranch Resort Spa Casino
2300 Paseo Verde Parkway
Henderson, Nevada 89052
(702) 617-7777
Website: www.greenvalleyranchresort.com

Room Reservations: (866) 782-9487
Rooms: 200 Price Range: $80-$280
Suites: 45 Price Range: $180-$750
Restaurants: 8 (1 open 24 hours)
Buffets: B-$12.99/$22.99 (Sun) L-$16.99
D- $22.99/$44.99 (Fri)/$25.99 (Sat)
Casino Size: 134,681 Square Feet
Other Games: SB, RB, B, MB, CSP,
PGP, LIR, TCP
Senior Discount: Various Wed if 50+
Overnight RV Parking: No
Special Features: Buffet discount for Players Club members.

Jokers Wild
920 N. Boulder Highway
Henderson, Nevada 89011
(702) 564-8100
Website: www.jokerswildcasino.com

Restaurants: 2 (1 open 24 hours)
Casino Size: 23,698 Square Feet
Other Games: SB, K
Overnight RV Parking: No
Senior Discount: Various Tue/Wed if 55+
Special Features: Affiliated with Boyd Gaming. $1 craps and $3 blackjack

M Resort • Spa • Casino
12300 Las Vegas Blvd South
Henderson, Nevada 89044
(702) 797-1000
Website: www.themresort.com

Toll-free Number: (877) 673-7678
Rooms: 355 Price Range: $125-$265
Suites: 35 Price Range: $149-$599
Restaurants: 7 (1 open 24 hours)
Buffet: B- $24.99 (Sat/Sun)
L- $17.99/$24.99 (Fri)
D- $24.99/$41.99 (Fri-Sun)
Casino Size: 97,357 Square Feet
Other Games: RB, SB, PGP, MB, LIR, TCP
Senior Discount: Various Tue if 50+

Railroad Pass Hotel & Casino
2800 S. Boulder Highway
Henderson, Nevada 89002
(702) 294-5000
Website: www.railroadpass.com

Toll-Free Number: (800) 654-0877
Rooms: 100 Price Range: $69-$99
Suites: 20 Price Range: $119-$139
Restaurants: 3 (1 open 24 hours)
Buffets: B-$8.99/$10.99 (Sat/Sun)
L-$7.99
D-$10/$19.99 (Fri)/$12.99(Sat/Sun)
Casino Size: 12,803 Square Feet
Other Games: TCP, SB, RB
Overnight RV Parking: No

Skyline Hotel & Casino
1741 N. Boulder Highway
Henderson, Nevada 89011
(702) 565-9116
Website:www.skylinerestaurantandcasino.com

Rooms: 50 Price Range $69-$169
Restaurants: 1
Casino Size: 4,000 Square Feet
Other Games: BJ, P (Mon-Fri starting at 6pm),
SB, RB, no craps/roulette
Overnight RV Parking: No

Sunset Station Hotel and Casino
1301 W. Sunset Road
Henderson, Nevada 89014
(702) 547-7777
Website: www.sunsetstation.com

Toll-Free Number: (888) 319-4655
Rooms: 448 Price Range: $69-$169
Suites: 18 Price Range: $99-$369
Restaurants: 7 (1 open 24 hours)
Buffets: B-$10.99/$16.99 (Sun)
L-$13.99 D-$16.99
Casino Size: 89,443 Square Feet
Other Games: SB, RB, MB, PGP, K, BG
Overnight RV Parking: No
Senior Discount: Various Wedif 50+
Special Features: 13-screen movie theater. Kid's Quest childcare center. Food Court with five fast food stations. 72-lane Bowling Alley. Buffet discount for Players Club members.

Jackpot

Map Location: **#17** (Just S. of the Idaho border on Hwy. 93)

Barton's Club 93
1002 Highway 93
Jackpot, Nevada 89825
(775) 755-2341
Website: www.bartonsclub93.com

Toll-Free Number: (800) 258-2937
Rooms: 98 Price Range: $65-$85
Suites: 4 Price Range: $81-$151
Restaurants: 2
Buffets: B- $13.93 (Sat/Sun)
D- $20.93 (Fri/Sat)
Casino Size: 12,550 Square Feet
Other Games: LIR, PGP
Overnight RV Parking: No

Cactus Pete's Resort Casino
1385 Highway 93
Jackpot, Nevada 89825
(775) 755-2321
Website: www.cactuspetes.com

Rooms: 272 Price Range: $89-$199
Suites: 28 Price Range: $169-$219
Restaurants: 3 (1 open 24 hours)
Buffets: Brunch-$17.95 (Sun)
D- $17.95/$29.95 (Fri/Sat)
Casino Size: 24,727 Square Feet
Other Games: SB, RB, P, PGP, TCP, LIR, K
Overnight RV Parking: Must use RV park
Special Features: 91-space RV park ($20-$26 per night). 18-hole golf course.

Horseshu Hotel & Casino
1220 Highway 93
Jackpot, Nevada 89825
(775) 755-2321
Website: www.cactuspetes.com

Rooms: 110 Price Range: $59-$89
Suites: 10 Price Range: $79-$119
Restaurants: 1
Casino Size: 3,377 Square Feet
Other Games: no table games
Overnight RV Parking: No

Jean

Map Location: **#6** (22 miles S.W. of Las Vegas on I-15; 12 miles from the California border)

Terrible's Road House - Jean
1 Main Street
Jean, Nevada 89019
(702) 477-5000
Website: www.stopatjean.com

Rooms: 800 Price Range: $35-$66
Suites: 13 Price Range: $59-$119
Restaurants: 3 (1 open 24 hours)
Casino Size: 37,006 Square Feet
Other Games: MB, no craps
Overnight RV Parking: No
Special Features: Table games are open from 11am-3am. Denny's restaurant.

Lake Tahoe

Map Location: **#5** (directly on the Nevada/California border; 98 miles northeast of Sacramento and 58 miles southwest of Reno).

The area is best known for its many recreational activities with skiing in the winter and water sports in the summer. Lake Tahoe Airport is located at the south end of the basin. The next closest airport is in Reno with regularly scheduled shuttle service by bus.

Incline Village and Crystal Bay are on the north shore of Lake Tahoe, while Stateline is located on the south shore. For South Lake Tahoe information call the Lake Tahoe Visitors Authority at (800) 288-2463 and for North Lake Tahoe information call the Incline Village/Crystal Bay Convention & Visitors Authority at (800) 468-2463.

Here's information, as supplied by Nevada's State Gaming Control Board, showing the slot machine payback percentages for all of the south shore casinos for the fiscal year beginning July 1, 2018 and ending June 30, 2019:

Denomination	Payback %
1¢ Slots	88.94
5¢ Slots	N/A
25¢ Slots	91.24
$1 Slots	92.55
All Slots	93.33

And here's that same information for the north shore casinos:

Denomination	Payback %
1¢ Slots	92.81
5¢ Slots	N/A
25¢ Slots	91.40
$1 Slots	91.52
All Slots	94.29

These numbers reflect the percentage of money returned to the players on each denomination of machine. All electronic machines including slots, video poker and video keno are included in these numbers.

Optional games in the casino listings include: sports book (SB), race book (RB), Spanish 21 (S21), baccarat (B), mini-baccarat (MB), poker (P), pai gow poker (PGP), Caribbean stud poker (CSP), let it ride (LIR), three-card poker (TCP), four card poker (FCP), ultimate Texas hold 'em (UTH), Mississippi stud (MS), keno (K) and bingo (BG).

Cal-Neva Resort Spa & Casino
2 Stateline Road
Crystal Bay, Nevada 89402
(775) 832-4000
Website: www.calnevaresort.com

THIS CASINO WAS CLOSED AT PRESSTIME, BUT IS EXPECTED TO REOPEN AT A LATER DATE.

Reservation Number: (800) 225-6382
Rooms: 199 Price Range: $108-$179
Suites: 18 Price Range: $243-$269
Restaurants: 3
Overnight RV Parking: No
Special Features: Straddles California/Nevada state line on north shore of Lake Tahoe. European Spa. Three wedding chapels. Florist. Photo studio. Bridal boutique. Gift shop. Airport shuttle. Internet cafe.

Crystal Bay Club Casino
14 State Route 28
Crystal Bay, Nevada 89402
(775) 833-6333
Website: www.crystalbaycasino.com

Restaurants 2 (1 open 24 hours)
Casino Size: 14,020 Square Feet
Other Games: RB, SB
Overnight RV Parking: No

Grand Lodge Casino at Hyatt Regency
111 Country Club Drive
Incline Village, Nevada 89451
(775) 832-1234
Website: www.grandlodgecasino.com

Toll-Free Number: (800) 553-3288
Rooms: 412 Price Range: $210-435
Suites: 48 Price Range: $540-$1,400
Restaurants: 4 (1 open 24 hours)
Casino Size: 18,900 Square Feet
Other Games: SB, RB, P, LIR, TCP
Overnight RV Parking: No
Senior Discount: Food/room discounts if 62+
Special Features: On north shore of Lake Tahoe. Two Robert Trent Jones golf courses.

Hard Rock Hotel & Casino Lake Tahoe
50 Highway 50
Stateline, Nevada 89449
(844) 588-7625
Website: www.hardrockcasinolaketahoe.com

Toll-Free Number: (844) 588-7625
Rooms: 521 Price Range: $99-$289
Suites: 18 Price Range: $199-$399
Restaurants: 5
Casino Size: 25,000 square feet
Other Games: UTH, TCP, PGP, RB, SB
Senior Discounts: Various if 50+
Special Features: Display of rock and roll memorabilia

Harrah's Lake Tahoe
15 Highway 50
Stateline, Nevada 89449
(775) 588-6611
Website: www.harrahslaketahoe.com

Reservation Number: (800) 427-7247
Rooms: 463 Price Range: $109-$359
Suites: 62 Price Range: $199-$800
Restaurants: 7
Buffets: B-$21.99 (Sat/Sun)
D- $25.95/$31.99 (Fri)/$34.99 (Sat)
Casino Size: 89,244 Sq Ft (including Harvey's)
Other Games: SB, B, MB, P, PGP, LIR, TCP, K
Overnight RV Parking: No
Special Features: On south shore of Lake Tahoe. Health club. Pet kennel.

Harveys Resort Hotel/Casino - Lake Tahoe
18 Highway 50
Stateline, Nevada 89449
(775) 588-2411
Website: www.harveys.com

Toll-Free Number: (800) 553-1022
Rooms: 704 Price Range: $79-$279
Suites: 36 Price Range: $199-$679
Restaurants: 5 (1 open 24 hours)
Casino Size: 89,244 Sq Ft (including Harrah's)
Other Games: SB, RB, B, MB, P, PGP, LIR, TCP, K
Overnight RV Parking: No
Special Features: On south shore of Lake Tahoe. 2,000-seat amphitheater. Hard Rock Cafe. Owned by Harrah's. Lake cruises.

Lakeside Inn and Casino
168 Highway 50
Stateline, Nevada 89449
(775) 588-7777
Website: www.lakesideinn.com

Toll-Free Number: (800) 523-1291
Rooms: 124 Price Range: $79-$164
Suites: 8 Price Range: $129-$304
Restaurants: 2
Casino Size: 17,852 Square Feet
Other Games: SB, RB, P, K
Overnight RV Parking: No
Special Features: On south shore of Lake Tahoe. $6.99 breakfast 11pm-2:30pm.

Montbleu Resort Casino & Spa
55 Highway 50
Stateline, Nevada 89449
(775) 588-3515
Website: www.montbleuresort.com

Toll-Free Number: (888) 829-7630
Rooms: 403 Price Range: $89-$299
Suites: 37 Price Range: $159-$999
Restaurants: 5
Casino Size: 45,000 Square Feet
Other Games: SB, RB, MB, P, LIR, TCP, PGP
Overnight RV Parking: No
Special Features: On south shore of Lake Tahoe. Health spa.

Tahoe Biltmore Lodge & Casino
5 Highway 28
Crystal Bay, Nevada 89402
(775) 831-0660
Website: www.tahoebiltmore.com

Reservation Number: (800) 245-8667
Rooms: 106 Price Range: $109-$149
Suites: 7 Price Range: $139-$189
Restaurants: 2
Buffets: B- $9.95 (Sun)
Casino Size: 10,398 Square Feet
Other Games: SB, RB
Overnight RV Parking: Free/RV Dump: No
Senior Discount: Various Tue if 50+
Special Features: On north shore of Lake Tahoe.

See page 257 for a story on "The Best Places to Gamble in Reno/Tahoe"

Las Vegas

Map Location: **#1**

Las Vegas is truly the casino capital of the world! While many years ago the city may have had a reputation as an "adult playground" run by "shady characters," today's Las Vegas features many world-class facilities run by some of America's most familiar corporate names.

Las Vegas has more motel/hotel rooms - 150,000 - than any other city in the U.S. and it attracts more than 42 million visitors each year. The abundance of casinos in Las Vegas forces them to compete for customers in a variety of ways and thus, there are always great bargains to be had, but only if you know where to look.

H. Scot Krause is a 25-year Las Vegas veteran. He is a freelance writer, gaming industry analyst and researcher who writes the weekly Vegas Values column that appears on the American Casino Guide Book website.

Here are Scot's picks for the best deals available for a Las Vegas visitor.

Best Appetizer Bargain:
Shrimp Cocktail:
Fremont Casino (Lanai Express): $.99
Skyline Casino (Main Bar) (Henderson): $1.99

With the closing of Du-Par's inside the Golden Gate in 2017, the honor of best shrimp cocktails now moves to Henderson. The Skyline Casino in Henderson offers theirs for a mere $1.99 (up 50 cents from last year). For a best price bargain downtown, it's the Fremont's 99-cent shrimp cocktail at the Lanai Express counter.

Best Steak Deal:
*Ellis Island, $7.99**
*Arizona Charlie's Boulder & Decatur, Steak & Eggs, $5.99**

You may find other steak deals in Las Vegas, but the steak special at Ellis Island Casino & Brewery still remains the leader in steak bargains. It's not on the menu but available for the asking 24 hours a day, 7 days a week. For $12.99 (you can get it to down to $7.99*) you get a generous cut of tenderloin cooked to your liking, bread, salad, vegetable of the day and choice of potato. *With your Passport Player's Card you can get it down to $7.99 with a $3 discount voucher printed from a kiosk, plus if you play $5 through any machine you can get an additional $1 off and then print out a coupon from a Passport Central kiosk for a voucher. This is not a menu item! Ask your server for the special and they will be happy to take care of you! Another good deal is the steak & eggs at Arizona Charlie's (*with players card.) The deal comes with hash browns and toast.

Best Place to Play Slots:
Rampart Casino
Downtown
South Point (See "Best Video Poker" for info.)

Rampart Casino inside the J.W. Marriott in Summerlin recently shared and boasted the payback percentages on all of their slot machines. Numbers are among the best paybacks in Las Vegas, if not the best. They claim to be "up to 36% looser than the Strip." Few seem to have challenged them or the numbers, but luck can happen anywhere. Your mileage may vary, but if you're a slot player, I'd try Rampart. Downtown Las Vegas is also a hotbed of activity for slot players and generally the downtown casinos yield a higher payback percentage overall than the Strip. The nice thing about downtown is that you can pop in and out of all of the casinos with ease until you find your lucky casino or machine! You'll even find a few old coin-dropper slots still left downtown for that "old-time" Vegas feel. Others with a good track record for slot payouts include The Palms and South Point.

Best Video Poker:
South Point
Downtown

South Point's gaming amenities include more than 2,563 of the most popular slot and video poker machines featuring ticket-in, ticket-out technology. They (arguably) offer the most video poker machines with paybacks over 99% of any casino in the city. Combine that with slot club benefits and year-round good promotions and you've got a winning play! Generally, if a casino offers good video poker it follows that the slots may be set to higher payouts too. They want your business, so both tend to be better. Most all Downtown casinos also feature higher paytables for video poker.

Best Bargain Shows:
Mac King, Harrah's
Adam London, D Las Vegas

The plaid-suited magician is hilarious and talented and cheap enough to take the whole family. Normally priced around $25-30, tickets can usually be found for far less using coupons, including FREE tickets (usually with the price of a drink.) Great afternoon bargain show! See him again for the first time! Comedy-magician Adam London at the D Las Vegas is also a great afternoon show. This afternoon comedy magic show is hilarious and highly engaging. London's tricks have a mix of whimsy and wit with clever slight of hand magic. Priced at $49.95; get 40% off with the ACG book coupon!

Best Free Attractions:
Bellagio Fountains and Conservatory
Silverton Casino (Aquarium)

Everyone has their favorite free attraction but the water show at Bellagio is by far a fan favorite for tourists as well as locals. It's quite a dazzling display. Some call it "romantic." While you're there, don't miss the Conservatory inside the hotel. Beautiful displays of flowers, gardens and scenery are changed four times a year depicting the seasons. Often breathtaking and definitely aromatic! I personally like the free Aquarium attraction at the Silverton Casino. It's up-close, relaxing and intriguing.

Best Buffet(s)

Generally, the "best buffets" are not exactly "bargains." Usually considered to be among the best (but also pricey) by popular opinion are the buffets at Caesars Palace, Wynn, Bellagio, Cosmopolitan and Planet Hollywood. For a locals casino, Studio B Buffet at M Resort rivals the Strip's best buffets and is much less expensive. You can even get it comped for minimal play! (See the player's club for details.) My new favorite is…ready for it? Palace Station! Palace Station, the original Las Vegas locals' casino, debuted its all-new Feast Buffet as part of a $192 million modernization in late 2018. Located on the new casino floor, the new Feast Buffet boasts a 14,000 square-foot buffet experience and allows seating for up to 394 guests in a dining hall setting. Feast Buffet features an eclectic menu of greatest hits and contemporary twists on traditional favorites, available at seven stations presenting global cuisine in a contemporary and relevant fashion, grouped by cooking techniques. Inspired by its sister concept A.Y.C.E Buffet at Palms Las Vegas (but more expensive than Palace Station), the new buffet allows guests to sample its reasonably sized stove pots and serving trays, individual plates and ramekins, carved-to-order proteins, as well as a series of made-to-order options – allowing for the ultimate feast. The quality and variety is top-notch! Not bad on the wallet either compared to others! Other favorites for me personally include Seasons Buffet at Silverton, Main Street Station and Fremont Downtown, and Rampart's Buffet. Thursday's New York Deli nights at Rampart are always excellent and the dessert station is always aces!

Unlike New Jersey, the Nevada Gaming Control Board does not break down its slot statistics by individual properties. Rather, they are classified by area.

The annual gaming revenue report breaks the Las Vegas market down into two major tourist areas: the Strip and downtown. There is also a very large locals market in Las Vegas and those casinos are shown in the gaming revenue report as the Boulder Strip and North Las Vegas areas.

When choosing where to do your slot gambling, you may want to keep in mind the following slot payback percentages for Nevada's fiscal year beginning July 1, 2018 and ending June 30, 2019:

1¢ Slot Machines
The Strip - 88.33%
Downtown - 88.96%
Boulder Strip - 90.53%
N. Las Vegas - 90.79%

5¢ Slot Machines
The Strip - 91.96%
Downtown - 93.32%
Boulder Strip - 96.30%
N. Las Vegas - 95.24%

25¢ Slot Machines
The Strip - 89.34%
Downtown - 93.91%
Boulder Strip - 95.77%
N. Las Vegas - 96.27%

$1 Slot Machines
The Strip - 92.34%
Downtown - 94.12%
Boulder Strip - 95.49%
N. Las Vegas - 95.62%

$1 Megabucks Machines
The Strip - 87.31%
Downtown - 86.40%
Boulder Strip - 87.61%
N. Las Vegas - 86.98%

All Slot Machines
The Strip - 91.84%
Downtown - 92.22%
Boulder Strip - 94.26%
N. Las Vegas - 93.34%

These numbers reflect the percentage of money returned to the players on each denomination of machine. All electronic machines including slots, video poker and video keno are included in these numbers and the highest-paying returns are shown in bold print.

As you can see, the machines in downtown Las Vegas pay out more than those located on the Las Vegas Strip.

Returns even better than the downtown casinos can be found at some of the other locals casinos along Boulder Highway such as Sam's Town and also in the North Las Vegas area. Not only are those numbers among the best returns in the Las Vegas area, they are among the best payback percentages for anywhere in the United States.

This information is pretty well known by the locals and that's why most of them do their slot gambling away from the Strip unless they are drawn by a special players club benefit or promotion.

If you are driving an RV to Las Vegas and want to stay overnight for free in a casino parking lot the only casino that will allow you to do that is Bally's.

Other games in the casino listings include: sports book (SB), race book (RB), Spanish 21 (S21), baccarat (B), mini-baccarat (MB), pai gow (PG), poker (P), pai gow poker (PGP), Caribbean stud poker (CSP), let it ride (LIR), three-card poker (TCP), Mississippi stud (MS), ultimate Texas hold em (UTH), four card poker (FCP), big 6 wheel (B6), sic bo (SIC), keno (K) and bingo (BG).

The Alamo Casino
8050 Dean Martin Drive
Las Vegas, Nevada 89139
(702) 361-1176
Website: www.thealamo.com

Other Games: No craps/roulette
Casino Size: 3,000 Square Feet
Special Features: Truck stop. Burger King restaurant.

Aria Resort & Casino
3730 Las Vegas Boulevard South
Las Vegas, Nevada 89109
(702) 590-7757
Website: www.aria.com

Rooms: 3,436 Price Range: $139-$600
Suites: 568 Price Range: $335-$1500
Self-Parking: $15 (1-4 hours), $18 (4-24 hours)
Valet Parking: $21 (0-2 hours)/$24 (2-4 hours)/ $30 (4 to 24 hours)
Restaurants: 15
Buffets: B- $25.99/$34.99 (Sat/Sun)
L- $34.99
D- $39.99/$44.99 (Fri-Sun)
Casino Size: 150,000 Square Feet
Other Games: SB, RB, B, MB, P, PG, PGP, TCP, UTH, B6, CW
Special Features: Located within 76-acre City Center project. Adjacent to 500,000-square foot Crystals shopping/entertainment complex. 80,000-square foot Spa.

Arizona Charlie's - Boulder
4575 Boulder Highway
Las Vegas, Nevada 89121
(702) 951-9000
Website: www.arizonacharliesboulder.com

Rooms: 300 Price Range: $32-$130
Restaurants: 4 (1 open 24 hours)
Buffets: B-$7.9/$12.99 (Sun) L-$9.99
D-$12.99/$13.99 (Wed)/ $13.99(Fri-Sun)
Casino Size: 47,541 Square Feet
Other Games: No table games
Senior Discounts: Various on Mon if 50+
Special Features: 239-space RV park ($34 per night). Buffet discount for players club members

Arizona Charlie's - Decatur
740 S. Decatur Boulevard
Las Vegas, Nevada 89107
(702) 258-5200
Website: www.arizonacharliesdecatur.com

Rooms: 245 Price Range: $45-$99
Suites: 10 Price Range: $55-$135
Restaurants: 5 (1 open 24 hours)
Buffets: B- $9.32 (Fri/Sat)/$15.99 (Sun)
L- $11.32/$15.99 (Sun)
D- $9.99/$13.32 (Fri/Sat)
Casino Size: 55,227 Square Feet
Other Games: SB, RB, P, PGP, K, BG
Special Features: Buffet discount with players club card.

Bally's Las Vegas
3645 Las Vegas Boulevard S.
Las Vegas, Nevada 89109
(702) 739-4111
Website: www.ballyslv.com

Toll-Free Number: (800) 722-5597
Rooms: 2,814 Price Range: $89-$219
Suites: 265 Price Range: $259-$449
Restaurants: 9 (1 open 24 hours)
Buffets: Brunch-$89.99 (Sat/Sun)
Self-Parking: $7 (1-4 hours) $12 (4-24 hours)
Valet Parking: $15 (0-4 hours) $20 (4-6 hours) $24 (6-24 hours)
Casino Size: 66,187 Square Feet
Other Games: SB, RB, B, MB, P, PGP, CSP, LIR, TCP, K, BG, CW, PG, UTH
Overnight RV Parking: Free/RV Dump: No
Senior Discount: Various if 55+
Special Features: 20 retail stores. Brunch buffet is $85 with Players Club card.

Bellagio
3600 Las Vegas Boulevard S.
Las Vegas, Nevada 89109
(702) 693-7111
Website: www.bellagioresort.com

Rooms: 2,688 Price Range: $169-$398
Suites: 308 Price Range: $402-$695
Self-Parking: $15 (1-4 hours) $18 (4-24 hours)
Valet Parking: $21 (0-2 hours), $24 (2-4 hours)
$30 (4 to 24 hours)
Restaurants: 14 (2 open 24 hours)
Buffets: B- $25.99/$34.99 (Sat/Sun)
L- $29.99/$34.99 (Sat/Sun)
D- $39.99/$44.99 (Fri/Sat)
Casino Size: 156,000 Square Feet
Other Games: SB, RB, B, MB, P, PG,
PGP, CSP, LIR, TCP
Special Features: Lake with nightly light and water show. Shopping mall. Two wedding chapels. Beauty salon and spa. Cirque du Soleil's "O" stage show.

Binion's Gambling Hall
128 E. Fremont Street
Las Vegas, Nevada 89101
(702) 382-1600
Website: www.binions.com

Toll-Free Number: (800) 937-6537
Rooms: 81 Price range: $99-$199
Restaurants: 4 (1 open 24 hours)
Casino Size: 79,400 Square Feet
Other Games: SB, RB, MB, P, PGP,
LIR, TCP, B6
Special Features: Historic 81- room Apache Hotel. Steak House on 24th floor offers panoramic views of Las Vegas. Free souvenir photo taken in front of $1,000,000 cash.

Boulder Station Hotel & Casino
4111 Boulder Highway
Las Vegas, Nevada 89121
(702) 432-7777
Website: www.boulderstation.com

Toll-Free Number: (800) 981-5577
Reservation Number: (800) 683-7777
Rooms: 300 Price Range: $33-$139
Restaurants: 5 (1 open 24 hours)
Buffets: B-$10.99/$16.99 (Sat/Sun)
L-$13.99/$16.99 (Sat/Sun)
D-$16.99/$17.99 (Fri/Sat)
Casino Size: 89,443 Square Feet
Other Games: SB, RB, MB, B, P,
PGP, TCP, K, BG
Special Features: 11-screen movie complex. Kid Quest childcare center. Buffet discount for slot club members.

Caesars Palace
3570 Las Vegas Boulevard S.
Las Vegas, Nevada 89109
(702) 731-7110
Website: www.caesarspalace.com

Toll-Free Number: (800) 634-6001
Rooms: 3,349 Price Range: $109-$500
Petite Suites: 242 Price Range: $378-$1,340
Nobu Rooms: $159-$379
Nobu Suites: $609-$1,560
Suites: 157 Price Range: $609-$1,600
Restaurants: 14 (1 open 24 hours)
Self-Parking: $12 (1-2 hours), $15 (2-4 hours)
$18 (4-24 hours)
Valet Parking: $21 (0-2 Hours), $24 (2-4 hours)
$30 (4-24 hours)
Buffets: B- $30.99 L- $38.99 D- $54.99
Casino Size: 136,415 Square Feet
Other Games: SB, RB, B, MB, PG, P, PGP,
LIR, MS, UTH, TCP, K
Special Features: Health spa. Beauty salon. Shopping mall with 125 stores and interactive attractions.

California Hotel & Casino
12 Ogden Avenue
Las Vegas, Nevada 89101
(702) 385-1222
Website: www.thecal.com

Reservation Number: (800) 634-6505
Rooms: 781 Price Range: $50-$220
Suites: 74 Price Range: Casino Use Only
Restaurants: 3 (1 open 24 hours)
Casino Size: 35,848 Square Feet
Other Games: P, SB, PGP, LIR, TCP, K
Senior Discounts: Wednesdays if 50+
Special Features: Offers charter packages from Hawaii.

Casino Royale Hotel & Casino
3411 Las Vegas Boulevard S.
Las Vegas, Nevada 89109
(702) 737-3500
Website: www.casinoroyalehotel.com

Toll-Free Number: (800) 854-7666
Rooms: 151 Price Range: $129-$209
Suites: 3 Price Range: $299-$399
Restaurants: 3 (1 open 24 hours)
Casino Size: 22,000 Square Feet
Other Games: TCP
Special Features: No resort fee. Outback, Denny's, White Castle and Subway. Refrigerator in every room.

Circus Circus Hotel & Casino
2880 Las Vegas Boulevard S.
Las Vegas, Nevada 89109
(702) 734-0410
Website: www.circuscircus.com

Rooms: 3,770 Price Range: $25-$159
Suites: 122 Price Range: $89-$269
Self-Parking: Free
Valet Parking: $12 (0-2 hours), $14 (2-4 hours)
$16 (4-24 hours)
Restaurants: 7
Buffets: B/L- $19.99/$22.99 (Sat/Sun)
D-$21.99/$24.99 (Fri/Sat)/
$23.99 (Sun)
Casino Size: 118,928 Square Feet
Other Games: MB, SB, RB, P, PGP, TCP, UTH
Special Features: Free circus acts 11 am-midnight. Wedding chapel. Midway and arcade games. Indoor Adventuredome theme park. 170-space RV park ($36-$58 per night).

The Cosmopolitan of Las Vegas
3708 Las Vegas Boulevard South
Las Vegas, Nevada 89109
(702) 698-7000
Website: www.cosmopolitanlasvegas.com

Toll-free Number: (877) 551-7778
Rooms: 2,600 Price Range: $150-$500
Suites: 395 Price Range: $289-$1,299
Restaurants: 21
Buffets: B/L- $28.00/$36.00 (Fri-Sun)
Self Parking: $10 (1-4 hours), $15 (4-24 hours)
Valet Parking: $15 (0-4 hours)
$20 (4-24 hours)
Buffet: D- $42.00/$49.00 (Fri-Sun)
Casino Size: 100,890 Square Feet
Other Games: B, MB, UTH, PGP,
TCP, CW, RB, SB

The Cromwell Las Vegas
3595 Las Vegas Boulevard S.
Las Vegas, Nevada 89109
(702) 777-3777
Website: www.thecromwell.com

Toll-Free Number: (844) 426-2766
Rooms: 186 Price Range: $99-$309
Suites: 12 Price Range: $339-$1,250
Restaurants: 2
Self Parking: $9 (1-2 hours), $12 (2-4 hours)
$15 (4-24 hours)
Valet Parking: $15 (0-2 hours), $20 (2-4 hours)
$24 (4-24 hours)
Casino Size: 40,000 Square Feet
Other Games: P, PGP, MB, UTH, MS,
LIR, TCP, SB
Special Features: Drai's Nightclub and Beach Club. 100x odds on craps.

The D Las Vegas
301 Fremont Street
Las Vegas, Nevada 89101
(702) 388-2400
Website: www.thed.com

Toll-Free Number: (855) 264-2046
Reservation Number: (800) 274-5825
Rooms: 624 Price Range: $29-$179
Suites: 14 Price Range: $85-$270
Restaurants: 3
Casino Size: 42,251 Square Feet
Other Games: SB, K
Special Features: *Defending the Caveman* stage show.

The Best Places To Play In Las Vegas

Roulette- There are 10 casinos in Las Vegas that offer single-zero roulette: Aria, Bellagio, Cromwell, Encore, Mandalay Bay, MGM Grand, Mirage, Palazzo, Venetian and Wynn. This game has a 2.70% edge as compared to the usual 5.26% edge on a double-zero roulette wheel. Be aware that all of these casinos offer single-zero wheels at just some of their roulette games and not all of them. The minimum bet starts at $25 and can go as high as $100.

Craps- 100X odds is the highest offered in Las Vegas and there is only one casino offering that game: The Cromwell. The next best game offers 20x odds and it can be found at Sam's Town, as well as at Main Street Station.

Blackjack- All recommendations in this section apply to basic strategy players. You should always look for casinos that pay the standard 3-to-2 for blackjacks. Some casinos only pay 6-to-5 for blackjack and this increases the casino edge to around 1.5% and they should be avoided.

The best single-deck game can be found at the El Cortez which offers the following rules: dealer hits soft 17, double down on any first two cards, split any pair, re-split any pair (except aces), and no doubling after splitting. The casino edge in this game is .18% and the minimum bet is $5.

Silverton offers a similar single-deck game, but they only allow you to double down on two card totals of 10 or more, and this raises the casino edge to 0.44%

There are six casinos with two-deck games offering the following rules: dealer stands on soft 17, double down on any first two cards, re-split any pair (except aces) and doubling allowed after splitting. The casinos that offer it are: Aria, Bellagio, MGM Grand, Mirage, Park MGM and Treasure Island. The casino edge in these games is .19% with minimum bets of $50 to $200.

The best double-deck game, however, is offered at M Resort. This game has the same rules as the above games except it allows the re-splitting of aces and that brings the casino edge down to .14% The minimum bet at this game is $25.

The remaining best two-deckers in Las Vegas can be found at some casinos that have the same rules as above, with two exceptions: the dealer hits soft 17 and aces can be re-split. The casino advantage is .35% and the game can be found at Palms, Tropicana and Westgate. The minimum bet at these casinos is $5 to $25.

For six-deck shoe games the best casinos have these rules: dealer stands on soft 17, double after split allowed, late surrender offered and re-splitting of aces allowed. The casino edge in this game works out to .26% and you can find it at many major casinos: Aria, Bellagio, Caesars Palace, Encore, M Resort, MGM Grand, Mirage, Palazzo, Palms, Rio, SLS, Treasure Island, Tropicana, Wynn and the Venetian. The minimum bet at these casinos is usually at least $50, with some at $100.

Almost all of these casinos also offer this same game with identical rules except that they will hit soft 17. The minimums in this game are lower, usually $25, but the casino's mathematical edge is raised to .46%.

Cosmopolitan (Cosmo), Mandalay Bay, Mirage, NYNY, Park MGM, SLS, and Treasure Island offer eight deck games that have the same rules as the .26% six-deck game and the casino advantage is .49% with minimum bets of $10 to $25. Cosmo also offers this game where the dealer stands on soft 17. The casino edge is .28% and the minimum bet is $100.

Video Poker- Smart video poker players know that some of the best machines to look for are: 9/6 Jacks or Better (99.54% return), 8/5 Bonus Poker (99.17% return), 10/7 Double Bonus (100.17% return), full-pay Deuces Wild (100.76% return), 10/6 Double Double Bonus (100.07% return) and Not So Ugly Deuces (99.73% return). These games rarely exist at Las Vegas Strip casinos, but they are usually widely available at "locals" casinos along Boulder Highway, or in Henderson or North Las Vegas.

Following is a list of casinos offering some of these better paying video poker games. The abbreviations used for each listing are JB (9/6 jacks or better - 99.54%), BP (8/5 bonus poker - 99.17%), DB (10/7 Double Bonus - 100.17%), DDB (10/6 double double bonus - 100.07%), FPDW (full-pay deuces wild - 100.76%) and NSUD (not so ugly deuces - 99.73%).

Strip-area Casinos
Aria: JB - $5 to $100; *BP* - $1 to $100
Bellagio: JB - $5 to $10; BP - quarter to $100
Caesars Palace: JB $5 to $100; BP $5 to $100
Circus Circus: BP - quarter and $1 (some with progressives)
Cosmopolitan: BP - quarter to $100; JB - fifty cents to $25
Cromwell: JB - quarter; NSUD - quarter; BP - quarter
Ellis Island: JB - nickel to $5; NSUD - nickel to $5; BP - nickel to $5
Gold Coast: JB - quarter to $2; NSUD - quarter to $1; BP - quarter to $10
Hard Rock: BP - $1 to $25
Mandalay Bay: BP $2 to $100
MGM Grand: JB - $1 to $25; BP - $1 to $100
Mirage: BP $5 to $100
New York New York: JB $5 to $10; BP $10
Orleans: BP - quarter to $2; NSUD - quarter
Palace Station: JB- quarter to $1; DB - nickel to $1; DDB - nickel to $1; FPDW - nickel; NSUD - quarter to $1
Palms: BP - quarter to $100; DB - quarter to $1; DDB - quarter to $1; FPDW- quarter
Paris: JB $5 to $100; BP $5 to $100
Park MGM: BP $1 to $5
Rio: JB $5 to $100; BP - $1 to $100
Silver Sevens: JB quarters; BP - quarter to $1
SLS: BP - $1 to $5
Treasure Island: JB - $1; BP - $1
Tuscany: BP - quarter to $1
Westgate: BP - $0.50 and $1
Wynn/Encore: JB - $5 to $100; BP - $5 to $100; NSUD - $5 to $100

Downtown Casinos
Binion's: BP - quarter to $1
California: JB - quarter to $1; BP - nickel to $0.50; DB - quarter to $1; NSUD - nickel to fifty-cents
The D: BP - quarter to $2
Downtown Grand: BP - nickel to $1; DB quarter to $1; DDB quarter to $10
El Cortez: DB - quarter; BP - quarter to $5
Four Queens: JB - quarter to $1; DB - quarter and $1
Fremont: NSUD - quarter and $1; BP - quarter to $5
Golden Gate: BP - quarter to $1
Main Street Station: JB - quarter to $1; NSUD - quarter; DB - quarter to $1
Plaza: JB - quarter to $2; BP - quarter to $5; DB - quarter to $1

Locals Casinos- If you are looking for the best video poker in Las Vegas then you may want to make a side trip to some of the casinos along Boulder Highway, as well as in Henderson or North Las Vegas. Most of these casinos offer all of the games listed above in a variety of denominations. The casino company that operates the most locals properties is Station Casinos which owns: Palms, Sunset Station, Boulder Station, Texas Station, Santa Fe Station, Palace Station, Green Valley Ranch, Red Rock, Fiesta Henderson and Fiesta Rancho. The other major player is Boyd Gaming, which operates Aliante, Sam's Town, Gold Coast, Orleans, Suncoast, California, Cannery, Eastside Cannery, Fremont and Main Street Station. All of these locals casinos will offer good video poker games, coupled with a good players club that will allow you to redeem your points at any of their company-owned casinos.

Downtown Grand Casino
206 North 3rd Street
Las Vegas, Nevada 89101
(855) 384-7263
Website: www.downtowngrand.com

Toll-Free Number: (855) 384-7263
Rooms: 626 Price Range: $39-$119
Suites: 8 Price Range: Casino use only
Restaurants: 6
Casino Size: 35,000 square Feet
Other Games: P, PGP, SB, RB
Special Features: eSports Arena

Eastside Cannery
5255 Boulder Highway
Las Vegas, Nevada 89122
(702) 856-5300
Website: www.eastsidecannery.com

Rooms: 190 Price Range: $49-$119
Suites: 20 Price Range: $99-$169
Restaurants: 1
Casino Size: 62,479 Square Feet
Other Games: SB, RB, PGP
Senior Discount: Food discounts if 55+
Special features: Tables open 11:00am-3:00am/9:00am-3:00am (Saturday/Sunday)

El Cortez Hotel & Casino
600 E. Fremont Street
Las Vegas, Nevada 89101
(702) 385-5200
Website: www.elcortezhotelcasino.com

Reservation Number: (800) 634-6703
Rooms: 299 Price Range: $22-$119
Suites: 10 Price Range: $80-$159
Restaurants: 3
Casino Size: 45,300 Square Feet
Other Games: TCP, UTH, SB, RB, K
Senior Discount: Various on Wed if 50+
Special Features: Video arcade. Gift shop and ice cream parlor. Barber shop. Beauty salon.

Ellis Island Casino & Brewery
4178 Koval Lane
Las Vegas, Nevada 89109
(702) 733-8901
Website: www.ellisislandcasino.com

Restaurants: 3
Rooms: 289 Price Range: $55-$129
Suites: 12 Price Range: $105-$189
Casino Size: 13,916 Square Feet
Other Games: SB, RB
Special Features: $7.99 steak dinner for players club members (not on menu, must ask for it). #1 Microbrewery in Nevada as voted by the state's Brewers Association.

Encore Las Vegas
3131 Las Vegas Boulevard S.
Las Vegas, Nevada 89109
(702) 770-7800
Website: www.encorelasvegas.com

Suites: 1,800 Price Range: $169-$549
Tower Suites: 234 Price Range: $299-$1700
Restaurants: 9
Valet Parking: $21 (up to 2 hours)/
$24 (2-4 hours)/
$30 (4-24 hours)
Casino Size: 186,187 Sq. Ft. (Includes Wynn)
Other Games: SB, RB, B, MB, P, PG, CW,
PGP, CSP, LIR, TCP, B6
Special Features: Le Reve stage show. Beach club with three pools. Attached to Wynn Las Vegas.

Excalibur Hotel/Casino
3850 Las Vegas Boulevard S.
Las Vegas, Nevada 89109
(702) 597-7777
Website: www.excalibur.com

Rooms: 4,008 Price Range: $31-$299
Suites: 46 Price Range: $130-$499
Self-Parking: First hour free, $8 (1-4 hours), $10 (4 to 24 hours)
Valet Parking: $16 (0 to 2 hours), $18 (2-4 hours) $24 (4 to 24 hours)
Self-Parking: $5 (1-4 hours), $8 (4-24 hours)
Restaurants: 5 (1 open 24 hours)
Buffets: B- $19.99/$23.99 (Sat/Sun)
L- $20.49/$23.99 (Sat/Sun)
D- $24.99/$28.499 (Fri-Sun)
Casino Size: 99,960 Square Feet
Other Games: SB, RB, P, PGP, K
Special Features: Canterbury wedding chapel. Strolling Renaissance entertainers. Video arcade and midway games. Food Court with fast food outlets. Nightly Tournament of Kings dinner show. *Australian Bee Gees* show. *Thunder from Down Under* show.

Flamingo Las Vegas
3555 Las Vegas Boulevard S.
Las Vegas, Nevada 89109
(702) 733-3111
Website: www.flamingolasvegas.com

Rooms: 3,545 Price Range: $47-$240
Suites: 215 Price Range: $140-$905
Restaurants: 6
Buffets: B/L- $24.99/$29.99 (Sat/Sun)
D- $31.99 (Fri/Sat)
Self Parking: $9 (1-2 Hours), $12 (2-4 hours) $15 (4-24 hours)
Valet Parking: $15 (0-2 hours), $20 (2-4 hours) $24 (4-24 hours)
Casino Size: 76,763 Sq Ft (includes O'Shea's)
Other Games: SB, RB, MB, P, PGP, LIR, TCP
Special Features: Health Spa. Shopping arcade. Jimmy Buffet's Margaritaville restaurant.

Four Queens Hotel/Casino
202 Fremont Street
Las Vegas, Nevada 89101
(702) 385-4011
Website: www.fourqueens.com

Rooms: 690 Price Range: $49-$169
Suites: 48 Price Range: $139-$269
Restaurants: 3
Casino Size: 27,389 Square Feet
Other Games: SB, RB, UTH, LIR, TCP, K
Special Features: No resort fee charged.

Fremont Hotel & Casino
200 E. Fremont Street
Las Vegas, Nevada 89101
(702) 385-3232
Website: www.fremontcasino.com

Toll-Free Number: (800) 634-6460
Rooms: 428 Price Range: $52-$120
Suites: 24 Price Range: Casino Use Only
Restaurants: 4
Buffets: B- $9.99/$14.99 (Sat/Sun)
L- $10.99/$14.99 (Sat/Sun)
D- $16.69/$26.99 (Tue/Fri)
Casino Size: 30,244 Square Feet
Other Games: SB, RB, PGP, LIR, TCP, K
Special Features: 99-cent shrimp cocktail at snack bar. Buffet discount for Players Club members. Only Tony Roma's restaurant in Nevada.

Gold Coast Hotel & Casino
4000 W. Flamingo Road
Las Vegas, Nevada 89103
(702) 367-7111
Website: www.goldcoastcasino.com

Toll-Free Number: (888) 402-6278
Rooms: 750 Price Range: $45-$255
Suites: 27 Price Range: $165-$450
Restaurants: 6
Buffets: B-$9.99/$16.99 (Sun)
L-$12.99/$16.99 (Sun)
D-$16.99/$21.99 (Fri)
Casino Size: 88,915 Square Feet
Other Games: SB, RB, MB, PGP, LIR, TCP, K, BG
Special Features: 70-lane bowling center. Showroom. Buffet discount with Player Club card.

Free Things To See In Las Vegas!

Fremont Street Experience

This $70 million computer-generated sound and light show takes place 90 feet in the sky over a pedestrian mall stretching four city blocks in downtown Las Vegas and in mid-2004 the entire system was upgraded with new LED modules to provide even crisper and clearer images. It's like watching the world's largest plasma TV with larger-than-life animations, integrated live video feeds, and synchronized music.

There are five differently themed shows nightly. Starting times vary, beginning at dusk, but then begin on the start of each hour through midnight.

Golden Gate Hotel & Casino
One Fremont Street
Las Vegas, Nevada 89101
(702) 385-1906
Website: www.goldengatecasino.com

Rooms: 106 Price Range: $19-$129
Restaurants: 2 (2 open 24 hours)
Casino Size: 9,596 Square Feet
Other Games: SB, RB, LIR, TCP
Special Features: $2.99 shrimp cocktail. Oldest hotel in Vegas (opened 1906).

The Golden Nugget
129 E. Fremont Street
Las Vegas, Nevada 89101
(702) 385-7111
Website: www.goldennugget.com

Toll-Free Number: (800) 634-3403
Rooms: 1,805 Price Range: $49-$199
Suites: 102 Price Range: $149-$450
Restaurants: 8
Buffets: B- $15.99/$22.99 (Sat/Sun)
L- $16.99/$22.99 (Sat/Sun)
D- $23.99/$24.99 (Thu/Sat)/ $28.99 (Fri)/$25.99 (Sun)
Casino Size: 47,796 Square Feet
Other Games: SB, RB, MB, P, PGP, LIR, TCP, MS, K
Special Features: World's largest gold nugget (61 pounds) on display. Health spa. Swimming pool with shark tank. Buffet closed Mon/Tue.

Hard Rock Hotel & Casino
4455 Paradise Road
Las Vegas, Nevada 89109
(702) 693-5000
Website: www.hardrockhotel.com

Toll-Free Number: (800) 473-7625
Rooms: 340 Price Range: $49-$389
Suites: 28 Price Range: $99-$429
Restaurants: 8
Casino Size: 59,125 Square Feet
Games: SB, RB, B, MB, PGP, LIR, TCP, UTH
Special Features: Rock and Roll memorabilia display. Spa, Beach Club with cabanas and sandy beaches. Lagoon with underwater music. Planned rebranding in late 2020 to become **Virgin Hotels Las Vegas**.

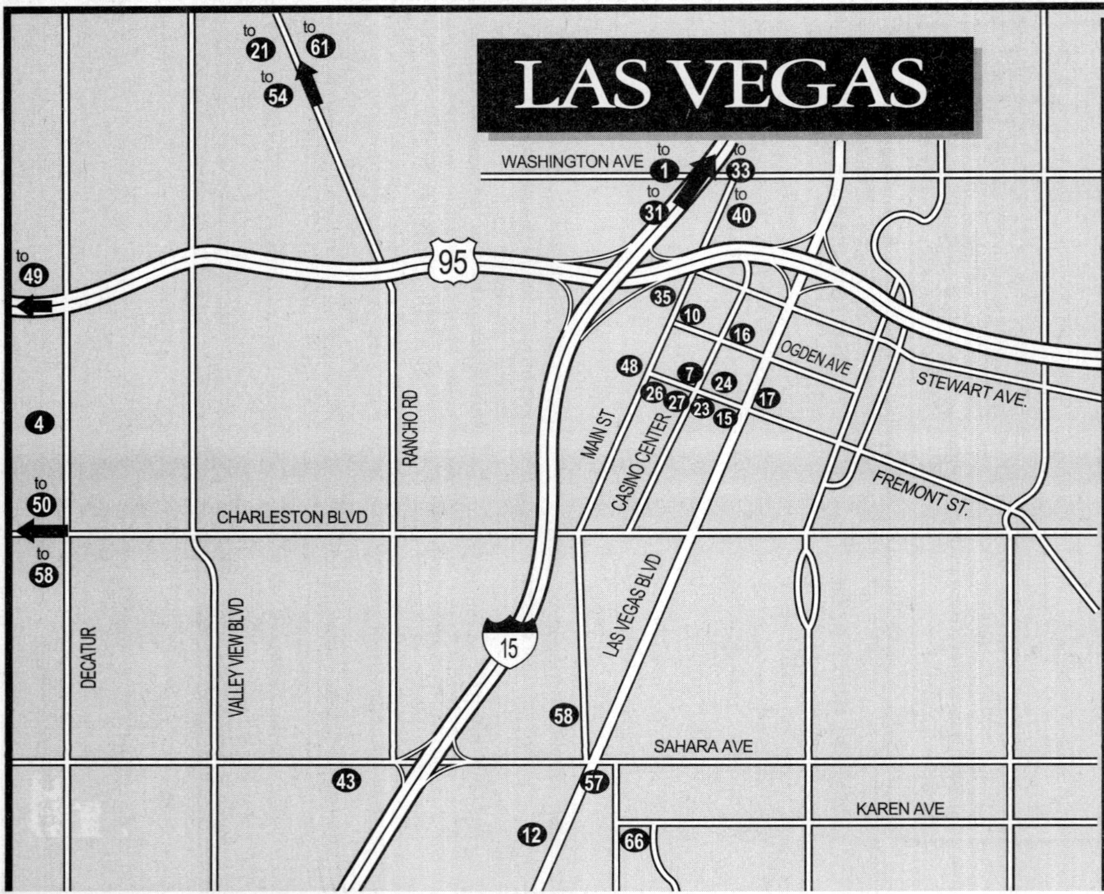

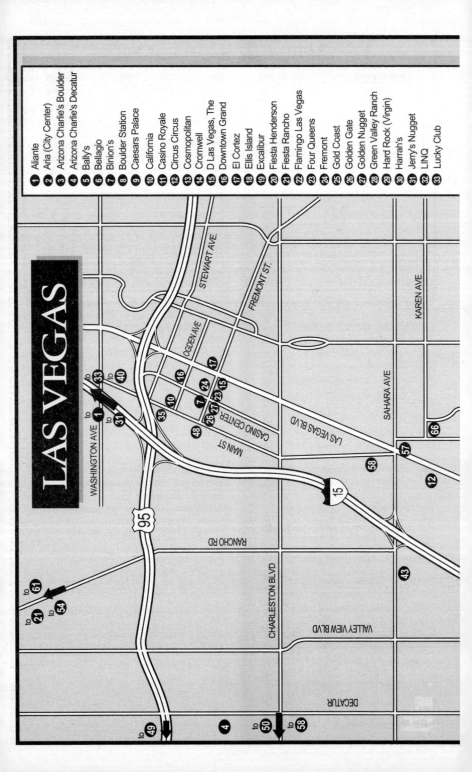

1 Aliante
2 Aria (City Center)
3 Arizona Charlie's Boulder
4 Arizona Charlie's Decatur
5 Bally's
6 Bellagio
7 Binion's
8 Boulder Station
9 Caesars Palace
10 California
11 Casino Royale
12 Circus Circus
13 Cosmopolitan
14 Cromwell
15 D Las Vegas, The
16 Downtown Grand
17 El Cortez
18 Ellis Island
19 Excalibur
20 Fiesta Henderson
21 Fiesta Rancho
22 Flamingo Las Vegas
23 Four Queens
24 Fremont
25 Gold Coast
26 Golden Gate
27 Golden Nugget
28 Green Valley Ranch
29 Hard Rock (Virgin)
30 Harrah's
31 Jerry's Nugget
32 LINQ
33 Lucky Club

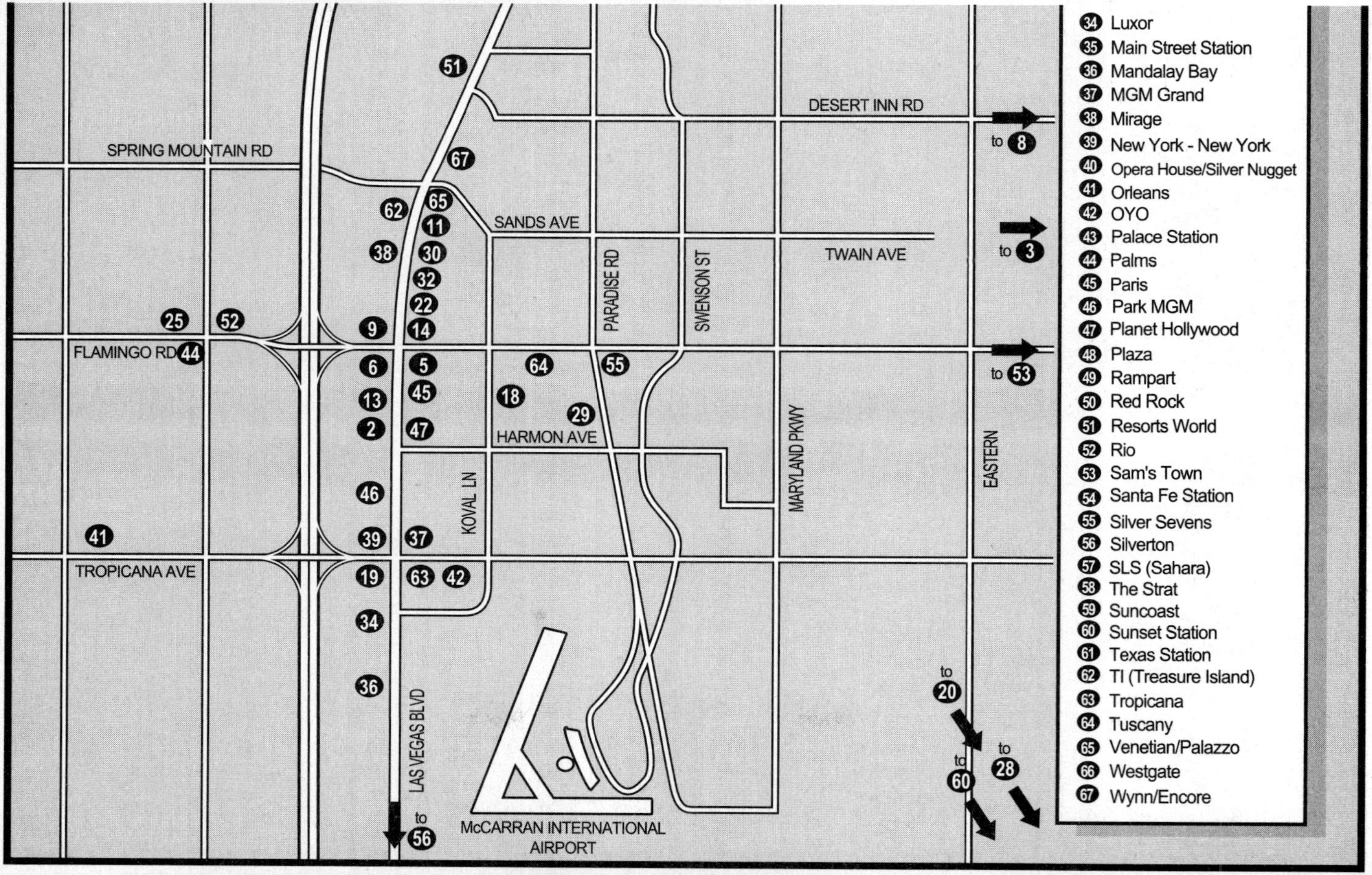
SPRING MOUNTAIN RD
FLAMINGO RD
TROPICANA AVE
DESERT INN RD
SANDS AVE
TWAIN AVE
PARADISE RD
SWENSON ST
HARMON AVE
KOVAL LN
MARYLAND PKWY
EASTERN
LAS VEGAS BLVD
McCARRAN INTERNATIONAL AIRPORT
to 8
to 3
to 53
to 20
to 28
to 60
to 56
34 Luxor
35 Main Street Station
36 Mandalay Bay
37 MGM Grand
38 Mirage
39 New York - New York
40 Opera House/Silver Nugget
41 Orleans
42 OYO
43 Palace Station
44 Palms
45 Paris
46 Park MGM
47 Planet Hollywood
48 Plaza
49 Rampart
50 Red Rock
51 Resorts World
52 Rio
53 Sam's Town
54 Santa Fe Station
55 Silver Sevens
56 Silverton
57 SLS (Sahara)
58 The Strat
59 Suncoast
60 Sunset Station
61 Texas Station
62 TI (Treasure Island)
63 Tropicana
64 Tuscany
65 Venetian/Palazzo
66 Westgate
67 Wynn/Encore

Harrah's Las Vegas
3475 Las Vegas Boulevard S.
Las Vegas, Nevada 89109
(702) 369-5000
Website: www.caesars.com

Toll-Free Number: (800) 392-9002
Reservation Number: (800) 427-7247

Toll-Free Number: (800) 392-9002
Rooms: 2,672 Price Range: $60-$210
Suites: 94 Price Range: $110-$595
Restaurants: 4
Buffets: B-$21.99/$30.99 (Sat/Sun)
L- $25.99 D- $31.99/$34.99 (Fri/Sat)
Self Parking: $9 (1-2 hours), $12 (2-4 hours)
$15 (4-24 hours)
Valet Parking : $15 (0-2 hours), $20 (2-4 hours)
$24 (4-24 hours)
Casino Size: 90,637 Square Feet
Other Games: SB, RB, MB, B, P, PG, PGP,
LIR, CW, UTH, TCP, K
Special Features: Mardi Gras-themed casino. Mac King comedy show. Fulton Street Food Hall with nine different food stations.

Jerry's Nugget
See North Las Vegas section

The LINQ Hotel & Casino
3535 Las Vegas Boulevard S.
Las Vegas, Nevada 89109
(702) 731-3311
Website: www.thelinq.com

Toll-Free Number: (800) 351-7400
Rooms: 1,088 Price Range: $49-$325
Suites: 225 Price Range: $115-$485
Restaurants: 5
Self Parking: $9 (1-2 hours), $12 (2-4 hours)
$15 (4-24 hours)
Valet Parking: $15 (0-2 hours), $20 (2-4 hours)
$24 (4-24 hours)
Casino Size: 118,000 Square Feet
Other Games: SB, RB, PGP, LIR, P, TCP, B6
Special Features: *The Auto Collections*, (admission charge). Video arcade. Wedding chapel. 550-foot tall *High Roller* ferris wheel.

Longhorn Casino
5288 Boulder Highway
Las Vegas, Nevada 89122
(702) 435-9170
Website: www.longhorncasinolv.com

Rooms: 150 Price Range $27-$69
Restaurants: 1 (open 24 hours)
Casino Size: 4,825 Square Feet
Other Games: SB, RB, no craps/roulette
Special Features: $11.99 Monster Burger and other restaurant specials.

Luxor Las Vegas
3900 Las Vegas Boulevard S.
Las Vegas, Nevada 89119
(702) 262-4000
Website: www.luxor.com

Rooms: 4,204 Price Range: $37-$269
Suites: 473 Price Range: $97-$335
Self-Parking: First hour free, $8 (1-4 hours)
$10 (4 to 24 hours)
Valet Parking: $16 (0-2 hours), $18 (2-4 hours)
$24 (4-24 hours)
Restaurants: 6
Buffets: B- $19.99/$23.99 (Sat/Sun)
L- $20.49
D- $24.99/$28.49 (Fri/Sat)
Casino Size: 120,000 Square Feet
Other Games: SB, RB, MB, P, PGP,
LIR, TCP, UTH
Special Features: 30-story pyramid-shaped hotel with Egyptian theme. *Carrot Top* comedy show. *Blue Man Group* stage shows. *R.U.N.* by Cirque du Soleil. Hyper X eSports arena.

The Best Vegas Values

By H. Scot Krause

Welcome to "Vegas Values!" It's an exclusive weekly column found only at: americancasinoguidebook.com, the companion website to this book. The column is updated weekly with some of the best casino promotions found throughout Las Vegas. Below are examples from the "Vegas Values" column. Remember, promotions are subject to change and may be cancelled at anytime. Call ahead to verify before making a special trip.

Arizona Charlie's Boulder and Decatur: New members can sign up and earn slot points within the first 24 hours of sign-up and get free slot play or dining comps. This can be done at either Arizona Charlie's or Boulder, but not both, since the club is linked. The 24 hour "Take the Challenge" promotion works like this: Earn 200 slot points = $5 free slot play or $10 dining comp, Earn 400 slot points = $10 free slot play or $20 dining comp, Earn 800 slot points = $20 free slot play or $40 dining comp, Earn 1,000 slot points = $50 free slot play, Earn 2,000 slot points = $100 free slot play. Keep your earned points too. You'll need your ace/PLAY card for the café's excellent $5.55 breakfast special of steak or ham, eggs, hash browns & toast. You must present your players card to your server.

Casino Royale: Slot and video poker players can get daily rebates of $20 in free slot play for every $100 in losses.

D Las Vegas: New member sign up bonus: Earn $5 in free slot play for every 50 points earned during first 3 days of sign-up up to $100.

El Cortez: Have an IRS tax refund check you're ready to cash? Get a 5% free slot bonus for it. Cash your IRS check (or any government issued check) at the El Cortez main cage and you'll receive an extra 5% (up to $50) in FREE slot play money. The offer generally runs year round. Also, Earn 1,941 points in a day and receive your choice of a FREE pack of cigarettes, a $10 dining voucher at Siegel's 1941, two slices of pizza and a soft drink or draft beer at Pizza Lotto, a $6 Subway voucher or $10 in free slot play. Limit of one redemption per day.

Ellis Island Casino & Brewery: Known for their off-the-menu-great steak special. You get a generous cut of tenderloin cooked to your liking, bread, salad, vegetable of the day, and choice of potato. The regular price is $12.99, but Passport Players Card members can get it down to $7.99 by jumping through a few hoops. Everyone can swipe their players card to get $3 off for $9.99. Whereas you used to be able to get an additional $2 off by playing $1 in a machine, that requirement has been raised to $5. This steak special is not on the menu. Ask your server for it!

Jerry's Nugget: Players who join the Jerry's Nugget MoreClub earn free introductory gifts all on their first day's play. Based on slot points earned from 12 a.m. to 11:59 p.m. on the day they sign up, new members receive the following: 50 base points - $5 comp, 100 base points - Jerry's Nugget t-shirt, 250 base points - $20 comp, and 500 base points - $40 dining reward. New members earning 1,000 base points get $100 Free Play. Multiple prizes will be awarded based on the points earned categories. No points will be deducted.

M Resort: Comp Buffet Promotion: Must earn points the same day the comp buffet is used - prior to 8 pm to qualify. Offer does not include a line pass. Limit one meal per Marquee Rewards member. Offer not valid during holiday periods. Management reserves all rights to alter or cancel any promotion at any time. Lunch (Mon – Fri): 300 points on Reel Slots, 850 points on Video Poker. Dinner (Mon–Thu): 450 points on Reel Slots, 1,300 points on Video Poker. Seafood Dinner Buffet (Fri–Sun): 700 points on Reel Slots, 2,000 points on Video Poker.

Main Street Station: "Score with Four" promotion. Hit any four-of-a-kind, straight flush or royal flush and receive a scratch card for additional cash. Most cards are of the $2, $3 to $5 variety, but they do offer cards valued at $20, $50 and $100, as well as the extremely rare $5,000 cards.

Silverton: All new Silverton Rewards Club members will receive a half off dining offer and a free gift when signing up for the Rewards Club and will begin participating in the new sign-up program. Guests that earn 100 points on the same day that they sign up will receive a free buffet at Seasons Buffet. All new Silverton Rewards Club members will receive up to $200 in free slot play based on the points earned on their first visit. See Silverton Rewards Club for complete rules and details.

Station & Fiesta Casinos: For guests 50 years and older, "MyGeneration" offers special benefits every Wednessday, including: $4 Movie Matinées – Present your Boarding Pass at Regal Cinemas or Century Theatres to redeem your offer. Valid before 6 pm. Half-Point Bingo – Visit the Rewards Center to receive half-point bingo. Half-Point Bowling – Visit the Rewards Center to receive half-point bowling. $108,000 Free Slot Tournaments – 10AM – 7PM. $3,000 at each casino. $1,000 top prize. First entry free. Just earn 50 base points for each additional entry (up to 4). Additional specials (including multiple bonus point offers) may be offered at each participating casino and they can vary from month to month. (Note: Palms is not included in "MyGeneration" promotions.)

TI (Treasure Island): New Member Sign ups earn 100 slot points and spin to win $20-$100 in free slot play.

Tuscany Casino: Offering new members signing up for the slot club a randomly selected amount of free play, from $5 up to $500, plus a good little Fun Book.

Wynn Las Vegas: Offering new members signing up for a Wynn Las Vegas Get $10 in free slot play when you sign up. After earning first 300 points, spin a wheel for a prize ranging from $10 to $10,000 in free slot play, buffets, show tickets and more. Red Card is the same for Encore. Enroll at one or the other, not both.

Main Street Station Hotel & Casino
200 N. Main Street
Las Vegas, Nevada 89101
(702) 387-1896
Website: www.mainstreetcasino.com

Toll-Free Number: (800) 713-8933
Rooms: 406 Price Range: $45-$150
Suites: 14 Price Range: Casino Use Only
Restaurants: 2 (1 open 24 hours)
Buffets: B- $10.99/$15.99 (Sat/Sun)
L- $11.99
D- $14.99/$17.99 (Tue/Sat)/ $29.99 (Fri)
Casino Size: 26,918 Square Feet
Other Games: PGP, LIR, TCP
Special Features: 200-space RV park ($22-$30 per night). Buffet discount for Players Club members.

Mandalay Bay
3950 Las Vegas Boulevard S.
Las Vegas, Nevada 89119
(702) 632-7777
Web Site: www.mandalaybay.com

Rooms: 3,220 Price Range: $79-$399
Suites: 424 Price Range: $169-$649
Restaurants: 16
Self-Parking: $12 (1-4 hours), $15 (4-24 hours)
Valet Parking: $16 (0-2 hours), $18 (2-4 hours) $24 (4-24 hours)
Buffets: B- $19.99/$25.99 (Fri-Sun)
L- $21.99/$25.99 (Sun) D- $32.99
Casino Size: 160,344 Square Feet
Other Games: SB, RB, B, MB, P, PG, PGP, LIR, TCP, B6
Special Features: Four Seasons Hotel on 35th-39th floors. House of Blues restaurant. Sand and surf beach with lazy river ride. Shark Reef exhibit (admission charge). Spa. Michael Jackson *ONE* Cirque du Soleil show.

Free Things To See In Las Vegas!

The Fountains at Bellagio

More than one thousand fountains dance in front of the Bellagio hotel, creating a union of water, music and light. The display spans more than 1,000 feet, with water soaring as high as 240 feet. The fountains are choreographed to music ranging from classical and operatic pieces to songs from Broadway shows.

Showtimes are every 30 minutes from 3 p.m (noon on Sat/Sun) until 8 p.m. After 8 p.m. the shows start every 15 minutes until midnight. A list of all musical selections is available on the Bellagio website at: www.bellagio.com.

MGM Grand Hotel Casino
3799 Las Vegas Boulevard S.
Las Vegas, Nevada 89109
(702) 891-1111
Website: www.mgmgrand.com

Toll-Free Number: (800) 929-1111
Rooms: 5,005 Price Range: $66-$351
Suites: 752 Price Range: $114-$441
Skylofts: 51 Price Range: $790-$10,000
Self-Parking: $12 (1-4 hours), $15 (4-24 hours)
Valet Parking: $16 (0-2 hours), $18 (2-4 hours)
$24 (4-24 hours)
Restaurants: 22
Buffets: B/L-$21.99/$29.99 (Fri-Sun)
D-$32.99/$39.99 (Fri-Sun)
Casino Size: 156,023 Square Feet
Other Games: SB, RB, B, MB, PG, PGP, P, LIR, TCP, B6, CW
Special Features: Largest hotel in America. Topgolf driving range. Cirque du Soleil Ka stage show.

The Mirage
3400 Las Vegas Boulevard S.
Las Vegas, Nevada 89109
(702) 791-7111
Website: www.themirage.com

Rooms: 3,044 Price Range: $79-$329
Suites: 281 Price Range: $299-$1,500
Self-Parking: $12 (1-4 hours), $15 (4-24 hours)
Valet Parking: $16 (0-2 hours), $18 (2-4 hours)
$24 (4-24 hours)
Restaurants: 12
Buffets: B- $19.99/$31.99 (Sat/Sun)
L- $23.99/$31.99 (Sat/Sun)
D- $32.99/$34.99 (Fri-Sun)
Casino Size: 97,550 Square Feet
Other Games: SB, RB, B, MB, PG, P, PGP, LIR, TCP, B6, UTH
Special Features: Secret Garden and Dolphin Habitat (admission charge). Aquarium display at check-in desk. Simulated volcano with periodic 'eruptions'. Terry Fator and Cirque du Soleil's Love stage shows. Shin Lim's Limitless show.

New York-New York Hotel & Casino
3790 Las Vegas Boulevard S.
Las Vegas, Nevada 89109
(702) 740-6969
Website: www.nynyhotelcasino.com

Rooms: 2,024 Price Range: $59-$289
Suites: 12 Price Range: $114-$685
Self-Parking: $12 (1-4 hours), $15 (4-24 hours)
Valet Parking: $16 (0-2 hours), $18 (2-4 hours) $24 (4-24 hours)
Restaurants: 12
Casino Size: 84,000 Square Feet
Other Games: SB, RB, MB, PGP, LIR, TCP, B6
Special Features: Replica Statue of Liberty and Empire State Building. The Big Apple roller coaster. Cirque du Soleil's Zumanity stage show.

The Orleans Hotel & Casino
4500 West Tropicana Avenue
Las Vegas, Nevada 89103
(702) 365-7111
Website: www.orleanscasino.com

Rooms: 1,828 Price Range: $45-$135
Suites: 58 Price Range: $199-$499
Restaurants: 10
Buffets: B- $11.99/$20.99 (Sun) L- $14.99 D- $20.99/$25.99 (Fri)
Casino Size: 137,000 Square Feet
Other Games: SB, RB, MB, P, PGP, TCP, K, LIR
Special Features: 70-lane bowling center. 18-screen movie theater. Childcare center. 9,000-seat arena. Free shuttle to Gold Coast and Cromwell.

OYO Casino Hotel
115 East Tropicana Avenue
Las Vegas, Nevada 89109
(702) 739-9000
Website: www.hooterscasinohotel.com

Toll-Free Number: (866) 584-6687
Rooms: 694 Price Range: $39-$195
Suites: 17 Price Range: $205-$500
Restaurants: 4 (1 open 24 hours)
Casino Size: 27,528 Square Feet
Games Offered: SB, RB, TCP

Palace Station Hotel & Casino
2411 West Sahara Avenue
Las Vegas, Nevada 89102
(702) 367-2411
Website: www.palacestation.com

Rooms: 949 Price Range: $40-$195
Suites: 82 Price Range: $70-$485
Restaurants: 6 (1 open 24 hours)
Buffets: B-$13.99/$22.99 (Sun) L-$15.99 D-$22.99
Casino Size: 84,000 Square Feet
Other Games: SB, RB, B, MB, PG, P, PGP, TCP, K, BG
Senior Discount: Various Wed if 50+
Special Features: Buffet discount with Players Club card.

The Palazzo
3355 Las Vegas Boulevard S.
Las Vegas, Nevada 89109
(702) 607-7777
Website: www.palazzo.com

Suites: 3,025 Price Range: $119-$599
Restaurants: 17
Casino Size: 138,684 square feet
Other Games: SB, RB, B, MB, P, PG, PGP, CSP, LIR, TCP, B6
Special Features: Property is owned and located adjacent to The Venetian. Recreates city of Venice with canals, gondoliers and replica of Campanile Tower, St. Mark's Square, Doges Palace and Rialto Bridge. 90 retail stores. Madame Tussaud's Wax Museum. Canyon Ranch Spa.

Free Things To See In Las Vegas!

Volcano at The Mirage

Another fun Vegas attraction that won't cost you anything is the iconic volcano at the Mirage. The volcano first opened in 1989, but received a $25 million update in 2008. The volcano's choreographed, fire eruptions occur nightly and feature an original soundtrack put together by Grateful Dead drummer Mickey Hart and Indian composer Zakir Hussain. This, combined with sounds from actual volcanic eruptions create a truly thrilling experience. The volcano is located outside the Mirage (you can't miss it!) and "eruptions" occur at 8 p.m. and 9 p.m. Sunday-Thursday and 8 p.m., 9 p.m. and 10 p.m. Friday and Saturday.

The Palms
4321 Flamingo Road
Las Vegas, Nevada 89103
(702) 942-7777
Website: www.palms.com

Toll Free Number: (866) 942-7777
Rooms: 447 Price Range: $99-$329
Suites: 60 Price Range: $203-$419
Specialty Suites: 9 Prices: $2,500-$40,000
Restaurants: 8
Buffets: B-$15.99/$24.99 (Sat/Sun)
L-$17.99/$24.99 (Sat/Sun)
D-$24.99
Casino Size: 94,136 Square Feet
Other Games: SB, RB, MB, P, PGP, TCP, UTH, B6, CW
Special Features: 14-theater cineplex. IMAX theater. Tattoo shop. Childcare center.

Paris Casino Resort
3655 Las Vegas Boulevard S.
Las Vegas, Nevada 89109
(702) 946-7000
Website: www.parislasvegas.com

Toll-Free Number: (877) 796-2096
Rooms: 2,916 Price Range: $75-$379
Suites: 300 Price Range: $460-$989
Restaurants: 11 (1 open 24 hours)
Buffets: B/L- $21.99/$23.99 (Sat)/$30.99 (Sun)
D-$32.99
Self Parking: $9 (1-2 hours), $12 (2-4 hours)
$15 (4-24 hours)
Valet Parking $15 (0-2 hours), $20 (2-4 hours)
$24 (4-24 hours)
Casino Size: 95,263 Square Feet
Other Games: SB, RB, MB, B, TCP, PGP, PG, LIR, K
Special Features: Replicas of Paris landmarks. 50-story Eiffel Tower with restaurant/observation deck. *Anthony Cools* stage show.

Park MGM Las Vegas
3770 Las Vegas Boulevard S.
Las Vegas, Nevada 89109
(702) 730-7777
Website: www.parkmgm.com

Rooms: 3,002 Price Range: $45-$285
Suites: 259 Price Range: $125-$385
Self-Parking: First hour free, $5 (1-4 hours) $8 (4 to 24 hours)
Valet Parking: $8 (0-4 hours), $13 (4-24 hours)
Restaurants: 12 (1 open 24 hours)
Buffets: B-$18.99/$21.99 (Fri-Sun)
L-$19.99
D-$24.99/$27.99 (Fri-Sun)
Casino Size: 102,197 Square Feet
Other Games: SB, RB, MB, B, P, PGP, LIR, TCP, FCP, B6
Special Features: Food court. Microbrewery. Pool with lazy river ride. Health spa.

Planet Hollywood Resort & Casino
3667 Las Vegas Boulevard S.
Las Vegas, Nevada 89109
(702) 785-5555
Website: www.planethollywoodresort.com

Rooms: 1,878 Price Range: $87-$353
Parlor Rooms: 466 Price Range: $259-$369
Suites: 223 Price Range: $229-$689
Restaurants: 10 (1 open 24 hours)
Buffets: B/L-$18.99/$23.99 (Sat/Sun)
D-$35.99
Self Parking: Free
Valet Parking: $15 (0-2 hours), $20 (2-4 hours) $24 (4-24 hours)
Casino Size: 90,425 Square Feet
Other Games: SB, RB, B, MB, PGP, LIR, TCP
Special Features: 130-store retail mall. 7,000-seat Theater of the Performing Arts. Health spa and salon. V-theater located in the Miracle Mile Shops offers a variety of stage shows. Buffet discount for Players Club members.

Plaza Hotel & Casino
1 Main Street
Las Vegas, Nevada 89101
(702) 386-2110
Website: www.plazahotelcasino.com

Rooms: 1,037 Price Range: $35-$219
Suites: 60 Price Range: $69-$189
Restaurants: 5
Casino Size: 57,436 Square Feet
Other Games: K, SB, RB, PGP, LIR, TCP, UTH, BG, P
Special Features: Firefly Restaurant offers full view of Fremont Street Experience. Food court.

Rampart Casino
221 N. Rampart Boulevard
Las Vegas, Nevada 89145
(702) 507-5900
Website: www.rampartcasino.com

Rooms: 440 Price Range: $159-$229
Suites: 70 Price Range: $209-$399
Restaurants: 6
Buffets: L- $11.99/$16.99 (Sat/Sun)
D- $15.99/$18.99 (Thu)/$25.99 (Sat)
Casino Size: 56,750 Square Feet
Other Games: B, MB, SB, RB, PGP, TCP, FCP, UTH, BG
Senior Discount: Buffet discount if 50+
Special Features: Hotel is JW Marriott. Golf course. Spa. Buffet discount for Players Club members.

Red Rock Resort Spa Casino
11011 W. Charleston Boulevard
Las Vegas, Nevada 89135
(702) 797-7777
Website: www.redrocklasvegas.com

Toll-Free Number: (866) 767-7773
Rooms: 366 Price Range: $85-$305
Suites: 48 Price Range: $285-$1180
Restaurants: 8
Buffets: B-$12.99/$22.99 (Sun)
L- $16.99/$22.99 (Sun)
D- $22.99/$25.99 (Fri/Sat)
Casino Size: 119,309 Square Feet
Other Games: SB, RB, MB, B, PGP, TCP, LIR, K, BG
Special Features: 16-screen movie complex. Childcare center. Full-service spa. Buffet discount for Players Club members.

Free Things To See In Las Vegas!

Conservatory at Bellagio

Looking for some greenery during your Las Vegas stay? The Bellagio Conservatory has got you covered and is completely free! Every season, the Bellagio's 140 expert horticulturists create a breathtaking new scene made up of intricate floral arrangements, gazebos, bridges, and ponds for guests to explore. The themes begin with the Chinese New Year in January and change for summer, fall, and winter. The conservatory is located inside the Bellagio and is open 24 hours, with live music offered from 5-6pm daily in the south garden.

Resorts World - Las Vegas
3000 Las Vegas Boulevard South
Las Vegas, Nevada 89109

Rooms: 3,400 Price Range: Not set at press time
Casino Size: 110,000 Square Feet
Special Features: Chinese-themed casino with baccarat as dominant table game. **Expected to open late-2020**

Rio Suites Hotel & Casino
3700 W. Flamingo Road
Las Vegas, Nevada 89103
(702) 252-7777
Website: www.playrio.com

Toll-Free Number: (800) 752-9746
Suites: 2,563 Price Range: $68-$250
Restaurants: 11
Buffets: B/L-$29.99 (Sat/Sun)
D-$34.99/$34.99 (Fri/Sat)
Casino Size: 117,330 Square Feet
Other Games: SB, RB, MB, P, PG, PGP, LIR, TCP, UTH, MS, K
Overnight RV Parking: Free/RV Dump: No
Special Features: Kiss mini-golf. Outdoor zipline between hotel towers. *Penn and Teller* stage show.

Sam's Town Hotel & Gambling Hall
5111 Boulder Highway
Las Vegas, Nevada 89122
(702) 456-7777
Website: www.samstownlv.com

Toll-Free Number: (800) 897-8696
Rooms: 620 Price Range: $52-$119
Suites: 30 Price Range: $144-$265
Restaurants: 4
Buffets: B-$9.99/$15.99 (Sun) L-$12.99
D-$15.99/$20.99 (Fri)
Casino Size: 126,681 Square Feet
Other Games: SB, RB, P, LIR, TCP, UTH, PGP, K, BG
Senior Discounts: Various Wed if 50+
Special Features: 500-space RV park ($30 to $80 per night). Food court with 4 fast food options. Indoor promenade with free laser-light show. 24-hour 56-lane bowling center. 18-theater cinema complex. Childcare center. Buffet discounts for Players Club members.

Santa Fe Station Hotel & Casino
4949 North Rancho Drive
Las Vegas, Nevada 89130
(702) 658-4900
Website: santafestation.sclv.com

Rooms: 200 Price Range: $49-$149
Restaurants: 7
Buffets: B- $11.99/$17.99 (Sun)
L- $13.99
D- $17.99/$22.99 (Fri/Sat)
Casino Size: 156,401 Square Feet
Other Games: P, SB, RB, MB, PGP, TCP, UTH, K, BG
Senior Discounts: Various Wed if 50+
Special Features: 60-lane bowling center. 16-screen cinema. Childcare center. Buffet discount for Players Club members.

Silver Sevens Hotel and Casino
4100 Paradise Road
Las Vegas, Nevada 89169
(702) 733-7000
Website: www.silversevenscasino.com

Rooms: 370 Price Range: $39-$159
Restaurants: 2
Buffets: D- $21.99 (Fri)/$23.99 (Sat)
Casino Size: 27,225 Square Feet
Other Games: SB, RB, TCP, BG
Senior Discounts: Various Mon if 50+
Special features: Buffet discounts for players club members.

Silverton Casino Hotel Lodge
3333 Blue Diamond Road
Las Vegas, Nevada 89139
(702) 263-7777
Website: www.silvertoncasino.com

Toll-Free Number: (800) 588-7711
Rooms: 292 Price Range: $49-$139
Suites: 8 Price Range: $188-$388
Restaurants: 9
Buffets: L- $11.99/$19.99 (Sun)
D- $16.99/$39.99 (Fri)/$23.99 (Sat)
Casino Size: 73,213 Square Feet
Other Games: SB, RB, PGP, TCP, UTH
Senior Discount: Various Mon if 50+
Special Features: Starbucks coffee house. Johnny Rockets. Bass Pro Shops. 117,000 gallon aquarium with live mermaid shows.

Slots-A-Fun Casino
2890 Las Vegas Boulevard S.
Las Vegas, Nevada 89109
(702) 734-0410

Restaurants: 1 Subway and Pizza Shop
Casino Size: 16,733 Square Feet
Other Games: No table games
Special Features: Affiliated with Circus Circus Casino.

SLS Hotel & Casino (Sahara)
2535 Las Vegas Boulevard S.
Las Vegas, Nevada 89109
(702) 761-7000
Website: www.slslasvegas.com

Rooms: 1,350 Price Range: $49-$219
Suites: 250 Price Range: $179-$515
Restaurants: 5
Casino Size: 60,000 Square Feet
Other Games: B, MB, PGP, CW, UTH, TCP, SB, RB
Special Features: Spa. Expected to change name to **Sahara Las Vegas** by early 2020

South Point Hotel and Casino
9777 Las Vegas Boulevard S.
Las Vegas, Nevada 89183
(702) 796-7111
Website: www.southpointcasino.com

Toll-Free Number: (866) 796-7111
Rooms: 1,325 Price Range: $56-$159
Suites: 25 Price Range: $150-$950
Restaurants: 11
Buffets: B-$11.95/$20.95 (Sat/Sun)
L-$13.95
D-$20.95/$31.95 (Fri/Sat)
Casino Size: 137,232 Square Feet
Other Games: SB, RB, MB, P, PGP, TCP, MS, UTH, BG
Senior Discounts: Various Mon if 50+
Special Features: 16-screen movie complex. Equestrian center with 4,400-seat arena and 1,200 stalls. 64-lane bowling center. Childcare facility. Health spa.

Free Things To See In Las Vegas!

Welcome to Las Vegas Sign

Located on the Las Vegas Strip just south of Mandalay Bay is the historic "Welcome to Fabulous Las Vegas" sign. The sign, which was built in 1959 and has since become a well-known Vegas landmark, reads "Welcome to Fabulous Las Vegas, Nevada" on the front and "Drive Carefully" and "Come Back Soon" on the back.

The sign has its own 12-car parking lot and photos can be taken near the sign with ease. The parking lot also has room for two buses and there is access for individuals with disabilities. Parking is free and the sign can be accessed 24 hours a day.

In order to access the "Welcome to Las Vegas" sign parking lot, you must be heading south on Las Vegas Boulevard going away from Mandalay Bay and toward the Las Vegas Outlet Center.

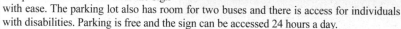

The Strat
2000 Las Vegas Boulevard S.
Las Vegas, Nevada 89104
(702) 380-7777
Website: www.thestrat.com

Rooms: 2,427 Price Range: $76-$129
Suites: 250 Price Range: $119-$340
Restaurants: 7
Buffets: B/L-$17.99/$24.99 (Sat-Sun)
D-$23.99
Casino Size: 80,000 Square Feet
Other Games: P, PGP, LIR, B6, CSP, TCP
Senior Discount: Tower discount if 55+
Special Features: 109 story Indoor/Outdoor Observation Deck (admission charge). *SkyPod* and *SkyJump* attractions. Revolving restaurant at top of tower. 50 retail stores. Comedy club.

Suncoast Hotel and Casino
9090 Alta Drive
Las Vegas, Nevada 89145
(702) 636-7111
Website: www.suncoastcasino.com

Toll-Free Number: (866) 636-7111
Rooms: 432 Price Range: $79-$139
Suites: 40 Price Range: $156-$324
Restaurants: 8
Buffets: B-$11.99/$17.99 (Sun)
L-$12.99
D-$13.99/$16.99 (Fri/Sun)/
$21.99 (Sat)
Casino Size: 95,898 Square Feet
Other Games: SB, RB, MB, PGP,
TCP, UTH, BG
Senior Discount: Various on Wed if 50+
Special Features: 64-lane bowling center. 16-screen movie theater. Family arcade. Free shuttles to airport, Strip and other Coast properties. $5 buffet discount for Players Club members.

Treasure Island (TI)
3300 Las Vegas Boulevard S.
Las Vegas, Nevada 89109
(702) 894-7111
Website: www.treasureisland.com

Rooms: 2,665 Price Range: $56-$259
Suites: 220 Price Range: $213-$279
Restaurants: 7
Buffets: B- $23.45/$30.45 (Sat/Sun)
L- $25.95/$30.45 (Sat/Sun)
D- $29.95/$35.45 (Fri/Sat)
Casino Size: 50,335 Square Feet
Other Games: SB, RB, B, MB, PG, PGP, LIR, TCP, B6
Special Features: Health spa/salon. Cirque du Soleil's *Mystere* stage show. *Marvel Avengers S.T.A.T.I.O.N.* attraction.

Tropicana Resort & Casino
3801 Las Vegas Boulevard S.
Las Vegas, Nevada 89109
(702) 739-2222
Website: www.troplv.com

Rooms: 1,877 Price Range: $59-$329
Suites: 115 Price Range: $189-$599
Restaurants: 6
Buffet: B/L- $23.99
Casino Size: 66,200 Square Feet
Other Games: SB, RB, MB, PGP, UTH
Special Features: Legends in Concert tribute show.

Tuscany Suites & Casino
255 East Flamingo Road
Las Vegas, Nevada 89169
(702) 893-8933
Website: www.tuscanylv.com

Suites: 760 Price Range: $31-$205
Restaurants: 4
Casino Size: 22,450 Square Feet
Other Games: SB, RB
Senior Discounts: Various Thu if 50+
Special Features: All suite hotel

The Venetian Resort Hotel Casino
3355 Las Vegas Boulevard S.
Las Vegas, Nevada 89109
(702) 414-1000
Website: www.venetian.com

Suites: 4,046 Price Range: $129-$900
Restaurants: 39
Casino Size: 138,684 Square Feet
Other Games: SB, RB, B, MB, P, PG, PGP, CSP, LIR, TCP, B6, S21, MS, UTH
Special Features: Stadium version of blackjack. Recreates city of Venice with canals, gondola rides and replica Campanile Tower, St. Mark's Square, Doge's Palace and Rialto Bridge. 90 retail stores. Madame Tussaud's Wax Museum. Canyon Ranch Spa. Human Nature stage show.

Westgate Las Vegas Resort & Casino
3000 Paradise Road
Las Vegas, Nevada 89109
(702) 732-5111
Website: www.westgatedestinations.com

Reservation Number: (888) 796-3564
Rooms: 2,956 Price Range: $50-$189
Suites: 305 Price Range: $179-$2,500
Restaurants: 10
Buffets: B- $19.00/$26.00 (Sat/Sun)
L-$22.00 D- $27.00
Casino Size: 74,676 Square Feet
Other Games: SB, RB, P, B, MB.
Special Features: Benihana Restaurant. *Barry Manilow* stage show. *George Wallace* comedy show. World's largest race and sports book. Health club. Jogging track.

Wild Wild West Casino
3330 West Tropicana Avenue
Las Vegas, Nevada 89103
(702) 740-0000
Website: wildfire.sclv.com

Rooms: 260 Price Range: $39-$149
Restaurants: 1 (open 24 hours)
Casino Size: 11,250 Square Feet
Other Games: SB, no table games
Special Features: Hotel is a Days Inn. Part of Station Casinos group. Denny's restaurant. 15-acre truck plaza.

Wynn Las Vegas
3131 Las Vegas Boulevard S.
Las Vegas, Nevada 89109
(702) 770-7000
Website: www.wynnlasvegas.com

Toll-Free Number: (888) 320-7123
Rooms: 2,359 Prices: $179-$559
Suites: 351 Prices: $309-$5,000
Restaurants: 19
Valet Parking: $21 (up to 2 hours)/
$24 (2-4 hours)/
$30 (4-24 hours)
Buffets: B- $26.99/$29.99 (Sat/Sun)
L- $26.99
D- $42.99/$49.99 (Fri/Sat)
Casino Size: 186,187 Square Feet
Other Games: SB, RB, B, MB, P, PG, PGP, LIR, TCP, UTH, CW, B6
Special Features: 150-foot man-made mountain with five-story waterfall. 18-hole golf course. *Le Reve* stage show. Spa and salon.

Laughlin

Map location: **#2** (on the Colorado River, 100 miles south of Las Vegas and directly across the river from Bullhead City, Arizona)

Laughlin is named after Don Laughlin, who owns the Riverside Hotel & Casino and originally settled there in 1966. The area offers many water sport activities on the Colorado River as well as at nearby Lake Mojave.

For Laughlin tourism information call: (800) 452-8445. You can also visit their Website at: www.visitlaughlin.com.

Here's information, as supplied by Nevada's State Gaming Control Board, showing the slot machine payback percentages for all of Laughlin's casinos for the fiscal year beginning July 1, 2018 and ending June 30, 2019:

Denomination	Payback %
1¢ Slots	89.11
5¢ Slots	92.59
25¢ Slots	93.44
$1 Slots	93.92
$1 Megabucks	88.27
$5 Slots	94.33
All Slots	92.15

These numbers reflect the percentage of money returned to the players on each denomination of machine. All electronic machines including slots, video poker and video keno are included in these numbers.

Optional games in the casino listings include: sports book (SB), race book (RB), Spanish 21 (S21), baccarat (B), mini-baccarat (MB), poker (P), pai gow poker (PGP), Caribbean stud poker (CSP), let it ride (LIR), three-card poker (TCP), four card poker (FCP), ultimate Texas hold'em (UTH), Texas hold'em bonus (THB), keno (K), sic bo (SIC), Mississippi stud (MS), big 6 wheel (B6) and bingo (BG).

Aquarius Casino Resort
1900 S. Casino Drive
Laughlin, Nevada 89029
(702) 298-5111
Website: www.aquariuscasinoresort.com

Rooms: 1,900 Price Range: $39-$89
Suites: 90 Price Range: $109-$299
Restaurants: 6 (1 open 24 hours)
Buffets: B/L- $16.00/$18.00 (Sun)
D-$20.00/$30.00 (Fri)/$28.00 (Sat)
Casino Size: 57,070 Square Feet
Other Games: RB, SB, MB, PGP, LIR, TCP
Overnight RV Parking: No
Special Features: Fast Food court. Outback Steakhouse. 3,300-seat amphitheater. Buffet discount for Players Club members.

Colorado Belle Hotel Casino Resort
2100 S. Casino Drive
Laughlin, Nevada 89029
(702) 298-4000
Website: www.coloradobelle.com

Rooms: 1,124 Price Range: $25-$55
Suites: 49 Price Range: $105-$175
Restaurants: 3
Buffets: B/L- $15.99 (Sat)/$19.99 (Sun)
L-$8.99/$12.99 (Sun)
D- $16.99/$24.99 (Fri/Sat)
Casino Size: 48,268 Square Feet
Other Games: SB, RB, TCP, LIR
Overnight RV Parking: No
Special Features: Video arcade. Microbrewery. Spa.

Don Laughlin's Riverside Resort Hotel & Casino
1650 S. Casino Drive
Laughlin, Nevada 89029
(702) 298-2535
Website: www.riversideresort.com

Rooms: 1,405 Price Range: $49-$89
Executive Rooms: 93 Price Range: $79-$399
Restaurants: 6
Buffets: B-$8.99 L-$9.99/$16.99 (Sun)
D- $15.99/$20.99 (Fri)
Casino Size: 86,106 Square Feet
Other Games: SB, RB, P, LIR, PGP, TCP, UTH, K, BG
Overnight RV Parking: Must use RV park
Special Features: 740-space RV park ($25-$35 per night). Six-screen cinema. Free classic car exhibit. 34-lane bowling center. Childcare center.

Edgewater Hotel Casino
2020 S. Casino Drive
Laughlin, Nevada 89029
(702) 298-2453
Website: www.edgewater-casino.com

Toll-Free Number: (800) 289-8777
Rooms: 1,420 Price Range: $24-$89
Suites: 23 Price Range: $95-$155
Restaurants: 3
Buffets: B- $11.99/$15.99 (Sun)
D- $16.99/$24.99 (Fri-Sat)
Casino Size: 45,927 Square Feet
Other Games: SB, RB, PGP, TCP, LIR
Overnight RV Parking: No

Golden Nugget Laughlin
2300 S. Casino Drive
Laughlin, Nevada 89029
(702) 298-7111
Website: www.goldennugget.com

Rooms: 300 Price Range: $45-$129
Suites: 4 Price Range: $150-$300
Restaurants: 4
Casino Size: 32,600 Square Feet
Other Games: SB, RB, PGP, TCP
Overnight RV Parking: Free/RV Dump: No
Special Features: Suites must be booked through casino marketing. Gift shop.

Harrah's Laughlin Casino & Hotel
2900 S. Casino Drive
Laughlin, Nevada 89029
(702) 298-4600
Website: www.harrahslaughlin.com

Rooms: 1,451 Price Range: $46-$320
Suites: 115 Price Range: $146-$495
Restaurants: 4
Buffets: B-$13.99/$18.99 (Sun)
L-$15.99
D-$17.99/$28.99 (Fri)/$23.99 (Sat)/ $21.99 (Sun)
Casino Size: 56,357 Square Feet
Other Games: SB, RB, P, PGP, TCP, LIR, K
Overnight RV Parking: No
Special Features: Salon and day spa. Beach and pools. 300-seat showroom. 3,000-seat amphitheater. McDonald's. Baskin-Robbins. Cinnabon. Starbucks.

Laughlin River Lodge
2700 S. Casino Drive
Laughlin, Nevada 89029
(702) 298-2242
Website: www.laughlinriverlodge.com

Toll-Free Number: (800) 835-7904
Rooms: 995 Price Range: $50-$97
Suites: 8 Price Range: $192-$249
Restaurants: 1
Casino Size: 30,087 Square Feet
Other Games: BG, no table games
Overnight RV Parking: Free/RV Dump: No
Special Features: Denny's restaurant. Health spa.

Pioneer Hotel & Gambling Hall
2200 S. Casino Drive
Laughlin, Nevada 89029
(702) 298-2442
Website: www.pioneerlaughlin.com

Rooms: 416 Price Range: $30-$90
Suites: 20 Price Range: $112-$129
Restaurants: 1
Casino Size: 16,300 Square Feet
Other Games: No table games
Overnight RV Parking: Free/RV Dump: No
Special Features: Western-themed casino. Western wear store. Liquor/cigarette store.

Tropicana Laughlin
2121 S. Casino Drive
Laughlin, Nevada 89029
(702) 298-4200
Website: www.troplaughlin.com

Toll-Free Number: (800) 343-4533
Rooms: 1,501 Price Range: $45-$139
Suites: 55 Price Range: $79-$179
Restaurants: 5
Casino Size: 53,000 Square Feet
Other Games: PGP, TCP, MS, SB, RB, BG
Overnight RV Parking: Free/RV Dump: No
Senior Discounts: Various Mon if 50+
Special Features: Train-shaped swimming pool

Lovelock

Map Location: **#18** (92 miles N.E. of Reno on I-80)

C Punch Inn & Casino
1440 Cornell Avenue
Lovelock, Nevada 89419
(775) 273-2971
Website: www.cpunchinnandcasino.com

Rooms: 74 Price Range: $79-$99
Spa Rooms: 2 Price Range: $99-$119
Restaurants: 1
Casino Size: 7,000 Square Feet
Other Games: SB, no table games
Overnight RV Parking: Free/RV Dump: No
Special Features: Fully operational cattle and alfalfa farm.

Mesquite

Map Location: **#19** (77 miles N.E. of Las Vegas on I-15 at the Arizona border)

Here's information, as supplied by Nevada's State Gaming Control Board, showing the slot machine payback percentages for all of the Mesquite area casinos for the fiscal year beginning July 1, 2018 and ending June 30, 2019:

Denomination	Payback %
1¢ Slots	90.16
5¢ Slots	95.48
25¢ Slots	95.52
$1 Slots	95.19
$1 Megabucks	87.77
All Slots	93.80

These numbers reflect the percentage of money returned on each denomination of machine and encompass all electronic machines including slots, video poker and video keno.

CasaBlanca Hotel-Casino-Golf-Spa
950 W. Mesquite Boulevard
Mesquite, Nevada 89027
(702) 346-7529
Website: www.casablancaresort.com

Rooms: 500 Price Range: $39-$79
Suites: 18 Price Range: $69-$199
Restaurants: 3
Buffets: B/L -$8.99 (Sat/Sun)
D-$18.99 (Fri/Sat)
Casino Size: 27,000 Square Feet
Other Games: SB, RB, PGP, TCP, LIR
Overnight RV Parking: Must use RV park
Special Features: 45-space RV park ($30-$40 per night). 18-hole golf course. Health spa.

Eureka Casino & Hotel
275 Mesa Boulevard
Mesquite, Nevada 89027
(702) 346-4600
Website: www.eurekamesquite.com

Rooms: 192 Price Range: $79-$139
Suites: 18 Price Range: $149-$265
Restaurants: 4
Buffets: B-$8.99 L- $9.99
D- $14.99/$21.99 (Fri)/$18.99 (Sat)
Casino Size: 40,285 Square Feet
Other Games: P, PGP, TCP, UTH, BG
Overnight RV Parking: No
Senior Discounts: Various on Tuesdays if 55+
Special Features: Buffet discount with Players Club card.

Virgin River Hotel/Casino/Bingo
100 E. Pioneer Boulevard
Mesquite, Nevada 89027
(702) 346-7777
Website: www.virginriver.com

Toll-Free Number: (877) 438-2929
Rooms: 720 Price Range: $27-$68
Restaurants: 2
Buffets: B-$6.99/$11.99 (Sun)
L-$9.99/$11.99 (Sun)
D- $13.99/$15.99 (Tue/Sat)/
$17.99 (Fri)
Casino Size: 37,000 Square Feet
Other Games: SB, RB, PGP, TCP,
UTH, K, BG
Overnight RV Parking: No
Special Features: 24-lane bowling center. Family arcade.

Minden

Map Location: **#14** (42 miles S. of Reno on Hwy. 395)

Carson Valley Inn
1627 Highway 395 N.
Minden, Nevada 89423
(775) 782-9711
Website: www.cvinn.com

Hotel Rooms: 146 Price Range: $119-$159
Lodge Rooms: 75 Price Range: $79-$119
Restaurants: 2
Casino Size: 22,800 Square Feet
Other Games: SB, RB, P, TCP, no roulette
Overnight RV Parking: Free/Dump; $5
Senior Discount: Various discounts if 50+
Special Features: 59-space RV park ($39-$60 per night). 24-hour convenience store. Wedding chapel. Childcare center.

North Las Vegas

Map Location: **#20** (5 miles N.E. of the Las Vegas Strip on Las Vegas Blvd. N.)

Aliante Casino Hotel & Spa
7300 Aliante Parkway
North Las Vegas, Nevada 89084
(702) 692-7777
Website: www.aliantegaming.com

Toll-Free Number: (877) 477-7627
Rooms: 202 Price Range: $89-$179
Restaurants: 5
Buffets: B-$8.99/$16.99 (Sun)
L- $11.99/$14.99 (Sat/Sun)
D- $15.99/$21.99 (Fri/Sat)
Casino Size: 125,000 Square Feet
Other Games: SB, RB, TCP, PGP, UTH, BG
Overnight RV Parking: No
Special Features: 16-screen Regal Theater. Spa. 650-seat showroom.

Bighorn Casino
3016 E. Lake Mead Boulevard
N. Las Vegas, Nevada 89030
(702) 642-1940

Restaurants: 1
Casino Size: 3,740 Square Feet
Other Games: SB, no craps/roulette
Overnight RV Parking: No

Cannery Hotel & Casino
2121 E Craig Road
N. Las Vegas, Nevada 89030
(702) 507-5700
Website: www.cannerycasino.com

Toll-Free Number: (866) 999-4899
Rooms: 201 Price Range: $89-$169
Restaurants: 6
Buffets: B- $15.99 (Sat/Sun)
L- $11.99/$15.99 (Sat/Sun)
D- $15.99/$17.99 (Thu-Sat)
Casino Size: 80,375 Square Feet
Other Games: SB, RB, P, PGP, BG
Overnight RV Parking: No
Special Features: Property is themed to resemble a 1940's canning factory. Buffet discount for players club members.

Fiesta Rancho Casino Hotel
2400 N. Rancho Drive
N. Las Vegas, Nevada 89130
(702) 631-7000
Website: www.fiestarancholasvegas.com

Rooms: 100 Price Range: $35-$145
Restaurants: 2
Buffets: B- $15.99 (Sat/Sun) L- $12.99
D- $15.99/$16.99 (Sat)
Casino Size: 59,951 Square Feet
Other Games: SB, RB, PGP, K, BG
Overnight RV Parking: Yes/Dump: No
Senior Discount: Various on Wed if 50+
Special Features: Ice skating arena. Coffee bar. Buffet discount for slot club members.

Jerry's Nugget
1821 Las Vegas Boulevard North
N. Las Vegas, Nevada 89030
(702) 399-3000
Website: www.jerrysnugget.com

Restaurants: 1
Casino Size: 32,511 Square Feet
Other Games: SB, RB, K, BG
Overnight RV Parking: No
Senior Discount: Various on Tue if 50+
Special Features: Bakery

Lucky Club Casino
3227 Civic Center Drive
N. Las Vegas, Nevada 89030
(702) 399-3297
Website: www.luckyclublv.com

Rooms: 92 Price Range: $49-$99
Suites: 3 Price Range: $200
Restaurants: 1
Casino Size: 16,000 Square Feet
Games Offered: SB, RB, no roulette
Overnight RV Parking: No
Special Features: Closest hotel/casino to Las Vegas Motor Speedway. $9.99 steak & lobster dinner.

The Poker Palace
2757 Las Vegas Blvd. North
N. Las Vegas, Nevada 89030
(702) 649-3799
Website: www.pokerpalace.net

Restaurants: 1
Casino Size: 25,900 Square Feet
Other Games: SB, RB, P, BG, no craps/roulette
Overnight RV Parking: No

Silver Nugget
2140 Las Vegas Boulevard North
N. Las Vegas, Nevada 89030
(702) 399-1111
Website: www.silvernuggetlv.com

Restaurants: 1
Casino Size: 22,395 Square Feet
Other Games: SB, RB, no craps/roulette
Overnight RV Parking: No
Special Features: 24-lane bowling center.

Texas Station Gambling Hall & Hotel
2101 Texas Star Lane
N. Las Vegas, Nevada 89032
(702) 631-1000
Website: www.texasstation.com

Toll-Free Number: (800) 654-8804
Rooms: 200 Price Range: $59-$89
Restaurants: 4
Buffets: B-$10.99/$16.99 (Sun) L-$13.99
D-$16.99/$18.99 (Fri)
Casino Size: 123,045 Square Feet
Other Games: SB, RB, PGP, K, BG
Overnight RV Parking: No
Senior Discount: Various on Wed if 50+
Special Features: 18-screen movie theater. 60-lane bowling center. Childcare center. Food court. Wedding chapels. Video arcade. 2,000-seat events center. Buffet discount for slot club members.

Pahrump

Map Location: **#21** (59 miles W. of Las Vegas on Hwy. 160)

Gold Town Casino
771 S. Frontage Road
Pahrump, Nevada 89048
(775) 751-7777
Website: www.gtowncasino.com

Toll Free Number: (888) 837-7425
Restaurants: 1
Casino Size: 15,057 Square Feet
Other Games: RB, SB, K, BG
Overnight RV Parking: Free/RV Dump: No
Special Features: General store and gas station.

Pahrump Nugget Hotel & Gambling Hall
681 S. Highway 160
Pahrump, Nevada 89048
(775) 751-6500
Website: www.pahrumpnugget.com

Toll Free Number: (866) 751-6500
Rooms: 70 Price Range: $59-$89
Suites: 5 Price Range: $149-$179
Restaurants: 2
Casino Size: 19,259 Square Feet
Other Games: SB, RB, FCP, UTH, BG
Overnight RV Parking: No
Special Features: 24-lane bowling center. Video arcade.

Saddle West Hotel/Casino & RV Park
1220 S. Highway 160
Pahrump, Nevada 89048
(775) 727-1111
Website: www.saddlewest.com

Rooms: 148 Price Range: $49-$85
Suites: 10 Price Range: $89-$129
Restaurants: 2 (1 open 24 hours)
Buffets: B- $9.95 L- $8.95
D- $12.95 (Sun-Wed)/$13.95 (Thu)/ $15.95 (Fri)/$17.95 (Sat)
Casino Size: 16,115 Square Feet
Other Games: SB, RB, BG
Overnight RV Parking: Free/RV Dump: No
Special Features: 80-space RV park ($32 per night). Closest casino to Death Valley Park.

Primm

Map Location: **#6** (25 miles S.W. of Las Vegas on I-15; 9 miles from the California border)

Buffalo Bill's Resort & Casino
31700 Las Vegas Boulevard S.
Primm, Nevada 89019
(702) 382-1212
Website: www.primmvalleyresorts.com

Toll-Free Number: (800) 386-7867
Rooms: 1,242 Price Range: $34-$94
Restaurants: 3
Casino Size: 62,130 Square Feet
Other Games: SB, RB, P, MS, TCP
Overnight RV Parking: Free/RV Dump: No
Special Features: 3 Roller coasters. Flume ride. Two water slides. Movie theater. Video Arcade. 6,500-seat arena. 24-hour bus shuttle connects to Whiskey Pete's and Primm Valley.

Primm Valley Resort & Casino
31900 Las Vegas Boulevard S.
Primm, Nevada 89019
(702) 382-1212
Website: www.primmvalleyresorts.com

Rooms: 661 Price Range: $34-$104
Restaurants: 3
Buffets: B/L-$17.95 (Fri-Sun)
D-$19.95 (Fri-Sun)
Casino Size: 38,049 Square Feet
Other Games: SB, RB, TCP, MS
Overnight RV Parking: Free/RV Dump: No
Special Features: 24-hour bus shuttle connects to Whiskey Pete's and Buffalo Bill's.

Whiskey Pete's Hotel & Casino
100 Primm Boulevard West
Primm, Nevada 89019
(702) 382-1212
Website: www.primmvalleyresorts.com

Rooms: 777 Price Range: $35-$145
Restaurants: 2
Casino Size: 36,400 Square Feet
Other Games: SB, RB, P
Overnight RV Parking: Free/RV Dump: No
Special Features: Al Capone's car and Bonnie & Clyde's "death" car on display. 24-hour bus shuttle connects to Primm Valley and Buffalo Bill's. Starbucks.

Reno

Map Location: **#4** (near the California border, 58 miles N.E. of Lake Tahoe and 32 miles N. of Carson City).

Reno may be best known for its neon arch on Virginia Street which welcomes visitors to "The Biggest Little City in the World." The current arch is actually the fourth one since the original arch was built in 1927. The area also houses the nation's largest car collection at the National Automobile Museum.

For Reno information call the Reno/Sparks Convention & Visitors Authority at (800) 367-7366 or go to: www.visitrenotahoe.com.

Overnight parking of an RV in a casino parking lot is prohibited in Reno.

Here's information, as supplied by Nevada's State Gaming Control Board, showing the slot machine payback percentages for all of the Reno area casinos for the fiscal year beginning July 1, 2018 and ending June 30, 2019:

Denomination	Payback %
1¢ Slots	92.69
5¢ Slots	95.10
25¢ Slots	92.16
$1 Slots	95.38
$1 Megabucks	87.40
$5 Slots	95.06
All Slots	94.56

These numbers reflect the percentage of money returned on each denomination of machine and encompass all electronic machines including slots, video poker and video keno.

Optional games in the casino listings include: sports book (SB), race book (RB), Spanish 21 (S21), baccarat (B), mini-baccarat (MB), pai gow (PG), poker (P), pai gow poker (PGP), Caribbean stud poker (CSP), let it ride (LIR), three-card poker (TCP), four card poker (FCP), ultimate Texas hold'em (UTH), Texas hold'em bonus (THB), big 6 wheel (B6), keno (K) and bingo (BG).

Atlantis Casino Resort
3800 S. Virginia Street
Reno, Nevada 89502
(775) 825-4700
Website: www.atlantiscasino.com

Rooms: 975 Price Range: $69-$219
Suites: 120 Price Range: $99-$325
Restaurants: 8 (1 open 24 hours)
Buffets: B- $16.99/$29.99 (Sat)/$32.99 (Sun)
L- $18.99/$29.99 (Sat)/$32.99 (Sun)
D- $25.99/$36.99 (Fri/Sat)
Casino Size: 63,814 Square Feet
Other Games: SB, RB, MB, P, PGP, LIR, TCP, K, BG
Senior Discount: 10% off buffet if 55+
Special Features: Health spa and salon. Buffet discount for Players Club members.

Bonanza Casino
4720 N. Virginia Street
Reno, Nevada 89506
(775) 323-2724
Website: www.bonanzacasino.com

Restaurants: 2
Casino Size: 12,484 Square Feet
Other Games: SB, RB, no roulette

Circus Circus Hotel Casino/Reno
500 N. Sierra Street
Reno, Nevada 89503
(775) 329-0711
Website: www.circusreno.com

Toll-Free Number: (888) 682-0147
Rooms: 1,464 Price Range: $55-$155
Suites: 108 Price Range: $115-185
Restaurants: 5
Casino Size: 65,959 Square Feet
Other Games: SB, RB, electronic table games
Special Features: Free circus acts. Carnival games. 24-hour gift shop/liquor store.

Club Cal-Neva
38 E. Second Street
Reno, Nevada 89501
(775) 323-1046
Website: www.clubcalneva.com

Restaurants: 2
Casino Size: 40,140 Square Feet
Other Games: TCP, SB, P, K, no craps/roulette
Special Features: Hot dog and beer or taco and beer specials.

Diamond's Casino
1010 E. 6th Street
Reno, Nevada 89512
(775) 786-5151
Website: www.diamondscasinoreno.com

Rooms: 280 Price Range: $65-$109
Suites: 6 Price Range: $330
Restaurants: 1
Casino Size: 8,000 Square Feet
Other Games: SB, RB, no craps/roulette
Special Features: Hotel is Ramada Inn.

Eldorado Hotel Casino
345 N. Virginia Street
Reno, Nevada 89501
(775) 786-5700
Website: www.eldoradoreno.com

Toll-Free Number: (800) 879-8879
Rooms: 817 Price Range: $60-$139
Suites: 127 Price Range: $130-$240
Restaurants: 9
Buffets: B- $16.99/$21.99 (Sat)/$27.99 (Sun)
L- $17.99
D- $24.99/$35.99 (Fri/Sat)
Casino Size: 76,500 Square Feet
Other Games: SB, RB, B, MB, PG, PGP, P, K
Special Features: In-house coffee roasting. Microbrewery. Bakery.

Grand Sierra Resort & Casino
2500 E. Second Street
Reno, Nevada 89595
(775) 789-2000
Website: www.grandsierraresort.com

Rooms: 1,847 Price Range: $69-$219
Suites: 154 Price Range: $184-$319
Restaurants: 7
Buffets: B/L- $18.99/$27.99 (Sat/Sun)
D- $24.99/$34.99 (Fri/Sat)
Casino Size: 80,000 Square Feet
Other Games: SB, RB, PG, PGP, TCP, K, P
Senior Discount: Various Tue/Wed if 55+
Special Features: 50-lane bowling center. 174-space RV park ($45-$60 summer/$35-$50 winter). 50-lane bowling center. Health club. Shopping mall. Family amusement center. Laketop golf driving range. Indoor simulated golf. Five-screen movie theater. Ice skating rink. Family arcade and kart racing.

The Best Places To Play in Reno/Tahoe

Roulette- The house edge on a single-zero wheel cuts the house edge from 5.26% down to a more reasonable 2.70%. Unfortunately, there are no casinos in Reno/Tahoe that offer single-zero roulette.

Craps- Almost all Reno/Tahoe area casinos offer double odds, or 3x/4x/5x on their crap games. The casino offering the highest odds is The Lakeside Inn in Lake Tahoe which offers 10X odds.

Blackjack- All recommendations in this section apply to basic strategy players. You should always look for casinos that pay the standard 3-to-2 for blackjack. Some casinos may pay 6-to-5 for blackjack and this increases the casino edge to around 1.5% and they should be avoided.

There's good news and bad news for blackjack players in Northern Nevada. The good news is that there is an abundance of single-deck and double-deck games available. The bad news is that all casinos in the Reno/Tahoe area hit soft 17. This results in a slightly higher advantage (.20%) for the casinos. Additionally, some casinos may also restrict your double-downs to two-card totals of 10 or 11 only.

The best single-deck games can be found at Boomtown and Western Village where they allow you to double down on any first two cards, split any pair and resplit any pair (except aces). The casino edge in this game is .18%. (NOTE: There are numerous casinos that offer a game similar to this one except they will only allow you to double down on totals of 10 or more. This raises the casino edge in this game to .44%).

There are seven Reno-area casinos that tie for best place to play double-deck blackjack: Atlantis, Cal-Neva, Eldorado, Grand Sierra, Nugget, Peppermill and Silver Legacy. Their two-deck games have the following rules: double down on any first two cards, split any pair, and resplit any pair (except aces). This works out to a casino edge of .53%.

The best six-deck game can be found in Reno at the Silver Legacy. The game's edge is .32% with these rules: double down on any two or more cards, split any pair, resplit any pair (including aces) and double allowed after split.

Next best is a game found at five Lake Tahoe casinos: Harrah's, Hard Rock, Harveys, Hyatt Regency and Lakeside Inn. The casino edge here is .56% with the following rules: double down on any two cards, split any pair, resplit any pair (including aces) and double allowed after split.

If you take away resplitting of aces from the previous game then you have a game with a casino edge of .63% which is offered at most other casinos, including: Atlantis, Eldorado, Grand Sierra, Nugget, the Peppermill and Sands Regency.

Video Poker- Smart video poker players know that some of the best varieties of machines to look for are: 8/5 Bonus Poker (99.17 % return), 9/6 Jacks or Better (99.54% return), 10/6 Double Double Bonus (100.07% return), 10/7 Double Bonus (100.17% return) and full-pay Deuces Wild (100.76% return).

All of these games are available in Northern Nevada, with the exception of full-pay Deuces Wild, which is hard to find. A slightly lesser-paying version, known as Not So Ugly Deuces (NSUD), which returns 99.73%, however, is widely available.

Following is a list of casinos offering the better paying video poker games. The abbreviations used for each listing are BP (8/5 Bonus Poker), JB (9/6 Jacks or Better), DDB (10/6 Double Double Bonus), DB (10/7 Double Bonus), FPDW (Full-Pay Deuces Wild) and NSUD (Not So Ugly Deuces).

Reno/Sparks Casinos:
Atlantis: JB - nickel to 50-cents (some with progressives); BP - nickel to $10 (some with progressives); NSUD - nickel to $10 (some with progressives)
Bonanza: JB - $1 to $5; BP - $1 to $5
Club Cal Neva: JB - 50-cents, $1 and $5; BP - 50-cents and $1
Eldorado: JB - quarter to $5 (some with progressives); NSUD - quarter to $1; BP - quarter
Grand Sierra: JB - quarter to $10 (some with progressives); BP - quarter to $10; NSUD - quarter to $10
Harrah's Reno: JB - $1 to $5; BP - nickel to $5 (some with progressive)
Nugget: JB - nickel to 50-cent; BP - two-cents an nickel
Peppermill: JB - penny to $100 (some with progressives); NSUD - nickel to $5 (some with progressives); BP - nickel to $100
Rail City: JB - quarter to $1; BP quarter to $1
Silver Legacy: JB - nickel to $25; NSUD - quarter and $1; BP - quarter to $25 (some with progressives)
Western Village: JB - penny to $1; NSUD - penny to $1

Lake Tahoe Casinos:
Harrah's Lake Tahoe: JB - quarter to $100; BP - quarter to $100
Harvey's: JB - $5 to $100; BP - $1 to $100 (one with progressive)
Tahoe Biltmore: JB- quarter to $5; BP- $1; NSUD - $1

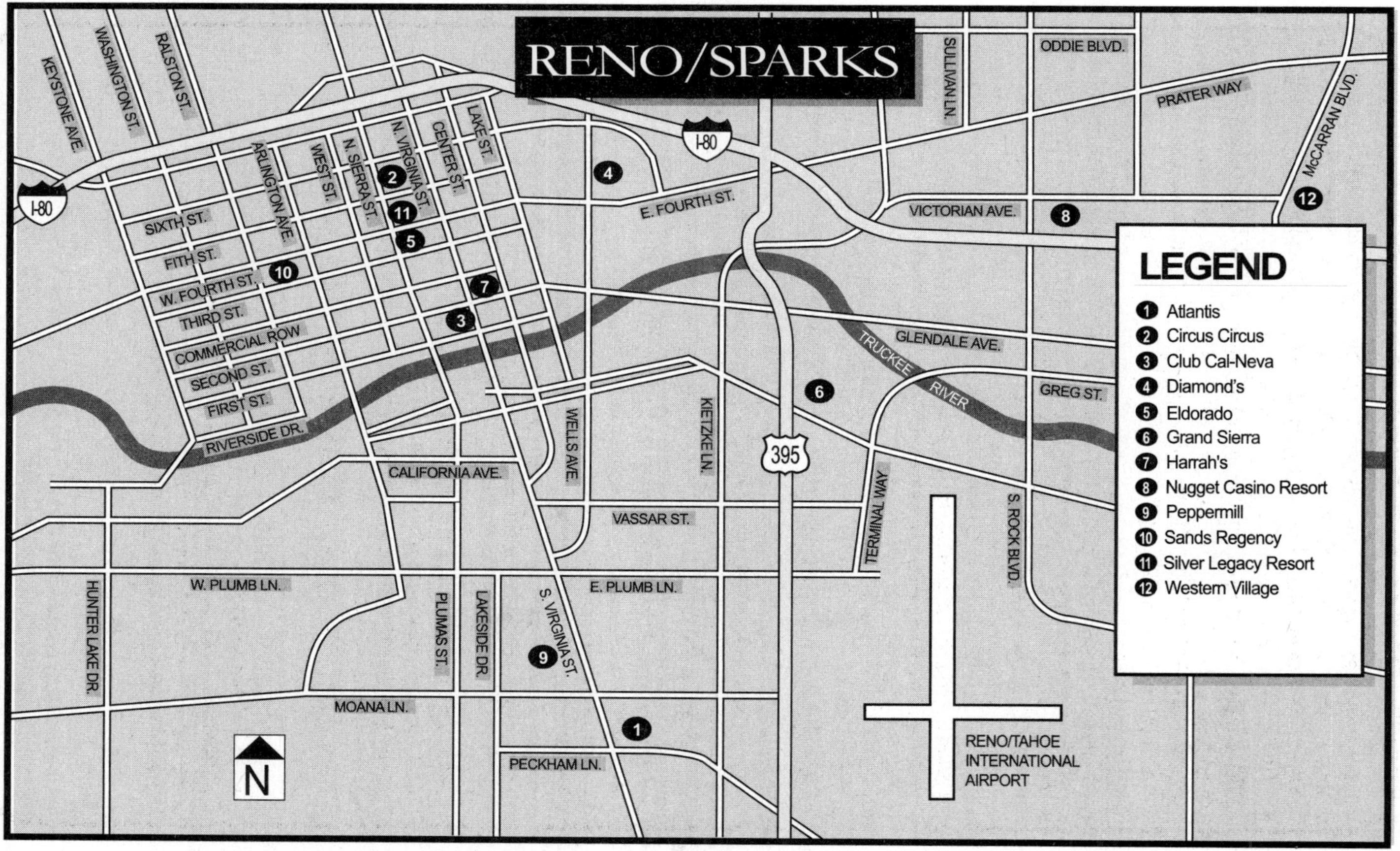
RENO/SPARKS
LEGEND
1 Atlantis
2 Circus Circus
3 Club Cal-Neva
4 Diamond's
5 Eldorado
6 Grand Sierra
7 Harrah's
8 Nugget Casino Resort
9 Peppermill
10 Sands Regency
11 Silver Legacy Resort
12 Western Village
KEYSTONE AVE.
WASHINGTON ST.
RALSTON ST.
I-80
SIXTH ST.
FITH ST.
W. FOURTH ST.
THIRD ST.
COMMERCIAL ROW
SECOND ST.
FIRST ST.
RIVERSIDE DR.
ARLINGTON AVE.
WEST ST.
N. SIERRA ST.
N. VIRGINIA ST.
CENTER ST.
LAKE ST.
E. FOURTH ST.
WELLS AVE.
KIETZKE LN.
395
CALIFORNIA AVE.
VASSAR ST.
W. PLUMB LN.
E. PLUMB LN.
HUNTER LAKE DR.
PLUMAS ST.
LAKESIDE DR.
S. VIRGINIA ST.
MOANA LN.
PECKHAM LN.
N
SULLIVAN LN.
ODDIE BLVD.
PRATER WAY
McCARRAN BLVD.
VICTORIAN AVE.
GLENDALE AVE.
TRUCKEE RIVER
GREG ST.
TERMINAL WAY
S. ROCK BLVD.
RENO/TAHOE
INTERNATIONAL
AIRPORT

The arch in downtown Reno that welcomes visitors to "The Biggest Little City in the World" is the city's most famous landmark.

Harrah's Reno
219 N. Center Street
Reno, Nevada 89501
(775) 786-3232
Website: www.harrahsreno.com

Toll-Free Number: (800) 423-1121
Rooms: 886 Price Range: $49-$200
Suites: 60 Price Range: Casino use only
Restaurants: 5
Buffets: B/L- $20.99 (Sun)
D- $21.99/$29.99 (Fri/Sat)
Casino Size: 41,600 Square Feet
Other Games: SB, RB, MB, PGP, TCP, K
Senior Discount: 2-for-1 buffet if 55+

Peppermill Hotel Casino Reno
2707 S. Virginia Street
Reno, Nevada 89502
(775) 826-2121
Website: www.peppermillreno.com

Toll-Free Number: (800) 648-6992
Rooms: 1,070 Price Range: $70-$199
Suites: 185 Price Range: $140-$3,600
Restaurants: 7
Buffets: B- $17.99/$22.99 (Sat)/$31.99 (Sun)
L- $19.99/$22.99 (Sat)/$31.99 (Sun)
D- $26.99/$38.99 (Fri/Sat)/
$29.99 (Sun)
Casino Size: 77,058 Square Feet
Other Games: SB, RB, MB, P, PGP, PG,
LIR, TCP, FCP, UTH, K
Senior Discount: Various food discounts if 55+

The Sands Regency Hotel Casino
345 North Arlington Avenue
Reno, Nevada 89501
(775) 348-2200
Website: www.sandsregency.com

Rooms: 811 Price Range: $35-$159
Restaurants: 4
Buffets: D- $18.99 (Sun-Thu)/$27.99 (Fri-Sat)
Casino Size: 25,791 Square Feet
Other Games: SB, BG
Senior Discounts: Various Tue if 50+

Silver Legacy Resort Casino
407 N. Virginia Street
Reno, Nevada 89501
(775) 325-7401
Website: www.silverlegacy.com

Toll-Free Number: (800) 687-8733
Rooms: 1,720 Price Range: $50-$195
Restaurants: 4
Casino Size: 89,200 Square Feet
Other Games: B, SB, RB, PG, PGP,
LIR, TCP, UTH, K
Special Features: Simulated mining machine above casino floor. Rum bar.

Searchlight

Map Location: **#22** (58 miles S. of Las Vegas on Hwy. 95)

Terrible's Road House - Searchlight
100 N. Highway 95
Searchlight, Nevada 89046
(702) 297-1201

Casino Size: 3,260 Square Feet
Other Games: No Table Games
Overnight RV Parking: Free/RV Dump: No

Sparks

Map Location: **#4** (Sparks is a suburb of Reno and is located one mile east of Reno on I-80)

Here's information, as supplied by Nevada's State Gaming Control Board, showing the slot machine payback percentages for all of the Sparks area casinos for the fiscal year beginning July 1, 2018 and ending June 30, 2019:

Denomination	Payback %
1¢ Slots	92.98
5¢ Slots	97.19
25¢ Slots	95.43
$1 Slots	96.17
All Slots	94.55

These numbers reflect the percentage of money returned on each denomination of machine and encompass all electronic machines including slots, video poker and video keno.

Alamo Casino & Travel Center
1950 East Greg Street
Sparks, Nevada 89431
(775) 355-8888
Website: www.thealamo.com

Rooms: 64 Price Range: $79-$129
Suites: 7 Price Range: $104-$174
Restaurants: 1 (open 24 hours)
Casino Size: 7,150 Square Feet
Other Games: SB, RB, P, no roulette
Overnight RV Parking: Free/RV Dump: No
Special Features: Motel is Super 8. Truck stop. Video arcade. Post office and gas station

Nugget Casino Resort
1100 Nugget Avenue
Sparks, Nevada 89431
(775) 356-3300
Website: www.nuggetcasinoresort.com

Toll-Free Number: (800) 648-1177
Rooms: 1,450 Price Range: $33-$129
Suites: 150 Call for pricing
Restaurants: 7
Buffets: L- $11.99/$19.99 (Sat/Sun)
D- $16.99/$24.99 (Fri/Sat)
Casino Size: 82,600 Square Feet
Overnight RV Parking: Check with security/ RV Dump: No
Other Games: SB, RB, P, PGP, UTH, TCP, K, BG
Senior Discounts: Various Thu if 50+
Special Features: Wedding chapel. Fitness Center. 8,500-seat event center.

Rail City Casino
2121 Victorian Avenue
Sparks, Nevada 89431
(775) 359-9440
Website: www.railcity.com

Restaurants: 2
Buffets: D- $21.99
Casino Size: 18,120 Square Feet
Other Games: SB, K, no craps/roulette
Overnight RV Parking: No
Special Features: Buffet discount for Players Club members.

Western Village Inn & Casino
815 Nichols Boulevard
Sparks, Nevada 89434
(775) 331-1069
Website: www.westernvillagesparks.com

Rooms: 147 Price Range: $60-$139
Restaurants: 4
Casino Size: 26,452 Square Feet
Other Games: SB
Overnight RV Parking: No/RV Dump: No
Senior Discount: Food discount in Bellini Cafe if 55+

Verdi

Map Location: **#4** (4 miles W. of Reno on I-80 at the California border)

Boomtown Hotel & Casino
2100 Garson Road
Verdi, Nevada 89439
(775) 345-6000
Website: www.boomtownreno.com

Toll-Free Number: (800) 648-3790
Rooms: 318 Price Range: $89-$129
Suites: 20 Price Range: $105-$265
Restaurants: 4 (1 open 24 hours)
Buffets: D- $9.99 (Thu-Fri)/$36.99 (Sun)
Casino Size: 38,675 Square Feet
Other Games: SB, RB, P, PGP, TCP, K, BG (Wed)
Overnight RV Parking: Free (1 night only)
Special Features: 203-space RV park ($34-$50 per night). 24-hour mini-mart. Indoor family fun center with rides and arcade games. Buffet discount for Players Club members.

Gold Ranch Casino & RV Resort
350 Gold Ranch Road
Verdi, Nevada 89439
(775) 345-6789
Website: www.goldranchrvcasino.com

Restaurants: 1
Casino Size: 8,000 Square Feet
Other Games: SB, no table games
Overnight RV Parking: Must use RV park
Special Features: 105-space RV park ($45-$48 per night). 24-hour mini-mart.

Wells

Map Location: **#23** (338 miles N.E. of Reno on I-80)

Alamo Casino Wells
1440 6th Street
Wells, Nevada 89835
(775) 752-3344
Website: www.thealamo.com

Restaurants: 1
Casino Size: 6,100 Square Feet
Other Games: SB, no table games
Overnight RV Parking: Free/RV Dump: No

West Wendover

Map Location: **#24** (Just W. of the Utah border on I-80)

Here's information, as supplied by Nevada's State Gaming Control Board, showing the slot machine payback percentages for all of the Wendover area casinos for the fiscal year beginning July 1, 2018 and ending June 30, 2019:

Denomination	Payback %
1¢ Slots	93.41
25¢ Slots	93.34
$1 Slots	95.86
$5 Slots	96.39
All Slots	94.32

These numbers reflect the percentage of money returned on each denomination of machine and encompass all electronic machines including slots, video poker and video keno.

Montego Bay Casino Resort
680 Wendover Boulevard
W. Wendover, Nevada 89883
(775) 664-4800
Website: www.wendoverfun.com

Toll-Free Number: (877) 666-8346
Reservation Number: (800) 537-0207
Rooms: 437 Price Range: $79-$109
Suites: 75 Price Range: $139-$259
Restaurants: 4
Buffets: B- $17.95 (Sat/Sun) L- $15.95 D- $18.95/$31.95 (Fri)/$25.95 (Sat)
Casino Size: 49,400 Square Feet
Other Games: P, PGP, TCP, LIR
Overnight RV Parking: Free/RV Dump: No
Special Features: Connected by sky bridge to Wendover Nugget. Liquor Store. Golf packages.

Peppermill Inn & Casino
680 Wendover Boulevard
W. Wendover, Nevada 89883
(775) 664-4800
Website: www.wendoverfun.com

Reservation Number: (800) 217-0049
Rooms: 302 Price Range: $69-$129
Suites: 42 Price Range: $119-$189
Restaurants: 2 (1 open 24 hours)
Casino Size: 30,577 Square Feet
Other Games: SB, RB, PGP, LIR, TCP
Overnight RV Parking: Free/RV Dump: No
Special Features: Affiliated with Montego Bay and Rainbow casinos.

Rainbow Hotel Casino
1045 Wendover Boulevard
W. Wendover, Nevada 89883
(775) 664-4800
Website: www.wendoverfun.com

Toll-Free Number: (800) 217-0049
Rooms: 379 Price Range: $59-$139
Suites: 50 Price Range: $119-$209
Restaurants: 3
Buffets: B-$16.95 (Sat/Sun)
L- $13.95/$16.95 (Sat/Sun)
D-$16.95/$29.95 (Fri)/$23.95 (Sat)
Casino Size: 57,360 Square Feet
Other Games: P, PGP, LIR, TCP
Overnight RV Parking: Free/RV Dump: No
Special Features: Affiliated with Peppermill Inn and Montego Bay casinos.

Red Garter Hotel & Casino
1225 Wendover Boulevard
W. Wendover, Nevada 89883
(775) 664-2111
Website: www.redgartercasino.com

Toll-Free Number: (800) 982-2111
Rooms: 46 Price Range: $68-$104
Restaurants: 1 (open 24 hours)
Casino Size: 16,124 Square Feet
Other Games: SB, TCP, LIR, PGP
Overnight RV Parking: No
Special Features: Affiliated with Wendover Nugget Hotel & Casino

Wendover Nugget Hotel & Casino
101 Wendover Boulevard
W. Wendover, Nevada 89883
(775) 664-2221
Website: www.wendovernugget.com

Toll-Free Number: (800) 848-7300
Rooms: 500 Price Range: $64-$79
Suites: 60 Price Range: $112-189
Restaurants: 3 (1 open 24 hours)
Buffets: B-$16.95 (Sat/Sun)
L-$12.95/$16.95 (Sat/Sun)
D-$16.95/$27.95 (Fri/Sat)
Casino Size: 40,089 Square Feet
Other Games: SB, RB, P, TCP, LIR, PGP, K
Overnight RV Parking: Must use RV park
Senior Discount: Room/food discounts if 55+
Special Features: 18-space RV park ($35 per night). Sky bridge to Montego Bay. Truck stop

Winnemucca

Map Location: **#25** (164 miles N.E. of Reno on I-80)

Model T Hotel/Casino/RV Park
1130 W. Winnemucca Boulevard
Winnemucca, Nevada 89445
(775) 623-2588
Website: www.modelt.com

Reservation Number: (800) 645-5658
Rooms: 75 Price Range: $98-$130
Restaurants: 1
Casino Size: 7,053 Square Feet
Other Games: SB, TCP
Overnight RV Parking: Free/RV Dump: No
Special Features: Hotel is Quality Inn. 58-space RV park ($30 per night). Table games Wed-Sun only.

Winnemucca Inn
741 W. Winnemucca Boulevard
Winnemucca, Nevada 89445
(775) 623-2565
Website: www.winnemuccainn.com

Reservation Number: (800) 633-6435
Rooms: 105 Price Range: $91-$119
Restaurants: 1
Casino Size: 3,000 Square Feet
Other Games: SB, RB, No table games
Overnight RV Parking: No

Winners Inn Casino
185 W. Winnemucca Boulevard
Winnemucca, Nevada 89445
(775) 623-2511
Website: www.winnersinn.com

Reservation Number: (800) 648-4770
Rooms: 123 Price Range: $69-$89
Restaurants: 1
Casino Size: 10,340 Square Feet
Other Games: SB, TCP
Overnight RV Parking: Free/ Dump: No
Senior Discount: Room discount if 55+

Yerington

Map Location: **#26** (60 miles S.E. of Reno on Hwy. Alt. 95)

Pioneer Crossing Casino
11 N. Main Street
Yerington, Nevada 89447
(775) 463-2481
Website: www.pioneercrossingcasino.com

Restaurants: 1 (open 24 hours)
Casino Size: 4,950 Square Feet
Other Games: P, no craps/roulette
Overnight RV Parking: Free/RV Dump: No
Special Features: Movie theater. 12-lane bowling alley. Wednesday night Weiner Buffet. Table games open Friday and Saturday.

Indian Casinos

Avi Resort & Casino
10000 Aha Macav Parkway
Laughlin, Nevada 89029
(702) 535-5555
Website: www.avicasino.com
Map Location: **#2**

Toll-Free Number: (800) 284-2946
Rooms: 426 Price Range: $49-$89
Suites: 29 Price Range: $65-$140
Restaurants: 4 (1 open 24 hours)
Buffets: B-$10.99/$11.99 (Sat)/$16.99 (Sun)
L- $10.99 (Thu/Fri)$11.99 (Sat)/ $22.99 (Sun)
D- $16.99/$25.99 (Fri)/$21.99 (Sat)
Casino Size: 25,000 Square Feet
Other Games: SB, RB, P, TCP, PGP, LIR, K, B
Overnight RV Parking: Free/RV Dump: No
Special Features: 260-space RV park ($30-$60 per night). On Colorado River with boat dock, launch and private beach. Fast Food Court. 8-screen cinema. Smoke shop. Kid's Quest childcare center. Buffet discount for Players Club members

Moapa Travel Plaza
Interstate 15, Exit 75
Moapa, Nevada 89025-0340
(702) 864-2601
Website: www.moapapaiutes.com
Map Location: **#27** (65 miles N.E. of Las Vegas)

Other Games: Gaming Machines Only
Overnight RV Parking: No
Special Features: Located in travel plaza with gas station and convenience store.

NEW JERSEY

Map Location: **#1** (on the Atlantic Ocean in southeast New Jersey, 130 miles south of New York City and 60 miles southeast of Philadelphia)

All Atlantic City casinos are located along the boardwalk, except for three: Borgata, Harrah's and Golden Nugget. Those three are located in the marina section.

Following is information from the New Jersey Casino Control Commission regarding average slot payout percentages for the 12-month period from July 1, 2018 through June 30, 2019:

CASINO	PAYBACK %
Harrah's	91.79
Borgata	91.66
Caesars	91.03
Resorts	90.78
Bally's A.C.	90.76
Golden Nugget	90.57
Ocean	90.49
Hard Rock	90.41
Tropicana	90.35

These figures reflect the total percentages returned by each casino for all of their electronic machines which include slot machines, video poker, etc.

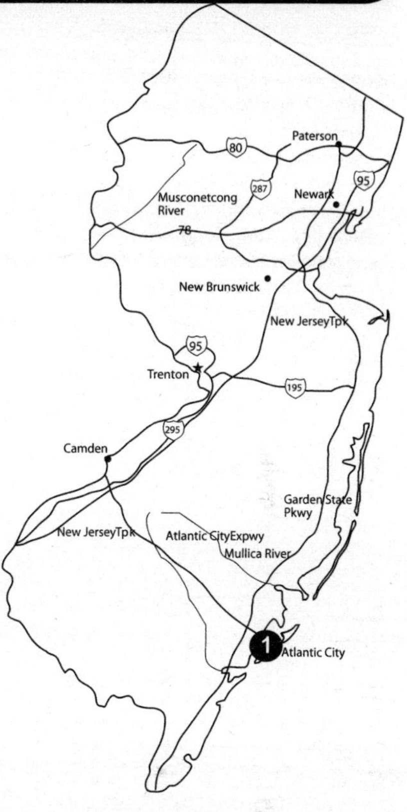

All Atlantic City casinos are open 24 hours and, unless otherwise noted, the games offered at every casino are: slots, video poker, craps, blackjack, Spanish 21, roulette, mini-baccarat, three card poker, four card poker, let it ride, pai gow tiles and pai gow poker. Additional games offered include: sic bo (SIC), keno (K), baccart (B), casino war (CW), poker (P), off-track betting (OTB), Caribbean stud poker (CSP), Texas hold 'em bonus (THB), Mississippi stud (MS), ultimate Texas hold 'em (UTH), big six wheel (B6) and sports betting (SB). The minimum gambling age is 21.

For more information on visiting New Jersey you can contact the state's Travel & Tourism Department at (800) 537-7397 or go to: www.visitnj.com.

For information only on Atlantic City call (800) 847-4865 or go to: www.atlanticcitynj.com.

Bally's Atlantic City
1900 Pacific Avenue
Atlantic City, New Jersey 08401
(609) 340-2000
Website: www.ballysac.com

Toll-Free Number: (800) 772-7777
Rooms: 1,611 Price Range: $92-$389
Suites: 146 Price Range: $210-$620
Restaurants: 18
Self Parking: $20/$25 (Fri-Sun)
Valet Parking: $30/$40 (Friday-Sunday)
Buffets: (located at Wild Wild West)
B- $19.99 (Saturday-Mon)
L- $19.99/$34.99 (Sun/Mon)
D- $34.99/$39.99 (Fri/Sat)
Casino Size 127,247 Square Feet
Other Games: SIC, B6, CSP, THB,
UTH, CW, SB
Special Features: Southern walkway connects to **Wild Wild West Casino**. Parking discount for players club members.

Borgata Hotel Casino and Spa
One Borgata Way
Atlantic City, New Jersey 08401
(609) 317-1000
Website: www.theborgata.com

Toll-Free Number: (866) 692-6742
Rooms: 2,200 Prices Range: $209-$359
Suites: 600 Price Range: $309-$699
Restaurants: 10
Self Parking: $5 Valet Parking: $10
Buffets: B-$17.95/$27.95 (Sun)
L-$20.95/$27.95 (Sun) D-$34.95
Casino Size: 136,771 Square Feet
Other Games: B6, B, CSP, THB, RB, SB
Special Features: 3,700-seat events center. 1,000-seat music theater. $5 parking discount for players club members. Comedy club. Health spas, salon, barber shop.

Caesars Atlantic City
2100 Pacific Avenue
Atlantic City, New Jersey 08401
(609) 348-4411
Website: www.caesarsac.com

Toll-Free Number: (800) 443-0104
Rooms: 979 Price Range: $119-$499
Suites: 198 Price Range: $199-$800
Restaurants: 12
Self Parking: $10/$25 (Friday-Sunday)
Valet Parking: $20/$30 (Friday-Sunday)
Buffets: B- $32.00 (Sat/Sun)
L- $25.00
D- $34.99/$44.00 (Sat/Sun)
Casino Size: 115,924 Square Feet
Other Games: SIC, B6, B, CSP, THB,
OTB, UTH, MS, SB
Special Features: Roman themed hotel and casino. Parking and buffet discounts for players club members. Health spa. Shopping arcade. Unisex beauty salon.

Golden Nugget Atlantic City
Huron Avenue & Brigantine Boulevard
Atlantic City, New Jersey 08401
(609) 441-2000
Website: www.goldennugget.com

Reservation Number: (800) 365-8786
Toll-Free Number (800) 777-8477
Rooms: 568 Price Range: $99-$419
Suites: 160 Price Range: $175-$999
Restaurants: 9
Self Parking: Free
Valet Parking: $10/$15 (Fri-Sun)
Buffets: B-$16.99 L-$19.99
D-$25.99/$34.99 (Friday)
Casino Size: 78,464 Square Feet
Other Games: UTH, MS, SB
Special Features: Adjacent to marina with 640 slips. 3-acre recreation deck with pools, jogging track, tennis courts, miniature golf course and health club. 1,500-seat event center.

The Best Places To Play in Atlantic City

Blackjack- All recommendations in this section apply to basic strategy players. You should always look for casinos that pay the standard 3-to-2 for blackjacks. Some casinos may pay 6-to-5 for blackjack and this increases the casino edge to around 1.5% and they should be avoided.

The blackjack games offered at Atlantic City casinos are pretty much all the same for low-limit players: eight-deck shoe games with double down on any first two cards, dealer hits soft 17, pairs can be split up to three times and doubling after splitting is allowed. This works out to a casino edge of .67% against a player using perfect basic strategy and every casino in Atlantic City offers this game. The Golden Nugget, Hard Rock and Resorts have some tables where the dealers stand on soft 17. These are the best eight-deck games in the city and the casino advantage is .44% with a minimum bet of $25.

If you're willing to make higher minimum bets you can find slightly better games. All casinos offer six-deck games with minimum bets of $25, $50 or $100 per hand where the dealers stand on soft 17 and the casino edge in these games is lowered to .42%. It is offered at every casino in the city. The Golden Nugget and Hard Rock offer the city's best six-deck game because they add late surrender to the above rules, which brings their house advantage down to .34%. The minimum bet on this game is usually $50.

Roulette: When choosing roulette games it's usually best to play in a casino offering a single-zero wheel because the casino advantage is 2.70% versus a double-zero wheel which has a 5.26% advantage. However, that situation is somewhat different in Atlantic City because of certain gaming regulations. On double-zero wheels the casinos can only take one-half of a wager on even money bets (odd/even, red/black, 1-18/19-36) when zero or double-zero is the winning number. This lowers the casino edge on these particular bets to 2.63%, while the edge on all other bets remains at 5.26%. This rule is not in effect on single-zero wheels and virtually all bets on that game have a 2.70% house edge. There are five casinos that have single-zero roulette wheels: Harrah's, Bally's, Borgata, Tropicana and Caesars. You should be aware, however, that almost all of these games are only open on weekends (or by special request) and they require $25-$100 minimum bets.

Craps: All craps tables at Bally's, as well as one table at Golden Nugget, offer 10x odds while all other casinos offer 5x odds.

Video Poker: The opening of two new casinos in the summer of 2018 did little to improve video-poker opportunities in Atlantic City. One of the properties – the Hard Rock – has no full-pay video poker, and pickings are slim at Ocean Resort.

While Atlantic City is a far cry from the video-poker Nirvana it was a decade or so ago, decent plays are still available. The gaming halls are quite stingy with the comps and cashback on these machines, so most players will not be able to gain an advantage unless they play exclusively on promotion days. But skilled recreational players can extend their playing time and limit their losses.

Jacks or Better with a 9/6 paytable (99.54%) is the most prolific full-pay game in Atlantic City, and is available at about half the casinos in town. But only Borgata, Caesars, and Bally's have it in denominations lower than $1.

The best selection of 9/6 Jacks, in denominations of 25 cents and up, can be found at Borgata, but be careful when selecting a machine, as short-pay versions are in abundance.

Multi-denomination games: Most video poker is found on multi-denomination machines, where the player can choose to play for a quarter on up.

Borgata has several banks of machines with 9/6 Jacks or Better. They can be found at the B Bar, which is a smoking area with drinks comped for players. It's best to go early in the day before the bar gets crowded and noisy. Another bank of six slant-tops is near the Amphora lounge. It is a non-smoking area, but near a smoking section. Another row of slant-tops with 9/6 Jacks or Better is in a smoking section near the front entrance to the B Bar. The sign above the machines says 50 cents, but there are some quarter games in the mix. For Multi Strike Poker enthusiasts, Borgata has a few quarter machines with 9/6 Jacks or Better near the entrance to the buffet.

Bally's has a bank of four machines with 9/6 Jacks or Better, 8/5 Bonus Poker (99.16%), 9/7 Double Bonus Poker (99.11%), 9/6 Double Double Bonus (98.985) and Aces & Faces versions of Bonus Poker and Double Bonus. The machines are against a wall on the Boardwalk end of the casino in a smoking area alongside other video poker games, and can be played from 25 cents to $2. Note that it takes $50 in play to earn one Total Rewards credit, instead of $10 a point for short-pay games. (One Total Rewards credit equals a penny in comps.)

Resorts has 8/5 Bonus Poker in several banks of machines around the casino, from a quarter on up. Comps and cashback have been reduced in recent years, but a moderate gaming session will probably generate free play and room offers, especially in the off-season.

Harrah's has three carousels of machines with 9/6 Double Double Bonus from quarters to $2 near the Total Rewards booth. Unlike most full-pay games, these still offer one Total Rewards credit for every $10 played. The other games on these machines are all short-pay.

Quarter Games: The best quarter game in Atlantic City is at the Tropicana. A row of five full-pay (99.59%), Five-Joker progressive games can be found in a video-poker alcove near the back entrance to a women's restroom. They are somewhat more difficult to find since the Trop reconfigured the casino floor, but they're there. The seats are almost always occupied – especially when the jackpot is high - so unless you arrive late at night or early in the morning, you'll probably have to wait for a chance to play. Look for Sigma machines with a purple face glass.

Caesars has a six-machine bank of progressive quarter 9/6 Jacks or Better slant-tops in the video poker area (smoking) toward the center of the casino. The jackpot rises slowly, and it takes $50 of play to earn one Total Rewards credit.

Bally's has another good quarter play in the form of 8/5 Bonus Poker Triple Play progressives. A group of eight machines is in the video-poker area (smoking) in the south corner of the casino. Since the amount of play to earn a point was raised to $50 a few years ago, it is easy to get a seat, except maybe on multiplier days.

Dollar and Higher Games: The three Caesars Entertainment properties - Bally's, Caesars, and Harrah's – all have banks of upright full-pay machines in their video-poker areas, with 9/6 Jacks or Better, 8/5 Bonus, 9/7 Double Bonus, 9/6 Double Double Bonus and Aces & Faces versions. The dollar machines offer one Total Rewards credit for every $20 played. Another bank of these machines can be found in the Diamond Cove high-limit area at Harrah's.

Bally's has three triple-play dollar machines with 9/6 Jacks or Better and 8/5 Bonus Poker, along with other games, located in the Diamond Pointe high-limit area off the hotel lobby.

Golden Nugget has several $1 9/6 Double Double Bonus games in and near the high-limit area. One machine in the high-limit area has 9/6 Jacks or Better and 9/7 Double Bonus that can be played from $1 to $5.

Borgata has numerous machines with dollar and up 9/6 Jacks or Better in and near the high-limit slot area.

Ocean Resort has 9/6 Jacks or Better on several machines in the high-limit area along the left wall after entering the room. They can be played from $1 to $25.

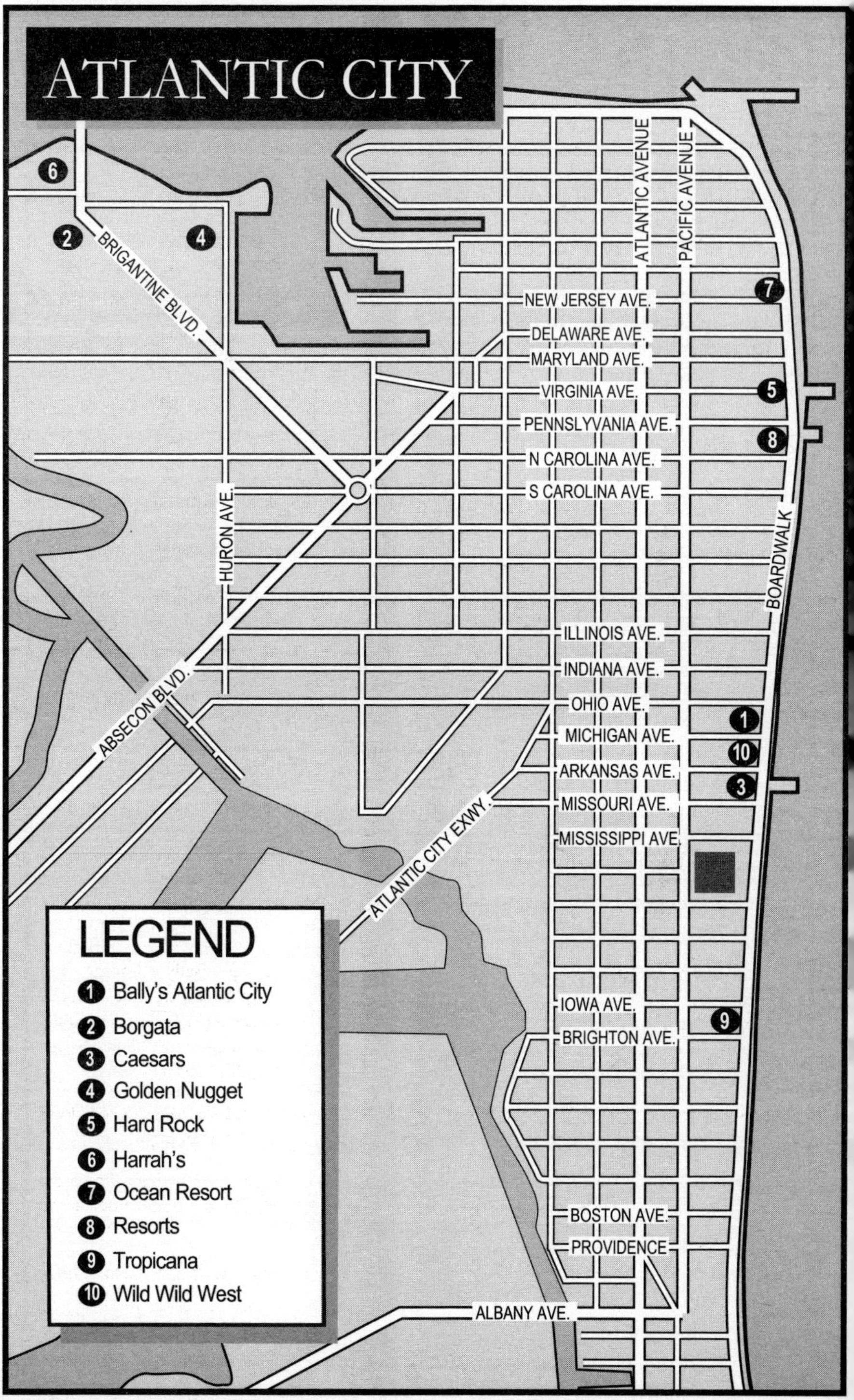
ATLANTIC CITY
BRIGANTINE BLVD.
ATLANTIC AVENUE
PACIFIC AVENUE
NEW JERSEY AVE.
DELAWARE AVE.
MARYLAND AVE.
VIRGINIA AVE.
PENNSLYVANIA AVE.
N CAROLINA AVE.
S CAROLINA AVE.
HURON AVE.
BOARDWALK
ILLINOIS AVE.
INDIANA AVE.
ABSECON BLVD.
OHIO AVE.
MICHIGAN AVE.
ARKANSAS AVE.
MISSOURI AVE.
ATLANTIC CITY EXWY.
MISSISSIPPI AVE.
IOWA AVE.
BRIGHTON AVE.
BOSTON AVE.
PROVIDENCE
ALBANY AVE.
LEGEND
1 Bally's Atlantic City
2 Borgata
3 Caesars
4 Golden Nugget
5 Hard Rock
6 Harrah's
7 Ocean Resort
8 Resorts
9 Tropicana
10 Wild Wild West

Hard Rock Casino Hotel Atlantic City
1000 Boardwalk at Virginia Avenue
Atlantic City, New Jersey 08401
Website: www.hardrockhotelatlanticcity.com

Rooms: 1,795 Price Range: $119-$469
Suites: 300 Price Range: $349-$599
Restaurants: 8
Self Parking: $10 Valet Parking: $15
Buffets: B- $19.99 L- $19.99 D- $29.99
Casino Size: 122,771 Square Feet
Other Games: B6, THB, SB
Special Features: Spa & salon. Gas station and car wash. 7,000-seat events center. Parking discount for Players Club members.

Harrah's Resort Atlantic City
777 Harrah's Boulevard
Atlantic City, New Jersey 08401
(609) 441-5000
Website: www.caesars.com

Reservation Number: (800) 242-7724
Rooms: 2,010 Price Range: $89-$299
Suites: 616 Price Range: Casino Use Only
Restaurants: 8
Self Parking: $5 Valet Parking: $10
Buffets: B- $24.99 (Sat/Sun)
D- $34.99
Casino Size: 156,284 Square Feet
Other Games: B6, CSP, THB, MS, K, RB, SB
Special Features: Parking and buffet discounts for players club members. 65-slip marina. Beauty salon. Miniature golf course (in season).

Ocean Casino Resort
500 Boardwalk
Atlantic City, New Jersey 08401
(609) 783-8777
Website: www.theoceanac.com

Rooms: 1,399 Price Range: $139-$389
Suites: 300 Price Range: $179-$509
Self Parking: $5/$10 (Fri-Sun)
Valet Parking: $10/$15 (Fri-Sun)
Restaurants: 10
Casino Size: 132,185 Square Feet
Other Games: SB
Special Features: Health spa. Six-store shopping arcade. Topgolf Swing Suite virtual driving range.

Resorts Casino Hotel
1133 Boardwalk
Atlantic City, New Jersey 08401
(609) 344-6000
Website: www.resortsac.com

Toll-Free Number: (800) 334-6378
Rooms: 879 Price Range: $95-$375
Suites: 79 Price Range: $209-$1,000
Restaurants: 10
Self Parking: $20 Valet Parking: $20
Casino Size: 79,009 Square Feet
Other Games: SIC, THB, SB
Special Features: Indoor/outdoor pools. Health spa. 1,350-seat theater. Comedy club. Beachfront bar. Parking discount for players club members.

Tropicana Casino & Resort
2831 Boardwalk
Atlantic City, New Jersey 08401
(609) 340-4000
Website: www.tropicana.net

Toll-Free Number: (800) 843-8767
Rooms: 1,426 Price Range: $99-$399
Suites: 340 Price Range: $179-$675
Restaurants: 10
Self Parking $10 Valet Parking: $15
Buffets: B $19.95/$27.95 (Sat-Sun)
L- $20.95 D- $33.95
Casino Size: 121,909 Square Feet
Other Games: CSP, THB, CW, SB
Special Features: Features "The Quarter", a dining/entertainment complex with 30 stores. Buffet is closed Wednesdays and Thursdays. Parking discount for Players Club members.

NEW MEXICO

New Mexico's Indian casinos offer an assortment of table games and electronic gaming machines. Additionally, slot machines are allowed at the state's racetracks as well as at about 40 various fraternal and veterans clubs.

New Mexico gaming regulations require that electronic machines at racetracks and fraternal/veterans organizations return a minimum of 80%.

New Mexico's Indian tribes do not make their slot machine payback percentages a matter of public record but the terms of the compact between the state and the tribes require all electronic gaming machines to return a minimum of 80%.

Unless otherwise noted, all New Mexico Indian casinos are open 24 hours and offer: blackjack, craps, roulette, video slots and video poker. Some casinos also offer: Spanish 21 (S21), mini-baccarat (MB), poker (P), pai gow poker (PGP), three card poker (TCP), four card poker (FCP), Caribbean stud poker (CSP), let it ride (LIR), ultimate Texas hold 'em (UTH), Mississippi stud (MS), casino war (CW), big 6 wheel (B6), keno (K), bingo (BG) and off track betting (OTB). The minimum gambling age is 21 for the casinos and 18 for bingo or pari-mutuel betting.

Sports betting was introduced at the Santa Ana Star Casino in October 2018. Although it has never been legalized by the state's legislature, sports betting is slowly being introduced at more New Mexico casinos because the state's gaming compact does not specifically prohibit it.

Please note that all New Mexico casinos are prohibited from serving alcohol on the casino floor. If a casino serves alcohol it can only be consumed at the bar and not in the casino itself.

For information on visiting New Mexico call the state's tourism department at (800) 733-6396 or go to: www.newmexico.org.

Apache Nugget Travel Center and Casino
US Highway 550 and NM Highway 537
Dulce, New Mexico 87528
(575) 289-2486
Website: www.apachenugget.com
Map: **#15** (on Jicarilla reservation at intersection of Hwys 550 and 537 near Cuba)

Restaurants: 1 Liquor: No
Casino Hours: 8am-12am/1am (Thu)/ 2am (Fri-Sat)
Casino Size: 12,000 Square Feet
Games Offered: Gaming Machines Only
Overnight RV Parking: Free (check in with security first)/RV Dump: No

Black Mesa Casino
25 Hagan Road
Algodones, New Mexico 87001
(505) 867-6700
Website: www.sanfelipecasino.com
Map: **#6** (17 miles N. of Albuquerque)

Toll-Free Number: (877) 867-6700
Restaurants: 1 Liquor: No
Hours: 8am-4am/24 Hours (Fri-Sat)
Other Games: P, TCP
Overnight RV Parking: Must use RV park
Special Features: 100-space RV park ($20 per night).

Buffalo Thunder Resort & Casino
20 Buffalo Thunder Trail
Santa Fe, New Mexico 87506
(505) 455-5555
Website: www.buffalothunderresort.com
Map: **#2**

Room Reservations: (877) 848-6337
Rooms: 350 Price Range: $109-$229
Suites: 45 Price Range: $229-$279
Restaurants: 4 Liquor: Yes
Casino Hours: 8am-4am/24 hours (Thu-Sat)
Other Games: P, TCP, OTB, SB
Casino Size: 61,000 Square Feet
Special Features: Hotel is Hilton. Health Spa. Retail shopping area. Native American art gallery.

Casino Apache Travel Center
25845 U.S. Highway 70
Ruidoso, New Mexico 88340
(575) 464-7777
Website: www. casinoapachetravelcenter.com
Map: **#4** (90 miles N.E. of Las Cruces)

Restaurants: 1 Liquor: Yes
Other Games: UTH, No craps
Casino Size: 10,000 Square Feet
Overnight RV Parking: Free/RV Dump: No
Special Features: Free shuttle service to Inn of the Mountain Gods Casino. Truck stop. Discount smoke shop.

Casino Express
14500 Central Avenue SW
Albuquerque, New Mexico 87120
(505) 552-7777
Map: **#3** (I-40 at exit 140)

Toll-Free Number: (866) 352-7866
Other Games: No Table Games
Overnight RV Parking: Free/RV Dump: No
Special Features: Adjacent to, and affiliated with, Route 66 Casino.

Cities of Gold Casino Hotel
10-B Cities of Gold Road
Santa Fe, New Mexico 8750
(505) 455-3313
Website: www.citiesofgold.com
Map: **#2** (Intersection of Hwys 84/285/502)

Toll-Free Number: (800) 455-3313
Rooms: 122 Price Range: $59-$109
Suites: 2 Price Range: $136
Restaurants: 3 Liquor: Yes
Casino Size: 40,000 Square Feet
Other Games: No table games, BG (Wed-Sun)
Overnight RV Parking: No
Special Features: They also operate the Cities of Gold Sports Bar which is one block away from main casino. 27-hole golf course.

Dancing Eagle Casino and RV Park
Interstate 40, Exit 108
Casa Blanca, New Mexico 87007
(505) 552-7777
Website: www.dancingeaglecasino.com
Map: **#1** (40 miles W. of Albuquerque)

Toll-Free Number: (877) 440-9969
Restaurants: 1 Liquor: No
Casino Size: 21,266 Square Feet
Other Games: No Table Games, BG (Sat/Sun)
Senior Discount: Various Mon-Thu if 50+
Overnight RV Parking: Free/RV Dump: No
Special Features: Located on I-40 at exit 108. Truck stop. 35-space RV park ($17 per night).

Fire Rock Navajo Casino
249 Route 66
Church Rock, New Mexico 87311
(505) 905-7100
Website: www.firerocknavajocasino.com
Map: #**16** (8 miles E of Gallup)

Toll-Free Number: (866) 941-2444
Restaurants: 2 Liquor: No
Hours: 8am-4am/24 hours (Thu-Sat)
Casino Size: 64,000 square Feet
Other Games: P, BG
Senior Discount: Various Tue if 50+

Flowing Water Navajo Casino
2710 East Highway 64
Shiprock, New Mexico 87421
(505) 368-2300
Website: www.flowingwater.com
Map: #**17** (105 miles N of Gallup)

Restaurants:1
Casino Size: 11,000 square Feet
Other Games: Only Gaming Machines
Senior Discount: Various Tue if 50+

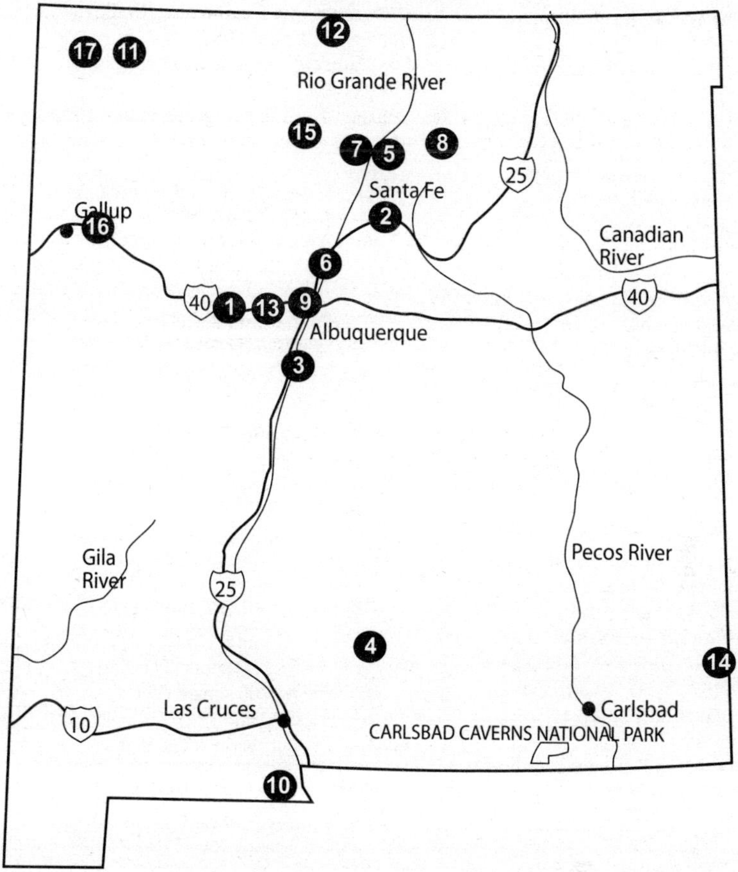

Inn of the Mountain Gods Resort & Casino
287 Carrizo Canyon Road
Mescalero, New Mexico 88340
(575) 464-7059
Website: www.innofthemountaingods.com
Map: **#4** (90 miles N.E. of Las Cruces)

Toll-Free Number: (800) 545-9011
Rooms: 250 Price Range: $149-$249
Suites: 23 Price Range: $269-$399
Restaurants: 5 Liquor: Yes
Buffets: B- $9.99/$13.99 (Sat/Sun)
L- $10.99/$17.99 (Sat/Sun)
D- $12.99/$20.99 (Thu)/
$20.99 (Fri-Sun)
Casino Size: 38,000 Square Feet
Other Games: MB, P, PGP, LIR, TCP,
FCP, UTH, SB
Overnight RV Parking: Free/RV Dump: No
Senior Discount: Buffet discount if 55+
Special Features: 18-hole golf course.

Isleta Resort Casino
11000 Broadway S.E.
Albuquerque, New Mexico 87105
(505) 724-3800
Website: www.isleta.com
Map: **#3**

Toll-Free Number: (877) 475-3827
Rooms: 201 Price Range: $99-$199
Restaurants: 6 Liquor: Yes
Casino Size: 30,000 Square Feet
Other Games: P, LIR, TCP, PGP, MB, B
Overnight RV Parking: Free/RV Dump: No
Special Features: Convenience store. Gas station. Three nine-hole golf courses. Alcohol is only served at sports bar in casino. 50-space RV park ($37/night).

Nambe Falls Casino
17730 US 84 Fronteg
Santa Fe, New Mexico 87501
(505) 820-5030
Map: **#2**

Casino Size: 7,310 Square Feet
Other Games: No Table Games
Overnight RV Parking: Free/RV Dump: No
Special Features: Located in travel plaza with convenience store.

Northern Edge Casino
2752 Navajo Route 36
Fruitland, New Mexico 87416
(505) 960-7000
Website: www.northernedgenavajocasino.com
Map: **#11** (150 miles N.W of Sante Fe)

Toll-free Number: (877) 241-7777
Rooms: 124 Price Range: $89-$209
Restaurants: 1 Liquor: Yes
Buffets: B- $7.95 (Sat)/$10.95 (Sun)
D- $10.95 (Wed)
Hours: 8am-4am/24 hours (Fr-Sun)
Casino Size: 36,000 square feet
Other Games: TCP, PGP, P
Overnight RV Parking: No
Senior Discount: Various Tuesdays if 50+
Special Features: Food court with fast food outlets.

Ohkay Casino Resort
68 New Mexico 291
Ohkay Owingeh, New Mexico 87566
(505) 747-1668
Website: www.ohkay.com
Map: **#5** (24 miles N. of Santa Fe)

Room Reservation (877) 747-1668
Rooms: 101 Price Range: $84-$104
Suites: 24 Price Range: $114-$134
Restaurants: 2 Liquor: Yes
Buffets: B- $9.99 L- $12.99 (Sun)
D- $10.99/$28.99 (Fri/Sun)/
$12.99 (Sat)
Other Games: Only gaming machines
Casino Size: 30,000 Square Feet
Overnight RV Parking: Free/RV Dump: No
Senior Discount: Various Wednesdays if 55+
Special Features: Hotel is Best Western. Sporting clays club. Buffet discount for players club members.

Palace West Casino
2S State Road NM-45
Albuquerque, New Mexico 87105
(505) 846-1930
Map: **#3** (at Coors & Isleta Road)

Hours: 8am-2am Daily
Other Games: Only gaming machines
Overnight RV Parking: Free/RV Dump: No
Special Features: Completely non-smoking.

Route 66 Casino Hotel
14500 Central Avenue SW
Albuquerque, New Mexico 87121
(505) 352-7866
Website: www.rt66casino.com
Map: **#13** (20 miles W. of Albuquerque)

Toll-Free Number: (866) 352-7866
Rooms: 154 Rates: $89-$129
Restaurants: 2 Liquor: No
Buffets: L- $12.99/$14.99 (Sun)
D- $14.99 (Sun-Thu)/$34.99 (Fri)/
$29.99 (Sat)
Other Games: P, PGP, TCP, BG
Overnight RV Parking: Free/RV Dump: No
Special Features: Johnny Rockets restaurant. Adjacent to, and affiliated with, Casino Express. Buffet discount for Players Club members. 100-space RV park ($55-$75 per night)

Sandia Resort & Casino
30 Rainbow Road NE
Albuquerque, New Mexico 87113
(505) 796-7500
Website: www.sandiacasino.com
Map: **#9**

Toll-Free Number: (800) 526-9366
Rooms: 198 Price Range: $195-$226
Suites: 30 Price Range: $269-$339
Restaurants: 4 Liquor: Yes
Buffets: B- $9.95 L- $11.95/$14.95 (Sun)
D- $14.50/$34.95 (Fri/Sat)
Hours: 8am-4am/24 Hours (Thu-Sun)
Casino Size: 65,000 Square feet
Other Games: MB, P, CSP, LIR,
TCP, PGP, K, BG
Overnight RV Parking: Free/RV Dump: No
Special Features: 4,200-seat amphitheater. 18-hole golf course, smoke-free slot room.

Santa Ana Star Casino Hotel
54 Jemez Canyon Dam Road
Santa Ana Pueblo, New Mexico 87004
(505) 867-0000
Website: www.santaanastar.com
Map: **#6** (17 miles N. of Albuquerque)

Rooms: 204 Price Range $105-$245
Restaurants: 5 Liquor: Yes
Buffets: B- $10.95 (Fri)/ L- $10.60
D- $10.60/$10.95 (Thu)/
$29.95 (Fri-Sat)
Casino Size: 19,000 Square Feet
Other Games: B, PGP, P, LIR, TCP, UTH, SB.
Overnight RV Parking: Free/RV Dump: No
Senior Discount: Various Mondays if 50+
Special Features: 36-lane bowling alley. 18-hole golf course. Spa. Smoke shop. 3,000-seat event center. Buffet closed Sundays, Tuesdays and Wednesdays.

Santa Claran Hotel Casino
460 North Riverside Drive
Espanola, New Mexico 87532
(505) 367-4500
Website: www.santaclaran.com
Map: **#7** (25 miles N of Sante Fe)

Rooms: 124 Price Range: $159-$129
Suites: 19 Price Range: $169-$189
Restaurants: 4 Liquor: Yes
Hours: 8am-4am/24 hours (Fri-Sat)
Casino Size: 27,000 square feet
Other Games: No Craps
Overnight RV Parking: No
Special Features: 24 lane bowling alley

Sky City Casino Hotel
Interstate 40, Exit 102
Acoma, New Mexico 87034
(505) 552-6123
Website: www.skycity.com
Map: **#1** (50 miles W. of Albuquerque)

Toll-Free Number: (888) 759-2489
Rooms: 132 Price Range: $79-$99
Suites: 15 Price Range: $119-$169
Restaurants: 3 Liquor: Yes
Buffets: B- $6.99/$8.99 (Sat/Sun)
L-$7.99/$8.99 (Sat/Sun)
D-$13.99/$12.99 (Tue/Wed)/
$20.99 (Fri)/$14.99 (Sat)/
$10.99 (Sun)
Casino Size: 30,000 Square Feet
Other Games: TCP, BG
Overnight RV Parking: Free/RV Dump: No
Senior Discount: Various Fridays if 55+
Special Features: 42-space RV park ($22+ per night)

Taos Mountain Casino
700 Veterans Highway
Taos, New Mexico 87571
(575) 737-0777
Website: www.taosmountaincasino.com
Map: **#8** (50 miles N.E. of Santa Fe)

Toll-Free Number: (888) 946-8267
Restaurants: 1 Deli Liquor: No
Hours: 8am-1am/2am (Thursday-Saturday)
Other Games: Only gaming machines
Overnight RV Parking: No
Special Features: Entire casino is nonsmoking.

Tesuque Casino
17486-A Highway 84/285
Santa Fe, New Mexico 87504
(505) 984-8414
Website: www.tesuquecasino.com
Map: **#2**

Toll-Free Number: (800) 462-2635
Restaurants: 1 Liquor: No
Hours: 8am-2am/24 Hours (Thu-Sat)
Casino Size: 60,000 Square Feet
Other Games: PGP
Overnight RV Parking: Free/RV Dump: No
Senior Discount: Various on Tue/Thu if 49+

Wild Horse Casino & Hotel
13603 US Highway 64
Dulce, New Mexico 87528
(575) 759-3663
Website: www.apachenugget.com
Map: **#12** (95 miles N.W. of Santa Fe)

Rooms: 41 Price Range: $75-$95
Restaurants: 1 Liquor: Yes
Hours: 11am-1am/9am-1am (Thu)/
9am-2am (Fri/Sat)/9am-12am (Sun)
Other Games: Only gaming machines

Pari-Mutuels

The Downs Racetrack and Casino
145 Louisiana Boulevard NE
Albuquerque, New Mexico 87108
(505) 767-7171
Website: www.abqdowns.com
Map: **#9**

Restaurants: 2
Hours: 9am-12am/4am (Fri-Sat)
Other Games: Only gaming machines
Overnight RV Parking: No
Special Features: Live horse racing seasonally. Daily simulcasting of horse racing.

Ruidoso Downs & Billy The Kid Casino
26225 U.S. Highway 70 East
Ruidoso Downs, New Mexico 88346
(575) 378-4431
Website: www.ruidownsracing.com
Map: **#4** (90 miles N.E. of Las Cruces)

Restaurants: 2
Hours: 10am-11pm/12am (Fri/Sat)
Other Games: Only gaming machines
Overnight RV Parking: No
Senior Discount: Various Wed 2pm-9pm if 55+
Special Features: Live horse racing seasonally. Daily simulcasting of horse racing.

Sunland Park Racetrack & Casino
1200 Futurity Drive
Sunland Park, New Mexico 88063
(575) 874-5200
Website: www.sunland-park.com
Map: **#10** (5 miles W. of El Paso, TX)

Restaurants: 4
Hours: 10am-1am/2am (Thu)/4am (Fri/Sat)
Other Games: Only gaming machines
Overnight RV Parking: Free/$5 w/hookups
Senior Discount: Various Mon/Wed if 50+
Special Features: Live thoroughbred and quarter-horse racing seasonally. Daily simulcasting of horse racing.

SunRay Park and Casino
#39 Road 5568
Farmington, New Mexico 87401
(505) 566-1200
Website: www.sunraygaming.com
Map: **#11** (150 miles N.W. of Santa Fe)

Restaurants: 1
Hours: 11am-2am/3am (Thu)/4am (Fri)
10am-4am (Sat)/10am-2am (Sun)
Other Games: Only gaming machines
Overnight RV Parking: No
Special Features: Live horse racing seasonally. Daily simulcasting of horse racing.

Zia Park Casino • Hotel • Racetrack
3901 W. Millen Drive
Hobbs, New Mexico 88240
(575) 492-7000
Website: www.ziaparkcasino.com
Map: **#14** (70 miles N.E. of Carlsbad)

Toll-Free Number: (888) 942-7275
Rooms: 154 Price Range: $99-$199
Restaurants: 3
Hours: 10am-1am/10am-3am (Fri-Sat)/
9am-2am (Sun)
Other Games: Only gaming machines
Overnight RV Parking: Free/RV Dump: No
Special Features: Live horse racing seasonally. Daily simulcasting of horse racing.

NEW YORK

In late 2013 New York passed legislation allowing up to four destination casino resorts in upstate New York.

All casinos offer: blackjack, roulette, craps, slots and video poker. Some casinos also offer: mini-baccarat (MB), poker (P), pai gow poker (PGP), Caribbean stud poker (CSP), let it ride (LIR), big 6 wheel (B6), bingo (BG), keno (K), Mississippi stud (MS), three card poker (TCP), four card poker (FCP) and Spanish 21 (S21). Sports betting is also allowed at these four upstate casinos. The Rivers Casino in Schenectady opened its sports book in July 2019 and the other three casinos are expected to offer it by early 2020.

Here's information, as supplied by the New York Gaming Commission, showing the slot machine payback percentages for all of the casinos for the fiscal year from April 1, 2018 through March 31, 2019:

LOCATION	PAYBACK %
Tioga Downs	91.62
Resorts World Catskills	91.40
Del Lago	90.94
Rivers Casino Schenectady	90.50

The minimum gambling age is 21. All casinos are open 24 hours, except for Tioga Downs.

Del Lago Resort & Casino
1133 State Route 414
Waterloo, New York 13165
(315) 946-1777
Website: www.dellagoresort.com
Map: **#16** (50 miles S.W. of Syracuse)

Rooms: 205 Rates: $119 - $229
Restaurants: 8
Buffets: B- $13.95/$21.95 (Sun)
L- $17.95 D- $23.95
Casino Size: 94,000 Square Feet
Other Games: P, S21, LIR, TCP, MS,
UTH, MB, CSP, B6
Special Features: Spa. Buffet discount for players club members.

Resorts World Catskills
888 Resorts World Drive
Monticello, New York 12701
(833) 586-9358
Website: www.rwcatskills.com
Map: **#18** (100 miles N.W. of New York City)

Suites: 332 Price Range: $119-$499
Casino Size: 100,000 Square Feet
Restaurants: 8
Other Games: P, PG, B, PGP, LIR, UTH, CW
Special Features: Spa, 2,000-seat theater. Top Golf Swing Suite.

Rivers Casino & Resort Schenectady
1 Rush Street
Schenectady, New York 12305
(518) 579-8800
Website: www.riverscasinoandresort.com
Map: **#17**

Rooms: 165 Rates: $140-$279
Restaurants: 6
Casino Size: 50,000 Square Feet
Other Games: P, TCP, LIR, S21, PGP, MB, MS, CW, SB

Tioga Downs
2384 West River Road
Nichols, New York 13812
(888) 946-8464
Website: www.tiogadowns.com
Map: **#14** (30 miles W. of Binghamton)

Rooms: 161 Rates: $129-$289
Toll-Free: (888) 946-8464
Restaurants: 6
Buffets: L- $9.99/$15.99 (Sun)
D- $11.99/$25.99 (Thu)/
$19.99 (Fri/Sat)/$15.99 (Sun)
Casino Size: 19,000 Square Feet
Other Games: MB, LIR, TCP, B6,
PGP, P, MS, SB
Senior Discount: $6.99 All Day Buffet
Tue/ Wed if 50+
Overnight RV Parking: Free
Special Features: Live harness racing seasonally. Daily simulcasting of thoroughbred and harness racing.

Indian Casinos (Class III)

There are five Indian casinos located in upstate New York which offer traditional Class III casino gambling.

All of these casinos are open 24 hours and offer the following games: slot machines, video poker, blackjack, craps, and roulette. Some casinos also offer: Spanish 21 (S21), baccarat (B), mini-baccarat (MB), big six wheel (B6), keno (K), poker (P), pai gow poker (PGP), let it ride (LIR), caribbean stud poker (CSP), three-card poker (TCP), sic bo (SIC), four-card poker (FCP), Mississippi stud (MS), Texas hold'em bonus (THB), ultimate Texas hold'em (UTH) and casino war (CW).

The minimum gambling age is 21 at the three Seneca casinos and 18 at the other two casinos. For more information on visiting New York call the state's travel information center at (800) 225-5697 or go to: www.iloveny.com.

Akwesasne Mohawk Casino Resort
873 State Route 37
Hogansburg, New York 13655
(518) 358-2222
Website: www.mohawkcasino.com
Map: **#2** (65 miles W. of Champlain)

Toll-Free Number: (877) 992-2746
Rooms: 145 Price Range: $119-$229
Suites: 5 Price Range: $175-$500
Restaurants: 3 Liquor: Yes
Valet Park: Free
Buffets: B- $14.00 (Sat-Sun)
L- $12.00/$14.00 (Sat-Sun)
D- $19.00/$26.00 (Fri)/$21.00 (Sat)
Casino Size: 40,000 Square Feet
Other Games: S21, LIR, TCP, PGP, CSP, MS, BG
Overnight RV Parking: Free/RV Dump: No
Special Features: 19-space RV park ($32/day).

Point Place Casino
450 Route 31
Bridgeport, New York 13030
(315) 366-9610
Website: www.pointplacecasino.com
Map: **#8** (15 miles N.E. of Syracuse)

Restaurants: 2 Liquor: Yes
Casino Size: 65,000 Square Feet
Other Games: B6, TCP, S21, MS, SB
Special features: Gambling age is 18. Non-smoking casino.

Seneca Allegany Casino & Hotel
777 Seneca Allegany Boulevard
Salamanca, New York 14779
(716) 945-9300
Website: www.senecaalleganycasino.com
Map: **#12** (65 miles S. of Buffalo)

Toll-Free Number: (877) 553-9500
Rooms: 413 Price Range: $129-$349
Suites: 23 Price Range: $219-$449
Restaurants: 6 (1 open 24 hours)
Liquor: Yes Valet Park: Free
Buffets: L -$17.00/$23.00 (Sat/Sun)
D- $21.00/$23.00 (Sat/Sun)
Casino Size: 48,000 Square Feet
Other Games: CSP, P, TCP, FCP, LIR, S21, B6, MS
Overnight RV Parking: No
Special Features: Buffet discount for players club members.

Seneca Buffalo Creek Casino
1 Fulton Street
Buffalo, New York 14204
(716) 853-7576
www.senecabuffalocreekcasino.com
Map: **#3**

Restaurants: 2 Liquor: Yes
Valet Park: Free
Casino Size: 65,000 Square Feet
Other Games: MS, S21, LIR, TCP, THB
Overnight RV Parking: No

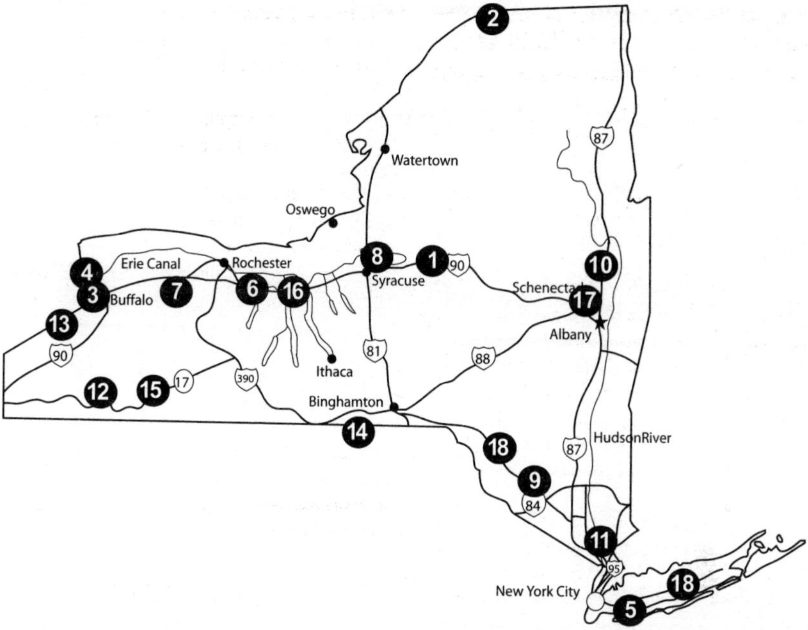

Seneca Niagara Casino
310 Fourth Street
Niagara Falls, New York 14303
(716) 299-1100
Website: www.senecaniagaracasino.com
Map: **#4**

Toll-Free Number: (877) 873-6322
Rooms: 574 Price Range: $189-$295
Suites: 30 Price Range: $305-$455
Restaurants: 6 Liquor: Yes
Valet Park: Free
Buffets: B- $15.00 (Sat/Sun) L- $17.00
D- $18.95
Other Games: CSP, S21, MB, P, PGP, TCP, LIR, FCP, K, MS, B6
Overnight RV Parking: No
Special Features: Buffet discount for slot club members.

Turning Stone Casino Resort
5218 Patrick Road
Verona, New York 13478
(315) 361-7711
Website: www.turning-stone.com
Map: **#1** (adjacent to NY State Thruway exit 33 at Verona, off Route 365, 30 miles E. of Syracuse)

Toll-Free Number: (800) 771-7711
Rooms: 572 Price Range: $179-$289
Suites: 143 Price Range: $279-$595
Restaurants: 10 Liquor: Yes
Buffets: B-$21.95 (Sat-Sun)
L- $16.95/$21.95 (Sat/Sun)
D- $20.95/$22.95 (Tue)/
$25.95 (Fri/Sat)/$23.95 (Sun)
Casino Size: 122,000 Square Feet
Other Games: CSP, B, MB, P, LIR, SIC, PGP, B, TCP, FCP, K, B6, CW, S21, SB
Overnight RV Parking: No
Special Features: Three golf courses. Gift shop. Discount smoke shop. 800-seat showroom. 175-space RV park ($40-$60 per night).

Yellow Brick Road Casino
800 West Genesee St
Chittenango, New York 13037
(315) 366-9400
Website: www.yellowbrickroadcasino.com
Map: **#1** (15 miles E. of Syracuse)

Restaurants: 3 Liquor: Yes
Casino Size: 67,000 Square Feet
Other Games: S21, LIR, TCP, MS, B6

Indian Casinos (Class II)

There are some Indian casinos that offer Class II gambling which consist of electronic gaming machines which look like slot machines, but are actually games of bingo and the spinning video reels are for "entertainment purposes only." No public information is available concerning the payback percentages on the video gaming machines.

All of these casinos have a cashless system whereby you have to go to a cashier cage, or a kiosk, get a "smart" card and deposit money to that card's account. The machines will then deduct losses from, or credit wins to, your account.

Additionally, after playing don't forget to cash out because all remaining credits on cards will be forfeited at the end of the day.

Some of these casinos also offer high-stakes bingo and poker, as shown in the "Other Games" listings.

Lakeside Entertainment
271 Cayuga Street
Union Springs, New York 13160
(315) 889-5416
Website: www.lakesidegaming.com
Map: **#15** (55 miles S. W. of Syracuse)

Restaurants: None Liquor: No
Valet Park: No
Hours: 10am-10pm Daily
Overnight RV Parking: Free/RV Dump: No

Seneca Gaming - Irving
11099 Route 5
Irving, New York 14081
(716) 549-4389
Website: www.senecagames.com
Map: **#13** (38 miles S.W. of Buffalo)

Toll-Free Number: (800) 421-2464
Restaurants: 1 Liquor: No Valet Park: No
Hours: 9:30am-2am/4:30am (Fri/Sat)
Overnight RV Parking: Free (must check in with security first)/RV Dump: No
Special Features: Discount smoke shop.

Seneca Gaming - Oil Spring
5374 West Shore Road
Cuba, New York 14727
(716) 780-8787
Website: www.senecagames.com
Map: **#15** (80 miles SW of Buffalo)

Casino Hours: 10:30am-11pm Daily
Senior Discount: Various Tuesdays if 55+

Seneca Gaming - Salamanca
768 Broad Street
Salamanca, New York 14779
(716) 945-4080
Website: www.senecagames.com
Map: **#12** (65 miles S. of Buffalo)

Toll-Free Number: (877) 860-5130
Restaurants: 1 Liquor: No Valet Park: No
Hours: 9:30am-1am/2am (Fri/Sat)
Overnight RV Parking: Free (must check in with security first)/RV Dump: No

Pari-Mutuels

New York allows slot machine-type video lottery machines at all New York racetracks, as well as one off-track betting facility. Officially referred to as Video Gaming Machines (VGM's), they are regulated by the New York Lottery.

All VGM's offer standard slot machine-type games, plus keno in denominations from five cents to $10.

The VGM's do not operate like regular slot machines or video poker games. Instead, they are similar to scratch-off-type lottery tickets with a pre-determined number of winners. The legislation authorizing the VGM's states, "the specifications for video lottery gaming shall be designed in such a manner as to pay prizes that average no less than ninety percent of sales."

All racetrack casinos also offer electronic versions of roulette, craps and baccarat, except for three racinos in western New York: Hamburg Gaming, Finger Lakes and Batavia Downs.

Here's information, as supplied by the New York Lottery, showing the video gaming machine payback percentages for each of the state's racetracks for the fiscal year from April 1, 2018 through March 31, 2019:

LOCATION	PAYBACK %
Resorts World	94.16
Jake's 58	93.73
Empire City	93.06
Monticello	92.40
Saratoga	92.35
Finger Lakes	92.12
Vernon Downs	91.74
Batavia Downs	91.66
Fairgrounds	91.66

All Video Gaming Machine facilities are alowed to be open for 20 hours a day, with varrying hours. Some are open 8am-4am, some are open 9am-5am, etc. and all are non-smoking. Please call to confirm hours if necessary. Admission is free to all facilities and the minimum gambling age is 18 for playing VGM's, as well as for pari-mutuel betting.

Batavia Downs Gaming & Hotel
8315 Park Road
Batavia, New York 14020
(585) 343-3750
Website: www.bataviadownsgaming.com
Map: **#7** (35 miles E. of Buffalo)

Toll-Free: (800) 724-2000
Hours: 8am-4am
Restaurants: 4
Overnight RV Parking: No
Senior Discount: Various Mon if 55+
Special Features: Live harness racing seasonally. Daily simulcasting of thoroughbred and harness racing. Hall of Fame Running Back Thurman Thomas' Sports Bar with Buffalo Bills Memorabilia, HD TVs and Live Entertainment most weekends.

Empire City Casino
810 Yonkers Avenue
Yonkers, New York 10704
(914) 968-4200
Website: www.empirecitycasino.com
Map: **#11** (20 miles N. of Manhattan)

Restaurants: 3
Valet: $15
Special Features: Year-round live harness racing select evenings. Daily simulcasting of thoroughbred and harness racing.

Finger Lakes Gaming & Racetrack
5857 Route 96
Farmington, New York 14425
(585) 924-3232
Website: www.fingerlakesgaming.com
Map: **#6** (25 miles S. of Rochester)

Hours: 8am-4am
Restaurants: 5
Buffets: B- $18.95 (Sun) L- $16.95 D- $20.95
Casino Size: 28,267 Square Feet
Overnight RV Parking: Call for permission
Senior Discount: Various Tuesday if 50+
Special Features: Live thoroughbred horse racing seasonally. Daily simulcasting of harness and thoroughbred racing. Buffet closed Mondays and Tuesdays.

Hamburg Gaming at The Fairgrounds
5820 South Park Avenue
Hamburg, New York 14075
(716) 646-6109
Website: www.the-fairgrounds.com
Map: **#3** (20 miles S. of Buffalo)

Toll-Free: (800) 237-1205
Casino Hours: 8am-4am
Restaurants: 2 Valet Parking: No
Buffets: B- $16.99 (Sun)
L - $15.99/$16.99 (Sun)
D- $20.99
Casino Size: 27,000 Square Feet
Overnight RV Parking: Yes
Special Features: Live harness racing seasonally. Simulcasting Wed-Sun of thoroughbred and harness racing. $2 buffet discount for Players Club members. Buffet closed Mon & Tue.

Jake's 58 Hotel & Casino
3635 Express Drive North
Islandia, New York 11749
(631) 232-3000
Website: jakes58.com
Map: **#18** (50 miles E. of Manhattan)

Rooms: 200 Price Range:$179 - $225
Suites: 28 Price range: $329 - $429
Restaurants: 2
Casino Hours: 8am - 4am Daily
Casino Size: 100,000 Square Feet
Overnight RV Parking: No
Special Features: Off Track Betting on thoroughbred and harness racing.

Resorts World Casino New York City
110-00 Rockaway Boulevard
Jamaica, New York 11420
(718) 215-2828
Website: www.rwnewyork.com
Map: **#5** (15 miles E. of Manhattan)

Toll-Free Number: (888) 888-8801
Restaurants: 1
Special Features: Live thoroughbred racing seasonally. Daily simulcasting of thoroughbred racing. 6-outlet food court.

Saratoga Casino Hotel
342 Jefferson Street
Saratoga Springs, New York 12866
(518) 584-2110
Website: www.saratogacasino.com
Map: **#10** (25 miles N. of Schenectady)

Toll-Free: (800) 727-2990
Rooms: 103 Price Range: $155-$435
Suites: 13 Price Range: $205-$600
Casino Hours: 8am-4am Daily
Restaurants: 5 Valet Parking: $3
Buffets: L- $13.95 D- $15.95
Casino Size: 55,000 Square Feet
Overnight RV Parking: Free
Senior Discount: Buffet Tue $6.95 if 55+
Special Features: seasonally. Daily simulcasting of thoroughbred and harness racing. Buffet discounts for players club members.

Vernon Downs Casino Hotel
4229 Stuhlman Road
Vernon, New York 13476
(315) 829-2201
Website: www.vernondowns.com
Map: **#1** (30 miles E. of Syracuse)

Toll-Free Number: (877) 888-3766
Room Reservations: (866) 829-3400
Suites: 175 Price Range: $59-$159
Restaurants: 1 Valet Parking: $3
Buffets: L- $7.77
D- $7.77/$18.99 (Fri)/$14.99 (Sun)
Casino Size: 28,000 Square Feet
Overnight RV Parking: Free/RV Dump: No
Special Features: Live harness racing seasonally. Daily simulcasting of thoroughbred and harness racing.

Canadian Casinos

If you are traveling to the Buffalo area there are two nearby Canadian casinos just across the border in Niagara Falls, Ontario.

Both of these casinos are open 24 hours and offer the following games: slot machines, video poker, blackjack, craps and roulette. Optional games include: Spanish 21 (S21), Casino War (CW), Mississippi stud (MS), three card poker (TCP), poker room (P). baccarat (B), mini-baccarat (MB), big six wheel (B6), keno (K), pai gow poker (PGP), pai gow tiles (PG), let it ride (LIR), caribbean stud poker (CSP), sic bo (SIC), four-card poker (FCP), Texas hold'em bonus (THB) and ultimate Texas hold'em (UTH).

All winnings are paid in Canadian currency and the minimum gambling age is 19.

Casino Niagara
5705 Falls Avenue
Niagara Falls, Ontario L2E 6T3
(905) 374-3589
Website: www.casinoniagara.com
Map: **#4**

PRICES ARE IN CANADIAN DOLLARS
Toll-Free Number: (888) 946-3255
Restaurants: 6
Buffets: L/D- $27.00
Casino Size: 100,000 Square Feet
Other games: S21, B, PGP, LIR, CW,
MS, P, SB
Overnight RV Parking: Free/RV Dump: No
Senior Discount: Various Wed if 55+
Special Features: Buffet discount for Players Club members.

Fallsview Casino Resort
6380 Fallsview Boulevard
Niagara, Ontario L2G 7X5
(905) 358-3255
Website: www.fallsviewcasinoresort.com
Map: **#4**

PRICES ARE IN CANADIAN DOLLARS
Toll-Free Number: (888) 325-5788
Rooms: 340 Price Range: $209-$350
Suites: 28 Price Range: $359-$559
Restaurants: 10 Valet Parking: $20
Buffets: B-$22.00/$34.00 (Sun) L/D-$34.00
Games Offered: PG, CW, SIC, P
Casino Size: 200,000 Square Feet
Overnight RV Parking: No
Special Features: Buffet discounts for players club members. Spa/fitness center. 1,500-seat theatre. Additional Hilton hotel connected by walkway.

NORTH CAROLINA

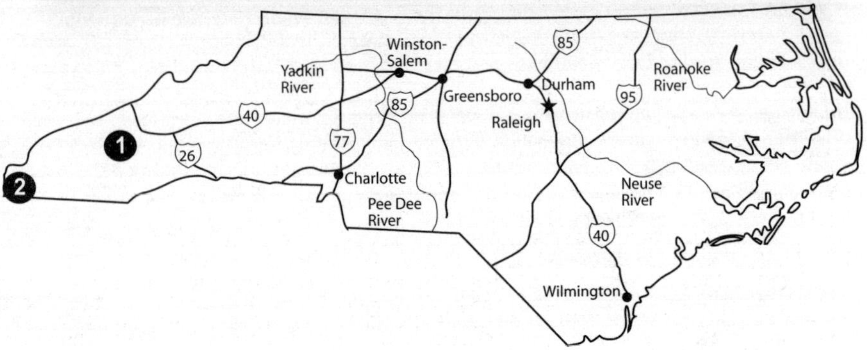

North Carolina has two Indian casinos and they are not required to release information on the payback percentages of their games. However, according to the terms of their compact with the state, the video machines are required to return a minimum of 83% to a maximum of 98%.

Both casinos offer: slots, video poker, video keno, blackjack, roulette and craps. Optional games include: mini-baccarat (MB), poker (P), let it ride (LIR), Mississippi stud (MS) and three card poker (TCP). Both casinos are open 24 hours and the minimum gambling age is 21.

In July 2019, the North Carolina legislature approved sports betting for both casinos and it is expected to be offered at both by early 2020.

For more information on visiting North Carolina call the state's division of travel & tourism at (800) 847-4862 or go to: www.visitnc.com.

Harrah's Cherokee Casino
777 Casino Drive
Cherokee, North Carolina 28719
(828) 497-7777
Website: www.harrahscherokee.com
Map: **#1** (50 miles W. of Asheville)

Toll-Free Number: (800) 427-7247
Rooms 1,108 Price Range: $149-$499
Suites: 107 Price Range: Casino Use Only
Restaurants: 6 Liquor: Yes
Buffets: L/D- $28.49(Mon-Sat)/$34.99 (Sun)
Other Games: MB, LIR, TCP, P
Overnight RV Parking: No
Special Features: 1,500-seat entertainment pavilion. Buffet closed Tue/Wed.

Harrah's Cherokee Valley River Casino & Hotel
777 Casino Parkway
Murphy, North Carolina 28906
(828) 422-7777
Map: **#2** (108 miles S.W. of Asheville)

Rooms: 300 Price Range: $299-$619
Restaurants: 5 fast food outlets
Casino Size: 50,000 sq ft
Other Games: TCP

NORTH DAKOTA

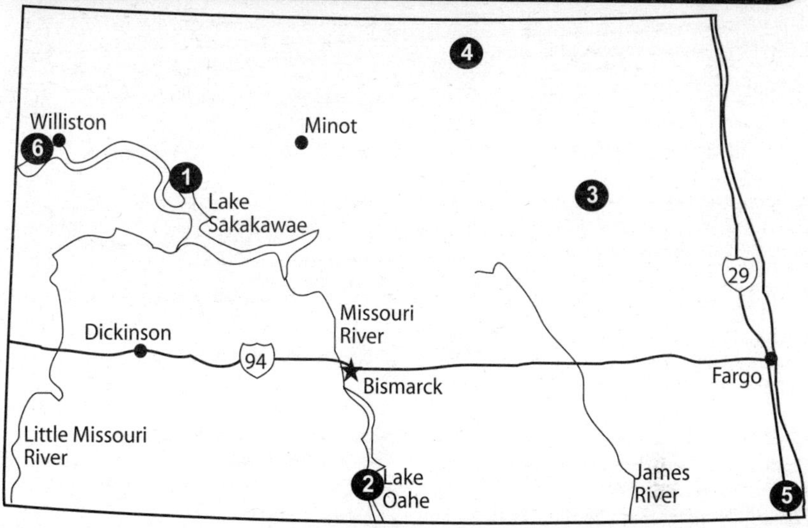

North Dakota has more than 800 sites throughout the state that offer blackjack, with betting limits of $1-$25, for the benefit of charities.

There are also Indian casinos in North Dakota which are limited by law to the following maximum bet limits: blackjack-$100 (two tables in a casino may have limits up to $250), craps-$60, roulette-$50, slots/video poker-$25 and poker-$50 per bet, per round with a maximum of three rounds.

The terms of the state's compact with the tribes require gaming machines to return a minimum of 80% and a maximum of 100%. However, if a machine is affected by skill, such as video poker or video blackjack, the machines must return a minimum of 83%.

All casinos are open 24 hours and offer: blackjack, craps, slots, video poker and video keno. Optional games include: Roulette (R), Spanish 21 (S21), Caribbean stud poker (CSP), let it ride (LIR), ultimate Texas hold em (UTH), poker (P), three-card poker (TCP), keno (K), bingo (BG), big-6 wheel (B6) and off-track betting (OTB).

The minimum age requirement is 21 for casino gambling and 18 for bingo. Legislation to legalize sports betting was proposed in 2019, but it did not pass. However, it may be introduced again in 2020.

For information on visiting North Dakota call the state's tourism office at (800) 435-5663 or go to: www.ndtourism.com.

Dakota Magic Casino Resort
16849 102nd Street SE
Hankinson, North Dakota 58041
(701) 634-3000
Website: www.dakotamagic.com
Map: **#5** (50 miles S. of Fargo)

Toll-Free Number: (800) 325-6825
Rooms: 111 Price Range: $79-$129
Suites: 8 Price Range: $150-$240
Restaurants: 4 Liquor: Yes
Valet Parking: No
Buffets: L- $12.95/$15.95 (Sat/Sun)
D- $15.95/$24.95 (Mon)/
$29.95 (Fri)/$18.95 (Sat)
Casino Size: 24,000 Square Feet
Overnight RV Parking: Free/RV Dump: Fee
Senior Discount: Various on Wednesday if 55+
Special Features: 10% off rooms for seniors.

Four Bears Casino & Lodge
202 Frontage Road
New Town, North Dakota 58763
(701) 627-4018
Website: www.4bearscasino.com
Map: **#1** (150 miles N.W. of Bismarck)

Toll-Free Number: (800) 294-5454
Rooms: 190 Price Range: $109-129
Suites: 30 Price Range: $149-179
Restaurants: 3 Liquor: Yes
Valet Parking: No
Buffets: B- $9.95 L- $10.95 D- $22.95
Other Games: R, P
Overnight RV Parking: Free/RV Dump: No
Senior Discount: Various Tue if 55+
Special Features: 115-space RV park ($25 per night). Nearby marina. 1,000-seat event center.

Grand Treasure Casino
4418 147th Avenue NW
Trenton, North Dakota 58553
(701) 572-2690
Website: www.grandtreasurecasino.net
Map: **#6** (120 miles N.W of Dickinson)

Restaurants: 2 Liquor: Yes
Casino Size: 5,000 sq ft
Other Games: Slots only
Senior Discount: Various Mondays if 55+

Prairie Knights Casino & Resort
7932 Highway 24
Fort Yates, North Dakota 58528
(701) 854-7777
Website: www.prairieknights.com
Map: **#2** (60 miles S. of Bismarck)

Toll-Free Number: (800) 425-8277
Rooms: 188 Price Range: $100
Suites: 12 Price Range: $150
Restaurants: 2 Liquor: Yes
Buffets: L/D 12.95
Valet Parking: No
Casino Size: 42,000 Square Feet
Overnight RV Parking: Free/RV Dump: Free
Special Features: 12-space RV park ($15 per night) at casino. 32-space RV park ($15 per night) at marina. Free RV dump at marina. Room discount for players club members. Convenience store. Table games open at noon.

Sky Dancer Hotel Casino & Resort
3965 Sky Dancer Way N.E.
Belcourt, North Dakota 58316
(701) 244-2400
Website: www.skydancercasino.com
Map: **#4** (120 miles N.E. of Minot)

Toll-Free Number: (866) 244-9467
Rooms: 70 Price Range: $65-$101
Suites: 27 Price Range: $111-$121
Restaurants: 2 Liquor: Yes
Buffets: B- $7.77 L- $10.95
D-$16.95 (Fri/Sat)
Casino Size: 25,000 Square Feet
Other Games: No Craps, P, LIR,
FCP, OTB(Wed-Sun)
Overnight RV Parking: Free/RV Dump: Free
Special Features: Gift shop.

Spirit Lake Casino & Resort
7889 ND Highway 57
St. Michael, North Dakota 58370
(701) 766-4747
Website: www.spiritlakecasino.com
Map: **#3** (6 miles S. of Devil's Lake)

Toll-Free Number: (800) 946-8238
Rooms: 108 Price Range: $89-$129
Suites: 16 Price Range: $115-$159
Restaurants: 3 Liquor: No
Valet Parking: Free
Buffets: B- $9.95 (Sun)
L- $6.95/$9.95 (Sun)
D- $10.95 (Mon)/$7.95 (Tue)/
$30.00 (Wed)/$5.95 (Thu)/
$10.95 (Fri/Sun)/$11.95 (Sat)
Casino Size: 45,000 Square Feet
Other Games: P, TCP, UTH,
LIR, BG (Wed-Sun)
Overnight RV Parking: Must use RV park
Senior Discount: Various on Mon if 55+
Special Features: 15-space RV park ($30-$35 per night). Gift shop. Discount smoke shop. 32-slip marina. Room discount for players club members.

OHIO

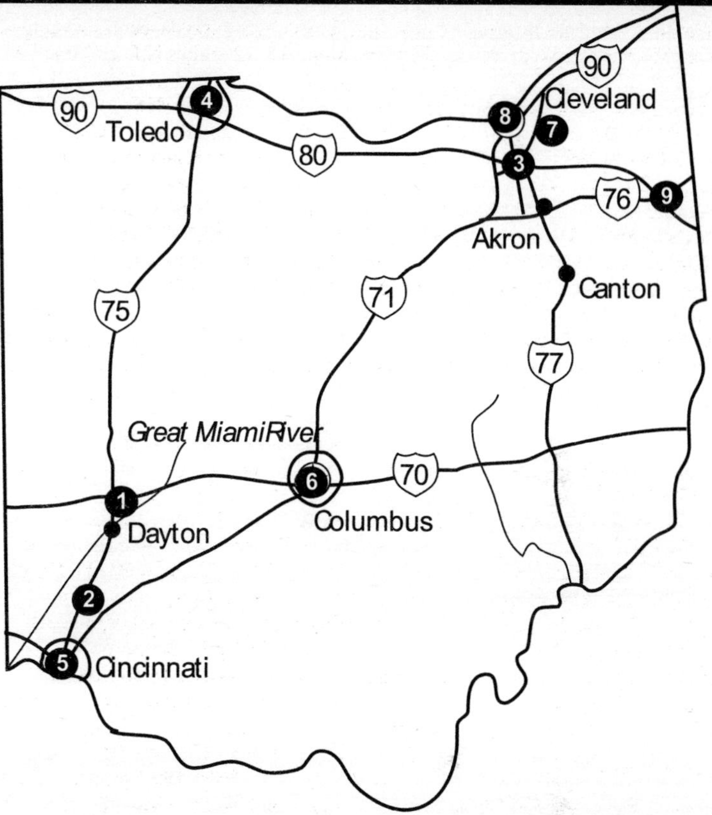

Ohio has casinos in four cities: Cleveland, Cincinnati, Columbus and Toledo. All of the casinos are non-smoking, open 24 hours and the minimum gambling age is 21.

Unless otherwise noted, all Ohio casinos offer: blackjack, craps, roulette, slots and video poker. Some casinos also offer: mini-baccarat (MB), baccarat (B), poker (P), pai gow poker (PGP), Mississippi stud (MS), sic-bo (SIC), let it ride (LIR), three card poker (TCP), four card poker (FCP), casino war (CW), big six (B6) and bingo (BG). Legislation to legalize sports betting was proposed in 2019, but it did not pass. However, it may be introduced again in 2020.

If you want to order a drink while playing, be aware that Ohio gaming regulations do not allow casinos to provide free alcoholic beverages. Additionally, casinos are not allowed to serve any alcohol between the hours of 2 a.m. and 6 a.m.

NOTE: If you happen to win a jackpot of $1,200 or more in Ohio, the casino will withhold approximately 5% of your winnings for the Ohio Department of Taxation. The $1,200 threshold also applies to any cash prizes won in casino drawings or tournaments.

Additionally, the casino will withhold another approximate 2.5% of your winnings for city taxes in Columbus, Cleveland and Cincinatti. In Toledo, the city tax won't be withheld until you win $2,000, or more. The $1,200 and $2,000 thresholds would also apply to any cash prizes won in casino drawings or tournaments.

Here's information from the Ohio Casino Control Commission regarding the payback percentages for each racino and casino's electronic machines for the twelve-month period from July 1, 2018 through June 30, 2019:

CASINO	PAYBACK %
JACK Cleveland	92.16
Hollywood Columbus	92.09
JACK Cincinatti	91.87
Belterra	91.15
MGM Northfield	91.09
Miami Valley	90.73
Hollywood Toledo	90.73
Eldorado Gaming	90.72
JACK Thistledown	90.61
Hollywood Dayton	90.27
Mahoning Valley	90.10

For tourism information, call the Ohio Division of Travel and Tourism at (800) 282-5393, or visit their website at www.discoverohio.com

Hollywood Casino - Columbus
200 Georgesville Road
Columbus, Ohio 43228
(614) 308-3333
Website: www.hollywoodcasinocolumbus.com
Map: #**6**

Toll-Free Number: (855) 617-4206
Restaurants: 4 Valet Parking: Free
Buffets: B- $16.99 (Sun) L-$13.99
D- $20.99 (Wed/Thu/Sun)/
$26.99 (Fri)/$24.99 (Sat)
Casino Size: 120,317 Square Feet
Other Games: TCP, FCP, LIR, CW, P, SIC,
MB, B6, PGP, UTH, MS
Overnight RV Parking: Free/RV Dump: No
Special Features: Buffet is Closed Mon/Tue. Stadium style table games.

Hollywood Casino - Toledo
777 Hollywood Boulevard
Toledo, Ohio 43605
(419) 661-5200
Website: www.hollywoodcasinotoledo.com
Map: #**4**

Toll-Free Number: (877) 777-9579
Buffets: B-$15.99 (Sun)
L-$15.99 (Tue-Sat)
D- $21.99/$15.99 (Thu)/
$39.99 (Fri/Sat)
Casino Size: 125,000 square feet
Other Games: MB, P, PGP, UTH, TCP, MS
Senior Discount: $9.99 buffet Tuesday and Wednesday if 48+.

JACK Cincinatti Casino
1000 Broadway Street
Cincinnati, Ohio 45202
(513) 252-0777
Website: www.jackentertainment.com
Map: #**5**

Restaurants: 5 Liquor: Yes
Valet Park: Free for Players Club Members: Non Members $15
Casino Size: 100,000 sq ft
Buffets: L- $17.99/$25.99 (Sat/Sun)
D- $25.99/$34.95 (Wed)/$39.99 (Sat)
Other Games: LIR, FCP, TCP, PGP, MS, P
Overnight RV Parking: No
Special Features: Buffet discount for players club members. Food court.

JACK Cleveland Casino
100 Public Square
Cleveland, Ohio 44113
(216) 297-4777
Website: www.jackentertainment.com
Map: #**8**

Toll-free Number: (855) 746-3777
Restaurants: 5
Buffet: B- $25.99 (Sun) L- $15.99
D- $25.99/$30.99 (Fri/Sat)
Casino Size: 96,000 Square Feet
Other Games: P, B, PGP, LIR, TCP, FCP, MS
Special features: Buffet discount for players club members. Stadium style table games available. Parking rates vary based on day of the week and level of play.

Pari-Mutuels

In Ohio, pari-mutuels are allowed to offer video lottery terminals that are regulated by the Ohio Lottery Commission.

All racetrack casinos (racinos) are open 24 hours and the minimum gambling age is 21. The minimum age for pari-mutuel betting is 18.

Belterra Park Gaming & Entertainment Center
6301 Kellogg Road
Cincinnati, Ohio 45230
(513) 232-8000
Website: www.belterrapark.com
Map: **#5**

Restaurants: 4
Buffets: L- $15.99/$21.99 (Sun)
D- $20.99/$27.99 (Wed/Fri/Sat)/
$24.99 (Sunday)
Senior Discount: Buy one buffet, get one free Tuesdays if 55+.
Special Features: Live horse racing seasonally. Daily simulcasting of horse and harness racing.

Eldorado Gaming at Scioto Downs
6000 S. High St
Columbus, Ohio 43207
(614) 295-4700
Website: www.sciotodowns.com
Map: #**6**

Restaurants: 1
Buffets: L- $15.99 D- $19.99
Special Features: Daily simulcasting of horse and harness racing. Live harness Racing seasonally.

Hollywood Gaming Dayton Raceway
3100 Needmore Road
Dayton, Ohio 45414
(937) 235-7800
Website: www.hollywooddaytonraceway.com
Map: #**1**

Restaurants: 3
Special Features: Live harness racing seasonally. Daily simulcasting of horse and harness racing.

Hollywood Gaming Mahoning Valley
655 North Canfield Niles Road
Austintown, Ohio 44515
(877) 788-3777
Website: www.hollywoodmahoningvalley.com
Map: #**9** (45 miles E. of Akron)

Restaurants: 4
Special Features: Live thoroughbred racing seasonally. Daily simulcasting of horse and harness racing.

JACK Thistledown Racino
21501 Emery Road
Cleveland, Ohio 44128
(216) 662-8600
Website: www.thistledown.com
Map: #**8**

Toll-free Number: (800) 289-9956
Restaurants: 1
Special Features: Live thoroughbred racing seasonally. Daily simulcasting of horse and harness racing.

MGM Northfield Park
10777 Northfield Road
Northfield, Ohio 44067
(330) 908-7625
Website: mgmnorthfieldpark.mgmresorts.com
Map: #**3** (10 miles SE. of Clevland)

Restaurants: 3
Buffets: L- $15.99/$19.99 (Sunday) D- $22.99
Senior Discounts: Various on Sun-Tue if 50+
Special Features: Live harness racing seasonally. Daily simulcasting of horse and harness racing.

Miami Valley Gaming
6000 State Route 63
Lebanon, Ohio 45036
(513) 934-7070
Website: www.miamivalleygaming.com
Map: #**2** (25 miles S. of Dayton)

Toll Free Number: (855) 946-6847
Restaurants: 3
Buffets: B- $18.99 (Sun)
L- $13.99/$15.99 (Tue/Sat)/
$18.99 (Sun)
D- $18.99/$24.99 (Friday-Saturday)
Special Features: Live harness racing seasonally. Daily simulcasting of horse and harness racing. Buffet discounts for players club members. Buffet closed Monday.

OKLAHOMA

All Oklahoma Indian casinos are allowed to offer both Class II and Class III gaming machines.

Most casinos offer only Class II machines which look like slot machines, but are actually games of bingo and the spinning video reels are for "entertainment purposes only." Some casinos also offer traditional Class III slots.

No public information is available concerning the payback percentages on gaming machines in Oklahoma.

Some casinos with card games such as blackjack, let it ride or three-card poker, etc., offer a player-banked version where players must pay a commission to the house on every hand they play. The amount of the commission charged varies, depending on the rules of each casino, but it's usually 50 cents to $1 per hand played. Call the casino to see if they charge a commission.

In mid-2018, traditional roulette and dice games were legalized in Oklahoma. The games are the same player-banked versions like above where players must pay a commission to the house on every spin in roulette or once for each point roll in craps.

There are also two horse racing facilities in Oklahoma which feature Class II gaming machines.

All Oklahoma Indian casinos offer gaming machines. Other games include: blackjack (BJ), craps (C), roulette (R), mini-baccarat (MB), poker (P), three-card poker (TCP), pai gow poker (PGP), ultimate Texas hold 'em (UTH), let it ride (LIR), Mississippi stud (MS), bingo (BG) and off-track betting (OTB).

No legislation to legalize sports betting in Oklahoma was proposed in 2019. However, it may be introduced in 2020.

Not all Oklahoma Indian casinos serve alcoholic beverages and the individual listings note which casinos do serve it.

Unless otherwise noted, all casinos are open 24 hours. The minimum gambling age is 18 at some casinos and 21 at others.

For more information on visiting Oklahoma call the Oklahoma Tourism Department at (800) 652-6552 or go to: www.travelok.com

Ada Gaming Center - East
1500 North Country Club Road
Ada, Oklahoma 74820
Website: www.adagaming.com
(580) 436-3740
Map: **#2** (85 miles S.E. of Oklahoma City)

Restaurants: 2 (1 snack bar) Liquor: Yes
Casino Size: 9,220 Square Feet
Other Games: BJ, UTH
Overnight RV Parking: No
Special Features: Located in travel plaza with gas station and convenience store.

Ada Gaming Center - West
201 Latta Road
Ada, Oklahoma 74820
(580) 310-0900
Website: www.chickasaw.net
Map: **#2** (85 miles S.E. of Oklahoma City)

Restaurants: 1 Snack Bar Liquor: No
Overnight RV Parking: No
Special Features: Located in travel plaza with gas station and convenience store.

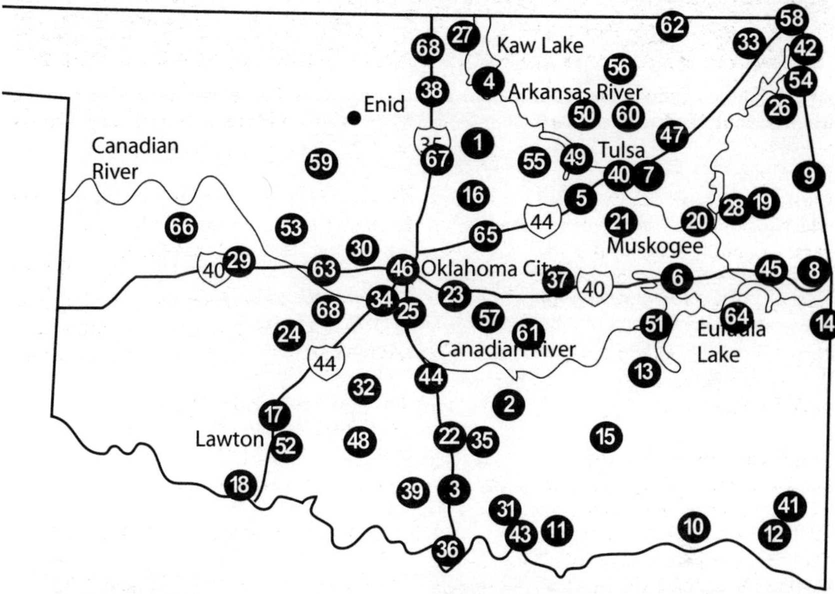

Apache Casino Hotel
2315 East Gore Boulevard
Lawton, Oklahoma 73501
(855) 248-5905
Website: www.apachecasinohotel.com
Map: **#17** (86 miles S.W. of Oklahoma City)

Rooms: 124 Price Range: $109-$187
Suites: 8 Price Range: $239-$297
Restaurants: 2 (1 snack bar) Liquor: Yes
Buffet: B- $29.99 (Sun)
Casino Size: 7,700 Square Feet
Other Games: BJ, R, UTH
Overnight RV Parking: Free/RV Dump: No
Special Features: Offers card versions of craps.

Artesian Hotel Casino Spa
1001 W. 1st Street
Sulphur, Oklahoma 73086
(580) 622-2156
Website: www.artesianhotel.com
Map: **#35** (84 miles S. of Oklahoma City)

Toll-Free Number: (855) 455-5255
Rooms: 81 Price Range: $149-$299
Restaurants: 2 Liquor: Yes
Other Games: BJ, LIR, UTH, BG(Sun-Tue)
Senior Specials: Bonus Free Play and food offers after earning 20 points.
Special Feature: Spa

Black Gold Casino
288 Mulberry Lane (on Route 70)
Wilson, Oklahoma 73463
(580) 668-4415
Website: www.myblackgoldcasino.com
Map: **#39** (112 miles S. of Oklahoma City)

Restaurants: 1 Snack Bar Liquor: No
Casino Size: 3,744 Square Feet
Overnight RV Parking: Free/RV Dump: No
Special Features: Located in travel plaza with gas station and convenience store.

Black Hawk Casino
42008 Westech Road
Shawnee, Oklahoma 74804
(405) 275-4700
Website: www.theblackhawkcasino.com
Map: **#23** (40 Miles E. of Okalhoma City)

Restaurants: 1 Liquor: Yes
Casino Size: 8,600 Square Feet
Other Games: BJ, C, MS, UTH
Tables open 4pm-12am daily
Overnight RV Parking: No

Border Casino
22953 Brown Springs Road
Thackerville, Oklahoma 73459
(580) 276-1727
Website: www.mybordercasino.com
Map: **#36** (124 miles S. of Oklahoma City)

Restaurants: 1 Liquor: Yes
Casino Size: 88,000 Square Feet
Overnight RV Parking: Free/RV Dump: No

Bordertown Casino and Arena
129 W. Oneida Street
Wyandotte, Oklahoma 74370
(918) 666-9401
Map: **#26** (90 miles N.E. of Tulsa)

Restaurants: 1
Special Features: Indoor arena

Buffalo Run Casino
1000 Buffalo Run Boulevard
Miami, Oklahoma 74354
(918) 542-7140
Website: www.buffalorun.com
Map: **#33** (89 miles N.E. of Tulsa)

Rooms: 88 Room Rates: $75-$99
Suites: 12 Room Rates: $85-$119
Restaurants: 3 Liquor: Yes
Other Games: BJ, TCP, UTH
Overnight RV Parking: Free/RV Dump: No
Special Features: 2,000-seat showroom.

Casino Oklahoma
220 E. Cummins Road
Hinton, Oklahoma 73047
(405) 542-4200
Website: www.casinooklahoma.com
Map: **#63** (55 miles W. of Oklahoma City)

Restaurants: 2 Liquor: Yes
Senior Discount: Various Thu at 11am if 55+
Overnight RV Parking: Free/RV Dump: No

Cherokee Casino - Ft. Gibson
107 N. Georgetown Road/US Highway 62
Ft. Gibson, Oklahoma 74434
(918) 684-5507
Website: www.cherokeecasino.com
Map: **#28** (55 miles S.E. of Tulsa)

Restaurants: 1 Liquor : Yes
Overnight RV Parking: No
Senior Discount: Various Tue if 55+

Cherokee Casino - Grove
Highway 59 and East 250 Road
Grove, Oklahoma 74344
(918) 786-1300
Website: www.cherokeecasino.com
Map: **#54** (100 miles N.E. of Tulsa)

Restaurants: 1 Liquor: Yes
Overnight RV Parking: Free/RV Dump: No
Senior Discount: Various Mon/Thu if 50+

Cherokee Casino - Ramona
31501 US 75 Highway
Ramona, Oklahoma 74061
(918) 535-3800
Website: www.cherokeecasino.com
Map: **#60** (30 miles N. of Tulsa)

Restaurants: 1 Liquor: Yes
Senior Discount: Food discounts on Mondays and Wednesdays if 55+

Cherokee Casino & Hotel - Roland
109 Cherokee Boulevard
Roland, Oklahoma 74954
(800) 256-2338
Website: www.cherokeecasino.com
Map: **#8** (175 miles E. of Oklahoma City)

Rooms: 98 Room Rates: $85-$136
Suites: 12 Room Rates: $139-$189
Restaurants: 2 Liquor: Yes
Buffet: L- $5.99 L- $6.99
D- $10.99/$14.99 (Fri/Sat)
Casino Size: 28,000 Square Feet
Other Games: BJ, R, TCP, UTH
Senior Discount: Various Thu if 50+
Overnight RV Parking: Free/RV Dump: No

Cherokee Casino - Sallisaw
1621 West Ruth Street
Sallisaw, Oklahoma 74955
(918) 774-1600
Website: www.cherokeecasino.com
Map: **#45** (160 miles E. of Oklahoma City)

Toll-Free Number: (800) 256-2338
Restaurants: 1 Liquor: Yes
Casino Size: 22,000 Square Feet
Other Games: OTB
Overnight RV Parking: Free/RV Dump: No

Cherokee Casino - South Coffeyville
1506 North Highway 169
South Coffeyville, Oklahoma 74072
(918) 255-4200
Website: www.cherokeecasino.com
Map: **#62** (70 miles N.E. of Tulsa)

Restaurants: 1 Liquor: Yes
Overnight RV Parking: No

Cherokee Casino - Tahlequah
16489 Highway 62
Tahlequah, Oklahoma 74464
(918) 207-3600
Website: www.cherokeecasino.com
Map: **#19** (83 miles S.E. of Tulsa)

Restaurants: 2 Liquor: Yes
Overnight RV Parking: Free/RV Dump: No
Senior Discount: Various Tuesday if 50+

Cherokee Casino & Hotel - West Siloam Springs
3426 US Highway 412
West Siloam Springs, Oklahoma 74338
(800) 754-4111
Website: www.cherokeecasino.com
Map: **#9** (85 miles E. of Tulsa)

Toll-Free Number: (800) 754-4111
Rooms: 140 Price Range: $99-$109
Suites: 7 Price Range $248-$381
Restaurants: 3 Liquor: Yes
Buffets: B-$6.99 L- $8.99
D-$11.99/$29.99 (Wed)
Other Games: BJ, P, R, TCP, OTB, UTH
Overnight RV Parking: Free/RV Dump: No
Senior Discount: Food discounts Tue if 55+
Special Features: Buffet discount for players club members.

Chisholm Trail Casino
7807 N. Highway 81
Duncan, Oklahoma 73533
(580) 255-1668
Website: www.chisholmtrailcasino.com
Map: **#48** (79 miles S. of Oklahoma City)

Casino Size: 22,000 Square Feet
Restaurants: 1 Liquor: Yes
Overnight RV Parking: Free/RV Dump: No
Senior Discount: Various Mondays if 50+
Special Feature: Virtual version of Blackjack.

Choctaw Casino - Broken Bow
1790 South Park Drive
Broken Bow, Oklahoma 74728
(580) 584-5450
Website: www.choctawcasinos.com
Map: **#41** (235 miles S.E. of Oklahoma City)

Restaurants: 1 Snack Bar Liquor: Yes
Other Games: BJ, TCP
Overnight RV Parking: Free/ RV Dump: No
Senior Discount: Various Wed if 50+

Choctaw Casino Resort - Durant
4216 South Highway 69/75
Durant, Oklahoma 74701
(580) 920-0160
Website: www.choctawcasinos.com
Map: **#11** (150 miles S.E. of Oklahoma City)

Toll-Free Number: (888) 652-4628
Rooms: 240 Price Range: $109-$279
Suites: 90 Price Range: $239-$750
Restaurants: 8 Liquor: Yes
Buffets: L- $17.99/$25.99 (Sun)
D- $21.99/$32.99 (Fri/Sat)
Casino Size: 36,000 Square Feet
Other Games: BJ, C, R, P, OTB,
TCP, LIR, PGP, MB
Senior Discount: Various Thu if 50+
Overnight RV Parking: Must use RV Park/ RV Dump: No
Special Features: Free shuttle buses from Dallas and Fort Worth. 77-space RV park ($45+ nightly). Buffet discount for Players Club members. Expansion that includes 1,000-room luxury hotel and expanded gaming floor scheduled to open in Spring, 2021.

Choctaw Casino Resort - Grant
1516 US Highway 271
Grant, Oklahoma 74738
(580) 326-8397
Website: www.choctawcasinos.com
Map: **#10** (200 miles S. of Oklahoma City)

Restaurants: 4 Deli Liquor: Yes
Rooms: 156 Price Range: $119-$189
Suites: 28 Price Range $199-$349
Buffets: B-$11.10/$15.00 (Sun) L-$11.10
D-$15.00/$24.99 (Fri/Sat)
Other Games: C, R, BJ, P
Overnight RV Parking: No
Special Features: No dinner buffet on Mon/ Tue. Buffet discount for slot club members.

Choctaw Casino - Idabel
1425 Southeast Washington Street
Idabel, Oklahoma 74745
(800) 634-2582
Website: www.choctawcasinos.com
Map: **#12** (240 miles S.E. of Oklahoma City)

Restaurants: 1 Liquor: Yes
Casino Size: 11,000 Square Feet
Overnight RV Parking: Must check-in at front desk/RV Dump: No
Senior Discount: Various Wed if 50+

Choctaw Casino - McAlester
1638 South George Nigh Expressway
McAlester, Oklahoma 74501
(918) 423-8161
Website: www.choctawcasinos.com
Map: **#13** (130 miles S.E. of Oklahoma City)

Toll-Free Number: (877) 904-8444
Restaurants: 1 Liquor: Yes
Other Games: BJ, UTH
Casino Size: 17,500 Square Feet
Overnight RV Parking: Free/RV Dump: No
Special Features: Blackjack games open at 4pm.

Choctaw Casino Hotel - Pocola
3400 Choctaw Road
Pocola, Oklahoma 74902
(918) 436-7761
Website: www.choctawcasinos.com
Map: **#14** (195 miles E. of Oklahoma City)

Rooms: 118 Price Range: $99-$119
Suites: 10 Price Range: $149-$279
Toll-Free Number: (800) 590-5825
Restaurants: 4 Liquor: No
Buffets: B- $15.95 (Sun)
D-$12.95 (Wed)$32.95 (Thu)/
$29.95 (Fri)/$15.95 (Sat)/
$13.95 (Sun)
Other Games: BJ, R, TCP, P, UTH, OTB, MS, MB
Overnight RV Parking: Free/RV Dump: No
Special Features: Buffet is closed Monday/ Tuesday. Buffet discount for Players Club members.

Choctaw Casino - Stringtown
895 North Highway 69
Stringtown, Oklahoma 74569
(580) 346-7862
Website: www.choctawcasinos.com
Map: **#15** (163 miles S.E. of Oklahoma City)

Restaurants: 1 Liquor: Yes
Hours: 8am-2am/4am (Thu-Sat)
Overnight RV Parking: Free/RV Dump: No

Cimarron Casino
821 W. Freeman Avenue
Perkins, Oklahoma 74059
(405) 547-5352
Website: www.cimarroncasino.com
Map: **#16** (60 miles N. of Oklahoma City)

Restaurants: 2 Liquor: Yes
Other Games: P, BJ, UTH
Overnight RV Parking: No
Senior Discount: Various Wed/Fri 8am-8pm if 50+

Comanche Nation Casino
402 Southeast Interstate Drive
Lawton, Oklahoma 73501
(580) 250-3030
Website: www.comanchenationcasinos.com
Map: **#17** (86 miles S.W. of Oklahoma City)

Toll-Free Number: (877) 900-7594
Restaurants: 2 Liquor: Yes
Other Games: BJ, TCP, P, UTH
Overnight RV Parking: Free, must get pass from front desk first (with hook ups)/ RV Dump: No
Senior Discount: Various Wed if 55+

Comanche Red River Hotel & Casino
Highway 36 and Highway 70
Devol, Oklahoma 73531
(580) 250-3060
Website: www.comanchenationcasinos.com
Map: **#18** (125 miles S.W. of Oklahoma City)

Toll-Free Number: (866) 280-3261
Rooms: 87 Price Range: $99-$129
Restaurants: 2 Liquor: Yes
Casino Size: 52,500 Square Feet
Other Games: BJ, P, TCP, MS, UTH
Overnight RV Parking: Check-in at front desk/RV Dump: No
Special Features: Drive-thru smoke shop.

Comanche Spur Casino
9047 US Highway 62
Eldon, Oklahoma 73538
(580) 250-3090
Website: www.comanchenationcasinos.com
Map: **#29** (75 miles S.W. of Oklahoma City)

Restaurants: 1 Snack Bar Liquor: No
Hours: 11am-12am/2am (Fri/Sat)
Overnight RV Parking: No
Senior Discount: Various Wed if 50+
Special features: Smoke shop. Convenience store.

Comanche Star Casino
263171 Highway 53
Walters, Oklahoma 73572
(580) 250-3100
Website: www.comanchenationcasinos.com
Map: **#52** (25 miles S.E. of Lawton)

Restaurants: 1 Liquor: No
Hours: 12pm-11pm/1am (Fri/Sat)
Casino Size: 7,000 Square Feet
Overnight RV Parking: No
Senior Discount: Various Tue if 50+

Creek Nation Casino - Bristow
121 West Lincoln
Bristow, Oklahoma 74010
(918) 367-2260
Website: www.creeknationbristow.com
Map: **#5** (60 miles N.E. of Oklahoma City)

Restaurants: 1 Liquor: No
Hours: 8am-6am
Overnight RV Parking: No

Creek Nation Casino - Checotah
830 North Broadway
Checotah, Oklahoma 74426
(918) 473-5200
Map: **#6** (120 miles E. of Oklahoma City)

Restaurants: 1
Hours: 8am-10pm/11pm Friday/Saturday
Gambling Age: 18
Casino Size: 12,000 Square Feet
Overnight RV Parking: No

Creek Nation Casino - Eufaula
806 Forest Avenue
Eufaula, Oklahoma 74432
(918) 689-9191
Map: **#51** (135 miles E. of Oklahoma City)

Restaurants: 1 Snack Bar Liquor: No
Hours: 8am-4am daily
Gamling Age: 21
Overnight RV Parking: No

Creek Nation Casino - Holdenville
211 East Willow Street
Holdenville, Oklahoma 74848
(405) 379-3321
Map: **#61** (75 miles S.E. of Oklahoma City)

Casino Hours: 12pm-12am/2am (Fri/Sat)/
10pm (Sun)
Overnight RV Parking: No
Gambling Age: 18

Creek Nation Casino - Muscogee
3420 West Peak Boulevard
Muskogee, Oklahoma 74403
(918) 683-1825
Website: www.creeknationcasino.net
Map: **#20** (50 miles S.E. of Tulsa)

Restaurants: 1 Liquor: Yes
Casino Size: 22,500 Square Feet
Overnight RV Parking: Free/RV Dump: No
Senior Discount: Various Mon if 55+
Gambling Age: 21

Creek Nation Casino - Okemah
1100 S. Woodie Guthrie Boulevard
Okemah, Oklahoma 74859
(918) 623-0051
Map: **#37** (72 miles E. of Oklahoma City)

Restaurants: 1 Snack Bar Liquor: No
Gambling age: 18
Overnight RV Parking: Free/RV Dump: No

Creek Nation Travel Plaza
Highway 75 and 56 Loop
Okmulgee, Oklahoma 74447
(918) 752-0090
Map: **#21** (45 miles S. of Tulsa)

Restaurants: 1 Snack Bar Liquor: No
Overnight RV Parking: Free/RV Dump: No
Special Features: Gas station and convenience store. Burger King.

Davis Trading Post
12218 Highway 7 West
Davis, Oklahoma 73030
(580) 369-5360
Website: www.chickasawtravelstop.com
Map: **#22** (75 miles S. of Oklahoma City)

Restaurants: 1 Liquor: No
Overnight RV Parking: Free/RV Dump: No

Downstream Casino Resort
69300 East Nee Road
Quapaw, Oklahoma 74363
(918) 919-6000
Website: www.downstreamcasino.com
Map: **#58** (On the border of OK, MO, and KS)

Toll-Free Number: (888) 396-7876
Rooms: 200 Price Range: $109-$159
Suites: 22 Price Range: $219-$289
Restaurants:5 Liquor: Yes
Buffet: B- $13.99 (Sun) L- $8.99
D- $17.95/$19.99 (Tue-Thu)/
$21.99 (Fri/Sat)
Gambling Age: 18
Casino size: 70,000 Square feet
Games Offered: P, C, R, BJ, TCP, MB, UTH
Special Features: Only Casino/Hotel in the country located in three States: Oklahoma, Missouri, and Kansas.

Duck Creek Casino
10085 Ferguson Road
Beggs, Oklahoma 74421
(918) 267-3468
Website: www.duckcreekcasino.com
Map: **#21** (35 miles S. of Tulsa)

Restaurants: 1 (open 24 hours) Liquor: No
Casino Size: 20,000 Square Feet
Overnight RV Parking: No
Senior Discount: Various Tuesdays if 55+

Fire Lake Casino
41207 Hardesty Road
Shawnee, Oklahoma 74801
(405) 878-4862
Website: www.winatfirelake.com
Map: **#23** (38 miles E. of Oklahoma City)

Restaurants: 2 Liquor: Yes
Buffets: B-$6.99 (Sat/Sun) L- $7.99
D- $9.99/$16.99 (Fri)
Other Games: BJ, P, BG, UTH
Overnight RV Parking: Free/RV Dump: No
Senior Discount: Various Sun if 55+

Gold Mountain Casino
1410 Sam Noble Parkway
Ardmore, Oklahoma 73401
(580) 223-3301
Website: www.mygoldmountaincasino.com
Map: **#3** (100 miles S. of Oklahoma City)

Liquor: No
Casino Size: 8,620 Square Feet
Overnight RV Parking: No

Gold River Casino
31064 S. Highway 281
Anadarko, Oklahoma 73005
(405) 247-4700
Website: www.goldriverok.com
Map: **#24** (60 miles S.W. of Oklahoma City)

Restaurants: 1 Liquor: Yes
Casino Size: 12,000 Square Feet
Casino Hours: 9am-4am/24 hrs (Fri/Sat)
Senior Discount: Various Tue if 55+
Overnight RV Parking: Free/RV Dump: No

Golden Pony Casino
109095 Okemah Street
Okemah, Oklahoma 74859
(918) 582-4653
Website: www.goldenponycasino.com
Map: **#37** (72 miles E. of Oklahoma City)

Toll-Free Number: (877) 623-0072
Restaurants: 1 Liquor: No
Overnight RV Parking: Free/RV Dump: No
Senior Discount: Various Mon if 50+

Goldsby Gaming Center
1038 West Sycamore Road
Norman, Oklahoma 73072
(405) 329-5447
Website: www.goldsbycasino.com
Map: **#25** (21 miles S. of Oklahoma City)

Restaurants: 1 Liquor: Yes
Other Games: BG
Casino Size: 23,007 Square Feet
Overnight RV Parking: No

Grand Casino Hotel & Resort
777 Grand Casino Boulevard
Shawnee, Oklahoma 74804
(405) 964-7263
Website: www.grandresortok.com
Map: **#23** (38 miles E. of Oklahoma City)

Rooms: 242 Price Range: $129-$179
Suites: 20 Price Range: $149-$199
Restaurants: 5 Liquor: Yes
Buffets: B- $14.45 (Sun)
L- $11.45/$14.45 (Sun)
D- $14.45/$24.95 (Fri/Sat)
Casino Size: 125,000 Square Feet
Other Games: BJ, C, R, P, K, UTH
Overnight RV Parking: Register at hotel lobby. 1st night is free.
Special Features: 3,000-seat event center.

Grand Lake Casino
24701 S. 655 Road
Grove, Oklahoma 74344
(918) 786-8528
Website: www.grandlakecasino.com
Map: **#26** (80 miles N.E. of Tulsa)

Toll-Free Number: (800) 426-4640
Rooms: 30 Price Range: $99-$129
Restaurants: 2 Liquor: Yes
Casino Size: 45,000 Square Feet
Overnight RV Parking: No
Special Features: Lodge is located 2 miles from the casino. Complimentary shuttle service is available 24/7.

Hard Rock Hotel & Casino Tulsa
770 W Cherokee Street
Catoosa, Oklahoma 74015
(800) 760-6700
Website: www.hardrockcasinotulsa.com
Map: **#7** (a suburb of Tulsa)

Rooms: 420 Price Range: $109-$199
Suites: 20 Price Range: $199-$600
Restaurants: 5 Liquor: Yes
Buffets: B-$8.95/$10.95 (Sat/Sun) L-$10.95
D-$17.95/$23.99 (Fri/Sat)
Casino Size: 80,000 Square Feet
Other Games: BJ, C, R, P, TCP, UTH
Overnight RV Parking: Free/RV Dump: No

High Winds Casino
61475 E. 100 Road
Miami, Oklahoma 74354
(918) 541-9463
Website: www.highwindscasino.com
Map: **#33** (89 miles N.E. of Tulsa)

Restaurants: 1 Liquor: Yes
Overnight RV Parking: Free/RV Dump: No

Indigo Sky Casino
70220 East US Highway 60
Wyandotte, Oklahoma 74370
(888) 992-7591
Website: www.indigoskycasino.com
Map: **#26** (90 miles N.E. of Tulsa)

Toll-Free Number: (888) 992-7591
Rooms: 100 Price Range: $119-$149
Suites: 17 Price Range: $149-$209
Restaurants: 3 Liquor: Yes
Other Games: BJ, P, TCP, P, OTB, UTH
Overnight RV Parking: Must use RV park
Special Features: 30-space RV park ($25 per night).

Ioway Casino
338445 East Highway 66
Chandler, Oklahoma 78349
(405) 258-0051
Website: www.iowaycasino.com
Map: **#65** (40 miles N. E. of Okla. City)

Restaurants: 1 Liquor: Yes
Casino Hours: 10am-2am/12am (Mon)/
24 hours (Fri/Sat)

Kickapoo Casino - Harrah
25230 East Highway 62
Harrah, Oklahoma 73045
(405) 964-4444
Website: www.kickapoo-casino.com
Map: **#23** (31 miles E. of Oklahoma City)

Restaurants: 1 Liquor: Yes
Hours: Noon-4am
Other Games: BJ, UTH
Overnight RV Parking: Free/RV Dump: No

Kickapoo Casino - Shawnee
38900 W. MacArthur Drive
Shawnee, Oklahoma 74804
(405) 395-0900
Website: www.kickapoo-casino.com
Map: **#23** (38 miles E. of Oklahoma City)

Restaurants: 1 Snack Bar Liquor: Yes
Overnight RV Parking: Free/RV Dump: No

Kiowa Casino - Carnegie
514 OK-9
Carnegie, Oklahoma 73015
(866) 370-4077
Website: www.kiowacasino.com
Map: **#24** (90 miles SW of Oklahoma City)

Toll-Free Number: (866) 370-4077
Restaurants: Snack Bar Liquor: Beer Only
Casino Hours: Mon-Thu 10am-2am/
24 hours (Fri/Sat)
Overnight RV Parking: Free/RV Dump: No

Kiowa Casino - Red River
198131 Highway 36
Devol, Oklahoma 73531
(580) 299-3333
Website: www.kiowacasino.com
Map: **#18** (125 miles SW of Oklahoma City)

Toll-Free Number: (866) 370-4077
Rooms: 63 Price Range: $99-$119
Casino Size: 60,000 Square Feet
Restaurants: 3 Liquor: Yes
Buffets: B-$11.50 (Sun)
L-$9.50/$11.50 (Sat/Sun)
D-$11.50/$29.00 (Fri/Sat)
Other Games: BJ, TCP
Overnight RV Parking: Free/RV Dump: No
Special Features: Tables open at 10am. No lunch buffet Friday.

Kiowa Casino - Verden
33165 County Street 2740
Verden, Oklahoma 73092
(866) 370-4077
Website: www.kiowacasino.com
Map: **#68** (55 miles S.W. of Oklahoma City)

Casino Hours: 10am-2am/ 24 hours (Fri-Sun)
Overnight RV Parking: Free/RV Dump: No

Lucky Star Casino - Canton
301 NW Lake Road
Canton, Oklahoma 73724
(580) 886-2490
Website: www.luckystarcasino.org
Map: **#59** (60 miles N. W. of Okla. City)

Restaurants: 1 Snack Bar Liquor: Beer
Hours: 10am-2am/24 hours (Fri/Sat)
Gambling Age: 18
Casino Size: 2,200 Square Feet
Overnight RV Parking: Free/RV Dump: No

Lucky Star Casino - Clinton
N2274 Road
Clinton, Oklahoma 73601
(580) 323-6599
Website: www.luckystarcasino.org
Map: **#29** (85 miles W. of Oklahoma City)

Restaurants: 1 Liquor: Beer
Other Games: BJ, TCP, UTH
Overnight RV Parking: Free/RV Dump: No
Special Features: Gambling age is 18.

Lucky Star Casino - Concho
7777 North Highway 81
Concho, Oklahoma 73022
(405) 422-6500
Website: www.luckystarcasino.org
Map: **#30** (35 miles N.W. of Oklahoma City)

Restaurants: 1 Liquor: Yes
Other Games: BJ, P
Gambling Age: 18
Casino Size: 40,000 Square Feet
Overnight RV Parking: Free/RV Dump: Free
Special Features: Free RV hookups (must register first).

Lucky Star Casino - Hammon
20413 Highway 33
Hammon, Oklahoma 73650
(580) 473-2010
Website: www.luckystarcasinos.com
Map: **#66** (120 miles W. of Okla. City)

Restaurants: 1 Deli Liquor: Beer Only
Hours: 10am-2am/24 hours (Fri/Sat)
Overnight RV Parking: Free/RV Dump: No
Special Features: Gambling age is 18.

Lucky Star Casino - Watonga
1407 S. Clarence Nash Boulevard
Watonga, Oklahoma 73772
(580) 623-7333
Website: www.featherwarrior.com
Map: **#53** (70 miles N. W. of Okla. City)

Restaurants: 1 Snack Bar Liquor: Beer
Hours: 11am-2am/10am-2am (Thu-Sat)
Casino Size: 2,200 Square Feet
Overnight RV Parking: Free/RV Dump: No
Special Features: Gambling age is 18.

Lucky Turtle Casino
64499 East Highway 60
Wyandotte, Oklahoma 74370
(918) 678-6450
Map: **#42** (90 miles N.E. of Tulsa)
Website: luckyturtle.wyandottecasinos.com

Restaurants: 1 Liquor: No
Casino Size: 4,000 Square Feet
Overnight RV Parking: No
Senior Discount: Various Wed if 50+
Special Features: Convenience store.

Madill Gaming Center
902 South First Street
Madill, Oklahoma 73446
(580) 795-7301
Website: www.madillgaming.com
Map: **#31** (122 miles S. of Oklahoma City)

Restaurants: 1 Liquor: No
Casino Size: 2,071 Square Feet
Overnight RV Parking: No
Special Features: Smoke shop. Closed 7am-8:30am daily.

Native Lights Casino
12375 N. Highway 77
Newkirk, Oklahoma 74647
(877) 468-3100
Website: www.nativelightscasino.com
Map: **#27** (106 miles N. of Oklahoma City)

Restaurants: 1 Liquor: Yes
Hours: 10am-12am/3am (Fri/Sat)
Casino Size: 5,700 Square Feet
Overnight RV Parking: Free/RV Dump: No

Newcastle Casino
2457 Highway 62 Service Road
Newcastle, Oklahoma 73065
(405) 387-6013
Website: www.newcastlecasino.com
Map: **#34** (19 miles S. of Oklahoma City)

Restaurants: 2 Liquor: Yes
Casino Size: 44,622 Sqaure Feet
Other Games: BJ, B, R, K, OTB,
TCP, MS, UTH
Overnight RV Parking: Free/RV Dump: No
Senior Discount: Various Sun if 50+

One Fire Casino
1901 North Wood Drive
Okmulgee, Oklahoma 74447
(918) 756-8400
Website: www.onefirecasino.com
Map: **#21** (45 miles S. of Tulsa)

Restaurants: 1 Liquor: Yes
Casino Size: 10,000 Square Feet
Overnight RV Parking: Free/RV Dump: No
Senior Discount: Various Tue if 50+

Osage Casino - Bartlesville
222 Allen Road
Bartlesville, Oklahoma 74003
(918) 699-7740
Website: www.osagecasinos.com
Map: **#56** (50 miles N. of Tulsa)

Toll-Free Number (877) 246-8777
Restaurants: 2 Liquor: No
Buffet: L- $9.99 (Sun)
D- $9.99/$27.99 (Fri)/$16.99 (Sat)
Other Games: BJ, TCP, UTH
Senior Discount: Various Mon/Tue
7am-10am if 50+
Overnight RV Parking: No

Osage Casino - Hominy
39 Deer Avenue
Hominy, Oklahoma 74035
(918) 699-7740
Website: www.osagecasinos.com
Map: **#49** (44 miles N.W. of Tulsa)

Toll-Free Number (877) 246-8777
Restaurants: 1 Liquor: Yes
Hours: 10am-2am/4am (Wed-Sat)
Senior Discount: Various promotions if 50+
Overnight RV Parking: Free/RV Dump:No

Osage Casino - Pawhuska
2017 E. 15th Street (at Highway 99)
Pawhuska, Oklahoma 74056
(918) 699-7740
Website: www.osagecasinos.com
Map: **#50** (a suburb of Tulsa)

Toll-Free Number (877) 246-8777
Restaurants: 1 Liquor: No
Hours: 10am-2am/4am (Thu-Sat)
Senior Discount: Various promotions if 50+
Overnight RV Parking: Free/RV Dump: No

Osage Casino - Ponca City
64464 U.S. Highway 60
Ponca City, Oklahoma 74601
(918) 699-7740
Website: www.osagecasinos.com
Map: **#5** (50 miles N.W. of Tulsa)

Toll-Free Number (877) 246-8777
Rooms: 46 Price Range: $89-$169
Suites: 2 Price Range: $189-$259
Restaurants: 1 Liquor: Yes
Senior Discount: Various promotions if 50+
Other Games: BJ
Overnight RV Parking: No

Osage Casino - Sand Springs
301 Blackjack Drive (on Highway 97T)
Sand Springs, Oklahoma 74063
(918) 699-7740
Website: www.osagecasinos.com
Map: **#40** (a suburb of Tulsa)

Toll-Free Number: (877) 246-8777
Restaurants: 1 Liquor: Yes
Senior Discount: Various promotions if 50+
Overnight RV Parking: No

Osage Casino - Skiatook
5591 West Rogers Boulevard
Skiatook, Oklahoma 74070
(918) 699-7740
Website: www.osagecasinos.com
Map: **#60** (17 miles N. of Tulsa)

Toll-Free Number (877) 246-8777
Restaurants:1 Liquor: Yes
Games Offered: Slots, Video Poker, Blackjack
Overnight RV Parking: No
Senior Discount: Various promotions if 50+

Osage Casino - Tulsa
951 W. 36th Street North
Tulsa, Oklahoma 74127
(918) 699-7740
Website: www.osagecasinos.com
Map: **#40**

Toll-Free Number: (877) 246-8777
Rooms: 160 $89-$124
Suites: 6 $199-$209
Restaurants: 4 Liquor: Yes
Casino Size: 47,000 Square Feet
Other Games: BJ, P, TCP
Senior Discount: Various promotions if 50+
Overnight RV Parking: Free/RV Dump: No

Outpost Casino
67901 East 100 Road
Wyandotte, Oklahoma 74370
(918) 666-6770
Map: **#42** (90 miles N.E. of Tulsa)

Restaurants: 1 Snack Bar Liquor: No
Casino Size: 3,000 Square Feet
Overnight RV Parking: No
Special Features: Gambling age is 18.

Prairie Moon Casino
202 South Eight Tribes Trail
Miami, Oklahoma 74354
(918) 542-8670
Website: www.miaminationcasinos.com
Map: **#33** (89 miles N.E. of Tulsa)

Restaurants: 1 Liquor: No
Overnight RV Parking: No
Special Features: Gambling age is 18.

Prairie Sun Casino
3411 P Street NW
Miami, Oklahoma 74354
(918) 541-2150
Website: www.miaminationcasinos.com
Map: # **33** (89 miles N.E. of Tulsa)

Restaurants: 1 Snack Bar Liquor: Yes
Casino Size: 11,000 Square Feet
Gambling age: 21
Overnight RV Parking: No

Quapaw Casino
58100 E. 64h Road
Miami, Oklahoma 74354
(918) 540-9100
Website: www.quapawcasino.com
Map: **#33** (89 miles N.E. of Tulsa)

Restaurants: 1 Liquor: Yes
Overnight RV Parking: Free up to 3 days/ RV Dump: No
Senior Discount: Various Wed if 50+

River Bend Casino Hotel
100 Jackpot Place
Wyandotte, Oklahoma 74370
(918) 678-4946
Website: www.riverbendcasino.com
Map: **#26** (90 miles N.E. of Tulsa)

Toll-Free Number: (866) 447-4946
Rooms: 80 Price Range $89-$119
Suites: 12 Price Range $109-$149
Restaurants: 2 Liquor: Yes
Other Games: BJ, TCP
Overnight RV Parking: Free/RV Dump: No
Special Features: Events Center offers bowling, billiards and special events.

River Spirit Casino Resort
8330 Riverside Parkway
Tulsa, Oklahoma 74137
(918) 299-8518
Website: www.riverspirittulsa.com
Map: **#40**

Toll-Free Number: (888) 748-3731
Rooms: 463 Price Range: $109-$239
Suites: 20 Price Range: $209-$329
Restaurants: 5 Liquor: Yes
Buffets: B-$21.95 (Sun)
L-$11.95/$21.95 (Sun)
D-$17.95/$24.95 (Thu)/ $21.95 (Fri)/$24.95 (Sat)
Casino Size: 81,000 Square Feet
Other Games: BJ, C, R, MB, TCP, P
Senior Discount: Buffet discount Mon-Sat if 50+
Overnight RV Parking: Free/RV Dump: No
Special Features: Separate non-smoking casino. Free shuttle to/from local hotels.

Riverwind Casino
1544 West State Highway 9
Norman, Oklahoma 73072
(405) 322-6000
Website: www.riverwind.com
Map: **#25** (21 miles S. of Oklahoma City)

Toll-Free Number: (888) 440-1880
Restaurants: 2 Liquor: Yes
Rooms: 100 Price Range: $109-$249
Buffets: B- $23.99 (Sat/Sun)
D- $19.99/$29.95 (Fri)/ $24.99 (Sat)/$18.99 (Sun)
Casino Size: 60,000 Square Feet
Other Games: BJ, P, TCP, B, UTH, OTB, K
Overnight RV Parking: Free/RV Dump: No
Senior Discount: Breakfast special Wed
Special Features: 1,500-seat showroom. Food court with three fast food outlets.

Sac and Fox Casino - Stroud
356120 E 926 Road
Stroud, Oklahoma 74079
(918) 968-2540
Website: www.snfcasino.com
Map: **#5** (60 miles N.E. of Oklahoma City)

Restaurants: 1 Liquor: Yes
Casino Hours: 10am-2am/12am (Sun/Mon)
Casino Size: 8,600 Sqaure Feet
Overnight RV Parking: No

Salt Creek Casino
1600 Highway 81
Pocasset, Oklahoma 73079
(405) 459-4000
Website: www.saltcreekcasino.com
Map: **#34** (50 miles S.W. of Oklahoma City)

Restaurants: 1 Liquor: Yes
Overnight RV Parking: No
Other Games: BJ, UTH

Seminole Nation Casino
11277 Highway 99
Seminole, Oklahoma 74868
(405) 217-0176
Website: www.snocasinos.com
Map: **#57** (60 miles S.E of Oklahoma City)

Restaurants: 1 Liquor: Yes
Overnight RV Parking: No

Seminole Nation Casino Konawa
14313 Old Highway 99
Konowa, Oklahoma 74849
(405) 217-0176
Website: www.snocasinos.com
Map: **#2** (75 miles S.E. of Oklahoma City)

Restaurants: 1
Casino Hours: 10am-12am/2am (Fri/Sat)
Gaming age: 18

Seminole Nation Trading Post
36625 Highway 270
Wewoka, Oklahoma 74884
(405) 217-0176
Website: www.snocasinos.com
Map: **#57** (60 miles E. of Oklahoma City)

Restaurants: 1 Snack Bar Liquor: No
Casino Size: 3,424 Square Feet
Overnight RV Parking: No
Hours: 10am-12am/2am (Fri/Sat)
Senior Discount: Various Sun if 55+
Special Features: Convenience store.

Seven Clans Gasino - Chilocco
12901 N. Highway 77
Newkirk, Oklahoma 74647
(580) 448-3210
Website: www.sevenclans.com
Map: **#27** (106 miles N. of Oklahoma City)

Restaurants: 1 Deli Liquor: Yes
Overnight RV Parking: No

Seven Clans Casino Hotel - First Council
12875 North Highway 77
Newkirk, Oklahoma 74647
(877) 725-2670
Website: www.sevenclans.com
Map: **#27** (Just south of the Kansas state line)

Toll-Free: (877) 725-2670
Rooms: 126 Price Range: $109-$179
Suites: 20 Price Range: $239-$339
Restaurants: 4 Liquor: Yes
Casino Size: 125,000 Square Feet
Other Games: BJ, C, R, P, UTH, MS, TCP
Overnight RV Parking: Free/RV Dump: No
Special Features: 3,000-seat event center and indoor waterpark (available to hotel guests only).

Seven Clans - Paradise
7500 Highway 177
Red Rock, Oklahoma 74651
(580) 723-4005
Website: www.firstcouncilcasinohotel.com
Map: **#1** (82 miles N. of Oklahoma City)

Toll-Free Number: (866) 723-4005
Restaurants: 1 Liquor: Yes
Casino Size: 23,000 Square Feet
Other Games: BJ, P, UTH, MS
Senior Discounts: Mon 12pm-6pm if 50+
Overnight RV Parking: Must use RV park
Special Features: 7-space RV park ($10 per night). Convenience store and gas station.

Seven Clans Casino - Perry
5111 Kaw Street
Perry, Oklahoma 73077
(580) 336-7260
Website: www.sevenclans.com
Map: **#67** (65 miles N. of Okla. City)

Restaurants: 1 Liquor: Yes
Overnight RV Parking: Free/RV Dump: No
Casino Size: 4,500 Square Feet
Special Features: Drive-through smoke shop.

Seven Clans Gasino - Red Rock
8401 Highway 177
Red Rock, Oklahoma 74651
(580) 723-1020
Website: www.sevenclans.com
Map: **#1** (82 miles N. of Oklahoma City)

Restaurants: 1 Deli Liquor: Yes
Overnight RV Parking: No

Southwind Casino - Braman
9695 N. Highway
Braman, Oklahoma 74632
(580) 385-2441
Website: www.southwindcasino.com
Map: **#27** (106 miles N. of Okla. City)

Restaurants: 1 Liquor: Yes
Other Games: OTB
Overnight RV Parking: Free/RV Dump: No

Southwind Casino - Kanza
9601 U.S. 177
Braman, Oklahoma 74632
(580) 385-2444
Website: www.southwindcasino.com
Map: **#27** (106 miles N. of Okla. City)

Casino Hours: 8am-12am/2am (Fri/Sat)
Overnight RV Parking: Free/RV Dump: No
Special Features: Located in a truck stop. Located one block from Braman Casino.

Southwind Casino - Newkirk
5640 North LaCann Drive
Newkirk, Oklahoma 74647
(580) 362-2578
Website: www.southwindcasino.com
Map: **#27** (106 miles N. of Oklahoma City)

Toll-Free Number: (866) 589-24646
Restaurants: 1 Liquor: Yes
Hours: 9am-2am/24 hrs (Fri/Sat)
Other Games: BJ, BG (Thu-Sun), OTB
Senior Discount: Various Mon/Wed if 55+
Overnight RV Parking: Free/RV Dump: No

The Stables Casino
530 H Street Southeast
Miami, Oklahoma 74354
(918) 542-7884
Website: www.the-stables.com
Map: **#33** (89 miles N.E. of Tulsa)

Toll-Free Number: (877) 774-7884
Restaurants: 1 Liquor: Yes
Overnight RV Parking: No
Senior Discount: Various if 55+

Stone Wolf Casino & Grill
54251 S 349 Road
Pawnee, Oklahoma 74058
(918) 454-7777
Website: www.stonewolfcasino.com
Map: **#55** (57 miles N.W. of Tulsa)

Restaurants: 1 Liquor: Yes
Hours: 8am-2am/24hrs (Fri-Sun)
Senior Discount: Various Thu if 55+

Sugar Creek Casino
5304 North Broadway
Hinton, Oklahoma 73047
(405) 542-2946
Website: www.sugarcreekcasino.net
Map: **#63** (55 miles W. of Oklahoma City)

Restaurants: 3 Liquor: Yes
Other Games: BJ, UTH
Overnight RV Parking: No
Senior Discount: Various Mon if 55+

Texoma Gaming Center
1795 Highway 70 East
Kingston, Oklahoma 73439
(580) 564-6000
Website: www.mytexomacasino.com
Map: **#43** (130 miles S. of Oklahoma City)

Restaurants: 1 Liquor: Yes
Casino Size: 8,800 Square Feet
Overnight RV Parking: No
Special Features: Convenience store.

Thunderbird Casino - Norman
15700 East State Highway 9
Norman, Oklahoma 73026
(405) 360-9270
Website: www.playthunderbird.com
Map: **#25** (21 miles S. of Oklahoma City)

Toll-Free Number: (800) 259-5825
Restaurants: 1 Liquor: Yes
Other Games: BJ, R, BG
Casino Size: 40,000 Square Feet
Overnight RV Parking: Free

Thunderbird Casino - Shawnee
2051 S. Gordon Cooper Drive
Shawnee, Oklahoma 74801
(405) 273-2679
Website: www.playthunderbird.com
Map: **#23** (38 miles E. of Oklahoma City)

Toll-Free Number: (800) 259-5825
Restaurants: 1 Deli Liquor: Yes
Hours: 9am-12am/2am (Fri/Sat)

Tonkawa Gasino
10700 Allen Drive
Tonkawa, Oklahoma 74653
(580) 628-2624
Website: www.tonkawacasino.com
Map: **#38** (91 miles N. of Oklahoma City)

Toll-Free Number: (877) 648-2624
Restaurant: No Liquor: No
Hours: 11am-11pm Daily
Overnight RV Parking: Free/RV Dump: No
Special Features: Convenience store. Gas station.

Tonkawa Hotel & Casino
16601 W. South Avenue
Tonkawa, Oklahoma 74653
(877) 648-2624
Website: www.tonkawacasino.com
Map: **#38** (91 miles N. of Oklahoma City)

Rooms: 58 Price Range $109-$149
Suites: 8 Price Range $119-$169
Restaurants: 1 Liquor: Yes
Other Games: BJ, TCP, UTH, C, R
Overnight RV Parking: Free/RV Dump: No

Trading Post Casino - Pawnee
291 Agency Road
Pawnee, Oklahoma 74058
(918) 762-4466
Map: **#55** (57 miles N.W. of Tulsa)

Restaurants: 1 Liquor: No
Casino Size: 3,600 Square Feet
Hours: 7am-2am/11pm (Sun)
Overnight RV Parking: No
Special Features: Convenience store. Gas station.

Treasure Valley Casino
12252 Ruppe Road
Davis, Oklahoma 73030
(580) 369-2895
Website: www.treasurevalleycasino.com
Map: **#22** (75 miles S. of Oklahoma City)

Rooms: 60 Price Range: $104-$119
Restaurants: 2 Liquor: Yes
Casino Size: 19,666 Square Feet
Other Games: BJ, TCP, UTH
Overnight RV Parking: Free/RV Dump: No
Special Features: Gambling age is 18.

Washita Casino
30639 Highway 145
Paoli, Oklahoma 73074
(405) 484-7777
Website: www.washitacasino.com
Map: **#44** (52 miles S. of Oklahoma City)

Restaurants: 1 Liquor: Yes
Casino Size: 6,335 Square Feet
Overnight RV Parking: No
Special Features: Convenience store.

Wilson Travel Plaza
288 Mulberry Lane
Wilson, Oklahoma 73463
(580) 668-9248
Map: **#39** (112 miles S. of Oklahoma City)

Restaurants: 1 Snack Bar Liquor: No
Overnight RV Parking: Free/RV Dump: No
Special Features: Convenience store. Gas station.

WinStar World Casino and Resort
777 Casino Avenue
Thackerville, Oklahoma 73459
(580) 276-4229
Website: www.winstarworldcasino.com
Map: **#36** (124 miles S. of Oklahoma City)

Toll-Free Number: (800) 622-6317
Rooms: 1,159 Price Range: $99-$279
Suites: 240 Price Range:$129-$399
Restaurants: 10 Liquor: Yes
Buffets: L- $18.99/$23.99 (Sun)
D- $23.99/$29.99 (Fri-Sun)
Other Games: BJ, C, R, MB, P, MS, LIR, TCP, UTH, PGP, OTB, K
Casino Size: 169,824 Square Feet
Overnight RV Parking: Free/RV Dump: No
Senior Discount: Free buffet Wed/Thu if 50+
Special Features: 153-space RV ($30/$40 per night)

Pari-Mutuels

Oklahoma has two horse tracks which offer Class II electronic video gaming machines as well as pari-mutuel betting on horse races. Admission is free to the casinos, but there is an admission charge for horse racing. The minimum gambling age is 18.

Cherokee Casino Will Rogers Downs
20900 S. 4200 Road
Claremore, Oklahoma 74019
(918) 283-8800
Website: www.cherokeecasino.com
Map: **#47** (30 miles N.E. of Tulsa)

Self-Parking: Free
Restaurants: 1
Hours: 11am-1am/4am (Friday)
10am-4am(Saturday)/1am (Sunday)
Overnight RV Parking: Must use RV park
Senior Discount: Various Wed 3pm-7pm if 50+
Special Features: Live horse racing seasonally. Daily simulcasting of horse racing. 400-space RV park ($32 per night/$10 without hookups).

Remington Park Racing • Casino
One Remington Place
Oklahoma City, Oklahoma 73111
(405) 424-1000
Website: www.remingtonpark.com
Map: **#46**

Toll-Free Number: (800) 456-4244
Restaurants: 1
Overnight RV Parking: No
Senior Discount: Various Tue if 55+
Special Features: Live horse racing seasonally. Daily simulcasting of horse racing. Buffet discount for players club members.

OREGON

Oregon law permits bars and taverns to have up to six video lottery terminals that offer various versions of video poker. Racetracks are allowed to have no more than 10 machines. The maximum bet allowed is $2.50 and the maximum single payout on any machine is capped at $600.

These machines are the same as regular video gaming devices but are called lottery terminals because they are regulated by the state's lottery commission which receives a share of each machine's revenue.

According to figures from the Oregon Lottery, during its fiscal year from June 28, 2018 through June 25, 2019, the VLT's had an approximate return of 92.34%.

There is also one racetrack, Portland Meadows, which offers instant racing betting machines. While these machines may appear to be regular slot machines, they are actually based on unidentified past horse races and the reels are for entertainment purposes only.

There are nine Indian casinos in operation in Oregon. According to the governor's office which regulates the Tribe's compacts, "there is no minimum payback percentage required on the Tribe's machines. Each Tribe is free to set their own limits on their machines."

All casinos offer blackjack, slots and video poker. Some casinos also offer: craps (C), roulette (R), poker (P), Pai Gow Poker (PGP), Spanish 21 (S21), let it ride (LIR), three card poker (TCP), four card poker (FCP), big 6 wheel (B6), bingo (BG), keno (K) and off track betting (OTB). Unless otherwise noted, all casinos are open 24 hours and the minimum gambling age is 21 (18 for bingo).

Sports betting through the Oregon Lottery was legalized in mid-2019. However, it may also start to be offered at Oregon's Indian casinos by early 2020.

For Oregon tourism information call (800) 547-7842 or go to: www.traveloregon.com.

Chinook Winds Casino Resort
1777 N.W. 44th Street
Lincoln City, Oregon 97367
(541) 996-5825
Website: www.chinookwindscasino.com
Map: **#4** (45 miles W. of Salem)

Toll-Free Number: (888) 244-6665
Rooms: 227 Price Range: $89-$184
Suites: 81 Price Range: $184-$264
Restaurants: 7 Liquor: Yes
Buffets: B- $12.00/$24.95 (Sun)
L- $12.00/$24.95 (Sun)
D- $18.00 (Sun-Thu)/$24.95 (Fri-Sat)
Other Games: C, R, P, LIR, TCP, PGP, BG
Overnight RV Parking: Must be a Winners Circle Member and earn 20 points to receive parking pass.
Senior Discount: Meal discounts if 55+
Special Features: Childcare center. Video arcade. 18-hole golf course.

Indian Head Casino
3636 Highway 26
Warm Springs, Oregon 97761
(541) 460-7777
Website: www.indianheadgaming.com
Map: **#5** (100 miles E. of Portland)

Toll-Free Number: (800) 554-4786
Restaurants: 2 Liquor: Yes
Casino Size: 25,000 Square Feet
Hours: 8:30am-2am/ 4am (Fri/Sat)
Other Games: P
Overnight RV Parking: Free/RV Dump: No

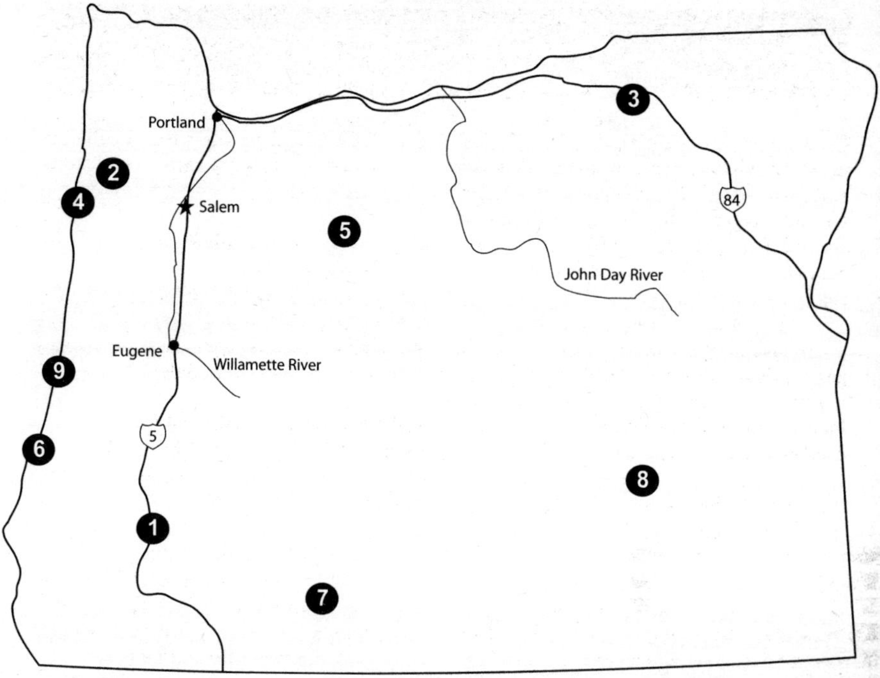

Kla-Mo-Ya Casino
34333 Highway 97 North
Chiloquin, Oregon 97624
(541) 783-7529
Website: www.klamoyacasino.com
Map: **#7** (20 miles N. of Klamath Falls)

Toll-Free Number: (888) 552-6692
Restaurants: 2 Liquor: No
Overnight RV Parking: Free/RV Dump: No
Senior Discount: Various on Mon. if 55+.
Special Features: Tables closed Mon and Tue.

The Mill Casino Hotel
3201 Tremont Avenue
North Bend, Oregon 97459
(541) 756-8800
Website: www.themillcasino.com
Map: **#6** (75 miles S.W. of Eugene)

Toll-Free Number: (800) 953-4800
Rooms: 109 Price Range: $129-$199
Suites: 3 Price Range: $149-$239
Restaurants: 4 Liquor: Yes
Buffet: D- $18.99 (Sun)/$14.99 (Mon)/ $22.99 (Fri/Sat)
Other Games: C, R, PGP
Overnight RV Parking: Free/RV Dump: No
Senior Discount: 10% off food if 55+
Special Features: 65-space RV park ($37-$72 per night spring/summer; $25-$35 fall/winter). Free local shuttle. Room and food discounts for players club members. Table games open at 3pm.

Seven Feathers Hotel & Casino Resort
146 Chief Miwaleta Lane
Canyonville, Oregon 97417
(541) 839-1111
Website: www.sevenfeathers.com
Map: **#1** (80 miles S. of Eugene)

Toll-Free Number: (800) 548-8461
Rooms: 146 Price Range: $69-$109
Restaurants: 4 Liquor: Yes
Buffets: L- $9.99 (Sat-Sun)
D- $13.99(Mon-Thu)/$27.99 (Fri)/
$23.99 (Sat)/$18.99 (Sun)
Casino Size: 27,300 Square Feet
Other Games: C, R, LIR, PGP, TCP,
FCP, K, BG
Senior Discount: $2 off buffet Thu-Sun if 50+
Overnight RV Parking: Free/RV Dump: No
Special Features: 191-space RV park ($36-$69 per night). 18-hole golf course. Buffet discount for Players Club members.

Spirit Mountain Casino
27100 Salmon River Highway
Grand Ronde, Oregon 97347
(503) 879-2350
Website: www.spiritmountain.com
Map: **#2** (85 miles S.W. of Portland)

Toll-Free Number: (800) 760-7977
Reservation Number: (888) 668-7366
Rooms: 94 Price Range: $89-$169
Suites: 6 Price Range: $169-$219
Restaurants: 5 Liquor: Yes
Buffets: B-$10.95 L-$11.95/$18.95 (Sun)
D-$16.95/$26.95 (Fri)/
$20.95 (Sat-Sun)
Other Games: C, R, P, PGP, LIR, TCP, K, BG
Overnight RV Parking: Free/RV Dump: Free
Special Features: Childcare center. Video arcade. Players club members receive a $20 room discount.

Three Rivers Casino & Hotel
5647 US Highway 126
Florence, Oregon 97439
(541) 997-7529
Website: www.threeriverscasino.com
Map: **#9** (61 miles W. of Eugene)

Toll-Free Number: (877) 374-8377
Rooms: 90 Price Range: $89-$139
Suites: 4 Price Range: $190- $250
Restaurants: 5 Liquor: Yes
Other Games: C, R, P, LIR, PGP, TCP,
UTH, K, BG
Overnight RV Parking: Free/RV Dump: No

Three Rivers Casino Coos Bay
1297 NW Ocean Boulevard
Coos Bay, Oregon 97420
(877) 374-8377
Website: www.threeriverscasino.com
Map: **#6** (75 miles S.W. of Eugene)

Restaurants: 1
Special Features: This casino offers Class II gambling which consist of electronic gaming machines which look like slot machines, but are actually games of bingo and the spinning video reels are for "entertainment purposes only."

Wildhorse Resort & Casino
72777 Highway 331
Pendleton, Oregon 97801
(541) 278-2274
Website: www.wildhorseresort.com
Map: **#3** (211 miles E. of Portland)

Toll-Free Number: (800) 654-9453
Rooms: 300 Price Range: $70-$199
Suites: 37 Price Range: $100-225
Restaurants: 7 Liquor: Yes
Buffets: B/L- $13.95 (Sat)/$15.95 (Sun)
D- $16.95/$26.95 (Thu)/$31.95 (Fri)
Casino Size: 40,000 Square Feet
Other Games: S21, C, R, P, TCP, K, BG
Overnight RV Parking: Free/RV Dump: Yes
Senior Discount: Various if 55+
Special Features: 100-space RV park ($31-$41 per night). Cultural Institute. 18-hole golf course. Health spa. Child care center, 5-screen cineplex.

PENNSYLVANIA

In July 2004 the Pennsylvania legislature authorized the legalization of slot machines at 14 locations throughout the state: seven racinos, five stand-alone casinos, and two hotel resorts. All casinos can have up to 5,000 machines, except the resort licensees, which are allowed up to 600. As of late 2019 all locations had opened, except for one racino and one stand-alone casino.

The final stand-alone license was awarded to Live! Hotel and Casino which is building a $700 million project housing a 200,000-square-foot gaming floor, a 220-room hotel and a 1,000-seat music venue. The resort will be located at 900 Packer Avenue in South Philadelphia and it is expected to open by mid-2020.

In October 2017 legislation was passed to allow up to 10 mini-casinos. Each casino can have between 300 and 750 slot machines and 30 table games. After being open for one year each casino can petition the Pennsylvania Gaming Control Board to add 10 more table games. The earliest any of the mini-casinos is expected to open is early 2020.

Unless otherwise noted, all casinos offer: slots, video poker, craps, blackjack, roulette, three card poker, mini-baccarat and Pai-gow poker. Optional games include: baccarat (B), poker (P), ultimate Texas hold 'em (UTH), Texas hold'em bonus (THB), let it ride (LIR), pai gow (PG), big 6 wheel (B6), Spanish 21 (S21), four card poker (FCP), Sic-Bo (SIC), Mississippi stud (MS) and casino war (CW).

Additionally, sports betting was legalized for Pennsylvania casinos in mid-2019 and it is expected to be offered at most of the state's casinos by early 2020.

Pennsylvania gaming regulations require that gaming machines return a minimum of 85%. Following is information from the Pennsylvania Gaming Control Board regarding average slot payout percentages for the one-year period from July 1, 2018 through June 30, 2019:

CASINO	PAYBACK %
Parx Casino	90.70
Valley Forge	90.68
Mount Airy	90.31
The Meadows	90.14
Wind Creek Bethlehem	90.09
Sugar House	90.03
Mohegan Sun at PD	89.90
The Rivers	89.87
Harrah's Philadelphia	89.82
Hollywood Casino at PN	89.38
Lady Luck Nemacolin	89.34
Presque Isle	89.31

The minimum gambling age is 18 for pari-mutuel betting and 21 at casinos. All casinos are open 24 hours and admission is free. However, the casinos at the two hotel resorts are not open to the general public. You must be a guest of the resort in order to play at their casinos. However, you can buy a guest pass for temporary admission.

For more information on visiting Pennsylvania call their Office of Tourism at (800) 237-4363 or visit their website at www.visitpa.com.

Lady Luck Nemacolin
4067 National Pike
Farmington, Pennsylvania 15437
(724) 329-7500
Website: www.nemacolin.com/casino
Map: **#11** (60 miles S.E. of Pittsburgh)

Room Reservations: (800) 422-2736
Rooms: 300 Price Range: $259-$579
Suites: 27 Price Range: $379-$3,299
Restaurants: 9
Other Games: MS, UTH, no PGP
Special Features: Located near Nemacolin Woodlands Resort. Casino is affiliated with Isle of Capri Casinos. All room rates do not include $20 daily resort fee. You must be a guest of the resort for admittance to the casino.

Mount Airy Resort & Casino
312 Woodland Road
Mount Pocono, Pennsylvania 18344
(570) 243-4800
Website: www.mounttairycasino.com
Map: **#8** (30 miles S.E. of Scranton)

Toll-Free Number: (877) 682-4791
Rooms: 175 Price Range: $139-$359
Suites: 25 Price Range: $239-$459
Restaurants: 5
Buffets: B-$24.99 (Sat/Sun) L- $16.99
D- $19.99/$25.99 (Fri/Sun)
Casino Size: 68,000 Square Feet
Other Games: PG, LIR, B, B6, P, FCP, S21
Special Features: 18-hole golf course. Spa. Buffet discount for Players Club members.

Rivers Casino
777 Casino Drive
Pittsburgh, Pennsylvania 15212
(412) 231-7777
Website: www.theriverscasino.com
Map: **#9**

Toll-free Number: (877) 558-0777
Parking: Free Valet: $6
Restaurants: 5
Buffets: B - $14.99 (Sat/Sun) L- $14.99
D- $19.99
Other Games: P, B6, SB.
Special Features: Free parking for players club members who play and put points on card. 219-Room hotel expected to open in 2021.

Sugar House Casino
1001 N Delaware Avenue
Philadelphia, Pennsylvania 19125
(877) 477-3715
Website: www.sugarhousecasino.com
Map: **#10**

Restaurants: 8
Casino Size: 45,000 Square Feet
Other Games: SIC, CW, FCP, P, B, PG, S21, UTH, SB

Valley Forge Casino Resort
1160 First Avenue
King of Prussia, Pennsylvania 19406
(610) 354-8118
Website: www.vfcasino.com
Map: **#10** (15 miles N.W of Philadelphia)

Room Reservations: (610)354-8118
Rooms: 485 Price Range: $99-$389
Restaurants: 5
Casino Size: 33,000 Square Feet
Other Games: UTH, SB
Special Features: Two hotels attached to convention center: Radisson Tower and the Casino Tower.

Wind Creek Bethlehem
77 Sands Boulevard
Bethlehem, Pennsylvania 18015
Website: www.pasands.com
Map: **#7** (60 miles N of Philadelphia)

Toll-Free number: (877) 727-3777
Rooms: 288 Price Range: $129-$349
Suites: 22 Price Range: $249-$349
Restaurants: 10
Buffets: L- $18.95/$22.95 (Sat)/$25.95 (Sun)
D-$18.95/$33.95 (Fri/Sat)/
$25.95 (Sun)
Other Games: B, PG, P, CSP, CW, B6, SIC
Special Features: Stadium gaming versions of baccarat, roulette and blackjack. Previously known as Sands Casino Resort Bethlehem.

Pari-Mutuels

Harrah's Philadelphia Casino & Racetrack
777 Harrah's Boulevard
Chester, Pennsylvania 19013
(800) 480-8020
Website: www.harrahsphilly.com
Map: **#5** (8 miles S. of Philadelphia airport)

Valet Parking: $5/$10 (Fri-Sun)
Restaurants: 5
Other Games: P, LIR, FCP, S21, SIC, B6, UTH, SB
Special Features: Live harness racing seasonally. Daily simulcast of harness and thoroughbred racing. No lunch buffet Mon/Tue.

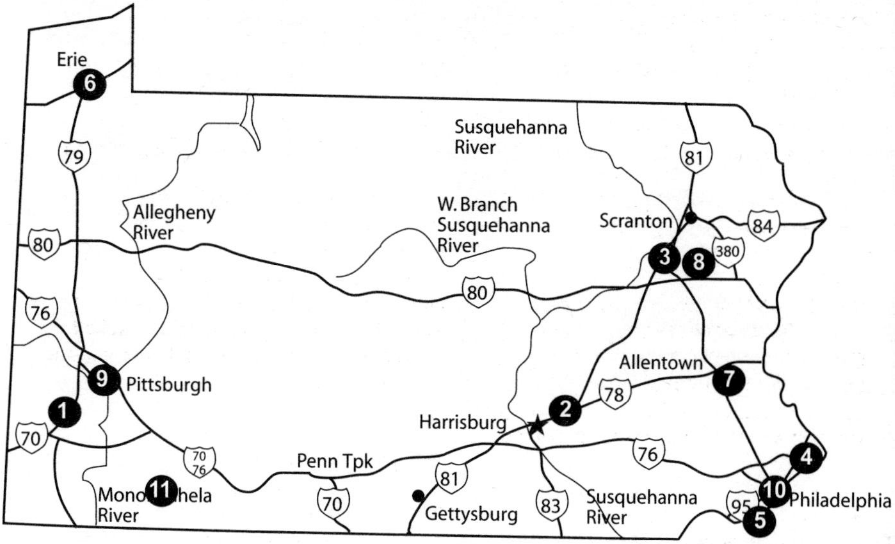

Hollywood Casino at Penn National
777 Hollywood Boulevard
Grantville, Pennsylvania 17028
(717) 469-2211
Website: www.hollywoodpnrc.com
Map: #2 (16 miles N.E. of Harrisburg)

Restaurants: 9
Buffets: B-$16.99 (Sun) L-$14.99
D-$14.99 (Thu)/$36.99 (Fri)/
$26.99 (Sat)/$16.99 (Sun)
Casino Size: 45,000 Square Feet
Other Games: FCP, P, PG, UTH, S21, B6
Special Features: Live thoroughbred horse racing Wed-Sat evenings all year long. Daily simulcast of harness and thoroughbred racing. Buffet closed Monday-Wednesday.

Mohegan Sun at Pocono Downs
1280 Highway 315
Wilkes-Barre, Pennsylvania 18702
(570) 831-2100
Website: www.mohegansunpocono.com
Map: **#3** (20 miles S.W. of Scranton)

Valet Parking: Not Offered
Rooms: 238 Price Range: $119-$329
Restaurants: 8
Buffets: B-$22.99 (Sun) L- $16.99
D-$19.99 (Sun)/$25.99 (Fri/Sat)
Other Games: LIR, S21, P, B6
Special Features: Live harness racing seasonally. Daily simulcast of harness and thoroughbred racing. Buffet open Friday-Sunday.

The Meadows Racetrack & Casino
210 Racetrack Road
Washington, Pennsylvania 15301
(877) 824-5050
Website: www.meadowsgaming.com
Map: **#1** (25 miles S.W. of Pittsburgh)

Rooms: 140 Price Range: $109 $159
Suites: 15 Price range: $143-$209
Restaurants: 5
Other Games: B, FCP, MS, LIR, P, B6
Special Features: Live harness racing various evenings all year long. Daily simulcast of harness and thoroughbred racing. Hotel is a Hyatt Place.

Parx Casino and Racing
2999 Street Road
Bensalem, Pennsylvania 19020
(800) 588-7279
Website: www.parxcasino.com
Map: **#4** (18 miles N.E. of Philadelphia)

Toll-Free Number: (888) 588-7279
Restaurants: 5
Other Games: SIC, FCP, P, B6, PGP, SB
Special Features: Thoroughbred horse racing seasonally. Daily simulcast of harness and thoroughbred racing.

Presque Isle Downs & Casino
8199 Perry Highway
Erie, Pennsylvania 16509
(814) 860-8999
Website: www.presqueisledowns.com
Map: **#6**

Toll-Free Number: (866) 374-3386
Valet Parking: $3
Restaurants: 4
Buffets: L-$14.99 (Fri-Sun)
D-$14.99 (Fri-Sun)
Other Games: FCP, LIR, P, SB.
Special Features: Live thoroughbred horse racing seasonally. Daily simulcast of harness and thoroughbred racing. Buffet discount for players club members.

RHODE ISLAND

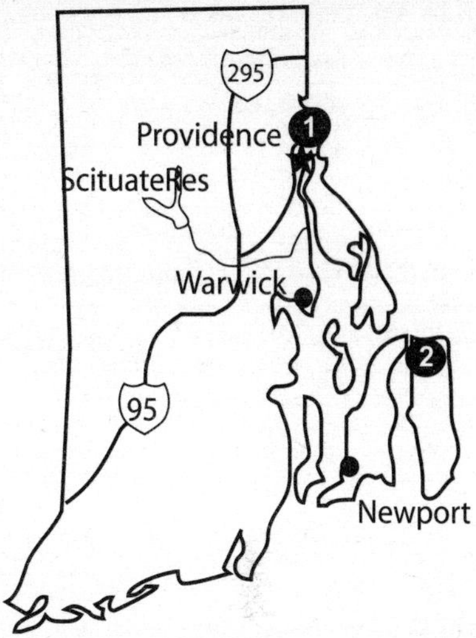

Rhode Island has two casinos which both feature video lottery terminals (VLT's). These machines are the same as regular video gaming devices but are called lottery terminals because they are regulated by the state's lottery commission which receives a share of each machine's revenue.

All VLT's are programmed to play at least six different games: blackjack, keno, slots and three versions of poker (jacks or better, joker poker and deuces wild).

According to figures from the Rhode Island Lottery for the one-year period from July 1, 2018 through June 30, 2019 the average VLT return at Twin River was 92.10% and at Tiverton it was 91.63%.

Both casinos are open 24 hours and offer the following games: slot machines, video poker, video keno, blackjack, craps, roulette, baccarat, three-card poker, Spanish 21, let it ride, pai gow poker and sports betting. The minimum gambling age is 21 and both casinos also offer simulcast betting on horse racing and dog racing.

For information on visiting Rhode Island call the state's tourism division at (800) 556-2484 or go to: www.visitrhodeisland.com.

Tiverton Casino Hotel
777 Tiverton Casino Boulevard
Tiverton, Rhode Island 02878
(401) 849-5000
Website: www.twinrivertiverton.com
Map: **#2** (15 miles S.E of Warwick)

Toll-Free Number: (888) 722-7662
Hotel Reservations: (800) 874-3669
Rooms: 84 Price Range: $109-$169
Restaurants: 3
Special Features: Food Court with three fast food outlets.

Twin River Casino
100 Twin River Road
Lincoln, Rhode Island 02865
(401) 723-3200
Website: www.twinriver.com
Map: **#1** (10 miles N. of Providence)

Toll-Free Number: (877) 827-4837
Restaurants: 5
Other Games: Poker Room
Overnight RV Parking: No
Special Features: Daily (except Tuesday) simulcasting of horse and dog racing. Three food courts with 10 fast food outlets.

SOUTH CAROLINA

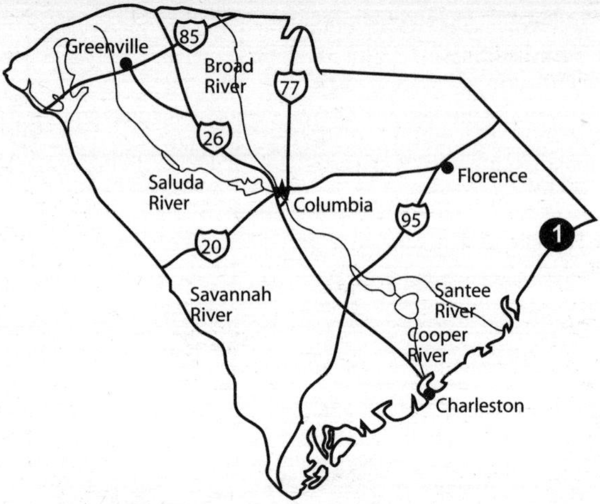

South Carolina has one casino boat which sails three miles out into international waters where casino gambling is permitted.

Big M Casino offers: blackjack, craps, roulette, three card poker, let it ride, slots and video poker. Due to security restrictions, you must present a photo ID or you will not be allowed to board.

For more information on visiting South Carolina go to: www.discoversouthcarolina.com or call their tourism department at (800) 872-3505.

The Big "M" Casino
4491 Waterfront Avenue
Little River, South Carolina 29566
(843) 249-9811
Website: www.bigmcasino.com
Map Location: **#1** (35 miles N. of Myrtle Beach)

Reservation Number: (877) 250-5825
Ship's Registry: U.S. Gambling Age: 21
Buffet: $13 am cruise/ $18 pm cruise
Schedule:
Ship I AM Monday 11:00am/4:30pm
Ship II AM Tuesday-Sunday 11:00am/4:30pm
Ship II PM Tuesday-Sunday 6:30pm/11:30pm
Price: $20 am/$25 pm/$30 Sat pm
Port Charges: Included Parking: Free
Special Features: Big M Casino Ship I and II sail from Little River waterfront. Optional buffet and cash bar offered. Must be 21 or older to board. Select cruises offer Live Entertainment.

SOUTH DAKOTA

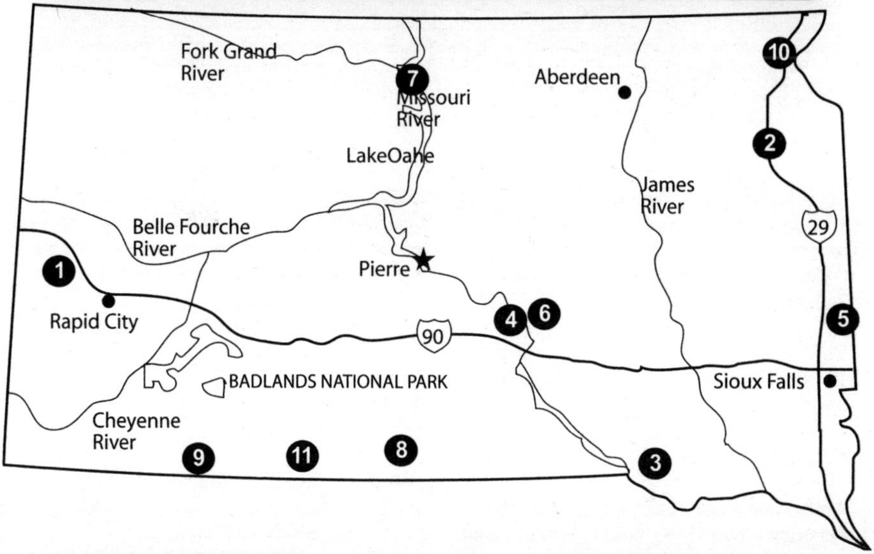

South Dakota's bars and taverns are allowed to have up to 10 video lottery terminals (VLT's) that offer the following games: poker, keno, blackjack and bingo.

These machines are the same as regular video gaming devices but are called lottery terminals because they are regulated by the state's lottery commission which receives a share of each machine's revenue.

The maximum bet is $2 and the maximum payout allowed is $1,000.

Slot machines, as well as blackjack, roulette, craps and poker are only permitted at Indian casinos and in Deadwood.

Deadwood was once most famous for being the home of Wild Bill Hickok who was shot to death while playing cards in the No. 10 Saloon. The hand he held was two pairs: black aces and black eights, which is now commonly referred to as a "dead man's hand." Wild Bill is buried in the local cemetery along with another local celebrity: Calamity Jane.

The first casinos in Deadwood opened on November 1, 1989. All of the buildings in the downtown area are required to conform with the city's authentic 1880's architecture. Many of the casinos are located in historic structures but there are also some new structures which were designed to be compatible with the historic theme of the town. The old No. 10 Saloon is still operating and you can actually gamble in the same spot where old Wild Bill bit the dust!

South Dakota law limits each casino licensee to a maximum of 30 slot machines and no one person is allowed to hold more than three licenses. Some operators combine licenses with other operators to form a cooperative which may look like one casino but in reality it's actually several licensees operating under one name.

The state's gaming laws originally limited blackjack, poker, let it ride and three-card poker bets to a maximum of $5, however, in July 2012 the law was changed to allow maximum bets of $1,000.

In addition to the Deadwood casinos, there are also nine Indian casinos in South Dakota. These casinos are also subject to the $1,000 maximum bet restrictions.

Here are statistics from the South Dakota Commission on Gaming for the payback percentages on all of Deadwood's slot machines for the one-year period from July 1, 2018 through June 30, 2019:

Denomination	Payback %
1¢ Slots	90.73
5¢ Slots	93.56
25¢ Slots	91.18
$1 Slots	92.53
$5 Slots	92.51
All	91.05

Unless otherwise noted, all casinos are open 24 hours.

The Deadwood Trolley runs a scheduled shuttle service to all of the casinos that operates from 8 am to 12am weekdays and 8 am to 3 am on weekends. The cost is $1 per ride, or $5 for an all-day pass.

Unless otherwise noted, all casinos offer slot machines and video poker. Some casinos also offer: blackjack (BJ), craps (C), roulette (R), let it ride (LIR), three-card poker (TCP), ultimate Texas hold 'em (UTH), Mississippi stud (MS) and poker (P). Most of the Indian casinos also offer bingo (BG).

Legislation to legalize sports betting was proposed in 2019, but it did not pass. However, it may be introduced again in 2020.

The minimum gambling age is 21 at all Deadwood and Indian casinos (18 for bingo at Indian casinos). South Dakota's casinos have very liberal rules about allowing minors in casinos and virtually all of the casinos will allow children to enter with their parents until about 8 p.m. Additionally, South Dakota is the only jurisdiction that will allow children to stand next to their parents while they are gambling.

For South Dakota tourism information call (800) 732-5682. For information on visiting Deadwood call the city's Chamber of Commerce at (800) 999-1876, or visit their website at www.deadwood.com

Deadwood

Map: **#1** (in the Black Hills, 41 miles N.W. of Rapid City. Take I-90 W. Get off at the second Sturges exit and take Hwy. 14-A into Deadwood)

Best Western Hickok House
137 Charles Street
Deadwood, South Dakota 57732
(605) 578-1611
Website: www.bestwesternhickokhouse.com

Best Western Reservations: (800) 837-8174
Rooms: 38 Price Range: $79-$280
Restaurants: 1
Special Features: Hot tub and sauna.

Buffalo-Bodega Gaming Complex
658 Main Street
Deadwood, South Dakota 57732
Website: www.buffalobodega.com
(605) 578-1162

Restaurants: 1
Special Features: Oldest bar in Deadwood. Steakhouse restaurant. Live entertainment Fridays and Saturdays.

Bullock Hotel
633 Main Street
Deadwood, South Dakota 57732
(605) 578-1745
Website: www.historicbullock.com

Reservation Number: (800) 336-1876
Rooms: 26 Price Range: $119-$229
Suites: 2 Price Range: $239-$259
Restaurants: 1
Hours: 24 Hours Daily
Special Features: Deadwood's oldest hotel.

Nestled in the Black Hills of South Dakota, the entire city of Deadwood has been designated a national historic landmark. Free historic walking tours are offered daily.

Cadillac Jack's Gaming Resort
360 Main Street
Deadwood, South Dakota 57732
(605) 578-1500
Website: www.cadillacjacksgaming.com

Toll Free Number: (866) 332-3966
Rooms: 92 Price Range: $89-$179
Suites: 11 Price Range: $179-$349
Restaurants: 4
Hours: 24 Hours Daily
Casino Size: 10,000 Square Feet
Games Offered: BJ, TCP, MS, UTH, P, K
Special Features: Hotels are Doubletree Hilton network, and Springhill Suites. Free valet parking.

Deadwood Comfort Inn & Suites
225 Cliff Street
Deadwood, South Dakota 57732
(605) 578-7550
Website: www.deadwoodcomfortinn.com/

Reservation Number: (800) 961-3096
Rooms: 66 Price Range: $129-$190
Suites: 5 Price Range: $199-$219
Restaurants: 1
Special Features: Family amusement arcade and mini-golf. Affiliated with Choice Hotels.

Deadwood Dick's Saloon and Gaming Hall
51 Sherman Street
Deadwood, South Dakota 57732
(605) 578-3224
Website: www.deadwooddicks.com

Toll Free Number: (877) 882-4990
Rooms: 5 Price Range: $89-$199
Suites: 6 Price Range: $119-$299
Restaurants: 1
Games Offered: Slots
Special Features: Antique mall with 25 dealers.

Deadwood Gulch Gaming Resort
304 Cliff Street
Deadwood, South Dakota 57732
(605) 578-1294
Website: www.deadwoodgulch.com

Reservation Number: (800) 695-1876
Rooms: 95 Price Range: $99-$199
Suites: 5 Price Range $225-$299
Restaurants: 2
Hours: 24 Hours Daily
Casino Size: 7,500 Square Feet

Deadwood Gulch Saloon
560 Main Street
Deadwood, South Dakota 57732
(605) 578-1207

Hours: 9am-11:30pm Daily

Deadwood Mountain Grand
1906 Deadwood Mountain Drive
Deadwood, South Dakota 57732
(605) 559-0386
Website: www.deadwoodmountaingrand.com

Toll-free Number: (877) 907-4726
Rooms: 90 Price Range: $129-$179
Suites: 8 Price Range: $189-$389
Restaurants: 2
Hours: 24 Hours Daily
Casino Size: 7,500 Square Feet
Other Games: BJ, TCP
Senior Discount: Various Tue 12pm-4pm if 50+
Special Features: 2,500-seat entertainment center.

Deadwood Station Bunkhouse and Gambling Hall
68 Main Street
Deadwood, South Dakota 57732
(605) 578-3476
Website: www.deadwoodstation.com

Toll-Free Number: (855) 366-6405
Rooms: 28 Price Range: $99-$129
Restaurants: 1

First Gold Hotel & Gaming
270 Main Street
Deadwood, South Dakota 57732
(605) 578-9777
Website: www.firstgold.com

Rooms: 101 Price Range: $79-$119
Suites: 1 Price Range: $99-$219
Restaurants: 2
Buffets: B/L- $11.00 (Sat-Sun)
D- $34.42 (Friday/Saturday)
Hours: 24 Hours Daily
Casino Size: 11,000 Square Feet
Other Games:BJ, TCP, MS
Senior Discount: 10% off room if 55+
Special Features: RV park located next door. Includes **Blackjack** and **Horseshoe** casinos.

Gold Country Inn Gambling Hall and Cafe
801 Main Street
Deadwood, South Dakota 57732
(605) 578-2393
Website:www.goldcountrydeadwood.com

Reservation Number: (800) 287-1251
Rooms: 53 Price Range: $79-$129
Restaurants: 1

Gold Dust Casino & Hotel
688 Main Street
Deadwood, South Dakota 57732
(605) 578-2100
Website: www.golddustdeadwood.com

Rooms: 56 Price Range: $119-$209
Suites: 22 Price Range: $129-$219
Restaurants: 1
Hours: 24 Hours Daily
Casino Size: 30,000 Square Feet
Other Games: BJ, TCP
Senior Discount: $1 off buffets if 55+
Special Features: Hotel is Holiday Inn Express. Largest gaming complex in Deadwood with eleven casinos. Indoor pool, gym, whirlpool, arcade. Includes **French Quarter**, **Legends** and **Silver Dollar** casinos.

Hickok's Hotel and Casino
685 Main Street
Deadwood, South Dakota 57732
(605) 578-2222
Website: www.hickoks.com

Rooms: 18 Price Range: $99-$129
Suites: 4 Price Range: $139-$189
Restaurants: 1 Snack Bar
Special Features: Includes **B.B. Cody's.**

Iron Horse Inn
27 Deadwood Street
Deadwood, South Dakota 57732
(605) 717-7530
Website: www.ironhorseinndeadwood.com

Toll Free Number: (877) 815-7974
Rooms: 19 Price Range: $97-$159
Suites: 4 Price Range: $129-$269
Hours: 24 Hours Daily
Casino Size: 1,000 Square Feet

The Lodge at Deadwood
100 Pine Crest Lane
Deadwood, South Dakota 57732
(605) 571-2132
Website: www.deadwoodlodge.com

Toll-Free Number: (877) 393-5634
Rooms: 100 Price Range: $129-$199
Suites: 40 Price Range: $230-$380
Restaurants: 2
Hours: 24 Hours Daily
Casino Size: 11,000 Square Feet
Other Games: BJ, TCP, P, PGP, MS
Special Features: Electronic version of roulette. Hotel has indoor water playland.

Lucky 8 Gaming Hall/Super 8 Motel
196 Cliff Street
Deadwood, South Dakota 57732
(605) 578-2535

Rooms: 47 Price Range: $49-$129
Suites: 4 Price Range: $99-$149
Restaurants: 1 Snack Bar
Special Features: Video arcade. Free continental breakfast for hotel guests.

Martin & Mason Hotel
33 Deadwood Street
Deadwood, South Dakota 57732
(605) 722-3456
Website: www.martinmasonhotel.com

Rooms: 6 Prices: $149-$180
Suites: 2 Prices: $230-$389
Restaurants: 1
Special Features: Includes **Wooden Nickel Casino & Lee Street Station.**

Mineral Palace Hotel & Gaming
601 Main Street
Deadwood, South Dakota 57732
(605) 578-2036
Website: www.mineralpalace.com

Reservation Number: (800) 847-2522
Rooms: 71 Price Range: $79-$179
Suites: 4 Price Range: $139-$389
Restaurants: 1
Other Games: BJ, R, TCP

Mustang Sally's
634 Main Street
Deadwood, South Dakota 57732
(605) 578-2025
Website: www.mustangsallys.biz

Restaurants: 1

Old Style Saloon #10
657 Main Street
Deadwood, South Dakota 57732
(605) 578-3346
Website: www.saloon10.com

Toll-Free Number: (800) 952-9398
Restaurants: 1
Casino Size: 4,000 Square Feet
Casino Hours: 9am-2am Daily
Other Games: BJ, P, TCP
Special Features: May through October there is a reenactment of the "Shooting of Wild Bill Hickok" at 1, 3, 5 and 7 p.m. Wild Bill's chair and other Old West artifacts on display. Italian restaurant. Includes **The Utter Place** card room.

Oyster Bay/Fairmont Hotel
628 Main Street
Deadwood, South Dakota 57732
(605) 578-2205
Website: www.deadwoodbrotheltours.com

Restaurants: 1
Special Features: Historic restoration of 1895 brothel, spa and underground jail cell. Oyster bar. Ghost tours.

Silverado - Franklin Historic Hotel & Gaming Complex
709 Main Street
Deadwood, South Dakota 57732
(605) 578-3670
Website: www.silveradofranklin.com

Toll-Free Number: (800) 584-7005
Rooms: 80 Price Range: $69-$129
Suites: 15 Price Range: $109-$209
Restaurants: 2
Buffets: B/L $13.95/$16.95 (Sun)
D- $19.95/$30.95 (Fri/Sat)
Hours: 24 Hours Daily
Casino Size: 20,000 Square Feet
Other Games: BJ, P, LIR, TCP, CSP, FCP, MS, CW
Senior Discount: Various promotions on Wednesdays if 50+

Tin Lizzie Gaming
555 Main Street
Deadwood, South Dakota 57732
(605) 578-1715
Website: www.tinlizzie.com

Toll-Free Number: (800) 643-4490
Rooms: 59 Price Range: $69-$149
Suites: 5 Price Range: $159-$249
Restaurants: 3
Casino Size: 8,300 Square Feet
Other Games: BJ, C, R, LIR, TCP, UTH
Senior Discount: Various if 50+
Special Features: Hotel is Hampton Inn.

Veterans of Foreign War
10 Pine Street
Deadwood, South Dakota 57732
(605) 722-9914

Hours: 9:30am-12am Daily

Indian Casinos

Dakota Connection
46102 County Highway 10
Sisseton, South Dakota 57262
(605) 698-4273
Website: www.dakotaconnection.com
Map: **#10** (165 miles N. of Sioux Falls)

Toll-Free Number: (800) 542-2876
Restaurants: 1 Liquor: No
Buffets: B- $10.99 (Sat/Sun)
Hours: 8am-2am/24 (Fri/Sat)
Overnight RV Parking: Free must register at players club/RV Dump: No

Dakota Sioux Casino & Hotel
16415 Sioux Conifer Road
Watertown, South Dakota 57201
(605) 882-2051
Website: www.dakotasioux.com
Map: **#2** (104 miles N. of Sioux Falls)

Toll-Free Number: (800) 658-4717
Rooms: 88 Price Range: $65-$99
Suites: 2 Price Range: $89-$199
Restaurants: 2 Liquor: Yes
Buffets: B/L- $9.95 (Sat/Sun)
D- $12.95 (Sun)/$24.95 (Sat)
Other Games: BJ, P
Overnight RV Parking: Free/RV Dump: Free
Senior Discount: Various Mon if 50+
Special Features: 9-space RV park ($10 per night). Room discount for players club members.

East Wind Casino
US Highway 18
Martin, South Dakota 57551
(605) 685-1140
Website: www.eastwindcasino.com
Map: **#11** (150 miles S.W. of Pierre)

Restaurants: 1 Deli Liquor: No
Senior Discount: Various Wed if 55+

Fort Randall Casino Hotel
38538 East Highway 46
Pickstown, South Dakota 57367
(605) 487-7871
Website: www.fortrandallcasino.com
Map: **#3** (100 miles S.W. of Sioux Falls)

Room Reservations: (800) 362-6333
Rooms: 57 Price Range: $65-$81
Suites: 2 Price Range: $115
Restaurants: 1 Liquor: Yes
Other Games: BJ, R (Fri/Sat), P (Wed/Fri/Sat), BG (Thu-Sun)
Overnight RV Parking: Free/RV Dump: Free
Senior Discount: Various Wed if 50+
Special Features: Room discount for players club members.

Golden Buffalo Casino
321 Sitting Bull Street
Lower Brule, South Dakota 57548
(605) 473-5577
Website: www.thegoldenbuffalocasino.com
Map: **#4** (45 miles S.E. of Pierre)

Rooms: 38 Price Range: $55-$80
Restaurants: 1 Liquor: Yes
Hours: 8am-12:30am/2am (Fri/Sat)
Casino Size: 9,000 Square Feet
Overnight RV Parking: Free/RV Dump: Free

Grand River Casino and Resort
2 U.S. 12
Mobridge, South Dakota 57601
(605) 845-7104
Website: www.grandrivercasino.com
Map: **#7** (240 miles N.E. of Rapid City)

Toll-Free Number: (800) 475-3321
Rooms: 38 Price Range: $80-$105
Suites: 2 Price Range: $150-$200
Restaurants: 1 Liquor: Yes
Buffets: B- $8.95 (Sat/Sun) D- $10.50
Hours: 24 Hours Daily
Other Games: BJ, P (Thu)
Overnight RV Parking: Free/RV Dump: No
Senior Discount: 20% off dining Mon if 55+
Special Features: 10-space RV park ($20 per night). Room discount for players club members.

Lode Star Casino & Hotel
1003 SD Highway 47
Fort Thompson, South Dakota 57339
(605) 245-6000
Website: www.thelodestarcasino.com
Map: **#6** (150 miles N.W. of Sioux Falls)

Restaurants: 1 Liquor: Yes
Rooms: 50 Price Range: $50-$75
Overnight RV Parking: Free/RV Dump: No

Prairie Wind Casino & Hotel
112 Casino Drive
Oglala, South Dakota 57764
(605) 867-6300
Website: www.prairiewindcasino.com
Map: **#9** (85 miles S.E. of Rapid City)

Toll-Free Number: (800) 705-9463
Rooms: 78 Price Range: $60-$99
Suites: 6 Price Range: $116-$156
Restaurants: 1 Liquor: No
Buffet: D- $25.95 (Thu)
Hours: 24 Hours Daily
Other Games: BJ, P, B
Overnight RV Parking: Free/RV Dump: No
Senior Discount: Various Thu 9am-2pm if 50+

Rosebud Casino
370421 Highway 83 (on SD/NE stateline)
Valentine, Nebraska 69201
(605) 378-3800
Website: www.rosebudcasino.com
Map: **#8** (22 miles S. of Mission)

Toll-Free Number: (800) 786-7673
Rooms: 58 Price Range: $94-$109
Suites: 2 Price Range: $109-$139
Restaurants: 2 Liquor: Yes
Hours: 24 Hours Daily
Other Games: BJ, P, UTH, BG (Thu-Sat)
Overnight RV Parking: Free/RV Dump: No
Senior Discount: Various promotions if 55+
Special Features: Hotel is Quality Inn. 10-space RV park ($20 per night).

Royal River Casino & Hotel
607 S. Veterans Street
Flandreau, South Dakota 57028
(605) 997-3746
Website: www.royalrivercasino.com
Map: **#5** (35 miles N. of Sioux Falls on I-29)

Toll-Free Number: (877) 912-5825
Rooms: 108 Price Range: $69-$89
Suites: 12 Price Range: $90-$105
Restaurants: 2 Liquor: Yes
Buffets: B- $5.99 (Sat)/$10.99 (Sun)
L-$8.99/$10.99 (Sun)
D- $9.99/$16.99 (Fri)/$14.99 (Sat)/
$7.99 (Sun)
Hours: 24 Hours Daily
Casino Size: 17,000 Square Feet
Other Games: BJ, R, P(Thu-Sun)
Overnight RV Parking: Free/RV Dump: No
Senior Discount: Various on Thu if 55+
Special Features: 21-space RV park ($15 per night).

Turtle Creek Crossing Casino
28281 US Highway 18
Mission, South Dakota 57555
(605) 856-2329
Map: **#8** (100 miles S. of Pierre)

Casino Hours: 8am-8pm
Games Offered: Gaming Machines Only

TEXAS

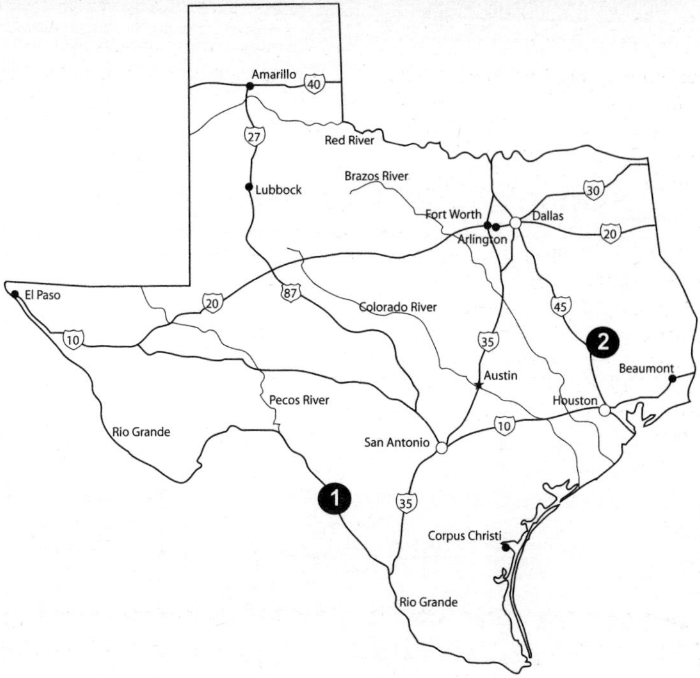

Texas has two Indian casinos which offer class II gaming machines based on bingo. One of them also offers pull tab machines, bingo and poker. The minimum gambling age is 21 and the casinos are open 24 hours daily.

Class II video gaming devices look like slot machines, but are actually bingo games and the spinning reels are for "entertainment purposes only." No public information is available concerning the payback percentages on any gaming machines in Texas' Indian casino.

For more information on visiting Texas call (800) 888-8839 or go to: www.traveltex.com.

Kickapoo Lucky Eagle Casino Hotel
794 Lucky Eagle Drive
Eagle Pass, Texas 78852
(830) 758-1936
Website: www.luckyeagletexas.com
Map: **#1** (140 miles S.W. of San Antonio)

Toll-Free Number: (888) 255-8259
Rooms: 240 Price Range: $139-$189
Suites: 9 Price Range: $239-$269
Restaurants: 3 Liquor: Yes
Valet Parking: No
Casino Size: 16,000 Square Feet
Overnight RV Parking: Free/RV Dump: Free
Senior Discount: Various on Thursday if 55+
Special Features: 20-space RV park ($15/day, including hookups).

Naskila Gaming
540 State Park Road 56
Livingston, Texas 77351
(936) 563-2946
Website: www.naskilagaming.com
Map: **#2** (75 miles N.E. of Houston)

Restaurants: 1
Buffet: B-$12.99 (Sunday)
Valet Parking: Free
Casino Size: 30,000 square feet
Games Offered: Class II Gaming Machines based on bingo

WASHINGTON

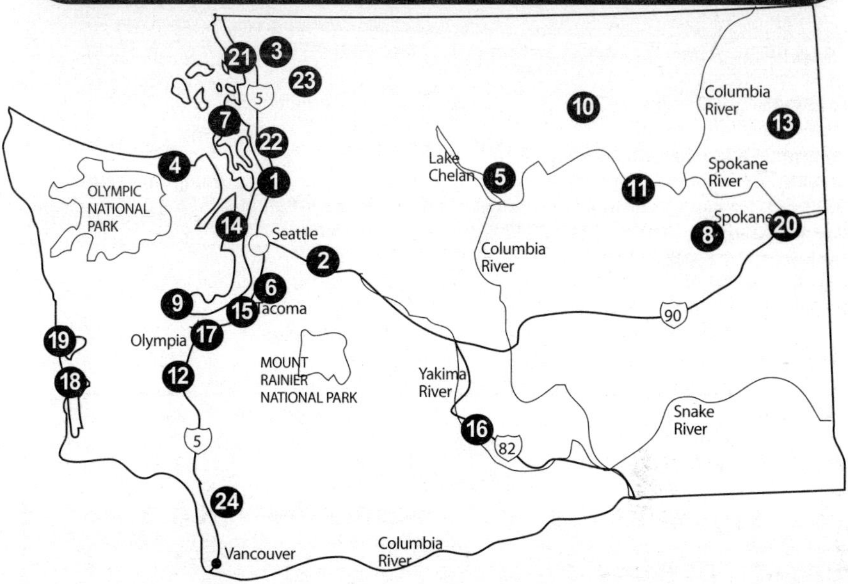

The Indian casinos operating in Washington all have compacts with the state allowing them to offer table games, as well as electronic 'scratch' ticket games which use a finite number of tickets with a predetermined number of winners and losers.

These video gaming machines have a maximum bet of $20.

The Tribes are not required to release information on their slot machine percentage paybacks. However, according to the terms of the compact between the Tribes and the state, the minimum prize payout for electronic 'scratch' ticket games is 75%.

Most Washington casinos are open on a 24-hour basis. The hours of operation are noted in each casino's listing for those not open 24 hours.

All casinos offer blackjack, craps, roulette, slots, video poker and pull tabs. Optional games offered include: baccarat (B), mini-baccarat (MB), poker (P), pai gow poker (PGP), Caribbean stud poker (CSP), three-card poker (TCP), ultimate Texas hold em (UTH), four card poker (FCP), Spanish 21 (S21), big 6 wheel (B6), keno (K), Off-Track Betting (OTB) and bingo (BG).

Legislation to legalize sports betting was proposed in 2019, but it did not pass. However, it may be introduced again in 2020.

The minimum gambling age is 21 at most casinos (at some it's 18) and 18 for bingo or pari-mutuel betting. Look in the "Special Features" listing for each casino to see which allow gambling at 18 years of age.

Although most of the casinos have toll-free numbers be aware that some of these numbers will only work for calls made within Washington.

For more information on visiting Washington call their tourism department at (800) 544-1800 or go to: www.experiencewashington.com.

Angel of the Winds Casino
3438 Stoluckquamish Lane
Arlington, Washington 98223
(360) 474-9740
Website: www.angelofthewinds.com
Map: **#22** (50 miles N. of Seattle)

Rooms: 125 Price Range: $114-$279
Restaurants: 1 Liquor: Yes
Casino Size: 84,000 square feet
Buffets: B- $10.99/$16.99 (Sat/Sun) L- $11.99
D- $16.99/$27.99 (Fri-Sun)
Other Games: P, PGP, TCP, FCP, K
Overnight RV Parking: Free with hotel room/ RV Dump: No
Special Feature: Electric vehicle charging station

BJ's Bingo
4411 Pacific Highway East
Fife, Washington 98424
(253) 922-0430
Website: www.bjs-bingo.com
Map: **#15** (a suburb of Tacoma)

Restaurants: 1
Other games: BG, No table games
Overnight RV Parking: Call ahead
Senior Discount: Various Sun/Mon if 55+

Chewelah Casino
2555 Smith Road
Chewelah, Washington 99109
(509) 935-6167
Website: www.chewelahcasino.com
Map: **#13** (50 miles N. of Spokane)

Toll-Free Number: (800) 322-2788
Restaurants: 1 Liquor: Yes
Buffets: B-$11.99 (Sun) L-$10.99 (Wed)
Hours: 8am-2am
Casino Size: 22,000 Square Feet
Other Games: S21
Overnight RV Parking: Free/RV Dump: No
Senior Discount: Various Wed if 55+
Special Features: One block from Double Eagle Casino. 10-space RV park ($20 per night). Gambling age is 21.

Coulee Dam Casino
515 Birch Street
Coulee Dam, Washington 99116
(509) 633-0766
Website: www.colvillecasinos.com
Map: **#11** (85 miles N.W of Spokane)

Toll-Free Number: (800) 556-7492
Restaurants: 1 Liquor: Yes
Hours: 10am-3am/24 hours (Fri/Sat)
Other Games: Only Gaming Machines
Overnight RV Parking: Free/RV Dump: No
Special Features: Gambling age is 18.

Elwha River Casino
631 Stratton Road
Port Angeles, Washington 98363
(360) 452-3005
Website: www.elwharivercasino.com
Map: **#4** (70 miles N.W. of Seattle via ferry)

Restaurants: 1 Liquor: No
Other Games: Only Gaming Machines
Hours: 10am-12am/2am (Fri/Sat)

Emerald Queen Hotel & Casino at Fife
5700 Pacific Highway East
Fife, Washington 98424
(253) 922-2000
Website: www.emeraldqueen.com
Map: **#15** (a suburb of Tacoma)

Toll-Free Number: (888) 820-3555
Rooms: 130 Price Range: $109-$139
Suites: 10 Price Range: $179-$239
Restaurants: 1 Liquor: Yes
Buffets:L- $13.95/$19.95 (Sun) D- $19.95
Other Games: Only Gaming Machines
Senior Discount: $2 off buffet if 60+
Overnight RV Parking: No

Emerald Queen Casino at I-5
2024 East 29th Street
Tacoma, Washington 98404
(253) 594-7777
Website: www.emeraldqueen.com
Map: **#15**

Toll-Free Number: (888) 831-7655
Restaurants: 4 Liquor: Yes
Buffets: L- $15.95/$24.95 (Sun) D- $24.95
Other Games: S21, PGP, LIR, TCP
Overnight RV Parking: Free/RV Dump: No
Senior Discount: $2 off buffet if 60+
Special Features: Sports bar. Free shuttle to Emerald Queen Fife.

ilani Casino Resort
1 Cowlitz Way
Ridgefield, Washington 98642
(877) 464-5264
Website: www.ilaniresort.com
Map: #**24** (20 miles N. of Vancouver, WA)

Restaurants: 8 Liquor: Yes
Casino Size: 100,000 square feet
Games Offered: MB, S21, PGP, TCP, UTH
Special Feature: 2,500 seat entertainment venue.

Kalispel Casino
420 Qlispe River Road
Cusick, Washington 99119
(833) 881-7492
Website: www.kalispelcasino.com

Restaurants: 2 Liquor: Yes
Other Games: Machines Only
Hours: 10am-12am/2am (Friday/Saturday)
Special Features: Two fast-food outlets. Convenience store. 33-space RV park ($35-$55 per night). Eight rental cabins ($120-$160 per night).

Little Creek Casino Resort
91 West Highway 108
Shelton, Washington 98584
(360) 427-7711
Website: www.little-creek.com
Map: **#9** (23 miles N. of Olympia off Hwy 101/108 interchange)

Toll-Free Number: (800) 667-7711
Rooms: 92 Price Range: $89-$139
Suites: 6 Price Range: $139-$229
Restaurants: 5 Liquor: Yes
Buffets: B- $8.95/$16.95 (Sat/Sun) L- $12.95
D- $16.95/$24.95 (Fri/Sat)
Casino Size: 30,000 Square Feet
Hours: 8am-5am/24 hours (Fri/Sat)
Other Games: S21, P, PGP, K, BG, FCP
Overnight RV Parking: Free/RV Dump: No
Senior Discount: Various Mon-Wed if 50+
Special Features: Indoor pool. Gift shop. 44-space RV park.

Lucky Dog Casino
19330 N. Highway 101
Skokomish, Washington 98584
(360) 877-5656
Website: www.myluckydogcasino.com
Map: **#9** (23 miles N. of Olympia)

Toll-Free Number: (877) 582-5948
Restaurants: 2 Liquor: Yes
Hours: 9am-12am/2am (Fri/Sat)/1am (Sun)
Casino Size: 2,500 Square Feet
Other Games: Only Gaming Machines
Special Features: 20-space RV park ($34-$39 per night).

Lucky Eagle Casino
12888 188th Avenue SW
Rochester, Washington 98579
(360) 273-2000
Website: www.luckyeagle.com
Map: **#12** (26 miles S. of Olympia)

Toll-Free Number: (800) 720-1788
Rooms: 65 Price Range: $99-$135
Suites: 4 Price Range: $138-$265
Restaurants: 5 Liquor: Yes
Buffets: L-$15.95/$17.95 (Sun)
D-$19.95/$25.95 (Fri/Sat)
Hours: 8am-4am/24 hours (Fri/Sat)
Casino Size: 75,000 Square Feet
Other Games: P, PGP, TCP, S21, K, BG
Overnight RV Parking: No
Senior Discount: Various specials Mon if 50+
Special Features: 20-space RV park ($25 per night). Buffet discount if 50+.

Mill Bay Casino
455 Wapato Lake Road
Manson, Washington 98831
(509) 687-2102
Website: www.colvillecasinos.com
Map: **#5** (200 miles N.E. of Seattle on the N. shore of Lake Chelan)

Toll-Free Number: (800) 648-2946
Restaurants: 1 Liquor: Yes
Overnight RV Parking: Free/RV Dump: No
Other Games: S21, PGP, TCP, FCP
Senior Discount: Various Tue 10am-2pm if 55+
Special Features: Gambling age is 18.

Muckleshoot Casino
2402 Auburn Way South
Auburn, Washington 98002
(253) 804-4444
Website: www.muckleshootcasino.com
Map: **#6** (20 miles S. of Seattle)

Toll-Free Number (800) 804-4944
Restaurants: 5 Liquor: Yes
Buffets: B-$12.95/$18.95 (Sat/Sun)
L-$14.95/$18.95 (Sat/Sun)
D-$19.95/$29.95 (Fri/Sat/Sun)
Other Games: S21, B, MB, P, PGP, CSP, TCP, FCP
Overnight RV Parking: Free/RV Dump: No
Special Features: Two casinos in separate buildings, one is non-smoking. Buffet discount for players club members. 400-room hotel expected to open in 2021.

Nooksack Northwood Casino
9750 Northwood Road
Lynden, Washington 98264
(360) 734-5101
Website: www.northwoodcasino.com
Map: **#3** (14 miles N. of Bellingham)

Toll-Free Number (877) 777-9847
Restaurants: 2 Liquor: Yes
Buffets: B-$9.99 (Sun)
D-$14.95 (Wed)/$4.99 (Thu)/
$16.95 (Fri/Sat)
Hours: 9am-3am/4am (Fri/Sat)
Casino Size: 20,000 Square Feet
Other Games: P, S21, PGP, UTH
Overnight RV Parking: Free/RV Dump: No
Special Features: RV hook-ups available for $30 per night/$7 for players club members. Buffet closed Monday and Tuesday.

Northern Quest Resort & Casino
100 N Hayford Road
Airway Heights, Washington 99001
(509) 242-7000
Website: www.northernquest.com
Map: **#20** (10 miles W. of Spokane)

Toll-Free Number (888) 603-7051,
Rooms: 200 Prices $179-$219
Suites: 50 Prices: $239-$539
Restaurants: 5 Liquor: Yes
Buffets: L- $12.95/$16.95 (Sun)
D- $16.95/$29.95 (Wed)/
$27.99 (Fri)/$21.95 (Sat)
Casino Size: 21,500 Square Feet
Other Games: S21, P, PGP, TCP, K, OTB, BG
Overnight RV Parking: Free/RV Dump: No
Senior Discount: Various on Tue if 55+
Special Feature: 67-spot RV park ($60-$75 per night) with 18 cottages $177-$217 per night.)

The Point Casino
7989 Salish Lane NE
Kingston, Washington 98346
(360) 297-0070
Website: www.the-point-casino.com
Map: **#14** (18 miles W. of Seattle via Bainbridge Ferry)

Toll-Free Number (866) 547-6468
Rooms: 85 Price Range: $119-$159
Suites: 9 Price Range: Call for Rates
Restaurants: 2 Liquor: Yes
Buffets: B-$14.95 (Sun)
D-$17.95 (Wed-Fri)/$24.95 (Sat)
Casino Size: 18,500 Square Feet
Other Games: C, R, S21, PGP, P
Overnight RV Parking: Free/RV Dump: No
Senior Discount: Various on Sunday if 55+
Special Features: $15 off Seattle and Edmonds Ferry fees reimbursed after one hour of play. Table games open at 2pm/10am (Fri-Sun).

Quil Ceda Creek Nightclub & Casino
6410 33rd Avenue N.E.
Tulalip, Washington 98271
(360) 716-1700
Website: www.quilcedacreekcasino.com
Map: **#1** (30 miles N. of Seattle)

Toll-Free Number: (888) 272-1111
Restaurants: 1 Liquor: Yes
Casino Size: 52,000 Square Feet
Other Games: S21, PGP, TCP, UTH
Overnight RV Parking: Free/RV Dump: No
Special Features: One mile from Tulalip Casino.

Quinault Beach Resort and Casino
78 Route 115
Ocean Shores, Washington 98569
(360) 289-9466
Website: www.quinaultbeachresort.com
Map: **#19** (90 miles W. of Tacoma)

Toll-Free Number: (888) 461-2214
Rooms: 159 Price Range: $149-$229
Suite: 9 Price Range: $289-$449
Restaurants: 4 Liquor: Yes
Buffets: B- $9.95 D- $16.95/$29.95 (Fri)
Casino Size: 16,000 Square Feet
Other Games: C, R, S21, P, PGP, TCP
Overnight RV Parking: Call toll-free number to register/RV Dump: No
Senior Discount: Various Wednesdays if 50+

Red Wind Casino
12819 Yelm Highway SE
Olympia, Washington 98513
(360) 412-5000
Website: www.redwindcasino.com
Map: **#17**

Toll-Free Number: (866) 946-2444
Restaurants: 4 Liquor: Yes
Buffets: B- $15.00 (Sat)/$23.00(Sun)
L- $16.00 D- $23.00/$30.00 (Sun)
Casino Size: 64,000 Square Feet
Games Offered: C, R, S21, FCP, PGP,
TCP, LIR, UTH, K
Overnight RV Parking: Free/RV Dump: No
Senior Discount: 25% food discount if 55+

7 Cedars Casino
270756 Highway 101
Sequim, Washington 98382
(360) 683-7777
Website: www.7cedarscasino.com
Map: **#4** (70 miles N.W. of Seattle via ferry)

Toll-Free Number: (800) 458-2597
Restaurants: 2 Liquor: Yes
Hours: 9am-3am/4am (Friday/Saturday)
Other Games: S21, P, PGP, LIR, TCP, UTH, K, BG, OTB (Wed-Mon)
Senior Discount: Various on Monday, if 50+
Overnight RV Parking: Free (Must check-in at casino cage first)/RV Dump: No
Special Feature: Construction underway on 100-room hotel that is scheduled to open Summer of 2020.

Shoalwater Bay Casino
4112 Highway 105
Tokeland, Washington 98590
(360) 267-2048
Website: www.shoalwaterbaycasino.com
Map: **#18** (75 miles S.W. of Olympia)

Toll-Free Number: (888) 332-2048
Restaurants: 2 Liquor: Yes
Hours: 10am-Midnight/2am (Fri/Sat)
Casino Size: 10,000 Square Feet
Other Games: S21
Overnight RV Parking: Free (check with security first)
Senior Discount: Various on Tue if 55+
Special Features: Table games are open Thu-Sun beginning at 2pm.

Silver Reef Hotel • Casino • Spa
4876 Haxton Way
Ferndale, Washington 98248
(360) 383-0777
Website: www.silverreefcasino.com
Map: **#21** (7 miles N. of Bellingham)

Toll-Free Number: (866) 383-0777
Rooms: 105 Price Range: $129-$159
Suites: 4 Price Range: $279-$319
Restaurants: 4 Liquor: Yes
Buffets: L-$12.95/$16.95 (Sun)
D-$18.95/$23.95 (Fri)/$19.95(Sat)
Casino Size: 48,000 Square Feet
Other Games: S21, PGP, TCP, FCP, UTH
Senior Discount: Various on Mon if 50+
Overnight RV Parking: Free/RV Dump: No
Special Features: Buffet closed Wednesday.

Skagit Valley Casino Resort
5984 N. Darrk Lane
Bow, Washington 98232
(360) 724-7777
Website: www.theskagit.com
Map: **#7** (75 miles N. of Seattle)

Toll-Free Number: (877) 275-2448
Rooms: 74 Price Range: $1199-$189
Suites: 29 Price Range: $179-$219
Restaurants: 3 Liquor: Yes
Buffets: B- $17.00 (Sat/Sun) L- $12.00
D- $17.00/$30.00 (Fri/Sat)
Hours: 9am-3am/5am (Friday/Saturday)
Casino Size: 26,075 Square Feet
Other Games: C, R, PGP, TCP, S21, K
Overnight RV Parking: No
Special Features: Two 18-hole golf courses. Health spa.

Snoqualmie Casino
37500 SE North Bend Way
Snoqualmie, Washington 98065
(425) 888-1234
Website: www.snocasino.com
Map: **#2** (30 miles E. of Seattle)

Restaurants: 5 Liquor: Yes
Buffets: L-$15.95/$18.95 (Sat/Sun)
D-$28.95/$44.95 (Tue)/$25.95 (Mon)
Other Games: S21, B, PGP, P

Spokane Tribe Casino
14300 W SR-2 Hwy
Airway Heights, Washington 99001
(425) 888-1234
Website: www.spokanetribecasino.com
Map: **#2** (30 miles E. of Seattle)

Toll-Free Number: (877) 786-9467
Restaurants: 2 Liquor: Yes
Hours: 24 Hours Daily
Casino Size: 38,000 Square Feet
Overnight RV Parking: Free/RV Dump: No
Senior Discount: Various Tuesday if 55+
Special Features: Gambling age is 18.

Suquamish Clearwater Casino Resort
15347 Suquamish Way NE
Suquamish, Washington 98392
(360) 598-8700
Website: www.clearwatercasino.com
Map: **#14** (15 miles W. of Seattle via Bainbridge Ferry)

Toll-Free Number: (800) 375-6073
Room Reservations: (866) 609-8700
Rooms:70 Room Rates: $139-$189
Suites: 15 Room Rates: $169-$219
Restaurants: 3 Liquor: Yes
Casino Size: 22,000 Square Feet
Other Games: C, R, P, PGP, TCP, LIR, K
Overnight RV Parking: Free/RV Dump: No
Senior Discount: Various Mondays if 55+
Special features: Food hall with 6 dining options available. Seattle and Edmonds Ferries fee reimbursed with qualified play. Gambling age is 18.

Swinomish Casino & Lodge
12885 Casino Drive
Anacortes, Washington 98221
(360) 293-2691
Website: swinomishcasinoandlodge.com
Map: **#7** (70 miles N. of Seattle, between I-5 and Anacortes on Hwy. 20)

Toll-Free Number: (888) 288-8883
Rooms: 94 Price Range: $129-$179
Suites: 4 Price Range: $279-$349
Restaurants: 5 Liquor: Yes
Casino Size: 23,000 Square Feet
Other Games: C, R, P, PGP, TCP, FCP, UTH, K
Overnight RV Parking: Must use RV park
Senior Discount: Various on Tuesday if 50+
Special Features: 35-space RV park ($27-$35 per night). Gift shop.

Tulalip Casino
10200 Quil Ceda Boulevard
Tulalip, Washington 98271
(360) 716-6000
Website: www.tulalipcasino.com
Map: **#1** (30 miles N. of Seattle)

Toll-Free Number: (888) 272-1111
Rooms: 370 Room Rates: $149-$249
Suites: 23 Room Rates: $235-$389
Restaurants: 8 Liquor: Yes
Buffets: B- $12.95 L- $14.50/$18.95 (Sat/Sun)
D- $19.95/$21.95 (Fri-Sun)
Casino Size: 45,000 Square Feet
Other Games: C, R, S21, B, MB, P, PGP, TCP, FCP, UTH, LIR, K, BG
Overnight RV Parking: Free/RV Dump: No
Senior Discount: Various on Tue if 50+
Special Features: 3,000-seat amphitheatre. One mile from Quil Ceda Creek Casino.

12 Tribes Casino
28968 US Highway 97
Omak, Washington 98841
(509) 422-4646
Website: www.colvillecasinos.com
Map: **#10** (165 miles N.E. of Seattle)

Toll-Free Number: (800) 559-4643
Rooms: 68 Price Range: $99-$189
Suites: 12 Price Range: $179-$229
Restaurants: 2
Casino Size: 56,000 Square Feet
Senior Discount: Various Tue if 55+
Special Features: 21-space RV park ($30 per night). Spa.

Yakama Legends Casino
580 Fort Road
Toppenish, Washington 98948
(509) 865-8800
Website: www.legendscasino.com
Map: **#16** (20 miles S. of Yakima)

Toll-Free Number: (877) 726-6311
Rooms: 200 Price Range: $139-$159
Restaurants: 2 Liquor: No
Buffets: B-$17.99 (Sun)
L-$13.99/$21.99 (Thu)
D- $17.99/$32.95 (Thu)/$16.99 (Sun)
Hours: 9am-4am/5am (Fri/Sat)
Casino Size: 45,000 Square Feet
Other Games: C, R, S21, P, PGP, K
Overnight RV Parking: Free/RV Dump: No
Senior Discount: Various on Tuesdays if 55+
Special Features: Indoor waterfall. Gambling age is 18.

Card Rooms

Card rooms have been legal in Washington since 1974. Initially limited to just five tables per location, the law was changed in 1996 to allow up to 15 tables. One year later, a provision was added to allow house-banked games. Permissible games include: blackjack, Caribbean stud poker, pai gow poker, let it ride, casino war and numerous other card games. Baccarat, craps, roulette and keno are not allowed.

The maximum bet at each card room is dependent on certain licensing requirements and is capped at either $25 or $100. Additionally, the rooms can be open no more than 20 hours per day. These card rooms are now commonly called "mini-casinos." The minimum gambling age in a card room is 18.

Each city and county has the option to ban the card rooms so they are not found in every major city (Seattle has none). Due to space limitations we don't list all of the Washington card rooms in this book.

For a list of card rooms, we suggest that you contact the Washington State Gambling Commission at (360) 486-3581, or visit their website at: www.wsgc.wa.gov

WEST VIRGINIA

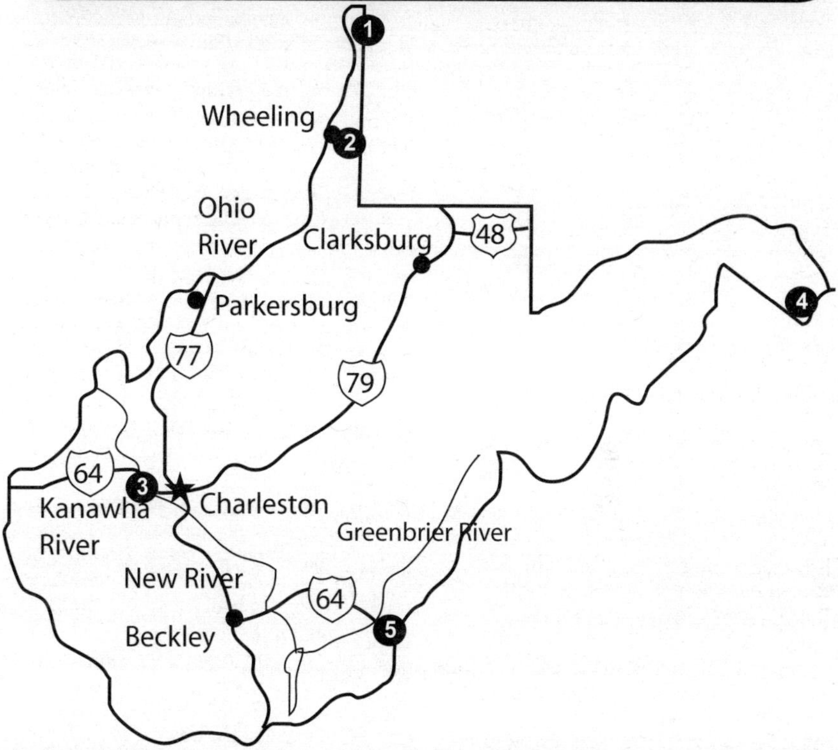

West Virginia has four pari-mutuel facilities and one resort hotel that feature video lottery terminals. The VLT's are the same as regular video gaming devices but are called lottery terminals because they are regulated by the state's lottery commission which receives a share of each machine's revenue.

West Virginia law requires that VLT's return a minimum of 80% to a maximum of 95%. VLT games include: slots, blackjack, keno and numerous versions of poker. The minimum gambling age is 21.

For the one-year period from July 1, 2018 through June 30, 2019 the average return on VLT's was: 88.97% at Mountaineer Park, 90.81% at Mardi Gras, 89.46% at Wheeling Island, 89.53% at Charles Town Races.

West Virginia law also allows bars, as well as restaurants that serve alcohol, to have up to five VLT's. Fraternal organizations are also allowed to have up to 10 VLT's. All of these machines are identical to the machines found at the racetracks.

All West Virgina casinos offer sports betting, plus the following table games: blackjack, craps, roulette and three card poker. Optional games offered include: poker (P), pai gow poker (PGP), four card poker (FCP), Caribbean stud poker (CSP), mini-baccarat (MB), Spanish 21 (S21), Mississippi stud (MS) and big 6 wheel (B6).

All casinos are open 24 hours, except for the Greenbriar facility. For West Virginia tourism information call (800) 225-5982 or go to: www.callwva.com.

The Casino Club at The Greenbrier
300 W. Main Street
White Sulphur Springs, West Virginia 24986
(304) 536-1110
Website: www.greenbrier.com
Map: **#5** (120 miles S.E. of Charleston)

Toll-free Number: (855) 453-4858
Rooms: 238 Price Range: $209-$499
Restaurants: 6
Hours:11am-3am/4am(Fri/Sat)/1pm-3am(Sun)
Casino Size: 75,000 square Feet
Other Games: B, MB, P
Special Features: Casino only open to hotel guests, sporting club or golf/tennis club members, or convention/event attendees. Dress code enforced. Men required to wear jackets after 7 p.m.

Hollywood Casino at Charles Town Races
750 Hollywood Drive
Charles Town, West Virginia 25414
(304) 725-7001
Website: hollywoodcasinocharlestown.com
Map: **#4** (320 miles N.E. of Charleston)

Toll-Free Number: (800) 795-7001
Rooms: 132 Price Range: $119-$189
Suites: 18 Price Range: $219-$329
Restaurants: 6
Buffets: L- $14.99/$15.99 (Sat)/$21.99 (Sun)
D- $18.99/$19.99 (Fri)/
$25.99 (Sat)/$21.99 (Sun)
Other Games: FCP, LIR, MB, B6, PGP
Overnight RV Parking: Free/RV Dump: No
Special Features: Live thoroughbred racing Wednesday-Sunday. Daily simulcasting of horse and dog racing. Food court with five fast-food outlets.

Mardi Gras Casino & Resort
1 Greyhound Drive
Cross Lanes, West Virginia 25313
(304) 776-1000
Website: www.mardigrascasinowv.com
Map: **#3** (10 miles N.W. of Charleston)

Toll-Free Number: (800) 224-9683
Rooms: 132 Price Range: $149-$169
Suites: 21 Price Range: $189-$219
Restaurants: 3
Casino Size: 90,000 Square Feet
Other Games: B6, P, MS
Overnight RV Parking: Free/RV Dump: No
Senior Discount: Various Tue if 50+
Special Features: Live dog racing seasonally. Daily simulcasting of horse and dog racing.

Mountaineer Casino Racetrack & Resort
1420 Mountaineer Circle
New Cumberland, West Virginia 26047
(304) 387-2400
Website: www.moreatmountaineer.com
Map: **#1** (35 miles N. of Wheeling)

Toll-Free Number: (800) 804-0468
Rooms: 238 Price Range: $79-$169
Suites: 20 Price Range: $179-$239
Restaurants: 5
Buffets: B-$12.99 (Sun)L-$12.99
D-$18.99/21.99 (Fri)
Other Games: S21, P, FCP, LIR, MS
Overnight RV Parking: Free/RV Dump: No
Special Features: Live thoroughbred racing seasonally. Daily simulcasting of horse/dog racing. 18-hole golf course. Spa and fitness center.

Wheeling Island Hotel Casino & Racetrack
1 S. Stone Street
Wheeling, West Virginia 26003
(304) 232-5050
Website: www.wheelingisland.com
Map: **#2**

Toll-Free Number: (877) 946-4373
Room Reservations: (877) 943-3546
Rooms: 142 Price Range: $135-$169
Suites: 9 Price Range: $169-$250
Restaurants: 2
Buffets: B-$9.99 (Sat)/$18.99 (Sun)
L-$15.99/$30.99 (Fri)/
$19.99(Sat)/$18.99(Sun)
D-$17.99/$25.99 (Fri)/$19.99 (Sat)
Hours: 24 Hours Daily
Casino Size: 50,000 Square Feet
Other Games: P, PGP, LIR, SB
Overnight RV Parking: Free/RV Dump: No
Senior Discount: Various on Wed if 50+
Special Features: Live dog racing seasonally. Daily simulcasting of horse and dog racing.

WISCONSIN

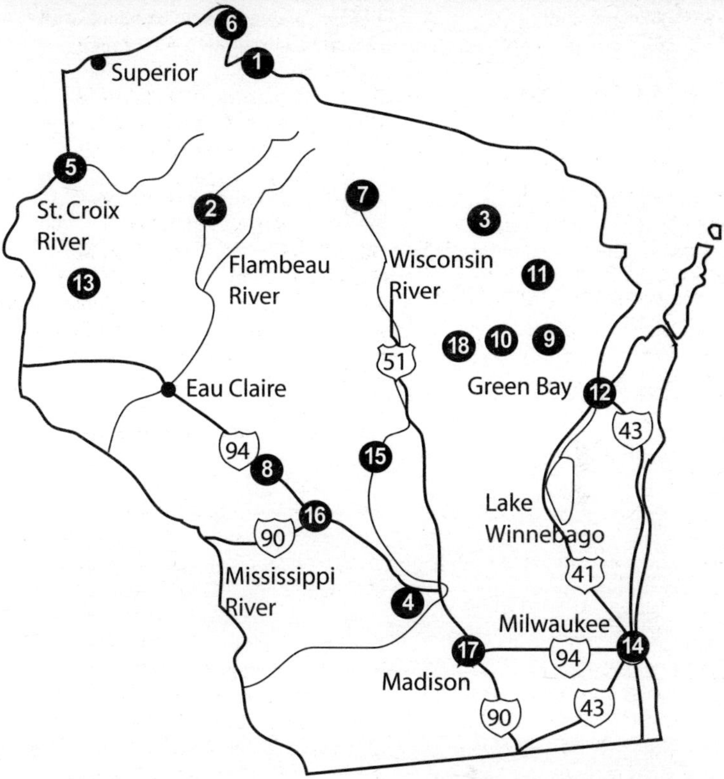

All Wisconsin casinos are located on Indian reservations.

The Tribes are not required to release information on their slot machine percentage paybacks, but according to the terms of the compact between the state and the tribes "for games not affected by player skill, such as slot machines, the machine is required to return a minimum of 80% and a maximum of 100% of the amount wagered."

All casinos offer blackjack, slots and video poker. Some casinos also offer: craps (C), roulette (R), mini baccarat (MB), Mississippi stud (MS), poker (P), Pai Gow Poker (PGP), three card poker (TCP), four card poker (FCP), let it ride (LIR), ultimate Texas hold 'em (UTH), big 6 wheel (B6), bingo (BG), keno (K) and off-track betting (OTB). Unless otherwise noted, all casinos are open 24 hours and the minimum gambling age is 21 (18 for bingo).

Sports betting is not allowed in Wisconsin and there were no legislative efforts made to legalize it in 2019.

For visitor information contact the state's department of tourism at (800) 432-8747 or their website at: www.travelwisconsin.com.

Bad River Lodge Casino
73370 U.S. Highway 2
Odanah, Wisconsin 54861
(715) 682-7121
Website: www.badriver.com
Map: **#1** (45 miles east of Duluth, MN)

Toll-Free Number: (800) 777-7449
Lodge Reservations: (800) 795-7121
Rooms: 42 Price Range: $79-$89
Suites: 8 Price Range: $85-$99
Restaurants: 2 Liquor: Yes
Casino Size: 19,200 Square Feet
Hours: 8am-2am Daily
Other Games: P, TCP, LIR
Overnight RV Parking: Free/RV Dump: Free
Senior Discount: Various dining specials if 55+
Special Features: 20-space RV park ($10/$20). Gas station. Grocery store.

Grindstone Creek Casino
13394 West Trepania Road
Hayward, Wisconsin 54843
(715) 634-6630
Map: **#2** (55 miles S.E. of Duluth, MN)

Restaurants: 1 Liquor: No
Hours: 9am-10pm Daily
Special Features: Gambling age is 18. Located in LCO Commercial Center. Gas station. Grocery store. Four miles from Sevenhills Casino, Lodge & Convention Center.

Ho-Chunk Gaming Black River Falls
W9010 Highway 54 East
Black River Falls, Wisconsin 54615
(715) 284-9098
Website: www.ho-chunkgaming.com
Map: **#8** (110 miles N.W. of Madison)

Toll-Free Number: (800) 657-4621
Rooms: 60 Price Range: $88-$129
Suites: 6 Price Range: $130-$199
Restaurants: 2 Liquor: Yes
Buffets: L-$9.95/$10.99 (Fri/Sat)/$12.95 (Sun)
D-$14.95/$21.95 (Fri/Sat)
Size: 35,000 Square Feet
Other Games: MS, UTH, TCP, BG
Overnight RV Parking: Free/RV Dump: No
Senior Discount: Various Mondays if 50 or older.
Special Features: 10% off food/hotel for slot club members.

Ho-Chunk Gaming Madison
4002 Evan Acres Road
Madison, Wisconsin 53718
(608) 223-9576
Website: www.ho-chunkgaming.com
Map: **#17**

Toll-Free Number: (888) 248-1777
Restaurants: 1 Liquor: Yes
Casino Size: 22,000 Square Feet
Other Games: Class II Gaming machines
Based on Bingo
Senior Discount: $5 free play on Wed if 50+
Special Features: Smoke-free casino. Free valet parking.

Ho-Chunk Gaming Nekoosa
949 County Road G
Nekoosa, Wisconsin 54457
(715) 886-4560
Website: www.ho-chunkgaming.com
Map: **#15** (50 miles S. of Wausau)

Toll-Free Number: (800) 782-4560
Restaurants: 2 Liquor: Yes
Overnight RV Parking: Free (must check-in
first with security)/RV Dump: No
Senior Discount: Various on Thu if 50+
Special Features: Smoke and gift shop. Convenience store. Electronic table games including Blackjack, Roulette, Three Card Poker and Mississippi Stud.

Ho-Chunk Gaming Tomah
27867 Highway 21
Tomah, Wisconsin 54660
(608) 372-3721
Website: www.ho-chunkgaming.com
Map: **#16** (3 miles E. of Tomah on Hwy 21)

Toll-Free Number: (866) 880-9822
Restaurants: 1 Snack Bar Liquor: No
Hours: 8am-Midnight/2am (Fri/Sat)
Casino Size: 2,000 Square Feet
Other Games: Only Gaming Machines
Special Features: Convenience store. Open 24 hours Fri-Sat during the summer.

Ho-Chunk Gaming Wisconsin Dells
S3214 Highway 12
Baraboo, Wisconsin 53913
(608) 356-6210
Website: www.ho-chunkgaming.com
Map: **#4** (40 miles N. of Madison.)

Toll-Free Number: (800) 746-2486
Room Reservations: (800) 446-5550
Rooms: 295 Price Range: $119-$195
Suites: 20 Price Range: $279-$299
Restaurants: 5 Liquor: Yes
Buffets: B-$9.99 (Sat/Sun)
L- $11.99 (Sat/Sun)
D-$12.99/$32.99 (Fri/Sat)
Casino Size: 90,000 Square Feet
Other Games: C, R, P, TCP, OTB, UTH, BG (Tue-Sun)
Overnight RV Parking: Must use RV Park
Senior Discount: Various Tue if 50+
Special Features: Smoke shop. Free local shuttle. Kid's Quest childcare center. 49-space RV park ($35-$75 per night).

Ho-Chunk Gaming Wittenberg
N7198 US Highway 45
Wittenberg, Wisconsin 54499
(608) 372-3721
Website: www.ho-chunkgaming.com
Map: **#18** (3 miles E. of Tomah on Hwy 21)

Restaurants: 2 Liquor: Yes
Casino Size: 19,000 Square Feet
Other Games: Gaming Machines only
Overnight RV Parking: Yes/RV Dump: No
Special Features: Convenience store.

IMAC Casino/Bingo
2100 Airport Drive
Green Bay, Wisconsin 54313
920-494-4500
Website: www.oneidacasino.net
Map: **#12**

Restaurants: 1 Liquor: Yes
Overnight RV Parking: $15/night. Register with Players Club.
Hours: 8am-12am/2am (Fri/Sat)
Special features: Free Shuttle Service to Oneida's Main Airport Casino and West Mason Casino.

Lake of the Torches Resort Casino
510 Old Abe Road
Lac du Flambeau, Wisconsin 54538
(715) 588-7070
Website: www.lakeofthetorches.com
Map: **#7** (160 miles N.W. of Green Bay)

Toll-Free Number: (800) 258-6724
Rooms: 88 Price Range: $95-$155
Suites: 13 Price Range: $135-$195
Restaurants: 2 Liquor: Yes
Buffets: B-$7.95/$12.95 (Sun)
L- $9.75/$12.95 (Sun)
D-$15.95/$9.95 (Thu)/$16.95 (Fri)/ $24.95 (Tue/Sat)
Other Games: C, R, P, BG (Wed-Sun)
Overnight RV Parking: Free/RV Dump: No
Special Features: Players club members get 20% off rooms and other discounts.

Legendary Waters Resort & Casino
37600 Onigaming Drive
Red Cliff, Wisconsin 54814
(715) 779-3712
Website: www.legendarywaters.com
Map: **#6** (70 miles E. of Duluth, MN)

Toll-Free Number: (800) 226-8478
Rooms: 40 Price Range: $90-$199
Suites: 7 Price Range: $149-$229
Restaurants: 1 Liquor: Yes
Hours: 10am-2:30am Daily
Other Game: P
Overnight RV Parking: Must use RV park
Special Features: Campground and 34-space RV park ($45 per night). 45-slip marina.

Menominee Casino Resort
N277 Highway 47/55
Keshena, Wisconsin 54135
(715) 799-3600
Website: www.menomineecasinoresort.com
Map: **#9** (40 miles N.W. of Green Bay)

Toll-Free Number: (800) 343-7778
Rooms: 100 Price Range: $112-$169
Suites: 8 Price Range: $159-$189
Restaurants: 2 Liquor: Yes
Buffets: B/L- $14.00 (Sun)
D- $17.00 (Fri)/$21.00 (Sat)
Casino Size: 33,000 Square Feet
Games Offered: C, R, P, LIR, TCP, BG, UTH, MS
Overnight RV Parking: Free/RV Dump: No
Special Features: 60-space RV park ($20 per night). Gift shop. Smoke shop. No Bingo on Tue.

Mole Lake Casino & Lodge
3084 Highway 55
Mole Lake, Wisconsin 54520
(715) 478-5290
Website: www.molelake.com
Map: **#3** (100 miles N.W. of Green Bay)

Toll-Free Number: (800) 236-9466
Lodge Rooms: 65 Price Range: $89-$109
Lodge Suites: 10 Price Range: $129-$150
Restaurants: 1 Liquor: Yes
Hours: 7am-2am/3am (Fri/Sat)
Other Games: BG (Fri-Tue)
Overnight RV Parking: Free/RV Dump: No
Special Features: Blackjack tables closed Wednesdays. Motel is two blocks from casino.

North Star Mohican Casino Resort
W12180 County Road A
Bowler, Wisconsin 54416
(715) 787-3110
Website: www.northstarcasinoresort.com
Map: **#10** (50 miles N.W. of Green Bay)

Toll-Free Number: (800) 775-2274
Rooms: 130 Price Range: $59-$119
Restaurants: 2 Liquor: Yes
Casino Size: 66,000 Square Feet
Other Games: C, R, LIR, TCP, UTH, BG (Sun/Tue-Fri)
Overnight RV Parking: Free/ RV Dump: At RV park.
Special Features: 57-space RV park ($29-$39 per night). Smoke shop. $10 freeplay with stay at RV park.

Oneida Bingo & Casino
2020 Airport Drive
Green Bay, Wisconsin 54313
(920) 494-4500
Website: www.oneidacasino.net
Map: **#12**

Toll-Free Number: (800) 238-4263
Rooms: 408 Price Range: $105-$159
Suites: 40 Price Range: $195-$449
Restaurants: 3 Liquor: Yes
Buffets: L-$12.99/$14.99 (Sat/Sun)
D-$16.99/$21.99 (Wed)
Hours: 10am-4am (Tables)/24 Hours (Slots)
Other Games: C, R, P, LIR, TCP, FCP, MB, BG
Overnight RV Parking: Free/RV Dump: No
Special Features: Two casinos. One is connected to Radisson Inn where hotel rooms are located. Free local shuttle. Smoke shop.

Oneida Casino - Mason Street
2522 W. Mason Street
Green Bay, Wisconsin 54313
(920) 494-4500
Website: www.oneidacasino.net
Map: **#12**

Toll-Free Number: (800) 238-4263
Restaurant: 2
Casino Size: 38,000 square feet
Other games: Gaming Machines Only
Overnight RV Parking: Free/RV Dump: No

Oneida Casino One-Stop Packerland
3120 S. Packerland Drive
Green Bay, Wisconsin 54303
(920) 496-5601
Website: www.oneidacasino.net
Map: **#12**

Restaurant: 1 Snack Bar Liquor: No
Casino Size: 5,000 Square Feet
Other Games: gaming machines only
Overnight RV Parking: No

Oneida Casino Travel Center
5939 Old Highway 29 Drive
Pulaski, Wisconsin 54313
(920) 865-7919
Website: www.oneidacasino.net
Map: **#12**

Restaurant: 1
Casino Size: 5,800 Square Feet
Hours: 8am-12am/2am (Fri/Sat)
Other Games: gaming machines only
Overnight RV Parking: Free/RV Dump: No

Potawatomi Carter Casino Hotel
618 Highway 32
Wabeno, Wisconsin 54566
(800) 487-9522
Website: www.cartercasino.com
Map: **#11** (85 miles N. of Green Bay)

Toll-Free Number: (800) 487-9522
Rooms: 98 Price Range: $98-$113
Suites: 10 Price Range: $190-$255
Restaurants: 2 Liquor: Yes
Casino Size: 25,000 Square Feet
Other Games: C, R, LIR, TCP, MS, UTH, BG (Wed-Sun)
Overnight RV Parking: Free. Must register with Guest Services.
Special Features: Conference space available, 24 hour gas station and convenience store located across the street

Potawatomi Hotel & Casino
1721 W. Canal Street
Milwaukee, Wisconsin 53233
(414) 645-6888
Website: www.paysbig.com
Map: **#14**

Toll-Free Number: (800) 729-7244
Rooms: 381 Price Range: $129-$239
Suites: 10 Price Range: Casino Use Only
Restaurants: 6 Liquor: Yes
Buffets: B-$18.00 (Sun) L-$15.00
D-$15.00 (Tue/Thu)/
$41.00 (Wed/Fri)/$24.00 (Sat)
Casino Size: 38,400 Square Feet
Other Games: C, R, P, PGP TCP, FCP, LIR, BG. OTB, S21, CW, B
Overnight RV Parking: Free/RV Dump: No
Special Features: Smoke-free casino on 2nd floor. No dinner buffet Sunday or Monday.

Sevenwinds Casino, Lodge & Convention Center
13767 W County Highway B
Hayward, Wisconsin 54843
(715) 634-5643
Website: www.sevenwindscasino.com
Map: **#2** (55 miles S.E. of Duluth, MN)

Toll-Free Number: (833)479-4637
Room Reservations: (800) 526-5634
Rooms: 53 Price Range: $59-$89
Suites: 22 Price Range: $80-$130
Restaurants: 2 Liquor: Yes
Buffets: B-$10.95 (Sat/Sun L-$11.95
D-$13.95/$16.95 (Fri)
Casino Size: 35,000 Square Feet
Other Games: C, R, P, BG (Tue-Fri/Sun)
Overnight RV Parking: Free (must register first at customer service)/RV Dump: No
Special Features: Nearby 8-space RV park ($25 per night). Sports lounge. Gift shop.

St. Croix Casino Danbury
30222 State Road 35 - 77
Danbury, Wisconsin 54830
(715) 656-3444
Website: www.stcroixcasino.com
Map: **#5** (26 miles E. of Hinckley, MN)

Toll-Free Number: (800) 238-8946
Rooms: 47 Price Range: $58-$199
Suites: 1 Price Range: $80
Restaurants: 1 Liquor: Yes
Buffets: B- $10.99 (Sat/Sun)/$6.99 (Fri)
L- $9.99
D- $12.99/$19.99 (Wed-Sat)
Gambling Age: 21
Casino Size: 22,500 Square Feet
Other Games: C, R
Overnight RV Parking: Must use RV park
Special Features: Craps and Roulette only offered on Friday and Saturday. 35-space RV park ($22 per night). $10 off room for players club members.

St. Croix Casino - Hertel Express
4384 State Road 70
Webster, Wisconsin 54893
(715) 349-5658
Website: www.stcroixcasino.com
Map: **#5** (26 miles E. of Hinckley, MN)

Restaurants: 1 Liquor: No
Other Games: Gaming machines only
Overnight RV Parking: Must use RV park
Special Features: Gambling age is 21. 16-space RV park ($27 per night).

St. Croix Casino - Turtle Lake
777 US Highway 8/63
Turtle Lake, Wisconsin 54889
(800) 846-8946
Website: www.stcroixcasino.com
Map: **#13** (105 miles S. of Duluth, MN)

Rooms: 153 Price Range: $85-$119
Suites: 8 Price Range: $132-$157
Restaurants: 2 Liquor: Yes
Buffets: B-$14.99 L-$7.99 D-$12.99
Gambling Age: 21
Casino Size: 95,000 Square Feet
Other Games: C, R, P
Overnight RV Parking: Must use RV park
Special Features: 20% off rooms for slot club member. 18-space RV park ($15/$25 for electricity & water per night).

WYOMING

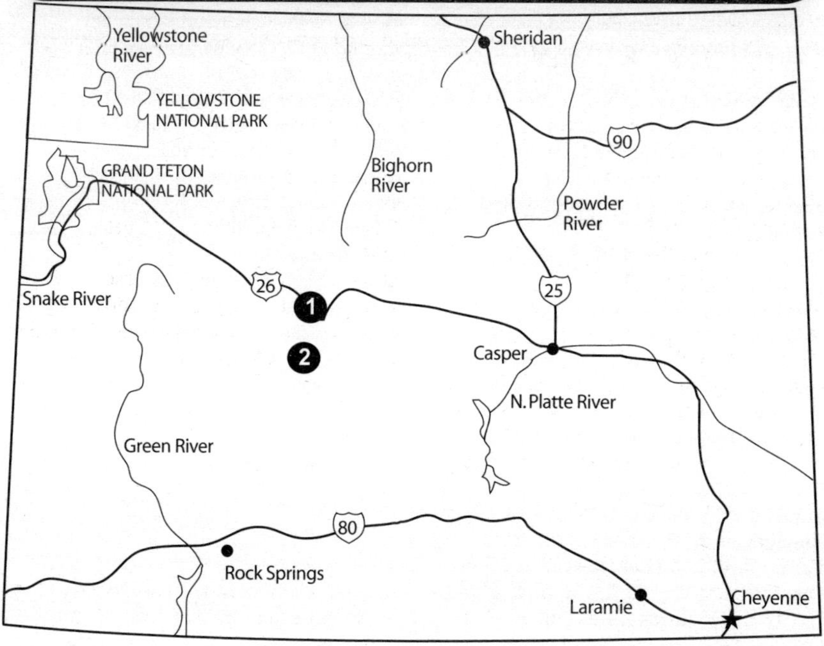

Wyoming's Indian casinos offer Class II bingo-type gaming machines, plus traditional Class III slot machines. Two of the casinos also offer some table games.

On some machines you can make bets via a cashless system whereby you get a "smart" card and deposit money to that card's account. The machines will then deducts losses from, or credit wins to, your account.

No public information is available regarding the payback percentages on Wyoming's gaming machines. Unless otherwise noted, the casinos are open 24 hours and the minimum gambling age is 18.

Sports betting is not allowed in Wyoming and there were no legislative efforts made to legalize it in 2019.

For Wyoming tourism information call (800) 225-5996 or visit their website at: www.wyomingtourism.org

789 Casino
10369 Highway 789
Riverton, Wyoming 82501
(307) 857-9451
Website: www.play789casino.com
Map: **#1** (125 miles W. of Casper)

Restaurants: 1 Liquor: No
Casino Size: 7,000 Square Feet
Other Games: Bingo
Overnight RV Parking: No
Senior Discount: Various Tue if 55+

Little Wind Casino
800 Blue Sky Highway
Ethete, Wyoming 82520
(307) 438-7000
Website: www.littlewindcasino.com
Map: **#2** (140 miles W. of Casper)

Restaurants: 1 Liquor: No
Casino Size: 1,920 Square Feet
Overnight RV Parking: Free/RV Dump: No
Senior Discount: Various on Tue if 55+
Special Features: Convenience store. Gas station.

Shoshone Rose Casino & Hotel
5690 U.S. Highway 287
Lander, Wyoming 82520
(307) 828-1975
Website: www.shoshonerose.com
Map: **#2** (140 miles W. of Casper)

Rooms: 55 Price Range: $99-$149
Suites: 5 Price Range: $229-249
Restaurants: 1 Liquor: No
Casino Size: 7,000 Square Feet
Other Games: Blackjack, Ultimate Texas Hold 'Em
Overnight RV Parking: No
Senior Discount: Various Mon if 55+

Wind River Hotel and Casino
10269 Highway 789
Riverton, Wyoming 82501
(307) 885-2600
Website: www.windrivercasino.com
Map: **#1** (125 miles W. of Casper)

Toll-Free Number: (866) 657-1604
Rooms: 80 Price Range: $85-$155
Suites: 10 Price Range: $250-$300
Restaurants: 2 Liquor: No
Other Games: Blackjack, Craps, Roulette, Poker, Three Card Poker, Ultimate Texas Hold 'Em
Casino Size: 8,000 Square Feet
Senior Discount: Various Tue if 55+
Special Features: Smoke shop. Gas station and 24-space RV park ($25/night).

Casino Index

D

E

I

J

K

T

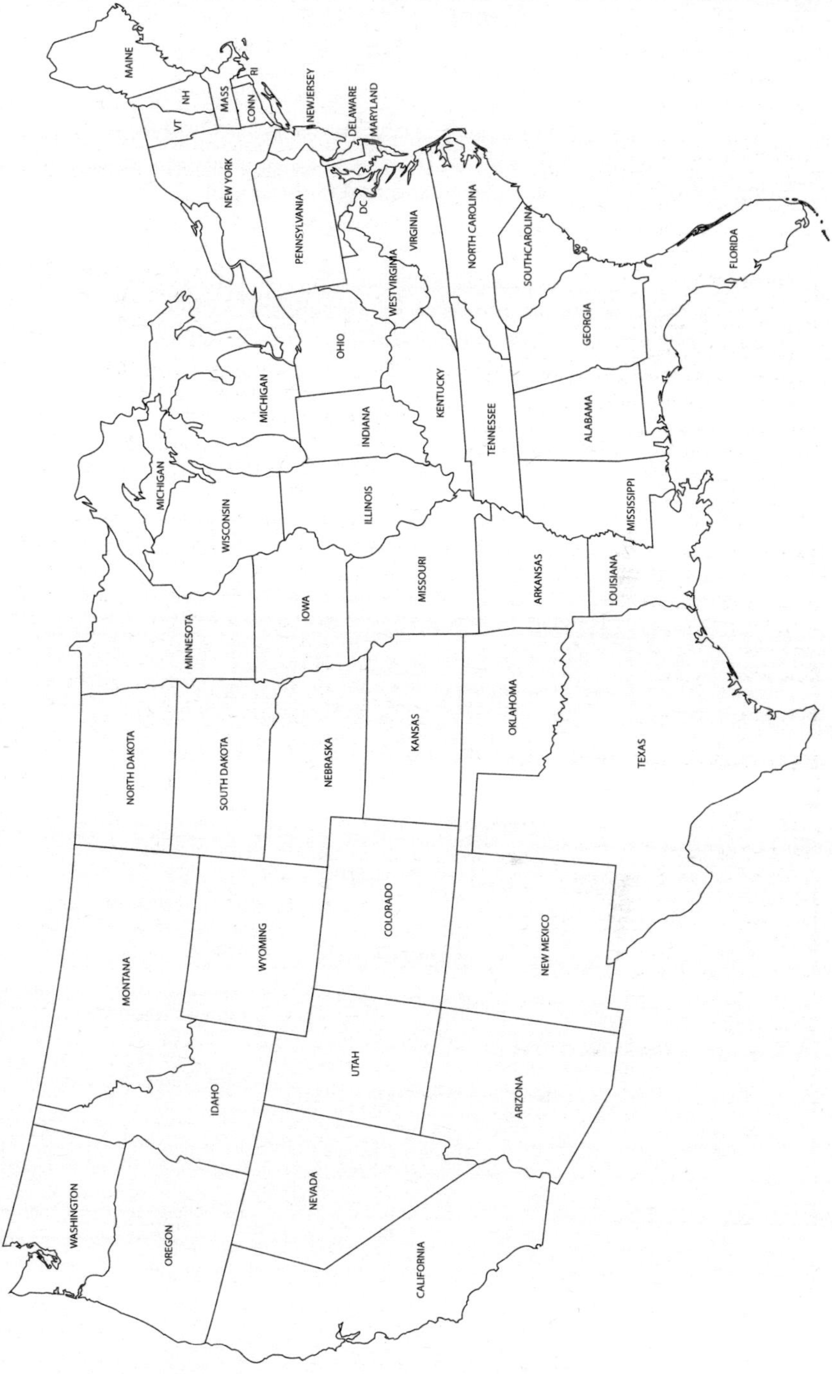
MAINE
NH
VT
MASS
CONN
RI
NEWJERSEY
DELAWARE
MARYLAND
NEW YORK
PENNSYLVANIA
DC
VIRGINIA
WESTVIRGINIA
NORTH CAROLINA
SOUTHCAROLINA
FLORIDA
GEORGIA
OHIO
MICHIGAN
KENTUCKY
TENNESSEE
ALABAMA
INDIANA
MICHIGAN
WISCONSIN
ILLINOIS
MISSISSIPPI
MISSOURI
ARKANSAS
LOUISIANA
IOWA
MINNESOTA
OKLAHOMA
TEXAS
KANSAS
NEBRASKA
SOUTH DAKOTA
NORTH DAKOTA
COLORADO
NEW MEXICO
WYOMING
MONTANA
UTAH
ARIZONA
IDAHO
NEVADA
WASHINGTON
OREGON
CALIFORNIA

Notice

Casino Vacations Press, Inc. and/or its parent or subsidiaries, will not be responsible if a participating merchant refuses to honor a coupon offer in this book. However, we will try to secure compliance. Additionally, Casino Vacations Press, Inc. and/or its parent or subsidiaries, disclaims all alleged liability, for bodily injury or property damage resulting from any accident, event or occurrence on, or resulting from the use of the premises of the participating merchants. Casino Vacations Press, Inc. and/or its parent or subsidiaries, disclaims all warranties, expressed or implied, or otherwise imposed by law, regarding the condition of those premises or the safety of same. Casino Vacations Press, Inc. and/or its parent or subsidiaries, disclaims all alleged vicarious liability for bodily injury or property damage resulting from the acts or ommissions of the participating merchants.

Coupon Directory

COUPON CHANGES

Coupon offers can change without notice.
To see a list of any coupon changes, go to:
americancasinoguidebook.com/changes.html

We will list any coupon changes on that page.

AMERICAN CASINO GUIDE

DOUBLE EAGLE
HOTEL & CASINO
CRIPPLE CREEK, CO

Play $30 Get $10 FREE!

Play $30 and receive $10 in CasinoPlay. Must be a Premier Club member. Offer expires December 31, 2020. See reverse for full details.

A current American Casino Guide Discount Card must be presented when redeeming this coupon, or offer is void

AMERICAN CASINO GUIDE

MONARCH
CASINO • BLACK HAWK

2-4-1 Lunch Buffet

Present this coupon with your Monarch Rewards card to the cashier at The Buffet and receive one free lunch buffet with the purchase of a second buffet at the regular price. See back for details.

A current American Casino Guide Discount Card must be presented when redeeming this coupon, or offer is void

AMERICAN CASINO GUIDE

Harrah's
JOLIET

Buy One Buffet Get One FREE

Present this coupon at Flavors The Buffet, along with your Caesars Rewards® card, to receive one FREE buffet with the purchase of one buffet. All ages welcome. See reverse for full details.

A current American Casino Guide Discount Card must be presented when redeeming this coupon, or offer is void

americancasinoguidebook.com

DOUBLE EAGLE
HOTEL & CASINO
CRIPPLE CREEK, CO

442 E. Bennett Avenue
Cripple Creek, CO 80813
www.decasino.com
(800) 711-7234
(719) 689-5000

Must present coupon. Limit one coupon per customer per day. Not valid for use with any other coupons, ads or promotions. Must be 21 years of age and a Premier Club Member. Membership in Premier Club is free. Management reserves the right to cancel or change this promotion at any time. Valid through December 31, 2020.

Offer void if coupon is copied or sold

americancasinoguidebook.com

MONARCH
CASINO • BLACK HAWK
P.O. Box 9 | 488 Main St.
Black Hawk, CO 80422 | 303.582.1000

Expires December 30, 2020. Valid daily. Excludes holidays or special events. No cash value. Gratuity not included. Must be 21. Not valid in combination with any other offer. Non-transferable. Management reserves all rights. Must be a Monarch Rewards member. Not a Monarch Rewards member? Join today! It's fun, it's easy, it's free.

Monarch Rewards # ________________

Offer Code #ACG2020C1

Offer void if coupon is copied or sold

americancasinoguidebook.com

Harrah's
JOLIET

151 N. Joliet Street
Joliet, IL 60432
(815) 740-7800
harrahsjoliet.com

Offer valid on cash purchases only. Valid for dine in only. Alcohol and gratuity not included. Some restrictions apply. Not valid at any other outlet. See Caesars Rewards for complete details. Valid Caesars Rewards card required. In some cases a valid government issued picture ID may also be required. Subject to rules available at venue. This offer is non-transferable, non-negotiable, subject to availability, cannot be combined with any other discount, promotion or complimentary offer. Alteration, duplication or unauthorized use voids this offer. Some blackout dates may apply. Harrah's reserves the right to change or cancel this program at any time upon IGB approval. Harrah's employees and their immediate families are not eligible. Must be 21 years or older to gamble. Know When Stop Before You Start® If you or someone you know has a gambling problem, crisis counseling and referral services can be accessed by calling 1-800-GAMBLER (1-800-426-2537). ©2019, Caesars License Company, LLC. All rights reserved. Offer expires 12/30/20.

Offer void if coupon is copied or sold

AMERICAN CASINO GUIDE

SILVER SLIPPER

Buy One Buffet Get One Free!

(or 50% off when dining alone)

Buy one lunch or dinner at Jubilee Buffet and get one free (or 50% off when dining alone). See reverse for details.

A current American Casino Guide Discount Card must be presented when redeeming this coupon, or offer is void

AMERICAN CASINO GUIDE

EIGHT75®

Free Well Drink or Domestic Beer

Get a complimentary well drink or domestic beer at EIGHT75! Valid 4pm-8pm daily. See reverse for full details.

A current American Casino Guide Discount Card must be presented when redeeming this coupon, or offer is void

AMERICAN CASINO GUIDE

HOLLYWOOD Casino® TUNICA, MS

Buy One Epic Buffet and Get One Free!

Enjoy two buffets for the price of one at Hollywood's Epic Buffet! Dine and play among movie memorabilia in an authentic Hollywood atmosphere 7 days a week! See reverse for details.

Exp: 12/31/20 #87005

A current American Casino Guide Discount Card must be presented when redeeming this coupon, or offer is void

americancasinoguidebook.com

Present this coupon to Players Services to redeem offer. Must be a Slipper Rewards member to participate. Membership is free; must be 21 years or older. Not valid on holidays or holiday weekends.

Limit one coupon, per person for the duration of the promotion. Not valid with any other offer. Management reserves all rights. Offer expires 12/24/20.

5000 South Beach Blvd.
Bay St. Louis, MS 39520
www.silverslipper-ms.com
1-866-SLIPPER

2020ACG

Offer void if coupon is copied or sold

americancasinoguidebook.com

RESORT & CASINO · BILOXI

An MGM Resorts Luxury Destination

875 Beach Boulevard
Biloxi, MS 39530
(228) 386-7111 • (888) 567-6667
www.beaurivage.com

Present this coupon to your server at EIGHT75, before ordering, to receive one FREE well drink or domestic beer. No cash value, no change given. Offer valid 4pm-8pm daily. Must be 21 years of age or older. Management reserves right to change or cancel offer at any time. Limit one coupon per person, per 30-day period. Excludes Express Comp purchases and cannot be combined with any other offers. Expires 12/15/2020.

Offer void if coupon is copied or sold

americancasinoguidebook.com

Sign up for a MyChoice® card at the Player Services Counter. MyChoice cards are free with valid, state issued ID. Then present this coupon at the Epic Buffet along with your MyChoice card to receive your buy-one-get-one-free Epic Buffet® offer. Must be 21 years of age or older to redeem.

Hollywood Casino Tunica reserves the right to modify or cancel this promotion at anytime without prior notice. Offer not valid on Friday or Saturday. This coupon cannot be combined with any other promotion. Valid only at Hollywood Casino Tunica. Not transferable. One coupon per Player account. Offer void if sold. Offer expires 12/31/20.

TUNICA, MS

1150 Casino Strip Resorts Blvd.
Tunica Resorts, MS 38664
(800) 871-0711
(662) 357-7700
hollywoodcasinotunica.com

Offer void if coupon is copied or sold

AMERICAN CASINO GUIDE

HOLLYWOOD Casino®
TUNICA, MS

Room Rates From $59 (Sun-Thu)

Special packages available! Call 1-800-871-0711 for reservations. See reverse for details.

Exp: 12/31/20

A current American Casino Guide Discount Card must be presented when redeeming this coupon, or offer is void

AMERICAN CASINO GUIDE

GRAND LODGE CASINO
AT HYATT REGENCY LAKE TAHOE

$10 FREE Slot Play

Present this coupon at the Players Advantage Club® booth, sign up for a card, or present your current card, and receive $10 in FREE slot play. See reverse for more details.

A current American Casino Guide Discount Card must be presented when redeeming this coupon, or offer is void

AMERICAN CASINO GUIDE

$10 Match Play

Present this coupon at the Backstage Pass/Bank to receive $10 in Match Play for table games. See reverse for more details.

Group 10077

A current American Casino Guide Discount Card must be presented when redeeming this coupon, or offer is void

americancasinoguidebook.com

Offer valid for American Casino Guide readers. Must be 21 years of age or older. Subject to availability. Valid for one night only, must present coupon.

Offer subject to change or cancellation at any time without prior notice. Valid only at Hollywood Casino Tunica. Not transferable. One coupon per Player account. Offer void if sold. Offer expires 12/31/20.

HOLLYWOOD Casino

TUNICA, MS

1150 Casino Strip Resorts Blvd.
Tunica Resorts, MS 38664
(800) 871-0711
(662) 357-7700

hollywoodcasinotunica.com

Offer void if coupon is copied or sold

americancasinoguidebook.com

GRAND LODGE CASINO
AT HYATT REGENCY LAKE TAHOE

111 Country Club Drive
Incline Village, NV 89451
(775) 832-1234
(800) 327-3910

Must be 21 years of age, or older. Valid once per account per calendar year. One offer per account. Management reserves the right to alter or change promotion at any time. Expires 12/31/20.

Offer void if coupon is copied or sold

americancasinoguidebook.com

Hard Rock Hotel & Casino Lake Tahoe
50 Highway 50, Stateline, NV 89449
(844) 588-7625
www.hardrockcasinolaketahoe.com

Must be a Backstage Pass member to redeem; membership is free. Present voucher to Backstage Pass/Bank to enroll. Cannot be redeemed for cash. Non-negotiable. Not valid with any other offer. Must be 21 or older, with valid ID, to redeem. No photocopies accepted. One time use. Management reserves all rights. Offer expires December 30, 2020.

Offer void if coupon is copied or sold

AMERICAN CASINO GUIDE

$10 Free Play

Present this coupon at the Backstage Pass/Bank to receive $10 in Free Slot Play. See reverse for more details.

Group 10076

A current American Casino Guide Discount Card must be presented when redeeming this coupon, or offer is void

AMERICAN CASINO GUIDE

Medley BUFFET

TWO FOR ONE BUFFET

Must be a B Connected member. Must purchase one Medley Buffet at regular price, to receive a second buffet, of equal or lesser value, for free or 50% off a single buffet. See reverse for full details.

A current American Casino Guide Discount Card must be presented when redeeming this coupon, or offer is void

AMERICAN CASINO GUIDE

Medley BUFFET

TWO FOR ONE BUFFET

Must be a B Connected member. Must purchase one Medley Buffet at regular price, to receive a second buffet, of equal or lesser value, for free or 50% off a single buffet. See reverse for full details.

A current American Casino Guide Discount Card must be presented when redeeming this coupon, or offer is void

americancasinoguidebook.com

Hard Rock Hotel & Casino Lake Tahoe
50 Highway 50, Stateline, NV 89449
(844) 588-7625
www.hardrockcasinolaketahoe.com

Must be a Backstage Pass member to redeem; membership is free. Present voucher to Backstage Pass/Bank to enroll. Cannot be redeemed for cash. Non-negotiable. Not valid with any other offer. Must be 21 or older, with valid ID, to redeem. No photocopies accepted. One time use. Management reserves all rights. Offer expires December 30, 2020.

Offer void if coupon is copied or sold

americancasinoguidebook.com

Aliante™
CASINO + HOTEL + SPA

7300 Aliante Parkway
North Las Vegas, NV 89084
702-692-7777
aliantegaming.com

Present this coupon to receive a buy one, get one free buffet at Medley Buffet or 50% off a single buffet. Must be a B Connected member. Membership is free. Gratuity not included. No cash value. Must be 21 years of age or older to redeem. Not valid with any other offer. Valid Sunday dinner, Monday through Thursday breakfast; lunch or dinner, except holidays. Present this coupon to receive a buy one, get one free buffet at Medley Buffet or 50% off a single buffet. Management reserves all rights. Expires 12/30/2020. Settle to 50045

Offer void if coupon is copied or sold

americancasinoguidebook.com

Aliante™
CASINO + HOTEL + SPA

7300 Aliante Parkway
North Las Vegas, NV 89084
702-692-7777
aliantegaming.com

Present this coupon to receive a buy one, get one free buffet at Medley Buffet or 50% off a single buffet. Must be a B Connected member. Membership is free. Gratuity not included. No cash value. Must be 21 years of age or older to redeem. Not valid with any other offer. Valid Sunday dinner, Monday through Thursday breakfast; lunch or dinner, except holidays. Present this coupon to receive a buy one, get one free buffet at Medley Buffet or 50% off a single buffet. Management reserves all rights. Expires 12/30/2020. Settle to 50045

Offer void if coupon is copied or sold

AMERICAN CASINO GUIDE

$10 MATCH PLAY

Must be a B Connected member. Present this original coupon at the Pit to redeem. No cash value. See reverse for more details.

A current American Casino Guide Discount Card must be presented when redeeming this coupon, or offer is void

AMERICAN CASINO GUIDE

Arizona Charlie's Boulder

2-For-1 Buffet

Present this coupon to the True Rewards Center at Arizona Charlie's Boulder to receive one FREE buffet when you purchase one buffet at the regular price. See reverse for details.

True Rewards card # ____________________

A current American Casino Guide Discount Card must be presented when redeeming this coupon, or offer is void

AMERICAN CASINO GUIDE

Arizona Charlie's Decatur

2-For-1 Buffet

Present this coupon to the True Rewards Center at Arizona Charlie's Decatur to receive one FREE buffet when you purchase one buffet at the regular price. See reverse for details.

True Rewards card # ____________________

A current American Casino Guide Discount Card must be presented when redeeming this coupon, or offer is void

americancasinoguidebook.com

Aliante™
CASINO + HOTEL + SPA

7300 Aliante Parkway
North Las Vegas, NV 89084
702-692-7777
aliantegaming.com

No cash value. This offer is non-transferable. One coupon per person per day. Coupon is good for one bet, win or lose. Even money table game bets and coupon only pays even money. Must be 21 years of age. Void if copied or altered. Must present B Connected card and valid photo I.D. to redeem. Valid only on Blackjack: main bets only. Roulette: outside even money bets only. Craps: pass or don't pass, and/or field. Please gamble responsibly. See Players Club for complete details. Management reserves all rights. Expires 12/30/2020.

Offer void if coupon is copied or sold

americancasinoguidebook.com

Arizona Charlie's Boulder

4575 Boulder Highway
Las Vegas, NV 89121
702.951.5800
800.362.4040
ArizonaCharliesBoulder.com

Must be 21 years of age or older. Must present True Rewards card and surrender the original coupon (no photocopies) to the True Rewards Center representative for a voucher. Resale prohibited. No cash value. Maximum two people per coupon. Not valid Tuesdays or holidays. Tax and tip are not included. Not valid for takeout. Management reserves the right to change or cancel this promotion at any time without notice.

Valid January 2 - December 19, 2020.

Offer void if coupon is copied or sold

americancasinoguidebook.com

Arizona Charlie's Decatur

740 S. Decatur Boulevard
Las Vegas, NV 89107
702.258.5200
800.342.2695
ArizonaCharliesDecatur.com

Must be 21 years of age or older. Must present True Rewards card and surrender the original coupon (no photocopies) to the True Rewards Center representative for a voucher. Resale prohibited. No cash value. Maximum two people per coupon. Not valid Tuesdays or holidays. Tax and tip are not included. Not valid for takeout. Management reserves the right to change or cancel this promotion at any time without notice.

Valid January 2 - December 19, 2020.

Offer void if coupon is copied or sold

AMERICAN CASINO GUIDE

Arizona Charlie's Decatur

$10 Match Play

Make a $10 even-money bet on blackjack or craps with this coupon and your True Rewards card and receive a $10 Match Bet! See reverse for details.

True Rewards card # ______________________

A current American Casino Guide Discount Card must be presented when redeeming this coupon, or offer is void

AMERICAN CASINO GUIDE

A current American Casino Guide Discount Card must be presented when redeeming this coupon, or offer is void

AMERICAN CASINO GUIDE

X Rocks™

2-FOR-1 TICKETS

Redeem at the Bally's Box Office for 2-for-1 tickets to X Rocks. See reverse for details.

A current American Casino Guide Discount Card must be presented when redeeming this coupon, or offer is void

americancasinoguidebook.com

Arizona Charlie's Decatur

740 S. Decatur Boulevard
Las Vegas, NV 89107
702.258.5200
800.342.2695
ArizonaCharliesDecatur.com

Make a $10 even-money bet at any blackjack or craps game, with this original coupon (no photocopies), and your True Rewards card to receive a $10 Match Bet. Good for one decision on even money bets only. Win or lose, coupon is claimed by the house. If you tie, then coupon may be re-bet. No cash value. Management reserves all rights. Valid once per account.
Valid January 2 - December 19, 2020.

Offer void if coupon is copied or sold

americancasinoguidebook.com

The Twilight Zone By Monster Mini Golf
@ Bally's, Las Vegas
Open Daily, 10AM till Midnight

Contact Information:

Address:
Bally's Hotel & Casino
3645 S. Las Vegas Blvd.
Las Vegas, NV 89109

Phone: (702) 333-2121
Email: tzone@MonsterMiniGolf.com
Website: Syfyminigolf.com

Other Locations:
KISS by Monster Mini Golf at Rio Hotel & Casino
3700 W. Flamingo Rd. Las Vegas, NV 89103
(702) 558-6256
KISS@MonsterMiniGolf.com

All other Monster Mini Golf locations visit
MonsterMiniGolf.com

Expires 12/30/20

Offer void if coupon is copied or sold

americancasinoguidebook.com

BALLY'S
LAS VEGAS

3645 Las Vegas Blvd. S.
Las Vegas, NV 89109
702-967-4111
BallysLasVegas.com
xshowslasvegas.com

Present coupon at time of purchase to redeem. Must be 18 or older. Limit 4 per coupon. No cash value. Not valid on previously purchased tickets. Cannot be combined with any other offer. Subject to availability. Blackout dates may apply. Management reserves all rights. Offer subject to change or cancellation without notification. Offer expires 12/30/20

Offer void if coupon is copied or sold

AMERICAN CASINO GUIDE

KEVIN LEPINE HYPNOSIS UNLEASHED

2-for-1 Show Tickets

Buy one general admission ticket to the Hypnosis Unleashed Show and receive a second one FREE. See reverse for more details.

A current American Casino Guide Discount Card must be presented when redeeming this coupon, or offer is void

AMERICAN CASINO GUIDE

Downtown Las Vegas Since 1951
Binion's
Gambling Hall & Hotel

Double Points (Up to 500) for members of Club Binion's

Double your Club Binion's points (up to 500) with this coupon! See reverse for more details.

A current American Casino Guide Discount Card must be presented when redeeming this coupon, or offer is void

AMERICAN CASINO GUIDE

Downtown Las Vegas Since 1951
Binion's
Gambling Hall & Hotel

2-for-1 Binion's Famous Hamburger at Binion's Café

Buy one of Binion's famous hamburgers at Binion's Café and get one FREE! See reverse for more details.

A current American Casino Guide Discount Card must be presented when redeeming this coupon, or offer is void

Downtown Las Vegas Since 1951
Binion's
Gambling Hall & Hotel

128 East Fremont St.
Las Vegas, NV 89101
800.937.6537 • 702.382.1600
www.binions.com

Show recommended for ages 18+. Must be 21 to redeem coupon. Must redeem coupon at the Binion's Gambling Hall Box Office to receive second ticket for free with purchase of one at full price. Coupon is void if altered or duplicated. Not valid with any other offers or discounts. **Show times: 8:30pm Friday-Tuesday.** Subject to availability. Management reserves the right to cancel or modify offer at any time. Coupon has no cash value. Offer expires December 31, 2020.

Offer void if coupon is copied or sold

americancasinoguidebook.com

Downtown Las Vegas Since 1951
Binion's
Gambling Hall & Hotel

128 East Fremont St.
Las Vegas, NV 89101
800.937.6537 • 702.382.1600
www.binions.com

Strictly limited to one coupon per person per 12 month period. Coupon has no cash value. Must be 21 years or older. Points must be earned on day of redemption. Offer valid for Club Binion's members only. Double points will be added to account within 48 hours. Not valid with any other offers. Management reserves the right to cancel or modify offer at any time without notice. Coupon is void if altered or duplicated. Offer expires December 27, 2020.

Offer void if coupon is copied or sold

americancasinoguidebook.com

Downtown Las Vegas Since 1951
Binion's
Gambling Hall & Hotel

128 East Fremont St.
Las Vegas, NV 89101
800.937.6537 • 702.382.1600
www.binions.com

Strictly limited to one coupon per person per 12 month period. Must be 21 years or older. Must redeem coupon at Club Binion's to receive voucher for Binion's Café. Purchase one hamburger (of equal or greater value) to receive the second one free. Offer valid only at Binion's Café. Coupon is void if altered or duplicated. Not valid on takeout orders. Tax, alcoholic beverages and gratuity are not included. Not valid with any other offers or discounts. Management reserves the right to cancel or modify offer at any time. Coupon has no cash value. Offer expires December 27, 2020.

Offer void if coupon is copied or sold

AMERICAN CASINO GUIDE

Bonanno's®
NEW YORK PIZZERIA

Buy Any Slice or Stromboli, Get One Free

Present this coupon at Bonanno's New York Pizzeria listed on the back. Purchase you choice of any slice or stromboli and receive your choice of a second one of equal or lesser value FREE. See reverse for details.

A current American Casino Guide Discount Card must be presented when redeeming this coupon, or offer is void

AMERICAN CASINO GUIDE

BOULDER STATION

2-For-1 Buffet

or 50% off when dining alone
(Monday-Thursday)

Buy one Feast Buffet and get the second Feast Buffet free (or 50% off when dining alone). Offer valid Monday-Thursday. See reverse for more details.

A current American Casino Guide Discount Card must be presented when redeeming this coupon, or offer is void

AMERICAN CASINO GUIDE

CALIFORNIA®
HOTEL CASINO LAS VEGAS

$10 Table Games Match Play

Present this original coupon and B Connected Card to the B Connected Club for a match play voucher. Voucher and equal wager of real chips or cash should be presented to the dealer. See reverse side for details.

A current American Casino Guide Discount Card must be presented when redeeming this coupon, or offer is void

americancasinoguidebook.com

MGM Grand Food Court
Luxor Food Court
Flamingo Food Court
Mandalay Bay Food Court
Venetian Hotel Grand Canal Shops

Please present coupon to cashier prior to making purchase. Offer has no cash value. Not valid with any other offer or discount. One coupon per person. Subject to change or cancellation without prior notice. Offer valid through December 31, 2020.

Offer void if coupon is copied or sold

americancasinoguidebook.com

BOULDER STATION

4111 Boulder Highway • Las Vegas, NV 89121 • (702) 432-7777
www.boulderstation.sclv.com

This voucher entitles bearer to one free breakfast, lunch or dinner in the Feast Buffet when accompanied by a cash paying guest, or 50% off when dining alone. Tax and gratuity not included. One voucher per person/subscriber. Voucher must be presented to cashier. Vouchers are not transferable and are not redeemable for cash. Must be 21 or older. Not a line pass. Not valid on holidays. Not valid with any other offer. Offer may be changed or discontinued at any time at the discretion of management. Original vouchers only. Offer is void if sold. Offer expires December 20, 2020. Settle to: #88-942

Offer void if coupon is copied or sold

americancasinoguidebook.com

CALIFORNIA
HOTEL CASINO LAS VEGAS

12 East Ogden Avenue
Las Vegas, NV 89101
(800) 634-6505
thecal.com

Must be 21 or older and have an active B Connected Card. Limit one coupon per person and limit one coupon per wager. Coupon good for play on any California casino table game. Good for one decision on even-money bets only. Win or lose, coupon is claimed by the house. If you tie then the coupon may be re-bet. This coupon has no cash value, cannot be combined with any other offer or used more than once. Reproduction, sale, barter or transfer are prohibited and render this coupon void. Management reserves the right to change or discontinue this offer without notice. Expires 12/30/20. Offer code: CAGT3Y9CX

Offer void if coupon is copied or sold

AMERICAN CASINO GUIDE

CALIFORNIA HOTEL CASINO LAS VEGAS

2-For-1 Breakfast or Lunch Buffet

(or 50% off when dining alone)

Buy one breakfast or lunch buffet and get a second one FREE (or 50% off when dining alone) at the Garden Court Buffet located at Main Street Station. Excludes holidays and Brunch buffet. Coupon has no cash value, must be 21 years of age or older. Must be a B Connected member to redeem. See reverse for full details.

A current American Casino Guide Discount Card must be presented when redeeming this coupon, or offer is void

AMERICAN CASINO GUIDE

CALIFORNIA HOTEL CASINO LAS VEGAS

MAIN STREET STATION CASINO BREWERY HOTEL

FREMONT HOTEL & CASINO

$10 Off Dining Purchase of $30 or More

Present this original coupon and B Connected Card to the B Connected Club for a $10 off voucher. Coupon has no cash value, must be 21 years of age or older. Must be a B Connected member to redeem. See reverse for full details.

A current American Casino Guide Discount Card must be presented when redeeming this coupon, or offer is void

AMERICAN CASINO GUIDE

Cannery CASINO • HOTEL

2-For-1 Buffet

Purchase one buffet at regular price and receive a second buffet of equal or lesser value free. See reverse for more details.

A current American Casino Guide Discount Card must be presented when redeeming this coupon, or offer is void

americancasinoguidebook.com

CALIFORNIA
HOTEL CASINO LAS VEGAS

12 East Ogden Avenue
Las Vegas, NV 89101
(800) 634-6505
thecal.com

Present this coupon to Garden Court Buffet cashier. Tax and Gratuity is not included. Original coupon (no photocopies) must be presented at time of purchase. This offer is not valid with any other offer or promotion and is not valid on holidays or for Brunch buffet. This offer is void if sold. Management reserves the right to change or cancel this offer at anytime. Offer expires 12/30/20. Offer code: MSFC8TSD4

Offer void if coupon is copied or sold

americancasinoguidebook.com

California Hotel Casino
12 East Ogden Avenue
Las Vegas, NV 89101
(800) 634-6505
thecal.com

Fremont Hotel & Casino
200 Fremont St
Las Vegas, NV 89101
(800) 634-6460
fremontcasino.com

Main Street Station
200 North Main Street
Las Vegas, NV 89101
(800) 713-8933
mainstreetcasino.com

Present the $10 off voucher to one of the following participating restaurants cashiers: California Noodle House, Garden Court Buffet, Lanai Express, Market Street Café, Paradise Buffet/Café, Redwood Steakhouse, Second Street Grill or Triple 7. Tax and Gratuity is not included. This offer is not valid with any other offer or promotion and is not valid on holidays. This offer is void if sold. Management reserves the right to change or cancel this offer at any time. Offer expires 12/30/20. Offer Code: FRFCX2VT9

Offer void if coupon is copied or sold

americancasinoguidebook.com

Cannery
CASINO • HOTEL

2121 E. Craig Road
N. Las Vegas, NV 89030
(702) 507-5700
(866) 999-4899
www.cannerycasino.com

Must present Players Club card, valid photo ID and coupon to cashier to redeem. Coupon has no cash value, must be 21 or older to redeem. Limit one coupon redemption per person. Excludes holidays. Cannot be combined with any other offer or discount. Valid at Cannery on Craig Road only. Management reserves all rights. Offer expires 12/30/20.

Settle to comp: 90600

Offer void if coupon is copied or sold

AMERICAN CASINO GUIDE

the D LAS VEGAS

Get out of Blackjack Hand for Free (push your bet on 22)

Redeem this coupon at Club One desk and have your bet pushed when you get a 22. Maximum $25 bet. See reverse side for full details.

A current American Casino Guide Discount Card must be presented when redeeming this coupon, or offer is void

AMERICAN CASINO GUIDE

the D LAS VEGAS

$25 Match Play

Bet $25 on any even-money bet and we'll pay you $50 if you win. Present this coupon at Club One to receive your free $25 match play. See reverse side for full details.

A current American Casino Guide Discount Card must be presented when redeeming this coupon, or offer is void

AMERICAN CASINO GUIDE

the D LAS VEGAS

Up to $100 Free Play

Earn $5 in free play for every 50 points earned on slots or video poker. Maximum bonus of $100. See reverse side for full details.

A current American Casino Guide Discount Card must be presented when redeeming this coupon, or offer is void

americancasinoguidebook.com

the D LAS VEGAS

301 E. Fremont Street
Las Vegas, NV 89101
(702) 388-2400
www.TheD.com

Voucher must be redeemed at Club One prior to play. Offer valid for blackjack only (not valid on Super Fun 21). Bonus is not paid on double downs or pair splits. Limit one offer per account per calendar year. Maximum bonus payout not to exceed $25. A minimum buy-in of $100 is required.

Valid government issued ID required to join Club One. Must be 21 or older. Membership is free. Management reserves all rights. No cash value. Offer expires December 29, 2020.

Offer void if coupon is copied or sold

americancasinoguidebook.com

the D LAS VEGAS

301 E. Fremont Street
Las Vegas, NV 89101
(702) 388-2400
www.TheD.com

Voucher must be surrendered to Club One to receive free match play offer. Good for one bet only, win or lose, (pushes play again). Limit one offer per account per calendar year.

Valid government issued ID required to join Club One. Must be 21 or older. Membership is free. Management reserves all rights. No cash value. Offer expires December 29, 2020.

Offer void if coupon is copied or sold

americancasinoguidebook.com

the D LAS VEGAS

301 E. Fremont Street
Las Vegas, NV 89101
(702) 388-2400
www.TheD.com

Voucher must be redeemed at Club One prior to play. Receive $5 free slot play for every 50 points earned up to a $100 maximum bonus. Any bonus must be redeemed within the first 24-hours of play and can be redeemed one time only. Player keeps points earned. Limit one offer per account per calendar year. Cannot be used in conjunction with Club One new member sign-up bonus.

Valid government issued ID required to join Club One. Must be 21 or older. Membership is free. Management reserves all rights. No cash value. Offer expires December 29, 2020.

Offer void if coupon is copied or sold

AMERICAN CASINO GUIDE

Marriage can be Murder
A Comedy-Murder Mystery Dinner Show!
VEGAS BORN 20 YEARS ANNIVERSARY

FRIENDS! The Musical Parody

Up to $20 Off Tickets

Present this coupon at The D box office to receive $10 off regular tickets or $20 off VIP tickets to Marriage Can Be Murder or FRIENDS! The Musical Parody. See reverse for more details.

A current American Casino Guide Discount Card must be presented when redeeming this coupon, or offer is void

AMERICAN CASINO GUIDE

DEFENDING THE CAVEMAN.
A COUPLE THAT LAUGHS TOGETHER STAYS TOGETHER

Jokesters COMEDY CLUB

2-for-1 Tickets

Buy one ticket to Defending the Caveman or Jokesters Comedy Club and get a second ticket FREE! See reverse for more details.

A current American Casino Guide Discount Card must be presented when redeeming this coupon, or offer is void

AMERICAN CASINO GUIDE

COMEDY MAGICIAN ADAM LONDON LAUGHTERNOON

$40 Off Regular Tickets

Get $40 off when purchasing regular tickets to see Adam London's Laughternoon. See reverse for more details.

A current American Casino Guide Discount Card must be presented when redeeming this coupon, or offer is void

americancasinoguidebook.com

the D LAS VEGAS

301 E. Fremont Street
Las Vegas, NV 89101
(702) 388-2400
www.TheD.com

Coupon must be redeemed at the D Las Vegas Box Office. Based on availability. Cannot be combined with other offers or discounts. No cash value. Management reserves all rights. All tickets plus tax and service fee. Expires December 31, 2020.

Offer void if coupon is copied or sold

americancasinoguidebook.com

the D LAS VEGAS

301 E. Fremont Street
Las Vegas, NV 89101
(702) 388-2400
www.TheD.com

Coupon must be redeemed at the D Las Vegas Box Office. Based on availability. Cannot be combined with other offers or discounts. No cash value. Management reserves all rights. All tickets plus tax and service fee. Expires December 31, 2020.

Offer void if coupon is copied or sold

americancasinoguidebook.com

the D LAS VEGAS

301 E. Fremont Street
Las Vegas, NV 89101
(702) 388-2400
www.TheD.com

Coupon must be redeemed at the D Las Vegas Box Office. Based on availability. Cannot be combined with other offers or discounts. No cash value. Management reserves all rights. All tickets plus tax and service fee. Expires December 31, 2020.

Offer void if coupon is copied or sold

AMERICAN CASINO GUIDE

DOWNTOWN GRAND HOTEL & CASINO

$10 Matchplay

Redeem at Grand Rewards Players Club.
See reverse for details.

A current American Casino Guide Discount Card must be presented when redeeming this coupon, or offer is void

AMERICAN CASINO GUIDE

DOWNTOWN GRAND HOTEL & CASINO

Earn 25 Points and receive $10 in Free Slot Play

Redeem at Grand Rewards Players Club.
See reverse for details.

A current American Casino Guide Discount Card must be presented when redeeming this coupon, or offer is void

AMERICAN CASINO GUIDE

DOWNTOWN GRAND HOTEL & CASINO

Buy One Get One FREE Cocktail at Furnace Bar

Redeem at Grand Rewards Players Club.
See reverse for details.

A current American Casino Guide Discount Card must be presented when redeeming this coupon, or offer is void

DOWNTOWN GRAND HOTEL & CASINO

206 N. 3rd Street
Las Vegas NV 89101
(855) DT-GRAND
www.downtowngrand.com

Must be a GRAND REWARDS member and at least 21 or older to redeem. Maximum of one (1) coupon per GRAND REWARDS member per year. Must present at GRAND REWARDS Players Club for redemption. Match bet must be given with ten dollars in cash to be played. May be used on table game's even money bets only. If won, the player will receive $20 in winnings. Coupon has no cash value and are nontransferable. Downtown Grand Hotel & Casino has the right to modify or cancel the offer at any time. Cannot be combined with any other offers. Management reserves all rights. Coupon expires 12/29/20.

DOWNTOWN GRAND HOTEL & CASINO

206 N. 3rd Street
Las Vegas NV 89101
(855) DT-GRAND
www.downtowngrand.com

Must be a GRAND REWARDS member and at least 21 or older to redeem. Maximum of one (1) coupon per GRAND REWARDS member per year. Points must be earned same day. Free Slot Play will be valid for 72 hours from time earned. Offer is non-transferable and has no cash value. Downtown Grand Hotel & Casino has the right to modify or cancel the offer at any time. Cannot be combined with any other offers. Management reserves all rights. Coupon expires 12/29/20

DOWNTOWN GRAND HOTEL & CASINO

206 N. 3rd Street
Las Vegas NV 89101
(855) DT-GRAND
www.downtowngrand.com

Must be a GRAND REWARDS member and at least 21 or older to redeem. Maximum of one (1) coupon per GRAND REWARDS member per year. Receive one (1) free drink with purchase of a drink of equal or lesser value. Valid at Furnace Bar. Gratuity not included. Downtown Grand Hotel & Casino has the right to modify or cancel the offer at any time. Cannot be combined with any other offers. Offer is non-transferable and has no cash value. Management reserves all rights. Coupon expires 12/29/20

AMERICAN CASINO GUIDE

DOWNTOWN GRAND HOTEL & CASINO

FREE Appetizer with purchase of an Entrée at Triple George Grill

Redeem at Grand Rewards Players Club.
See reverse for details.

A current American Casino Guide Discount Card must be presented when redeeming this coupon, or offer is void

AMERICAN CASINO GUIDE

Eastside Cannery CASINO · HOTEL

$15 Off at Chinese Restaurant

Present this original coupon and Players Club card to the server before ordering to receive $15 off a check total of $30, or more, excluding alcohol and tax. See reverse side for details.

A current American Casino Guide Discount Card must be presented when redeeming this coupon, or offer is void

AMERICAN CASINO GUIDE

Eastside Cannery CASINO · HOTEL

$5 Off at The Deli

Present this original coupon and Players Club card to the server before ordering to receive $5 off a check total of $10, or more, excluding alcohol and tax. See reverse side for details.

A current American Casino Guide Discount Card must be presented when redeeming this coupon, or offer is void

americancasinoguidebook.com

DOWNTOWN
GRAND
HOTEL & CASINO

206 N. 3rd Street
Las Vegas NV 89101
(855) DT-GRAND
www.downtowngrand.com

Must be a GRAND REWARDS member and at least 21 or older to redeem. Maximum of one (1) coupon per GRAND REWARDS member per year. Valid at Triple George Grill only. Free Appetizer with the purchase of an Entrée. Maximum value $15. Valid for dine-in only. Gratuity not included. Downtown Grand Hotel & Casino has the right to modify or cancel the offer at any time. Cannot be combined with any other offers. Offer is non-transferable and has no cash value. Management reserves all rights. Coupon expires 12/29/20

Offer void if coupon is copied or sold

americancasinoguidebook.com

Eastside Cannery
CASINO · HOTEL

5255 Boulder Highway
Las Vegas, Nevada 89122
(702) 856-5300
eastsidecannery.com

Limit one coupon per table. Present coupon along with Players Club card and valid photo ID to the server for redemption. Dine-in only and cannot be used in conjunction with any other offer. Original coupon (no photocopies) must be presented at time of purchase. Gratuity not included. Management reserves the right to change or cancel this offer at anytime. Expires 12/30/20. #97036

Offer void if coupon is copied or sold

americancasinoguidebook.com

Eastside Cannery
CASINO · HOTEL

5255 Boulder Highway
Las Vegas, Nevada 89122
(702) 856-5300
eastsidecannery.com

Limit one coupon per table. Present coupon along with Players Club card and valid photo ID to the server for redemption. Dine-in only and cannot be used in conjunction with any other offer. Original coupon (no photocopies) must be presented at time of purchase. Gratuity not included. Management reserves the right to change or cancel this offer at anytime. Expires 12/30/20. #97036

Offer void if coupon is copied or sold

AMERICAN CASINO GUIDE

Eastside Cannery CASINO · HOTEL

Free Breakfast at Snaps 24/7 Restaurant

Purchase an "Early to Rise" breakfast and a beverage to receive a second "Early to Rise" breakfast free. Offer valid at Eastside Cannery. See reverse side for details.

A current American Casino Guide Discount Card must be presented when redeeming this coupon, or offer is void

AMERICAN CASINO GUIDE

Eldorado℠ CASINO
HENDERSON, NEVADA

2-for-1 Entrée at Mary's Diner

(or 50% off when dining alone)

Purchase one entrée at regular price and receive a second entrée of equal or lesser value free. Dine in only. Gratuity not included. Excludes holidays. See reverse side for details.

A current American Casino Guide Discount Card must be presented when redeeming this coupon, or offer is void

AMERICAN CASINO GUIDE

Eldorado℠ CASINO
HENDERSON, NEVADA

New Members Play $10 Get $10

Present this coupon when signing up for a new Players Club card to be eligible for Play $10 and Get $10 Slot Dollars. See reverse side for details.

A current American Casino Guide Discount Card must be presented when redeeming this coupon, or offer is void

Eastside Cannery Casino · Hotel

5255 Boulder Highway
Las Vegas, Nevada 89122
(702) 856-5300
eastsidecannery.com

Limit one coupon per table. Present coupon along with Players Club Card and valid photo ID to the server for redemption. Dine-in only and cannot be used in conjunction with any other offer. Original coupon (no photocopies) must be presented at time of purchase. Management reserves the right to change or cancel this offer at anytime. Gratuity not included. Expires 12/30/20. #97036

americancasinoguidebook.com

Eldorado CASINO HENDERSON, NEVADA

140 S Water Street
Henderson, NV 89015
(702) 564-1811
www.eldoradocasino.com

Valid at Eldorado Casino only. Must be a Players Card member and show valid I.D. Must be 21 years or older. Coupon has no cash value and cannot be combined with any other offer or discount. Management reserves all rights. Expires 12/30/20.

Offer void if coupon is copied or sold

americancasinoguidebook.com

Eldorado CASINO HENDERSON, NEVADA

140 S Water Street
Henderson, NV 89015
(702) 564-1811
www.eldoradocasino.com

Must be 21 years or older and show valid I.D. Coupon is non-transferable and cannot be used with any other offer. Slot Dollars reward must be redeemed by midnight on date of issue. Unused Slot Dollars will expire in 48 hours of date issued. Expired Slot Dollars will not be replaced. Management reserves all rights. Expires 12/30/20.

Offer void if coupon is copied or sold

AMERICAN CASINO GUIDE

Eldorado CASINO
HENDERSON, NEVADA

FREE Bingo Blue Pack

Present this coupon to Bingo Agent to receive one free blue pack in Bingo. $1 Validation charge not included.

See reverse side for details.

A current American Casino Guide Discount Card must be presented when redeeming this coupon, or offer is void

AMERICAN CASINO GUIDE

ellis island
CASINO • HOTEL • BREWERY

Play $10 and get up to $100 free play

(with your Passport Players Club Card)

Play $10 on slots or video poker and get up to $100 free play. Upon playing $10 through any Ellis Island slot or video poker machine, you will be enrolled into the Spin and Win promotion. See reverse for details.

Name ____________________ PPC ____________________

A current American Casino Guide Discount Card must be presented when redeeming this coupon, or offer is void

AMERICAN CASINO GUIDE

ellis island
CASINO • HOTEL • BREWERY

Play $20 and Receive an Ellis Island T-Shirt

Present this coupon, along with your Passport Players Club Card, to the promotions booth after playing $20 to receive your exclusive limited edition t-shirt. See reverse for more details.

Name ____________________ PPC ____________________

A current American Casino Guide Discount Card must be presented when redeeming this coupon, or offer is void

americancasinoguidebook.com

Eldorado CASINO
HENDERSON, NEVADA

140 S Water Street
Henderson, NV 89015
(702) 564-1811
www.eldoradocasino.com

No purchase necessary. Must be a Players Card member and show valid I.D. Must be 21 years or older. Coupon has no cash value and cannot be combined with any other offer or discount. Management reserves all rights. Expires 12/30/20.

Offer void if coupon is copied or sold

americancasinoguidebook.com

ellis island
CASINO • HOTEL • BREWERY

4178 Koval Lane
Las Vegas, NV 89169
(702) 733-8901
www.ellisislandscasino.com

Must be playing with Passport Player's Club card, membership is free. Upon playing $10 through any slot or video poker machine, present this coupon at the Passport Players Club, you will be "Enrolled" into the spin and win promotion at the passport Central Kiosk. Participate in the promotional game where you can win $10 - $100 in Slot free play. Free play will automatically post in your account same day. Free play must be played through once to cash out. Limit one voucher per customer. One time only. No cash value. Not valid in conjunction with any other offer. Must be 21 years or older to redeem. Management reserves the right to cancel or change this offer at any time. Offer expires December 30, 2020.

Offer void if coupon is copied or sold

americancasinoguidebook.com

ellis island
CASINO • HOTEL • BREWERY

4178 Koval Lane
Las Vegas, NV 89169
(702) 733-8901
www.ellisislandscasino.com

Must be 21 years of age or older. Original coupon must be presented (no photocopies) along with your Passport Players Club Card. Membership in Passport Players Club must be in good standing. Resale prohibited. Limit one offer per calendar year per person. Management reserves the right to cancel or alter this coupon without prior notice. Offer expires 12/30/20

Offer void if coupon is copied or sold

Here is your
American Casino Guide
Discount Card.

Cut out this card
and carry it with you!

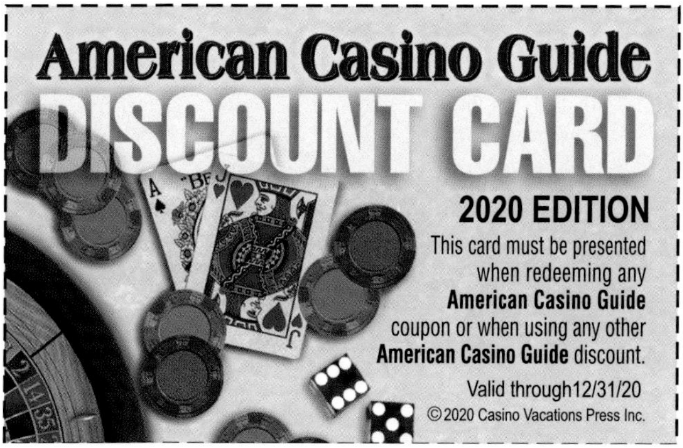

You <u>must</u> present this card to a merchant whenever you redeem an *American Casino Guide* coupon.

Do not lose this card.
No replacements will be given.

This card identifies you as the purchaser of an ***American Casino Guide*** and it entitles you to all of the benefits offered through our coupon program.

Print Name

Valid through December 31, 2020

This card ***must be presented*** when redeeming any *American Casino Guide* coupon or when using any other *American Casino Guide* discount.

AMERICAN CASINO GUIDE

ellis island
CASINO • HOTEL • BREWERY

$10 Match Play for Any Even-Money Table Game Bet

Present this coupon, along with your Passport Players Club Card, to the promotions booth to receive your $10 Match Play coupon.

See reverse for more details.

Name____________________ PPC________________

A current American Casino Guide Discount Card must be presented when redeeming this coupon, or offer is void

AMERICAN CASINO GUIDE

FIESTA
HENDERSON

2-For-1 Buffet

or 50% off when dining alone (Monday-Thursday)

Buy one Festival Buffet and get the second Festival Buffet free (or 50% off when dining alone). Offer valid Monday-Thursday.

See reverse for more details.

A current American Casino Guide Discount Card must be presented when redeeming this coupon, or offer is void

AMERICAN CASINO GUIDE

FIESTA
RANCHO

2-For-1 Buffet

or 50% off when dining alone (Monday-Thursday)

Buy one Festival Buffet and get the second Festival Buffet free (or 50% off when dining alone). Offer valid Monday-Thursday.

See reverse for more details.

A current American Casino Guide Discount Card must be presented when redeeming this coupon, or offer is void

americancasinoguidebook.com

ellis island
CASINO • HOTEL • BREWERY

4178 Koval Lane
Las Vegas, NV 89169
(702) 733-8901
www.ellisislandscasino.com

Must be 21 years of age or older. Original coupon must be presented (no photocopies) along with your Passport Players Club Card. Membership in Passport Players Club must be in good standing. Resale prohibited. Limit one offer per calendar year per person. Management reserves the right to cancel or alter this coupon without prior notice. Offer expires 12/30/20

Offer void if coupon is copied or sold

americancasinoguidebook.com

FIESTA
HENDERSON

777 W Lake Mead Pkwy
Henderson, NV 89015
(702) 558-7000
www.fiestahenderson.sclv.com

This voucher entitles bearer to one free lunch or dinner in the Festival Buffet when accompanied by a cash paying guest, or 50% off when dining alone. Tax and gratuity not included. One voucher per person/ subscriber. Voucher must be presented to cashier. Vouchers are not transferable and are not redeemable for cash. Must be 21 or older. Not a line pass. Not valid on holidays. Not valid with any other offer. Offer may be changed or discontinued at any time at the discretion of management. Original vouchers only. Offer is void if sold. Offer expires 12/20/20. Settle to: #88-942

Offer void if coupon is copied or sold

americancasinoguidebook.com

FIESTA
RANCHO

2400 N Rancho Dr
N. Las Vegas, NV 89130
(702) 631-7000
www.fiestarancho.sclv.com

This voucher entitles bearer to one free lunch or dinner in the Festival Buffet when accompanied by a cash paying guest, or 50% off when dining alone. Tax and gratuity not included. One voucher per person/ subscriber. Voucher must be presented to cashier. Vouchers are not transferable and are not redeemable for cash. Must be 21 or older. Not a line pass. Not valid on holidays. Not valid with any other offer. Offer may be changed or discontinued at any time at the discretion of management. Original vouchers only. Offer is void if sold. Offer expires 12/20/20. Settle to: #88-942

Offer void if coupon is copied or sold

AMERICAN CASINO GUIDE

Grand Canyon Helicopter Tours – Fly Below the Rim!

$75 OFF Grand Canyon West Rim Helicopter Tour

5 STAR HELICOPTER TOURS

180 Degree Panoramic Views

First Class/VIP Configuration

Mercedes-Benz Hotel Transfers

A current American Casino Guide Discount Card must be presented when redeeming this coupon, or offer is void

AMERICAN CASINO GUIDE

WORLD FAMOSO MEXICAN GRILL & FIESTA
Carlos'n Charlie's MR
LAS VEGAS

Second Round
of Frozen House Margarita free
Classic, Strawberry or Mango

Order your Frozen House Margarita, and the second round is on us. Gratuity not included. Coupon holds no cash value. Cannot be combined with another offer. Not valid if reproduced. Any attempts to sell or auction shall nullify this offer. Management reserves all rights. Must present offer at the time of order.

A current American Casino Guide Discount Card must be presented when redeeming this coupon, or offer is void

AMERICAN CASINO GUIDE

Jimmy Buffett's MARGARITAVILLE.
LAS VEGAS

Buy One
Who's To Blame Margarita
Get One FREE!

Present this coupon to your server, before ordering, and receive two Who's To Blame Margaritas for the price of one. See reverse for details.

A current American Casino Guide Discount Card must be presented when redeeming this coupon, or offer is void

americancasinoguidebook.com

Ask about our Extended Air Tour or our 30 min, 1 hour and 2 Hour Landing and Adventure Tours.

Grand Canyon West Rim

$75 OFF!

Secure your seats NOW!
Call 7a-10p, mention "ACG"
5StarHelicopterTours.com

5 STAR Grand Canyon West Rim Helicopter Tours Include:

- ★ *Luxury Mercedes-Benz Motorcoach Hotel Pickup*
- ★ *Complimentary Refreshments at Our Air Terminal*
- ★ *Luxurious State-of-the-Art Jet Helicopters*
- ★ *All Forward-facing Leather Seats with 180° Panoramic Views*
- ★ *Narrated Pilot Commentary and In-flight Music*

702-565-7827

All Tours Include Luxury Mercedes-Benz Las Vegas Area Hotel Pickup & Drop-off!

Must mention CODE "ACG" at time of booking to receive discount. Must call direct. Not valid with any other offer or discount.
Copyright © 5 STAR Grand Canyon Helicopter Tours, LLC. FAA Certified Air Carrier No. 5S9A1230. Follow us on

Offer expires 12/30/20

Offer void if coupon is copied or sold

americancasinoguidebook.com

WORLD FAMOSO MEXICAN GRILL & FIESTA
Carlos'n Charlie's MR
LAS VEGAS

3555 Las Vegas Blvd. South Las Vegas, NV, 89109. Caesars Entertainment License Company, LLC, Ph (702) 522 9254.
Inside the Flamingo Hotel
www.carlosncharlieslv.com

Must be 21 or older to gamble. Know When To Stop Before You Start. ®Gambling Problem? Call 1-800-522-4700. ©2012, Caesars Entertainment License Company, LLC. Expiration date of 12/30/20.

Offer void if coupon is copied or sold

americancasinoguidebook.com

Jimmy Buffett's MARGARITAVILLE®
LAS VEGAS

Located at The Flamingo
3555 Las Vegas Blvd. S.
Las Vegas, NV 89109
702-733-3302
www.margaritaville.com

Coupon must be presented upon ordering. Must be 21 or older. Gratuity not included. Limit one per person. Coupon has no cash value. May not be combined with any other offer. Management reserves all rights. Expires 12/29/20.

Offer Code: BOGOMACG

Offer void if coupon is copied or sold

AMERICAN CASINO GUIDE

Uno
salon • barber
blow dry bar

$10 Off Any Service of $50 or More

Redeem at the Uno Salon at the Flamingo Las Vegas for $10 off any service of $50 or more. See reverse for details.

A current American Casino Guide Discount Card must be presented when redeeming this coupon, or offer is void

AMERICAN CASINO GUIDE

4 QUEENS HOTEL • CASINO LAS VEGAS

Double Points (Up to 500) for members of the Royal Players Club™

Double your Royal Players Club™ points (up to 500) with this coupon! See reverse for more details.

A current American Casino Guide Discount Card must be presented when redeeming this coupon, or offer is void

AMERICAN CASINO GUIDE

4 QUEENS HOTEL • CASINO LAS VEGAS

2-for-1 Lunch or Dinner Entrée in Magnolia's

Buy one lunch or dinner entrée in Magnolia's and get one entrée FREE! See reverse for more details.

A current American Casino Guide Discount Card must be presented when redeeming this coupon, or offer is void

americancasinoguidebook.com

Flamingo
FOREVER FABULOUS

3555 Las Vegas Blvd. S.
Las Vegas, NV 89109
702-733-3111
Flamingo.com

Limit 1 coupon per guest. No cash value. Not valid on previously purchased services. Cannot be combined with any other offer. Subject to availability. Blackout dates may apply. Management reserves all rights. Offer subject to change or cancellation without notification. Offer expires 12/30/20.

Offer void if coupon is copied or sold

americancasinoguidebook.com

4 QUEENS
HOTEL • CASINO
LAS VEGAS

202 Fremont Street
Las Vegas, NV 89101
(702) 385-4011
(800) 634-6045
www.fourqueens.com

Strictly limited to one coupon per person per 12 month period. Coupon has no cash value. Must be 21 years or older. Points must be earned on day of redemption. Offer valid for Royal Players Club™ members only. Double points will be added to account within 48 hours. Management reserves the right to cancel or modify offer at any time without notice. Not valid with any other offer. Coupon is void if altered or duplicated. Offer expires December 27, 2020.

Offer void if coupon is copied or sold

americancasinoguidebook.com

4 QUEENS
HOTEL • CASINO
LAS VEGAS

202 Fremont Street
Las Vegas, NV 89101
(702) 385-4011
(800) 634-6045
www.fourqueens.com

Strictly limited to one coupon per person per 12 month period. Must be 21 years or older. Must redeem coupon at the Royal Players Club to receive voucher for Magnolia's. Purchase one lunch or dinner entrée (equal or greater value) to receive the second one free. Offer valid only in Magnolia's. Coupon is void if altered or duplicated. Not valid on takeout orders. Tax, alcoholic beverages and gratuity are not included. Not valid with any other offers or discounts. Management reserves the right to cancel or modify offer at any time. Coupon has no cash value. Offer expires December 27, 2020.

Offer void if coupon is copied or sold

AMERICAN CASINO GUIDE

Mike Hammer Show

comedy & magic

2-for-1 Show Tickets

Buy one ticket to the Mike Hammer Comedy Magic Show and receive a second one FREE.

See reverse for more details.

A current American Casino Guide Discount Card must be presented when redeeming this coupon, or offer is void

AMERICAN CASINO GUIDE

Spirit of the King

Elvis Tribute Show

2-for-1 Show Tickets

Buy one ticket to the Spirit of the King Elvis Tribute Show and receive a second one FREE.

See reverse for more details.

A current American Casino Guide Discount Card must be presented when redeeming this coupon, or offer is void

AMERICAN CASINO GUIDE

FREMONT HOTEL & CASINO

$10 Table Games Match Play

Present this original coupon and B Connected Card to the B Connected Club for a match play voucher. Voucher and equal wager of real chips or cash should be presented to the dealer.

See reverse side for details.

A current American Casino Guide Discount Card must be presented when redeeming this coupon, or offer is void

americancasinoguidebook.com

4 QUEENS HOTEL • CASINO LAS VEGAS

202 Fremont Street
Las Vegas, NV 89101
(877) 935-2844
mikehammershow.com

Show open to ages 13+. Must be 21 to redeem coupon.Must redeem coupon at the Four Queens Box Office to receive second ticket for free with purchase of one at full price. Coupon is void if altered or duplicated. Tax and box office fees are not included. Not valid with any other offers or discounts. **Show times: 7pm Tuesday-Saturday.** Subject to availability. Management reserves the right to cancel or modify offer at any time. Coupon has no cash value. Offer expires December 29, 2020.

Offer void if coupon is copied or sold

americancasinoguidebook.com

4 QUEENS HOTEL • CASINO LAS VEGAS

202 Fremont Street
Las Vegas, NV 89101
(877) 935-2844
mikehammershow.com

Show open to ages 13+. Must be 21 to redeem coupon.Must redeem coupon at the Four Queens Box Office to receive second ticket for free with purchase of one at full price. Coupon is void if altered or duplicated. Tax and box office fees are not included. Not valid with any other offers or discounts. **Show times: 9pm Tuesday-Saturday**. Subject to availability. Management reserves the right to cancel or modify offer at any time. Coupon has no cash value. Offer expires December 29, 2020.

Offer void if coupon is copied or sold

americancasinoguidebook.com

FREMONT HOTEL & CASINO

200 Fremont St
Las Vegas, NV 89101
(800) 634-6460
fremontcasino.com

Must be 21 or older and have an active B Connected Card. Limit one coupon per person and limit one coupon per wager. Coupon good for play on any Fremont casino table game. Good for one decision on even-money bets only. Win or lose, coupon is claimed by the house. If you tie then the coupon may be re-bet. This coupon has no cash value, cannot be combined with any other offer or used more than once. Reproduction, sale, barter or transfer are prohibited and render this coupon void. Management reserves the right to change or discontinue this offer without notice. Expires 12/30/20. Offer code: FRGTVP2M2

Offer void if coupon is copied or sold

AMERICAN CASINO GUIDE

FREMONT HOTEL & CASINO

2-For-1 Breakfast or Lunch Buffet

(or 50% off when dining alone)

Buy one breakfast or lunch buffet and get a second one FREE (or 50% off when dining alone) at the Paradise Buffet located at Fremont. Excludes holidays and Brunch buffet. Coupon has no cash value, must be 21 years of age or older. Must be a B Connected member to redeem. See reverse for full details.

A current American Casino Guide Discount Card must be presented when redeeming this coupon, or offer is void

AMERICAN CASINO GUIDE

CALIFORNIA HOTEL CASINO LAS VEGAS

MAIN STREET STATION CASINO BREWERY HOTEL

FREMONT HOTEL & CASINO

$10 Off Dining Purchase of $30 or More

Present this original coupon and B Connected Card to the B Connected Club for a $10 off voucher. Coupon has no cash value, must be 21 years of age or older. Must be a B Connected member to redeem. See reverse for full details.

A current American Casino Guide Discount Card must be presented when redeeming this coupon, or offer is void

AMERICAN CASINO GUIDE

GAMBLERS GENERAL STORE

THE WORLD'S LARGEST GAMBLING SUPERSTORE! OPEN 7 DAYS A WEEK!

PERSONALIZED POKER CHIPS • CARDS • ROULETTE • BLACKJACK • CRAPS
GAMBLING TABLES • RAFFLE DRUMS • AWARD WHEELS • BOOKS • VIDEOS

10% Off Your Purchase!

Save 10% on your order from the largest Gambling Superstore in the world! We are located in Las Vegas, Nevada and offer genuine casino quality gaming products that can be used in casinos, homes, offices or parties.

A current American Casino Guide Discount Card must be presented when redeeming this coupon, or offer is void

FREMONT HOTEL & CASINO

200 Fremont St
Las Vegas, NV 89101
(800) 634-6460
fremontcasino.com

Present this coupon to Paradise Buffet cashier. Tax and Gratuity not included. Original coupon (no photocopies) must be presented at time of purchase. This offer is not valid with any other offer or promotion and is not valid on holidays or for Brunch buffet. This offer is void if sold. Management reserves the right to change or cancel this offer at anytime. Offer expires 12/30/20. Offer code: FRFCX2VT9

Offer void if coupon is copied or sold

americancasinoguidebook.com

California Hotel Casino	Main Street Station	Fremont Hotel & Casino
12 East Ogden Avenue	200 North Main Street	200 Fremont St
Las Vegas, NV 89101	Las Vegas, NV 89101	Las Vegas, NV 89101
(800) 634-6505	(800) 713-8933	(800) 634-6460
thecal.com	mainstreetcasino.com	fremontcasino.com

Present the $10 off voucher to one of the following participating restaurants cashiers: California Noodle House, Garden Court Buffet, Lanai Express, Market Street Café, Paradise Buffet/Café, Redwood Steakhouse, Second Street Grill or Triple 7. Tax and Gratuity is not included. This offer is not valid with any other offer or promotion and is not valid on holidays. This offer is void if sold. Management reserves the right to change or cancel this offer at any time. Offer expires 12/30/20. Offer Code: FRFCX2VT9

Offer void if coupon is copied or sold

americancasinoguidebook.com

9:00AM-5:30PM
Monday-Saturday
9:00AM-4:30PM
Sunday

Call: (702) 382-9903 or (800) 522-1777

727 South Main Street Las Vegas, Nevada 89101

Email: info@ggslv.com **Web: gamblersgeneralstore.com**

Limit one coupon per order. Not valid with any other offer. Must present coupon at store, or mention code "ACG" when ordering by telephone or on our website. Valid through 12/31/20.

Offer void if coupon is copied or sold

AMERICAN CASINO GUIDE

GOLD COAST®
HOTEL & CASINO · LAS VEGAS

2-For-1 Buffet

(or 50% off when dining alone)

2 for 1 Buffet or 50% off when dining alone. Must be a B Connected Member. Present this coupon to cashier to redeem. See reverse for complete details.

A current American Casino Guide Discount Card must be presented when redeeming this coupon, or offer is void

AMERICAN CASINO GUIDE

GOLD COAST®
HOTEL & CASINO · LAS VEGAS

Get $20 off when you spend $40 in Cornerstone

Present this coupon to your server, before ordering, to get $20 off any check total of $40 or more at Cornerstone, the Classic American Steakhouse. See reverse for details.

A current American Casino Guide Discount Card must be presented when redeeming this coupon, or offer is void

AMERICAN CASINO GUIDE

GOLD COAST®
HOTEL & CASINO · LAS VEGAS

$10 Match Play

Present this original coupon and B Connected Card to the B Connected Club for a match play voucher. Voucher and equal wager of real chips or cash should be presented to the dealer. See reverse side for details.

A current American Casino Guide Discount Card must be presented when redeeming this coupon, or offer is void

americancasinoguidebook.com

GOLD COAST
HOTEL & CASINO · LAS VEGAS

Gold Coast Hotel & Casino
4000 W. Flamingo Road
Las Vegas, NV 89103
(702) 367-7111 • (800) 331-5334
www.goldcoastcasino.com

Must be 21 or older and an active B Connected member. Not valid on holidays. Limit one coupon per person. This coupon has no cash value, cannot be combined with any other offer or used more than once. Reproduction, sale, barter, or transfer are prohibited and render this coupon void. Management reserves the right to change or discontinue this offer without notice. Expires 12/30/20.

Offer void if coupon is copied or sold

americancasinoguidebook.com

GOLD COAST
HOTEL & CASINO · LAS VEGAS

Gold Coast Hotel & Casino
4000 W. Flamingo Road
Las Vegas, NV 89103
(702) 367-7111 • (800) 331-5334
www.goldcoastcasino.com

Must present B Connected Card with valid ID to redeem. B Connected membership is free. Dining area only. $20 dining credit applied to minimum check total of $40 or more. Valid through December 30, 2020. Excludes holidays. Limit one offer per check. Cannot be combined with any other offer. Gratuity not included. Must be 21 years or older to redeem.

Offer void if coupon is copied or sold

americancasinoguidebook.com

GOLD COAST
HOTEL & CASINO · LAS VEGAS

Gold Coast Hotel & Casino
4000 W. Flamingo Road
Las Vegas, NV 89103
(702) 367-7111 • (800) 331-5334
www.goldcoastcasino.com

Must be 21 or older and have an active B Connected Card. Limit one coupon per person and limit one coupon per wager. Coupon good for play on any Gold Coast casino table game but excludes live poker. Good for one decision on even-money bets only. Win or lose, coupon is claimed by the house. If you tie then the coupon may be re-bet. This coupon has no cash value, cannot be combined with any other offer or used more than once. Reproduction, sale, barter or transfer are prohibited and render this coupon void. Management reserves the right to change or discontinue this offer without notice. Expires 12/30/20.

Offer void if coupon is copied or sold

AMERICAN CASINO GUIDE

GOLDEN GATE
HOTEL & CASINO

Up to $100 Free Play

Earn $5 in free play for every 50 points earned on slots or video poker. Maximum bonus of $100. See reverse side for full details.

A current American Casino Guide Discount Card must be presented when redeeming this coupon, or offer is void

AMERICAN CASINO GUIDE

GOLDEN GATE
HOTEL & CASINO

$25 Match Play

Bet $25 on any even-money bet and we'll pay you $50 if you win. Present this coupon at Club One to receive your free $25 match play. See reverse side for full details.

A current American Casino Guide Discount Card must be presented when redeeming this coupon, or offer is void

AMERICAN CASINO GUIDE

GOLDEN NUGGET®

2-FOR-1 TICKETS

Redeem at the Golden Nugget Box Office for 2-for-1 tickets to the 52 Fridays concert series. See reverse for details.

A current American Casino Guide Discount Card must be presented when redeeming this coupon, or offer is void

americancasinoguidebook.com

GOLDEN GATE
HOTEL & CASINO

One Fremont Street
Las Vegas, NV 89101
(702) 385-1906
Reservations (800) 426-1906

Voucher must be redeemed at Club One prior to play. Receive $5 free slot play for every 50 points earned up to a $100 maximum bonus. Any bonus must be redeemed within the first 24-hours of play and can be redeemed one time only. Player keeps points earned. Limit one offer per account per calendar year. Cannot be used in conjunction with Club One new member sign-up bonus.

Valid government issued ID required to join Club One. Must be 21 or older. Membership is free. Management reserves all rights. No cash value. Offer expires December 29, 2020.

Offer void if coupon is copied or sold

americancasinoguidebook.com

GOLDEN GATE
HOTEL & CASINO

One Fremont Street
Las Vegas, NV 89101
(702) 385-1906
Reservations (800) 426-1906

Voucher must be surrendered to Club One to receive free match play offer. Good for one bet only, win or lose, (pushes play again). Limit one offer per account per calendar year.

Valid government issued ID required to join Club one. Must be 21 or older. Membership is free. Management reserves all rights. No cash value. Offer expires December 29, 2020.

Offer void if coupon is copied or sold

americancasinoguidebook.com

GOLDEN NUGGET®

129 East Fremont St
Las Vegas, NV 89101
702-385-7111
GoldenNugget.com

Visit the Box Office for redemption. Offer valid for one free ticket to the 52 Fridays Concert Series with the purchase of a second ticket of equal or greater value. Full tax and service fee will be applied to both tickets. Not valid with any other offers, on previously purchased tickets, or on Golden Circle seating. Based on availability and may be discontinued for any show without notice. Not valid 12/4 & 12/11. Management reserves the right to alter or cancel this promotion at any time. Expires 12/31/20. Promo Code: ACG20

Offer void if coupon is copied or sold

AMERICAN CASINO GUIDE

GVR
GREEN VALLEY RANCH™

2-For-1 Buffet

or 50% off when dining alone (Monday or Tuesday)

Buy one Feast Buffet and get the second Feast Buffet free (or 50% off when dining alone). Offer valid Monday or Tuesday.

See reverse for more details.

A current American Casino Guide Discount Card must be presented when redeeming this coupon, or offer is void

AMERICAN CASINO GUIDE

Häagen-Dazs®

Buy One Get One Free

Present this coupon at any Haagen Dazs shop listed on the back. Purchase your choice of any menu item and receive your choice of a second menu item of equal or lesser value free!

A current American Casino Guide Discount Card must be presented when redeeming this coupon, or offer is void

AMERICAN CASINO GUIDE

JERRY'S NUGGET CASINO

$10 Table Games Match Play

Redeem at The MoreClub and receive a $10 table games match play. See reverse for details.

A current American Casino Guide Discount Card must be presented when redeeming this coupon, or offer is void

americancasinoguidebook.com

GVR

GREEN VALLEY RANCH™

2300 Paseo Verde Pkwy
Las Vegas, NV 89052
(702) 617-7777
www.greenvalleyranch.sclv.com

This voucher entitles bearer to one free breakfast, lunch or dinner in the Feast Buffet when accompanied by a full price, cash paying guest, or 50% off when dining alone. Not valid with any Boarding Pass discounts or comps. Tax and gratuity not included. One voucher per person/subscriber. Voucher must be presented to cashier. Vouchers are not transferable and are not redeemable for cash. Not a line pass. Not valid on holidays. Not valid with any other offer. Offer may be changed or discontinued at any time at the discretion of management. Original vouchers only. Offer is void if sold. Offer expires 12/19/20. Settle to: #88-942

Offer void if coupon is copied or sold

americancasinoguidebook.com

MGM Grand Hotel - Food Court
New York New York Hotel

Please present coupon to cashier prior to making purchase. Offer has no cash value. Not valid with any other offer or discount. One coupon per person. Subject to change or cancellation without prior notice. Offer valid through December 31, 2020.

Offer void if coupon is copied or sold

americancasinoguidebook.com

JERRY'S NUGGET CASINO

1821 Las Vegas Boulevard North
N. Las Vegas, NV 89030
(702) 399-3000 • www.jerrysnugget.com

Limit one coupon per customer from January 1, 2020 thru December 31, 2020. Must be a MoreClub member. MoreClub membership is free. Present original coupon to The MoreClub and receive a $10 table games match play. No photocopies will be honored. A $10 minimum bet is required. Match play surrendered after first hand. Good for one hand, one wager. Player rating required at time of play. Cannot be redeemed for cash. Not valid with any other offer. Must be 21 years of age or older to redeem. Management reserves all rights. Offer expires December 31, 2020.

Offer void if coupon is copied or sold

AMERICAN CASINO GUIDE

JERRY'S NUGGET CASINO

$10 Bingo Bucks added to $10 Required Bingo Buy-In

Redeem at The MoreClub and receive $10 bingo bucks added to your $10 bingo buy-in. See reverse for details.

A current American Casino Guide Discount Card must be presented when redeeming this coupon, or offer is void

AMERICAN CASINO GUIDE

JERRY'S NUGGET CASINO

$10 Free Slot Play

Redeem at The MoreClub and receive $10 free slot play. See reverse for details.

A current American Casino Guide Discount Card must be presented when redeeming this coupon, or offer is void

AMERICAN CASINO GUIDE

Johnny Rockets THE ORIGINAL HAMBURGER

FREE Milkshake With Purchase

Present this coupon at any Johnny Rockets listed on the back. Purchase any burger and receive a milkshake FREE! Applies to Non-alcoholic milkshakes only. See reverse for details.

A current American Casino Guide Discount Card must be presented when redeeming this coupon, or offer is void

JERRY'S NUGGET CASINO

1821 Las Vegas Boulevard North
N. Las Vegas, NV 89030
(702) 399-3000 • www.jerrysnugget.com

Limit one coupon per customer from January 1, 2020 thru December 31, 2020. Must be a MoreClub member. MoreClub membership is free. Present original coupon to The MoreClub and receive $10 bingo bucks at the Jerry's Nugget Bingo Hall with $10 bingo buy-in. No photocopies will be honored. Valid for one bingo session. Minimum $10 bingo buy-in required. Cannot be redeemed for cash. Not valid with any other offer. Must be 21 years of age or older to redeem. Management reserves all rights. Offer expires December 31, 2020.

JERRY'S NUGGET CASINO

1821 Las Vegas Boulevard North
N. Las Vegas, NV 89030
(702) 399-3000 • www.jerrysnugget.com

Limit one coupon per customer from January 1, 2020 thru December 31, 2020. Must be a MoreClub member. MoreClub membership is free. Present original coupon to The MoreClub to receive $10 free slot play. No photo copies will be honored. Free slot play will be activated when you play at any eligible game. Free slot play valid for 48 hours. Cannot be redeemed for cash. Not valid with any other offer. Must be 21 years of age or older to redeem. Management reserves all rights. Offer expires December 31, 2020.

Fashion Show Mall • Bally's Hotel & Casino
Venetian Hotel Grand Canal Shops • Luxor Food Court
Excalibur Hotel Casino • Mandalay Bay Food Court
Flamingo Hotel Food Court • MGM Grand Food Cour

Please present coupon to cashier prior to making purchase. Does not apply to alcoholic milkshakes. Offer has no cash value. Not valid with any other offer or discount. One coupon per person. Subject to change or cancellation without prior notice. Offer valid through December 31, 2020.

AMERICAN CASINO GUIDE

Johnny Rockets THE ORIGINAL HAMBURGER

Buy One Get One Free

Present this coupon at any Johnny Rockets listed on the back. Purchase your choice of any menu item and receive your choice of a second menu item of equal or lesser value FREE! See reverse for details.

A current American Casino Guide Discount Card must be presented when redeeming this coupon, or offer is void

AMERICAN CASINO GUIDE

JOKER WILD CASINO HENDERSON, NEVADA

2-for-1 Entrée at the Court Cafe

(or 50% off when dining alone)

Purchase one entrée at regular price and receive a second entrée of equal or lesser value free. Dine in only. Gratuity not included. Excludes holidays. See reverse side for details.

A current American Casino Guide Discount Card must be presented when redeeming this coupon, or offer is void

AMERICAN CASINO GUIDE

JOKER WILD CASINO HENDERSON, NEVADA

Up to $10 Match Play

Present this coupon to the dealer at the Pit to receive your match play bet. See reverse side for details.

A current American Casino Guide Discount Card must be presented when redeeming this coupon, or offer is void

americancasinoguidebook.com

Fashion Show Mall • Bally's Hotel & Casino
Venetian Hotel Grand Canal Shops • Luxor Food Court
Excalibur Hotel Casino • Mandalay Bay Food Court
Flamingo Hotel Food Court • MGM Grand Food Court

Please present coupon to cashier prior to making purchase. Offer has no cash value. Not valid with any other offer or discount. One coupon per person. Subject to change or cancellation without prior notice. Offer valid through December 31, 2020.

Offer void if coupon is copied or sold

americancasinoguidebook.com

JOKERS WILD® CASINO
HENDERSON, NEVADA

920 N Boulder Hwy
Henderson, NV 89011
(702) 564-1811
www.jokerswildcasino.com

Valid at Jokers Wild Casino only. Must be a Players Card member and show valid I.D. Must be 21 years or older. Coupon has no cash value and cannot be combined with any other offer or discount. Management reserves all rights. Expires 12/30/20.

Offer void if coupon is copied or sold

americancasinoguidebook.com

JOKERS WILD® CASINO
HENDERSON, NEVADA

920 N Boulder Hwy
Henderson, NV 89011
(702) 564-1811
www.jokerswildcasino.com

Valid at Jokers Wild Casino only. Must be a Players Card member and show valid I.D. Must be 21 years or older. Coupon has no cash value and cannot be combined with any other offer. Even money bets only. Management reserves all rights. Expires 12/30/20.

Offer void if coupon is copied or sold

AMERICAN CASINO GUIDE

JOKERS WILD CASINO
HENDERSON, NEVADA

New Members Play $10 Get $10

Present this coupon when signing up for a new Players Club card to be eligible for Play $10 and Get $10 Slot Dollars.

See reverse side for details.

A current American Casino Guide Discount Card must be presented when redeeming this coupon, or offer is void

AMERICAN CASINO GUIDE

KLONDIKE CASINO

Earn 1,000 Points and Receive $20 Free Slot Play

Earn 1,000 points in one day and receive $20 in free slot play.

See reverse for more details.

A current American Casino Guide Discount Card must be presented when redeeming this coupon, or offer is void

AMERICAN CASINO GUIDE

KLONDIKE CASINO

2-for-1 Entrée at Sarah's Kitchen

(With Purchase of 2 drinks)

Buy one entrée at Sarah's Kitchen and receive another one FREE with the purchase of any two beverages.

See reverse for more details.

A current American Casino Guide Discount Card must be presented when redeeming this coupon, or offer is void

americancasinoguidebook.com

JOKER WILD CASINO
HENDERSON, NEVADA

920 N Boulder Hwy
Henderson, NV 89011
(702) 564-1811
www.jokerswildcasino.com

Must be 21 years or older and show valid I.D. Coupon is non-transferable and cannot be used with any other offer. Slot Dollars reward must be redeemed by midnight on date of issue. Unused Slot Dollars will expire in 48 hours of date issued. Expired Slot Dollars will not be replaced. Management reserves all rights. Expires 12/30/20.

Offer void if coupon is copied or sold

americancasinoguidebook.com

KLONDIKE CASINO

Klondike Sunset Casino
444 W. Sunset Rd.
Henderson, NV 89011
702.826.3866
www.klondikesunset.com

Must be 21 years of age or older and present a valid photo ID. Must be a Player's Card member or sign up as a new member to receive offer. Player's Club membership is free. Not valid on machine marked as non-promotional. Valid one time only. No cash value. Management reserves all rights. Expires 12/31/20

Offer void if coupon is copied or sold

americancasinoguidebook.com

KLONDIKE CASINO

Klondike Sunset Casino
444 W. Sunset Rd.
Henderson, NV 89011
702.826.3866
www.klondikesunset.com

This coupon entitles bearer to one free entrée in Sarah's Kitchen at the Klondike Sunset Casino with the purchase of an equal or greater value entrée. Tax and gratuity not included. One voucher per guest. Non-transferrable. No Cash Value. Cannot be combined with any other coupon or offer. Management reserves all rights. Must be 21 or older. Expires 12/31/2020.

Offer void if coupon is copied or sold

AMERICAN CASINO GUIDE

L.A. SUBS and Salads

Buy One Get One Free

Present this coupon at any L.A. Subs, purchase your choice of any sub sandwich or salad and get a second sub sandwich or salad of equal or lesser value free! See reverse for details.

A current American Casino Guide Discount Card must be presented when redeeming this coupon, or offer is void

AMERICAN CASINO GUIDE

ameriCAN beer & cocktails

2-For-1 Cocktail

Present this coupon at ameriCAN to receive two well cocktails for the price of one before 9 p.m. See reverse for details.

A current American Casino Guide Discount Card must be presented when redeeming this coupon, or offer is void

AMERICAN CASINO GUIDE

ameriCAN beer & cocktails

2-For-1 Draft Beer

Present this coupon at ameriCAN to receive two draft beers for the price of one before 9 p.m. See reverse for details.

A current American Casino Guide Discount Card must be presented when redeeming this coupon, or offer is void

americancasinoguidebook.com

L.A. SUBS and Salads

Luxor Food Court
Flamingo Hotel Food Court

Please present coupon to cashier prior to making purchase. Offer has no cash value. Not valid with any other offer or discount. One coupon per person. Subject to change or cancellation without prior notice. Offer valid through December 31, 2020.

Offer void if coupon is copied or sold

americancasinoguidebook.com

ameriCAN beer & cocktails

The Promenade at The Linq
3535 S Las Vegas Blvd
Las Vegas, NV 89109

Valid on any well drink. Free drink of equal or lesser value. Gratuity not included. Limit one per person. Coupon has no cash value. May not be combined with any other offer. Must be 21 years of age or older. Management reserves all rights. Expires 12/29/20.

Offer void if coupon is copied or sold

americancasinoguidebook.com

ameriCAN beer & cocktails

The Promenade at The Linq
3535 S Las Vegas Blvd
Las Vegas, NV 89109

Valid on any draft beer. Free drink of equal or lesser value. Gratuity not included. Limit one per person. Coupon has no cash value. May not be combined with any other offer. Must be 21 years of age or older. Management reserves all rights. Expires 12/29/20.

Offer void if coupon is copied or sold

AMERICAN CASINO GUIDE

CHAYO
MEXICAN KITCHEN + TEQUILA BAR
LAS VEGAS

Buy One Get One FREE On Breakfast Entrées!

Present this coupon to your server, before ordering, and receive two breakfast entrées for the price of one. Valid 8am - 2pm. See reverse for details.

A current American Casino Guide Discount Card must be presented when redeeming this coupon, or offer is void

AMERICAN CASINO GUIDE

Lucky Club CASINO

Free Deck of Cards

Present this coupon at guest services and receive a free deck of cards. See reverse for more details.

A current American Casino Guide Discount Card must be presented when redeeming this coupon, or offer is void

AMERICAN CASINO GUIDE

Lucky Club CASINO

Buy One Entrée Get One Free

(or 50% one entrée when dining alone)

Purchase one entrée at Lucy's Bar & Grill and get a second entrée for FREE, or get 50% off one entrée when dining alone. See reverse for details.

A current American Casino Guide Discount Card must be presented when redeeming this coupon, or offer is void

americancasinoguidebook.com

CHAYO

MEXICAN KITCHEN + TEQUILA BAR

LAS VEGAS

The LINQ Hotel and Casino
3545 S Las Vegas Blvd #4
Las Vegas, NV 89109
(702) 691-3773

Coupon must be presented upon ordering. Gratuity not included. Limit one per person.

Coupon has no cash value. May not be combined with any other offer. Management reserves all rights. Expires 12/29/20.

Offer void if coupon is copied or sold

americancasinoguidebook.com

Lucky Club

CASINO

(702) 399-3297 • (877) 333-9291
3227 Civic Center Drive
N. Las Vegas, NV 89030

Present this coupon to the Lucky Club Players' Club for redemption. Valid for new and existing members. Limit one per calendar year. Offer is non-transferrable and has no cash value. Offer cannot be combined with any other offer. Management reserves all rights. Must be 21 years or older with a valid ID. Offer expires December 30, 2020.

Offer void if coupon is copied or sold

americancasinoguidebook.com

Lucky Club

CASINO

(702) 399-3297 • (877) 333-9291
3227 Civic Center Drive
N. Las Vegas, NV 89030

Present this original coupon to your server in Lucy's Bar & Grill, along with your My Points Las Vegas Club card, to receive one FREE entree with the purchase of another entree at the regular price, or 50% off a single entree when dining alone. The FREE entree must be of equal or lesser value. Not valid for to-go orders. Limit: one coupon per customer, per month. No cash value. Must be 21 years of age or older. Tax and gratuity not included. Management reserves all rights. Offer expires December 30, 2020.

Offer void if coupon is copied or sold

AMERICAN CASINO GUIDE

Lucky Club CASINO

$10 Table Games Match Bet

Place a $10 even-money bet with this voucher at Lucky Club, along with your players' card, and get an extra $10 if you win! See reverse for more details.

A current American Casino Guide Discount Card must be presented when redeeming this coupon, or offer is void

AMERICAN CASINO GUIDE

BODIES
THE EXHIBITION

30% Off Admission

Located insidc the Luxor Hotel and Casino, this Exhibition showcases real human bodies and specimens meticulously dissected, preserved through an innovative process and respectfully presented, giving visitors the opportunity to view the beauty and complexity of their own organs and systems. Present this coupon at the Luxor box office to receive 30% off each adult admission for up to 4 people.

A current American Casino Guide Discount Card must be presented when redeeming this coupon, or offer is void

AMERICAN CASINO GUIDE

TITANIC
THE ARTIFACT EXHIBITION

30% Off Admission

Located inside the Luxor Hotel and Casino, this Exhibition takes guests back in time to April 1912. Guests receive a replica boarding pass, assume the role of a passenger and follow a journey through life on Titanic. The Exhibition features more than 300 artifacts and historical items as well as room re-creations. Present this coupon at the Luxor box office to receive 30% off each adult admission for up to 4 people.

A current American Casino Guide Discount Card must be presented when redeeming this coupon, or offer is void

americancasinoguidebook.com

Lucky Club
CASINO

(702) 399-3297 • (877) 333-9291
3227 Civic Center Drive
N. Las Vegas, NV 89030

Present this coupon to the Lucky Club Players' Club for redemption. Valid for new and existing members. Limit one per calendar year. Offer is non-transferrable and has no cash value. Offer cannot be combined with any other offer. Management reserves all rights. Must be 21 years or older with a valid ID. Offer expires December 30, 2020.

Offer void if coupon is copied or sold

americancasinoguidebook.com

BODIES
THE EXHIBITION

The BODIES exhibition is open daily at 10 a.m. with last admission at 9 p.m. For more information and pricing, please call 702-262-4400 or visit www.bodieslasvegas.com. Located inside the Luxor Hotel and Casino on Las Vegas Boulevard (The Strip). Management reserves all rights. Not valid with any other discount. Expires December 31, 2020. **Offer Code: AYD**

Offer void if coupon is copied or sold

americancasinoguidebook.com

TITANIC
THE ARTIFACT EXHIBITION

The Titanic exhibition is open daily at 10 a.m. with last admission at 9 p.m. For more information and pricing, please call 702-262-4400 or visit www.titaniclasvegas.com. Located inside the Luxor Hotel and Casino on Las Vegas Boulevard (The Strip). Management reserves all rights. Not valid with any other discount. Expires December 31, 2020. **Offer Code: AYD**

Offer void if coupon is copied or sold

AMERICAN CASINO GUIDE

$10 Table Games Match Play

Present this original coupon and B Connected Card to the B Connected Club for a match play voucher. Voucher and equal wager of real chips or cash should be presented to the dealer. See reverse side for details.

A current American Casino Guide Discount Card must be presented when redeeming this coupon, or offer is void

AMERICAN CASINO GUIDE

2-For-1 Breakfast or Lunch Buffet

(or 50% off when dining alone)

Buy one breakfast or lunch buffet and get a second one FREE (or 50% off when dining alone) at the Garden Court Buffet located at Main Street Station. Excludes holidays and Brunch buffet. Coupon has no cash value, must be 21 years of age or older. Must be a B Connected member to redeem. See reverse for full details.

A current American Casino Guide Discount Card must be presented when redeeming this coupon, or offer is void

AMERICAN CASINO GUIDE

$10 Off Dining Purchase of $30 or More

Present this original coupon and B Connected Card to the B Connected Club for a $10 off voucher. Coupon has no cash value, must be 21 years of age or older. Must be a B Connected member to redeem. See reverse for full details.

A current American Casino Guide Discount Card must be presented when redeeming this coupon, or offer is void

MAIN STREET STATION CASINO BREWERY HOTEL

200 North Main Street
Las Vegas, NV 89101
(800) 713-8933
mainstreetcasino.com

Must be 21 or older and have an active B Connected Card. Limit one coupon per person and limit one coupon per wager. Coupon good for play on any Main Street Station casino table game. Good for one decision on even-money bets only. Win or lose, coupon is claimed by the house. If you tie then the coupon may be re-bet. This coupon has no cash value, cannot be combined with any other offer or used more than once. Reproduction, sale, barter or transfer are prohibited and render this coupon void. Management reserves the right to change or discontinue this offer without notice. Expires 12/30/20. Offer code: MSGT6BYCZ

MAIN STREET STATION CASINO BREWERY HOTEL

200 North Main Street
Las Vegas, NV 89101
(800) 713-8933
mainstreetcasino.com

Present this coupon to Garden Court Buffet cashier. Tax and Gratuity is not included. Original coupon (no photocopies) must be presented at time of purchase. This offer is not valid with any other offer or promotion and is not valid on holidays or for Brunch buffet. This offer is void if sold. Management reserves the right to change or cancel this offer at anytime. Offer expires 12/30/20. Offer code: MSFC8TSD4

California Hotel Casino
12 East Ogden Avenue
Las Vegas, NV 89101
(800) 634-6505
thecal.com

Fremont Hotel & Casino
200 Fremont St
Las Vegas, NV 89101
(800) 634-6460
fremontcasino.com

Main Street Station
200 North Main Street
Las Vegas, NV 89101
(800) 713-8933
mainstreetcasino.com

Present the $10 off voucher to one of the following participating restaurants cashiers: California Noodle House, Garden Court Buffet, Lanai Express, Market Street Café, Paradise Buffet/Café, Redwood Steakhouse, Second Street Grill or Triple 7. Tax and Gratuity is not included. This offer is not valid with any other offer or promotion and is not valid on holidays. This offer is void if sold. Management reserves the right to change or cancel this offer at any time. Offer expires 12/30/20. Offer Code: FRFCX2VT9

AMERICAN CASINO GUIDE

GUINNESS® STORE *Las Vegas*

$5 Off The Perfect Pint Experience

Receive $5 off the Individual Perfect Pint Experience, offered at $20 per person. See reverse for more details.

A current American Casino Guide Discount Card must be presented when redeeming this coupon, or offer is void

AMERICAN CASINO GUIDE

GUINNESS® STORE *Las Vegas*

10% Off All GUINNESS® Merchandise After Spending $50

Receive a 10% discount on all GUINNESS® official merchandise inside the Guinness Store Las Vegas after spending $50 on full price items only. See reverse for details.

A current American Casino Guide Discount Card must be presented when redeeming this coupon, or offer is void

AMERICAN CASINO GUIDE

HOUSE OF BLUES RESTAURANT & BAR

Buy One Drink Get One FREE

Buy one drink at the House of Blues Restaurant & Bar and get a second drink FREE. See reverse for full details.

A current American Casino Guide Discount Card must be presented when redeeming this coupon, or offer is void

americancasinoguidebook.com

GUINNESS STORE Las Vegas

The Shoppes at Mandalay Place
3930 Las Vegas Blvd S. #129
Las Vegas, NV 89119
(702) 632-7773

Receive $5 off the Individual Perfect Pint Experience, offered at $20 per person. Guests who take advantage of this offer receive a 20-ounce official Guinness glass filled with a pint of Guinness, personalized certificate and framed photograph. Must be 21 or older. This offer cannot be combined with other promotions. No cash value. Must present original coupon (no photocopies).Management reserves all rights. Valid through 12/30/20.

Offer void if coupon is copied or sold

americancasinoguidebook.com

GUINNESS STORE Las Vegas

The Shoppes at Mandalay Place
3930 Las Vegas Blvd S. #129
Las Vegas, NV 89119
(702) 632-7773

Receive a 10% discount on all GUINNESS® official merchandise inside the Guinness Store Las Vegas after spending $50 on full price items only. This offer cannot be combined with other promotions. No cash value. Must present original coupon (no photocopies).Management reserves all rights. Valid through 12/30/20.

Offer void if coupon is copied or sold

americancasinoguidebook.com

HOUSE OF BLUES

Located at
Mandalay Bay Hotel & Casino
3950 Las Vegas Blvd South
Las Vegas, NV 89119
702-632-7600
www.houseofblues.com/lasvegas

Good for one domestic beer, well drink or house wine, valid at the bar only. Free drink must be of equal or lesser value. Must present this coupon when ordering drink. Limit one coupon per customer. Not valid with any other offers or holidays. Offer is non-transferable and has no cash value. Must be 21+ with valid ID. Management reserves all rights. Expires 12/30/20

Offer void if coupon is copied or sold

AMERICAN CASINO GUIDE

HOUSE OF BLUES®

Complimentary Hat at HOB Gear Shop

Receive a complimentary baseball cap at the House of Blues Company Store with the purchase of a t-shirt of $30 or more. See reverse for full details.

A current American Casino Guide Discount Card must be presented when redeeming this coupon, or offer is void

AMERICAN CASINO GUIDE

World Famous Gospel Brunch at House of Blues

Family & Friends 50% Off Adult Ticket to Gospel Brunch

Present this coupon when booking your Gospel Brunch ticket to receive the 50% discount. See reverse for details.

A current American Casino Guide Discount Card must be presented when redeeming this coupon, or offer is void

AMERICAN CASINO GUIDE

RíRá IRISH PUB & RESTAURANT

15% Off Full Price Menu Items

Present this coupon to your server, before ordering, to receive 15% off full price food items on the Breakfast, Brunch, Lunch, Dinner and Dessert menus. See reverse for more details.

A current American Casino Guide Discount Card must be presented when redeeming this coupon, or offer is void

americancasinoguidebook.com

Located at
Mandalay Bay Hotel & Casino
3950 Las Vegas Blvd South
Las Vegas, NV 89119
702-632-7600
www.houseofblues.com/lasvegas

T-shirt purchase of $30 or more required. Free baseball cap is a $20 value. Must present this coupon when purchasing retail item. Limit one coupon per customer. Not valid with any other offers. Not valid on previous purchases. Offer is non-transferable and has no cash value. Management reserves all rights. Expires 12/30/20

Offer void if coupon is copied or sold

americancasinoguidebook.com

Located at
Mandalay Bay Hotel & Casino
3950 Las Vegas Blvd South
Las Vegas, NV 89119
702-632-7600
www.houseofblues.com/lasvegas

Subject to availability. Must present coupon when booking adult Gospel Brunch ticket to receive discounted offer. Limit one coupon per customer. Not valid with any other offers or on holidays. Offer is non-transferable and has no cash value. Management reserves all rights. Expires 12/30/20

Offer void if coupon is copied or sold

americancasinoguidebook.com

RíRá
IRISH PUB & RESTAURANT

The Shoppes at
Mandalay Place
3930 Las Vegas Blvd S.
Las Vegas, NV 89119
(702) 632-7771
rira.com/lasvegas

This offer cannot be combined with other promotions. Limit: one coupon per customer, per calendar month.

No cash value. Must be 21 years of age or older. Tax and gratuity not included. Resale prohibited. Management reserves all rights. Offer expires 12/30/20.

Offer void if coupon is copied or sold

AMERICAN CASINO GUIDE

CSI: THE EXPERIENCE®

BUY 1 GET 1 FREE

CODE: ACG

A current American Casino Guide Discount Card must be presented when redeeming this coupon, or offer is void

AMERICAN CASINO GUIDE

THE HUNGER GAMES
THE EXHIBITION

35% Off Admission

Receive 35% off on admission tickets to The Hunger Games: The Exhibition at The District, MGM Grand. See Reverse for Details.

Code: CasinoGuide

A current American Casino Guide Discount Card must be presented when redeeming this coupon, or offer is void

AMERICAN CASINO GUIDE

The MINT TAVERN

2-For-1 Draft Beer

Present this coupon at The Mint Tavern to receive two draft beers for the price of one before 9 p.m. See reverse for details.

A current American Casino Guide Discount Card must be presented when redeeming this coupon, or offer is void

americancasinoguidebook.com

CSI: THE EXPERIENCE®

LOCATED INSIDE MGM GRAND

3799 Las Vegas Blvd South Las Vegas, Nevada 89109

702-891-5749 • LasVegasCSIexhibit.com

Redeem coupon at CSI: The Experience upon ticket purchase. Limit 4 per person. No cash value. Not valid on previously purchased tickets. May not be combined with other offers or discounts. Management reserves all rights. Offer expires 12/29/20.

Offer void if coupon is copied or sold

americancasinoguidebook.com

THE HUNGER GAMES
THE EXHIBITION

3799 Las Vegas Blvd S
LAS VEGAS, NV 89109
(702) 410-9899
www.thehungergamesexhibition.com

Present coupon at time of purchase to redeem. Cannot be combined with any other offers. No cash value. Not valid on previously purchased tickets. Blackout dates may apply. Management reserves all rights. Service fees and taxes apply. Expires December 30, 2020.

Offer void if coupon is copied or sold

americancasinoguidebook.com

The MINT TAVERN

332 W. Sahara Avenue
Las Vegas, NV 89102
(702) 776-3313
www.themintlv.com

Valid on any draft beer. Free drink of equal or lesser value. Gratuity not included. Limit one per person. Coupon has no cash value. May not be combined with any other offer. Must be 21 years of age or older. Management reserves all rights. Expires 12/29/20.

Offer void if coupon is copied or sold

AMERICAN CASINO GUIDE

The MINT TAVERN

2-For-1 Cocktail

Present this coupon at The Mint Tavern to receive two well cocktails for the price of one before 9 p.m. See reverse for details.

A current American Casino Guide Discount Card must be presented when redeeming this coupon, or offer is void

AMERICAN CASINO GUIDE

THE MOB MUSEUM

National Museum of Organized Crime & Law Enforcement®

$4 Off Adult Admission

Receive $4 off a full-price adult general admission ticket at The Mob Museum in downtown Las Vegas. See reverse for details.

A current American Casino Guide Discount Card must be presented when redeeming this coupon, or offer is void

AMERICAN CASINO GUIDE

Nathan's® SINCE 1916 FAMOUS

Buy One Get One Free

Present this coupon at any Nathan's listed on the back. Purchase your choice of any menu item and receive your choice of a second menu item of equal or lesser value free!

A current American Casino Guide Discount Card must be presented when redeeming this coupon, or offer is void

The MINT TAVERN

332 W. Sahara Avenue
Las Vegas, NV 89102
(702) 776-3313
www.themintlv.com

Valid on any well drink. Free drink of equal or lesser value. Gratuity not included. Limit one per person. Coupon has no cash value. May not be combined with any other offer. Must be 21 years of age or older. Management reserves all rights. Expires 12/29/20.

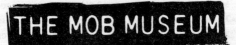

THE MOB MUSEUM

National Museum of Organized Crime & Law Enforcement®

300 Stewart Ave Las Vegas, Nevada 89101 • (702) 229-2734
www.themobmuseum.org

Receive $4 off the purchase of a full-price adult general admission ticket at The Mob Museum in Downtown Las Vegas. Good for up to two people. Cannot be combined with any offers, discounts or promotions. No cash value. Management reserves all rights. Original coupon must be presented (no photocopies). Offer expires December 31, 2020. Promo code: **AmericanCasinoGuide**

MGM Grand Hotel
New York New York Hotel and Casino
Luxor Hotel • Flamingo Food Court
Bally's Hotel • Mandalay Bay Hotel and Casino

Please present coupon to cashier prior to making purchase. Offer has no cash value. Not valid with any other offer or discount. One coupon per person. Subject to change or cancellation without prior notice. Offer valid through December 31, 2020.

AMERICAN CASINO GUIDE

NEW YORK PRETZEL

Buy One Get One Free

Present this coupon at any New York Pretzel listed on the back. Purchase your choice of any menu item and receive your choice of a second menu item of equal or lesser value free!

A current American Casino Guide Discount Card must be presented when redeeming this coupon, or offer is void

AMERICAN CASINO GUIDE

Original CHICKEN TENDER

Free Hand Battered Chicken Tenders & Fresh Cut Fries

Present this coupon at Original Chicken Tender. Buy any meal and receive a second meal of equal or lesser value free!

See reverse for details.

A current American Casino Guide Discount Card must be presented when redeeming this coupon, or offer is void

AMERICAN CASINO GUIDE

The ORLEANS℠

HOTEL & CASINO · LAS VEGAS

$10 Table Games Match Play

Present this original coupon and B Connected Card to the B Connected Club for a match play voucher. Voucher and equal wager of real chips or cash should be presented to the dealer.

See reverse side for details.

A current American Casino Guide Discount Card must be presented when redeeming this coupon, or offer is void

americancasinoguidebook.com

MGM Grand Underground
New York New York Hotel - MGM Entrance

Please present coupon to cashier prior to making purchase. Offer has no cash value. Not valid with any other offer or discount. One coupon per person. Subject to change or cancellation without prior notice. Offer valid through December 31, 2020.

Offer void if coupon is copied or sold

americancasinoguidebook.com

Original CHICKEN TENDER

Luxor Food Court
MGM Grand Food Court

Please present coupon to cashier prior to making purchase. Offer has no cash value. Not valid with any other offer or discount. One coupon per person. Subject to change or cancellation without prior notice. Offer valid through December 31, 2020.

Offer void if coupon is copied or sold

americancasinoguidebook.com

The ORLEANS℠
HOTEL & CASINO · LAS VEGAS

4500 W. Tropicana Ave.
Las Vegas, NV 89103
(702) 365-7111
(800) ORLEANS
www.orleanscasino.com

Must be 21 or older and have an active B Connected Card. Limit one coupon per person and limit one coupon per wager. Coupon good for play on any Orleans casino table game but excludes live poker. Good for one decision on even-money bets only. Win or lose, coupon is claimed by the house. If you tie then the coupon may be re-bet. This coupon has no cash value, cannot be combined with any other offer or used more than once. Reproduction, sale, barter or transfer are prohibited and render this coupon void. Management reserves the right to change or discontinue this offer without notice. Expires 12/30/20.

Offer void if coupon is copied or sold

AMERICAN CASINO GUIDE

The ORLEANS℠

HOTEL & CASINO · LAS VEGAS

Two Showroom Tickets For The Price of One

This coupon entitles the bearer to one free ticket of equal value for purchase of one ticket to any show in The Orleans Showroom. Present coupon at The Orleans Showroom box office. See reverse side for details.

A current American Casino Guide Discount Card must be presented when redeeming this coupon, or offer is void

AMERICAN CASINO GUIDE

The ORLEANS℠

HOTEL & CASINO · LAS VEGAS

Get $15 off when you spend $30 in Bailiwick

Present this coupon to your server, before ordering, to get $15 off any check total of $30 or more at Bailiwick, the Hub of Bites, Sips & Sounds. See reverse for details.

A current American Casino Guide Discount Card must be presented when redeeming this coupon, or offer is void

AMERICAN CASINO GUIDE

OYO

Play $10 Get $10 in Free Play

Play $10 on reel or video reel slot machines and get $10 in Free Play. $10 in Free Play will be credited to your rewards club account once you have played $10 on any reel or video reel slot machine. See reverse for full Details.

Name________________ Club #________________

A current American Casino Guide Discount Card must be presented when redeeming this coupon, or offer is void

americancasinoguidebook.com

The ORLEANS℠
HOTEL & CASINO · LAS VEGAS

4500 W. Tropicana Ave.
Las Vegas, NV 89103
(702) 365-7111
(800) ORLEANS
www.orleanscasino.com

Bearer must be at least 21 years of age and prepared to present a photo ID. Limit one coupon per person. Coupon has no cash value and cannot be combined with any other offer or used more than once. Reproduction, sale, barter and transfer are prohibited and render this coupon void. Management reserves all rights. Offer expires December 31, 2020.

Offer void if coupon is copied or sold

americancasinoguidebook.com

The ORLEANS℠
HOTEL & CASINO · LAS VEGAS

4500 W. Tropicana Ave.
Las Vegas, NV 89103
(702) 365-7111
(800) ORLEANS
www.orleanscasino.com

Must present B Connected Card with valid ID to redeem. B Connected membership is free. Dining area only. $15 dining credit applied to minimum check total of $30 or more. Valid through December 30, 2020. Excludes holidays. Limit one offer per check. Cannot be combined with any other offer. Gratuity not included. Must be 21 years or older to redeem.

Offer void if coupon is copied or sold

americancasinoguidebook.com

OYO

115 East Tropicana Avenue
Las Vegas, Nevada 89109
(702) 739-9000
(800) 726-7366

Coupon must be presented to the rewards club prior to play beginning. $10 in play must be recorded on rewards club card. Membership is free. Once the $10 in play threshold on a reel or video reel slot machine has been met, $10 in free play will be downloaded onto your rewards club card. Free Play must be played through once to cash out. Free Play cannot be used on any Wide Area Progressives, electronic table games or poker games. Limit one voucher per customer. Offer can only be used once per calendar year. No cash value. Not valid in conjunction with any other offer. Must be 21 years of age or older to redeem. Management reserves the right to alter, change or cancel without notice. A current American Casino Guide Discount Card must be presented when redeeming this coupon or offer is void. Offer expires December 30, 2020.

Offer void if coupon is copied or sold

AMERICAN CASINO GUIDE

OYO

$10 Match Play for Any Even-Money Table Game Bet

Make a $10 even-money bet at blackjack, craps or roulette with this coupon and your rewards club card and receive a FREE $10 Match Bet! See reverse for details.

A current American Casino Guide Discount Card must be presented when redeeming this coupon, or offer is void

AMERICAN CASINO GUIDE

HOOTERS

Buy 10 Wings Get 10 FREE!

Present this coupon to your server in the Hooters Restaurant inside OYO Hotel and Casino to receive 10 FREE wings when you buy 10 wings at regular price. See Reverse for full details.

Offer Code: 20587

A current American Casino Guide Discount Card must be presented when redeeming this coupon, or offer is void

AMERICAN CASINO GUIDE

PALACE STATION

2-For-1 Buffet

or 50% off when dining alone

(Monday-Thursday)

Buy one Feast Buffet and get the second Feast Buffet free (or 50% off when dining alone). Offer valid Monday-Thursday. See reverse for more details.

A current American Casino Guide Discount Card must be presented when redeeming this coupon, or offer is void

OYO

115 East Tropicana Avenue
Las Vegas, Nevada 89109
(702) 739-9000
(800) 726-7366

Must be 21 years of age or older and a rewards club member. Make a $10 minimum even-money bet at any blackjack, craps or roulette game, along with this original coupon (no photocopies), and receive a $10 Match Bet. Good for one decision on even-money bets only. Win or lose, coupon is claimed by the house. If you tie, then coupon may be re-bet. No cash value. Limit one voucher per customer. Offer can only be used once per calendar year. Not valid with any other offer. Management reserves the right to alter, change or cancel without notice. Offer expires December 30, 2020.

Offer void if coupon is copied or sold

OYO

115 East Tropicana Avenue
Las Vegas, Nevada 89109
(702) 739-9000
(800) 726-7366

Present this coupon to your server in the Hooters Restaurant inside OYO Hotel and Casino, Las Vegas. Gratuity not included. Non-transferable. Dine in only. Must be a rewards club member. One offer per rewards club member. One offer per table. Offer good at Hooters Restaurant insode OYO Hotel and Casino only. Management reserves the right to alter, change or cancel without notice. Offer expires December 30, 2020.

Offer void if coupon is copied or sold

PALACE STATION

2411 W Sahara Avenue • Las Vegas, NV 89102 • (702) 367-2411
www.palacestation.sclv.com

This voucher entitles bearer to one free breakfast, lunch or dinner in the Feast Buffet when accompanied by a cash paying guest, or 50% off when dining alone. Tax and gratuity not included. One voucher per person/subscriber. Voucher must be presented to cashier. Vouchers are not transferable and are not redeemable for cash. Must be 21 or older. Not a line pass. Not valid on holidays. Not valid with any other offer. Offer may be changed or discontinued at any time at the discretion of management. Original vouchers only. Offer is void if sold. Offer expires December 20, 2020. Settle to: #88-942

Offer void if coupon is copied or sold

AMERICAN CASINO GUIDE

PALMS®

2-For-1 Buffet
or 50% off when dining alone
(Monday-Saturday)

Buy one A.Y.C.E Buffet and get the second one free, (or 50% off when dining alone). Offer valid Monday-Saturday. See reverse for details.

A current American Casino Guide Discount Card must be presented when redeeming this coupon, or offer is void

AMERICAN CASINO GUIDE

PALMS®

$10 off $25 at Lucky Penny

Get $10 off your bill when you spend $25 or more at Lucky Penny. See reverse for more details.

A current American Casino Guide Discount Card must be presented when redeeming this coupon, or offer is void

AMERICAN CASINO GUIDE

Pan Asian EXPRESS

Buy one Two-Entree Meal Get One Free

Present this coupon at Pan Asian Express. Purchase any two entree meal and get a second one free! See reverse for details.

A current American Casino Guide Discount Card must be presented when redeeming this coupon, or offer is void

PALMS®

(702) 942-7777 • 1-866-942-7777
On Flamingo West of the Strip
Easy Access Convenient Parking
ww.palms.com

This voucher entitles bearer to one free breakfast, lunch or dinner in the A.Y.C.E Buffet when accompanied by a full price, cash paying guest, or 50% off when dining alone. Tax and gratuity not included. One voucher per person/subscriber. Voucher must be presented to cashier. Vouchers are not transferable and are not redeemable for cash. Must be 21 or older. Not a line pass. Not valid on holidays. Not valid with any other offer. Offer may be changed or discontinued at any time at the discretion of management. Original vouchers only. Offer is void if sold. Offer expires 12/20/20. Settle to: 41308

Offer void if coupon is copied or sold

americancasinoguidebook.com

PALMS®

(702) 942-7777 • 1-866-942-7777
On Flamingo West of the Strip
Easy Access Convenient Parking
ww.palms.com

Valid at Palms only. Receive $10 off when you spend $25 at Lucky Penny. Tax and gratuity not included. One voucher per person/subscriber. Voucher must be presented to cashier. Vouchers are not transferable and are not redeemable for cash. Must be 21 or older. Not a line pass. Not valid on holidays. Not valid with any other offer. Offer may be changed or discontinued at any time at the discretion of management. Original vouchers only. Offer is void if sold. Offer expires 12/20/20. Settle to: 41307

Offer void if coupon is copied or sold

americancasinoguidebook.com

Bally's Hotel & Casino
MGM Grand Food Court
Flamingo Food Court
Mandalay Bay Food Court

Please present coupon to cashier prior to making purchase. Offer has no cash value. Not valid with any other offer or discount. One coupon per person. Subject to change or cancellation without prior notice. Offer valid through December 31, 2020.

Offer void if coupon is copied or sold

AMERICAN CASINO GUIDE

Jeff Civillico COMEDYinACTION

2-for-1 Show Tickets

Buy one general admission ticket to the Jeff Civillico Comedy in Action show and receive a second one FREE. See reverse for more details.

A current American Casino Guide Discount Card must be presented when redeeming this coupon, or offer is void

AMERICAN CASINO GUIDE

EIFFEL TOWER VIEWING DECK

2-For-1 Daytime Tickets

Redeem at the Paris Box Office for 2-for-1 admission to the Eiffel Tower Viewing Deck. See reverse for details.

Offer code: ETACGDAY

A current American Casino Guide Discount Card must be presented when redeeming this coupon, or offer is void

AMERICAN CASINO GUIDE

Anthony Cools

Free Upgrade to VIP Seating

Get a FREE upgrade to VIP seating with the purchase of a regular price ticket to the Anthony Cools Hypnotism show. Valid for up to two tickets. Coupon must be presented at the box office. See back for full details.

A current American Casino Guide Discount Card must be presented when redeeming this coupon, or offer is void

americancasinoguidebook.com

Paris Las Vegas Casino & Hotel
3655 Las Vegas Boulevard S.
Las Vegas, NV 89109
(702) 946-7000 or visit
www.parislasvegas.com

Show open to all ages. Must redeem coupon at the Paris Las Vegas Box Office to receive second ticket for free with purchase of one at full price. Coupon is void if altered or duplicated. Not valid with any other offers or discounts. Subject to availability. Management reserves the right to cancel or modify offer at any time. Coupon has no cash value. Offer expires December 31, 2020.

Offer void if coupon is copied or sold

americancasinoguidebook.com

3655 Las Vegas Blvd. S
Las Vegas, NV 89109
702-946-7000
EiffelTowerLV.com

Present coupon at time of purchase to redeem. Limit 4 per coupon. Offer is only good on adult daytime tickets. No cash value. Not valid on previously purchased tickets or Express Pass Tickets. Cannot be combined with any other offer. Subject to availability. Service fees apply. Blackout dates may apply. Management reserves all rights. Offer subject to change or cancellation without notification. Offer expires 12/30/20

Offer void if coupon is copied or sold

americancasinoguidebook.com

Paris Las Vegas Casino & Hotel
3655 Las Vegas Boulevard S.
Las Vegas, NV 89109
(702) 946-7000 or visit
www.parislasvegas.com

Subject to availability. Show times subject to change. Offers cannot be combined. Coupon must be presented at time of purchase and is only available through the box office. Management reserves all rights. Not for resale. Valid through 12/30/20. Offer Code: ACAMCAS2018

Offer void if coupon is copied or sold

AMERICAN CASINO GUIDE

FREE COUPON BOOK

SAVINGS VALUED AT $2,000 IS YOURS!

Get your Shop-Dine-Save coupon book featuring exclusive offers from more than 75 retailers. A $2,000 value! Visit the Miracle Mile Shops Customer Service desk to receive your FREE coupon book.

MIRACLE MILE SHOPS
AT PLANET HOLLYWOOD RESORT & CASINO LAS VEGAS

A current American Casino Guide Discount Card must be presented when redeeming this coupon, or offer is void

AMERICAN CASINO GUIDE

PBR ROCK BAR & GRILL LAS VEGAS

2-For-1 Cocktail or Draft Beer

Present this coupon at PBR Rock Bar to receive two well cocktails or domestic draft beers for the price of one before 9pm. See reverse for details.

A current American Casino Guide Discount Card must be presented when redeeming this coupon, or offer is void

AMERICAN CASINO GUIDE

PBR ROCK BAR & GRILL LAS VEGAS

Free Appetizer with Purchase of Two Entrées

Present this coupon to your server before ordering to receive one complimentary appetizer with the purchase of two entrées at PBR Rock Bar & Grill. See reverse for more details.

A current American Casino Guide Discount Card must be presented when redeeming this coupon, or offer is void

americancasinoguidebook.com

MIRACLE MILE SHOPS
AT PLANET HOLLYWOOD RESORT & CASINO LAS VEGAS

OVER 200 SHOPS, TEMPTING RESTAURANTS & LIVE ENTERTAINMENT
Located center Strip at Planet Hollywood Resort & Casino, adjacent to Paris, across from Bellagio, The Cosmopolitan and Aria.

702-866-0710 | MIRACLEMILESHOPSLV.COM

While supplies last. Expires 12/31/2020

Offer void if coupon is copied or sold

americancasinoguidebook.com

PBR ROCK BAR & GRILL LAS VEGAS

Miracle Mile Shops at Planet Hollywood
3663 S Las Vegas Blvd #730
Las Vegas, Nevada 89109

Valid on any well drink, or domestic draft beer. Free drink of equal or lesser value. Gratuity not included. Limit one per person. Coupon has no cash value. May not be combined with any other offer. Must be 21 years of age or older. Management reserves all rights. Expires 12/29/20.

Offer void if coupon is copied or sold

americancasinoguidebook.com

PBR ROCK BAR & GRILL LAS VEGAS

Miracle Mile Shops at Planet Hollywood
3663 S Las Vegas Blvd #730
Las Vegas, Nevada 89109

Blackout dates apply. Gratuity not included. Limit one coupon per table. Coupon has no cash value. May not be combined with any other offer. Must be 21 years of age or older. Management reserves all rights. Expires 12/29/20.

Offer void if coupon is copied or sold

AMERICAN CASINO GUIDE

V THEATER SAXE THEATER

2-for-1 Show Tickets

Offer valid for ANY show including:

Beatleshow • The Mentalist • Hitzville The Show
Popovich Comedy Pet Theater • and more than 10 other shows!

Present this coupon when you buy 1 full price General Admission ticket and receive a second ticket of equal or lesser value FREE (or 50% off the price of a retail show ticket). See back for full details.

ACGF4ADG-001

A current American Casino Guide Discount Card must be presented when redeeming this coupon, or offer is void

AMERICAN CASINO GUIDE

V THEATER

V THE ULTIMATE VARIETY SHOW

2-for-1 Show Tickets to V - The Ultimate Variety Show

Present this coupon when you buy 1 full price General Admission ticket and receive a second ticket of equal or lesser value FREE (or 50% off the price of a retail show ticket). See back for full details.

ACGF4ADG-001

A current American Casino Guide Discount Card must be presented when redeeming this coupon, or offer is void

AMERICAN CASINO GUIDE

Vegas! The Show

SAXE THEATER

2-for-1 Show Tickets to VEGAS! The Show

Present this coupon when you buy 1 full price General Admission ticket and receive a second ticket of equal or lesser value FREE (or 50% off the price of a retail show ticket). See back for full details.

ACGF4ADG-001

A current American Casino Guide Discount Card must be presented when redeeming this coupon, or offer is void

americancasinoguidebook.com

V THEATER SAXE THEATER

In the Miracle Mile Shops at Planet Hollywood - 3663 Las Vegas Blvd.
For show information call (866) 932-1818

Valid on General Admission only, upgrades available at the box office. May not be combined with any other offer or applied to prior purchase. Applicable tax & service fees will apply. No cash value. Subject to availability, management reserves all rights. Offer only valid at the V Theater & Saxe Theater Box Office. Offer expires December 31, 2020.

Offer void if coupon is copied or sold

americancasinoguidebook.com

V THEATER

V The Ultimate Variety Show

In the Miracle Mile Shops at Planet Hollywood - 3663 Las Vegas Blvd.
For show information call (866) 932-1818

Valid on General Admission only, upgrades available at the box office. May not be combined with any other offer or applied to prior purchase. Applicable tax & service fees will apply. No cash value. Subject to availability, management reserves all rights. Offer only valid at the V Theater & Saxe Theater Box Office. Offer expires December 31, 2020.

Offer void if coupon is copied or sold

americancasinoguidebook.com

Vegas! The Show SAXE THEATER

In the Miracle Mile Shops at Planet Hollywood - 3663 Las Vegas Blvd.
For show information call (866) 932-1818

Valid on General Admission only, upgrades available at the box office. May not be combined with any other offer or applied to prior purchase. Applicable tax & service fees will apply. No cash value. Subject to availability, management reserves all rights. Offer only valid at the V Theater & Saxe Theater Box Office. Offer expires December 31, 2020.

Offer void if coupon is copied or sold

AMERICAN CASINO GUIDE

VCARD THE VEGAS NIGHTCLUB PASS

2-for-1 Vegas Nightclub Pass

Present this coupon to the V Theater or Saxe Theater Box office to get two V Card Vegas Nightclub Passes for the price of one. See reverse for full details.

A current American Casino Guide Discount Card must be presented when redeeming this coupon, or offer is void

AMERICAN CASINO GUIDE

Plaza HOTEL • CASINO • BINGO

Buy One Grilled Cheese Get One Free

Present this coupon to Royal Rewards to redeem.
Must be Royal Rewards member. See reverse for details.

A current American Casino Guide Discount Card must be presented when redeeming this coupon, or offer is void

AMERICAN CASINO GUIDE

Plaza HOTEL • CASINO • BINGO

15% Off Whole Pizza Pies

Present this coupon to Royal Rewards to redeem.
Must be Royal Rewards member. See reverse for details.

A current American Casino Guide Discount Card must be presented when redeeming this coupon, or offer is void

americancasinoguidebook.com

V THEATER SAXE THEATER

In the Miracle Mile Shops at Planet Hollywood - 3663 Las Vegas Blvd.
For information call (866) 932-1818 or visit vcardlasvegas.com

Please present this coupon to the V Theater or Saxe Theater Box office to receive one V Card Vegas Nightclub Pass with the purchase of another at full price. Not valid with any other offer or applied to prior purchase. Management reserves all rights. Box office hours 9 a.m. - 9 p.m. Offer expires December 30, 2020.

Offer void if coupon is copied or sold

americancasinoguidebook.com

Plaza
HOTEL • CASINO • BINGO

1 Main Street
Las Vegas, NV 89101
(702) 386-2110
(800) 634-6575
www.PlazaHotelCasino.com

Once coupon is redeemed at Royal Rewards, present redemption voucher at Brightside Breakfast & Burgers, before ordering. Purchase one grilled cheese to receive a second one, of equal or lesser value, free. Gratuity not included. Limit one per person per calendar year. Coupon has no cash value. May not be combined with any other offers or promotions. Management reserves all rights. Offer expires 12/29/20.

Settle to #89219

Offer void if coupon is copied or sold

americancasinoguidebook.com

Plaza
HOTEL • CASINO • BINGO

1 Main Street
Las Vegas, NV 89101
(702) 386-2110
(800) 634-6575
www.PlazaHotelCasino.com

Once coupon is redeemed at Royal Rewards, present redemption voucher to Pop Up Pizza before ordering. Valid for dine in only. Gratuity not included. Limit one per person per calendar year. May not be combined with any other offer or promotion. Must present coupon before ordering. Coupon has no cash value. Management reserves all rights. Offer expires 12/29/20.

Offer void if coupon is copied or sold

AMERICAN CASINO GUIDE

Plaza HOTEL • CASINO • BINGO

$25 Bingo Match Play

Present this coupon to Royal Rewards to redeem.
Must be Royal Rewards member. See reverse for details.

A current American Casino Guide Discount Card must be presented when redeeming this coupon, or offer is void

AMERICAN CASINO GUIDE

Plaza HOTEL • CASINO • BINGO

$10 Match Play

Redeem this coupon at the Royal Rewards Center for validation. Must be Royal Rewards member.
See reverse for details.

A current American Casino Guide Discount Card must be presented when redeeming this coupon, or offer is void

AMERICAN CASINO GUIDE

Plaza HOTEL • CASINO • BINGO

Free Glass of Wine at Oscar's Steakhouse

Present this coupon to Royal Rewards to redeem.
Must be Royal Rewards member. See reverse for details.

A current American Casino Guide Discount Card must be presented when redeeming this coupon, or offer is void

americancasinoguidebook.com

Plaza
HOTEL • CASINO • BINGO

1 Main Street
Las Vegas, NV 89101
(702) 386-2110
(800) 634-6575
www.PlazaHotelCasino.com

Once coupon is redeemed at Royal Rewards, present redemption voucher to Bingo room before ordering. Coupon has no cash value. Not valid towards purchase of Special Games. May not be combined with any other offers or promotions. Limit one per person per calendar year. One coupon per person. Offer expires 12/29/20.

Offer void if coupon is copied or sold

americancasinoguidebook.com

Plaza

1 Main Street
Las Vegas, NV 89101
(702) 386-2110
(800) 634-6575
www.PlazaHotelCasino.com

Coupon must be in its original format and may not be copied in any way. Present validated voucher to any table game prior to the start of the hand. Valid on straight up Blackjack, Craps & Roulette. Valid for even money bets only. Coupons are nontransferable and cannot be combined. Must be 21 years of age or older. Limit one per person per calendar year. No cash value. Win or lose, coupon is claimed by the house. If you tie, coupon may be re-bet. Management reserves all rights. Offer expires 12/29/20

Offer void if coupon is copied or sold

americancasinoguidebook.com

Plaza

1 Main Street
Las Vegas, NV 89101
(702) 386-2110
(800) 634-6575
www.PlazaHotelCasino.com

Once coupon is redeemed, present redemption voucher to Oscar's Steakhouse bar before ordering. Coupon must be surrendered to server before ordering. Must be 21 or older to redeem. Gratuity not included. Coupon only valid with purchase of an entrée. House wine sold by the glass only. Not applicable to group bookings. May not be combined with any other offer. Limit one per person per calendar year. Coupon has no cash value. Reservations recommended. Management reserves all rights. Offer expires 12/29/20

Offer void if coupon is copied or sold

AMERICAN CASINO GUIDE

Plaza HOTEL • CASINO • BINGO

2-For-1 Drink

Present this coupon to Royal Rewards to redeem. Must be Royal Rewards member. See reverse for details.

A current American Casino Guide Discount Card must be presented when redeeming this coupon, or offer is void

AMERICAN CASINO GUIDE

HISTORIC RAILROAD PASS HOTEL, CASINO, & TRAVEL CENTER

$5 Freeplay & Free Buffet (For New Members)

Enroll in The Players Junction Club and receive $5 Free Play and a Free Buffet! See reverse for details.

A current American Casino Guide Discount Card must be presented when redeeming this coupon, or offer is void

AMERICAN CASINO GUIDE

RAMPART CASINO AT THE RESORT AT SUMMERLIN

$10 Match Play for Any Even-Money Table Game Bet

Make a $10 even-money bet on blackjack, craps or roulette with this coupon and your Rampart Rewards card and receive a $10 Match Bet! See reverse for details.

A current American Casino Guide Discount Card must be presented when redeeming this coupon, or offer is void

americancasinoguidebook.com

Plaza

1 Main Street
Las Vegas, NV 89101
(702) 386-2110
(800) 634-6575
www.PlazaHotelCasino.com

Once coupon is redeemed, present redemption voucher to any casino bar before ordering. Valid on well drinks, domestic beers, house wines, soda or water. Free drink of equal or lesser value. Gratuity not included. Limit one per person. Must be 21 years of age or older. Coupon has no cash value. May not be combined with any other offers or promotions. Limit one per person per calendar year. Management reserves all rights. Settle to #82200. Offer expires 12/29/20

Offer void if coupon is copied or sold

americancasinoguidebook.com

HISTORIC RAILROAD PASS HOTEL, CASINO, & TRAVEL CENTER

1500 Railroad Pass Casino Rd
Henderson, NV 89002
(702) 294-5000
www.railroadpass.com

Must be 21 years of age or older to redeem. Present this coupon at the Players Junction Club to receive $5 freeplay and one (1) free buffet after signing up. Players Junction Club cards are free with valid, state issued ID. No cash value. Not valid with any other offer. Management reserves the right to alter, change or cancel without notice. Offer expires December 30, 2020.

Offer void if coupon is copied or sold

americancasinoguidebook.com

RAMPART CASINO AT THE RESORT AT SUMMERLIN

221 N. Rampart Boulevard
Las Vegas, NV 89128
(702) 507-5900
(877) 869-8777
www.RampartCasino.com

Must be 21 or older and a Rampart Rewards member. Make a $10 even-money bet at any blackjack, craps or roulette game, with this original coupon (no photocopies), and your Rampart Rewards card to receive a $10 Match Bet. Good for one decision on even money bets only. Win or lose, coupon is claimed by the house. If you tie, then coupon may be re-bet. No cash value. Limit: one coupon per customer, per year. Not valid with any other offer. Management reserves all rights. Valid through 12/30/20.

Offer void if coupon is copied or sold

AMERICAN CASINO GUIDE

RAMPART BUFFET

2-For-1 Buffet

(or 50% off when dining alone)

Buy one buffet and get a second one FREE (or 50% off when dining alone). When using as 2-for-1 coupon both buffets must be redeemed on same visit. See reverse for more details.

A current American Casino Guide Discount Card must be presented when redeeming this coupon, or offer is void

AMERICAN CASINO GUIDE

SPA AQUAE AT THE JW MARRIOTT, LAS VEGAS

30% Off Spa

Redeem at Spa Aquae at the Rampart Casino for 30% off any spa treatment. See reverse for details.

A current American Casino Guide Discount Card must be presented when redeeming this coupon, or offer is void

AMERICAN CASINO GUIDE

red rock℠

CASINO · RESORT · SPA

2-For-1 Buffet

or 50% off when dining alone

(Monday-Thursday)

Buy one Feast Buffet and get the second Feast Buffet free (or 50% off when dining alone). Offer valid Monday-Thursday. See reverse for more details.

A current American Casino Guide Discount Card must be presented when redeeming this coupon, or offer is void

RAMPART CASINO
AT THE RESORT AT SUMMERLIN

221 N. Rampart Boulevard
Las Vegas, NV 89128
(702) 507-5900
(877) 869-8777
www.RampartCasino.com

Present this coupon to the cashier at time of purchase. Must be 21 or older to reeem. Tax and gratuity not included. Coupon not redeemable for cash. Must have Rampart Rewards card. Original coupon (no photocopies) must be presented to the cashier. One coupon per customer. Not valid with any other coupon or offer. Management reserves all rights. Valid through 12/30/20.

Offer void if coupon is copied or sold

americancasinoguidebook.com

RAMPART CASINO
AT THE RESORT AT SUMMERLIN

221 N. Rampart Boulevard
Las Vegas, NV 89128
(702) 507-5900
(877) 869-8777
www.RampartCasino.com

Limit one treatment per coupon. No cash value. Not valid on previously purchased services or on waxing. Cannot be combined with any other offer, package or discount. Subject to availability. Blackout dates may apply. Management reserves all rights. Offer subject to change or cancellation without notification. Valid through 12/30/20.

Offer void if coupon is copied or sold

americancasinoguidebook.com

red rock℠
CASINO · RESORT · SPA

11011 W Charleston Blvd
Las Vegas, NV 89135
(702) 797-7777
www.redrock.sclv.com

This voucher entitles bearer to one free breakfast, lunch or dinner in the Feast Buffet when accompanied by a full price, cash paying guest, or 50% off when dining alone. Tax and gratuity not included. One voucher per person/subscriber. Voucher must be presented to cashier. Vouchers are not transferable and are not redeemable for cash. Must be 21 or older. Not a line pass. Not valid on holidays. Not valid with any other offer. Offer may be changed or discontinued at any time at the discretion of management. Original vouchers only. Offer is void if sold. Offer expires 12/20/20. Settle to: #88-942

Offer void if coupon is copied or sold

AMERICAN CASINO GUIDE

BUY 1 ROUND OF MINI GOLF GET 1 FREE W/ COUPON

REG. PRICE $11.95
CANNOT BE COMBINED WITH ANY OTHER OFFER

KISSminiGolf.com
Open daily 10am till Midnight
(702) 558-6256

A current American Casino Guide Discount Card must be presented when redeeming this coupon, or offer is void

AMERICAN CASINO GUIDE

CARNIVAL WORLD BUFFET

$5 Off

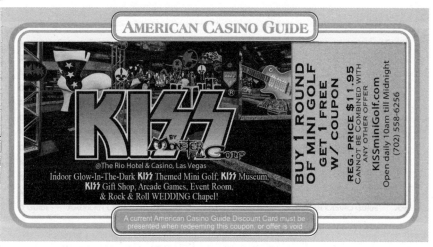

Redeem at the Carnival World Buffet® at Rio Las Vegas for $5 off buffet admission. See reverse for details.

Offer code: CB5TZ

A current American Casino Guide Discount Card must be presented when redeeming this coupon, or offer is void

AMERICAN CASINO GUIDE

VOODOO STEAK

$10 Off Entrée

Redeem at Voodoo Steak at Rio Las Vegas for $10 off your entrée. See reverse for details.

Offer code: ACGR1

A current American Casino Guide Discount Card must be presented when redeeming this coupon, or offer is void

americancasinoguidebook.com

AT THE RIO, LAS VEGAS
OPEN DAILY, 10AM TILL MIDNIGHT

Contact Information:

Address:
Rio Hotel & Casino
3700 W. Flamingo Rd.
Las Vegas, NV 89103

Phone: (702) 558-6256
Email: KISS@MonsterMiniGolf.com
Website: kissminigolf.com

Other Locations:
Twilight Zone by Monster Mini Golf at Bally's Hotel & Casino
3645 S. Las Vegas Blvd. Las Vegas, NV 89109
(702) 333-2121
tzone@MonsterMiniGolf.com

All other Monster Mini Golf locations visit
MonsterMiniGolf.com

Expires 12/30/20

Offer void if coupon is copied or sold

americancasinoguidebook.com

3700 W. Flamingo Rd.
Las Vegas, NV 89103
702-777-7777
RioLasVegas.com

Present coupon at time of purchase to redeem. Limit 4 per coupon. Excludes Buffet of Buffets passes. No cash value. Not valid on previously purchased tickets. Cannot be combined with any other offer. Subject to availability. Blackout dates may apply. Management reserves all rights. Offer subject to change or cancellation without notification. Offer expires 12/30/20

Offer void if coupon is copied or sold

americancasinoguidebook.com

3700 W. Flamingo Rd.
Las Vegas, NV 89103
702-777-7777
RioLasVegas.com

Minimum purchase of 2 entrees. Tax & gratuity not included. No cash value. Not valid on previously purchased services. Cannot be combined with any other offer. Subject to availability. Blackout dates may apply. Management reserves all rights. Offer subject to change or cancellation without notification. Offer expires 12/30/20

Offer void if coupon is copied or sold

AMERICAN CASINO GUIDE

SAM'S TOWN®

Earn 40 Tier Credits
Get a Free Buffet

Earn 40 tier credits playing slots or table games, then present this original coupon and B Connected Card to the B Connected Club and receive a voucher that will entitle bearer to one FREE breakfast, lunch or regular dinner buffet. See reverse side for details.

A current American Casino Guide Discount Card must be presented when redeeming this coupon, or offer is void

AMERICAN CASINO GUIDE

SAM'S TOWN®

Two FREE Drinks at any Casino Bar For NEW Members

Present this coupon when signing up for a new B Connected Card to receive two FREE well, call or draft beers at any casino bar. See reverse for more details.

Offer Validation Stamp Here

A current American Casino Guide Discount Card must be presented when redeeming this coupon, or offer is void

AMERICAN CASINO GUIDE

SAM'S TOWN®

One FREE Room Night

Pay for two nights and get a third night FREE! Good Sunday through Thursday. Holidays and convention periods excluded. Blackout dates may apply. Subject to availability. For reservations call 1-800-634-6371 and ask for offer "ACG20"

A current American Casino Guide Discount Card must be presented when redeeming this coupon, or offer is void

SAM'S TOWN®

Sam's Town Hotel & Gambling Hall
5111 Boulder Highway
Las Vegas, NV 89122
(702) 456-7777 • (800) 897-8696
www.samstownlv.com

Must be 21 or older and have an active B Connected Card. Not valid on holidays. Earn 40 tier credits playing slots or table games on same day original coupon is presented to B Connected Club to obtain voucher. Limit one coupon per person. Excludes specialty night dinners and brunch. This coupon has no cash value, cannot be combined with any other offer or used more than once. Reproduction, sale, barter or transfer are prohibited and render this coupon void. Management reserves the right to change or discontinue this offer without notice. Expires 12/30/20

SAM'S TOWN®

Sam's Town Hotel & Gambling Hall
5111 Boulder Highway
Las Vegas, NV 89122
(702) 456-7777 • (800) 897-8696
www.samstownlv.com

Present this coupon when signing up for a new B Connected card to receive two free well, call or draft beers at any casino bar. Must be 21 years of age or older. Coupon cannot be used in conjunction with any other offer. Management reserves right to change or cancel offer at any time. Must present B Connected Card with coupon for redemption. Coupon has no cash value. Expires 12/30/20. One per customer.

AM85994

SAM'S TOWN®

Sam's Town Hotel & Gambling Hall
5111 Boulder Highway
Las Vegas, NV 89122
(702) 456-7777 • (800) 897-8696
www.samstownlv.com

This voucher entitles the bearer to one free room night at Sam's Town Hotel & Casino, with the purchase of two nights at the prevailing rate. Must have advance reservations. Must present voucher upon check-in. Not valid in conjunction with any other offer. Management reserves the right to cancel this promotion at any time. Credit card or cash deposit required. Guest is responsible for all incidental charges. Must be 21 or older. Limit one free room per person. Offer expires 12/28/20

AMERICAN CASINO GUIDE

SANTA FE STATION

2-For-1 Buffet

or 50% off when dining alone
(Monday-Thursday)

Buy one Feast Buffet and get the second Feast Buffet free (or 50% off when dining alone). Offer valid Monday-Thursday. See reverse for more details.

A current American Casino Guide Discount Card must be presented when redeeming this coupon, or offer is void

AMERICAN CASINO GUIDE

SILVER NUGGET CASINO

Buy One Entrée Get One Free

(or 50% one entrée when dining alone)

Purchase one entrée at the Wrangler and get a second entrée for FREE, or get 50% off one entrée when dining alone. See reverse for details.

A current American Casino Guide Discount Card must be presented when redeeming this coupon, or offer is void

AMERICAN CASINO GUIDE

SILVER NUGGET CASINO

Free Deck of Cards

Present this coupon at guest services and receive a free deck of cards. See reverse for more details.

A current American Casino Guide Discount Card must be presented when redeeming this coupon, or offer is void

americancasinoguidebook.com

SANTA FE STATION

4949 N Rancho Drive • Las Vegas, NV 89130 • (702) 658-4900
www. santafestation.sclv.com

This voucher entitles bearer to one free breakfast, lunch or dinner in the Feast Buffet when accompanied by a cash paying guest, or 50% off when dining alone. Tax and gratuity not included. One voucher per person. Voucher must be presented to cashier. Vouchers are not transferable and are not redeemable for cash. Must be 21 or older. Not a line pass. Not valid on holidays or specialty nights. Not valid with any other offer. Offer may be changed or discontinued at any time at the discretion of management. Original vouchers only. Offer is void if sold. Offer expires December 20, 2020. Settle to: #88-942

Offer void if coupon is copied or sold

americancasinoguidebook.com

SILVER NUGGET CASINO

2140 Las Vegas Blvd. N.
N. Las Vegas, Nevada 89030
(702) 399-1111

Present this original coupon to your server in the Wrangler, along with your My Points Las Vegas Club card, to receive one FREE entree with the purchase of another entree at the regular price, or 50% off a single entree when dining alone. The FREE entree must be of equal or lesser value. Not valid for to-go orders. Limit: one coupon per customer, per month. No cash value. Must be 21 years of age or older. Tax and gratuity not included. Management reserves all rights. Offer expires December 30, 2020.

Offer void if coupon is copied or sold

americancasinoguidebook.com

SILVER NUGGET CASINO

2140 Las Vegas Blvd. N.
N. Las Vegas, Nevada 89030
(702) 399-1111

Present this coupon to the Silver Nugget Players' Club for redemption. Valid for new and existing members. Limit one per calendar year. Offer is non-transferrable and has no cash value. Offer cannot be combined with any other offer. Management reserves all rights. Must be 21 years or older with a valid ID. Offer expires December 30, 2020.

Offer void if coupon is copied or sold

SILVER NUGGET CASINO

$10 Table Games Match Bet

Place a $10 even-money bet with this voucher at Silver Nugget, along with your players' card, and get an extra $10 if you win! See reverse for more details.

A current American Casino Guide Discount Card must be presented when redeeming this coupon, or offer is void

SILVER SEVENS HOTEL & CASINO

Buy One Entrée Get One Free

(or 50% off one entrée when dining alone)

Purchase one entrée at the Sterling Spoon Café and get a second entrée for FREE, or get 50% off one entrée when dining alone. See reverse for details.

A current American Casino Guide Discount Card must be presented when redeeming this coupon, or offer is void

SILVER SEVENS HOTEL & CASINO

$10 Table Games Match Play

Redeem at the A-Play Club and receive a $10 table games match play. See reverse for details.

A current American Casino Guide Discount Card must be presented when redeeming this coupon, or offer is void

americancasinoguidebook.com

SILVER NUGGET CASINO

2140 Las Vegas Blvd. N.
N. Las Vegas, Nevada 89030
(702) 399-1111

Present this coupon to the Silver Nugget Players' Club for redemption. Valid for new and existing members. Limit one per calendar year. Offer is non-transferrable and has no cash value. Offer cannot be combined with any other offer. Management reserves all rights. Must be 21 years or older with a valid ID. Offer expires December 30, 2020.

Offer void if coupon is copied or sold

americancasinoguidebook.com

SILVER SEVENS HOTEL & CASINO

Not your average VEGAS

4100 Paradise Rd
Las Vegas, NV 89169
(702) 733-7000
www.silversevenscasino.com

Present A-Play Club coupon and A-Play® Club Card at the buffet or cafe when paying for meal. Must be 21 years or older. Tax and gratuity not included. Receive one FREE entrée of equal or lesser value with the purchase of one entrée at regular price or receive 50% off one entrée. Limit one coupon per day, per party. No cash value. May not be combined with any other coupon offer or discount; full retail pricing applies. Management reserves the right to cancel or discontinue this offer without prior notice. Not valid without A-Play® Club Card. Settle to: 465. Offer Expires 12/28/20.

Offer void if coupon is copied or sold

americancasinoguidebook.com

SILVER SEVENS HOTEL & CASINO

Not your average VEGAS

4100 Paradise Rd
Las Vegas, NV 89169
(702) 733-7000
www.silversevenscasino.com

Must be 21 or older and have an active A-Play Card. Limit one coupon per person and limit one coupon per wager. Good for one decision on even-money bets only. Win or lose, coupon is claimed by the house. If you tie then the coupon may be re-bet. This coupon has no cash value, cannot be combined with any other offer or used more than once. Reproduction, sale, barter or transfer are prohibited and render this coupon void. Management reserves the right to change or discontinue this offer without notice. Settle to: 37283. Offer expires 12/28/20.

Offer void if coupon is copied or sold

AMERICAN CASINO GUIDE

SILVERTON
Casino • Hotel • Las Vegas

2-For-1 Seasons Buffet

(or 50% off when dining alone)

Must be a Silverton Rewards Club member. Must purchase one Seasons buffet at regular price, to receive a second buffet, of equal or lesser value, for free. Good for one time use only. See reverse for more details.

A current American Casino Guide Discount Card must be presented when redeeming this coupon, or offer is void

AMERICAN CASINO GUIDE

WUHU NOODLE

Free Starter With Purchase Of An Entree

Must be a Silverton Rewards Club member. Present this coupon along with your Silverton Rewards card and valid photo ID at WuHu Noodle to redeem. See reverse for more details.

A current American Casino Guide Discount Card must be presented when redeeming this coupon, or offer is void

AMERICAN CASINO GUIDE

Su Casa
SUSHI MAS

$5 off when you spend $15

Must be a Silverton Rewards Club member. Present this coupon to your server, before ordering, to get $5 off any check total of $15 or more at Su Casa. See reverse for details.

A current American Casino Guide Discount Card must be presented when redeeming this coupon, or offer is void

SILVERTON

Casino • Hotel • Las Vegas

Silverton Casino Hotel
3333 Blue Diamond Road
Las Vegas, NV 89139
www.silvertoncasino.com
702-263-7777 • 866-946-4373

Receive one FREE lunch, brunch or dinner buffet with the purchase of a second lunch, brunch or dinner buffet at regular price. Present this coupon along with valid photo ID and Silverton Rewards card to the cashier at Seasons to redeem. Good for one time use only. Coupon has no cash value, gratuity not included. Cannot be combined with other discounts, offers, or promotions. Not valid on holidays. Multiple coupons, regardless of promotion, may not be used at one time. Must be 21 years of age or older. Management reserves all rights. Settle to #D148. Expires 12/28/20.

SILVERTON

Casino • Hotel • Las Vegas

Silverton Casino Hotel
3333 Blue Diamond Road
Las Vegas, NV 89139
www.silvertoncasino.com
702-263-7777 • 866-946-4373

Receive one Starter item with purchase of an entree. Present this coupon along with valid photo ID and Silverton Rewards card at WuHu Noodle to redeem. Maximum value $10. Good for one time use only. Coupon has no cash value, gratuity not included. Cannot be combined with other discounts, offers, or promotions. Multiple coupons, regardless of promotion, may not be used at one time. Must be 21 years of age or older. Management reserves all rights. Settle to #D148. Expires 12/28/20.

SILVERTON

Casino • Hotel • Las Vegas

Silverton Casino Hotel
3333 Blue Diamond Road
Las Vegas, NV 89139
www.silvertoncasino.com
702-263-7777 • 866-946-4373

Receive $5 off the check with a minimum purchase of $15. Present this coupon along with valid photo ID and Silverton Rewards card at Su Casa to redeem. Good for one time use only. Coupon has no cash value, gratuity not included. Cannot be combined with other discounts, offers, or promotions. Multiple coupons, regardless of promotion, may not be used at one time. Must be 21 years of age or older. Management reserves all rights. Expires 12/28/20.

AMERICAN CASINO GUIDE

South Point

Earn 300 points, Get Free Buffet (Keep the points)

Earn 300 points playing slots then present this original coupon and players club card to the players club, and receive a voucher that will entitle bearer to one FREE breakfast, lunch or regular dinner buffet. See reverse side for details.

A current American Casino Guide Discount Card must be presented when redeeming this coupon, or offer is void

AMERICAN CASINO GUIDE

South Point

FREE Appetizer With Purchase of Entrée at Don Vito's

Present this coupon to your server when ordering to get a FREE appetizer with the purchase of an entrée at Don Vito's Italian Restaurant located inside the South Point. See reverse for more details.

A current American Casino Guide Discount Card must be presented when redeeming this coupon, or offer is void

AMERICAN CASINO GUIDE

THE STRAT™ HOTEL • CASINO • SKYPOD

Two-For-One Tower Admission Tickets

Get one FREE Tower Admission ticket with the purchase of one Tower Admission ticket at full price.

(See back for full details.)

2000 Las Vegas Blvd. S. • Las Vegas, NV 89104 • 800.998.6937 • 702.380.7777

A current American Casino Guide Discount Card must be presented when redeeming this coupon, or offer is void

SOUTH POINT

9777 S Las Vegas Blvd
Las Vegas, NV 89183
(702) 796-7111• (866) 791-7626
www.southpointcasino.com

Must be 21 or older and have an active The Club Card. Not valid on Holidays. Earn 300 points playing slots on same day original coupon is presented to The Club to obtain voucher. Limit one coupon per person. Excludes brunch and seafood buffets. Gratuity not included. This coupon has no cash value, cannot be combined with any other offer or used more than once. Reproduction, sale, barter or transfer are prohibited and render this coupon void. Management reserves the right to change or discontinue this offer without notice. Expires 12/30/20. **Coupon Code 6452**

Offer void if coupon is copied or sold

americancasinoguidebook.com

SOUTH POINT

9777 S Las Vegas Blvd
Las Vegas, NV 89183
(702) 796-7111• (866) 791-7626
www.southpointcasino.com

Present this coupon to your server when ordering to get a FREE appetizer with the purchase of one entrée. Limit: one coupon per customer, per calendar month. No cash value. Must be 21 years of age or older. Tax and gratuity not included. Resale prohibited. Management reserves all rights. Offer expires 12/30/20. **Coupon Code 6453**

Offer void if coupon is copied or sold

americancasinoguidebook.com

THE STRAT™
HOTEL • CASINO • SKYPOD

OFFER CODE: ACG_TWR

To view special offers, go to StratosphereHotel.com

(Coupon must be presented at the Stratosphere Ticket Center.)

Management reserves all rights. Valid through December 30, 2020. Must be at least 18 years of age unless accompanied by an adult. Subject to availability. Offers cannot be combined.
Not for resale. Offer void if coupon is copied or sold.
Blackout dates apply. Not valid on New Year's eve.

Offer void if coupon is copied or sold

AMERICAN CASINO GUIDE

SUNCOAST

HOTEL & CASINO · LAS VEGAS

2-For-1 Breakfast or Lunch Buffet

(or 50% off when dining alone)

Buy one breakfast or lunch buffet and get a second one FREE (or 50% off when dining alone). Excludes holidays. Coupon has no cash value, must be 21 years of age or older. Must be a B Connected member to redeem. See reverse for full details.

A current American Casino Guide Discount Card must be presented when redeeming this coupon, or offer is void

AMERICAN CASINO GUIDE

SUNCOAST

HOTEL & CASINO · LAS VEGAS

2-For-1 Dinner Buffet

(or 50% off when dining alone)

Buy one dinner buffet and get a second one FREE (or 50% off when dining alone). Excludes holidays. Coupon has no cash value, must be 21 years of age or older. Must be a B Connected member to redeem. See reverse for full details.

A current American Casino Guide Discount Card must be presented when redeeming this coupon, or offer is void

AMERICAN CASINO GUIDE

SUNSET STATION

2-For-1 Buffet

or 50% off when dining alone

(Monday-Thursday)

Buy one Feast Buffet and get the second Feast Buffet free (or 50% off when dining alone). Offer valid Monday-Thursday. See reverse for more details.

A current American Casino Guide Discount Card must be presented when redeeming this coupon, or offer is void

SUNCOAST

HOTEL & CASINO · LAS VEGAS

(702) 636-7111 • 1-877-677-7111
9090 Alta Dr
www.suncoastcasino.com

Present this coupon to St. Tropez Buffet cashier. Tax and Gratuity is not included Original coupon (no photocopies) must be presented at the time of purchase. This offer is not valid with any other offer or promotion and is not valid on holidays. This offer is void if sold. Management reserves the right to change or cancel this offer at anytime. Offer expires 12/20/20

Comp Code: D9990

B Connected Membership # ____________

americancasinoguidebook.com

SUNCOAST

HOTEL & CASINO · LAS VEGAS

(702) 636-7111 • 1-877-677-7111
9090 Alta Dr
www.suncoastcasino.com

Present this coupon to St. Tropez Buffet cashier. Tax and Gratuity is not included Original coupon (no photocopies) must be presented at the time of purchase. This offer is not valid with any other offer or promotion and is not valid on holidays. This offer is void if sold. Management reserves the right to change or cancel this offer at anytime. Offer expires 12/20/20

Comp Code: D9990

B Connected Membership # ____________

Offer void if coupon is copied or sold

americancasinoguidebook.com

SUNSET STATION

1301 W Sunset Road • Henderson, NV 89014 • (702) 547-7777

www.sunsetstation.sclv.com

This voucher entitles bearer to one free breakfast, lunch or dinner in the Feast Buffet when accompanied by a cash paying guest, or 50% off when dining alone. Tax and gratuity not included. One voucher per person/subscriber. Voucher must be presented to cashier. Vouchers are not transferable and are not redeemable for cash. Must be 21 or older. Not a line pass. Not valid on holidays. Not valid with any other offer. Offer may be changed or discontinued at any time at the discretion of management. Original vouchers only. Offer is void if sold. Offer expires December 20, 2020. Settle to: #88-942

Offer void if coupon is copied or sold

AMERICAN CASINO GUIDE

TACOS & 'RITAS

50% Off Giant Margarita With Any Purchase

Present this coupon at Tacos & 'Ritas. Make any purchase and receive 50% off a giant 44oz frozen margarita in a souvenir glass! See reverse for details.

A current American Casino Guide Discount Card must be presented when redeeming this coupon, or offer is void

AMERICAN CASINO GUIDE

TEXAS STATION

2-For-1 Buffet

or 50% off when dining alone (Monday-Thursday)

Buy one Feast Buffet and get the second Feast Buffet free (or 50% off when dining alone). Offer valid Monday-Thursday. See reverse for more details.

A current American Casino Guide Discount Card must be presented when redeeming this coupon, or offer is void

AMERICAN CASINO GUIDE

MARVEL AVENGERS STATION INTERACTIVE EXHIBIT

35% Off Admission

Receive 35% off on admission tickets to the Marvel Avengers Station at Treasure Island. See Reverse for Details

Code: CasinoGuide

A current American Casino Guide Discount Card must be presented when redeeming this coupon, or offer is void

americancasinoguidebook.com

TACOS & 'RITAS

Venetian Hotel Casino Floor Food Court
MGM Grand Food Court

Please present coupon to cashier prior to making purchase. Offer has no cash value. Not valid with any other offer or discount. One coupon per person. Subject to change or cancellation without prior notice. Offer valid through December 31, 2020.

Offer void if coupon is copied or sold

americancasinoguidebook.com

TEXAS STATION

2101 Texas Star Lane • North Las Vegas, NV 89032 • (702) 631-1000
www.texasstation.sclv.com

This voucher entitles bearer to one free breakfast, lunch or dinner in the Feast Buffet when accompanied by a cash paying guest, or 50% off when dining alone. Tax and gratuity not included. One voucher per person/subscriber. Voucher must be presented to cashier. Vouchers are not transferable and are not redeemable for cash. Must be 21 or older. Not a line pass. Not valid on holidays. Not valid with any other offer. Offer may be changed or discontinued at any time at the discretion of management. Original vouchers only. Offer is void if sold. Offer expires December 20, 2020. Settle to: #88-942

Offer void if coupon is copied or sold

americancasinoguidebook.com

MARVEL AVENGERS STATION INTERACTIVE EXHIBIT

3300 Las Vegas Blvd S
Las Vegas, NV 89109
(702) 894-7626
www.stationattraction.com

Present coupon at time of purchase to redeem. Cannot be combined with any other offers. No cash value. Not valid on previously purchased tickets. Blackout dates may apply. Service fees and taxes apply. Management reserves all rights. Expires December 30, 2020.

Offer void if coupon is copied or sold

AMERICAN CASINO GUIDE

Señor Frog's®
FUN, FOOD & CLOTHES

FOOD ONLY

25* USD OFF

ON A 50 USD PURCHASE

TREASURE ISLAND RESORT & CASINO 3300 BLVD. SOUTH
702.337.7577 FROGSLASVEGAS

A current American Casino Guide Discount Card must be presented when redeeming this coupon, or offer is void

---

AMERICAN CASINO GUIDE

WORLD'S GREATEST LIVE TRIBUTE SHOW
Legends in Concert

2-FOR-1 TICKETS

Redeem at the Tropicana Box Office for 2-for-1 Preferred or GA tickets to Legends in Concert.

See reverse for details.

Offer code: LCACG

A current American Casino Guide Discount Card must be presented when redeeming this coupon, or offer is void

---

AMERICAN CASINO GUIDE

TUSCANY SUITES & CASINO

Earn 300 Points, Get $10 Free Slot Play

Present this coupon to the Tuscany Players Club after earning 300 same-day base points to receive $10 in free slot play. Valid for new or current members. See reverse side for details.

A current American Casino Guide Discount Card must be presented when redeeming this coupon, or offer is void

americancasinoguidebook.com

Señor Frog's® FUN, FOOD & CLOTHES

TERMS AND CONDITIONS

*MUST SPEND MINIMUN PURCHASE ON CERTIFICATE TO RECEIVE DISCOUNT

*ONLY ONE GIFT CERTIFICATE MAY BE REDEEMED PER PARTY, EVEN IF THE PARTY IS SEATED AT SEPARATE TABLES AND/OR RECEIVES MORE THAN ONE CHECK. NOT VALID ON TAXES, TIPS, MERCHANDISE OR PRIOR BALANCES.

*VALID AT THIS RESTAURANT ONLY. NOT VALID ON HOLIDAYS AND SPECIAL EVENTS.

*CANNOT BE COMEINED WITH ANY OTHER PROMOTIONS, COUPONS, OR SPECIAL OFFERS. DOES NOT EXPIRE.

Offer void if coupon is copied or sold

americancasinoguidebook.com

Tropicana LAS VEGAS

3801 Las Vegas Boulevard S
Las Vegas, Nevada
(800) GO2-TROP
www.troplv.com

Present coupon at time of purchase to redeem. Limit three free tickets per coupon. No cash value. Not valid on previously purchased tickets. Cannot be combined with any other offer. Subject to availability. Blackout dates may apply. Management reserves all rights. Offer subject to change or cancellation without notification. Offer expires 12/30/20.

Offer void if coupon is copied or sold

americancasinoguidebook.com

TUSCANY SUITES & CASINO

255 E Flamingo Road
Las Vegas, NV 89169
(702) 893-8933 • (877) 887-2261
www.tuscanylv.com

Base points only. No multipliers. Bearer must be at least 21 years of age and prepared to present a photo ID. Limit one coupon per person per 30-day period. Coupon has no cash value and cannot be combined with any other offer or used more than once. Reproduction, sale, barter and transfer are prohibited and render this coupon void. Management reserves all rights. Offer expires 12/31/20.

Offer void if coupon is copied or sold

AMERICAN CASINO GUIDE

TUSCANY SUITES & CASINO

2-for-1 Well Drink or Domestic Beer at Toscana Bar

Buy one well drink or select domestic beer, and receive one of equal or lesser value for free. See reverse for more details.

A current American Casino Guide Discount Card must be presented when redeeming this coupon, or offer is void

AMERICAN CASINO GUIDE

TUSCANY SUITES & CASINO

$10 Table Game Match Play

Bet $10 on any even-money bet and we'll pay you $20 if you win. Present this coupon at Tuscany Players Club to receive your free $10 table game match play. See reverse side for full details.

A current American Casino Guide Discount Card must be presented when redeeming this coupon, or offer is void

AMERICAN CASINO GUIDE

INDOOR SKYDIVE

$25 OFF

individual flight packages

Vegas Indoor Skydiving

A current American Casino Guide Discount Card must be presented when redeeming this coupon, or offer is void

americancasinoguidebook.com

TUSCANY SUITES & CASINO

255 E Flamingo Road
Las Vegas, NV 89169
(702) 893-8933 • (877) 887-2261
www.tuscanylv.com

Buy one well drink or select domestic beer, and receive one of equal or lesser value for free. Present coupon and Tuscany Players Club card to server for redemption. Valid only at Toscana Bar. Does not include tax or gratuity. Limit one per customer. Not valid with any other offer. No cash value. Management reserves all rights. Offer expires 12/31/20

Offer void if coupon is copied or sold

americancasinoguidebook.com

TUSCANY SUITES & CASINO

255 E Flamingo Road
Las Vegas, NV 89169
(702) 893-8933 • (877) 887-2261
www.tuscanylv.com

Voucher must be redeemed at Players Club to receive free match play offer. Good for one bet only, win or lose, (pushes play again). Limit one offer per account per calendar year. One per player. Must be a Tuscany Players Club member and have a valid photo ID to redeem. Offer is non-transferable and has no cash value. Cannot be combined with any other offer. Must be 21 or older. Membership is free. Management reserves all rights. Offer expires December 29, 2020.

Offer void if coupon is copied or sold

americancasinoguidebook.com

Vegas Indoor Skydiving

Located at
200 Convention Center Dr
Las Vegas, NV 89109
(702) 731-4768
VegasIndoorSkydiving.com

Use offer code: ACG20 to redeem $25 off. Good towards Learn To Fly or Fly For 5 Packages. Cannot be combined with any other offer. Call for more information. Expires 12/30/20.

Offer void if coupon is copied or sold

AMERICAN CASINO GUIDE

Madame Tussauds

LAS VEGAS

2-For-1 General Admission

Receive one FREE ticket with the purchase of a full-price adult general admission ticket at Madame Tussauds Interactive Wax Attraction located in front of the Venetian Resort on Las Vegas Boulevard. See reverse for details.

5106

A current American Casino Guide Discount Card must be presented when redeeming this coupon, or offer is void

AMERICAN CASINO GUIDE

PIZZERIA PRONTO!

Buy One Item Get One Free

Present this coupon at Pizzeria Pronto! Purchase any menu item and get a second menu item of equal or lesser value free! See reverse for details.

A current American Casino Guide Discount Card must be presented when redeeming this coupon, or offer is void

AMERICAN CASINO GUIDE

PRIMEBURGER

boutique burgers, crafted fries, spirits & shakes

Buy One Item Get One Free

Present this coupon at Primeburger in the Venetian Hotel Grand Canal Shoppes. Purchase any menu item and get a second menu item of equal or lesser value free! See reverse for details.

A current American Casino Guide Discount Card must be presented when redeeming this coupon, or offer is void

Madame Tussauds

LAS VEGAS

Who would you like to meet at the world famous Madame Tussauds Las Vegas? Featuring over 100 lifelike wax figures of your favorite celebrities, Madame Tussauds removes the velvet ropes and allows you to get up close to your favorite stars!

Madame Tussauds Las Vegas is open daily at 10 a.m. For more information and pricing, please call (866) 841-3739 or visit madametussauds.com. Located in front of the Venetian Resort on Las Vegas Blvd (The Strip). Not valid with any other discount promotion. Expires December 31, 2020.

PIZZERIA PRONTO!

Venetian Hotel Grand Canal Shoppes

Across From Tommy Bahama

Please present coupon to cashier prior to making purchase. Offer has no cash value. Not valid with any other offer or discount. One coupon per person. Subject to change or cancellation without prior notice. Offer valid through December 31, 2020.

PRIMEBURGER

boutique burgers, crafted fries, spirits & shakes

Venetian Hotel Grand Canal Shoppes

Please present coupon to cashier prior to making purchase. Offer has no cash value. Not valid with any other offer or discount. One coupon per person. Subject to change or cancellation without prior notice. Offer valid through December 31, 2020.

AMERICAN CASINO GUIDE

ROCKHOUSE

LAS VEGAS

2-For-1 Cocktail or Draft Beer

Present this coupon at Rockhouse to receive two well cocktails or domestic draft beers for the price of one before 9 p.m. See reverse for details.

A current American Casino Guide Discount Card must be presented when redeeming this coupon, or offer is void

AMERICAN CASINO GUIDE

ROCKHOUSE

LAS VEGAS

Free Pitcher of Domestic Draft Beer with $25 Purchase

Present this coupon at Rockhouse to receive a free pitcher of domestic draft beer with a purchase of $25 or more. See reverse for details.

A current American Casino Guide Discount Card must be presented when redeeming this coupon, or offer is void

AMERICAN CASINO GUIDE

ROYAL BRITANNIA GASTRO PUB

Buy One Item Get One Free

Present this coupon at Royal Britannia Gastro Pub. Purchase any menu item and get a second menu item of equal or lesser value free! See reverse for details.

A current American Casino Guide Discount Card must be presented when redeeming this coupon, or offer is void

americancasinoguidebook.com

ROCKHOUSE
LAS VEGAS

Grand Canal Shoppes at the Venetian
3355 S Las Vegas Blvd, #3200
Las Vegas, Nevada

Valid on any well drink, or domestic draft beer. Free drink of equal or lesser value. Gratuity not included. Limit one per person. Coupon has no cash value. May not be combined with any other offer. Must be 21 years of age or older. Management reserves all rights. Expires 12/29/20.

Offer void if coupon is copied or sold

americancasinoguidebook.com

ROCKHOUSE
LAS VEGAS

Grand Canal Shoppes at the Venetian
3355 S Las Vegas Blvd, #3200
Las Vegas, Nevada

Valid on any domestic draft only. Limit one coupon per table. Gratuity not included. Coupon has no cash value. Must be 21 years of age or older. Management reserves all rights. Expires 12/29/20.

Offer void if coupon is copied or sold

americancasinoguidebook.com

ROYAL BRITANNIA
GASTRO PUB

Venetian Hotel
Grand Canal Shoppes
Across From
Tommy Bahama

Please present coupon to cashier prior to making purchase. Offer has no cash value. Not valid with any other offer or discount. One coupon per person. Subject to change or cancellation without prior notice. Offer valid through December 31, 2020.

Offer void if coupon is copied or sold

AMERICAN CASINO GUIDE

BURGER San Gennaro

Buy One Get One Free

Present this coupon at the San Gennaro Burger in the Venetian Casino Floor Food Court. Purchase your choice of any menu item and receive your choice of a second menu item of equal or lesser value free!

A current American Casino Guide Discount Card must be presented when redeeming this coupon, or offer is void

AMERICAN CASINO GUIDE

Jennifer Romas Presents Sexxy® The Show

2-For-1 Tickets

Receive one FREE ticket with the purchase of a full-price ticket to Sexxy The Show located at Westgate Las Vegas Resort & Casino. See reverse for details.

KACGB

A current American Casino Guide Discount Card must be presented when redeeming this coupon, or offer is void

AMERICAN CASINO GUIDE

Wild West Horseback Adventures

$40 Off Sunset Dinner Ride

Present this coupon at time of purchase to receive $40 off the regular price of the sunset dinner ride. See reverse for details.

A current American Casino Guide Discount Card must be presented when redeeming this coupon, or offer is void

americancasinoguidebook.com

BURGER
San Gennaro

Venetian Hotel Casino Floor Food Court

Please present coupon to cashier prior to making purchase. Offer has no cash value. Not valid with any other offer or discount. One coupon per person. Subject to change or cancellation without prior notice. Offer valid through December 31, 2020.

Offer void if coupon is copied or sold

americancasinoguidebook.com

WESTGATE
LAS VEGAS
RESORT ♦ CASINO

3000 Paradise Rd
Las Vegas, NV 89109
(702) 732-5299
westgatelasvegas.com
sexxyshow.com

Present this coupon at the box office at Westgate Las Vegas to receive a FREE ticket to Sexxy The Show with the purchase of another ticket at full price. Not valid with any other offer or promotion. Must be 18 or older. 10:00 pm showtime, show days Wed-Sat. Westgate Las Vegas Resort & Casino reserves the right to change or cancel this promotion at any time. Offer expires 12/30/20 Code: KACGB

Offer void if coupon is copied or sold

americancasinoguidebook.com

Wild West Horseback Adventures

2470 Chandler Ave Suite 11
Las Vegas, NV 89120
(702) 792-5050
wildwesthorsebackadventures.com

Present this coupon at time of purchase to receive $40 off the regular price of the sunset dinner ride. No cash value. Offer valid for all party members.

This adventure includes roundtrip transportation, a 1.5 hour trail ride in beautiful Glendale, a mouthwatering steak BBQ dinner, spectacular views, and memories that will last a lifetime. Management reserves all rights and may change or cancel this promotion at any time without notice. Offer is valid through December 23, 2020.

Offer void if coupon is copied or sold

AMERICAN CASINO GUIDE

WILD GRILL
BREAKFAST • LUNCH
DINNER • LATE NIGHT

$20 For $10 at Wild Grill

Present this coupon to your server before ordering to receive $20 in food for only $10. Also valid at Brewer's Cafe at Barley's or Greens Lounge at The Greens. See reverse for more details.

A current American Casino Guide Discount Card must be presented when redeeming this coupon, or offer is void

AMERICAN CASINO GUIDE

William HILL
RACE & SPORTS BOOK

FREE $25 Mobile Sports Bet For New Members

Present this coupon at any Full Service William Hill Sports Book location in Nevada to receive a $25 Free Mobile Sports Bet with your new Mobile Sports account. See reverse for more details.

A current American Casino Guide Discount Card must be presented when redeeming this coupon, or offer is void

AMERICAN CASINO GUIDE

William HILL
RACE & SPORTS BOOK

FREE $2 Virtual Racing Bet For New Members

Present this coupon at participating Full Service William Hill Sports Book locations in Nevada to receive a $2 Free Virtual Racing Bet with your new Mobile Sports account or William Hill Rewards Club account. See reverse for more details.

A current American Casino Guide Discount Card must be presented when redeeming this coupon, or offer is void

WILDFIRE GAMING

For all locations please see:

www.wildfire.sclv.com

This voucher entitles bearer to $20 worth of Wild Grill Dining for only $10. **Offer is valid at any Wild Grill including Barley's, The Greens, Wildfire Anthem, Wildfire Boulder, Wildfire Lanes, Wildfire Rancho, Wildfire Sunset or Wildfire Valley View.** Tax and gratuity not included. One voucher per person/subscriber. Voucher must be presented to cashier. Vouchers are not transferable and are not redeemable for cash. Must be 21 or older. Not a line pass. Not valid on holidays. Not valid with any other offer. Offer may be changed or discontinued at any time at the discretion of management. Original vouchers only. Offer is void if sold. Offer expires 12/21/20. Settle to: #88-113

William HILL
RACE & SPORTS BOOK

For locations visit:
www.williamhill.us

Offer Expires December 31, 2020. Must be 21 years of age or older to participate. $25 minimum deposit required. Offer is non-transferable, may not be used in conjunction with any other offer or promotion and has no cash value. Member must not have previously established any William Hill Mobile Sports account. See official rules for details. Limit one coupon per person. Management reserves all rights.

William HILL
RACE & SPORTS BOOK

For participating locations visit:
www.williamhill.us

Must be 21 years of age or older to participate. Visit www.williamhill.us to find participating William Hill Sports Book offering Virtual Racing. Offer is non-transferable, may not be used in conjunction with any other offer or promotion and has no cash value. Member must not have previously established any William Hill Mobile Sports or Rewards Club account. See official rules for details. Limit one coupon per person. Management reserves all rights. Offer expires December 31, 2020.

AMERICAN CASINO GUIDE

Harrah's LAUGHLIN

FRESH MARKET SQUARE BUFFET

Buy One Buffet - Get One FREE!

Present this coupon and your Total Rewards® card at the Fresh Market Square Buffet at Harrah's Laughlin to buy one buffet (brunch or dinner) and receive one buffet FREE! Valid at Harrah's Laughlin only. Offer code: 176

A current American Casino Guide Discount Card must be presented when redeeming this coupon, or offer is void

AMERICAN CASINO GUIDE

Harrah's LAUGHLIN

Beach Café

Buy One Entree - Get One FREE!

Present this coupon and your Total Rewards® card at the Beach Cafe at Harrah's Laughlin at time of seating to buy one entree at the Beach Cafe and receive one entree of equal, or lesser value, FREE! Valid at Harrah's Laughlin only. Offer code: 176

A current American Casino Guide Discount Card must be presented when redeeming this coupon, or offer is void

AMERICAN CASINO GUIDE

PASSAGGIO ITALIAN GARDENS

2-for-1 Pasta Bowl Promo

Enjoy a 2-for-1 Pasta Bowl at Passaggio Italian Gardens at Tropicana Laughlin. Must purchase one Pasta Bowl at regular price to receive one free. Dine-in only. No sharing. Must be a Trop Advantage member. Offer excluded on holidays and blackout dates.

Coupon # 65

A current American Casino Guide Discount Card must be presented when redeeming this coupon, or offer is void

americancasinoguidebook.com

Harrah's LAUGHLIN

2900 South Casino Drive
Laughlin, Nevada 89029
(702) 298-4600 • (800) HARRAHS
www.harrahs.com

Management reserves the right to modify this offer at any time without prior notice. Original coupon must be presented (no photocopies), along with Total Rewards® card. Not valid on weekends (Friday/Saturday) or holidays. Cannot be used in conjunction with any other offer. Must be 21 or older to redeem. Coupon has no cash value. Limit one coupon per person per visit. Subject to availability. Gratuity not included. Expires December 30th, 2020. Must be 21 years or older to gamble. Know When To Stop Before You Start.® Gambling Problem? Call 1-800-522-4700. ©2019, Caesars License Company, LLC.

Offer void if coupon is copied or sold

americancasinoguidebook.com

Harrah's LAUGHLIN

2900 South Casino Drive
Laughlin, Nevada 89029
(702) 298-4600 • (800) HARRAHS
www.harrahs.com

Management reserves the right to modify this offer at any time without prior notice. Original coupon must be presented (no photocopies), along with Total Rewards® card. Not valid on weekends (Friday/Saturday) or holidays. Cannot be used in conjunction with any other offer. Must be 21 or older to redeem. Limit one coupon per person per visit. Subject to availability. Gratuity not included. Expires December 30th, 2020. Must be 21 years or older to gamble. Know When To Stop Before You Start.® Gambling Problem? Call 1-800-522-4700. ©2019, Caesars License Company, LLC.

Offer void if coupon is copied or sold

americancasinoguidebook.com

TROPICANA LAUGHLIN

Tropicana Laughlin Hotel & Casino
2121 South Casino Drive
Laughlin, NV 89029
www.troplaughlin.com
702-298-4200 • 1-800-343-4533

Receive ONE FREE PASTA BOWL at Passaggio Italian Gardens with purchase of ONE PASTA BOWL at regular price. CANNOT be combined with comps, players card discounts, other discounts or promos. Must be a Trop Advantage member. Dine in only. One Coupon per transaction. No cash value. Gratuity not included. No change given. Non-transferable. Management reserves all rights. Excludes holidays & special events. Must be 21+ Gambling problem? Call 1-800-522-4700. Offer valid Jan. 2, 2020 through Dec. 22, 2020.

Offer void if coupon is copied or sold

AMERICAN CASINO GUIDE

GOLD TOWN CASINO • PAHRUMP, NV

LAKESIDE CASINO & RV PARK PAHRUMP, NV

PAHRUMP NUGGET HOTEL • CASINO PAHRUMP, NV

2-for-1 Entrée

Present this coupon to the players club for a 2-for-1 entrée at the Pahrump Nugget Café, Gold Town Café or Lakeside Café. Not valid with any other offers. See reverse for more details.

A current American Casino Guide Discount Card must be presented when redeeming this coupon, or offer is void

AMERICAN CASINO GUIDE

GOLD TOWN CASINO • PAHRUMP, NV

LAKESIDE CASINO & RV PARK PAHRUMP, NV

PAHRUMP NUGGET HOTEL • CASINO PAHRUMP, NV

$10 in FREE Slot Play

New members only, present this coupon at the players club booth at the Pahrump Nugget, Gold Town or Lakeside casino and receive $10 in FREE slot play! See reverse for more details.

A current American Casino Guide Discount Card must be presented when redeeming this coupon, or offer is void

AMERICAN CASINO GUIDE

LAKESIDE CASINO & RV PARK PAHRUMP, NV

PAHRUMP NUGGET HOTEL • CASINO PAHRUMP, NV

One FREE Hotel or RV Night Stay!

Pay for one room night at the full rate and receive the second room night FREE at either the Pahrump Nugget or RV Space at Lakeside. See reverse side for more details.

A current American Casino Guide Discount Card must be presented when redeeming this coupon, or offer is void

GOLDEN™ CASINO GROUP
PAHRUMP NUGGET | GOLD TOWN | LAKESIDE

681 S. Highway 160
Pahrump, NV 89048
(775) 751-6500
(866) 751-6500
www.pahrumpnugget.com

Present this coupon to the players club. Excludes Nye County residents. Must be at least 21 years of age. Must show a valid photo I.D and a players club card.

Limit one coupon per person. Not valid with any other offer. Coupon has no cash value. Management reserves the right to cancel or modify this offer at any time. Max value $10. Resale prohibited. Expires 12/31/20

Offer void if coupon is copied or sold

GOLDEN™ CASINO GROUP
PAHRUMP NUGGET | GOLD TOWN | LAKESIDE

681 S. Highway 160
Pahrump, NV 89048
(775) 751-6500
(866) 751-6500
www.pahrumpnugget.com

This coupon is valid for new player club members only. Not valid with any other offer or discount. Limit one coupon per person. Excludes Nye County residents. Must be at least 21 years of age. Must show a valid photo I.D. Coupon has no cash value. Management reserves the right to cancel or modify this offer at any time. Offer expires 12/31/20

Offer void if coupon is copied or sold

GOLDEN™ CASINO GROUP
PAHRUMP NUGGET | GOLD TOWN | LAKESIDE

681 S. Highway 160
Pahrump, NV 89048
(775) 751-6500
(866) 751-6500
www.pahrumpnugget.com

Valid Sunday through Thursday for consecutive night stays in the same room or space. Excludes Nye county residents. Holidays and special events excluded. Subject to availability. Must have advance reservations by calling 866-751-6500 or 888-558-5253 and must advise the Pahrump Nugget Hotel agent or Lakeside RV agent that you are calling for the American Casino Guide offer. Must present and surrender this coupon upon check-in. No exceptions. Management reserves the right to modify or cancel this promotion at any time. Not valid with any other offer. Customer required to place credit card on file at check-in. Customer responsible for all other additional charges. Must be 21 or older. Limit one free room or RV Space per coupon. Expires 12/31/20

Offer void if coupon is copied or sold

AMERICAN CASINO GUIDE

PRIMM VALLEY
RESORT & CASINO

25% Off Hotel Room

Get 25% off your room rate by calling (888) 774-6668 to reserve and mention offer code TPCAS19. Must be 21 or older. Offer valid Sunday-Thursday. Not valid on holidays and subject to availability. Must present coupon at check-in. See reverse for full details.

A current American Casino Guide Discount Card must be presented when redeeming this coupon, or offer is void

AMERICAN CASINO GUIDE

PRIMM & PROPER

15% Off Entire Bill at Primm & Proper

Receive 15% off your entire bill at Primm & Proper located inside Primm Valley Resort & Casino. Offer is valid 7 days a week. Coupon must be presented at checkout. See reverse for full details.

A current American Casino Guide Discount Card must be presented when redeeming this coupon, or offer is void

AMERICAN CASINO GUIDE

Atlantis™
CASINO RESORT SPA • RENO

2-4-1 Breakfast or Lunch Buffet

in Toucan Charlie's Buffet & Grille

Present this coupon with your Monarch Rewards card to the cashier at Toucan Charlie's Buffet & Grille and receive one free breakfast or lunch buffet with the purchase of a second buffet at the regular price. See back for details.

A current American Casino Guide Discount Card must be presented when redeeming this coupon, or offer is void

americancasinoguidebook.com

PRIMMVALLEY
RESORT & CASINO

31900 Las Vegas Blvd S,
Primm, NV 89019
(702) 386-7867
www.primmvalleyresorts.com

Present coupon at check-in to receive 25% prevailing room rate. Blackout dates may apply. Offer cannot be combined with any other offer or promotional discount. No cash value. Resort fee applies on non-complimentary room nights. Credit card required when making reservation. Must be 21 years of age or older to redeem this offer. Management reserves all rights to modify, change or cancel this offer at any time without prior notice. Offer Expires 12/28/20.

Offer void if coupon is copied or sold

americancasinoguidebook.com

PRIMMVALLEY
RESORT & CASINO

31900 Las Vegas Blvd S,
Primm, NV 89019
(702) 386-7867
www.primmvalleyresorts.com

Present coupon at checkout to receive 15% off your food bill. Offer cannot be combined with any other offer or promotional discount. No cash value. Must be 21 years of age or older to redeem this offer. Management reserves all rights to modify, change or cancel this offer at any time without prior notice. Offer expires 12/28/20.

Settle to 1000

Offer void if coupon is copied or sold

americancasinoguidebook.com

Atlantis™
CASINO RESORT SPA • RENO

3800 S. Virginia St. | Reno NV 89502
800.723.6500 | atlantiscasino.com

Expires December 30, 2020. Valid Monday-Friday. Excludes holidays or special events. No cash value. Gratuity not included. Must be 21. Not valid in combination with any other offer. Non-transferable. Management reserves all rights. Must be a Monarch Rewards member. Not a Monarch Rewards member? Join today! It's fun, it's easy, it's free.

Monarch Rewards # ____________

Offer Code #20ACGTC

Offer void if coupon is copied or sold

AMERICAN CASINO GUIDE

Atlantis™
CASINO RESORT SPA • RENO

$5 wins $10 Match Play

Present this coupon with a $5 wager and receive $10 when you win an even money bet at any blackjack, roulette, craps, Pai Gow Poker game or Mini-Baccarat. *See back for details.*

A current American Casino Guide Discount Card must be presented when redeeming this coupon, or offer is void

AMERICAN CASINO GUIDE

Harrah's®
RENO

Buy One Carvings® Buffet Get One FREE!

Receive one Carvings Buffet FREE with the purchase of a full price Carvings Buffet. Present this coupon and Total Rewards® card to the Carvings Buffet cashier at Harrah's Reno prior to seating. Valid at Harrah's Reno only. See reverse for details. Coupon code: CG2F1

A current American Casino Guide Discount Card must be presented when redeeming this coupon, or offer is void

AMERICAN CASINO GUIDE

DUKES
CHOPHOUSE

$10 Off Purchase of $20 or More

Redeem at Dukes Chophouse at Rivers Casino & Resort Schenectady for $10 off your purchase of $20 or more.

See reverse side for details.

A current American Casino Guide Discount Card must be presented when redeeming this coupon, or offer is void